Photoshop CS

Photoshop® CS

STEPHEN ROMANIELLO

SAN FRANCISCO | LONDON

SYBEX®

Associate Publisher: DAN BRODNITZ
Acquisitions Editor: BONNIE BILLS
Developmental Editor: PETE GAUGHAN
Production Editor: DENNIS FITZGERALD
Technical Editor: STEPHEN MARSH
Copyeditor: SHARON WILKEY
Compositor: HAPPENSTANCE TYPE-O-RAMA
CD Coordinator: DAN MUMMERT
CD Technician: KEVIN LY
Proofreaders: DARCEY MAURER, LAURIE O'CONNELL, AMY RASMUSSEN, NANCY RIDDIOUGH, MONIQUE VAN DEN BERG
Indexer: TED LAUX
Cover, Interior, and Technical Illustration Designer: CARYL GORSKA
Cover Photographer: CHAD EHLERS, STONE

LIBRARY OF CONGRESS CARD NUMBER: 2003115543

ISBN: 0-7821-4280-X

SYBEX and the SYBEX logo are either registered trademarks or trademarks of SYBEX Inc. in the United States and/or other countries.

Screen reproductions produced with FullShot 99. FullShot 99 © 1991-1999 Inbit Incorporated. All rights reserved.
FullShot is a trademark of Inbit Incorporated.

Original stock images used in the book were provided courtesy of Corbis, Corel, EclectiCollections, Index Stock Imagery, and PhotoDisc. Images are for practice use only and cannot be used or reproduced for any other purpose. Image copyright remains with the original copyright holder.

The CD interface was created using Macromedia Director, COPYRIGHT 1994, 1997-1999 Macromedia Inc. For more information on Macromedia and Macromedia Director, visit http://www.macromedia.com.

TRADEMARKS: SYBEX has attempted throughout this book to distinguish proprietary trademarks from descriptive terms by following the capitalization style used by the manufacturer.

The author and publisher have made their best efforts to prepare this book, and the content is based upon final release software whenever possible. Portions of the manuscript may be based upon pre-release versions supplied by software manufacturer(s). The author and the publisher make no representation or warranties of any kind with regard to the completeness or accuracy of the contents herein and accept no liability of any kind including but not limited to performance, merchantability, fitness for any particular purpose, or any losses or damages of any kind caused or alleged to be caused directly or indirectly from this book.

MANUFACTURED IN THE UNITED STATES OF AMERICA

10 9 8 7 6 5 4 3 2

Dear Reader,

Thank you for choosing *Photoshop CS Savvy*. This book is part of a new wave of Sybex graphics books, all written by outstanding authors—artists and teachers who really know their stuff and have a clear vision of the audience they're writing for. It's also part of our growing library of truly unique Photoshop books, including *Photoshop CS at Your Fingertips*, *Photoshop Secrets of the Pros*, and *The Hidden Power of Photoshop CS*.

Founded in 1976, Sybex is the oldest independent computer book publisher. More than twenty-five years later, we're committed to producing a full line of consistently exceptional graphics books. With each title, we're working hard to set a new standard for the industry. From the paper we print on, to the writers and photographers we work with, our goal is to bring you the best graphics books available.

I hope you see all that is reflected in these pages. I'd be very interested to hear your comments and get your feedback on how we're doing. To let us know what you think about this, or any other Sybex book, please visit us at www.sybex.com. Once there, go to the product page, click on Submit a Review, and fill out the questionnaire. Your input is greatly appreciated.

Please also visit www.sybex.com to learn more about the rest of our graphics line.

Best regards,

Dan Brodnitz
Associate Publisher
Sybex Inc.

*For my students
who have taught
me so much.*

Acknowledgments

Writing a book of this kind is by no means a solitary venture. *Photoshop CS Savvy* was the result of many friends who contributed their time and expertise. First of all, Thanks are in order to David Fugate, my agent at Waterside Productions Inc. Thanks and kudos to the team at Sybex including Acquisitions Editor Bonnie Bills, Developmental Editor, Pete Gaughan, Production Editor Dennis Fitzgerald, and Copyeditor Sharon Wilkey, as well as Dan Mummert and Kevin Ly for help with the CD, and to Happenstance Type-O-Rama for layout. ■ Thanks is owed to my Technical Editor Stephen Marsh for his vast knowledge and attention to detail and to my contributors including color management guru Brian Lawler, Photoshop Web expert Mark Clarkson, digital video master Stephen Burns and Windows wiz David Barber. ■ My thanks to artist friends who provided images and inspiration including Andy Rush, Chris Mooney, and my daughter Leah. ■ I want to thank close friends Arnold Nelson, Margo Taylor, Steve Malkin, Carol Peterson Beach, Karen Brennan, Tim Fuller, Randal Williams, Mark Williams, Liisa Phillips, Charlotte Lowe, Debbie la Chapelle, Martin Levowitz and Margo Burwell, whose support helped me through some tough moments. ■ My gratitude is owed to my collegues at Pima Community College including Frank Pickard, Dennis Landry, Dave Wing, Patty Gardiner, and Mary Leffler, and of course to my students. ■ Many thanks to the Adobe Photoshop beta team, especially Stacy Strehlow for keeping me appraised of the many changes to the program during its development. Also, thanks to Image Stock, Corel, PhotoDisk, ImageIdeas and Eclectic Collections for providing images from their CD library. And thanks to Alien Skin, AutoFX, AutoEye and Maya PLE for contributing demos to the CD. ■ Thanks to my brother Chuck and my mom, Violette for their effusive enthusiasm. And special thanks is owed to Rebecca Peters for her incredible patience and support.

CONTENTS AT A GLANCE

Contents

The Spinning Wheel of Life

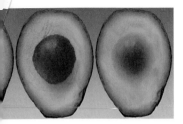

EL Jefe

I go where I please...

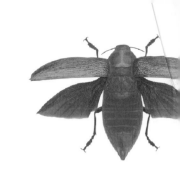

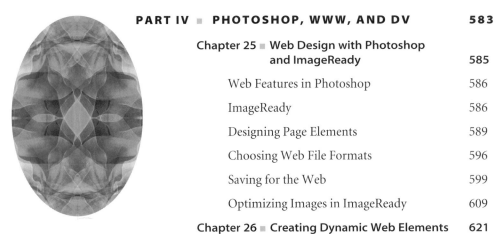

Introduction

The Image Transformed

Since its first release in 1990, Photoshop has emerged as the standard in image manipulation software. It has revolutionized the way we view and create images and has even undermined the veracity of once indisputable photographic evidence. It has become the chosen tool of the amateur and professional photographer, designer, artist, printer, and publisher. It is even used by scientists.

This latest version of Photoshop has many features that empower the novice and expert user alike to push the creative and technical envelope. *CS* stands for *Creative Suite*, and Photoshop is the cornerstone of the five new products that Adobe has recently released. These products are Illustrator CS for vector illustration, GoLive CS for Web design, InDesign CS for page layout, and Acrobat CS for online publishing, There is also the new Version Cue software that links all the CS products together with tools for workgroup and file management. The authors of these new versions have succeeded in creating a nexus that elegantly links technology and art.

There is a special emphasis on digital photography, an image technology that is rapidly emerging as the mainstream choice of the professional commercial photographer. The many new features and upgrades in this latest version satisfy the demands of a dynamic publishing industry, but are also crafted with the individual digital artist in mind.

If you are a beginner, you will find this book useful as a detailed introduction to the world's most powerful image manipulation software. If you are a seasoned user, then this book will serve as a guide to some of Photoshop's newest features and help you uncover its hidden secrets.

Photoshop CS Savvy: Who Should Use This Book

The immense popularity of Adobe Photoshop is in part attributable to the fact that it enables us to alter the reality of images. And who, after all, can resist the temptation to change the nature of what we see? *Photoshop CS Savvy* is for anyone who has ever unconsciously scribbled a mustache on a face in a magazine while talking on the telephone. It's for those of us who take photographs, draw, paint, and cut and paste pictures. It's for computer artists, graphic designers, Web designers, and printers. It is intended to help master the software, at whatever level you might be in the learning curve.

A Systematic, Comprehensive Approach

The focus of *Photoshop CS Savvy* is to present a complete and organized guide to the tools and operations of Adobe's amazing image-editing software. It offers descriptions, explanations, and techniques that will make all aspects of the software more accessible and familiar to you without oversimplifying or "dumbing down" the information. How you work in Photoshop will be defined by your specific output goals. The book explores the basic concepts that are fundamental to your understanding of the digital image. Each chapter contains information to help you master the Photoshop skills you need. Most chapters contain step-by-step modules, and the book is interspersed with Hands On projects, which will further enhance your capabilities so that you can ultimately apply the techniques to your own images.

Photoshop is an enormous software package with the capability to perform almost any imaging operation. When you consider the number of operations that Photoshop can execute, and how they might be combined, the image-editing possibilities become infinite. Making this information understandable and, above all, interesting to you, is the intent of *Photoshop CS Savvy*.

How to Become Photoshop Savvy

The Master in the art of living makes little distinction between work and play, labor and leisure, mind and body, education and recreation, love and religion. He simply pursues his vision of excellence in whatever he does, leaving others to decide whether he is working or playing. To him he is always doing both. —ZEN APHORISM

Becoming Photoshop savvy is more than learning where the tools and operations are and how to use them. The real knowledge comes from being able to creatively apply what you know. Although Photoshop is used by scientists and engineers for image manipulation and color correction, the majority of end users are interested in expressing visual ideas. Photoshop gives them the power to paint, color, synthesize, collage, composite, manipulate, and distort the reality of their pictures and fulfill the potential of their artistic vision.

Photoshop is like all visual art forms, in that the best work is created with love, passion, focus, and skill. The fundamentals of design, composition, and color apply to digital images just as they do to traditional drawings, paintings, and graphics. The basic principles of design are balance, proportion, unity, direction, and emphasis. Great images are *balanced* in that they carry an appropriate weight within a given space; the viewer's eye can move from one element to another with fluid ease. The *proportional* relations of elements create an optical rhythm throughout the composition that the viewer can sense, which effectively communicates the content of the image. The image is *unified* by a cohesive visual integrity that holds it together. The eye moves in a determined *direction* and does not wander aimlessly around looking for a place to rest. Elements are structured in a visual hierarchy, which *emphasizes* them in the order of their importance. The mood, color scheme, and ambiance are relevant to the content and message of the image.

Along with a cognizance of the importance of design, an innate sensitivity to the formal elements of the image—color, light, shadow, form, and perspective—is imperative. The knowledge of the potential and the limitations of the tools that are needed to produce the desired results are also critical. Pay attention to the minutest of details with the realization that the photographic image is relentless in its seamless portrayal of reality.

Finally, becoming Photoshop savvy means a commitment to the attainment of absolute perfection, but also an awareness of its elusiveness. Each new project presents a fresh opportunity to apply your knowledge, skills, and insights to the fulfillment of this exalted goal.

Photoshop CS Savvy takes the sting out of learning the program and makes the experience pleasant and interesting. It will be your tour guide and point out some of the remarkable landmarks and points of interest along the way, helping to make your journey absorbing and entertaining. Of course, merely reading this book is not enough. You must work through the step-by-step operations and Hands On tutorials until you understand the concepts, and then apply what you've learned to your images. You may need specific questions answered, and I hope *Photoshop CS Savvy* will provide all the answers you need.

Making the Most of *Photoshop CS Savvy*: What's Inside

Photoshop CS Savvy thoroughly covers the latest and greatest features of the software, from the from the File Browser's new enhancements to new tools and features for digital artists and photographers. Throughout the text I've identified features that are new to Photoshop CS with a "New" margin flag. If you're familiar with previous versions of

Photoshop and want to skim a topic for the latest changes, look for this marker. Photoshop's new features and operations are also summarized in Chapter 2.

Photoshop CS Savvy is for users on both the Mac and Windows platforms. Differences between the Mac and Windows versions of Photoshop are slight. One obvious difference is key commands, which vary in some cases because of differences between keyboards for the two platforms. When keys differ, both are given, with the Mac key first: ⌘/Ctrl, Option/Alt, Return/Enter, Delete/Backspace. When keys need to be pressed in combination, they are separated by a hyphen. For example, ⌘/Ctrl-S indicates that you should press ⌘ and S (Mac) or Ctrl and S (Win).

The primary content of *Photoshop CS Savvy* is distributed into several parts. There is also a special color section that provides the material you need to see in color, as well as a supporting CD-ROM containing the documents and images used in this book.

Part I: Photoshop Core

To put the phenomenon of Adobe Photoshop into a historical perspective, the introductory chapter presents the artistic foundations and technical innovations that have led to its emergence as the leading image-editing methodology in the world today. The sources are as diverse as the Impressionist movement and the development of the World Wide Web. In Chapter 2, I cover all of the new features that make this version a formidable upgrade.

The rest of Part I, which is by far the largest section of the book, explores the nuts and bolts of Photoshop. The fundamentals of digital imaging are explained to provide insight as to how Photoshop documents are created and structured. With this basic information under your belt, you will gain a working, hands-on knowledge of Photoshop's core tools and operations, knowledge enough to begin to apply them to real-world projects.

Part II: Photoshop Color

Part II presents techniques for managing and manipulating color. In this section you will learn how to manage color throughout the entire imaging process to ensure predictable results. Part II also delves into tonal adjustment and color correction. A variety of creative color-mapping and correction possibilities are explored, along with techniques for image enhancement and photo retouching.

Part III: Photoshop Savvy

You'll really flex your Photoshop muscles in Part III. Featured are advanced techniques to retouch photos, manage layers, make complex selections, apply creative enhancement filters, superimpose images, and automate the program.

Part IV: Photoshop, WWW, and DV

The Internet, being a fundamental aspect of communication in the 21st century, deserves an exclusive section of the book. Photoshop is universally used to create and edit images for the Web. You will explore techniques for Web page design in Photoshop and methods for optimizing and saving images for use on the Internet. You'll explore ImageReady, Adobe's Web image–preparation software that is bundled with Photoshop, and you'll learn to create spliced images, rollovers, and animations, and to save images for export to Flash.

This part of the book also covers the fine points of digital video and the integration of Photoshop images with nonlinear editing software.

Hands On: Comprehensive Tutorials

Among the chapters, you'll find in-depth tutorials called "Hands On." In these sections you'll get your hands dirty in complex, real-world projects that utilize a combination of the techniques discussed in previous chapters. Follow along using the image files on the CD.

Appendices

The appendices provide a reference to Photoshop CS. They include a description of some popular third-party plug-ins and an extensive list of Web resources. There are 4 bonus appendices on the CD, and these include a description of tools, file format information, explanations of blending modes, and an overview of key commands.

Glossary

The purpose of *Photoshop CS Savvy* is to demystify the software and make it more user-friendly and understandable to you. I have deliberately taken pains to avoid computerese wherever possible; however, in many instances it is not possible to explain certain concepts without using a specialized vocabulary. For this reason, I have included a comprehensive glossary for common (and uncommon) terminology that you might not be familiar with or that is needed to clarify a concept.

Color Material

The 32-page color section showcases color-oriented material from the chapters and Hands On sections. When you see a figure numbered C12, for example, within a chapter or tutorial, turn to the color section to see that image in full color.

The *Photoshop CS Savvy* CD

The CD that accompanies this book features the images and documents used in the book's step-by-step operations and Hands On sections. Images are contained within labeled folders for each chapter or Hands On tutorial. The CD also contains demo versions of some powerful Photoshop plug-ins and 4 bonus appendices.

How to Reach the Author

It gives me great pleasure to make the information I've gathered over the past 12 years available to you. I truly hope that *Photoshop CS Savvy* meets your needs and answers your questions. When I wrote *Photoshop 7 Savvy*, I was amazed at the incredible feedback for the book I received from all over the world. I appreciate your comments and would like to hear from you. You can reach me through the publisher at www.sybex.com.

Stephen Romaniello
Tucson, Arizona
December, 2003

Photoshop Core

The first part of *Photoshop CS Savvy* introduces you to the fundamental concepts of digital imaging. You'll see how Photoshop and digital image manipulation fit into the evolution of image technology. You'll explore Photoshop's newest features, its interface, its logic, and its techniques.

Part I also covers the key techniques of selections, layers, painting, and transformation— fundamental processes you'll use on almost every image. You'll work with Photoshop's paint engine, learn about digital color, and address resolution issues.

CHAPTER 1

The Foundations of Photoshop

Photoshop is the progeny of a lineage of artistic and technical methodologies that have evolved over the centuries. Painting, mosaic, photography, and printing have been the primary methods of producing two-dimensional images for many generations. The twentieth century saw the rapid emergence of new image technologies that extend and amplify the conventional ones. Photoshop combines these methods into a virtual interface that enables the user to experiment freely in a dynamic user-friendly environment.

This chapter will cover these topics:

- **Image technology defined**
- **The history of imaging, from prehistory to the present**
- **Painting, printing, collage, and photography**
- **The world of Photoshop and the Web**

Image Technology

Image technology is the method used to produce pictures. Since the first images were painted on the stone walls of caves with pigment extracted from natural materials, humans have invented new image technologies to visually express their ideas and experiences. The process of technical evolution was slow in preindustrial societies, so for thousands of years, techniques for creating images were primarily done by the skilled hands of artists and artisans. During and after the industrial revolution, however, image technology accelerated to the point that, today, we see new innovations on an almost daily basis.

The evolution of the visual image is due, in part, to the methods available to the artist. Artistic styles are an expression of the zeitgeist of the periods that produce them. As technology evolves, new ideas and visual idioms emerge that reflect the cultural ambiance of their times.

This idea was quite apparent in the twentieth century from the speed in which new technologies emerged. The obvious changes in aesthetic values can be observed decade by decade as cultural, political, and technological influences affected visual expression. Each decade of the twentieth century can be associated with distinct aesthetic styles that are part of the ongoing development of culture.

Figure 1.1

A mosaic from first-century B.C.E. Pompeii, The Defeated Persians under Darius (detail)

Mosaics

One significant milestone in the history of visual art was the ability to portray tonality. *Tonality* is the effect of changing light or color on an image. In the real world, we see a seamless continuum of blended color that defines our visual world in light and shadow, and produces a tangible, three-dimensional reality of color and form. Primitive artists made no attempt to express tonal differences, in part because the technology was unavailable to them.

If you think that tonal variations in digital images is a new phenomenon, however, think again. One of the first methods of simulating the effect of tonal variation was to place tiny individual units of slightly varied color next to each other. We see this technique commonly employed in mosaics from imperial Rome, such as the one in Figure 1.1. Each element of color is a separate glass or ceramic tile. The tiles, placed next to each other in a graduated sequence, produce the effect of varied tonality.

The mosaics of two thousand years ago are the predecessors of today's Photoshop images. Instead of tiles of glass, the digital artist uses squares of colored light called pixels (see Figure 1.2). Today's scanners can "see" and interpret color information from a continuous-tone image into these tiny units. When the image has been captured, we can, in Adobe Photoshop, select and change the color of pixels individually or in groups.

Painting

Creating images by applying color to a surface is one of the most basic forms of artistic expression; indeed, the history of the world can be viewed in the legacy of paintings that have been left behind by our talented predecessors. Throughout history, the technical and aesthetic qualities of painting have changed, various styles have emerged, and pictorial content has evolved.

Representational painting dominated the world for centuries. Paintings contained content that could be easily recognized, whether the subject matter was religious, histori-cal, or descriptive. Then in the late nineteenth century, artists began to abstract the tangible realities that they observed to produce art filtered through their personal experiences. Within 50 years, abstraction led to the creation of a totally nonobjective idiom in styles such as the Abstract Expressionism of the 1950s and the Minimalism of the 1960s.

Still, the tradition of representation coexisted with abstract painterly forms, but it was reinvented time and again as it reflected the zeitgeist in which it was

Figure 1.2

A close-up of a digital image displaying its pixels

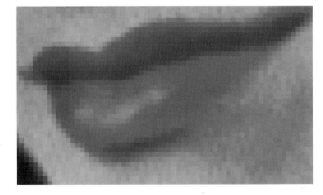

created. Pop Art of the 1960s, for example, introduced us to the idea that the objects and icons of popular culture could be assimilated and even elevated into the realm of "pure art." This concept was revolutionary because it changed the way we viewed the commonplace.

Though the imagery has changed, the painter's tools have remained pretty much the same over the centuries. Paint, palette, knife, brushes, solvent, paper, canvas, panel, and easel have been around for quite some time, having seen few refinements throughout history. (Even the airbrush evolved from an air-driven breath atomizer that has been in use since the eighteenth century.) The concept remains the same: mix colors on the palette, adding solvent if desired, and apply them to the painting surface with a brush or knife. Only recently have methods of applying color to a surface been substantially transformed.

Photoshop is a virtual art studio. Through Photoshop's graphical user interface, you can apply color to an image as if you were painting. Instead of pigment, however, you are mixing colors and painting with light. Photoshop has numerous tools, operations, and filters that enable you to make a photographic image appear as if it had been painted in virtually any style and with any paint medium (see Figure 1.3; for a full-color reproduction of this image, see Figure C1 in the color section). You have 16,777,216 colors to choose from and brushes of almost any size or shape with which to apply the color.

Figure 1.3

A photograph altered to look like a painting by using Photoshop's brushes and filters

PHOTO BY CHRIS MOONEY

Impressionism

In the nineteenth century, in an attempt to revive what was perceived to be the glories of the classical civilization of the Greeks and Romans, much of what was being produced in the art world consisted of the representational, idealized images of the Neoclassic style. In the latter part of the century, the nature of European art shifted. The Impressionist movement emerged with a fresh new approach to painting. Artists such as Claude Monet, Paul Cézanne, and Mary Cassatt produced paintings that were explorations of the quality and nature of light and color.

The importance of the Impressionists' contribution to the way we perceive color cannot be overstated. One particular group of Impressionists, the Pointillists—and particularly Georges Seurat and Paul Signac (see Figure 1.4, which is also Figure C3 in the color section)—most influenced the digital art we practice today. The Pointillists worked extensively with color theory and how one color affects the colors around it. They applied paint to the canvas in units, or little dots, not unlike the pixels on a Photoshop document or the halftone dots on a color separation. They experimented with how the eye mixes adjacent colors. Placing dots of two opposite colors—red and green, for example—next to each other will produce gray when seen from a distance. The relative density of the dots affects the darkness and lightness of the perceived color and its tint.

Pointillism influenced the development of process printing, which uses four colors to produce full-color images. Figure 1.5 presents a close-up view of such a four-color picture (for a color view of this image, see Figure C4 in color section). In

Figure 1.4

Paul Signac, *The Port at Sunset*, Saint-Tropez, Opus 236, 1892

Figure 1.5

Detail of a four-color process image

process printing, each color plate contains tiny dots of cyan, magenta, yellow, or black (CMYK). Like Pointillist painting, the densities of the colored dots on each plate influence the surrounding colors when the eye mixes them together.

Photoshop is the ultimate color separator. It can configure and generate process-color separations, and separate Duotones, Tritones, Quadtones and spot colors. In addition, Photoshop has filters that enable you to simulate Impressionist and other painterly effects.

Printing

Another significant change in the ability to produce images came about a thousand years ago with the emergence of woodcuts, which were used to print textiles. In the early fifteenth century, the use of woodcuts and wood engraving began to take hold in Europe as a method of producing pictures (see Figure 1.6). At about the same time, Johannes Gutenberg introduced the concept of movable type technology. Printing gave us the capability to produce multiples of the same image—the first big step in mass communication.

Of course, the printed image has evolved over the past five hundred years; we've invented numerous methods of imprinting ink on paper, monochromatically or in full color. In the case of traditional offset printing, the process involves separating colors into their ink components and transferring the information to a piece of film and then to a metal plate. The plate is mounted on a printing press where ink is applied to it. The image is transferred (offset) to a rubber blanket mounted on a cylinder which in turn contacts the paper and imprints the image. The process is repeated for each color component.

Figure 1.6

A woodcut from a Venetian edition of the fables of Aesop, published in 1491

Photoshop software is used to prepare images for almost any commercial printing technique, including offset lithography, silk screen, and digital press. Artists even use Photoshop to create and transfer images for traditional copper or zinc intaglio printing.

The most direct method of printing a Photoshop image is to a laser or ink-jet printer, but Photoshop files can also be output to film recorders to generate color slides, to imagesetters to produce high-resolution color separations on film, or directly to the printing plate. Exciting new output technologies have appeared within the last few years to print super-sized ink-jet images and continuous-tone photographic prints.

Photography

When you think of how many centuries passed in which images were created exclusively by hand, you can appreciate how revolutionary the photograph was. A crude type of camera called a camera obscura, which was invented in the beginning of the fourteenth century, captured and projected light on a surface. However, it wasn't until 1826 that the first true photograph was taken. Early photographers needed special equipment and a broad knowledge of chemistry to produce photographs (see Figure 1.7). As a result of the scientific and technical discoveries of the 19th and 20th centuries, cameras became more efficient and easier to operate. Now, millions of still photographs are taken and processed every day.

Figure 1.7

Lady Clemintina Hawarden, photograph of a model, 1860

A camera is very much like the human eye. Light rays enter a camera and are focused on a surface into an image. Film rests on the surface and is exposed, causing a chemical reaction. The exposed film is then bathed in certain chemicals in a process called developing. If the film is a negative, light passes through it onto a piece of photosensitive paper. The paper is developed, stopped, and fixed, producing a positive photographic image.

Several tools, filters, and operations are specially designed to make the photographer feel right at home in the digital Photoshop environment. In fact, Photoshop is a virtual darkroom that includes tools to dodge, burn, saturate, enlarge, crop, mask, and, of course, correct and adjust color. New digital printers are available that focus laser light on photosensitive materials to produce continuous-tone color prints and transparencies.

As a result of the popularity of computer programs such as Adobe Photoshop, digital cameras have become a recent addition to photo technology. Digital cameras create pictures that can be transferred to a computer or television set. The digital camera's lens focuses light on a light-sensitive mechanism, either a charge-coupled device (CCD), or to the newer complementary metal-oxide semiconductor (CMOS) chip. The electronic pictures can then be stored on disks or opened in a computer graphics program. With additional equipment, electronic images can also be sent over telephone lines or printed on paper.

Collage

In the early part of the twentieth century, the artistic revolution in Europe was shocking the world with images that had never before been seen. Instead of representational content, the pictorial sources came from an abstraction of physical reality or the realization of a personal, inner reality. Cubists, Dadaists, and Surrealists changed the face and meaning of art.

Before World War I, the Dada movement produced works of anti-art that deliberately defied reason. Growing principally out of Dada, Surrealism flourished in Europe between the world wars as a visual art and literary movement. Surrealist images had a dreamlike quality—time, space, and matter were completely malleable. Compelled by the idea that rational thought and behavior had brought the world close to the brink of annihilation, the Surrealists created images that were anti-rational and anti-bourgeois. Surrealist painters such as Jean Arp, Max Ernst, Salvador Dalí, Paul Delvaux, René Magritte, André Masson, Joan Miró, and Yves Tanguy created new worlds where the nature of reality depended only on the artist's unlimited imagination.

Hand in hand with this new aesthetic freedom came new image technologies. For artists concerned with the free association of images and the meaningful relation of unrelated objects, collage was the technique of choice. The recycling of printed graphics and text in the form of collage was developed to accommodate the Surrealists' need to create the visual non sequitur. For the first time, printed images from multiple sources were combined to produce a new pictorial reality. The Surrealist Max Ernst created a book called *Une semaine de bonté* (*A Week of Kindness*), a pictorial novel consisting entirely of recycled engravings from newspapers, magazines, and catalogs. This novel was a technical and aesthetic tour de force when it was published in 1933. It epitomized and refined the absurdist viewpoint of the Surrealists and the freedom and creativity in which they pursued their artistic vision.

Photomontage

New movements in art and graphic design blossomed in Europe in the 1920s and 1930s as a result of the instability brought about by the aftermath of World War I, the Great Depression, and the Russian Revolution. Constructivism, New Typography, Streamline, and Dada recycled photographic images, typography, and graphics as collage elements in a new process called photomontage.

Radical magazines and newspapers from the period, for example, *Simplicicimus, Der Knuppel,* and *Arbeiter-Illustrierte Zeitung* (*AIZ,* or *Worker's Illustrated Times*), published photomontage images as satirical cartoons to promote a socialist or anti-fascist political agenda. *Photomontage* is a collage of photographs that are carefully cut and pasted together to create a new visual reality. Often, type and other graphic elements are incorporated into the composition. These images synthesized the seamless pictorial realities of multiple photographic images into biting political metaphors and clever visual puns. Traditional cut-and-paste photomontage was an art form derived from the Cubist, Dadaist, and Surrealist movements, but was displayed in the commercial venue of magazine publications. It was the predecessor of the digital composite images we see in many of today's advertisements.

The ability to combine photographs, text, and graphics from multiple sources is one of Photoshop's strongest features. Images can be collected from a scanner, digital camera, or Photo CD, and be composited, superimposed, positioned, scaled, flipped, rotated, and distorted. In Photoshop, almost any effect is possible; the only limitation is your imagination.

The Web

Recently, the world has been transformed by a powerful new invention. This new communication technology is as revolutionary as the telephone and as ubiquitous as the automobile. Within a few years, it has embedded itself deeply in our lives and has affected how we communicate and how we do business. The World Wide Web (see Figure 1.8) is by far the most accessible communication medium in which to publish images or text. As a research tool, the Web gives us instant access to every conceivable form of information. The Web is the ultimate technical manifestation of democracy in that it embodies the essence of free speech and freedom of the press. Being the most unregulated of all publishing mediums, anyone can publish anything at any time.

Figure 1.8

An Adobe Web page

The Web has changed the nature of how we handle pictures. Images can be transmitted electronically and downloaded, making access to them almost instantaneous, even at a distance. Many art museums and libraries have placed digital files of their entire archives online, making them accessible to everyone. If you need a picture of a particular subject, the first and last place to look is now the Web.

Many tools and functions introduced with recent upgrades of Photoshop have been devoted to Web publishing. Methods for choosing, optimizing, and saving files in the appropriate format have been seamlessly integrated into the program, eliminating all guesswork. The Color Picker offers the choice of Web-compatible hexadecimal colors. ImageReady, which is bundled with Photoshop, empowers you to create dynamic Web pages that can include slices, hypertext, rollovers, and animations. This latest version of ImageReady provides new features like the ability to save documents in Flash (SWF) format, and a new Tables palette.

Photoshop

The introduction of new artistic idioms into our culture not only affects the world of art galleries and museums; it influences advertising, architecture, industrial design, and fashion. As new styles appear on the scene through commercial vehicles, they become an integral part of our everyday lives. The same is true of new image technologies: as new ones are introduced, they become embedded into the production cycle of our economy.

In our contemporary culture, images are everywhere. Pick up a book, magazine, or newspaper, and images dominate the layout. Take a walk or drive, and you'll see images on billboards, signs, and the sides of buildings. These pictures are the result of the work performed by artists, designers, illustrators, and photographers. The legacy of image technology is the primary influence on the images we see today. Its evolution has given us the foundation to create and manipulate images to visually communicate ideas in personal, commercial, or artistic venues.

Never in the history of art have we seen anything quite like Adobe Photoshop. Never has one single tool, studio, or machine combined so many powerful methods of working with images. Photoshop is the culmination of the development of image technology over thousands of years. It is a revolutionary new way of visually communicating ideas. It unites the vision of the artist with the technology of the moment. Since its first release, it has been the world's most popular imaging software, because it endows its users with so many possibilities for the creation and development of images for any form of publication. Photoshop presents those possibilities in the elegant, user-friendly environment of the virtual art studio, darkroom, or print shop, where images can be created and edited in almost any conceivable size, content, or configuration.

CHAPTER 2

What's New in Photoshop CS

One of the most important concepts of this new version of Photoshop is that it is part of a group of tools known as the Creative Suite, hence the *CS* after its name. Other Adobe products that are included in the standard edition are ImageReady, InDesign, Illustrator, and Version Cue (the premium edition of the Creative Suite adds GoLive and Acrobat. These programs are designed to work together to enable you to utilize tools for any publishing goals.

Photoshop CS is the cornerstone application of the Creative Suite, and it has been endowed with upgrades for superior image-editing capabilities and streamlined work flow. This chapter will cover new features such as:

- **System requirements**
- **File Browser improvements**
- **Photography features**
- **Video enhancements**
- **Design productivity upgrades**
- **Automation advancements**
- **Web tools**

System Requirements

The following lists indicate the hardware and operating system requirements for Windows and Macintosh:

Windows

- Windows 2000 with Service Pack 3, or Windows XP
- Intel Pentium III or Pentium 4 processor
- 192 MB of RAM (256 MB or more recommended)
- 280 MB of available hard-disk space
- Color monitor with 16-bit or greater video card
- 1024×768 or greater monitor resolution
- CD-ROM drive
- Internet or phone connection required for product activation

Macintosh

- Mac OSX 10.2.4 or higher
- PowerPC processor (G3, G4, or G5)
- 192 MB of RAM (256 MB or more recommended)
- 320 MB of available hard-disk space
- Color monitor with 16-bit or greater video card
- 1024×768 or greater monitor resolution
- CD-ROM drive

Adobe's minimum requirement of 192 MB of RAM is enough to launch and run the program, but its performance will be clunky. Purchase and install as much memory as you can. After you've installed the memory, be sure to allocate it to Photoshop.

File Browser

The File Browser (see Figure 2.1) has many new features that make locating and processing your images much easier. This is a next-generation version rather than a simple cosmetic update. The new features are as follows:

- A new button on the Options bar opens or closes the File Browser.
- The File Browser now has its own menu bar and toolbar.

- A customizable tabbed palette interface includes folders, preview, metadata, and keywords.
- The preview options have been upgraded.
- You can flag and unflag items for viewing and selecting.
- You can drag images in the File Browser to manually regroup them, as if your images were on a light box.
- You can apply actions and automations to images, including supported Camera Raw files.
- You can edit image metadata in the File Browser and you can apply saved metadata to multiple images.
- You can search for files via keywords.
- You can specify Favorites and Recent images in the File Browser.

Photography Features

Photoshop CS introduces these enhanced features that support the needs of photographers:

16-bit Editing   Most features now work on 16-bit images.

Camera Raw Support   The plug-in that supported Raw files made with professional digital cameras has been integrated into the program. Camera Raw settings can be applied to images selected in the File Browser.

Figure 2.1

The new File Browser contains many new features.

Camera Raw supports a wider range of cameras and has controls to create profiles to anticipate color shifts caused by unusual lighting situations.

Histogram Palette This new context-sensitive palette (see Figure 2.2) enables you to see brightness information on the fly with views of the histograms of individual color channels, before and after adjustment comparisons, and cached and uncached versions.

Match Color Feature You can sample color from one selection, layer, or an entire document and apply it to another selection, layer, or document.

Lens Blur Filter This new filter produces the effect of a narrow depth of field so that some areas are in focus while other areas are blurred. The highlights of a photo can conform to the shape of a variety of camera's lens iris.

Shadow/Highlight Correction This new adjustment feature (see Figure 2.3) can be used to correct silhouetted images that are backlit or images that are washed out by a camera's flash. It's also useful for brightening up areas of shadow in an otherwise well-lit image.

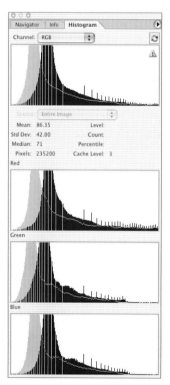

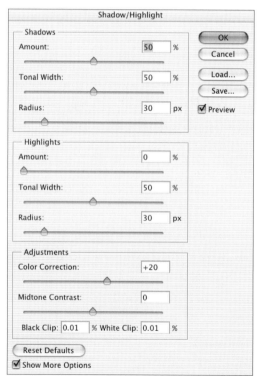

Figure 2.2

The context sensitive Histogram palette can display the changes to your image's individual channel information.

Figure 2.3

The Shadow/Highlight adjustment feature can correct backlit or washed out images.

Photo Filter The Photo Filter simulates colored filters used in traditional photography for color balance and color temperature. You can apply a preset color or you can specify a color from the Color Picker.

Replace Color Brush By using the Replace Color command, you can select specific colors in an image and replace them with hue, saturation, or brightness of the foreground color.

Video Features

Enhanced video features have been added to Photoshop's editing capabilities:

- Photoshop supports a variety of video formats and aspect ratios.
- Non-square ratio documents can be created in Photoshop's New dialog box.
- Photoshop automatically modifies the appearance and behavior of shapes, text, and brushes.
- The Pixel Aspect Correction feature simulates the appearance of non-square pixels but enables you to retain the proportion of common geometric shapes such as circles and squares.
- The New Document dialog box contains video-sized presets that control the document aspect ratio.

Design and Production Features

Photoshop CS features many new design and production tools that increase efficiency and accelerate work flow. They include:

Customizable Keyboard Shortcuts Custom Keyboard commands can be assigned to menu items and palette commands. You can print out the shortcuts to a list as a reference.

Text Enhancements You can put text on or inside of a path, (see Figure 2.4) and you can drag the insertion point of the text to change its position on the path.

Layer Comps Make multiple versions of your documents from its visible layers. Comps can be updated, renamed, or reverted.

Brush Tool Enhancements You can lock brushes. Brushes work on 16-bit images.

Metadata Features You can attach metadata to files. You can log your editing history to files and/or text files and print it. Included in Photoshop and ImageReady is the new Adobe-Standard File Info dialog box, which enables you to create custom File Info panels. Encrypted documents can contain unencrypted (read-only) Portable Document File (PDF) metatags.

Figure 2.4

You can now insert text directly on or inside of a path.

New Resampling Methods for Sizing Bicubic Sharper and Bicubic Smoother sizing algorithms are designed to produce better results when you increase or decrease the size of an image.

Layers Palette The enhanced Layers palette supports up to five levels of nested layer sets.

Increased Automation

Photoshop CS increases the power of automation to speed your work:

Photo Merge This new automation creates seamless panoramas from multiple images.

Crop and Straighten Photos This new File → Automate command looks for rectangular regions in a document, crops them, straightens them, and duplicates them into multiple documents. It's designed to quickly make separate documents from images that have been batch-scanned.

PDF Presentation You can save two or more images to multiple-page PDF files or create an automatic slide presentation complete with cool graphic transitions.

Web Photo Gallery New templates have been added to this automation.

Picture Package Enhancements You have the option of placing images from different sources on the same page. You can choose from a variety of new size and layout options for a picture package or create a custom picture package layout. See Figure 2.5.

Figure 2.5

The Picture package automation is fully customizable.

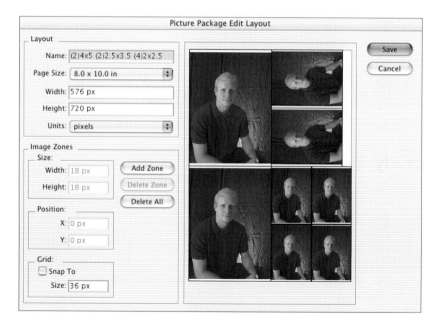

Other New Photoshop Features

Among the new features in Photoshop are a variety of items that make image editing easier and more user-friendly:

- A new welcome screen that gives you access to tutorials, and information about tips and tricks, color management, and new features by accessing both local and online links.

- The Healing Brush can now heal to transparent layers.

- The Patch tool source option now includes a live preview.

- You can create large format documents, up to 300,000 pixels in width and height, and up to a 4 GB file size.

- You can save document size presets to the New dialog box.

- An image can be moved in Full Screen mode.

- Photoshop supports up to 56 channels per document.

- You can "scrub" tool and palette values (for example, layer opacity) by clicking the label and dragging it left or right. Pressing the Shift key enables you to accelerate the value change by a factor of 10.

- Pressing the Shift key while scrolling or zooming will scroll or zoom all open documents.

- New Arrange options enable you to Match Zoom, Match Location, and Match Zoom And Location of all open documents.

- In the Window menu, palettes are organized alphabetically. Open documents are listed at the bottom of the menu.

- The new Filter Gallery (Figure 2.6) displays thumbnails of the results of the application of a filter. There is also a control panel and preview window.

- New filters include Render → Fibers and Blur → Average.

Image Ready Web Enhancements

New Web enhancements have been added to ImageReady, Photoshop's sidekick Web-authoring software. ImageReady is bundled with Photoshop and can be accessed by clicking the Edit In icon at the bottom of Photoshop's Tool palette.

User object-based interface enhancements

- Multiple objects can be selected on the canvas or on multiple layers by clicking the Direct Select mode button.

- Multiple objects can be grouped.

Figure 2.6

The filter gallery previews the effects of single or multiple filters.

- You can make noncontiguous selections on multiple layers by pressing ⌘/Ctrl.
- You can drag to select multiple objects.
- You can drag multiple layers to the trash simultaneously.
- You can drag layer and vector masks from one layer to another.
- Font settings of multiple text objects can be applied simultaneously.
- You can align selected objects or layers from the Options bar or with menu commands.

Streamlined performance

- Tools that are not used for Web production and are redundant with Photoshop have been eliminated.
- The enhanced Edit In (previously Jump To) command displays only the Photoshop or ImageReady document at one time.
- Edit In → ImageReady is in the Photoshop File menu and File Browser to increase its accessibility.

Flash export

- You can save to SWF Export for export to flash files.
- Vector information of text saved in SWF format is preserved.
- SWFs from ImageReady can contain dynamic text including embedded fonts.

Export layers

- You can save individual layers and layer sets as files.
- When saving, you can specify individual formats for individual layers.
- You can specify individual compression settings for each layer.

Enhanced tables

- The new Table palette (Figure 2.7) controls border, padding, and spacing values.
- Individual table cells can be specified in pixels or percent so that they will expand in a browser.
- You can specify how ImageReady generates HTML to favor COLSPAN or ROWSPAN settings.

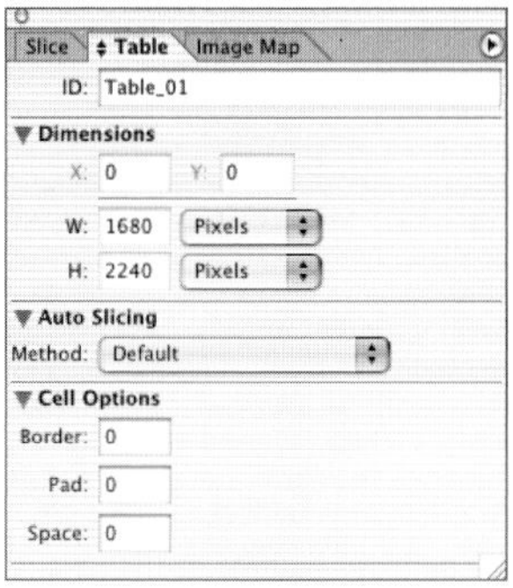

Figure 2.7

Image Ready's table palette enables you to easily define an HTML table.

MY FAVORITE NEW FEATURES

In the writing of this book I had the opportunity to test out all of the new features in the latest versions of Photoshop and ImageReady. I found that most of these features really improved the performance of the programs. I particularly like the Filter Gallery because it eliminates the guess work in the application of multiple filters—no more fiddling around with filter settings. It's presented in an elegant interface that quickly previews the results of filter combinations.

I've used the Crop and Straighten automation numerous times and believe me, it is a real time saver. I also like the new Picture Package Layout Editor for creating custom layouts. In the past, I spent a lot of time matching colors from one document to the other using the old Hue/Saturation workaround that was time consuming and produced dubious results. The new Match color dialog box is a godsend. It simplifies the process and greatly improves the results.

I like the Layer comps feature for the ability to quickly review multiple versions of a document. The File → Scripts command that automatically exports Layers to multiple documents, saves Layer comps to Files, PDF presentations, or to a fully interactive Web Gallery are excellent automations. I've created dozens of new key commands too and printed a list that I have attempted to memorize.

I think that you'll find that this upgrade of Photoshop is more than just a cosmetic facelift. Its automations can liberate you from many repetitive tasks. Its new or enhanced commands can endow you with more precision and unleash your creativity.

Improved rollovers and slices

- You can apply rollovers to an individual slice or you can apply them to multiple slices.

- You can create multiple slice sets in a document.

- Individual slice visibility can be toggled on and off. Invisible slices are not saved to HTML documents.

- Slices can be cut, copied, and pasted.

Better metadata

- You can embed metadata to GIFs, JPEGs, and PNGS.

- You can create "sidecar" metadata files to reduce file size.

Faster work flow

- ImageReady supports conditional logic in Actions. With the new Insert A Step button in the Actions palette, you can program an Action to scan for certain image characteristics and apply the Action only if the images meet the criteria.

- You can save your output settings to multiple files by using File → Output Settings.

CHAPTER 3

The Nature of the Beast

In order for Photoshop to maintain its position as the grand kahuna of all image-editing software, it needs frequent upgrades. Adobe's new release of Photoshop, currently in its eighth iteration, coincides with cutting-edge advances in digital photography and Web authoring. I think you'll find that there are several new whistles and bells that make the upgrade worthwhile (refer to Chapter 2, "What's new in Photoshop CS" for the full list).

Photoshop CS runs seamlessly on Mac OS X and Windows XP. It no longer runs on Mac OS 9 or Windows 98 or earlier. However, all the components of Photoshop 7 remain intact; the upgrade has either added to or improved those features. Users who were comfortable in 7 will feel even more at home in CS.

But Photoshop is not a soft and fuzzy program. It's big, it's powerful, and it will do almost anything for you if you ask it nicely. Before you jump into the world of Photoshop headfirst, you should understand its temperament. In this chapter, you'll learn about:

- **The anatomy of a digital image: vector and raster images**
- **Color channels**
- **Working wisely in Photoshop**
- **Opening, saving, and duplicating documents**
- **File formats and compatibility**

The Anatomy of a Digital Image

Graphics software uses two fundamentally different methods to construct images. First, vector graphics consist of objects constructed by mathematically defined points and curves. And second, raster images use a grid of squares, or pixels, to determine color variations.

Understanding Vector Graphics

Vector graphics use lines and objects to define their shapes. On a computer, you can draw hard-edged graphics that, when printed, produce clean, sharp lines and edges. This is particularly valuable for illustrators who want to create crisp, well-defined artwork. Vector software is also ideal for graphic designers who work with type, because type characters need razor-sharp edges with no "jaggies" (stair-step edges caused by a series of right angles trying to represent a curve).

Vector-based illustration software (such as Adobe Illustrator, Macromedia FreeHand, and CorelDRAW) and page-layout programs (such as QuarkXPress, Adobe PageMaker, and Adobe InDesign) are sometimes referred to as *object-oriented* software, because the primary technique requires building independent graphic lines or shapes ("objects") point by point, segment by segment, and stacking and arranging them until your drawing or page is complete.

To draw these objects, the artist uses a method of clicking and dragging the mouse, which deposits points, line segments, or shapes. The objects created in vector-based software are made from *Bezier curves,* like the ones in Figure 3.1. Bezier curves can even be straight lines, but what makes them different from the pixels used by raster images is that that they are composed of mathematically defined points and segments.

One advantage of using vectors is that the images are *resolution-independent,* which means that they automatically conform to the highest resolution of the output device on which they are printed, whether it's a desktop ink-jet, a laser printer, or a high-resolution imagesetter.

Because the data of vector-based images involves mathematical equations, a printer can read the formulas of each object transmitted in a printer language and convert the information into tiny dots. An image that is created at the size of a postage stamp can be resized and printed at the size of a billboard with no loss of quality. The complexity of a vector image, not its physical size, determines the file size; therefore, vector images take up much less space on a disk than raster images of comparable dimensions. Figure 3.2 shows raster and vector versions of the same image. The image on the left is composed of pixels; the image on the right is composed of objects surrounded by anchor points and line segments that define Bezier curves. The Bezier curves do not print. (See a color version of this image, as Figure C2, in the color section.)

Figure 3.1

Bezier curves

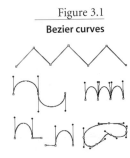

Figure 3.2

A raster image composed of pixels (left) and a vector version of the same image, composed of shapes constructed from Bezier curves (right)

Object-oriented software extends your capability to produce high-impact color graphics. Vector-based illustration software is appropriate for the creation of traditional logos, charts, graphs, maps, cartoons, highly detailed technical and architectural plans, and illustrations and images that require hard edges, smooth blends, and sumptuous color. Vector-based page-layout software is ideal for creating documents in which images and text are combined, as in books, pamphlets, brochures, and flyers.

Understanding Raster Images

Although Photoshop CS uses vector-based graphics in several of its operations (see the upcoming sidebar titled "Vector Tools in Photoshop"), it is primarily designed to edit

Figure 3.3

A close-up detail of an image composed of pixels

raster images. *Raster images,* sometimes called *bitmaps,* are fundamentally different from vector images in that they consist of a grid of little squares called pixels.

A *pixel* (short for *pixel element*) is an individual square of colored light and is the smallest editable unit in a digital image. Pixels are usually so small that, when seen on a monitor, their colors blend into what appears to be a continuous-tone image. Figure 3.3 is enlarged so you see the individual pixels that make up an image's overall effect.

VECTOR TOOLS IN PHOTOSHOP

Although Photoshop is primarily designed to select and edit pixels, it does offer several vector tools. The Pen tool, for example, uses Bezier curves to make accurate selections. Its operation is similar to the Pen tool in Adobe Illustrator. After you've created a curve or path, you can stroke or fill it, convert it into a selection for raster editing, or export it to a vector-based program. (The Pen tool is discussed in detail in Chapter 9, "Drawing Paths.")

The Photoshop Type tool creates type generated from your installed fonts. The type remains editable until you rasterize it or "flatten" the image. This tool is extremely powerful for creating display text and special text effects, and a new feature of Photoshop CS even enables you to enter text on a path. But it is not really designed to produce body copy (which usually is 12 points or smaller) on most documents. It is better to import your Photoshop image into a vector-based illustration or layout program and generate the body copy there. You'll find that you have more tools at your disposal and your file sizes will be much smaller. (See Chapter 8, "Working with Type," for more on the Type tool.)

Photoshop's Shape tools (described in Chapter 9) can also generate vectors. With these tools you can create standard shapes, such as rectangles, ellipses, and polygons, or you can construct, edit, and store custom vector-based shapes.

The quality of a raster image and how well it prints depend on the number of pixels the image contains, or its *resolution.* If you think of a pixel as the basic building block of an image, you can envision how a larger number of smaller blocks will define an edge or an area more precisely than fewer, larger blocks. The file sizes of raster images are usually quite large compared to other types of computer-generated documents, because information needs to be stored for every pixel in the entire document.

Raster-based software is best suited for editing, manipulating, and compositing scanned images; images from digital cameras and Photo CDs; continuous-tone photographs; realistic illustrations; hyperreal artwork including logos with subtle blends, soft edges, or shadow effects; and artistic filter effects such as impressionist or watercolor.

Color Channels

When you acquire an image, the color information that the scanner "sees" is separated into red, green, and blue components. Photoshop configures this information into a red, green, and blue color channel plus a composite RGB channel, which displays the entire image in full color. Think of each color channel as a separate, transparent color overlay consisting of red, green, or blue pixels. The combination of the three color values, when superimposed over each other, produces full color.

The channels can contain 256 possible shades of either red, green, or blue, because each pixel on the channel contains 8 bits of tonal information (see the upcoming sidebar titled "Bit Depth"). The computer processes the information in each channel as an independent grayscale image. Each pixel is assigned a specific numerical value, where the darkest shade (black) equals 0 and the lightest shade (white) equals 255.

By default, individual color channels are displayed in grayscale because the subtle variations in contrast are easier to see when looking at the channel in black-and-white. You can, however, see the independent components of an image in color. To see your channels in color follow these steps:

1. Choose Window → Channels.

2. Choose Photoshop (Mac)/Edit (Win) → Preferences → Display & Cursors.

3. In the Display options check the Color Channels In Color box.

4. In the Channels palette, click the thumbnail of the red, green, or blue color channel to display that color component of the image on-screen.

Working in Photoshop

If you think about it, the computer is really a megacalculator that crunches numbers at lightning speed. The graphical user interface, or GUI (pronounced "gooey"), of a raster software program such as Photoshop lets you perform virtual operations that mimic real-world tasks such as painting, compositing, or filtering. But what is actually happening behind the scenes is that the numeric color values of the pixels in each color channel are being changed.

Photoshop works as an image editor, color corrector, and photo compositor, but by no means is it limited to these tasks. Its primary purpose is to alter reality, and that is the ultimate reason for its popularity. There is something very compelling and empowering about changing the color of the sky in a landscape or replacing Uncle Herman's scowl with a smile from another photograph.

No matter how you alter an image, the sequence of procedures you employ is quite similar:

1. Capture the image by using a device such as a scanner or digital camera. These devices "see" the continuous-tone image and divide the information into pixels, which Photoshop can display and edit.

BIT DEPTH

A computer uses the binary number system to describe pixels. The simplest graphic images are 1 bit "deep." In these files, only 1 binary digit of information describes the pixel: 0 for off, 1 for on. Each pixel is one of two colors, either black or white.

Grayscale and indexed color images use an 8-bit system, in which any pixel can be one of 256 shades of gray or color, respectively. Each pixel contains 8 bits of information. Each bit can be either on (black) or off (white), which produces 256 possible combinations ($2^8 = 256$).

Full-color images are 24-bit color, using three 8-bit primary color channels—for red, green, and blue—each containing 256 colors. These three channels produce a potential 16.7 million colors ($256^3 = 16,777,216$). Photo-realistic images that consist of smooth gradations and subtle tonal variations require 24-bit color to be properly displayed.

Some scanners can produce images of 48-bit color. In this system, the information is being distributed into three 16-bit channels, each with 65,536 possible color combinations ($2^6 = 65,536$). These images can produce trillions of possible colors. Some professionals prefer these high-bit images because they offer an extended dynamic range and enhanced tonal variation. Photoshop can read images with 16 bits of information per channel, for example, a 48-bit RGB or a 64-bit CMYK color image. The file sizes of these images are much larger than 24 bit images. Although prior versions of Photoshop were very limited in their ability to edit high-bit images, the capabilities of this latest release have been greatly improved.

Even though images with higher bit depths contain more color information, they are displayed on the monitor at the bit depth capability of your video card, which in most cases is 24 bits. To see an image in 24-bit color depth on a Macintosh, the monitor should be set to Millions Of Colors; in Windows, the setting should be True Color.

The information from the image that you create in Photoshop is transmitted from the computer to the monitor. A color monitor consists of a grid of screen pixels that are capable of displaying three values of color simultaneously. In a CRT (cathode ray tube) monitor, there are three electron guns inside—a red, a green, and a blue—that scan the surface of the screen and fire streams of electrons at it. (LCD monitors use a different system. See Chapter 15, "Color Management and Printing.") The more electrons that hit the screen pixel, the brighter it glows. When all three guns are firing at full intensity, the screen pixel appears white; when all three guns are not firing, the pixel appears black. The variation of the intensities of red, green, and blue electrons striking the pixels is what produces the full range of color that you see on-screen. Of course, all of this happens much faster than your eye can perceive, so you see a stable image on your monitor.

2. Save the image to a disk. The image is stored on your disk media as a sequence of numbers that represent its pixel information.

3. Open the image in Photoshop and use one of Photoshop's selection techniques to isolate the part of the image that you want to affect. When you make a selection, you are telling Photoshop in advance where you would like to apply an operation.

4. Apply one of Photoshop's numerous tools or operations to the image to implement an edit.

Of course, this sequence can vary and can become extremely complex depending on the application's specialized selection techniques, multiple operations, or sophisticated layer methods, but, generally speaking, this is how you work in the program.

Developing Strategies

Because high-resolution images require large amounts of RAM and processing time, the digital artist or designer should develop a strategy for each job. A good production strategy should focus on four areas:

- Configuring and optimizing your system so that it runs smoothly
- Working wisely and efficiently in Photoshop
- Using shortcuts
- Communicating clearly with your client

Optimizing Your System

The following items are discussed in detail in Chapter 5, "Setting Up the Program," and Chapter 15, "Color Management and Printing," but here are some tips for optimizing your system:

- Increase the application memory.
- Assign the first scratch disk, the disk that stores the data during the editing process, to your fastest hard drive with the most disk space that is usually a secondary drive that is not being used to run the operating system. For the scratch disk, Photoshop requires three to five times the disk space of your largest open file. You can use additional scratch disks to increase the amount of virtual memory.
- Keep the Clipboard clear of large amounts of data.
- Install as much RAM as possible.
- Work on a calibrated system.
- Compress files whenever possible.
- Delete old files, back up data, and regularly optimize and defragment your disk with a program such as Norton Utilities.

Working Wisely

You'll want to keep the following items in mind when you are working in Photoshop. These items are discussed in more detail throughout the book:

- Create a low-resolution version of the document. Lay out the image and experiment with operations and effects. Then apply those same operations to a high-resolution version.
- Save your settings when adjusting color.
- Work on a duplicate of your image (Image → Duplicate) so that you can experiment freely.
- Save selections as paths or alpha channels whenever possible.
- Use layers to segregate parts of the image in order to keep the editing process dynamic.
- Apply filters to each channel individually when necessary.
- Learn default keyboard shortcuts or make custom key commands. Take advantage of the Actions and History palettes, Automations, and Scripting.
- Save tool and brush presets and your workspace by using the Save Workspace feature.
- Save your document often and back up your work.
- Archive your images to CD or other media to free up hard-disk space.

Using Shortcuts

While a good production strategy will smooth your workflow, numerous key commands and shortcut techniques can enhance your performance. In Photoshop, there are several ways to execute almost every operation, which can be confusing at first. Many of the same operations can be performed from a menu, by a key command, or from a palette, field, or button. As you develop knowledge of the program, however, you will begin to fashion a way of working that is unique to your personal style, and it will be only a matter of deciding which method suits you.

The quick-key list in Appendix D gives you a list of Photoshop's default key commands. It pays to learn as many of them as possible, particularly the ones that you use most frequently. Not only will this save you work time, but it can also be physically beneficial to try a new style of operating your computer. Photoshop CS enables you to create customized keyboard shortcuts and assign them to menu items, palette commands, and tools. You can read about this in detail in Chapter 23, "Automating the Process."

Finally, if you work on more than one operating system, be sure to read the section titled "Platform Compatibility" later in this chapter for more on keyboard shortcuts.

TAKING ADVANTAGE OF ACTIONS

You can record a Photoshop Action that you play by pressing a function key or clicking an icon. Actions automate one operation or a sequence of operations, and they enable you to perform multiple tasks quickly. One useful perk is that you can save Actions to a file. When you need a particular Action or Action sequence, you can play it and apply its operations to any image. Photoshop ships with some tasty default Actions that are really convenient to use. You can even run a Batch Action that will be applied to all of the images in a folder while you are sleeping, watching television, or eating a sandwich. For more about Actions, read Chapter 23.

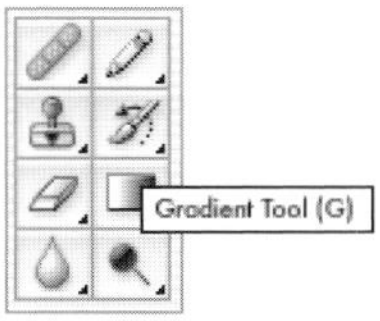

Figure 3.4
Tool labels

ACCESSING TOOLS

Photoshop's numerous tools are accessible by simply touching a letter key on the keyboard. Of course, you have to remember what tool each letter represents. Sometimes it's quite obvious—for example, M for the Marquee tool—but sometimes it's not, as in K for the Paint Bucket tool. Don't worry if you forget a tool's keyboard equivalent. Simply hold your cursor over any tool, and a little label called a *tool tip* will tell you the name of the tool and the key that represents it. As you can see in Figure 3.4, the shortcut key for the History Brush tool is Y.

SAVING ADJUSTMENTS, COLORS, AND BRUSHES

Color adjustment settings can be saved as a separate file and loaded for application to other documents. You can make a brush of virtually any shape, size, hardness, or angle and save it for use in any Photoshop document. You can create and save special Color palettes and apply the colors to any Photoshop image. These techniques are covered in detail in Chapter 10, "Creating and Applying Color," and Chapter 16, "Adjusting Tonality and Color."

Photoshop's interface is so well designed that the processes of saving and loading adjustments, colors, brushes, or Actions are all the same. When you've learned to save or load one, you've learned to save or load them all.

Communicating with Your Clients

Whether you're a professional designing for commercial customers or a volunteer producing images for nonprofits, many of you are using Photoshop to create images for clients. When you're working for a client, the creative process becomes a collaboration. Clear and open communication with your client is essential to maintaining a smooth work flow. Here are some keys to keeping your client satisfied:

- Make sure that you and your client have agreed on the job's objectives and specifications. Show your client your work in stages. Start with thumbnails and develop the project over time, getting your client's approval for each iteration before proceeding with the next. Determine how the finished image will be used. If you are going to output to print, determine film and print specifications such as paper, ink, and halftone screens. If it's going to be output to CD-ROM or the Web, be sure to find out the size and format specifications. Put all the job specifications in writing.

- Determine the nature of the job, what work is to be done, and what third-party vendors will be involved. Will you need to purchase high-end scans, or will desktop scans suffice? Are you responsible for output, or will your clients deal directly with the service bureaus, printers, or Internet providers?

- Define each component of the project and build a realistic schedule around this information. You will then be able to structure your time and make consistent progress on the project.

There are few software programs that end users love as much as Adobe Photoshop! Organizations of aficionados exist throughout the world. The National Association of Photoshop Professionals (NAPP) boasts thousands of members from 64 countries and is one of the largest graphics-related organizations in the world. NAPP holds annual conferences and training seminars in the U.S., the U.K., and several other European countries. See www.photoshopuser.com for more information.

Opening Documents

Most of your work in Photoshop will be performed on images that have been acquired by using some piece of digital technology that converts color information into pixels. After you've captured an image with a scanner or digital camera and stored it to a disk, you can open the file by choosing File → Open, which brings up the dialog box shown in Figure 3.5.

You are presented with a list of files on your disk. Highlight one by clicking it with your mouse. If the Show Preview button is clicked (it then becomes the Hide Preview button), the dialog box displays a thumbnail of the image.

Figure 3.5

The Open dialog box

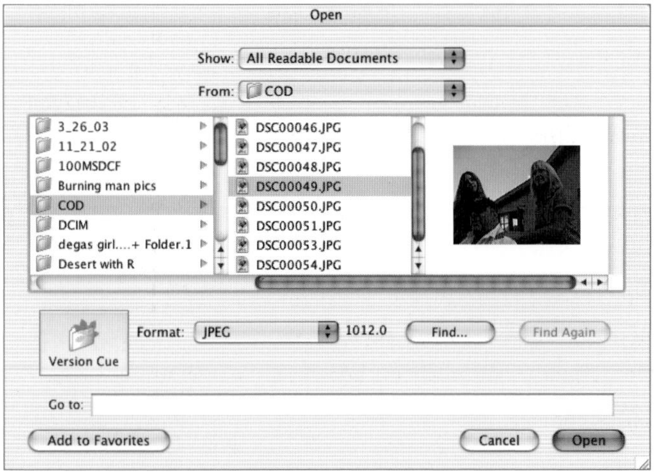

What if you swear that you saved an image to a particular disk, but it does not appear in the list? Well, the Photoshop Open dialog box might not display certain files when it doesn't recognize the file's type. On the Mac, a file's type code is four characters long and can be seen in its Get Info box. On Windows, the file type is represented by the filename extension, which is usually three characters long. For example, TIFF in Mac OS equates to .tif in Windows.

Windows displays a preview at the bottom of the Open dialog box. The Show/Hide Preview option is available only for Mac OS.

To display files regardless of their type code or extension, Macintosh users should select All Documents from the Show options pop-up list; Photoshop attempts to guess at the format in which it thinks the file has been saved. If you think Photoshop has guessed incorrectly, then click the Format options list and choose the correct format (as shown in Figure 3.6). If you get an error message, keep trying. If you've tried all the formats and can't open the image, it is either corrupt or incompatible with Photoshop.

Windows users should click the down arrow in Files Of Type and select All Formats. If the image won't open, try the Open As menu feature instead of the Open command and assign a format. Once again, if you've tried all the formats and can't open the image, it is either corrupt or incompatible with Photoshop.

Finding Files

In Photoshop for Mac OS, the Open command has a Find function built into it. If you can't find the file you're looking for, click the Find button. In the next dialog box, enter all or part of the filename, click Find, and the program will take you to the first item on your disk with the same name. If the Find function displays the wrong file, click the Find Again button until you locate what you're looking for.

Browsing Files

The File Browser provides a more convenient method of accessing files. You can preview the images in a folder or on a disk prior to opening them. To use this elegant feature, follow these steps:

1. Choose File → Browse. The browser window appears, displaying the contents of the selected folder (see Figure 3.7).

2. Choose the desired folder or disk from the drop down list or from the directory at the upper-left of the screen.

3. Click on a thumbnail of an image in the image list to see a larger version of it in the Preview field. The Preview area can be expanded or contracted by dragging its top and bottom borders. The field below the preview presents information about the image.

4. Double-click (Mac) or right-click (Win) an image to open it.

Figure 3.6

The Open dialog's Format list

Photoshop
BMP
Camera Raw
Cineon
CompuServe GIF
Photoshop EPS
Photoshop DCS 1.0
Photoshop DCS 2.0
EPS PICT Preview
EPS TIFF Preview
Filmstrip
JPEG
Large Document Format
Generic PDF
Generic EPS
PCX
Photoshop PDF
Acrobat TouchUp Image
Photo CD
Photoshop 2.0
✓ Photoshop Raw
PICT File
PICT Resource
Pixar
PNG
Scitex CT
Targa
TIFF
Wireless Bitmap

Figure 3.7

The File Browser

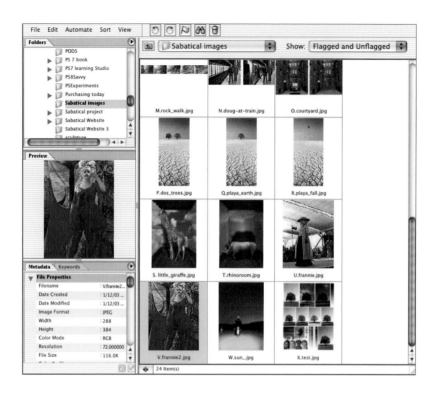

Several useful menu items at the top of the window enable you to access, sort, view, organize, rotate, and apply automated operations to your files. Many are redundant commands found in the main Photoshop interface. The File Browser's menu items are as follows:

File The items in the File Browser's File menu perform global operations to the files on your disk—including opening and searching capabilities, creating and deleting images and folders, closing files and images, and caching functions. These items are pretty self-explanatory except for the caching functions.

The Cache The cache stores thumbnail and file information to make loading times quicker when you return to a folder that you have previously viewed. The File menu contains commands to build a cache for the subfolders within a specific folder. You can also export a cache, which enables you to burn a CD without having to create thumbnails. To export the cache, choose Export Cache from the File menu. The cache is exported to the current folder in the File Browser. Purging the cache frees up disk space; choose Purge Cache from the File menu to purge a subfolder cache or choose Purge Entire Cache to purge all contents of the cache.

Edit The File Browser's Edit menu performs tasks that flag, rank, or rotate an image in the list. You can also access metadata from this menu or from the tab at the bottom of the File Browser display. Metadata describes the properties of the image.

Automate You can apply automations and batch Actions from this menu.

Sort Choose an option from this menu to organize the order in which the images are displayed in the File Browser.

View This menu lets you choose the types of files or folders that are displayed and the size of thumbnails. You can choose Details to reveal information about the image next to its thumbnail in the browser, as shown in Figure 3.8.

Figure 3.8 identifies the functions of the small icons to the right of the Browser's menu items.

At the bottom of the File Browser are the Metadata and Keywords tabs. The Metadata tab displays information about your images, including file properties, IPTC—the International Press Telecommunications Council that identifies text and images transmitted over the wire and the type of digital camera used to capture the image. When the Metadata tab is selected, the Options submenu to the right enables you to search for images and adjust font specifications of the File Browser's text. See Figure 3.9.

The Keywords tab enables you to attach keywords to an image to enhance your search capabilities.

Importing a Scanned Image

Scanner software often has a plug-in module that will work directly within Photoshop to scan an image. The module must be placed in the `Plug-Ins` folder in the `Adobe Photoshop CS` folder when the scanner software is installed. In most instances, the plug-in will automatically be placed in the `Plug-Ins` folder when it is installed. Choose File → Import to access the module. After the image is scanned, it will automatically appear in a new Photoshop window. (For more on this, see Chapter 14, "Capturing Images.")

Figure 3.8

**The File Browser
with the View →
Details option
selected**

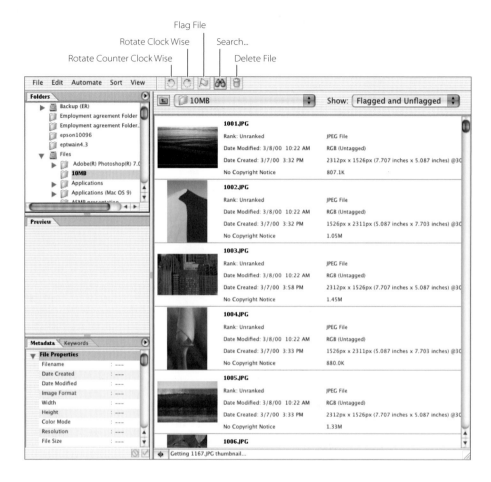

Creating New Documents

There are two ways to determine the size and specifications of a New Document in Photoshop. One is a blank canvas whose size is determined by entering or choosing preset specifications in the New document window. The other is from an image copied to the Clipboard.

Determining New Document Specifications

You can generate a new, empty document in Photoshop with specific characteristics that can be used as a blank canvas on which to paint or paste images from other sources.

To create a new document, follow these steps:

1. Choose File → New. The New dialog box (shown in Figure 3.10) appears.

2. In the Name field, type a name for the document, but remember that naming the document is not the same as saving it. Eventually you will need to save it to your disk.

3. On the bottom right of the menu, the image size in bytes is displayed. This will change depending on the height, width, resolution, and color mode you choose for the document. Enter a width and a height in the appropriate units or choose a preset size from the drop down list.

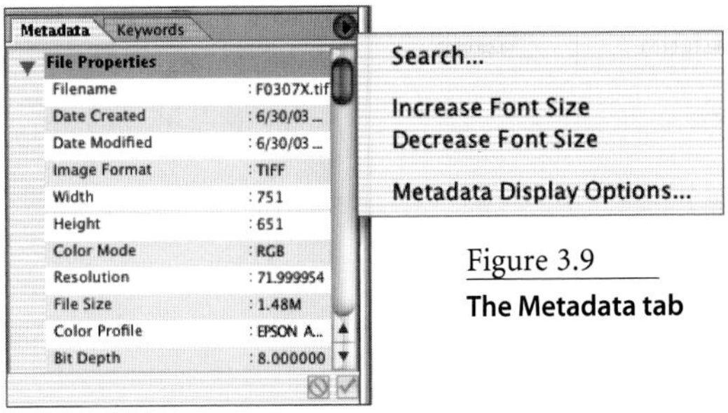

4. Type in the resolution of the document. This will depend on how the document will be output. (See Chapter 13, "Sizing and Transforming Images.")

5. Choose a mode from the Color Mode list, which indicates how the color information of the new document will be configured. Use Bitmap for line art and Grayscale for black-and-white images with tonality. RGB (red, green, blue), CMYK (cyan, magenta, yellow, and black), and Lab (Lightness, a, and b) modes will produce full-color images. (See Chapter 10 for more on color modes.)

6. In the Background Contents list, indicate the color of the background. You can choose White or choose the current background color in the Tool palette; these settings will produce a flattened image. If you choose Transparent, the background will become a regular layer (with a checkerboard pattern to indicate transparency), because the background cannot be transparent (see Chapter 7, "Layering Your Image").

7. Click OK.

The Photoshop CS New dialog box displays a menu (shown in Figure 3.10) with preset sizes, including standard image sizes for letter, legal, and tabloid paper, as well as metric ISO A sizes and typical pixel-size documents for display on monitors and the Web. Also, you can choose to match the size of any open document on the desktop by choosing it from the list, like the leafy_greens.jpg image.

Figure 3.9

The Metadata tab

Figure 3.10

The New dialog box

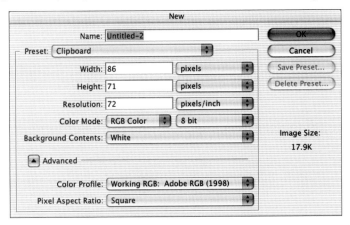

The Advanced mode in the New dialog box is new to Photoshop CS. To access it click the arrow next to the word Advanced. The dialog box will expand, displaying the features that enable you to assign a color profile to a new image (see Chapter 15, "Color Management and Printing). You can also choose a pixel aspect ratio for special video applications.

Also new to Photoshop CS is the ability to save and load a preset size from the New dialog box. To create a preset sized document follow these steps:

Choose File New, or press ⌘/Ctrl-N to display the New document window.

Enter the values for the height, width, resolution, color mode, and background contents for the new document. If desired, choose a color profile and if you're working on an image for digital video, choose a pixel aspect ratio.

Click the Save Preset button and the New Document Preset dialog box appears (Figure 3.11). The preset will be named the width and height of the document that you determined in the New dialog box. Check the features of the new document that you wish to preserve and click OK. The new name will now appear in the Preset list.

To Omit a preset, choose it from the Preset list and click the Delete Preset button.

Creating a Document from the Clipboard

You can create a document window from an image that has been copied to the Clipboard. To perform this operation, follow these steps:

1. Make a selection with one of the selection tools or choose Select → All to select the entire contents of a document.

2. Choose Edit → Copy to copy an image or the contents of a selection to the Clipboard.

3. Choose File → New. From the Preset list, choose Clipboard. Photoshop automatically displays a New Document dialog box with the dimensions of the copied image and its color mode.

4. Click OK. The new image window appears.

5. Choose Edit → Paste, and the image is pasted into the new document.

Saving Files

There are six methods for saving a Photoshop document to a disk—Save As, Save As A Copy, Save, Export → Paths To Illustrator, Save For Web, and the new Save A Version—which you can find in the File menu. They are affected by the options set under Edit → Preferences → File Handling (see Chapter 5). A description of each method follows.

Saving As

Use File → Save As to save your document to a designated location on your disk. You can name the document and choose a format for it. The newly named file will replace the document in the active window. These options are in the Save As dialog box (see Figure 3.12).

Checking or unchecking the boxes in the Save field of the Save As dialog box enables you to configure the document to your particular needs.

As A Copy When you select check As A Copy, the document is saved to a designated location on your disk but does not appear in the image window. Be sure to rename it so as not to replace the current image.

> Selecting the As A Copy option creates a new, identical document that is identical to the original. If you save as a copy with the same name to the same location, you replace the original file, defeating the make-two-versions purpose of the command and essentially just performing a plain save. Be sure to rename the file because it is possible to replace the previous document.

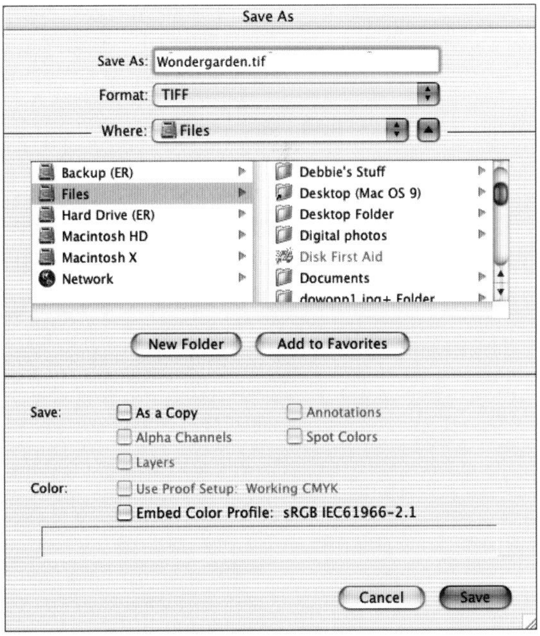

Alpha Channels If you're saving an image that contains alpha channels to a format that supports alpha channels, this box will be active. Formats that support alpha channels are Photoshop (PSD), Photoshop PDF, PICT, PICT Resource (Mac format only), Pixar, Raw, Targa, TIFF, and Photoshop DCS 2.0. JPEG 2000 (JPF) and Large Document Format. (See Chapter 12, "Using Alpha Channels and Quick Mask.")

Layers If you're saving an image that contains layers to a format that supports layers—TIFF, Photoshop PDF, or Photoshop (PSD) and for Large Document Format (PSB)— this box will be active. (See Chapter 7.)

Annotations If you've attached notes to your document with the Notes tool, you can include them in the saved version by checking the Annotation check box. Photoshop (PSD), Photoshop PDF, and TIFF are the only formats that support annotations. (See Chapter 4, "Navigation: Know Where to Go.")

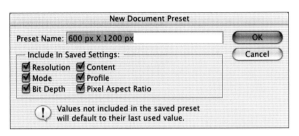

Figure 3.11

The New Document Preset dialog box

Figure 3.12

The Save As dialog box

Spot Colors Spot color channels can be saved by checking this box. Formats that support spot color are Photoshop (PSD), Photoshop PDF, TIFF, and Photoshop DCS 2.0. (See Chapter 18, "Duotones and Spot Color.")

The check boxes in the Color field of the Save As dialog box determine whether color management information will be saved with the document. (See Chapter 15.)

Use Proof Setup A soft proof is an on-screen document that appears as close as possible to what the image will look like if printed to a specific device. If you are saving the image as a Photoshop EPS, Photoshop PDF, or Photoshop DCS 1.0 or 2.0, you can convert the document to the soft proof profile, which you choose from the View → Proof Setup menu. (See Chapter 15.)

Embed Color Profile (Mac)/ICC Profile (Win) Checking this box embeds the RGB, CMYK, or grayscale profile currently in use for this image. You can select this option if you're saving to Photoshop (PSD), Photoshop PDF, JPEG, TIFF, EPS, DCS, or PICT formats. (See Chapter 15.)

Saving

Saving a document (File → Save) updates the file that you are working on and saves it to the current document. When working in Photoshop—or any software, for that matter—it is always a good idea to save frequently so you won't lose valuable time and effort should your system crash.

Saving for the Web

This option (File → Save For Web) was introduced in version 5.5 and serves as a convenient tool for preparing files for Web publication. On the Web, as in life, there is always a compromise between quality and speed. When you choose Save For Web, you choose the best combination of format characteristics for Web images (see Figure 3.13). You can compare the appearance and download times of up to four possible configurations for your image at a time. The Save For Web option is covered in detail in Chapter 26, "Web Design with Photoshop and ImageReady."

Version Cue

Adobe Version Cue is a group of features that manage files for increased productivity. Version Cue integrates the Adobe Creative Suite software which includes Adobe GoLive CS, Adobe Acrobat, Adobe Illustrator CS, Adobe InDesign CS, and Adobe Photoshop CS.

Adobe Version Cue streamlines the creation and maintenance of file versions, and enables file security on shared projects. It enhances browsing, searching, and reviewing file information.

Figure 3.13

**The Save For Web
dialog box**

You can use Version Cue Workspace for more advanced tasks too, including duplicating, exporting, backing up, and restoring projects. You can view information about projects and Import files to the workspace using FTP or WebDAV. You can also delete file versions and remove file locks. Version Cue's security features enable you to designate participants and limit or restrict their access privileges.

The complete Adobe Version Cue documentation is available in the Photoshop Help file.

Save a Version

This command is available for an image that is managed by a Version Cue Workspace. Versioning lets you save different versions of a file with attached comments and information. See the section on Version Cue earlier in this chapter.

Exporting Paths to Illustrator

The File → Export → Paths To Illustrator command lets you save paths created with Photoshop's vector tools as an Adobe Illustrator file. You can align and trace paths on an image in Photoshop and export them using Paths To Illustrator; when you open the document in Illustrator, they will be fully editable as Bezier curves. (See Chapter 8 for more about paths.)

Duplicating a Photoshop Document

You can duplicate a document on the fly. The Image → Duplicate function will produce an exact copy of the document along with its layers and alpha channels. It is useful for quick experimentation when you don't want to affect the original image. The new file, which by default is given the original filename plus the word *copy*, is unsaved and exists only in memory. If you plan to keep the duplicate file, it is wise to save it immediately. Click on the Duplicate Merged Layers Only check box if you want to combine the visible layers into one merged layer in the new document.

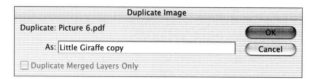

Understanding File Formats

Different file formats serve different purposes. Some formats compress data to make the file size smaller on the disk, whereas others are used to make a file compatible with another software program or the World Wide Web. The format you choose will depend on how the image will ultimately be used. It is important to know what saving an image to a specific format will do. At worst, saving a file to the wrong format can damage it; at the very least, it will inconvenience you by losing the ability to place the document into another program.

Photoshop CS can open 29 file formats on the Mac and 26 on Windows, and save to 18 file formats on the Mac and 16 on Windows. With the addition of plug-ins that attach to the Import and Export submenus, Photoshop supports even more, which means it is a great program for converting files to make them compatible with other software programs. A complete list of file formats, what they do, and how they operate can be found in Appendix B.

Platform Compatibility

In ancient computer times (less than a decade ago), a battle raged between Macintosh and Windows users. Amazingly, the passion and prejudice generated by proponents of one platform or the other bordered on religious fervor. What is it about a computer platform that generates such divisiveness in its adherents? I think it's because a personal computer is, in essence, an auxiliary brain. It stores information and ideas that can't fit into the limited storage capacity of our own gray matter and extends our ability to make calculations and perform complex tasks. A platform simulates the way we think and organize our reality. We can personalize the way each interface behaves and how it looks, to a certain extent, which increases our attachment to it.

The phenomenon of platform prejudice will, I'm sure, be a topic for social theorists to thoroughly investigate in the future. The battle has died down because of the capability of the different computers to read each other's data. The latest Macintosh operating system, Mac OS X, has a program called PC Exchange bundled into the system, which gives the computer the capability to read Windows disks. If you install a program such as MacOpener 2000 by DataViz (`www.dataviz.com`) on your Windows PC, it will read Macintosh disks. With the same data now readily accessible by both platforms, the barriers have come down.

> The one area of disparity between platforms remains the distinction between Mac and PC fonts, which has graphic designers and computer artists cringing when they have to work on more than one platform.

The platform issue has also diminished because of programs such as Photoshop that, for the most part, ignore platform differences. Photoshop is designed to be cross-platform compatible and to perform comparably in Windows and Macintosh environments. Photoshop will open documents from either platform, providing they have been saved in a format that supports cross-platform compatibility. The native Photoshop format is probably your best bet, because it supports layers. Photoshop PDF and TIFF (which also supports layers in recent versions), PICT, and EPS are good alternatives for flattened images, providing they are saved with cross-compatibility in mind. You can use JPEG or JPEG 2000 formats with their efficient compression scheme to archive images to CD and open them in either platform.

Photoshop performs equally well on Macintosh and Windows computers. For the most part, the Photoshop interface is similar for both versions of the software, with minor differences in appearance. Because Macintosh and Windows keyboards differ slightly, keyboard commands are different. Table 3.1 lists the parallel command keys of the two systems.

MACINTOSH	WINDOWS
⌘	Ctrl
Option	Alt
Delete	Backspace
Return	Enter

Table 3.1

Macintosh and Windows Keyboard Equivalents

Software Compatibility

In this age of information, publishing is indeed a universe unto itself. The process of creating an image for print, multimedia, video, or the Web can involve many steps that require specific tools. It is the task of the designer, image editor, desktop publisher, or computer artist to assemble the tools that best perform the necessary tasks. Photoshop does not exist in a vacuum, but works in concert with other computer programs to integrate the images, text, graphics, animations, digital video, and so forth, that compose the final publication.

Images created and edited in Photoshop integrate into all mainstream desktop-publishing, illustration, Web-authoring, and video-editing programs. Because of its capability to open and save in so many file formats, Photoshop is preferred by most design professionals as the essential image-editing software and is the mainstay in a suite of powerful publishing tools.

CHAPTER 4

Navigation: Know Where to Go

A computer-generated image is not really that complex. In fact, it exists most commonly as a series of positive and negative charges on a piece of magnetic media. Quite unlike a drawing, painting, or photograph for which you need only your eyes and a half-decent light source to see, viewing a digital image requires some very fancy electronic equipment, starting with a computer and a monitor. To seriously edit or manipulate the image, you need a big pixel-pusher program such as Adobe Photoshop.

Photoshop is big, all right—so big that it's quite possible to get confused or lost trying to determine where all the stuff is and what it means. Use this chapter as your road map, because it explains Photoshop's numerous navigation features that enable you to find your way around the program. In this chapter, you'll travel through the workspace, tour the menus and palettes, and zoom through Photoshop's viewing options. By the end of your journey, you'll be a seasoned Photoshop traveler.

In this chapter, you'll learn about:

- **Launching the program**
- **Using Photoshop's GUI**
- **Viewing Documents**
- **Accessing menus**
- **Working with palettes, rulers, guides, and grids**
- **Displaying an image**

Launching the Program

The code that runs Photoshop was produced by awesome programming wizardry and a comprehensive knowledge of the technical aspects of publishing. But let's not forget that Photoshop is primarily a creative environment. Whenever you feel the urge to express your visual ideas, you'll have all the necessary tools at your complete disposal. The splash screens and Photoshop's new Welcome screen are the first images you see when you launch the program. They are designed to make you feel right at home.

The Photoshop Folder

When you install Photoshop CS, you can access the program files from your Macintosh `Applications` folder on the hard disk or in Windows at `C:\Program Files\Adobe\Photoshop CS`. The `Adobe Photoshop CS` folder (see Figure 4.1 for the Mac version) contains icons that make Photoshop functional, plug-ins that extend its capabilities, and settings that contain Photoshop's preferences. Additional folders and the Install CD contain extras such as stock art, additional color palettes, custom brushes, and other freebies. The `Adobe Photoshop CS` folder also contains the Photoshop application (called Adobe Photoshop CS in Mac and Photoshop.exe in Windows). To launch the program, double-click its icon.

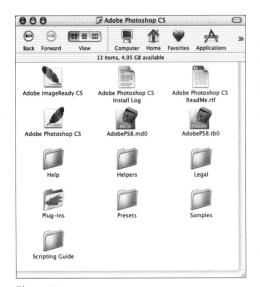

Figure 4.1

The Photoshop folder (Mac OS X version)

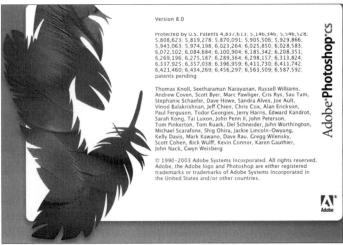

Figure 4.2

Photoshop's splash screen

The Splash Screens

When you double-click the Photoshop icon, the splash screen appears, telling you what components of the program are loading (see Figure 4.2). It also displays some of the data you entered when you loaded the program onto your computer, such as your name and the program's serial number. The splash screen contains a few amusing features worth mentioning, and I'll tell you about those in a moment. It is the signature piece of the designers and software engineers who contributed to the program's development.

As soon as the program finishes loading, the splash screen disappears. You can display it again by choosing About Photoshop from the Apple menu on a Macintosh or from the Help menu in Windows. Wait a moment, and the text starts to scroll. Hold down the Option key (Mac) or the Alt key (Win) to accelerate the scroll rate. If you wait for one complete scrolling cycle and then hover or Ctrl-click your cursor just above the large Adobe Photoshop CS title, you will see Adobe Transient Witticisms (ATWs), a series of one-liners created by Photoshop's program developers and engineers. The ATWs are very amusing—perfect for jaded Photoshop users in need of a chuckle—and provide an insight into the stressful life of the Photoshop development team. There is even a list of the music that the programmers listened to while crafting the beta. To make the splash screen disappear, click it.

After the splash screen closes you'll see the Adobe Photoshop Welcome Screen. This new feature gives you quick access to online tutorials, and tips and tricks from some of Photoshop's top experts. You'll also be able to set up color management from this screen

which is an important step in assuring consistency from on screen image to printed output and is discussed in detail in Chapter 15, "Color Management and Printing." There is also a What's New heading on the Welcome screen that displays PDF files of all of Photoshop's new features and a cool online movie. To complete the launching, click the Close button to display the Photoshop workspace.

The Adobe Online splash screen is another useful feature. The feather icon at the top of the Tool palette accesses the this splash screen, which launches your browser and takes you to the Adobe website at `http://www.adobe.com/ photoshop` for online help.

Using Photoshop's GUI

A Graphical User Interface or GUI (pronounced gooy) is a software program's way of communicating with you. The computer is really not much more than a machine that does really fast math, and each operation is a series of mathematical calculations. Imagine how labor-intensive it would be if you had to perform that math yourself. For example, suppose you had to change the RGB values of the pixels in 1 square inch of an image to be printed in a magazine. You would have to perform 90,000 calculations by hand. Talk about mathaphobia! Fortunately, software designers have set up an environment—the GUI—that makes it easy for you to perform complex calculations quickly and without even having to add 2 + 2. In fact, when you work in a program such as Photoshop, the GUI is so seamless that when you change the color of pixels, it feels as though you're working in a studio environment.

Figure 4.3

The Photoshop workspace in Mac OS X, showing default settings

Photoshop's GUI is easy to use after you learn what the tool icons, menus, and floating palettes represent and how they perform. The Photoshop GUI provides tools and operations that are used by many professionals who work with images, including designers, architects, photographers, artists, printers, and scientists. These virtual tools simulate the processes and operations performed by their real-life counterparts, and furnish a comfortable, familiar working environment.

The Photoshop interface, as shown on Mac OS X, looks like Figure 4.3. The Tool palette is displayed on the left side of the screen, and four palette clusters are displayed on the right side. At the top of the screen are the menus. From these three areas, you will access all of Photoshop's image-editing tools and operations.

Touring the Image Window

When you open or create an image, it is displayed in the *image window* (shown in Figure 4.4). To change the window's size, place your cursor on the lower-right corner, click the mouse button, and drag while holding it down.

> In the Windows interface, you can also enlarge or reduce any resizable window or palette by dragging any corner or edge.

To move the window, click the bar at the top of the window and drag. The scroll bars to the right and at the bottom enable you to scroll around images that appear larger than the size of the window.

The image window contains information about the document. The title bar gives the document's name, the percentage of the image's full size in pixels that you are viewing, the current layer and channel or mask, the color mode and the number 8 or 16 to indicate the image's bit depth. In the lower-left of the image window (on the Macintosh) or the Photoshop application window (in Windows) is the status bar. The leftmost field of the status bar shows, again, the view size as a percentage of the image, but this field is the magnification box where you can enter a specific percentage—to the hundredth of a percent—in which to view the image.

The second field at the bottom of the window shows, by default, two numbers divided by a slash, which is the document file size. The number to the left of the slash represents the base amount of uncompressed space that the file consumes on your disk, or the size of a flattened, uncompressed TIFF image. When you save the image in another format, the file size might shrink, because many formats

Figure 4.4

The image window labeled

Figure 4.5

Click the Status bar to show the position of your image on the paper size that you designated in Page Setup.

use a compression scheme to consolidate data. The number to the right of the slash indicates the size of the image with the addition of any alpha channels, paths, spot color channels, or layers you might have created. The second number, of course, better represents the actual size of the image.

Getting Information about Your Documents

Photoshop has options that show you important information about your document, your computer, and the program's current state of operation. All of this information is useful in determining how efficiently your file will process and print.

Clicking the Status Bar

You can quickly view information about your document when you click the Status Bar.

Image Position Simply clicking the Status bar displays a diagram of the image as it will appear on the paper, as specified in File → Page Setup (see Figure 4.5). Use this to ensure that the image will fit on your paper before you print it.

Size and Mode Info Option-click (Mac) or Alt-click (Win) the Status bar to display the image's size, resolution, color mode, and number of channels.

Tile Info ⌘-click/Ctrl-click to display the tile sizes of the document. Photoshop uses tiles to display and process images. When you display an image or when the image refreshes, you can sometimes see the image appear progressively as it tiles on-screen. This window tells you the number of tiles comprising the image and is of little practical use to most users.

CALCULATING FILE SIZE

A document's file size is calculated by multiplying its height and width in pixels by its bit depth, or the amount of memory each pixel consumes. For example, a full-color document that is 5″ tall by 7″ wide and has a resolution of 72 ppi (pixels per inch) is 504 pixels by 360 pixels.

Because the image is in full color, each pixel consumes 24 bits of space on the disk. For this information to be of use, you must convert it into bytes; there are 8 bits in a byte, so you divide 24 by 8 and get a factor of 3. You then multiply the height by the width by the bit-depth factor, or $504 \times 360 \times 3 = 544{,}320$ bytes. Because there are 1024 bytes in a kilobyte, you divide 544,320 by 1024 to get 531.56, or 532 kilobytes when rounded off to the nearest whole number.

The value derived from this formula is the raw file size. The file size might be further reduced when the image is saved to an image format with a compression scheme such as JPEG, TIFF, or PSD.

Clicking the Status Bar Pop-Up Menu

The status bar, by default, displays the current size of your document. But if you click the small black arrow at the right end of the bar, a pop-up menu enables you to select other information to be displayed:

✓ Document Sizes
Document Profile
Document Dimensions
Scratch Sizes
Efficiency
Timing
Current Tool

Doc:1.94M/1.94M
Untagged Gray
4.087 inches x 5.523 inches
Scr:46.8M/1.11G
Eff:100%*
0.0s
Rectangular Marquee

Document Profile This option displays the name of the color profile with which the image was saved or assigned when opening. The color profile affects how the image appears on-screen (see Chapter 15). In the case of untagged images (an image without a profile), the word *Untagged* will appear next to the color mode of the file.

Document Dimensions Here, the physical width and height of the document is displayed in the current units specified in the preferences.

Scratch Sizes The number to the left of the slash indicates the amount of memory needed to hold all current images open in RAM. The number to the right indicates the amount of memory Photoshop has been allocated (see the section on allocating memory in Chapter 5, "Setting Up the Program"). Because of Photoshop's capability to record events in its History palette, the number on the left grows every time you perform an operation, as RAM is being consumed. (See Chapter 11, "Altered States: History," to learn more about Photoshop's History features.)

Efficiency This option indicates what percentage of the last operation was performed in RAM. If this percentage drops below 80%, you might want to consider allocating more memory to Photoshop or installing more physical RAM. (See the section titled "Allocating Memory" in Chapter 5).

Timing If you select Timing, the information field tells you how long the last operation took to perform to the tenth of a second.

Current Tool This option displays the name of the currently selected tool.

Accessing Menus

You access the majority of Photoshop's most powerful operations through the pull-down menus at the top of the screen. Mac OS X offers ten menus (as illustrated in Figure 4.6); Windows has nine. The menus are quite logical and user-friendly, with related operations accessible from the same menu.

Commands on the menus apply various filters, effects, or operations to an image, directly or through dialog boxes. Some of the menus, such as the View menu or the Window menu, are used to display additional tools or palettes and to change how the image appears on-screen.

Figure 4.6

Photoshop's menus, with the Photoshop menu selected (in Mac OS X)

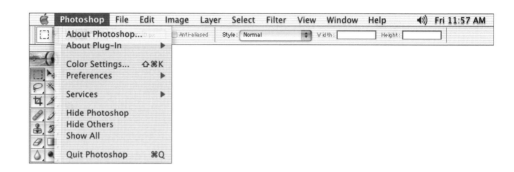

When applying an operation such as an image adjustment, you will see a dialog box that displays the items for that particular operation. You usually cannot perform any other operations until you implement or cancel the dialog. There are some exceptions: although the menus are accessible most of the items are grayed except for some items in the Edit, View, and Window menus which are still operational. You can access the Zoom tool while a dialog box is open (see "Navigation Shortcuts" later in this chapter), and you can hide the edges of the selection marquee by pressing ⌘-H/Ctrl-H (see Chapter 6, "Making Selections").

The dialog boxes are similar to each other in the way that they perform. To access options that are in a dialog box, follow these general steps:

1. Choose the desired operation from the menu. The dialog box appears.

2. Choose from the displayed options or enter values in the dialog box.

3. If there is a preview box, make sure it's checked to preview the result of the operation before closing the dialog box.

4. Make your changes, or abandon them, using these methods:

   • To undo the last operation inside a dialog box, press ⌘-Z/Ctrl-Z.

   • If you've entered values and wish to cancel the operation but keep the dialog box open, press the Option/Alt key, and the word *Cancel* changes to *Reset*. Click the Reset button.

   • Click Cancel to abort the operation and close the dialog without making any changes.

   • Click OK to implement the command.

Some menu commands such as Auto Levels do not display a dialog box. The three dots, that follow some of the menu commands such as Levels… for example, indicate that there are further options in a dialog box.

Pressing Opt/Alt when selecting a menu command that displays a dialog box will apply the last setting used during the work session.

Viewing Documents

The Window menu displays a list of the current images that are open on the desktop; this menu can be used to quickly navigate to a specific document.

At the top of the Window menu is the Arrange submenu. The Window → Arrange → New Window For *file name* command displays multiple windows of the same document. Multiple windows give you the ability to observe two or more views of your image simultaneously so that you can see both the close-up detail in which you are working and the global effect on the entire image. When you edit the image, you will see the changes on both views.

Choose Window → Arrange → Cascade to display multiple open documents on the desktop stacked and slightly offset. Use Window → Arrange → Tile to organize them in rows and columns.

Arrange → Match Zoom, Match Location, or Match Zoom And Location display all of the multiple windows at the same zoom ratio or position as the currently active one.

Organizing Your Workspace

The workspace controls, under the Window menu, give you the ability to organize and save a working environment. Specifically, the Workspace command enables you to save and restore palette locations and tool settings.

To use the Workspace command, follow these steps:

Figure 4.7

The Save Workspace dialog box

1. Choose Window → Workspace → Save Workspace to save the current environment.

2. In the dialog box that appears, name the workspace and click Save (see Figure 4.7). Its name then appears on the list in the Workspace dialog.

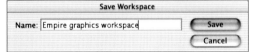

3. To restore Photoshop to the desired workspace, choose its name from the list.

To delete a Workspace, choose Delete Workspace from the list. In the dialog box that appears, choose the workspace you wish to remove from the menu and click OK/Delete.

This menu also enables you to restore the desktop to the default workspace. Choose Reset Palette Locations.

Working with Palettes

Many of Photoshop's tools and operations are displayed in a system of floating palettes, which appear on the desktop when you launch the program. These palettes let you efficiently apply operations directly to the image, thereby saving the time and hassle of following a sequence of windows to accomplish a task.

To display or hide a palette, click the Window menu and choose the palette's name. To hide or display all palettes simultaneously, press the Tab key. Press Shift-Tab to hide all palettes except for the Tool palette.

Using Palette Clusters

By default, palettes appear in clusters that can be separated or reconfigured according to how you might want to use them. To place a palette into a cluster, click the palette's tab and drag it into the cluster. When you see a heavy black outline appear around the cluster, release the mouse button. To separate a palette from a cluster, click its tab and drag it away from the cluster. The palette's new position is wherever you release the mouse.

Open palettes can be docked (joined) and moved as a unit. To dock a palette to another palette while keeping both visible, click the palette's tab, drag it, and place it on the bottom of the target palette. When you see a bold double line, release the mouse; the palette should snap to the bottom of the target palette. To move the palettes as a group, click the bar of the topmost palette and drag the set into position.

Organizing Palettes

Palettes can be organized to use the desktop space more efficiently. You can move a palette or a cluster by placing the cursor on the bar at the top of the palette and dragging it. You can reduce the size of a palette by clicking the Minimize button on the bar at the top of the palette. This method unfortunately conceals the tabs that identify the palette, and you will have to maximize the palette to see its contents. A more efficient method of decreasing a palette's size is to double-click the tab; the palette will collapse, but the name tab will remain visible, as shown in Figure 4.8.

After you've moved or separated the palettes, or changed the way they function, you might want to reset them to their original positions and reset their values to the original defaults of the program. You can accomplish this quickly and easily by choosing Window → Workspace → Reset Palette Locations.

If desired, you can save your current workspace before you reset the palette locations to their defaults. Choose Window → Workspace → Save Workspace.

Using the Palette Dock

Figure 4.8

The tab remains visible when you collapse the palette.

The Palette Dock provides a neat way to organize your palettes so that you can easily locate them. The dock is at the far right of the Options bar (discussed in the next section.) To place a palette in the Palette Dock, click its tab, drag it to the dock, and release the mouse. You can place as many palettes in the dock as you wish, but their names will become obscured if you place too many. To find a palette, drag over the dock and each palette's name will appear. Click to expand the palette, and click again to collapse it.

The Palette Dock is visible only at monitor resolutions of 1024×768 or greater. If palettes are docked and you decrease monitor resolutions, the palettes will be stacked in the workspace. Returning the monitor to a higher resolution will not redock them.

Using the Tool Palette

Photoshop's Tool palette displays the icons for 22 tools. Some of the tool icons expand to access tools that are not visible, bringing the entire number of tools to 56, plus paint swatches, Quick Mask icons, view modes, and the Edit In command. Figures 4.9 and 4.10 show the Tool palette with all of its pop-up tools and their shortcut keys. If you see a small black arrow next to the tool, click it with your mouse and hold down the mouse button, and the additional related tools will pop up.

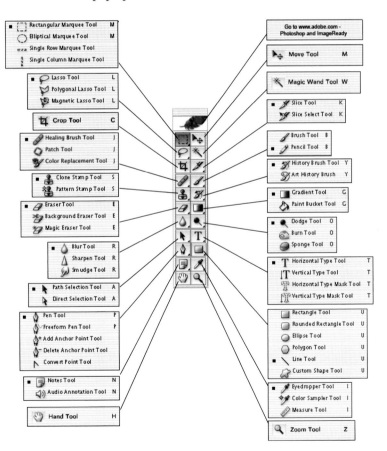

Figure 4.9

The Tool palette showing the expanded tools

Don't be intimidated by the Tool palette! When you place your cursor over a tool, a helpful label, or *tool tip*, identifies the tool, and its shortcut key appears within a few seconds. Photoshop extends the use of tool tips to describe the function of many of its operations inside palettes, toolbars, and dialog boxes, which can be an asset to obtaining a quick understanding of the program. To activate a tool tip, hover your cursor on the function or operation and wait a few seconds.

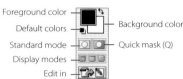

Foreground color
Default colors
Standard mode
Display modes
Edit in
Background color
Quick mask (Q)

Figure 4.10

The Tool palette, bottom portion

The Tool palette is divided into nine general sections. Under the Photoshop Online access logo, from top to bottom, the very broad categories include the selection tools, painting tools, editing tools, vector tools, and display tools. Below that are the foreground and background color swatches, Quick Mask options, display options, and (at the very bottom of the palette) the Edit In command.

Photoshop CS has only one new tool—the Color Replacement tool which is clustered with the Healing brush and the Patch tool. See Appendix A for a complete list of tools and descriptions of what they do and how they operate.

The Tool palette is designed to place all of the program's primary manual operations in full view on the desktop for easy access. Each tool is represented by a different cursor icon. To choose a tool, click its button on the Tool palette. Then place the cursor where you want to affect the image. Click the mouse, or click and drag (depending on the tool), to apply the tool's function to the image.

> You can access a tool by pressing its shortcut letter. To toggle through grouped sets of tools (for example, the three Lassos or Blur/Sharpen/Smudge), press Shift plus the shortcut letter repeatedly.

The Options Bar

Photoshop, by default, displays an Options bar at the top of the screen when you launch the program. This element is similar to the Options palette in earlier versions of the program, but more convenient because it is easier to locate. After you select a tool, its options become visible in the Options bar, and you can determine the behavioral characteristics of the tool. Figure 4.11 shows the Options bar with the Brush tool selected. A tool's performance can vary considerably with different options, so it's a good idea to check out the settings before you apply the tool to the image.

Figure 4.11

The Options bar (with the Brush tool selected)

Tool Presets

The tool icon on the far left side of the Options bar accesses the current Tool Preset menu (see Figure 4.12). This menu provides a handy way to save and access tool configurations that you frequently use. To access a tool, click the desired tool in the Tool palette. Place your cursor on the arrow next to the tool icon on the Options bar, and press the mouse button to display the list. Scroll down and choose a preset from the list.

To save a new tool preset, follow these steps:

1. Choose a tool from the Tool palette and set its characteristics in the Options bar.

2. Click the small arrow next to the tool icon on the Options bar to display the Tool Presets list.

3. Click the New Tool Preset icon in the upper-right of the palette, or click the small arrow at the upper-right side of the palette, to display the pull-down menu. Choose New Tool Preset.

4. In the dialog box that appears (see Figure 4.13), name the tool preset and click OK. It now appears in the Tool Preset list.

Figure 4.12

Photoshop's Tool Preset menu

When naming a preset, remember that descriptive names help you quickly locate a tool.

The Notes Tool

Two tools let you conveniently attach reminder notes to the image. You can create an annotation as either a sticky note or an audio recording.

To create a written annotation:

1. Click the Notes tool  in the Tool palette, or press N on the keyboard.

2. Click the image, and a yellow sticky note appears.

3. Enter the information, as shown in Figure 4.14, and click Close.

4. To access the information on the note, double-click the note icon on the image.

To record an audio annotation, you'll need a microphone and audio input capabilities.

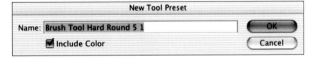

Figure 4.13

The New Tool Preset dialog box

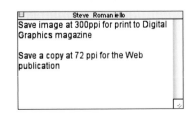

Figure 4.14

A written notation

Then follow these steps:

1. Click the Notes tool and hold down the mouse to expand the palette. Choose the Audio Annotation tool 🔊.

2. Click the image, and the Audio Notation dialog box appears.

3. Click the Start button to record; click Stop when you've completed the recording.

4. To play the annotation, double-click the audio icon on the image.

Displaying an Image

When you open an image in Photoshop, it is displayed to fit in the image window so that you can see the entire image regardless of its size. When working on an image, it's often necessary to vary the view size so that you can see changes to the document as a whole, concentrate on specific areas of the image, or work closely on details. Varying the size of the image display does not affect the physical size of the image. You can choose from several viewing methods.

The Zoom Tool

The Zoom tool 🔍 provides a fast way to take a closer look at an image and is probably the technique you'll use most frequently for changing the view. Choose the Zoom tool from the Tool palette by clicking it or press Z on the keyboard. Place your cursor on the area of the image that you want to see close-up; you will see the Zoom tool cursor (a magnifying glass) with a plus sign to indicate that the Zoom tool will enlarge the view. Click your mouse, and continue to click until the image appears at the desired magnification. Each time you click, the image appears larger, to a maximum view size of 1600%.

You can reduce the size of the displayed image by pressing the Option/Alt key. The Zoom tool displays a minus sign to indicate that it will reduce the view. Each time you click the mouse with the Option/Alt key held down, the image diminishes in size, all the way down to 1 screen pixel.

DISPLAY SIZE AND IMAGE RESOLUTION

The percentage at which you see an image in Photoshop depends on the ratio of the image resolution to the monitor's screen resolution. Macintosh monitors have a screen resolution of 72 ppi, whereas Windows monitors use 96 ppi to display an image.

When viewed at 100%, a document with an image resolution of 72 ppi will display at a ratio of 1:1 of its actual height and width dimensions on a Mac, and 33% larger on Windows. A resolution of 144 ppi will display an image at twice its print size on a Mac and, again, larger on a Windows machine when displayed at 100% viewing size. (See Chapter 13, "Sizing and Transforming Images," for more on monitor and image resolution.)

Scrolling

Scrolling tools and techniques let you move the image around the window when the image is larger than the image window:

Hand Tool Click the Hand tool 🖐 in the Tool palette or press the H key. Click the image and drag to move the image around.

Scroll Bars As in most software, the scroll bars are to the right and bottom of the image. Click and drag a scroll handle, or click an arrow at the end of a scroll bar, to scroll in the desired direction. Or click in the scroll bar section above or below the scroll handle to jump a full screen view up or down.

Keyboard You can use either a keyboard or an extended keyboard to scroll the image up, down, left, or right. Table 4.1 lists the commands.

Navigation Shortcuts

Clicking over and over again to display the image can become tiresome and consume precious time. As you become more proficient in Photoshop, you will want to consider alternative methods to speed the process of viewing your image at the right size. The following are a few techniques that will enhance your ability to see the image on-screen:

Centering an Image This technique centers and zooms in on an area of the image on-screen. It is the fastest way to closely see a detail of the image you are working on. Choose the Zoom tool, click in the image, drag a marquee around the portion of the image that you wish to enlarge, and release the mouse. The selected area enlarges to fill the window.

Restoring the Display to a 100% View Double-click the Zoom tool icon in the Tool palette.

SCROLL	MACINTOSH KEYBOARD	MAC EXTENDED KEYBOARD	WINDOWS ACTION KEYBOARD
Up	Control-K	PgUp	PgUp
Up slightly	Shift-Control-K	Shift-PgUp	Shift-PgUp
Down	Control-L	PgDn	PgDn
Down slightly	Shift-Control-L	Shift-PgDn	Shift-PgDn
Left	⌘-Control-K	⌘-Control-PgUp	Ctrl-PgUp
Left slightly	Shift-⌘-Control-K	Shift-⌘-Control-PgUp	Shift-Ctrl-PgUp
Right	⌘-Control-L	⌘-Control-PgDn	Ctrl-PgDn
Right slightly	Shift-⌘-Control-L	Shift-⌘-Control-PgDn	Shift-Ctrl-PgDn

Table 4.1

Keyboard Commands for Scrolling

Toggling to the Zoom Tool To toggle directly from any tool or dialog box to the Zoom tool, use one of these shortcuts:

- Hold down the ⌘/Ctrl key and the spacebar, and click the mouse to zoom in. Release the keys to resume using the tool.

- Hold down the Option/Alt key and the spacebar, and click the mouse to zoom out. Release the keys to resume using the tool.

Toggling to the Hand Tool To quickly access the Hand tool from any tool or dialog box, press the spacebar. Click and drag your mouse to scroll. The Hand tool lets you scroll around the image when it exceeds the size of the image window. Release the spacebar to resume using the tool.

The Navigator

When you are viewing an image close-up, it can be difficult to tell exactly what you are looking at and where you are in the image, especially if the image contains large areas of similar texture. The Navigator (see Figure 4.15) is a map of the image, displayed as a thumbnail, showing the exact location of what appears in the image window relative to the entire image.

When you launch Photoshop, the Navigator is displayed by default and offers the following navigational features:

View Box The red rectangle on the thumbnail indicates the image that is currently displayed in the image window. Place your cursor on the rectangle, click your mouse, and drag to scroll around the image. You can change the color of the View box by clicking the arrow in the upper-right corner of the palette and choosing Palette Options. You can then choose a color from the drop down list or click the swatch to choose a color from the Color Picker.

Zoom Slider You can zoom in on the image by moving the slider to the right, or zoom out by moving the slider to the left.

Zoom In and Zoom Out Buttons The button with the small mountains on the left of the slider zooms out, and the button with the large mountains to the right of the slider zooms in. The buttons use the same predefined increments as the Zoom tool.

Figure 4.15
The Navigator palette

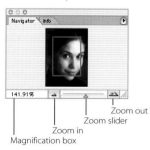

Zoom out
Zoom slider
Zoom in
Magnification box

Magnification Box At the bottom-left of the Navigator palette, you can enter a specific percentage at which to view your image.

Sizing Options On a Mac, you can drag the lower-right corner of the Navigator box to increase or decrease the size of the Navigator palette and its image thumbnail. In Windows, you can drag from any resizable edge.

The View Menu

After you get to know the program a little better, you will discover that many of its operations seem redundant, and working effectively becomes a matter of choosing your favorite method for achieving identical end results. For example, the View → Zoom In command achieves the same result as the keyboard shortcut ⌘/Ctrl-plus sign; using the Zoom Out command is the same as typing ⌘/Ctrl-minus sign. These techniques are identical to the Zoom tool and, of course, all of these commands are similar to the function of the Navigator and the magnification box, with slight variations.

The other options in the View menu include the following:

- Fit On-Screen displays the image at the maximum horizontal or vertical size that the monitor screen will accommodate.
- Actual Pixels displays the image in a 1:1 ratio with the monitor's screen resolution.
- Print Size accurately displays the height and width dimensions of the image.

Display Modes

Three icons on the Tool palette determine the display modes, or the way that you see the image on-screen. These modes act like electronic mattes. There are three options:

Standard Screen Mode The default view displays the image against the operating system's desktop or against the neutral gray Photoshop desktop in Windows, which obscures the operating system's desktop.

Full Screen Mode with Menu Bars The image takes up almost the entire surface of the monitor screen and displays menu bars across the top. When you zoom to a smaller display size, the image appears centered against a neutral gray background.

Full Screen Mode The image takes up the entire surface of the monitor screen. When you zoom to a smaller display size, the image appears centered against a black background.

The Full Screen display modes are ideal for displaying a view of your work unobstructed by other windows. It can be even more helpful to see an image in the Full Screen modes without any distracting palettes. To conceal or reveal all currently visible palettes, press the Tab key.

Using Rulers, Guides, and Grids

Rulers, guides, and grids are used to align image content. Alignment of visual elements is critical to maintaining a cohesive structure to the composition. A good composition gently guides the viewer's eye across its surface so that important elements are emphasized. Rulers, guides, and grids can assure the precise measurement and placement of image components.

Setting Preferences for Rulers and Guides

Photoshop can display a horizontal ruler across the top of the screen and a vertical ruler along the left side of the screen; to display them, choose View → Rulers. Rulers give you a visual reminder of the physical size of your image, which you might forget from time to time as you zoom in or out. You can change ruler units by choosing Edit → Preferences → Units & Rulers or double click either the horizontal or vertical rulers to display the preferences.

The *zero point*, or point of origin for all measurements, is in the upper-left corner of the image where the rulers intersect. The point of origin can be changed by placing your cursor on the crosshairs, clicking and dragging down and to the right, positioning to the desired location, and releasing the mouse. If you've changed the position of the point of origin, double-click on the origin point to reset the zero point.

Graphic designers use grids and guides to align elements within a layout. Aligning visual elements creates a compositional structure, which helps to control the viewer's eye. The importance of good composition in a Photoshop document cannot be stressed enough. The View menu contains the commands that let you create guides and display a grid, which are superimposed over the image to help you align elements within the composition. Neither guides nor grids print. You can change the color and properties of guides or grids by choosing Edit → Preferences → Guides, Grids, & Slices.

Chapter 5 goes into more detail on preference settings.

Using Guides

Figure 4.16

Guides on an image can be used for alignment.

Guides are horizontal or vertical lines that can be positioned anywhere on the image's surface. To create a horizontal or vertical guide, choose View → Rulers. Place your cursor on the ruler, click your mouse, and drag down or to the right, releasing the mouse wherever you want to place a guide (see Figure 4.16).

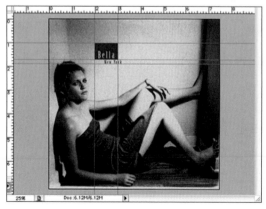

Use the following operations to position or move guides on your image:

Display or Conceal Guides You can hide or reveal guides with the Show command. Choose View → Show → Guides to toggle them on and off; if the box is checked, they'll be visible, and if it's not checked they'll be hidden.

Snap to Guides When moving a portion of a layer or a selected area of the image, you can snap it to a guide to assure the accuracy of its position by using the Snap To command. Choose View → Snap To → Guides to toggle snapping on and off.

Move a Guide With the Move tool selected, click the guide and drag. If another tool is selected, ⌘-click/Ctrl-click the guide and drag. The Move A Guide ⌘/Ctrl-click shortcut does not work with the Slice tool or the Hand tool.

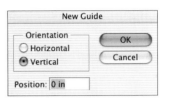

Figure 4.17

The New Guide dialog box

Delete a Guide Select the guide as if you were going to move it, and drag it out of the image window.

Delete All Guides Choose View → Clear Guides.

Lock a Guide Choose View → Lock Guides. This prevents accidentally moving a guide while you work.

New Guide Another method of generating a new guide is to choose View → New Guide (see Figure 4.17). The advantage of this method is that you can enter a value for the guide's exact location and can determine whether the guide is horizontal or vertical.

Change the Orientation of a Guide You can change a guide from horizontal to vertical or from vertical to horizontal. While in the Move tool, place your cursor on the guide. Hold down the Option/Alt key and click the guide.

Change Guide Characteristics The color and style of your guides can be modified by choosing Edit → Preferences → Guides, Grids, & Slices. Choose a color from the pull-down menu, or click the swatch to display the Color Picker. From the Style pull-down menu, choose either a dashed or solid line.

Using a Grid

A *grid* helps you see the global relationships between aligned elements on a page (as shown in Figure 4.18). A grid is a series of equally spaced horizontal and vertical lines that create a visual matrix. Like guides, grids do not print.

Figure 4.18

The Photoshop grid

Use the following operations to work with a grid:

Display or Conceal the Grid Choose View → Show → Grid.

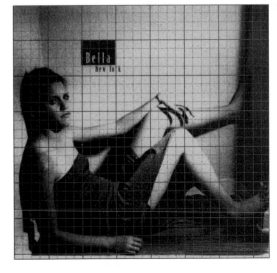

Snap to Grid When moving a portion of a layer or a selected area of the image, you can snap it to a horizontal or vertical grid line by using the Snap To command. Choose View → Snap To → Grid.

Grid Characteristics The color and style of the grid can be modified by choosing Photoshop/Edit → Preferences → Guides, Grids, & Slices. Choose a grid color from the drop down list, or click the swatch to display the Color Picker. From the Style drop down list, choose a dashed line, a solid line, or dots. You can also change the grid size by entering values in the Gridline and Subdivisions text fields.

Setting Up Photoshop

Before any job, there is always preparation. Let's say you are going to change the oil in your car. Before you crawl under it and loosen the plug, you'll need to move the car to an appropriate location—certainly not near your newly planted front lawn, and not on the side of a hill. You'll need to find a level spot and gather an oil filter, pan, pouring spout, and rag. A simple job, yes. But consider how difficult the task would be if any of the elements were missing. If you choose the wrong location, you might kill your grass; if you park on a hill, some of the old, dirty oil will stay in the crankcase. The pan is essential, because without it, the oil will spill onto the ground.

The point is, you need to choose the right workspace and prepare it with all of the things you need before you begin the job. In the case of Photoshop CS, that means setting up the program to run at its optimal level, customizing the interface to best suit your needs, and choosing the best color environment.

This chapter will describe:

- **Modifying settings and preferences**

- **Allocating memory**

- **Utilizing the Preset Manager**

- **Calibrating the monitor**

Modifying Photoshop's Settings

Photoshop's settings control how the program appears and behaves. On the Mac, settings are stored in files, folders, and directories with names such as Settings or Preferences. Windows has similar directories where settings are stored as well as having other settings stored deeper in the Registry. After you modify any setting and quit the program, the information is saved to these files.

When you launch Photoshop for the first time, a set of *preferences* is created. These are the factory default settings. Any changes you make in the appearance or the behavior of the program are recorded in the preferences file. After a work session, when you quit the program, these preferences are stored so that the next time you launch the program, the position of the palettes, the tool settings, the color of the guides or grid, and any other changes you made remain the same.

Restoring Preferences

If Photoshop starts behaving unpredictably or bombing frequently, it could indicate that the preferences are damaged. You should restore your preferences to the originally installed default settings. Re-creating your preferences file resets Photoshop to its defaults and can help troubleshoot problems.

> I recommend that as you begin each of the Hands On projects in this book, you discard your "prefs" file and restart Photoshop to create a clean set of options. This will make working through the exercises easier.

To restore your preferences, follow these steps:

1. Double-click the Photoshop program icon to launch the program.

2. Immediately after double-clicking, press Shift-Option-⌘ on a Macintosh or Shift-Alt-Ctrl on Windows.

3. A dialog box asks whether you want to discard the Photoshop's Settings file, as in Figure 5.1. Click Yes, and the program continues to launch.

Figure 5.1

The Discard Photoshop Settings dialog box

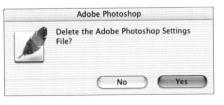

After Photoshop has launched in the Windows version, another dialog box appears stating that the both Photoshop and the operating system are using the same hard disk for virtual memory. Then, in both the Windows and Macintosh versions, a dialog box appears asking whether you want to change Photoshop's color settings. Click Yes or No depending on what you want to do. (See the section "Choosing a Color Working Space" later in this chapter and Chapter 15, "Color Management and Printing," for a comprehensive explanation of color management.) Finally, you'll see Photoshop's new welcome screen, which has hyperlinks to tutorials, tips and tricks, color management setup information, and a new features guide.

Allocating Memory

Processing graphics files requires large amounts of memory. Photoshop is a memory hog, so the often asked question, "How much memory do you need to best operate Photoshop?" is easily answered with another question: "How much memory can you afford?" The minimum hardware and software requirements for running Photoshop are as follows:

> **Mac OS 10.2.4, 10.2.5, 10.2.6:**

- PowerPC processor (G3, G4, or G5)
- 192 MB of RAM (256 MB recommended)
- 320 MB of available hard-disk space
- Color monitor with 16-bit or greater video card
- 1024×768 or greater monitor resolution
- CD-ROM drive

> **Microsoft Windows 2000 with Service Pack 3, or Windows XP:**

- Intel Pentium class III or 4 processor
- 192 MB of RAM (256 MB recommended)
- 280 MB of available hard-disk space
- Color monitor with 16-bit or greater video card
- 1024×768 or greater monitor resolution
- CD-ROM drive

Adobe's minimum requirement of 192 MB of RAM is enough to launch and run the program, but its performance will be clunky. Purchase and install as much memory as you can. After you've installed the memory, be sure to allocate it to Photoshop, using the following procedure.

To allocate memory, follow these steps:

1. With Photoshop running, in Mac OS X choose Photoshop → Preferences → Memory & Image Cache (bringing up the dialog box shown in Figure 5.2); in Windows, choose Edit → Preferences → Memory & Image Cache.

2. In the Maximum Used By Photoshop field, enter the proportion of available memory you want to dedicate to Photoshop. The 50% default setting is a good beginning for operating the software.

3. During a Photoshop work session, if the Efficiency setting (in the status bar at the bottom of the window) ever drops below 100%, increase the percentage of memory by 10% increments until the efficiency remains at the maximum 100%.

4. After you reset the memory allocation, you must quit and relaunch the program for the change to take effect.

Setting Preferences

When you change Photoshop's preferences, you affect the behavior or the appearance of the program, thereby customizing the interface to best suit your style of working. In the descriptions throughout this chapter, the illustrations are of the default preferences, but I recommend (in parentheses within the text) the preference configuration that is most suitable for the majority of working situations.

You access the preferences through the Photoshop → Preferences menu in the Mac and the Edit → Preferences menu in Windows, or type ⌘-K (Mac) or Ctrl-K (Win) to display Photoshop's Preferences dialog box. You also have the option of going directly to the preference category you want under the Preferences submenu.

From the dialog box, you can navigate to any of the preference categories by clicking the pop-up list at the top of the dialog box. You can also jump from category to category by clicking the Next or Prev buttons.

Figure 5.2

The Memory & Image Cache preferences in Mac OS X

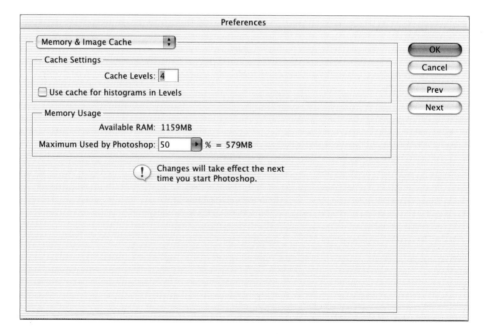

General Preferences

When you first open the Preferences dialog box, you see Photoshop's General preference settings (see Figure 5.3), which are global settings that affect most of your working environment.

Again: the illustrations are of the default preferences; the settings in parentheses within the text are my recommendation for the majority of working situations.

These settings include the following:

Color Picker (Adobe) You can specify which color picker to use when choosing a foreground or background color. The color picker you select is also used throughout the program to define preferences, such as the color of your guides and grids. In both Macintosh and Windows, you can choose between the Adobe Color Picker and the operating system's color picker.

Image Interpolation (Bicubic) This sets the global default for how Photoshop resamples, or sizes, images. When you resize an image, pixels are either added (if you increase the image size or resolution) or subtracted (if you reduce the image size or resolution). When adding pixels, the Nearest Neighbor setting, which is the fastest, makes an exact copy of the adjacent pixel. Bilinear uses an average of the two pixels above and below and the two pixels on either side to create gradations for smoother transitions. Bicubic averages the eight closest neighbors and adding a sharpening effect to increase the contrast.

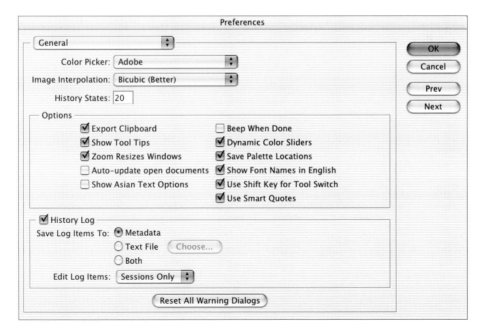

Figure 5.3

The General preferences

Two new interpolation algorithms have been added to Photoshop CS: Bicubic Smoother and Bicubic Sharper. These methods are designed to replace third-party plug-ins such as LizardTech's Genuine Fractals Print Pro. You can use these methods for upsizing an image with much better results than the original Bicubic resampling. Bicubic Smoother slightly blurs the edges of areas for a more sublimated continuous-tone look. Bicubic Sharper adds an additional sharpen algorithm to better enhance contrast. Both of these new methods require much less time than the third-party plug-in, but for best results, you should experiment and compare.

Nearest Neighbor is useful for increasing the size of a bitmap or line art image in which all the pixels are either black or white. Nearest Neighbor will preserve the absolute values without producing intermediate gray transitions or anti-aliasing. It's also good for maintaining the integrity of some screen captures when resampling up for print, as image quality might be reduced by the anti-aliasing effect of Bicubic interpolation. For virtually every other application, choose Bicubic interpolation.

History States (20) You can determine the maximum number of states that will appear in the History palette before the earliest one is discarded. History requires RAM to remember stages, or *states*, in the process of developing an image. Limit the number of states to the default so as not to compromise the efficiency of the program.

Export Clipboard (Off) If you are running more than one program, the content of Photoshop's Clipboard will be transferred to the system's Clipboard. When you switch to another program, those contents can be pasted into a document there. If you copy and paste images within Photoshop only, turn off this option to reduce the amount of time it takes to activate another program.

Show Tool Tips (On) The small, yellow identification tags on the Tool palette that display each tool's name and keyboard shortcut are turned on and off from this setting. The Tool palette displays the same information when the tool items are expanded, so the information is somewhat redundant. It's not a bad idea, however, to get a double hit of this information until you learn what the tools are and how to access them with shortcut key commands. Another reason to keep this check box selected is that the tool tips also appear as short descriptions on many of Photoshop's commands, giving you a clear idea of their purpose.

Zoom Resizes Windows (Off) This preference lets you resize the image window when you use the key commands for zooming in (⌘/Ctrl-plus sign) and zooming out (⌘/Ctrl-minus sign). The window will increase in size until it fills the screen vertically or horizontally.

Auto-Update Open Documents (Off) If an image is updated by another program outside of Photoshop, Photoshop will automatically reread and replace the open document with the updated version.

Show Asian Text Options (Off) Clicking this check box displays Chinese, Japanese, and Korean text options in the Paragraph palettes. You need this option only if you are working with Asian characters.

Beep When Done (Off) You can instruct Photoshop to emit a warning signal after it has performed an operation that displays a progress window. This can be helpful if you are away from your computer waiting for a long process (for example, a rotation or resize of a high-resolution image) to be completed.

Dynamic Color Sliders (On) When this check box is chosen, the bars on the Color palette preview the range of potential colors that can be designated, so that you know exactly where to move the sliders to designate a specific foreground or background color. Leave this check box selected to speed the process of determining your colors.

Save Palette Locations (On) If you choose this option, Photoshop will remember the position of your palettes when you quit and then relaunch the program. If the box is not checked, Photoshop restores the palette locations to the default positions.

Show Font Names in English (On) If you have any fonts on your system that do not use Roman characters, such as Asian fonts, their names will be displayed in English in the font list.

Use Shift Key for Tool Switch (Off) With this preference off, in order to switch to a tool or switch among grouped tools, you simply type the shortcut key for that group (L for the Lassos, E for the Erasers, and so forth). Checking this option adds the Shift key to the process, to prevent you from inadvertently switching while using a tool.

Use Smart Quotes (On) This preference instructs the Type tool to automatically place open quotation marks at the beginning of a quote and closed marks at the end of a quote.

Save Log Items To This new item lets you log your editing history to the metadata that is attached to the file, or to a separate text document, or both. Click the Choose button to establish a destination. If you choose Sessions from the list, the log begins and ends when you open and close files. Choose Concise for a brief description of the items in the History palette. Choose Detailed for a more comprehensive description of the steps. You can open the text file in a text editor such as Text Edit for Mac or Notepad for Windows and review the contents.

Reset All Warning Dialogs This option resets all warning dialog boxes that have a Don't Show Again check box chosen so that the dialogs will appear when activated.

File Handling

The File Handling preferences (see Figure 5.4) let you manage files when you save them either to your disk or to a workgroup server and let you designate whether your saved files will have previews or extensions.

These settings include the following:

Image Previews (Always Save) On the Macintosh, the Macintosh Thumbnail and Windows Thumbnail options create previews that will be displayed in the dialog box that you see when you open the image by using File → Open. There are two more options in Photoshop for Mac OS: Icon creates a tiny picture that you can view from the desktop for the purpose of identifying an image before you open it, and Full Size creates a preview that can be placed in a desktop-publishing program. These options are not available in the Windows File Handling preferences. The problem with previews is that they produce larger file sizes, so you need to decide whether the convenience of seeing the image prior to opening is worth the memory used.

Append File Extension (Always, Use Lower Case) On the Macintosh version, Append File Extension determines when to add an extension (for example, .tif, .psd, or .eps) to the filename; your options are Always, Never, or Ask When Saving. The Windows version automatically adds the three-character extension to the filename, and the extension won't hurt a Mac file, so choose Always. You will be able to readily identify the type of image even if it's in a folder on the desktop, and you don't have to worry about adding the extension when saving for a Windows computer or publication to the Web.

Figure 5.4

The File Handling preferences

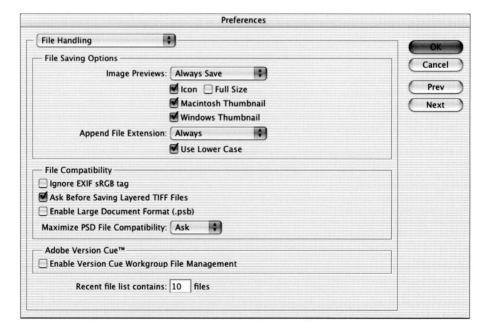

This option also enables you to select whether the extension is uppercase or lowercase. (Whichever way you choose here, you have the option to switch the extension's case for each given file as you use the Save dialog boxes.) I recommend that you choose the Use Lower Case option when saving files to the Web because of Unix servers' preference for lowercase extensions.

File Compatibility (On) Photoshop offers these options for maintaining compatibility with other software:

> **Ignore EXIF sRGB Tag (Off)** Digital cameras often embed metadata. Some of that metadata is EXIF data such as the camera make, model, date/time, shutter speed, flash, and so forth. One section of EXIF metadata is the EXIF Color Space tag. This is not an ICC profile, but an EXIF description of what ICC profile would be manually assigned to the file when opening the image in Photoshop. The EXIF specification has only two options: sRGB or Uncalibrated, with Uncalibrated standing for any color space that is not sRGB. Clicking this check box ignores the sRGB tag and assigns the Uncalibrated color space option to the file.

> **Ask Before Saving Layered TIFF Files (On)** Checking this box displays a reminder that your TIFFs are layered before you save them. Because layers increase file size, it's a good idea to keep this option on.

> **Enable Large Document Format (.psb) (Off)** Photoshop PSD is limited to 30,000×30,000 pixels. Large Document Format, or `.psb`, is essentially the same as PSD but supports up to 300,000×300,000 pixel resolution documents. This format is readable only by Photoshop CS.

> **Maximize PSD File Compatibility (Ask)** Selecting this preference saves a flattened preview with a PSD file. You can choose whether to Never or Always save the preview or to be asked each time you save. This feature is like insurance: it costs to use it but one day it might be needed. Turning it off might compromise compatibility with other software programs and future versions of Photoshop.

If you do decide to take out the "insurance" by saving a flat composite layer into the layered file, it is not immediately obvious how to access this flat layer—as Photoshop defaults to the layers and not this "hidden" composite used by other software. Choose File → Open or use the File Browser to select the file to open. Hold down Shift/Alt when opening the image to Read The Composite Data Instead of the layered data.

Within this you can choose Always, Never, or Ask when opening or updating images that reside on a managed file server. This pertains to workgroups who often use the same source image for publications. Choose Ask in both instances when checking out or updating to be sure that you don't automatically replace a file.

Recent File List Contains (10) Files You can find a list of the most recent files that have been opened under File → Open Recent. Enter a value for the number of the latest documents you would like to see displayed; the maximum is 30.

Display & Cursors

Use the Display & Cursors preferences (see Figure 5.5) to configure the way cursor icons and colors appear on-screen. These preferences do not affect the image data, but they do affect how you see the image.

These settings are as follows:

Color Channels in Color (Off) By default, color channels appear in black-and-white. Each color channel is actually an 8-bit grayscale image that supports 256 shades of gray. Photoshop will display a channel in red, green, or blue, depending on the color information it represents, if this check box is selected. The black-and-white information of the default is displayed more clearly and is probably more useful to you, so leave the check box unselected.

Use Diffusion Dither (On) This option is used to control the pattern of pixel blending on low-resolution color monitors, or if you're displaying anything less then Millions Of Colors (Mac) or True Color (Win). *Dithering* is a method of distributing pixels to extend the visual range of color on-screen.

Figure 5.5

The Display & Cursors preferences

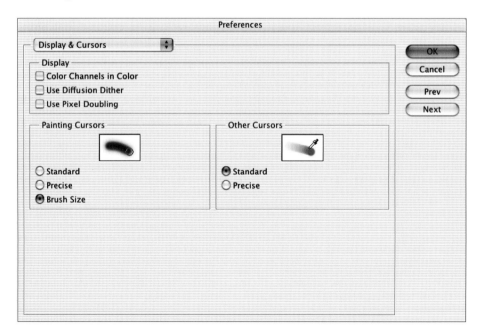

Use Pixel Doubling (On) When moving an image from one file to another, you can speed the process by reducing the resolution display. When you move an image with this box checked, the image will appear jagged and unrefined until it is in position and the operation is complete.

Painting Cursors (Brush Size) To change the display of the painting cursor, click the desired radio button. The Standard option displays the tool icon as the cursor. The Precise option displays crosshairs. Brush Size, the default, displays a cursor that is the size and shape of the brush for the currently selected tool.

Other Cursors (Standard) To change the display of tool cursors that do not use brushes, choose either Standard (the tool icon as the cursor) or Precise (a crosshair icon).

> If you use standard or brush size cursors, you can toggle back and forth to the precise cursor with your Caps Lock key.

Transparency & Gamut

These settings control the appearance of the transparency display of layers and the color of the CMYK gamut warning (see Figure 5.6).

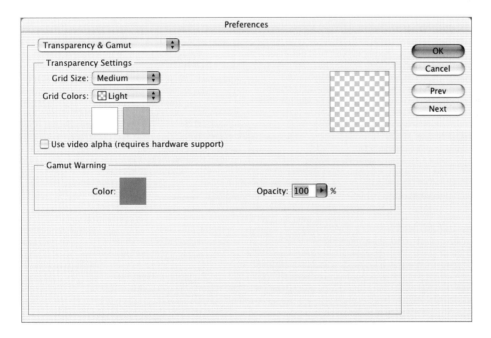

Figure 5.6

The Transparency & Gamut preferences

These settings include the following:

Transparency Settings (Medium, Light) With this option, you can set the default preferences for the transparency display on your layers. Sometimes the default gray checkerboard is not visible because of similar colors within the image. Under Grid Size, choose from a small, medium, or large grid. Grid Colors lets you select from a predefined list of color checkerboards. To choose specific grid colors, click either of the color swatches to display the Color Picker.

Use Video Alpha You can display alpha channels at a predefined opacity if you have the hardware that supports this type of display.

Gamut Warning (Default) When working on RGB images intended for four-color process printing, you'll want to preview the files before converting to CMYK. To see which colors are out of the CMYK gamut, choose View → Gamut Warning. The gamut warning displays a colored mask over the areas that are out of range. The Gamut Warning preferences let you determine the color of the mask. Click the color swatch to display the Color Picker. Choose an opacity percentage between 1 and 100 to affect the transparency of the mask.

Units & Rulers

You can establish settings for all measurement systems in Photoshop (see Figure 5.7).

Figure 5.7

The Units & Rulers preferences

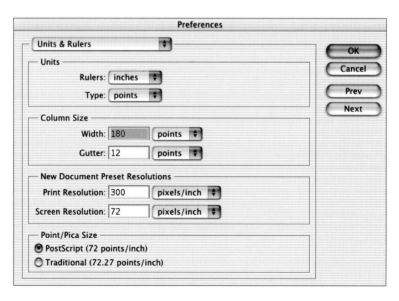

These settings include the following:

Rulers (Inches) The Rulers setting enables you to determine which measurement system will appear on the rulers when they are displayed. You can choose pixels, inches, centimeters, points, picas, or percent.

> A shortcut to this preference is to double-click the rulers within the Photoshop workspace.

Type (Points) You can determine how type size, leading, and other characteristics are displayed in the Options bar and in the Character and Paragraph palettes. Choose points, pixels, or millimeters.

Column Size (Default) If you're importing your image to a desktop-publishing program for publication to a newspaper, newsletter, or magazine, you might want to configure it to a specific column size. You can choose the width of the column and a gutter size so that your image will conform to the column size of the intended publication. You can determine the number of columns in the document when choosing File → New or Image → Image Size.

New Document Preset Resolutions (300 and 72) This preference enables you to determine the default print and screen resolutions for new documents.

Point/Pica Size (PostScript) This preference determines the size of your type characters. In PostScript type, there are 72 points per inch; in Traditional type, there are 72.27 points per inch. PostScript has clearly become the convention with the advent of desktop publishing and computer typography. Some purists still might prefer the Traditional type option, so it remains available.

Guides, Grid, & Slices

Graphic designers use guides and grids to align visual elements on a page (as described in Chapter 4, "Navigation: Know Where to Go"). *Slices* divide an image into pieces for faster display on the Web.

The Guides, Grid, & Slices preferences (see Figure 5.8) enable you to determine the color and style of your ruler guides and your grid. Under Color, choose from the options list or click the large swatch on the right side of the dialog box to select a specific color from the Color Picker. You can determine the matrix of your grid by entering a value in the Gridline Every field and can set the number of subdivisions in the grid by entering a value in the Subdivisions field. In the slice field, you can specify slice color and whether or not to display their designated number in the layout.

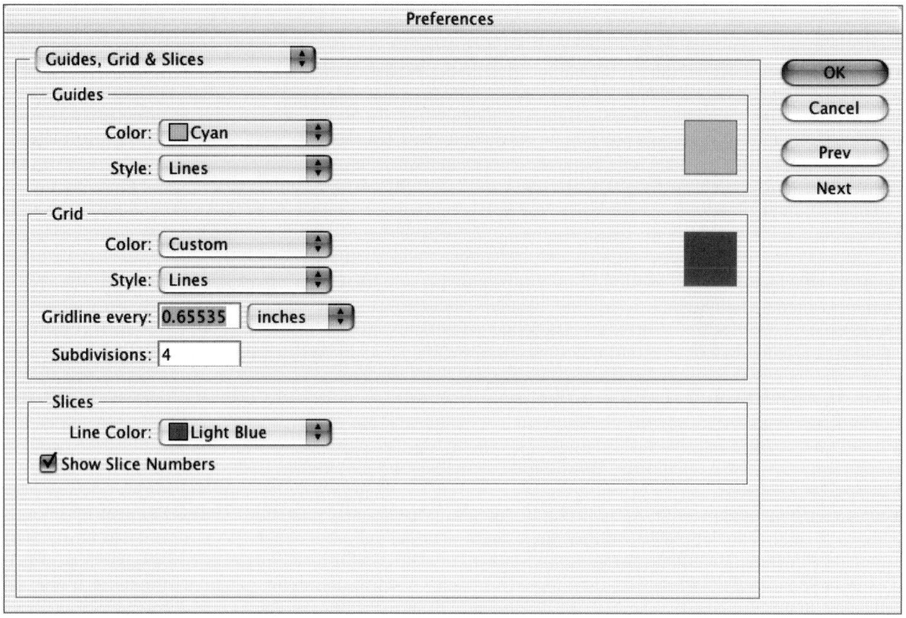

Figure 5.8

**The Guides, Grid, &
Slices preferences**

Figure 5.8

The Guides, Grid, & Slices preferences

Plug-Ins & Scratch Disks

Plug-ins are modular mini programs or filters that add functions to Photoshop. You can activate or deactivate third-party plug-ins from the Plug-Ins & Scratch Disks preferences (see Figure 5.9).

As you are aware, a scratch disk is hard-disk space used as memory. You can designate one or more hard disks in which to process images to increase the processing capabilities of your computer.

The settings in this dialog box include the following:

Additional Plug-Ins Folder (Off) Plug-ins extend Photoshop's capabilities; they include the filters, import/export modules, displacement maps, and third-party programs such as Kai's Power Tools. (See Appendix E for a list and descriptions of the most popular plug-ins.) You load or unload preferences from the Plug-Ins folder in the Photoshop application folder or any other folder on your disk. You can reorganize and load specific plug-ins into the program by checking this box, clicking the Choose button, and locating the desired folder on your disk.

Legacy Photoshop Serial Number Enter the serial number in this field if you use plug-ins that require an old-style Photoshop serial number.

Scratch Disks When Photoshop exceeds the amount of allocated memory, it uses a scratch disk as a source of virtual memory to process images. In the Scratch Disks field, assign the first scratch disk to your fastest hard drive with the most unused disk space. If you have additional hard drives, you can choose second, third, and fourth disks on which to allocate space. When the primary scratch disk is maxed out, the second one will kick in, then the third, and so on. Built-in memory is considerably faster than virtual memory, so you will experience a significant change in Photoshop's performance when you exceed the RAM allocation. Photoshop requires at least three to five times the file size for the amount of empty hard-disk space, so be sure to keep a block of space on your scratch disk(s) free of data. The disk should be defragmented and optimized regularly by using a utility program. Adobe recommends that you avoid working on removable media Zip disks, because they are less stable and much slower than hard disks.

A warning might appear at the bottom of the Plug-Ins & Scratch Disks dialog box that says changes to the options kick in only after you've quit and relaunched the program. If you anticipate the need to change the scratch disk, hold down the ⌘-Opt (Mac) or Ctrl-Alt (Win) keys while the program is launching and then respond to the dialog. If you want to add plug-ins to the program, press ⌘-Shift/Ctrl-Shift. The Plug-Ins folder will appear, where you can designate the plug-ins for your work session without having to quit and restart the program.

Figure 5.9

**The Plug-Ins &
Scratch Disks
preferences**

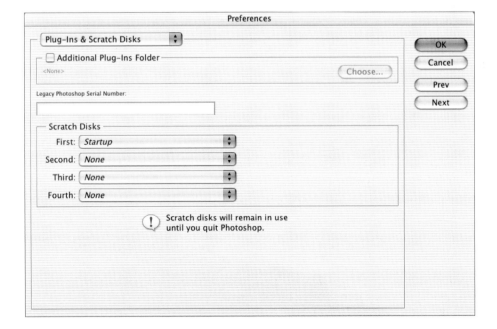

Memory & Image Cache

Image caching accelerates the screen redraw during the editing process. Control your use of this feature in the Memory & Image Cache preferences (shown in Figure 5.10).

The preference settings include the following:

Cache Levels (8) This setting specifies how many copies of your image are stored in memory to update the screen more quickly at reduced view sizes. For example, if you adjust the color of an image at 50% view, the adjustment happens much faster because the program has to change only 25% of the pixels. Experiment with the settings for images larger than 15 MB. Eight is the maximum setting, but high settings will deplete your system resources because the smaller previews are stored in memory. If you are working on large images and have sufficient RAM, as most computers do today, set the image cache to eight levels. For smaller images with less RAM, use lower settings.

Use Cache for Histograms in Levels (Off) This preference defines the Levels histogram based on the zoom ratio and the cumulative display of histograms throughout the work session, which compiles a histogram faster but with less accuracy. Do not check this option. For more on histograms, see Chapter 16, "Adjusting Tonality and Color."

Memory Usage (50%) This field displays the system's available RAM, the percentage of available RAM allocated to Photoshop, and the same amount in megabytes. The default setting of 50% is a good beginning to operating the software. During a Photoshop work session, if the Efficiency setting (in the status bar at bottom of the image window) ever drops below 100%, increase the percentage of memory by 10% increments until the efficiency remains at the maximum 100%. Never allocate, however, more than 90% of the memory. After you reset the memory allocation, you must quit and relaunch the program for the change to take effect.

PURGE MEMORY

Let's say you've been working on a file for the past 20 minutes, and you're about to apply the Unsharp Mask filter to give the image that final sparkle before sending it to the printer. You tweak the filter settings to perfection and click the OK button. A dialog box appears that tells you the filter cannot be applied because the scratch disk is full. Before you throw your shoe at the monitor in frustration, try purging the data stored on the scratch disks.

Choose Edit → Purge and choose data you would like to delete from the submenu. You can free up the Undo, Clipboard, and History memories individually, or choose All to dump

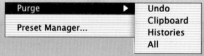

everything. Be careful, though; you cannot undo this operation.

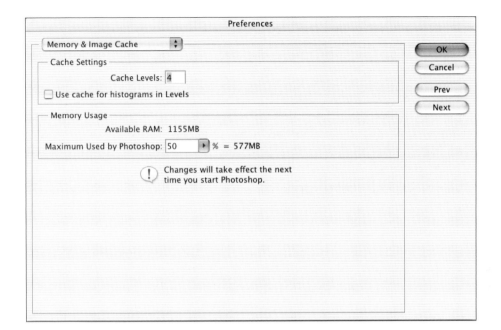

Figure 5.10

**The Memory &
Image Cache
preferences**

File Browser

The new File Browser preferences (see Figure 5.11) enable you to set specifications for the
File Browser display.

The options are as follows:

Do Not Process Files Larger Than (100 MB) It can be time-consuming for the File Browser
to create a thumbnail for an excessively large image. Enter a value for the maximum size
of an image for which the File Browser will display a thumbnail, extract metadata, or create previews. The default, 100 MB, is a good start.

Display Most Recently Used Folders In Location Popup (10) This setting determines the
number of folders to display in the Location pop-up list.

Custom Thumbnail Size (256 px) This option specifies the maximum width of a custom
File Browser thumbnail. 256 is a reasonable width for most monitors.

Allow Background Processing (Off) Selecting this option uses extra processing power to
regenerate metadata and preview information. Use it only if necessary or you may compromise performance.

High Quality Previews (Off) This setting creates better-quality previews, requiring more
disk space and RAM. Turn it on only if necessary or you may compromise performance.

Figure 5.11

Figure 5.11

**File Browser
Preferences**

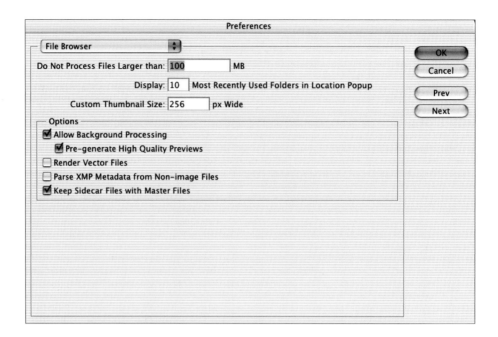

Render Vector Files (Off) Checking this box creates previews from EPS and Adobe PDF vector files. Use this only if you want the browser to display PDF 9Acrobat and EPS (Illustrator) previews.

Parse XMP Metadata from Non-Image Files (Off) Checking this box generates metadata from non-image files.

Keep Sidecar Files with Master Files (Off) This setting pertains to Sidecar files generated by XMP and THM formats. This feature enables you to copy, rename, batch rename, or move Sidecar files and keep them attached to their master files. A *sidecar* is a file in the same folder as the raw file with the same base name and an .xmp extension. This option is useful for long-term archiving of raw files with their associated settings, and for the exchange of raw files with associated settings in multiuser workflows.

Utilizing the Preset Manager

Photoshop gives you the ability to manage several libraries from a single dialog box. The Preset Manager is the storage unit for all of the elements that you might want to apply to the image, and it's a library of palettes that can be utilized by the program. As you add or delete items from the palettes, the currently loaded palette in the Preset Manager displays the changes. You can save the new palette and load any of the palettes on the system.

Choose Edit → Preset Manager to access its dialog box (Figure 5.12). From the Preset Type option list, choose the type of palette you wish to affect.

The small arrow to the right of the Preset Type list displays a pop-up menu that is divided into three groups of commands. The top group includes a list of display options for the items within the palette, which let you display the items as thumbnails or by their names. The second field lets you restore the current palette to the default or replace it with a previously saved palette. The third group lists additional palettes that can be readily accessed.

Adobe provides several palettes with Photoshop CS. If, for example, you are working on a document that will be used exclusively on the Web, you might want to load the Web Safe Swatches palette.

Calibrating Your Monitor

Part of the initial setup in Photoshop involves ensuring that your colors look right on-screen. A calibrated and ICC-profiled monitor is the foundation from which all other color settings are determined, and is the initial stage of color management that will ultimately provide consistency during each work session and predictable results from your printer. Calibration configures the best possible characteristics for a particular monitor so that the display is optimal. Calibration utilities are part of the Mac and Windows operating systems and will calibrate your monitor and record the resulting data to an ICC (International Color Consortium) profile.

Because these are visual calibration systems, they are inadequate for precision calibration. If you need precise calibration, use a device called a colorimeter, which sticks on the surface of your monitor's glass, measures the temperature of the phosphors, and records this state into an ICC profile. These devices are more accurate in that they measure the phosphor temperatures to determine the optimal settings for the monitor and don't rely on subjective visual decisions. (For a demonstration of ColorVision's hardware and software calibration system, refer to Chapter 15.)

Figure 5.12

The Preset Manager

Before calibrating, be sure that the monitor has been on for at least 30 minutes and that the ambient light in the room is set as you will use it during your work sessions—preferably low. Your monitor's bit depth should be set to Millions Of Colors (Mac) or True Color (Win), but see the following warning note. Turn off any background patterns or screen images, and change the background color to neutral gray. (The upcoming sidebar "Creating a Neutral Gray Desktop" shows how to do this.)

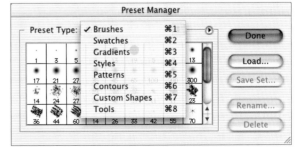

Do not attempt to change the screen bit depth of your monitor while running Photoshop on Windows systems. If you need to change the monitor's bit depth from 256 to True Color, for example, quit Photoshop, change the bit depth, and then launch Photoshop again.

Using Calibration Software

A monitor's gamma actually measures the contrast of the midtones of images displayed on-screen. Windows systems default to a higher gamma (2.2) than Macs (1.8), meaning that images will look slightly darker and have more contrast on a computer running Windows than on a Mac if they are not set to the same gamma value. To calibrate your monitor on the Macintosh, use the Display Calibrator Assistant (see Figure 5.13); from the control panel's utility, choose System Preferences → Displays → Color → Calibrate. On Windows, choose Start → Settings → Control Panel → Display. Follow the steps described in the utility to calibrate your monitor.

Using Adobe Gamma

Another calibration option for Windows users is Adobe Gamma software that bundles with Photoshop for Windows. You can learn about the Gamma utility in the Photoshop Help menu: choose Help → Help Contents → Search, and in the Search field, type **Adobe Gamma**.

To calibrate, choose the Adobe Gamma utility (see Figure 5.14) from the control panel. On Windows, choose Start → Settings → Control Panel → Adobe Gamma.

Figure 5.13

The Mac OS X Display Calibrator Assistant

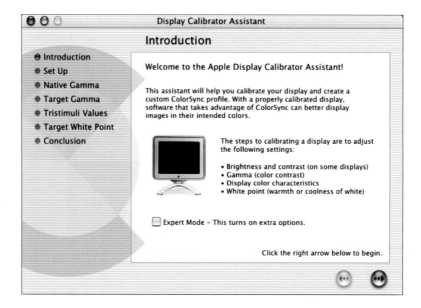

The first time you calibrate, choose the Gamma Wizard by clicking its radio button and then clicking Next. The wizard takes you by the hand and walks you through the calibration process, explaining the hows and whys of brightness and contrast, gamma, white point, and black point. (After you are familiar with its components, you can access the Control Panel version of Adobe Gamma.) As a starting point, click the Load button and select, as an ICC profile, Adobe Monitor or a manufacturer-supplied profile for your particular monitor. Click Next and follow the instructions and explanations as detailed by the Gamma Wizard. At the end of the session, compare the results by clicking the Before and After radio buttons, and then name and save the new profile.

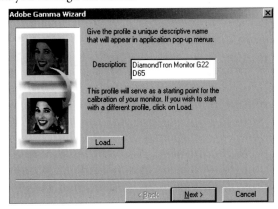

Figure 5.14

The Adobe Gamma utility

The Adobe Gamma utility has not been updated for Mac OS X but it does ship with the Windows version of Photoshop CS. I don't recommend calibrating in classic mode with an earlier version of Adobe Gamma on Mac OS X.

CREATING A NEUTRAL GRAY DESKTOP

Basic color theory teaches that your perception of a color is affected by the colors surrounding it. To ensure that your perception of color is unaltered by any ambient color or patterns, it's best to work with a completely neutral desktop.

Macintosh OS X

To create a neutral gray desktop in Mac OS X:

1. From System Preferences, choose Desktop.

2. Choose Collection → Solid Colors.

3. Click the medium-gray swatch.

Windows

To create a neutral gray desktop in Windows:

1. Choose Start → Settings → Control Panel. Launch the Display applet.

2. Click the Appearance tab.

3. From the Item list, choose Desktop.

4. From the color swatch pop-up list, choose Medium Gray (the color on the far right in the first row).

5. Click Apply to see the result or click OK to implement the operation.

The Adobe Gamma settings that you specify will automatically load each time your computer starts. Monitors deteriorate over time, so recalibrate weekly. If you find it impossible to calibrate your monitor to the standard settings, then it might be too old and faded and should be replaced.

Do not use the Adobe Gamma software and the System Calibration in the same session. Only one form of calibration should be in use at a time.

Choosing a Color Working Space

The next step in setting up the program is to choose a *color working space* to compensate for variables that occur as a result of different output devices. For example, an image intended for four-color process printing needs to look different on-screen than an image intended for the Web. Photoshop lets you work in RGB spaces other than those defined by your monitor.

To choose a color working space, choose Edit → Color Settings. In the Settings pop-up list, choose Web Graphics Defaults if you're preparing images for the Web or U.S. Prepress Defaults if you're prepping files for four-color printing (see Figure 5.15). See Chapter 15 for a more complete description of the Color Settings dialog box.

Figure 5.15

**The Photoshop
Color Settings
dialog box**

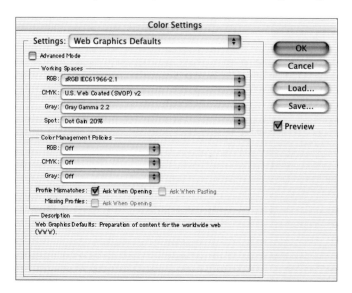

CHAPTER 6

Making Selections

Essential to image editing is the ability to isolate an area of the image so that an effect can be applied exclusively to that area. A selection serves two contradictory purposes: it affects and it protects. When you apply a Photoshop tool or operation, the area within the bounds of the selection marquee will be altered and the area outside the selection marquee will remain unaffected. Think of a selection simply as a hole through which you can alter the reality of your image.

Because there are so many variables to selecting an area, Photoshop provides several tools that facilitate the selection process. You'll encounter a wide range of methods, from the labor-intensive to the fully automatic, that enable you to select pixels for the ultimate purpose of altering their appearance.

This chapter will introduce you to the following:

- **Masking**

- **Using selection tools**

- **Applying selection techniques**

The Power of Masking

Masking, or the process of protecting portions of an image, used to be an entirely manual process. In ancient times—that is, prior to the introduction of Photoshop—one of the most common methods of altering a photograph was to paint it with an airbrush. Airbrushing required a person with a steady hand and a razor-sharp knife. A piece of transparent frisket film was placed over the entire image. The artist slowly, carefully, and gently (so as not to damage the photo) cut a hole in the frisket to expose the area of the photograph to be painted. The exposed portion of the image was painted, and the areas where the frisket remained were protected. The frisket was then peeled back to reveal the colored shape of the hole.

Photoshop CS offers an arsenal of tools and operations that give the user versatility and control unimagined in that bygone era. The selection tools range from purely manual, such as the Lasso, to semimanual, such as the Marquee, to semiautomatic, such as the Magnetic Lasso, to fully automatic, such as the Magic Wand. Each selection tool is designed to hasten the masking process, depending on the characteristics of the image. Because images vary in contrast, tonality, color, and content, Photoshop provides tools and methods that can be applied to every possible situation. Nevertheless, making selections is undoubtedly the most labor-intensive and time-consuming of all Photoshop operations. In many situations, one selection method is insufficient and several must be combined to define the target area. Often, other selection techniques will be employed in combination with the tools for greater accuracy or to isolate a tricky area.

Using Selection Tools

When you make a selection in Photoshop, an animated marquee defines the approximate boundaries of the selected area. This moving, dash-lined border is sometimes referred to as the "marching ants" because of its resemblance to a column of tiny insects on the move.

Figure 6.1

Photoshop's default selection tools

By default, three of Photoshop's selection tools are visible at the top of the Tool palette (see Figure 6.1). When you press and hold the mouse on the Rectangular Marquee tool, the palette expands to reveal all four marquee tools. When you expand the Lasso tool, all three free-form selection tools are revealed. With the Magic Wand tool, which resides alone, the total number of selection tools is eight.

Other methods can enhance the speed or accuracy of the selection process. The Pen tool, covered in Chapter 9, "Drawing Paths," uses Bezier curves to define edges. Quick Mask uses painting tools to select areas (see Chapter 12, "Using Channels and Quick Mask"). Color Range is an industrial-strength Magic Wand tool (see Chapter 21, "Making Difficult Selections").

The Selection Tool Options Bar

The Options bar, shown in Figure 6.2, displays the characteristics of the current selection tool. You can input values or choose options that will affect the selection tool's behavior.

When you choose a selection tool, the icon that represents it appears on the left end of the Options bar, which is also the Tool Preset menu. The next four icons represent selection options. These and other selection options on the Options bar are as follows:

New Selection Click this button to create a new selection with the chosen selection tool.

Add to Selection Click this button to add to an existing selection with the chosen selection tool. The addition can either expand a selection's boundaries or be used to select an unconnected area. You can perform the same function by holding down the Shift key as you drag with the selection tool.

Subtract from Selection Click this button to exclude a portion of an existing selection. You can perform the same function by holding down the Option (Macintosh) or Alt (Windows) key as you drag with the selection tool.

Intersect with Selection After making an initial selection and clicking this button, make a second selection overlapping the first. Only that portion of the image common to both selections will remain active. You can perform the same operation by pressing Shift-Option (Mac) or Shift-Alt (Win) as you use the second selection tool.

Feather Prior to drawing a selection, you can program a tool to produce a soft-edged selection by specifying a numerical value in the Feather field of the tool's Options bar.

Feathering creates a gradual transition between the inside and the outside of a border. When you apply an effect to a feathered selection, the areas of the effect at the edge of a selected area becomes gradually more transparent, producing a softening or blurring effect, as shown in Figure 6.3. Feathering a selection gives you the power to increase the credibility of your image by gradually blending colored pixels into each other and eliminating any evidence of a hard edge.

Figure 6.2

The Options bar showing the default options for the Rectangular Marquee tool

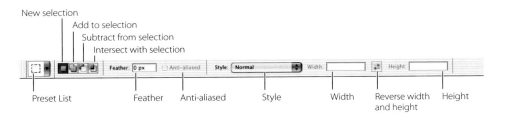

New selection
Add to selection
Subtract from selection
Intersect with selection

Preset List   Feather   Anti-aliased   Style   Width   Reverse width and height   Height

When you apply a feather to an existing selection border, sometimes you will see the border decrease in size or slightly change shape. This is because Photoshop displays selection borders only around areas that represent 50% transparency or more. You can select areas less than 50%, and you will notice a change when you apply an effect, but you will not see an outline around them.

> In addition to entering a value in the Options bar, you can also apply feathering to an existing selection outline by choosing Select → Feather. When you choose Select → Feather, a dialog box appears; enter a value in the Feather Radius field. The Feather Radius value extends the specified number of pixels into the selection outline (becoming increasingly more opaque) and outside the selection border (becoming increasingly more transparent). For example, if you enter a value of 10, the size of the feather will actually be 20 pixels, from the opaque pixels inside the selection border to absolute transparency outside the selection border.

Anti-Aliased An *anti-alias* is a 2- or 3-pixel border around an edge that blends into the adjacent color to create a small transition zone. It is intended to simulate depth of field in a photograph. Without the anti-alias, an image would look "aliased," or stair-stepped, without smooth transitions between colors. Anti-aliasing is different from feathering because the size of a feather transition can be controlled, whereas an anti-aliased edge is automatically applied when the option is chosen and is usually just a few pixels wide, depending on the resolution of the document (see Figure 6.4).

Figure 6.3

The Feather command softens the edge of a selection border. On the left, an image has been pasted into a selection. On the right, the same image has been pasted into a selection border with a 10-pixel feather radius.

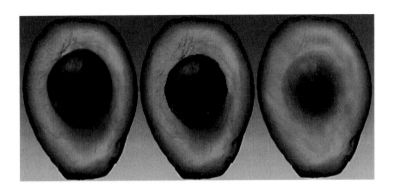

Figure 6.4

The effects of modifying an image through the various types of selection edges: the avocado pit has been pasted into (left) anti-aliased, (center) aliased, and (right) feathered selections.

Shape Selection Tools

You use the Rectangular Marquee tool and its fly-out, the Elliptical Marquee tool, primarily when you need to select a square, rectangular, circular, or elliptical shape within your image. Don't forget, however, that many more-complex shapes can be obtained with just these two tools when they are used in combination with the Add, Subtract, and Intersect options.

Within the Marquee fly-out (but for some reason not included in the Shift-M key shortcut when you cycle through it), you have two more options: the Single Column Marquee and the Single Row Marquee.

Rectangular Marquee

The Rectangular Marquee tool ⬚ is used to select rectangular or square areas of the image. Click in the image and drag in any direction to select a rectangular area of the image.

Elliptical Marquee

Use the Elliptical Marquee tool ⬭ to create ellipses or circles. It performs similarly to the Rectangular Marquee: click and drag in any direction to produce an elliptical, or circular, selection.

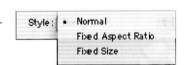

The Style menu in the Marquee tools' Options bar enables you to choose from three methods for sizing the Rectangular and Elliptical Marquees:

Normal I wish they would rename this *Manual* because that's precisely what it is—the setting for hands-on control of these Marquee tools. By choosing Normal, you determine the size and proportion of the marquee by dragging.

Fixed Aspect Ratio Enter numerical values for the proportion of the marquee in the Height and Width fields. Although you can change the *size* of the marquee by dragging, its *proportions* will remain constant.

Fixed Size The size of the marquee is determined by the values, in pixels, that you enter in the Height and Width fields. A marquee size is defined in pixels because it can't select anything smaller. If you want Photoshop to accept values in units other than pixels—inches, for example—then Control-click/right-click on the Width and Height fields and drag to your preferred units. Photoshop will create a marquee to the nearest pixel that you specify.

Table 6.1 describes the keyboard modifiers that you can use with the Rectangular and Elliptical Marquee tools to control the behavior of marquees as you draw them.

Single Row Marquee

The Single Row Marquee tool ▭ selects a single *horizontal* row of pixels. Click anywhere in the image, and a selection marquee appears around a single row of adjacent pixels that runs horizontally across the entire image.

Single Column Marquee

The Single Column Marquee tool ▯ selects a single *vertical* column of pixels. Click anywhere in the image, and a selection marquee appears around a single column of adjacent pixels that runs vertically from the top to the bottom of the image.

You can also use this tool to create stripes that can later be colorized to produce wood-grain effects. Here's how:

1. Open an RGB document with a white background.

2. Select a single column of pixels near the center of the image.

3. Choose Filter → Noise → Add Noise → 400, and click OK.

Table 6.1

Moving and Constraining Marquees

TASK	TECHNIQUE
Constrain to square or circle	Shift-dragging constrains the Rectangular Marquee selection to a square, or the Elliptical Marquee to a circle.
Draw from center	By default, a marquee originates from a corner point. To originate the marquee from its center, place your cursor in the center of the area and Option-drag/Alt-drag.
Reposition while dragging	While dragging out a marquee, hold down the spacebar and drag at any time to reposition it.
Reposition after drawing	While in the Marquee tool, place the cursor inside the marquee and drag to reposition it.
Combination techniques	You can combine any of these key command techniques. For example, press the Shift key and the mouse button, and drag to constrain the image to a circle or square. Then while dragging, press the Option/Alt key to radiate it from its center point.

4. Choose Edit → Transform → Scale. A bounding box appears. Drag the middle handle of the left and right side of the bounding box to the left and right edge of the image so that the noise fills the window. It will look like a series of colored stripes.

5. Press the Return/Enter key to initiate the transformation (or the Esc key to cancel it).

6. Choose Image → Adjustments → Hue/Saturation. Select the Colorize check box and move the sliders until the image changes to the desired color. Click OK.

Free-Form Selection Tools

Photoshop offers three tools for making irregularly shaped selections. The Lasso tool and its fly-outs, the Polygonal Lasso and the Magnetic Lasso, draw selections based on your mouse movements. Cycle through these tools by pressing Shift-L.

Lasso

The Lasso tool [icon] draws free-form selections. Click the edge of the area you want to select and drag to surround the area with the selection border. Close the marquee by placing the cursor on the starting point, or release the mouse to close the selection with a straight line.

Polygonal Lasso

The Polygonal Lasso tool [icon] is used to create straight-edged selection borders. Click and release the mouse. Then reposition the mouse to the next corner of the polygon, and click and release again. You can repeat the process until you return to the point of origin and close the marquee by clicking the starting point, or double-click to close the selection from the most recently established point. By holding down the Shift key, you can constrain line segments horizontally, vertically, or at 45-degree angles.

> When using either the Lasso or Polygonal Lasso, you can toggle between the two by pressing the Option/Alt key.

Magnetic Lasso

The Magnetic Lasso tool [icon] "intuitively" makes selections based on the contrast values of pixels. As you click and drag, the Magnetic Lasso deposits a path that is attracted to the edge of two contrasting areas. When you release the mouse, the path becomes a selection. The Magnetic Lasso tool rarely makes perfect selections, but it's a time-saver if combined with other selection tools.

The Magnetic Lasso selection tool takes a while to get used to. If you find that you've lost control over the path, double-click the mouse to complete the selection, deselect (using Select → Deselect or ⌘/Ctrl-D), and begin again.

The Magnetic Lasso tool has four settings in the Options bar that affect its behavior:

Width: 10 px	Edge Contrast: 10%	Frequency: 57	☑ Pen Pressure

Width This setting (in pixels) determines the distance from the path of the mouse within which pixels will be evaluated for contrast by the Magnetic Lasso.

Edge Contrast This is the minimum percentage of pixel contrast that the Magnetic Lasso will be attracted to. The higher the number, the smaller the range of contrast, hence the more selective the tool will be.

Frequency Enter a value for the frequency with which points are automatically deposited. The points create segments along the path that fix the previous segments and better control the tool's behavior. For even more control, I recommend that you also deposit extra points manually along the edge to be defined by clicking your mouse as you drag. Although these anchors are not editable like vector points, adding them can help guide the Magnetic Lasso when making a selection in an area where a clear outline is not present and your vision and the tool's "intuition" are at odds. (See Chapter 9 for a thorough discussion of editing anchor points while using Photoshop's vector-based tools.)

Pen Pressure Select this check box to increase the width of the tool by using stylus pressure when using a tablet.

The Magic Wand Tool

The Magic Wand tool ▨ (shortcut key Shift-W) makes "automatic" selections based on the similarity of pixel brightness. To use the Magic Wand, place your cursor on the area to be selected and click your mouse. Adjacent pixels of similar color will be included in the selection.

You can affect the range of pixels that are selected by adjusting the Tolerance setting in the tool's Options bar. Higher tolerance values include in the selection more pixels of greater color and brightness range. Lower values include fewer pixels in the selection.

The Eyedropper tool's sample size also plays a role in the Magic Wand selection. If the Eyedropper is set to a point sample, the Magic Wand will calculate its selection based on the tolerance of a single pixel. If it's set to a 3 × 3 or 5 × 5 average, then the tolerance is determined by the average brightness of 9 pixels or 25 pixels, respectively. For more about the Eyedropper tool see Chapter 16.

In the middle example in Figure 6.5, I entered a tolerance of 32 and clicked a pixel with a value of 128, or mid-gray. (I determined its value by looking at the Info palette.) The Magic Wand selection included all the pixels that are 32 steps lighter and all the pixels that are 32 steps darker than the sampled pixel—that is, all adjacent pixels with brightness values between 96 and 160 were selected.

> When selecting RGB color images with the Magic Wand tool, the range is determined by each of the red, green, and blue values of the sampled pixel.

Other choices in the Options bar enhance your ability to control the operation of the Magic Wand tool:

Contiguous By default, the Contiguous box is checked, which limits the Magic Wand selection to adjacent pixels. Click to uncheck this box, thereby selecting all the pixels in the image within the same tolerance range.

Use All Layers If this box is not checked, you will limit the Magic Wand selection to pixels within the same tolerance range on a single layer. Checking this box includes pixels within the same tolerance range on multiple layers. (Layers are covered in Chapter 7, "Layering Your Image.")

Applying Selection Techniques

You can modify a selection outline several ways; among them, you can conceal it, transform it, add to it, subtract from it, soften its edges, and eliminate it. These commands are important because they facilitate the process of masking. For example, if you draw a selection incorrectly, instead of redrawing it from scratch, it might be more efficient to make a few alterations to it. What follows are some indispensable outline-altering techniques.

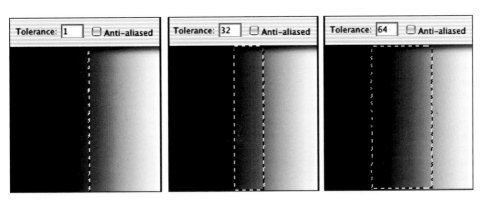

Figure 6.5

Tolerance determines the range of pixels that the Magic Wand selects.

Using the Select Menu

Some selection adjustments can be automatically applied by accessing them from the Select menu or applying a shortcut key command. You will find that you use these commands quite frequently, so in the interest of working efficiently, I recommend that you learn to use the shortcuts. Here are the Select Menu commands and their shortcuts:

Select All (⌘/Ctrl-A) This command selects the entire content of an image or a targeted layer. Because you can perform virtually any operation to the entire image in Photoshop when no specific area has been defined by a selection border, this command is used primarily to select the image prior to copying and pasting.

Deselect (⌘/Ctrl-D) Use Select → Deselect to deactivate the selection. Another method is to click off the selection anywhere on the image—except when using the Single Column and Single Row Marquee tools or the Magic Wand tool.

Reselect (Shift-⌘/Ctrl-D) Choose this command to reactivate the last deselected selection border.

Figure 6.6

After selecting the background (top), the Inverse command deselects that portion of the image and selects the masked portion (bottom).

Inverse (Shift-⌘/Ctrl-I) To deselect the selected portion of the image and select the masked portion, choose Select → Inverse. This technique can save time when an image has been photographed on a single-colored background. The background can be selected quickly with the Magic Wand and inverted to select the desired content, as in Figure 6.6.

Show/Hide Selection Edges Use View → Show → Selection Edges to conceal (and reveal) the marching ants from view while the selection remains active. You can then choose View → Extras (or ⌘/Ctrl-H) to perform the operation. This command is useful in seeing changes to the image without the distracting selection border.

> With the border invisible, you might forget that an area of the image is selected. Photoshop will not perform operations anywhere else on the image until the selection border is deactivated. If you find that the Paintbrush tool is not painting or the Smudge tool not smudging, press ⌘/Ctrl-D to deactivate the invisible selection.

Figure 6.7

The Border command selects only the outermost portion of your selection (here, the pixels immediately inward and outward from the edge of the plant).

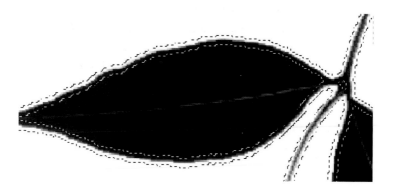

Modify After a selection has been made, you can alter its dimensions by choosing one of the Select ➝ Modify subcommands. Each command changes the selection marquee and alters its dimensions:

> **Border** frames the selection and deselects the inside area of the outline, producing a selected border of specific thickness (see Figure 6.7). When you choose Select ➝ Modify ➝ Border, you can determine the thickness of the border by entering a value in pixels in the Width field.
>
> **Smooth** rounds sharp corners of a selection, eliminating protrusions and stair-stepped areas of the selection border. Choose Select ➝ Modify ➝ Smooth, and then enter a sample radius value (larger values increase the effect). In Figure 6.8, the sample radius results in "cutting off" the left tip of the triangle.
>
> **Expand and Contract** both perform in the same way to enlarge or reduce the size of the selection by a specified number of pixels. This command is quite useful for trimming off stubborn, unwanted edge pixels (see the section on matting in Chapter 22, "Advanced Layer Techniques") or tightening up your selection a bit. Choose Select ➝ Modify ➝ Expand or Contract, and enter a value between 1 and 100 pixels. Click OK to implement the operation.

Figure 6.8

The Smooth command rounds off jagged corners, such as the tip of this triangle.

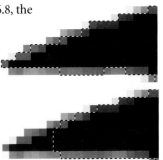

Grow The value entered in the Tolerance field of the Magic Wand's Options bar determines how much the selection will grow. When you choose Select ➝ Grow, the selection marquee expands to include adjacent pixels that are lighter or darker by no more than the tolerance range.

Similar To use this command, a selection must be active. When you choose Select ➝ Similar, Photoshop selects all pixels within the image that are the same colors as the pixels within the selected area. The amount selected is controlled by the Tolerance setting in the Magic Wand's Options bar.

Transforming a Selection

After you make a selection, you might want to alter its shape before applying one of Photoshop's many powerful operations to its content. Photoshop gives you the ability to scale, rotate, or move a selection border. To transform a selection, choose Select ➝ Transform Selection. A rectangular transformation box appears around the selection border. You can then transform the size, angle, or position of the selection border with the following procedures:

Move To move the selection, place your cursor within the rectangular transformation box; the Move cursor ▸ appears. Press your mouse button and drag the selection into position; then release the mouse.

The icon in the center of the transformation box represents the point of origin. You can move this icon prior to scaling or rotating the selection to change the point from which the selection will transform. When you want to move the box, however, you place your cursor anywhere in the selection *except* on the icon.

Scale To scale a selection border, place your cursor on one of the square handles on the corners or sides of the box. The Scale cursor appears. Press your mouse button and drag. To keep the selection border in its current proportion, press your Shift key while dragging.

Rotate To rotate a selection, place your cursor outside the box. The Rotate cursor appears. Press your mouse button and drag to rotate the selection. Holding down the Shift key enables precise rotation in 15-degree increments.

Scale and Rotate are demonstrated in Figure 6.9. To implement the transformation, click the check mark or press Return/Enter; the transformation box will disappear. To cancel the transformation, click the Cancel box or press the Esc key.

After you've chosen Select → Transform Selection and the transformation box is displayed, you can also apply many more transformations to the selection by choosing Edit → Transform. A list of options appears, including Skew, Distort, Perspective, and various precise Rotate commands. You perform these additional functions by repositioning the anchor points of the transformation box. The Flip Horizontal or Flip Vertical commands will mirror the marquee across a horizontal or vertical axis passing through its point-of-origin icon. See Chapter 13, "Sizing and Transforming Images" for more on this topic.

Figure 6.9

Transform Selection techniques: Scale (left) and Rotate (right)

Applying Other Selection Techniques

After a selection has been made, you can reposition the marquee with or without its contents by using the following techniques:

Move Selection Outline While in any selection tool, click inside the marquee and drag. After you've relocated the outline, release the mouse.

Nudge Selection Outline While in any selection tool, press the right, left, up, or down arrow keys to move a selection in increments of 1 pixel. Press Shift plus any of the arrow keys to move the selection outline 10 pixels at a time.

Move Selection Contents Choose the Move tool 🔖; click inside the marquee and drag. After you've relocated the marquee, release the mouse. You can also move the contents while in any selection tool: ⌘-click/Ctrl-click inside the marquee and drag. The icon 🔖 displays a symbol that looks like scissors, indicating that you are cutting the contents of the selection outline and moving them. After you've relocated the selection, release the mouse and then the key. The Move tool can be used for transformation operations such as scaling, rotating, and distorting You can read more about the Move tool in Chapter 13.

> After you've selected an area and moved it once, it "floats." That is, it can be moved again by placing a selection tool inside the marquee, pressing the mouse button, and dragging. You no longer need to press ⌘/Ctrl. The selection continues to float until you deselect it.

Nudge Selection Contents You can nudge the contents of a selection in 1-pixel increments: with the Move tool active, press the left, right, up, or down arrow keys. Press Shift and any of the arrow keys to move the selection contents 10 pixels at a time.

Duplicate Selection Contents With the Move tool active, hold down Option-Alt/⌘-Ctrl while you click and drag. You'll see a double Move cursor 🔖, which indicates that you are duplicating the selection. (Or, while any other tool is active, hold down ⌘/Ctrl while you drag.) After you've relocated the copy to the desired position, release the mouse.

Making Selections

When I was a kid, Mr. Potato Head was a special toy. It was one of the only objects in my toy chest that let me make real aesthetic choices. I would start with a potato and choose from dozens of plastic facial features that could attach to produce a unique character.

For this first Hands On exercise, Fred Photato Head is the virtual version of the popular toy. In the process of assembling a character from dozens of features, you will learn how to use Photoshop's selection tools. All of the elements are on a single document. You will choose a feature, select it, and drag it to the character. In this way, you will build your unique version of Fred Photato Head.

Making accurate selections is fundamental to maintaining the credibility of your image. Poorly drawn selections that are rough, inaccurate, or stair-stepped, or that contain unwanted edge pixels, are sure to destroy the illusion of a seamless reality. It's important, then, to familiarize yourself with the masking process and to hone your selection-making skills. That is what I hope this step-by-step section will accomplish.

Getting Started

Delete your preferences file before beginning this Hands On exercise. The "Modifying Photoshop's Settings" section in Chapter 5, "Setting Up the Program," details how to reset your preferences to Photoshop's defaults. After you have launched Photoshop with default preferences, here's how to begin the Hands On project:

1. Insert the *Photoshop CS Savvy* CD in your CD-ROM drive.

2. Choose File → Open; select and open `Fred_Photato_Head_Start.psd` in the `H01` folder on the CD (see Figure H1.1).

3. Save the file to your hard disk.

   Figure H1.2 shows one possible outcome.

See the color versions of Fred_Photato_Head_Start and Fred_Photato_Head_End—Figures C40 and C41—in the color section of this book.

Figure H1.1

The open Fred Photato Head file

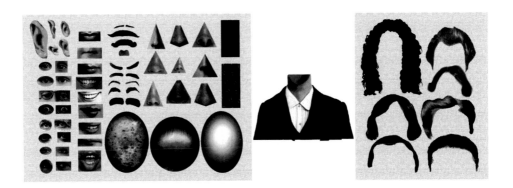

Moving the Mannequin

You'll use the Rectangular Marquee tool 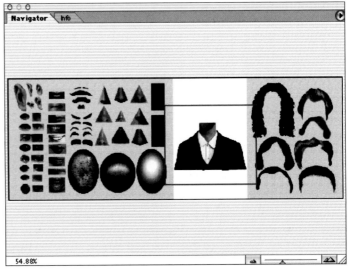 to move the mannequin into position:

1. Use the Navigator to zoom in or out so you can see all of the mannequin in the center of the screen (see Figure H1.3).

2. Choose the Rectangular Marquee tool. Place your cursor just below the lower-left corner of the mannequin. Click and drag to the upper-right corner to make your selection, as shown in Figure H1.4.

Figure H1.2

This is what I made out of the virtual elements, but yours might look quite different.

Figure H1.3

Use the Navigator palette to bring the mannequin into view.

Figure H1.4

Drag a rectangle around the mannequin.

Figure H1.5

The mannequin positioned at the bottom of the background

3. Choose the Move tool ![Move tool] . Place your cursor inside the marching ants. Click and hold the mouse button. Press the Shift key to constrain the vertical movement of the marquee as you drag down. Drag the mannequin until its ragged bottom edge is just outside the bottom of the white background, as shown in Figure H1.5. Then release the mouse.

4. Press ⌘-D (Mac) or Ctrl-D (Win) to deselect the mannequin.

Selecting a Head

You can choose among the potato, the onion, or the egg for the head. This exercise uses the egg. Follow these steps:

1. With the Navigator, zoom out so that you can see the egg, the onion, and the potato.

2. Press Shift-M to select the Elliptical Marquee tool ![Elliptical Marquee tool] or choose it from the Marquee fly-out in the Tool palette. Place your cursor in the approximate center of the egg. Press the Option/Alt key as you drag an ellipse from the center. As you near the edge, press the spacebar (but don't release the Option/Alt key!). Drag the marquee to accurately position it so that it just touches the edge. Release the spacebar to resize, and press it again to reposition the marquee until you've centered and positioned the selection outline on the edge of the egg. Release the mouse first and then the keys.

3. Choose the Move tool. Place the cursor inside the marquee and drag the egg to position it on the mannequin, as in Figure H1.6.

4. Press ⌘/Ctrl-D to deselect and ⌘/Ctrl-S to save the document.

Figure H1.6

The egg positioned on the mannequin

Selecting the Eyes

With the Elliptical Marquee tool still active, you will now select the eyes:

1. In the Options bar, from the Style pop-up list, choose Fixed Aspect Ratio. Enter **1.5** for the width and **1** for the height, as in Figure H1.7.

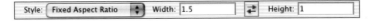

2. You'll find a group of eyes to the left of the mannequin. Zoom in on one of the left eyes and place your cursor in the center of it. Press the Option/Alt key and drag outward. Don't drag to the very edge, but stay a few pixels within the oval shape, as seen in Figure H1.8.

3. Choose Select → Feather. Enter a value of **2** pixels. This option lets you apply a feather to an existing selection.

4. Choose the Move tool. Drag the left eye and position it on the egg. Notice the seamless transition between the egg and the eye due to the feathered selection.

5. Choose the Elliptical Marquee tool. You will use the same fixed aspect ratio for the right eye.

6. In the Options bar, enter a value of **2** px for the feather. (Entering a value in the Options bar enables you to feather a selection before drawing it.)

7. Place your cursor on a right eye. Click your mouse and drag to position the fixed aspect ratio marquee.

8. Choose the Move tool. Drag the right eye and position it on the egg. Once again, there is a seamless transition between the egg and the eye due to the feathered selection, as shown in Figure H1.9.

9. Press ⌘/Ctrl-D to deselect and ⌘/Ctrl-S to save the document.

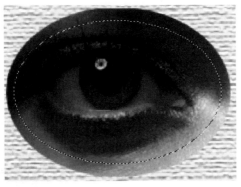

Figure H1.8

The selection of a left eye

Figure H1.9

The eyes positioned on the egg, with a feathered transition

Selecting a Nose

You'll use two variations of the Lasso tool 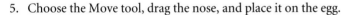 to select the nose:

1. Choose the Lasso tool. In the Options bar, set the feather radius to **2** px.

2. Choose a nose. Start at the lower-left of the nose and drag to the right around the curved shapes.

3. When you reach the side of the nose, press and hold the Option/Alt key. Release the mouse. The tool changes to the Polygonal Lasso. Drag a straight line up the right side of the nose. When you reach the top portion of the nose, press the mouse button, release the Option/Alt key, and drag the curve with the Lasso tool.

4. Press the Option/Alt key again. Release the mouse and drag a straight line down the left side of the nose. When you reach the curved portion of the left nostril, press the mouse button, release the key again, and drag the Lasso to close the selection. The selection should look like Figure H1.10.

5. Choose the Move tool, drag the nose, and place it on the egg.

6. Press ⌘/Ctrl-D to deselect and ⌘/Ctrl-S to save the document.

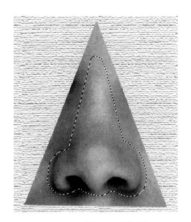

Figure H1.10
The selected nose

Selecting the Mouth

You will also select the mouth with the Lasso tool:

1. Choose the Lasso tool. Because the feather radius was set for the Lasso tool in the previous step, it doesn't need to be reset. Encircle one of the mouths as close to its edge as possible.

2. Choose the Move tool. In the Options bar, select the Show Bounding Box check box. Place the cursor inside the bounding box. Drag the mouth and place it on the egg. Press the Shift key while dragging to constrain the proportions.

3. To size the mouth, place your cursor on any one of the bounding box handles, and drag inward to decrease or outward to increase the size, as in Figure H1.11.

   Press the ⌘/Ctrl key to independently move the corner points of the bounding box to distort the mouth.

4. To rotate the mouth, place the cursor on the outside corner of the box until the rotate icon appears and then drag.

5. If you would like to see the mouth without the marquee to get a better idea of how it looks, choose View →Show → Selection Edges or press ⌘/Ctrl-H. The selection remains active, but the marquee becomes concealed. To display the marquee again, choose the same menu item or key command.

Figure H1.11
Sizing the mouth

6. In the Options bar, click the check mark to commit the transformation or the Cancel icon to cancel it 🚫 ✔.

7. Deselect and save the document.

Adding a Mustache

Use this fast technique of selecting the mustache by subtracting the area around it from the selection:

1. Choose the Rectangular Marquee tool.

2. Drag a rectangle around the mustache of choice.

3. Choose the Magic Wand tool. In the Options bar, set the tolerance to **24**.

4. Choose the Subtract From Selection icon 🖼 from the toolbar.

5. Click within the rectangular selection but not on the mustache. The mustache is automatically selected.

6. Choose Select → Feather. Enter a value of **1** px.

7. Choose the Move tool. Place the cursor inside the bounding box. Drag the mustache and place it between the mouth and the nose on the egg.

8. Size the mustache to fit the space.

9. Deselect and save.

Selecting the Eyebrows

To give Fred a little character, you will add eyebrows. There are some real whoppers to choose from. Here are the steps:

1. Choose the Magic Wand tool 🪄. In the Options bar, set the tolerance to **32**.

2. Click a right eyebrow. Only a portion of the eyebrow is selected, as shown in Figure H1.12. Depending on the eyebrow you select, you'll have to readjust the tolerance and reselect to make a complete selection, or you can click the Add To Selection icon in the Options bar and continue to click the unselected areas. Select the left eyebrow in the same way.

3. After the eyebrows are selected, choose Select → Feather. Enter a value of **1** px.

Figure H1.12

Only a portion of the eyebrows is selected.

4. Choose the Move tool. Place the cursor inside the bounding box. Drag the eyebrows and place them above the eyes on the egg. Resize them if desired.

5. Deselect and save.

Choosing the Hair

The easiest way to select a complex shape with an irregular edge and a lot of tonal variation is with the Magnetic Lasso tool. Here you'll use this tool to select the hair:

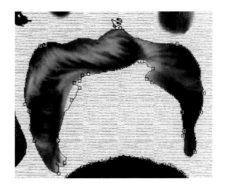

1. Choose the Magnetic Lasso tool ![icon]. In the Options bar, set the feather radius to **1** px. Use the other default settings in the Options bar to control the tool's performance.

2. Zoom in on one of the wigs. Place your cursor on the wig's edge. Drag slowly around it. A path is laid down as you drag, as demonstrated in Figure H1.13. For more control, add additional anchors by clicking your mouse as you drag.

Figure H1.13

The wig selected with the Magnetic Lasso tool. Notice the areas where some of the edge was not precisely selected. You can later refine these imperfect areas by subtracting them from the selection with the Lasso tool.

3. Completely surround the edge of the wig and connect the end point with the beginning point to close the selection. If you lose control of the tool, double-click, deselect, and begin again.

You might find that this tool does not make a perfect selection. Often it is necessary to refine the selection by adding or subtracting from the selection with the Lasso tool (see Figure H1.13).

1. You'll want to soften the edge of the hair. After the selection has been made, choose Select → Modify → Contract. Enter **2** pixels for the Contract By value (see Figure H1.14).

2. Zoom out. Choose the Move tool. Place the cursor inside the bounding box. Drag the wig and place it on the egg. Resize it for a perfect fit. Don't forget to commit the transformation by clicking the check mark in the Options bar.

3. Deselect and save.

Selecting and Duplicating the Ears

To select the ears, you will once again use the Magnetic Lasso tool:

1. Again, maintain the 1 px feather radius in the Options bar that you set in the previous step. Use the default settings in the Options bar to control the tool's performance.

2. Carefully drag along the edge of one of the ears to encircle it.

3. After you've entirely surrounded the edges with the magnetic selection outline, place your cursor on the original point and click your mouse to implement the selection.

Figure H1.14

The Contract Selection dialog box

Contract Selection		
Contract By: 2	pixels	OK
		Cancel

4. Choose the Move tool. Click inside the bounding box. Drag the ear and place it on the left side of Fred's head. Size the ear by dragging its corner points and then commit the transformation.

5. Click inside the bounding box again, but this time press Option/Alt as you drag to duplicate the ear. Position the ear on the right side of the egg and release the mouse.

6. Choose → Edit → Transform Flip Horizontal.

7. Reposition the ear.

8. Deselect and save.

Creating the Tie

First, you'll make a selection of the area where you want the tie. Then, you'll move the marquee onto the fabric, copy it, and deposit it on the mannequin to create a tie:

1. Choose the Lasso tool. In the Options bar, set the feather radius to **0** px.

2. On Fred's shirt, draw the shape of the tie, as shown in Figure H1.15.

3. Place your cursor in the center of the marching ants. Click the mouse and drag it to one of the material swatches.

4. Choose the Move tool. Place the cursor inside the selection outlines and drag the tie back onto the shirt.

5. Deselect and save.

You can enhance the tie, as I have done in Figure H1.16, by painting portions of it with a low-opacity black to produce a shadow effect. See Chapter 12, "Using Channels and Quick Mask," to learn about painting.

Figure H1.15

The outline of the tie

Figure H1.16

The completed tie, with a shadow for depth

Cropping the Image

Now that you've finished Fred, you can throw away any unwanted parts of the image:

1. Choose the Crop tool ▣ . Place your cursor on the lower-left corner of the white background. Click and drag up and to the right to encompass about seven-eighths of the vertical and the full horizontal dimension of the white background, as shown in Figure H1.17. Release the mouse.

2. Adjust the Crop bounding box by dragging its corner handles.

3. Click the check mark in the Options bar or press the Enter key to implement the crop.

4. Save the image.

Adding a Background

To finish this portrait off, you'll add a soft-edged background:

1. Choose the Magic Wand tool. Set the tolerance to **32**.

2. Click in the white background to select it.

3. Choose the Rectangular Marquee tool. In the Options bar, set the feather to **40** px.

4. Click the Subtract From Selection icon.

5. Click about a half-inch or so from the upper-left edge and drag down to the very bottom, about an inch or so from the lower-right edge, as shown in Figure H1.18.

Figure H1.17

The Crop bounding box in place

Figure H1.18

The feathered selection border

6. Click the Swatches tab in the Color/Swatches/ Styles palette cluster. Choose a color by clicking a swatch (see Figure H1.19).

7. Press Option-Delete/Alt-Backspace to fill the area with color.

8. Deselect and save.

Figure H1.19

Choosing a color in the Swatches palette

CHAPTER 7

Layering Your Image

Photoshop images appear on flat screens, but they are actually three-dimensional because of the power of layers. In the virtual world of the Photoshop work flow, layers are the third dimension. Beyond the height and width, they create depth.

Layers are critical to working dynamically in Photoshop. Fragments of an image saved on individual layers can be edited separately and moved independently of each other. The stacking order of layers can help determine the depth and position of visual elements within the picture plane. In short, working with layers gives you tremendous control over the image during the process of creating it.

This chapter will help you learn about the following:

- **Understanding the Layers palette**
- **Creating new layers**
- **Using layer styles**
- **Consolidating and blending layers**
- **Working with Type layers**

Creating the Illusion of Depth

The illusion of depth on a flat surface is created by techniques used to mimic what we see in the world. Artists have used these techniques for centuries to create realistic images that resemble our visual reality.

One technique, called *perspective,* achieves its effect by using converging lines that intersect at a horizon. An object whose contours align with the perspective lines appears to recede in space.

Another method involves modifying the relative scale of visual elements in an image. Larger objects appear closer to the viewer than smaller ones. Because this visual phenomenon is a naturally occurring characteristic of sight in the 3-D world, when we see it in a picture we subconsciously draw the conclusion that the objects exist in space when, in fact, the picture is two-dimensional.

The position of an object in an image also contributes to the illusion of depth. If one element blocks out part of another element, the obstructing element appears to be in front of the obstructed one.

Another common device, *atmospheric perspective,* uses tonality to simulate distance. As objects recede in space, they appear lighter and less distinct due to the presence of dust and haze in the air.

The fact remains, however, that no matter how many devices are used to produce three-dimensionality, and no matter how deep the picture appears, unless its surface is textured, it is as flat as a pancake.

Photoshop images are somewhat of an exception to the flat-as-a-pancake rule. They appear on-screen as flat images of colored light, and they have a specific height and width. But they can also have depth in the form of *layers.* A Photoshop layer is like a piece of clear glass (see Figure 7.1), and parts of the image can be pasted to the glass. If you have different parts of the image separated onto multiple layers, you can shuffle their position in the stack, enabling one part of the image to appear in front of another. Because the layers isolate each part of the image, you have the added advantage of being able to control the contents of each layer separately.

When a part of the image is isolated on an individual layer, it can be singled out and affected at any time. A layer can be moved horizontally or vertically, or repositioned anywhere in the stack, to help produce the illusion of depth. You can modify the color relationships of pixels on superimposed layers and adjust their level of opacity. Special layer styles can be applied to produce realistic shadows, embosses, textures, patterns, and glowing effects.

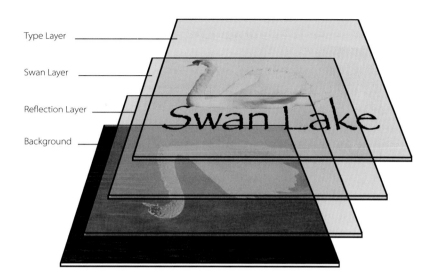

Figure 7.1

Layers in a Photo-shop document

Type Layer

Swan Layer

Reflection Layer

Background

Using the Layers Palette

At the heart of all this power is the Layers palette (shown in Figure 7.2). It is the control center from which you perform most layer operations. By default, the Layers palette is clustered with the Channels and the Paths palettes. If the Layers palette is not displayed, you can access it by choosing Window → Layers or by pressing F7 on an extended keyboard.

Each layer in the palette is separated from the one directly below it or above it by a thin line. Each layer's row includes a thumbnail of the layer's contents, the layer's name, and any layer styles, masks, or locks applied to that layer. In the far left column is a visibility indicator which, when displayed, indicates that the contents of the layer are visible. Immediately to the right of this visibility indicator is another column that displays a brush icon if the layer is targeted. A small chain icon appears to the right of the visibility indicator if the layer is linked, or a mask icon is visible if the layer is a Fill or Adjustment layer or if a Layer Mask is targeted. (For more about Layer Masks see Chapter 22.)

Above the layer stack are Lock icons, which enable you to lock the transparency, editing, and movement of layer contents. At the upper-left of the Layers palette is a list of blending modes that can alter the color relationships of layers in the stack. And to the right of the blending modes is the Opacity indicator, which controls the level of transparency of a targeted layer's contents. The Fill opacity control is just below the master opacity control.

Figure 7.2

The Layers palette

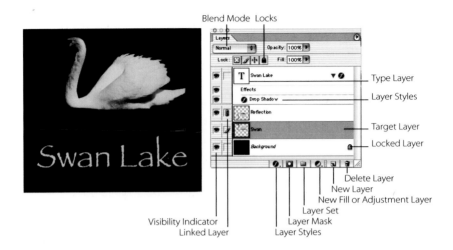

You can access many layer operations from the Layers Palette menu (shown in Figure 7.3). Clicking the small triangular icon on the upper-right of the palette reveals these options.

Working with the Background

When you scan or import an image from another program and open it in Photoshop, the Layers palette displays one thumbnail, labeled *Background*. You can think of the Background as an image mounted to a board. If you were to cut away a portion of the image

Figure 7.3

The Layers Palette menu

with an X-Acto knife, you would see the board underneath. In Photoshop, when you make a selection on the Background and delete it with the Delete key or erase it with the Eraser tool, the hole fills with the background color specified in the Tool palette.

The contents of all the layers float on top of the Background. Unlike a layer, the Background is opaque and cannot support transparency. If the document contains more than one layer, the Background is always at the bottom of the stack and cannot be moved or placed in a higher position. When new layers are added to the document, their content always appears in front of the Background.

> If your image is composed entirely of layers, you can convert one of your layers into a Background. Target a layer and choose Layer → New → Background From Layer. The Background will automatically be deposited at the bottom of the stack.

By default, the Background is locked. If you want to move its contents, adjust its opacity, or reposition it in the Layers stack, you need to convert it to a layer. As with many of Photoshop's operations, there is more than one way to perform this task:

To convert the Background into a layer **from the menu**, choose Layer → New → Layer From Background.

To convert the Background **from the Layers palette**, double-click the Background's name or thumbnail to display the New Layer dialog box. If you click OK, Photoshop names the converted layer Layer 0 by default. You can use the default name, or you can enter a name for the new layer in the Name field and click OK.

> The New Layer dialog box also lets you color-code a layer, adjust its opacity, and specify a blending mode. You can also group it with other layers if, for example, you're using it to make a clipping group. (Chapter 22, "Advanced Layer Techniques," describes clipping masks.)

To convert the Background **by using keyboard shortcuts**, Option-double-click (Macintosh) or Alt-double-click (Windows) the Background's name or thumbnail to automatically change it into a layer named Layer 0 (see Figure 7.4).

Naming Layers

Naming your layers is essential to establishing an efficient work flow. The default numbers that Photoshop assigns to new layers become quite anonymous when their content is too small to be recognized on the thumbnail or when there are 30 or 40 of them in the document. Instead of using the default name Layer 0, I recommend that you give the layer a name that readily identifies it. Naming each layer with a descriptive title is a fast way to organize the components of your image for easy identification.

To name or change the name of a layer, double-click the layer's current name next to the thumbnail in the Layers palette. A box will appear around it. Type in the new name.

Viewing Layers

You can conceal or reveal the content of a layer by clicking the visibility indicator in the first column of the Layers palette (it looks like an eye).

To reveal or conceal the contents of more than one layer at a time, click the eye next to each of the desired layers. To conceal all but one layer, press the Option/Alt key while clicking that layer's visibility icon. With the same key held down, click the icon again to reveal all layers.

Figure 7.4

The New Layer dialog box showing the layer name Layer 0

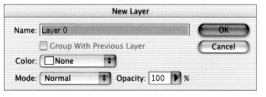

Choosing Your Thumbnail Size

The thumbnails that represent each layer display its content in miniature. You can choose from three sizes of thumbnails, or you can choose to display no thumbnail at all. To specify a thumbnail display, click the Layers Palette menu and choose Palette Options. In the dialog box that opens (Figure 7.5), click the radio button next to the desired thumbnail size and then click OK.

Targeting a Layer

You can apply a Photoshop operation to affect the contents of a layer, but first you must target the layer you want. A *targeted* layer is active and ready to be edited. To target a layer, click its name, which appears to the right of the thumbnail. You will see a colored highlight in the text field and a brush symbol to the left of the layer's thumbnail, in the second column (as in Figure 7.6). Only one layer can be targeted at a time; a targeted layer must be visible to be affected. Certain effects can be applied to multiple layers simultaneously by linking them (see the upcoming section titled "Linking Layers"), placing them in sets, or grouping them (see Chapter 22).

Understanding Transparency and Opacity

Because transparency is by nature invisible, it is graphically displayed in Photoshop as a gray and white checkerboard. If you see an area on a layer that is displayed as a checkerboard, then the area is totally transparent. This means that either it is void of pixels or the pixels are completely transparent. If it's displayed as a combination of image and checkerboard, then it is semitransparent; and if it's displayed totally as image, then it's opaque. Figure 7.7 illustrates the difference between opaque and semitransparent images.

If only one layer is displayed and its contents are surrounded by areas of transparency, the image will appear against a gray and white checkerboard. If the color of the image is predominantly gray and the checkerboard becomes difficult to see, the color and size of the checkerboard can be changed in Transparency & Gamut Preferences to better reveal the image.

Figure 7.5

The Layers Palette Options dialog box determines the size of the thumbnails that are displayed.

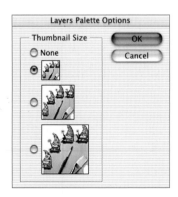

Controlling Opacity

The Opacity slider enables you to adjust the level of transparency of all the pixels on a targeted layer, so that you can see through the image to the underlying layers in the stack. Click the arrow next to the Opacity field on the Layers palette; a slider pops up, which you can drag right to increase, or left to decrease, opacity. Or enter a value from 0% to 100% directly in the box.

If any tool other than a painting or an editing tool is active, you can type any number between 01 and 100 to change the Opacity value of the targeted layer.

Setting Fill Opacity

The Fill opacity control enables you to add another opacity setting to a layer. Fill opacity affects a layer's pixels without affecting the opacity of any layer styles that have been applied to the layer. (Layer styles are discussed later in this chapter.)

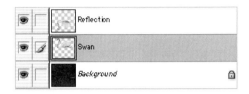

Changing Layer Order

The stacking order in the Layers palette determines the plane of depth where the visual elements appear. The content of the topmost layer in the Layers palette appears in the front of the image. The further down in the stack a layer is, the farther back its content appears, all the way back to the bottommost layer, or the Background.

You can change a layer's position in the stack and, consequently, its visual plane of depth in the image. In the Layers palette, click and drag the thumbnail or name of the layer that you wish to move. As you drag up or down, you will see the division line between layers become bold (as in Figure 7.8). The bold line indicates the new location where the layer will appear when the mouse is released.

Another method of changing the position of the layer in the stack is to choose an option under Layer → Arrange, or use the equivalent key command. The Arrange submenu presents you with four options, as shown in Table 7.1.

POSITION	MACINTOSH SHORTCUT	WINDOWS SHORTCUT	RESULT IN THE LAYERS PALETTE	RESULT TO THE IMAGE
Bring To Front	Shift-⌘-]	Shift-Ctrl-]	Moves the layer to the top of the stack.	Contents appear at the front of the picture plane.
Bring Forward	⌘-]	Ctrl-]	Moves the layer on top of the layer that was immediately above it.	Contents appear in front of the layer that was immediately above it.
Send Backward	⌘-[	Ctrl-[	Moves the layer under the layer that was immediately below it.	Contents appear behind of the layer that was immediately below it.
Send To Back	Shift-⌘-[	Shift-Ctrl-[	Moves the layer to the bottom of the stack one step above of the Background.	Contents appear in front of the Background but behind all of the other layers in the stack.

Figure 7.7

The swan at the left is displayed at 100% opacity; the swan at the right is displayed at 50% opacity.

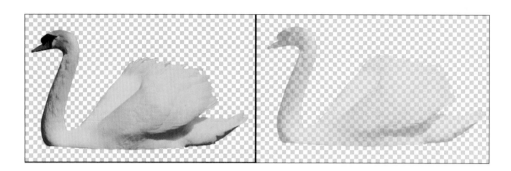

Linking Layers

Figure 7.8

You can change a layer's position in the stacking order.

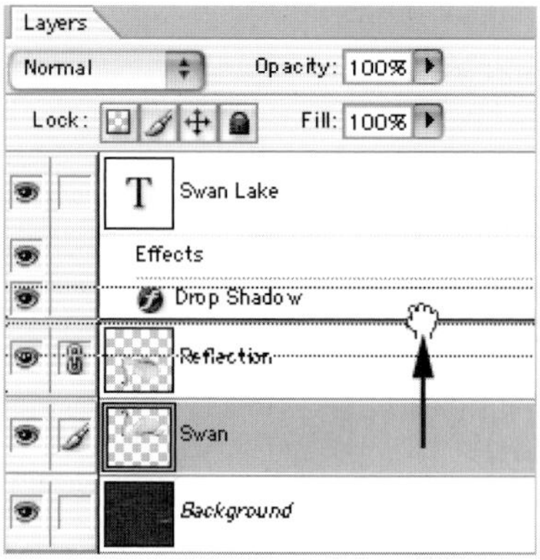

Let's say you've positioned two elements of a logo on separate layers, and you are satisfied with their visual relationship, except that they are a little too large and they need to be moved a half-inch to the left. You can transform or move two layers simultaneously by *linking* them.

To link one or more layers, target one of the layers. The target layer will display a brush icon. Click in the column to the immediate left of the thumbnail on the layers that you want link to the target layer. A chain icon appears, like the one next to the Reflection layer in Figure 7.9. You can then choose the Move tool or any transformation function (Edit → Transform), and the layers will scale, rotate, distort, and so forth as a group. (See Chapter 13, "Sizing and Transforming Images," for more on transformations.)

Linked layers are used primarily for transforming and moving multiple layers simultaneously. You can apply other effects to multiple layers by using specific layer-based operations. (These effects are described in more detail in later sections of this chapter or in later chapters of this book.)

These operations include the following:

Adjustment Layers You can control color, brightness, and contrast adjustments and for color mapping functions (see Chapter 16, "Adjusting Tonality and Color").

Figure 7.9

Linked layers are indicated by a chain icon.

Layer Masks You have the ability to conceal and reveal areas of layers in the stack (see Chapter 22).

Blending Modes Items for this list apply a preprogrammed color algorithm to affect the relationship between the pixels on a layer and the layer immediately below it in the stack (see companion CD).

Layer Sets You can group, control the opacity and the position of multiple layers in the stack, and transform or move multiple layers simultaneously (see the following section).

Layer Comps You can save different versions of an image to the Layer Comps palette and thereby avoid having to save multiple documents (see Chapter 22).

Fill Layers These operations apply a solid color, gradient, or pattern to an independent layer. When the opacity is adjusted, the Fill layer affects the underlying layer. A Fill layer also contains a layer mask, so that the color, gradient, or pattern can be superimposed onto a specific area of the image (see Chapter 10, "Creating and Applying Color").

Layer Content You can change the type of Adjustment or Fill layer and how it affects the layers below it in the stack (see Chapter 22).

Clipping Masks You can conform the content of one layer to the shape of the pixel content of the layer immediately below it (see Chapter 22).

Grouping Layers in Layer Sets

Photoshop supports an unlimited number of layers, with the amount of RAM being the only limiting factor. The potential to produce enormous quantities of layers makes a layer-management tool an absolute necessity.

Layer sets let you consolidate contiguous layers into a folder on the Layers palette. By highlighting the folder, you can apply certain operations to the layers as a group. The layers in a layer set, such as Swan and Reflection in Figure 7.10, can be simultaneously revealed or concealed by clicking the visibility indicator for the set in the Layers palette. The whole set can be repositioned in the stack, moved, and—like linked layers—transformed by using any of the transformation tools.

Although you can transform and reposition both layer sets and linked layers, layer sets differ from linked layers in that they contain contiguous layers—that is, layers that are sequenced immediately above or below each other in the stack. Layers that are linked can be anywhere in the stack.

There are a few ways to create a new layer set:

- From the Layer menu, choose New → Layer Set.
- From the Layers Palette menu, choose New Layer Set.
- Click the Create a New Set icon ▤ in the Layers palette. By default, the first layer set will be named Set 1.

Figure 7.10

The Swan and Reflection layers make up a layer set, which has been color-coded.

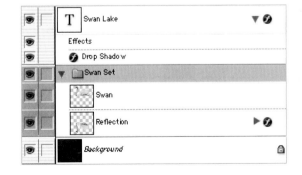

When using the first two methods, the New Layer Set dialog box appears (see Figure 7.11). You can name the layer set, color-code it, and specify the blending mode and opacity.

Layer Set Properties If you want to change the color properties of a targeted layer set, choose Layer → Layer Set Properties, or Layer Set Properties from the Layers palette menu. In the dialog box that appears (see Figure 7.12), select the check boxes to display the individual or combined color information of all the layers in the set. This dialog box also lets you color-code a layer.

Layer Sets from Linked Layers A fast way to create a layer set is to link the layers that you want in the set. Then choose Layer → New → Layer Set From Linked. All the linked layers will be consolidated into one set. When you convert linked layers into a layer set, however, they become contiguous and their positions in the stack might change.

Adding Layers to a Set To add a layer to a set, click and drag it to the Layer Set folder. Then, release the mouse. To reveal the layers within the set, click the triangle to the left of the folder so that it points down. To conceal the contents of the layer set to eliminate clutter, click the triangle so that it points to the right.

Nesting Layer Sets Photoshop CS enables you subdivide layer sets by nesting them within a layer set. Drag a layer set folder and drop it into another's folder or press ⌘/Ctrl when you click the Create a New Set icon to nest a new Layer set in the current targeted set.

Locking Layers

Photoshop offers four controls, or *locks*, in the Layers palette that prevent a layer from being modified (see Figure 7.13). Each lock is represented by an icon at the top of the palette. To lock a layer, target the layer and check the icon for the lock type you want.

The lock types include the following:

Lock Transparent Pixels This function is comparable to Preserve Transparency in earlier versions of the software. It protects the areas of the targeted layer that don't contain pixels from being edited. If you attempt to paint on a transparent area, for example, the tool will not respond, so in a sense, locking transparency works like a mask. The areas that do contain pixels will still respond to any Photoshop operation. Locking transparency does not protect transparent areas from the effects of transformations such as scaling, rotating, or moving.

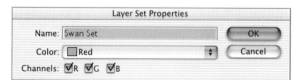

Figure 7.11

Creating a new layer set

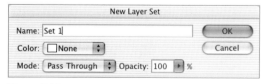

Figure 7.12

Determining layer set properties

Lock Image Pixels The entire targeted layer is protected from editing functions such as painting, color adjustments, or filters. You can, however, transform or move the content of a layer. Menu operations that you can't perform are grayed out. If you attempt to apply a tool function, you will be greeted by a circle with a line through it.

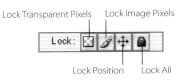

Lock Transparent Pixels   Lock Image Pixels

Lock Position   Lock All

Figure 7.13

Four locking controls

Lock Position Selecting this option prevents you from moving a targeted layer or applying Edit → Free Transform or any of the Edit → Transform operations such as Scale and Distort. When the Lock Position icon is locked, these menu items are grayed out.

Lock All You can protect a targeted layer from all editing functions by clicking the Lock All box.

Creating New Layers

It is often necessary to create a new layer, either to add new content to the image or to isolate an existing element. When a new layer is added, the file size of the document increases proportionately to the quantity of information on the new layer. Adding several new layers can significantly increase the amount of space the image consumes on your disk. This, however, is a small inconvenience for the power that layers deliver. As part of your work flow, though, you'll no doubt want to consolidate layers during the imaging process to decrease the file size (see "Consolidating Layers" later in this chapter).

Creating a New Empty Layer

Here is an another example of redundant Photoshop operations. Two of these operations produce identical results, and one produces similar results with a slight twist. All three create a new layer:

- From the Layer menu, choose New → Layer to bring up the New Layer dialog box. Name the layer and specify its characteristics. Click OK.

- From the Layers palette menu, choose New Layer to bring up the New Layer dialog box (see Figure 7.14). Name the layer and click OK.

- Click the New Layer icon ▣ (next to the trash icon at the bottom of the Layers palette). A new layer, named Layer 1, appears in the stack immediately above the targeted layer. To rename the new layer, double-click its name and enter the new name in the Name field. You can also access the Layer Properties dialog box from the Layer menu or from the Layers Palette menu to rename the layer. Opt/Alt-clicking the New Layer icon will also bring up the dialog box.

Figure 7.14

The New Layer dialog box

New Layer

Name: Layer 1   OK

☐ Group With Previous Layer   Cancel

Color: ☐ None ▾

Mode: Normal ▾   Opacity: 100 ▸ %

☐ (No neutral color exists for Normal mode.)

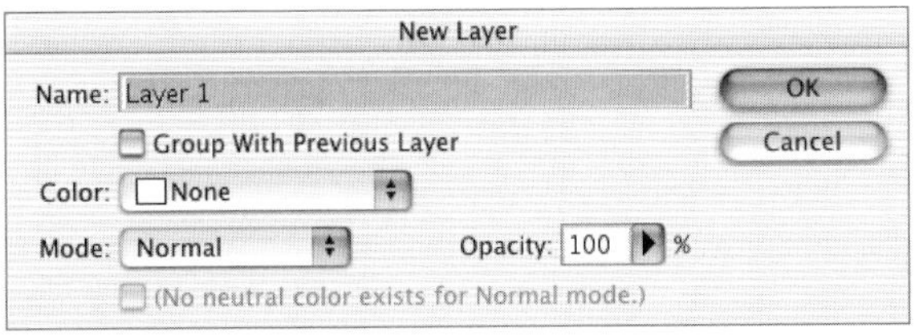

Creating a New Layer with Content

There are two potential sources for the content of new layers: elements cut or copied from another layer or Background, and elements dragged and dropped from another document. Whatever its source, the end result isolates the content onto a separate layer so that it can be moved, edited, or rotated in the stack.

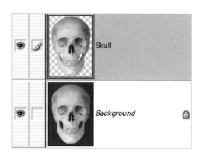

Figure 7.15

Layer → New → Layer Via Copy

Copying an Image to a New Layer

When you choose Layer → New → Layer Via Copy, the selected portion of the image is duplicated and moved to the same position on a new layer. By default, the first new layer you copy or cut is assigned a number that hasn't been used.

The name that Photoshop assigns to a new layer depends on the technique you choose to create the new layer and the existing content of the Layers palette. It will appear as Layer 0, Layer 1, or some other number. To avoid the confusion of inconsistent labels, rename your new layer immediately upon creating it.

To copy the contents of a layer to a new layer:

1. Target the layer or Background that you intend to copy.

2. Make an accurate selection of the area on the layer or Background by using one of the selection tools or techniques.

3. Choose Layer → New → Layer Via Copy, or press ⌘/Ctrl-J. The content within the selection marquee is copied to a new layer and is placed immediately above the layer from which it was copied. The new layer automatically becomes the target layer.

   In Figure 7.15, I selected just the skull on the Background and copied it to a new layer.

4. Double-click the layer name's text to rename the layer.

5. Press Return/Enter to commit the name.

> When you copy or cut to a new layer, inspect the image edges against a contrasting solid fill background. Use one of Photoshop's matting techniques (detailed in Chapter 22) to remove any stray edge pixels.

Cutting an Image to a New Layer

When you cut a selected portion of an image to a new layer, the content of the selection is either filled with the current background color (if it's on the Background) or replaced by transparency (if it's on a layer). It is transferred to the same position on a new layer.

To cut a portion of an image to a new layer:

1. Target the layer or Background with the element(s) that you intend to cut.

2. Make an accurate selection of the area by using one of the selection tools or techniques.

3. Choose Layer → New → Layer Via Cut, or press Shift-⌘/Ctrl-J. The content is cut to a new layer, leaving a transparent hole in the original layer or an area filled with the background color (if it was cut from the Background). The new layer is placed immediately above the targeted layer.

   Figure 7.16 shows the image of a skull cut to a new layer. On the left, I selected the skull on the Background and then cut it to a new layer. On the right, I selected the skull on a layer and cut it to a new layer.

4. Double-click the layer's name to rename the layer; then press Return/Enter.

Dragging a Layer from Another Document

A layer from an open document (and all of that layer's contents) can be copied to another open document simply by dragging and dropping it. The layer will appear immediately above the targeted layer in the stack. The *source* document is the document from which you will get the layer. The *destination* document is where you will put the layer.

To drag a layer from a document:

1. Open the source document and the destination document so that they both appear on-screen.

2. Target the layer or Background on the Layers palette of the source document.

3. Click and drag the layer name or thumbnail from the source to the destination document until you see an outline of the layer. Release your mouse (see Figure 7.17).

4. Name the layer by double-clicking its name.

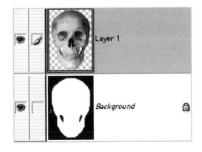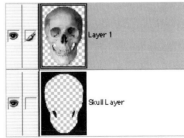

Figure 7.16

When the selection is made on the Background, the cut area fills with the background color (left). When the selection is made on a layer, the selected area creates a transparent hole (right).

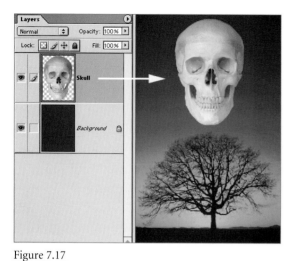

Figure 7.17

You can drag a layer from the Layers palette and drop it on an image that is open on the desktop.

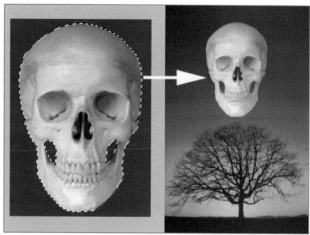

Figure 7.18

You can drag a selection from the image window and drop it on an image that is open on the desktop.

The new layer will appear immediately above the targeted layer on the destination document.

Dragging a Selection from Another Document

The contents of a selection can be copied from an open document and placed in another open document by dragging and dropping. When you drag and drop a selection, a new layer is automatically created in the destination document and will appear immediately above the targeted layer in the stack. Here are the steps:

1. Open the source document and the destination document so that they both appear on-screen.

2. Target the layer or Background on the Layers palette of the source document.

3. Make an accurate selection of the area to be moved.

4. Choose the Move tool. Click and drag the selection from the source document's image window to the destination document's image window until you see a rectangular outline. Release your mouse when the outline appears where you want the selection to be placed (see Figure 7.18).

5. Name the new layer.

Duplicating Layers

Two techniques produce identical results for creating an exact copy of a layer. When the copy is made, it appears directly above the original layer; its name is the name of the original plus the word *copy*. The new layer has the same opacity, styles, and blending mode settings as the original. To duplicate a layer, do *one* of the following:

- Target the layer to be copied. Choose Duplicate Layer from the Layer menu or from the Layers palette pop-up menu.

- Drag the layer's name or thumbnail to the New Layer icon in the Layers palette. If you Option/Alt-drag, you'll be able to name the new layer from the Duplicate Layer dialog box that automatically appears (see Figure 7.19). In the Destination field of the dialog box, you can designate any open document, or create a new document in which to duplicate the layer.

Figure 7.19

The Duplicate Layer dialog box

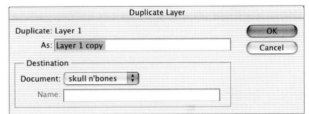

Removing Layers

You can eliminate layers by using the Layers palette (deleting the contents of that layer in the process). To discard a layer, do *one* of the following:

- Target the layer to be deleted. Choose Delete Layer from the Layer menu or from the Layers palette menu.

- Drag the layer's thumbnail or name to the trash icon in the Layers palette.

- Target the layer and then click the trash icon, which brings up a window to confirm the deletion (Figure 7.20).

- Target the layer and then Opt/Alt-click the trash icon to directly delete the layer.

Figure 7.20

The Delete Layer confirmation D ialog box

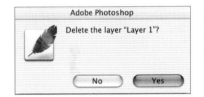

Blending Layers

Imagine having two color slides on a light table. Let's say you sandwich a red transparent gel between the two slides. The image you see would be a combination of the bottom slide and the top slide affected by the tint of the gel. But suppose that, instead of just the tinted image, you had the ability to slide in more complex, specific effects, such as color saturation, color inversion, or color bleaching.

That's how *blending modes* perform. They are preprogrammed effects that determine the color relationships between aligned pixels on two consecutive layers in the stack. Figure 7.21 demonstrates some of the many applications of blending. (A color version of this demonstration, Figure C6, is available in the color section.)

A blending mode can be assigned to a layer in a couple of ways:

- Target the layer and then use the Mode list at the top of the Layers palette (directly under the Palette Title tab) to choose the desired blending option.

- Opt/Alt-double-click the layer name or double-click the thumbnail to display the Layer Style dialog box (see Figure 7.22). From the list on the left, choose Blending Options: Custom. In the General Blending area, choose a blending mode and opacity level.

For a complete description of blending modes, refer to the book's companion CD.

The options in the General Blending area are identical to those in the Mode list at the top of the Layers palette. However, by using the General Blending area of the Layer Style dialog box, you have the additional ability to save the settings as a style and apply them to a different layer. (See "Using Layer Styles" later in this chapter.) When you adjust opacity and apply a blending mode from within the dialog box, the mode and opacity setting in the Layers palette change to reflect the adjustment.

Figure 7.21

**Examples of blend-
ing modes applied
to an image**

Advanced Blending

The Advanced Blending area of the Layer Style dialog box lets you control several characteristics of the color relationships between the targeted and the underlying layer:

Fill Opacity This value controls the interior opacity of the pixels in the layer. If, however, the image has a style applied to it (such as Drop Shadow), Fill Opacity does not affect the style. To set the fill opacity, move the slider to select a percentage between 0 and 100 or enter a value in the field.

Channels You can choose which channel to blend. Choosing any one or two of the channels excludes the color information from the others; consequently, the pixels on the layer will change color depending on their color content.

Knockout You can use this option to cut a hole through the content of the layer. Knockout works hand in hand with the Fill Opacity and Blend Modes options. As you move the Fill Opacity slider or change blending modes, Shallow knocks out the image just to the layer underneath it, and Deep punches a hole clear through all layers to the Background.

Blend Interior Effects as Group If you check box, the Fill Opacity and Blend If sliders affect any interior effects applied to the layer, for example, Inner Shadow or Inner Glow. If the box is not checked, the effects are excluded from blending.

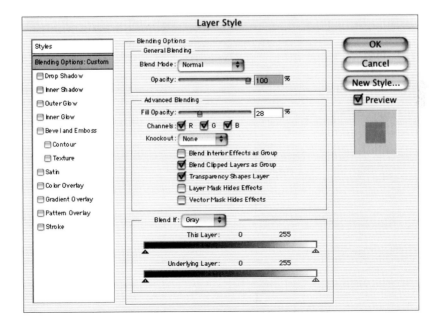

Figure 7.22

The Layer Style dialog box with Blending Options displayed

Blend Clipped Layers as Group   If you check this box, the Fill Opacity and Blend If sliders affect layers that are included in a clipping mask. This option, which is selected by default, causes the blending mode of the bottom layer in a clipping group to be applied to all layers within the group. Unchecking this option enables you to maintain the original blending mode and appearance of each layer individually. (Clipping groups are described in Chapter 22.)

Transparency Shapes Layer   This option uses the layer's transparency to determine the shape of the style and its interior effects.

Layer Mask/Vector Mask Hides Effects   Check these options to use a layer or vector mask to hide a layer style effect rather than shape the effect at the edges of the mask.

Blend If   You can choose the specific color components to be affected by the blend. Choose Blend If Gray to affect all the colors, or pick a specific color channel (or channels) to affect. The Blend If color sliders let you accurately adjust the highlight, midtone, and shadow areas to be blended. (See Chapter 24, "Overlay Techniques," for more on blending.)

Working with Layer Styles

Layer styles jazz up your images with realistic enhancements such as drop shadows, neon glowing edges, and deep embossing. These efficient, canned effects simplify operations that used to require tedious channel juggling and layer manipulation.

When a layer has been affected by a style, an italic *f* icon appears to the right of its name in the Layers palette (like the one next to the Pipe layer or the Sky B layer in Figure 7.23). The Layers palette can be expanded to reveal a list of the layer styles that have been applied, by clicking the small arrow to the left of the *f* icon. Double-clicking any one of these effects displays its controls so that you can modify it.

Layer styles apply their effects to the edges of the layer, so the content on the target layer should be surrounded by transparency.

Figure 7.23

Image with a Drop Shadow and a Bevel and Emboss effect

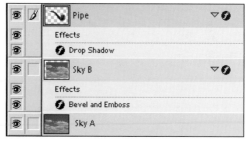

Using Layer Styles

If you want to create, define, or edit a layer style, access the Layer Style dialog box (see Figure 7.24) by doing *one* of the following. If a layer is targeted when you open this dialog, the style you choose will be applied to the layer. You cannot apply a layer style to the Background.

- Choose Layer → Layer Style. Choose a style from the list.

- Choose Blending Options from the Layer Options pull-down menu. Click on a layer style from the list to display its controls.

- Double-click the layer's thumbnail.

- Click the Layer Style icon at the lower-left of the Layers palette and drag to a layer style to display its controls.

From the Layer Style dialog box, you can also choose an effect. To display the extensive controls for each effect, click its name. Many of the controls have similarities, and experimentation with a live preview is the best way to see the result of your efforts. The swatch under the Preview check box demonstrates the effect on a square. This is very helpful in seeing the result of a combination of effects.

Figure 7.25 demonstrates several samples of the layer style effects. (A color version of this demonstration, Figure C5, is available in the color section.)

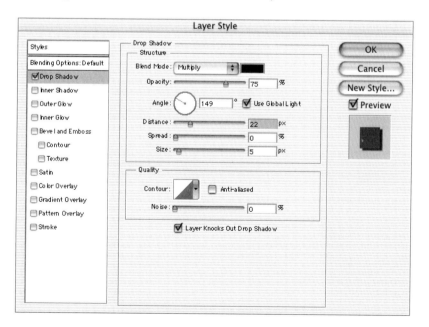

Figure 7.24

The Layer Style dialog box displaying Drop Shadow controls

Figure 7.25

Layer styles demonstrated

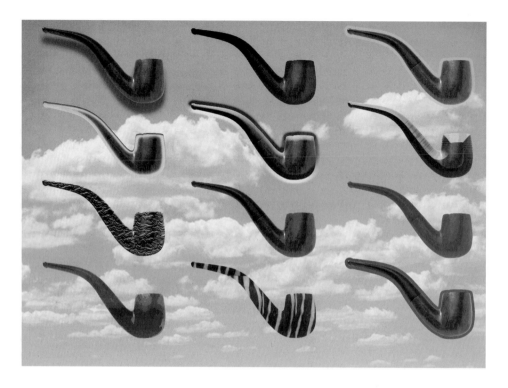

Each layer style provides a unique and potentially complex set of options. Experimentation with the controls and with combinations of styles is the key to producing the best possible effect for your particular image. Available options are as follows:

Drop Shadow Every object casts a shadow if placed in the path of a light source. Drop shadows are a key element in creating credible, realistic images. The drop shadow follows the same shape as the pixels on the target layer. This is a fast way to give your image a realistic look. There are two sets of controls:

> **Structure** determines the opacity, size, and position of the shadow.

> **Quality** determines the contour of its edges and its texture.

Inner Shadow As a drop shadow is cast outward, away from the layer content, an inner shadow is cast from the edge inward, toward its center. Use this style to model your image or to create inner depth. The settings are similar to Drop Shadow for controlling the structure and quality of the effect, except that Choke, a term used in the printing industry to indicate an inward expansion, replaces Spread, a term for outward expansion.

Outer Glow This style is perfect for a neon look. It creates a halo of a light color around the outside edge of the layer's content that can be as soft- or hard-edged as you like, depending on the settings you choose.

Inner Glow The best way to describe this effect is a soft-edged, light-colored stroke. Use Inner Glow to create a halo from the edge of the layer's content inward.

Bevel and Emboss The Bevel and Emboss style applies a highlight and a shadow to the layer content to create the illusion of three-dimensional relief. You can choose from five styles of embossing, each of which applies a different kind of sculptured surface. The Structure and Shading options let you minutely control the appearance of the effect. You also have these options:

Figure 7.26

The Contour controls

> **Contour** Control the shape of the edge of your Bevel and Emboss effect by editing its contour. Double-click the name Contour on the Styles list. Choose a contour from the pop-up list. Adjust the range of the contour with the Range slider (see Figure 7.26). A smaller percentage decreases the range of the contour relative to the bevel; a larger percentage increases the range.
>
> To create a new contour, click the Contour icon ◼ to display the Contour Editor (see Figure 7.27). Click the New button and name the contour. A dotted line on the graph displays the profile of the current contour. Edit the position of the anchor points by dragging them, or click the dotted line to place new anchor points. Click the Corner check box if you want a corner point, or deselect it if you want a smooth point. Drag the anchor points to modify the curve to the profile of the edge you want. The Input value represents the percentage of the horizontal position of an anchor point. Output represents the percentage of the vertical position of an anchor point. Click OK to save the new contour when you're satisfied with your settings. As you create a contour, a live preview in the image window will display the results on your image.
>
> **Texture** The Bevel and Emboss Texture option maps a textural surface to your layer's content. Display the texture controls by clicking Texture in the Styles list. Choose a pattern from the pop-up list. The Texture controls use the Pattern presets as a source

Figure 7.27

The Contour Editor

> for textures (see Chapter 10 for more on patterns). Essentially, the Texture controls applies the colorless texture of the pattern to the content of the layer. You can move the sliders to adjust the scale and depth of the texture. Clicking the Invert check box changes the appearance of the texture from emboss to relief.

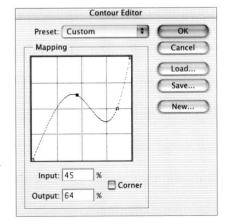

> You can reposition the texture while in the Texture dialog box by clicking the texture in the image window and dragging.
>
> Link the textural style to the layer by clicking the Link With Layer check box. If you move the layer, the texture moves along with it. If the box is not checked, the texture will remain in place while the layer moves.

Satin To produce the effect of light and shadow bouncing off a satiny surface, Photoshop applies a soft-edged shadow across the middle of the layer's content. Controls let you determine its size, position, opacity, and contour.

Color Overlay This style is a no-brainer. It simply fills the layer's content with a color that you select by clicking the swatch. You can control its opacity.

Gradient Overlay Similar to Color Overlay, Gradient Overlay applies a gradient to the pixels on the layer. You can choose a gradient from the current Gradient palette, or create one on-the-fly by clicking Gradient to display the Gradient Editor. (See Chapter 10 for more on gradients.) From the menu, you can control the opacity, style, angle, and scale of the gradient.

Pattern Overlay If you have one or more patterns stored in the current Patterns presets, you can overlay a pattern on the layer content as an effect. This is similar to the Bevel and Emboss Texture option. The difference is that Pattern overlay applies the colors as well as the texture of the pattern. You can control the opacity and scale of the pattern, and you can link the pattern to the layer so that it will accompany the layer if the layer is moved horizontally or vertically.

Stroke To apply an outline as an effect to the edge of the image, choose Stroke. You can determine the color and size of the stroke and whether it's placed on the inside, middle, or outside of the edge of the layer content. The best feature of this effect is Fill Type, which applies a gradient or pattern to the stroke; this is excellent incentive to use the Stroke layer style instead of the similar Edit → Stroke.

Applying Layer Styles

There are several ways to apply a layer style. If you have a style defined and wish to simply apply it, target the layer, click the Layer Style icon at the lower-left of the Layers palette, and choose the style from the list that pops up.

Use the Layer Style dialog box to apply a style by following one of these methods:

- Target the layer, choose Layer → Layer Style, choose a style by clicking its check box from the Layer Style dialog box, and click OK.
- Double-click the layer's thumbnail or title; select a style and click OK.
- Target the layer, click the Layer Style icon at the lower-left of the Layers palette, select a style, and click OK.

Clicking the style's check box in the Layer Style dialog box applies the style to the layer. To view the controls of a particular layer style, however, you must click the style's name.

Saving Layer Styles

If you've applied one or more styles or blending options to a layer and you're satisfied with the result, you might want to save the style so you can later apply it to a separate layer. To save a style, click the New Style button in the Layer Style dialog box. You'll be prompted to name your new style.

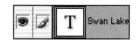

Figure 7.28

A capital *T* identifies a Type layer

Working with Type Layers

By default, when you enter type in Photoshop by using the Type tool, a new layer is automatically created. The layer is conveniently named with the text. Type layers are pretty much like any other layer in that they can be edited, transformed, reordered in the stack, and modified by applying styles to them. The thumbnail of a Type layer is identified by a capital *T*. If you've entered type and want to edit it, double-click the thumbnail to automatically highlight it, as in Figure 7.28.

Several Photoshop operations cannot be directly applied to Type layers, including color adjustments or filters that affect only pixels. Before a Type layer can be affected by these operations, it must first be *rasterized*. Rasterization converts the vector information of the type fonts into pixel-based information. After you've rasterized the type, you can no longer edit it with the Type tool. To rasterize a Type layer, target the layer and choose Layer → Rasterize → Type.

> For the big picture on generating and editing type, read Chapter 8, "Working with Type."

Consolidating Layers

At some point during the process of creating a digital image, you will probably have accumulated numerous layers.. This can present problems, because with the addition of each new layer, the size of your file will increase depending on the amount of information the layer contains. In the interest of streamlining your work flow, you should, from time to time, merge your layers. *Merging* layers combines the content of two or more layers into one. You can merge visible layers and linked layers, and you can merge down from a targeted layer. You can flatten the image so that all the layers are consolidated into a Background.

You can copy the contents of two or more layers onto a single layer. Hold down the Option/Alt key and select a Merge function from the Palette menu. This merges the content of the layers into the targeted layer but doesn't delete the original layers. By adding a new blank layer, holding Opt/Alt and using the Merge Visible command you can retain the original layers but 'stamp' them to the new layer.

Merging Visible Layers

This operation merges the content of all the visible layers into one layer. You will probably use this method more than any of the others, because you can see in the image window exactly what the new merged layer will look like. To merge visible layers, follow these steps:

1. Only the layers that you want to merge should be visible. In the Layers palette, click the visibility indicator next to any visible layer that you don't want to merge to conceal it from view.

2. Target one of the visible layers.

3. From either the Layer menu or the Layers Palette menu, choose Merge Visible.

The contents of the visible layers will be merged into the targeted layer. That layer will retain its original name.

Merging Linked Layers

This operation merges the content of all the linked layers into one layer:

1. In the Layers palette, click the second column to link the layers that you want to merge. Only the layers that you want to merge should be linked.

2. Target one of the linked layers.

3. From either the Layer menu or the Layers Palette menu, choose Merge Linked.

The images on the linked layers will be merged into the targeted layer, which keeps its original name.

Merging Down

This operation merges the content of the targeted layer and the layer immediately below it into one layer:

1. In the Layer palette, target a layer.

2. From either the Layer menu or the Layers Palette menu, choose Merge Down.
   The layer retains the name of the lower layer.

Flattening an Image

Flattening an image eliminates all layers and places all the content onto the Background. Because many other programs aren't able to read Photoshop's native layers format, you will usually need to flatten the image when you are saving your image to a format such as EPS (for use in a desktop-publishing program), GIF, or JPEG (both for use on the Web).

The TIFF format supports Photoshop layers. Even so, when saving your file as a TIFF to be imported to another program, remember that layered documents have much larger file sizes and will consequently take longer to print. It's a good idea to flatten a duplicate version of the document before saving it as a TIFF that will be imported elsewhere.

Before you flatten an image, be sure that you have finished editing its content and no longer need the layer operations. It is wise to flatten a duplicate version of the image instead of the original, because after the image has been saved and closed, it cannot be unflattened.

When you flatten an image, only the visible layers are included in the final results. If there are layers that are concealed, Photoshop displays a caution dialog box (Figure 7.29) asking whether you want to discard hidden layers.

Figure 7.29

The hidden layer caution dialog box

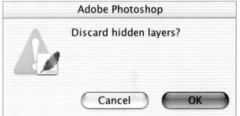

To flatten your image, follow these steps:

1. Be sure all of your layers are visible. Photoshop will discard layers that are not visible.

2. Choose Flatten Image from either the Layer menu or the Layers palette menu.

CHAPTER 8

Working with Type

Type is more than just written words. It is an important part of the visual gestalt of any layout. How a word looks can communicate to a viewer as much as or more than how it reads. Photoshop's powerful set of tools and palettes can precisely control all the characteristics of typography. Combined with the application of layer styles, the typographical options are limitless.

Many of Photoshop's type functions resemble those of page-layout programs, and you might be tempted to use Photoshop to create text documents. But don't try to drive a nail with a screwdriver! Use the right tool for the job. When generating body copy, it's better to import your image into a page-layout program and then create or manipulate the text there. Where Photoshop really shines is in its capability to produce cool text effects and large display type for headlines, subheads, and graphic text. This chapter will introduce you to these topics:

- Typography 101

- Using the Type tools

- Placing type on a path

- Applying character and paragraph specifications

- Working with Chinese, Japanese, and Korean type

- Warping text and rasterizing type

- Spell checking and using Find And Replace

Type in Photoshop

Photoshop's type functions give you the ability to generate fully editable type directly on the image. You have the ability to enter text in a bounding box to confine your text to a predefined area and to attribute paragraph characteristics such as indents and spaces to it. There is a Warp text feature that bends type into a variety of defined shapes, and Photoshop CS introduces a new feature that enables you to enter type on a curved path.

Many of the basic type functions—including orientation, font, style, size, anti-aliasing, alignment, and color—are accessed on the Options bar when the Type tool is selected. Additional type-specific characteristics—such as leading, tracking, horizontal and vertical scale, and baseline shift—are easily accessed from the Character and Paragraph palettes. You can set type attributes before you enter text, or edit selected characters after you enter them. In addition, you have a complete set of tools to create and edit Chinese, Japanese, and Korean characters.

Photoshop has a spell checker that ensures accurate spelling without having to thumb through your paper copy of Webster's each time you're unsure of a word. There is also a Find And Replace command that enables you to search for and change words or characters.

Don't be so dazzled by Photoshop's sophisticated type features that you use it for page layout. You'll find it much easier to import your image into a page-layout program (such as Adobe InDesign or QuarkXPress) and generate the body copy there. For one thing, the file size of your page-layout documents will be much smaller than equivalent documents in Photoshop. For another, Photoshop's performance in managing large amounts of text is pretty clunky, even on the fastest computers. It's best to concentrate Photoshop's type features where they'll do the most good: on spot text, headlines, and other display copy— any text where graphic enhancements are needed.

Typography 101

If you are going to create type on any software program, it's essential to understand the nature and terminology of type. Type has been around ever since humans decided to record their experiences as symbols. The conventions of typography have evolved over the centuries. Type is more than just words. It is a powerful visual element, capable of expressing ideas. Your eye perceives the character forms, and your brain freely associates what it sees with what it knows—it translates the unique visual relationships of the text symbols into a silent voice. The voice can have a gender; it can convey a particular time in history. It might have an accent from another language or culture. It can be humorous, serious, fluid, mechanical, or any other description. It can have a specific tempo and pitch.

Figure 8.1

Anatomy of type characters

Figure 8.1 identifies the traditional names for the key type features and dimensions that help define your type's voice. These characteristics, and many others, are explained in the following sections.

Font

Font is the name for the style or appearance of a complete set of characters. Your choice of font can greatly influence the appearance of a publication, as Figure 8.2 illustrates.

The five main categories of fonts include the following:

Serif fonts have a horizontal linear element on their extremities that guides the eye across the page.

Sans Serif fonts don't have the horizontal linear element.

Cursive (or Script) fonts are typographic versions of handwritten script.

Monotype characters are always evenly spaced, producing a mechanical appearance.

Display Letterforms are usually embellished with shapes or ornaments that endow them with a unique illustrative character.

Figure 8.2

The five main categories of fonts

Serif Type

Sans Serif Type

Cursive Type

Monotype

DISPLAY TYPE

Size

In traditional typography, the *type size* of a character is determined by the distance from the top of a capital letter to the bottom of a descender. Size is traditionally measured in *points*, with 72 points in an inch.

Style

By controlling the *style* of a character, you place a visual emphasis on its meaning. In Photoshop, style is chiefly a function of font *weight* (thickness or heaviness) and *obliqueness* (whether it leans). You can specify either of these two type characteristics by choosing a bold or italic typeface from a type family on your system or by applying faux styles from the Character palette. The weight or obliqueness of type creates emphasis or meaning when used in headlines, subheads, and character-based logos. A bold character headline, for example, might be used to indicate power or to simply ensure that it is the first thing seen by a viewer.

Alignment

Aligning text is an important step in maintaining readability. The *alignment* choices in traditional page layout are flush left, flush right, centered, and justified. Photoshop lets you apply these alignment options to horizontally or vertically oriented type. Alignment of text within an image reacts directly with the composition. It is a way to stabilize the viewer's eye movement by creating visible margins around the text blocks that establish clean, fluid lines and spaces. Aligning text to other visual elements frames the contents of the page so that there is ample, consistent space between the edge of the page and the content.

Leading

Leading is the typographic term that describes vertical spacing between lines; the word originates from the time when typesetters hand-set wooden or metal type. The space between lines was filled with lead slugs of specific sizes that controlled the vertical spacing. This term has been adopted throughout the industry as a way to describe the distance, in points from baseline to baseline, of rows of type characters. Software with a typography component (such as Photoshop) usually, by default, applies autoleading for body copy at 120% of the type's size.

Tracking and Kerning

These terms refer to the space between characters. *Tracking* is the global space between selected groups of characters, and *kerning* is the space between two individual characters. Because each letterform has specific visual characteristics, characters are optically spaced. For example, in the top line of type in Figure 8.3, the capital *T* next to the lowercase *y* needs less space than the capital *H* next to the lowercase *i* to appear the same distance apart. Sometimes Photoshop-generated text needs manual kerning.

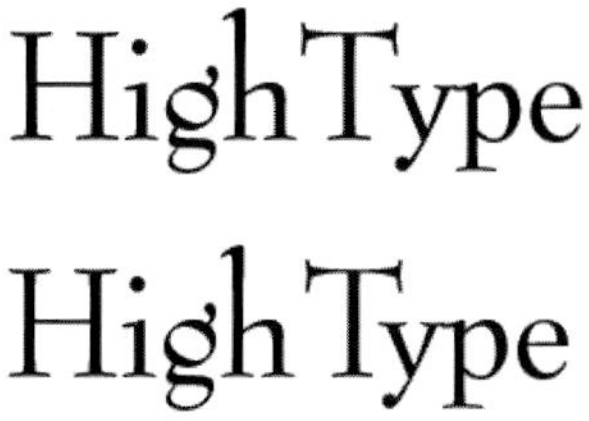

Horizontal and Vertical Scale

The horizontal and vertical *scale* of type can radically change its appearance, as seen in Figure 8.4. When you reduce the horizontal scale of a letterform (as in the second row of the example), you squeeze it from side to side. When you scale it "up" horizontally (to a percentage higher than 100), all of the vertical strokes appear fatter and the characters appear extended, as in the third row of type in the figure.

When you vertically scale a letterform (as in the fourth row of Figure 8.4), you stretch it from top to bottom. With scaling greater than 100%, the vertical strokes appear thinner and elongated relative to their size. The character appears condensed, even though it's at the normal horizontal width.

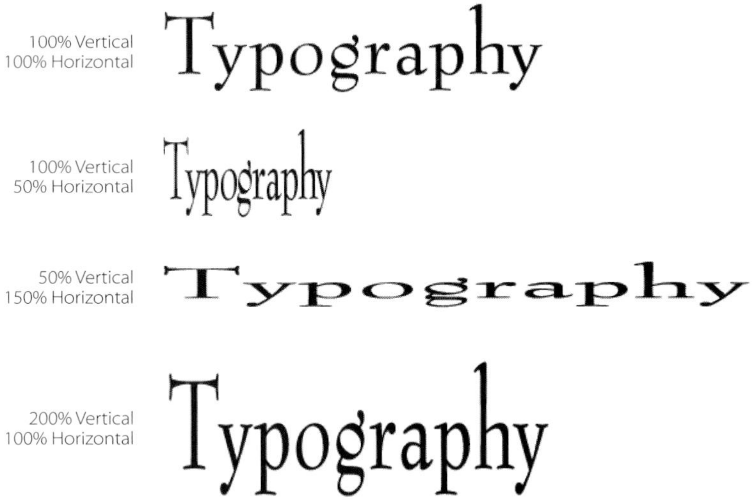

HighType

HighType

Figure 8.3

The characters in the top row are set by using Photoshop's default tracking. They seem to isolate the capital *T*. The text in the bottom row has been manually kerned to accommodate the optical spacing and to connect the capital *T* with the rest of the word.

100% Vertical
100% Horizontal

Typography

100% Vertical
50% Horizontal

Typography

50% Vertical
150% Horizontal

Typography

200% Vertical
100% Horizontal

Typography

Figure 8.4

Horizontal and vertical scale

Baseline Shift

Shifting the *baseline* of a character, as in Figure 8.5, moves it horizontally or vertically from its default starting position, or baseline. Unlike leading, which affects all the characters in a paragraph, baseline shift can target individual characters or a group of selected characters and move them up or down.

Figure 8.5

The effect of base-line shift on a single character

Typography

Type Conventions

Typography is an art that has evolved over thousands of years and, like any art form, it has common-sense rules of thumb. Type conventions act as guides to help the artist or designer achieve readable, well-emphasized character combinations. The conventions emphasize certain visual elements so that the viewer's eye is gently guided through the text.

For the sake of continuity and clarity, I mention these conventions here, because when designing with type, they are a good place to begin. Remember, however, that you can ignore the conventions, break the rules, and get wild and crazy in the anything-goes world of graphic design, providing you don't lose sight of your goal: to visually communicate your ideas clearly and efficiently.

Less Is More   Don't use more than two fonts, three sizes, or three styles in a design field. As a complicated example, a headline might be 36-point Gill Sans Bold, the subhead might be 20-point Gill Sans Demi, and the body text might be 12-point Garamond Medium.

Stick with Standard Leading   Normal leading equals 120% of the type size, so if a character is 10 points, for example, its normal leading is 12 points. If your leading is too tight and the lines are too close together, you lose readability; if your leading is too loose and the lines are too far apart, the reader's eye will wander instead of flowing smoothly from the end of one line to the beginning of the next.

No Faux Styles   Whenever possible, avoid using faux styles—that is, styles applied by a software program to the text. If you want to use a boldface style, use the bold style from that font's family, because there are subtle differences in the characters.

Kern and Track Your Text   Pay attention to the kerning and tracking of type. This is an area that is painfully neglected by many desktop publishers. Be sure the spacing looks natural. Although Photoshop auto-kerns its characters, it's wise to tweak the character spacing, *especially* when you apply warping or styles to the type. Look for consistent spacing of text by squinting your eyes. Correct gaps where the characters are too far apart or bunching where they are too close together.

Figure 8.6

The Type Tool cluster

Use Ligatures A *ligature* is a set of two characters that is designed to replace certain character combinations, such as *fl* and *fi*, to avoid spacing conflicts. Use ligatures whenever possible.

Using the Type Tools

To generate text, choose the Type tool $\boxed{\text{T}}$, click the point in the image where you want the text to appear, and enter the text from the keyboard. You can preprogram the Type tool prior to entering the text by entering values in the Options bar or in the Character or Paragraph palettes, or you can highlight the text after it has been entered and modify its specifications.

Use these functions to modify text:

- To highlight text so that it can be edited, click in front of it and drag over it.

- To select a word, double-click it.

- To select a line of text, triple-click it.

- To select all characters in a bounding box, quadruple-click anywhere in the box, or press ⌘/Ctrl-A (Select All).

When you select or format text on a Type layer, the Type tool shifts into edit mode. Before you can perform other operations, you must commit the changes by clicking the check mark or pressing Enter/Return, or cancel by clicking the Cancel icon or pressing Esc.

Choosing Horizontal or Vertical Type

There are four variations of the Type tool to choose from in the Type Tool cluster, as shown in Figure 8.6.

At the top is the basic Type tool, or Horizontal Type tool, which you'll use most of the time; it generates a Type layer. The variation immediately below it, the Vertical Type tool, generates a column of vertical characters, as seen in Figure 8.7. It too, creates a Type layer. Next are the Horizontal and Vertical Type Mask tools, which do not generate Type layers but instead produce a selection marquee in the shape of the specified character. When you enter text with these tools, it appears as a red mask until you commit the type. They can be used for generating type on existing layers or for pasting visual elements into the type to produce interesting type/image combinations, as shown in Figure 8.8.

All of the type on a layer must be either vertical or horizontal.

A R T S A V E S L I V E S

Figure 8.7

Text generated with the Vertical Type tool

Figure 8.8

**An image pasted
into a type mask**

Setting Type Characteristics

You can use the Type tool Options bar, shown in Figure 8.9, to set type characteristics. The Options bar displays these type characteristics:

Orientation The icon to the right of the Type tool Preset picker toggles between a horizontal and a vertical orientation of type.

Font Choose a font and style from the menus.

Size Choose a size in points from the list or enter a numeric value.

Anti-Alias This setting determines how the type blends into its background in varying degrees. The None option produces a jagged character; Strong makes a heavier character; Crisp, a sharper character; and Smooth, a softer character.

Alignment From the Options bar you can align either flush left, centered, or flush right. The type aligns to the insertion point. When the type is vertically oriented, the top, center, or bottom of the text aligns to the insertion point. To justify type, use the Paragraph palette discussed later in the chapter.

Color Click the swatch and select a fill color for the type from the Color Picker.

Warp Text You can place your text on a path, twist it, or bend it by using this function (see "Warping Text" later in this chapter).

Character/Paragraph This icon opens the Character and Paragraph palettes, where you can enter global specifications for your text.

Commit/Cancel After you input your type specs, click one of these buttons to commit the edit or to cancel it.

Figure 8.9

**The Type tool
Options bar**

Entering Type in a Bounding Box

There are three ways of entering type in Photoshop: from a point, on a vector path, or within a bounding box as a paragraph. The bounding box lets you control the flow of text (see Figure 8.10). As you enter text in the bounding box, it automatically inserts a soft return at the end of each line. After the bounding box has been drawn and the type entered, you can size the box to reflow the text by dragging its corner handles.

To enter text in a bounding box, follow these steps:

1. Choose the Type tool.

2. Click in your image and drag to the size you want the bounding box to be. Release the mouse, and the bounding box appears.

3. Set your type specifications in the Options bar and enter the text.

4. If needed, readjust the size of the bounding box by dragging any of the corner or side points.

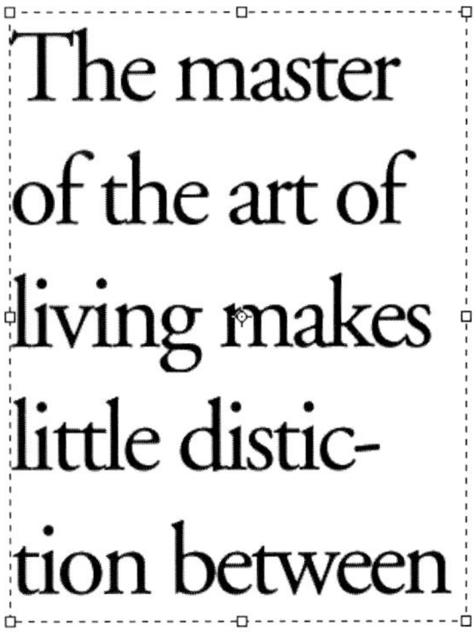

Figure 8.10

A bounding box around paragraph text

The master of the art of living makes little distic- tion between

> You can convert point text to paragraph text and vice versa. Target the Type layer and choose Layer → Type → Convert To Point Text or Convert To Paragraph Text. You can also convert the type to a work path or a shape (see Chapter 9 to learn more about paths).

Placing Type on a Path

This new feature lets you place type on a preexisting vector path as you would formerly have done in a program such as Adobe Illustrator, Macromedia FreeHand, or CorelDRAW. (See Chapter 9, "Drawing Paths," to learn more about paths.) The cross at the beginning of the text is the entry point or the leftmost extremity of the text. The circle at the end of the text is the rightmost extremity. A cross will appear in this circle to indicate that there is text that has over flowed and is not visible. These elements can be moved to alter the position of the text on the path. These two elements also determine the alignment of the text when a specific alignment option is applied.

To enter type on a path, follow these steps:

1. Draw either a shape layer or a path by using the Pen tool or any of the shape tools.

2. Choose any variation of the Type tool ⊤ . Click on the path or on the outside of the shape. Enter the text as in Figure 8.11.

3. If you want to move the text along the path or to the inside of the shape, choose the Path Selection tool ▶ . Click on the cross at the beginning of the text or the circle at the end of the text, depending on the alignment, and drag it into the desired position as in Figure 8.12.

Applying Character and Paragraph Specifications

Photoshop gives you two palettes that expand your capabilities for generating text above and beyond those readily available in the Tool palette. In these palettes you'll find controls for character and paragraph specifications and a compete set of Asian character controls. To access the palettes, select the Type tool and click the Palettes button in the Options bar. The Character and Paragraph palettes appear.

The Character Palette

This palette consolidates all the character attributes into one floating palette. To access the Character palette (see Figure 8.13), you can either choose Window → Character or, with the Type tool selected, click the Palettes button ▤ in the Options bar.

For most changes to the Character palette settings, you can click the Commit (check mark) button at the right end of the Options bar to apply your edits or the Cancel button if you change your mind. For most settings, pressing Return/Enter, choosing another tool, or targeting another layer will commit your changes. You can designate the following characteristics on the Character palette:

Size To designate the size in points prior to typing, enter a value or choose a size from the list. If the text has already been entered, highlight the text and then enter or choose a value.

Kerning This setting is measured in thousandths of an em space. (An *em space* is a standard for type measurement. The width of an em space depends on the size of the text; it's usually about the width of the letter *m*.) The Metrics setting uses the font's default spacing. To kern manually, place your insertion point between the two characters and enter a value or choose a width from the list. Negative values decrease the spacing between characters; positive values increase the spacing.

Figure 8.11

Type on a curved path

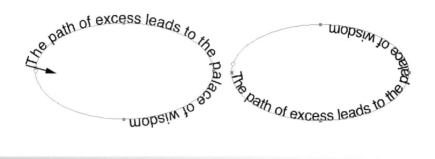

Figure 8.12

Moving type into a shape

If you need to work with other units when setting type, enter the number and then the unit abbreviation or name—inches (in), millimeters (mm), pixels (px), and so forth. Photoshop will automatically convert the value into the current type units specified in the preferences.

Tracking This option is akin to kerning and is also measured in thousandths of an em space. To change tracking, highlight the text, and then enter a value or choose a width from the list. As with kerning, negative values decrease the space between characters, and positive values increase the space.

Leading This is measured in points from baseline to baseline. To change the leading, highlight the text, and then enter a value or choose one from the list.

Vertical/Horizontal Scale This is measured as a percentage of normal scale. To change the horizontal or vertical scale, highlight the text and enter a value.

Baseline Shift This is measured in points. To change the baseline shift, highlight the text, and then enter a value or choose one from the list.

Color To change the color, click the swatch and choose a color from the Color Picker.

Style These icons let you apply faux styles to your type. They include bold, italic, all caps, small caps, superscript, subscript, underline, and strikethrough.

Language You can choose a language for hyphenation and spelling conventions on selected characters.

Anti-Alias Redundant with the anti-alias option on the Options bar, this feature lets you choose an anti-alias method from the menu.

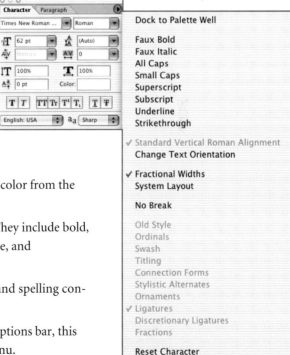

Figure 8.13

The Character palette

The Character Palette Menu

Click the arrow in the upper-right corner of the Character palette to access more commands and options for your type characters:

Faux Styles If you don't have a bold or italic type font, you can apply a faux style by choosing Faux Bold or Faux Italic.

Case Click on a case icon before typing: All Caps, Small Caps, Subscript, or Superscript. Or click on the icon after it has been entered by highlighting all or part of the text on a Type layer. This option is also available on the palette interface by clicking one of the icons. (Selecting Small Caps will have no effect on text that was originally typed as capital letters.)

Superscript, Subscript, Underline, and Strikethrough These traditional type styles are repeated in the palette menu. Superscript and subscript characters are smaller and shifted above or below the text baseline, respectively. Underline places a line of corresponding weight beneath the character, and Strikethrough places a line in the horizontal center of the characters.

Standard Vertical Roman Alignment Select the Standard Vertical Roman Alignment option to rotate a vertical character 90 degrees to be horizontal. This option is available only for vertical text; otherwise, it will be grayed out in the pull-down menu.

Change Text Orientation This option changes all the text on a layer to a vertical orientation if the type is horizontal, or horizontal if the type is vertical.

Fractional Widths The spacing between characters varies, with fractions of whole pixels between certain characters. Most of the time, fractional character widths provide the best spacing. Fractional widths, however, can cause small type to run together, making it difficult to read. To turn off this option so that the type is displayed in whole-pixel increments, choose Fractional Widths from the palette menu and clear the option.

System Layout This feature disables fractional-width spacing and the anti-aliasing option that might be applied to the text.

No Break Use No Break to prevent selected words from breaking at the end of lines, to preserve the intended meaning of these words.

The following features are only available on OpenType fonts as opposed to TrueType or PostScript Type One fonts) These items are will be grayed out unles your font supports them.

Old-Style Numerals If your font provides them, you can use old-style typographic numerals by choosing Old Style from the Character Palette menu.

Ordinals Ordinals are decorative characters that are often used on as paragraph markers, on title pages and as text dividers, or as bands and borders. Ordinals may include natural forms like flowers and leaves, or bullets, brackets, and contemporary graphic decorations.

Swash Swash capitals originated during the Italian Renaissance as calligraphy and were adopted as letterforms in the early sixteenth century. Swash capitals are used for expressive passages of text, or for titles and signs. They add a touch of elegance and refinement to the page.

Titling Titling capitals are ornate, inline, white-stroked or refined versions of regular capitals. They are used in all-capital settings or as initial capitals. Fonts with titling capitals may often include figures, monetary symbols, punctuation, and accented characters. Sometimes titling capitals are reversed and used as drop caps in book chapters or related paragraphs.

Connection Forms Some script typefaces use connecting forms to link characters together.

Stylistic Alternates Open Type fonts sometimes offer more than one option for a letterform. Choose this option to access the alternate characters.

Ornaments Some typefaces have ornamental characters. This option enables you to choose them.

Ligatures A *ligature* is a set of two characters that that replaces certain character combinations, such as *fl* and *fi*, to avoid spacing conflicts. You can add ligatures for a better appearance if your font supports them.

Discretionary Ligatures Discretionary ligatures are extra ligatures that aren't in widespread use, such as *st*. In order to use this feature, the font must support these ligatures.

Fractions This feature enables you to enter fractions if the font you are using supports them.

Reset Character Click this item to reset the Character palette to the defaults.

The Paragraph Palette

The Paragraph palette (see Figure 8.14) specifies options for an entire paragraph, which is defined by Photoshop as one or more characters followed by a hard return. Each line of text entered at a point is a separate paragraph because it's separated by a return. Photoshop won't wrap multiple lines in one paragraph unless you resize it with a bounding box.

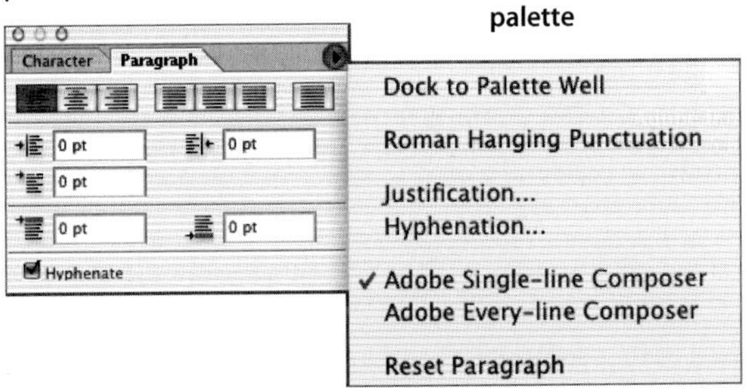

Figure 8.14

The Paragraph palette

You can access the Paragraph palette by choosing Window → Paragraph. Or, with the Type tool selected, click the Palettes button on the Options bar and then click the Paragraph tab.

Selecting Paragraphs

You can format a single paragraph, multiple paragraphs, or all paragraphs in a Type layer.

To Format This:	Do This:
A single paragraph	Choose the Type tool and click between any two characters in a paragraph.
Multiple paragraphs	Select the Type tool and drag to highlight the text range of the paragraphs you want to select.
A Type layer	Target the Type layer that you want to affect in the Layers palette.

Aligning and Justifying Type

You can *align* text to one edge or *justify* text to both edges. You can align point text and paragraph text; you can justify paragraph and path text but not point text.

To specify alignment for horizontally oriented text, click the Left Align, Center, or Right Align icons at the top of the Paragraph palette. For vertically aligned type, these become Top Align, Center, and Bottom Align.

In order to justify type, it has to be paragraph text (that is, in a bounding box) or path text (on a vector path or shape). When you choose a justification icon, the text is spread out so that both the left and right edges of the text align. The icons offer four options for aligning the last line of horizontally oriented type (Justify Last Left, Center, or Right, or Justify All) and, again, four options for vertically oriented type (Top, Center, Right, and Justify All).

Indenting Paragraphs

An *indent* is the space between the text and the insertion point or the edge of the bounding box. You specify a paragraph indent by entering a value in the indention fields. You can specify a left, right, or first-line indent:

Indent Left Margin indents the whole paragraph from the left edge of the bounding box.

Indent Right Margin indents the whole paragraph from the right edge of the bounding box.

Indent First Line indents the first line of text in the paragraph relative to the left indent.

Adding Space Before and After

Enter a value in the Add Space Before Paragraph or Add Space After Paragraph fields to add space between paragraphs. The values entered will be the units specified in the Units & Rulers preferences (described in Chapter 4, "Navigation: Know Where to Go").

The Paragraph Palette Menu

Click the arrow in the upper-right corner of the Paragraph palette to access commands that affect the punctuation, justification, hyphenation, and flow of the text.

Dock to Palette Well

This feature places the Paragraph Palette in the palette well for easy access.

Roman Hanging Punctuation

The Roman Hanging Punctuation option enhances the alignment of text by placing punctuation marks outside the margin. You can affect the following punctuation marks when this option is active: periods, commas, single and double quotation marks, apostrophes, hyphens, en and em dashes, colons, and semicolons.

    To hang punctuation marks, choose Roman Hanging Punctuation from the Paragraph Palette pull-down menu.

Justifying Text

Justification determines word- and letter-spacing defaults on justified text. To set justification options, choose Justification... from the Paragraph Palette menu. The dialog box in Figure 8.15 appears.

> Justification options are applied to the entire paragraph. If you want to increase or decrease space for a few characters, use the Kerning or Tracking functions.

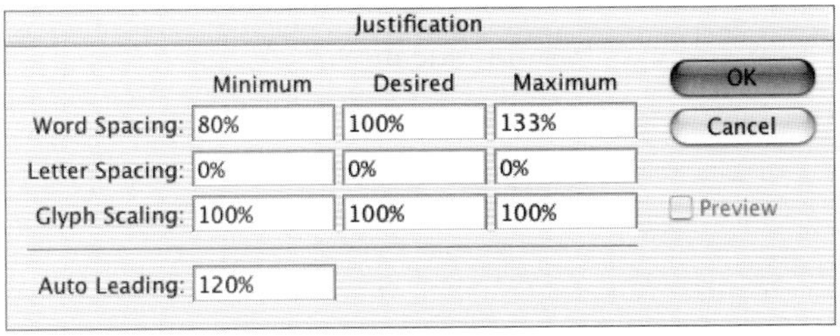

Figure 8.15

Use this dialog box to set justification options.

For the Word Spacing, Letter Spacing, and Glyph Spacing options, Photoshop will space text in order to stay between the Minimum and Maximum values, and will try to come as close to the Desired value as possible while balancing all the settings. The values you end up with are chosen not only by the spacing options, but also by factors such as the hyphenation settings and font size.

Word Spacing specifies the amount of space between words when the spacebar is pressed. Values range from 0% to 1000%; at 100% no additional space is added to the default spacing of the specified font.

Letter Spacing determines the normal distance between letters, which includes kerning and tracking values. Values range from 0 to 500%; at 100% no additional space is added to the default spacing of the specified font.

Glyph Scaling scales the actual width of characters to justify them. Input a Minimum value (50%), a Desired value, and a Maximum value (200%) to fit characters into a justified line of text.

Auto Leading is the normal distance between baselines of text—120% of the font size by default; enter a different value if desired.

Preview lets you see the result of your specification in selected text before closing the dialog box.

Hyphenating Text

Hyphenation options determine where a word breaks to be hyphenated. To activate automatic hyphenation, choose the Hyphenate… check box from the Paragraph palette. To set the following hyphenation options, choose Hyphenation from the palette pull-down menu to bring up the dialog box in Figure 8.16:

Figure 8.16

The Hyphenation dialog box

Words Longer Than specifies the minimum length, in letters, of a word to be hyphenated.

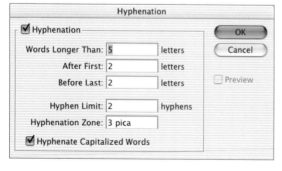

After First specifies the minimum number of letters at the beginning of a word before a hyphen.

Before Last specifies the minimum number of letters at the end of a word after a hyphen.

Hyphen Limit is the number of consecutive lines that can contain hyphens.

Hyphenation Zone is the distance at the end of a line of unjustified text that will cause a word break.

Hyphenate Capitalized Words does just that. Turn off this option to be sure headlines are not hyphenated. This works only with the Single-Line Composer.

Preview lets you see the result of your specifications on selected paragraphs before closing the dialog box.

Composing Text Lines

Composing methods determine possible line breaks, based on the hyphenation and justification settings. There are two composition methods and one option to choose from:

The Single-Line Composer composes text one line at a time. The result is more consistent spacing within a line but less consistent spacing and hyphenation among multiple lines. This option is preferable if you want to manually compose your type.

The Every-Line Composer looks ahead five lines to determine the line breaks. The result is more consistent spacing and less hyphenation. The Every-Line Composer is selected by default.

Reset Paragraph sets the paragraph to its previously formatted state before attributes from the Paragraph palette are applied.

Working with Asian Characters

If you have the proper fonts installed, Photoshop can manage Chinese, Japanese, and Korean text. To access these options in the Character and Paragraph palettes, choose Edit (Windows) Photoshop (Macintosh) → Preferences → General → Show Asian Text Options.

Tsume

The majority of Asian characters are *monospaced*, meaning that all the characters are the same width when using horizontal text and the same height when using vertical text. You can enter a percentage in the Tsume field in the Character palette (see Figure 8.17) to specify a character width for selected text. This decreases the size of each character but increases the proportional spacing between characters.

Figure 8.17

Specify a character width in the Tsume field.

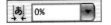

Tate-chuu-yoko

The *tate-chuu-yoko* system (also called *kumimoji* and *renmoji*) "flips" certain nontextual items. You can improve the readability of vertical text by rotating numerals and acronyms so that they are horizontally oriented. To do this, highlight the characters that you want to rotate and choose Tate-chuu-yoko from the Character Palette pull-down menu.

Japanese Composition

Spacing for Asian characters, numbers, and line breaks that can be applied to your Asian type fonts are determined by the following options, which are based on Japanese text standards.

MOJIKUMI

Mojikumi determines the composition of Japanese text, including character spacing between punctuation, symbols, and numbers, based on composition rules set forth in the Japanese Industrial Standards (JIS #4051).

Photoshop includes several mojikumi sets from which you can choose. They are accessible from the Paragraph palette's Mojikumi pop-up list.

KINSOKU SHORI

You can choose different methods for processing line breaks. *Kinsoku shori* are characters that cannot begin or end a line, based on composition rules set forth in the Japanese Industrial Standards. Choose JIS Weak or JIS Maximum from the Kinsoku Shori pop-up list. Oidashi and oikomi are line-break rules as applied to kinsoku shori:

Oidashi is push-out line breaking, which increases the number of characters on a line by reducing the space between letters.

Oikomi is push-in line breaking, which decreases the number of characters on a line by increasing the space between letters.

You can choose either of these options from the Paragraph Palette pull-down menu. A check mark indicates which option is selected.

Hanging Asian Punctuation

You can specify hanging punctuation in Asian text. Using hanging punctuation (called *burasagari*) forces punctuation marks to be placed outside the indent margins and evens the edges of the paragraph. Choose Burasagari from the Paragraph Palette menu. If the check box is selected, it is active.

Warping Text

You can bend type to conform to almost any type of curve. The Warp Text option 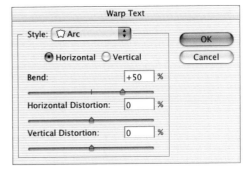 is accessible from the Type tool Options bar or from the Layer → Type menu. When you click the icon, the Warp Text dialog box appears (see Figure 8.18). You can choose from 15 styles (all demonstrated in Figure 8.19), each with its own set of precision controls.

There are so many combinations of styles and settings that it's impossible to list them all here. I'll show you how to warp a few lines of text in the Hands On project that follows this chapter, but play with these controls. Experiment with settings, sizes, and fonts so you'll be familiar with some of the wild, twisted type effects you can create.

Figure 8.18

The Warp Text dialog box

Rasterizing Type

Photoshop uses vector-based fonts that preserve the ability to edit the text throughout the imaging process. After you've generated the text, you can scale it and apply any layer style to it. You can also warp it or change its color. There are, however, certain operations such as filters and color adjustments that don't work on vector-based type. If you want to apply those effects, you'll have to *rasterize* the type, or convert it into pixels.

Figure 8.19

The 15 Warp Text styles

Pixel-based type has its advantages and disadvantages. The main disadvantage is that after you render your type, it appears at the same resolution as the document. This is

particularly problematic for small type on low-resolution documents, because there might not be enough pixels to do a decent job of smoothing the type's edges (as seen in the sample in Figure 8.20).

The advantage of pixel-based type is that it enables you to apply effects to the image as you please, such as pasting images into the type or applying a variety of filters to it. To render your type into pixels, target the Type layer and choose Layer → Rasterize → Type.

Using the Spell Checker

The spell checker will check the type on Type layers but will not check text that has been rasterized. To check your spelling, follow these steps:

1. Choose Edit → Check Spelling to display the spell checker (see Figure 8.21).

2. If a Type layer is targeted, you can check the text exclusively on that layer or select the Check All Layers check box.

3. The checker displays any words that are not in its dictionary and alternate spellings for the misspelled word. Click the correct spelling, or enter an alternate spelling in the Change To text box. Then click the Change or the Change All button to respell all instances of the word.

   If the checker doesn't recognize additional words, it continues to display alternate spellings.

Figure 8.21

The spell checker

4. If the word is spelled correctly and is not in the dictionary—a person's name, for instance—you can click Ignore or Ignore All.

5. To add an unrecognized word to the dictionary, click Add.

6. When the spell checker finishes, it displays a prompt that the spell checking is complete. Click OK (see Figure 8.22).

Using the Find and Replace Text Command

Find And Replace is a convenient method of locating and changing words in a document. It functions like the Find Change function in any word processor. The text needs to be on Type layers and not rasterized for this operation to work:

1. Choose Edit → Find And Replace. The dialog box in Figure 8.23 appears.

2. Enter the word you want to locate in the Find What text box, and the word you want to replace it with in the Change To text box.

3. Choose the following check boxes as needed:

   Search All Layers searches additional layers, other than the targeted layer.

   Forward moves forward through the document as you click the Find Next button.

   Case Sensitive ignores words that are not in the same case, even if they are spelled similarly.

   Whole Word Only finds and changes an entire word rather than a fragment.

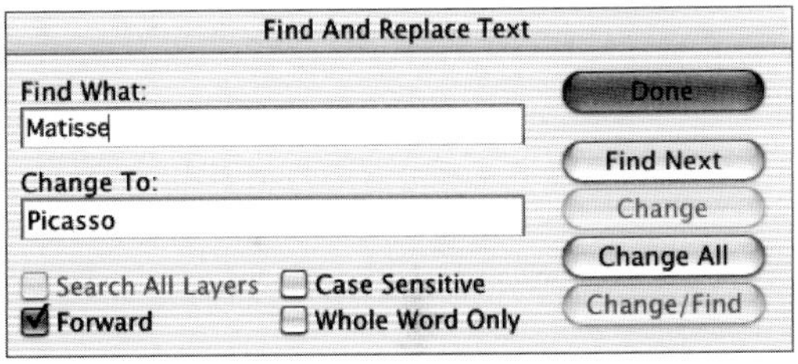

4. Click Find to locate the word and click Change to change it.

5. Click Find Next to locate additional instances of the word.

6. Click Change All to change all instances of the word. Click Done.

Figure 8.22

Spell checker prompt

Figure 8.23

The Find And Replace feature

Layers and Type

Layers greatly increase your power to manage your work. In this Hands On session, I'll put you through the moves of layers and type so that you can apply some of the powerful techniques from Chapter 7, "Layering Your Image," and Chapter 8, "Working with Type," to an actual project. You will see the advantage of organizing your layers into sets as you apply layer upon layer of digital images to produce a phantasmagoric poster. You will also take a crack at generating type, applying layer styles, and warping text.

Figure H2.1

The beginning Flying Women file showing the content of the poster

Getting Started

Before beginning this Hands On exercise, delete your preferences file. The section titled "Modifying Photoshop's Settings" in Chapter 5, "Setting Up Photoshop," details how to reset your preferences to Photoshop's defaults. After you have launched Photoshop with default preferences, here's how to begin the Hands On project:

1. Insert the *Photoshop CS Savvy* CD in your CD-ROM drive.

2. Choose File → Open; select and open `Flying_Women_start.psd` in the `HO2` folder on the CD.

3. Save the file to your disk as `Flying_Women.psd`. Figures H2.1 and H2.2 show the beginning and final images.

The color section in this book includes a color version of the first and last stages of the Amazing Flying Women poster (Figures C42 and C43).

Figure H2.2

The completed Flying Women poster

Arranging Layers

The Layers palette is the central control center for a layer's operations. From here you can view, move, link, and organize the components of an image. The following steps show you how.

Viewing Layers

Follow these steps to view your layers:

1. When you open the file Flying_Women_start.psd, you see only the transparency checkerboard, as shown in Figure H2.3. The Layers palette, however, reveals that the image contains two layer sets, seven additional layers, and the Background. To reveal the contents of the Background, click the first column next to its thumbnail. The layer visibility icon appears, and the Background image appears in the image window.

2. Reveal the contents of all layers: Option-click (Macintosh) or Alt-click (Windows) the visibility icon of the Background.

3. Conceal the layers that you don't need right now. Click the visibility icon next to the following layers or layer sets to conceal their content: Purple, Layer 1, Layer 2, and Blue. (Your image should look like Figure H2.4.)

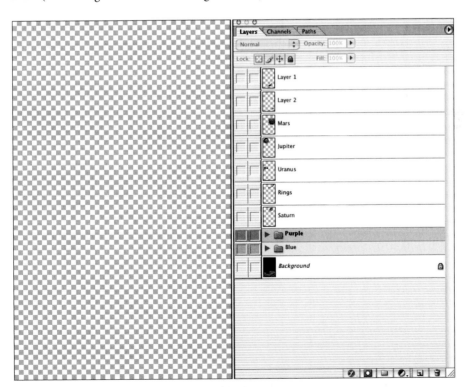

Figure H2.3

The image window and the Layers palette of the Flying Women document

Moving Layers

The contents of a layer can be repositioned horizontally or vertically within the image window. Follow these steps to move the planets into their vertical and horizontal positions on the image:

1. Choose View → Rulers to display the horizontal and vertical rulers.

2. Double-click the vertical or horizontal ruler to display the Units & Rulers preferences. Set the Units to Inches.

3. Target the Mars layer by clicking its thumbnail or its name, as shown in Figure H2.5.

4. Select the Move tool. In the Options bar, select Show Bounding Box. Place your cursor in the center of Mars, which is indicated by a little circle-cross. Click and drag until Mars aligns with the 12′ vertical and 8′ horizontal marks on the rulers (as in Figure H2.6). Release the mouse.

Figure H2.5

Targeting the Mars layer

5. Target the Jupiter layer. Using the same technique as in step 4, place the center of Jupiter on the 2′ vertical and the 8′ horizontal ruler marks.

6. Save your work (press ⌘/Ctrl-S or choose File → Save).

Moving Linked Layers

When items are linked, they can be moved or transformed simultaneously. You will link Saturn and its rings so they can be moved together into the correct position. Follow these steps to link and then move two layers:

1. Conceal the Jupiter and the Uranus layers by clicking their visibility icons in the Layers palette.

2. Target the Rings layer.

3. Click in the second column next to the Saturn layer. The chain icon appears to link the two layers.

4. With the Move tool, drag and place the center of Saturn and its rings at the 7.25′ vertical and 3′ horizontal marks.

5. Reveal the Jupiter layer by clicking the eye icon in the Layers palette. The image should look like Figure H2.7.

Figure H2.6

Aligning Mars on the ruler marks

Figure H2.7

The planets have been moved. Two layers (Saturn and Rings) are linked so that they can be moved as a unit. The bounding box surrounds the content of these two layers.

Naming Layers

To keep your document organized, name your layers:

1. Display Layer 1 and Layer 2 by clicking their eye icons. Double-click on the words *Layer 1*, and a box appears.

2. Type the words **Yellow Woman**.

3. Repeat the process for Layer 2, and rename it **Yellow Costume**.

Making a Layer Set

Layer sets organize your layers so that they can be easily managed. You will organize the flying women into color-coded layer sets for easy identification and repositioning.

1. Target the Yellow Woman layer. Click the Create A New Set icon  on the Layers palette. A new layer set folder appears above the targeted layer.

2. Option/Alt-double-click the layer set. The Layer Set Properties dialog box appears. Rename the layer set **Yellow**. For Color, choose yellow.

3. Click the Yellow Costume layer and drag it on top of the Yellow Layer Set icon. The layer becomes part of the set, as shown in Figure H2.8.

4. Drag the Yellow Woman layer on top of the Yellow layer set. Notice that the layers inside the folder have been automatically color-coded in yellow.

5. Save your work.

Moving Items within a Layer Set

You've created your layer set, but the costume is not on the yellow woman yet. She might be getting cold, flying around in deep space in her underwear, so you need to dress her. You can reposition the contents of a layer and change its stacking order within the layer set:

1. The costume is behind the yellow woman. In the Layers palette, drag the Yellow Costume layer above the Yellow Woman layer within the layer set.

2. Target the Yellow Costume layer, choose the Move tool, and drag the Yellow Costume onto the Yellow Woman until it is in position. Then release the mouse.

Changing the Order of Layers

You can change the position of all the layers within a layer set by dragging the layer set folder upward or downward in the layer stack. The stacking order in the Layers palette controls where the content is positioned. Layers at the top of the stack will appear in front of the other image elements. Layers at the bottom of the stack will appear behind the other image elements. You will perform this operation to move the blue lady and her costume in front of Mars.

Figure H2.8

The two layers are part of the color-coded layer set.

1. Make all the content of all layers visible by clicking all the visibility indicators. Notice that the Blue Woman is behind Mars.

2. To bring all the layers in the layer set forward, they must be moved up in the stack. Place your cursor on the Blue Layer Set folder or name. Click the layer set and drag it to the top of the stack until you see the line at the top of the stack become bold. The woman and her costume now appear in front of Mars.

3. Repeat the process with the Purple Layer Set to bring the purple woman to the front of Mars.

Using Layers to Create and Edit

Layers enable you to create and edit content. You will see how to create new layers from selected areas and affect their pixels with a few of Photoshop's powerful features.

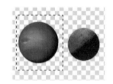

Figure H2.9

The contents of the Uranus layer appear against the transparent checkerboard.

Cutting and Copying Images to a New Layer

You can make new layers from the contents of existing layers. You'll cut a planet and copy it to a new layer.

1. Target the Uranus layer.

2. Option/Alt-click the eye icon of the Uranus layer to reveal only its contents against a transparent checkerboard, as in Figure H2.9.

3. Select the Rectangular Marquee tool ⬚ . Draw a marquee around the blue planet.

4. Choose Layer → New → Layer Via Copy, or press ⌘/Ctrl-J. The selected planet is copied onto a new layer. Double-click the default name and rename the layer **Galaxy**.

5. Target the Uranus layer again. Draw a rectangular marquee around the green planet.

6. Choose Layer → New → Layer Via Cut, or press Shift-⌘-J/Shift-Ctrl-J. The selected planet is cut to a new layer. Name the layer **Mercury** (see Figure H2.10).

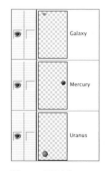

Figure H2.10

The new Mercury layer appears with the others.

Editing the Contents of a Layer

Follow these steps to edit the contents of your layers:

1. Target the Galaxy layer.

2. Option/Alt-click the eye icon of the Galaxy layer to reveal only its contents against a transparent checkerboard.

3. Select the Move tool. In the Options bar, select Show Bounding Box.

4. Click the upper-right handle of the bounding box (see Figure H2.11) and drag downward to squash the circular planet into an oval. Press Return/Enter or click the check mark on the Options bar to implement the transformation.

5. Choose Filter → Blur → Gaussian Blur → 4.4 pixels (as shown in Figure H2.12) to blur the edges of the oval.

6. Draw a rectangular marquee around the oval, as shown in Figure H2.13.

7. Choose Filter → Distort → Twirl, and set a value of 999 to twirl the oval into a galaxy (see Figure H2.14). The outcome of this operation depends on the size and shape of the rectangular marquee. Yours might vary from what is shown here.

8. Press ⌘/Ctrl-D to deselect.

9. With the Galaxy layer still targeted, select the Move tool and drag the Galaxy into the upper-left corner of the document so that its center aligns with the 1′ vertical and 2′ horizontal marks on the rulers.

10. View and target the Mercury layer. Press Shift as you drag Mercury to constrain its horizontal movement; reposition the planet so that its center aligns with the 6.5′ vertical and 8.75′ horizontal marks on the rulers.

11. Let's change the color of Mercury. Choose Image → Adjustments → Hue/Saturation. Move the Hue slider to the left until it reads –101. Move the Saturation slider to the right until it reads +29.

Figure H2.11

The bounding box

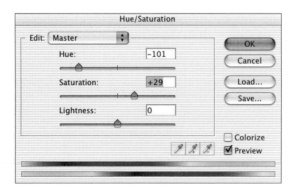

12. View and target the Uranus layer. Move Uranus so that its center aligns with the 14′ vertical, 2.25′ horizontal marks on the rulers.

13. Save the document.

Moving Layers from Another Document

You can easily move layers from one document to another. Here you will move two linked layers:

1. In the Flying_Women.psd file, click the visibility icon next to the Background and the Saturn and Ring layers to display them. Target the Saturn layer.

2. Open the file Red_Woman.psd from the H02 folder on the CD, and target the Red Costume layer.

3. In Red_Woman.psd, click in the second column next to the Red Woman layer to link it with Red Costume.

4. Place your cursor on the Red_Woman.psd image. Press your mouse, drag the image, and place it on the Flying_Women.psd document. Release the mouse, and two new layers appear between the Saturn layer and the Ring layer.

5. Select the Move tool and position the Red Woman and the Red Costume between Saturn and its rings.

There are three ways to drag layers and place them on another image. Make sure you use the right one:

- You can drag an individual layer from the Layers palette or from the image window to another image.

- To drag linked layers and maintain the linked relationship, you must target one of them and drag from the image window.

- To drag a layer set from an image, drag from the *name* or *folder* of the layer set in the Layers palette.

Applying a Style to a Layer

A drop shadow adds realism and depth to an image. Creating the drop shadow as a layer style is easy:

1. With the Red Woman layer targeted, double-click the layer thumbnail to bring up the Layer Style dialog box.

Figure H2.12

The Gaussian Blur filter applied to the Galaxy layer

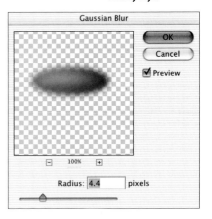

Figure H2.13

The Galaxy selected with the Rectangular Marquee tool

Figure H2.14

The Twirl filter applied to the Galaxy

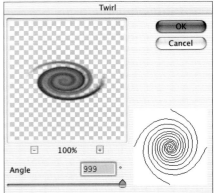

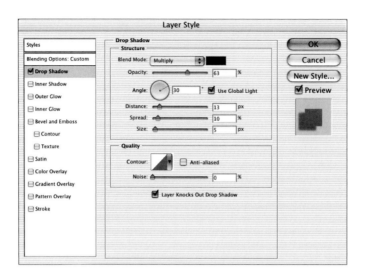

2. Click the Drop Shadow option to display its controls (see Figure H2.15).

3. Set the following specifications and then click OK. Your image should look like Figure H2.16.

Opacity	63%
Distance	13 px
Spread	10%
Size	5 px

Entering Type in a Bounding Box

The Type tool **T** can produce sophisticated text effects. Combined with Photoshop's layer styles, the graphic possibilities are endless. Follow these steps to place and manipulate the Amazing Flying Women from Outer Space text:

1. Display all the layers in the document by pressing the Option/Alt key and clicking the eye icon next to the Background.

2. Target the Purple layer set, which is topmost in the stack, to ensure that the Type layer you are about to create will appear above all the other layers.

3. Select the Type tool. Place your cursor on the image at the 1′ horizontal mark and the 2′ vertical mark. Drag downward and to the right to the 4.75′ vertical and 9′ horizontal mark to produce a bounding box. Enter the following text specifications in the Options bar:

Font	Times
Size	90 pt
Anti-Alias	Smooth
Alignment	Centered
Color	Red

4. Display the Character palette (Window → Character, or click the Palettes button on the Options bar); Set Leading field to 95 pt.

5. You'll see a blinking insertion point in the bounding box. Type this: **Amazing** <Return> **Flying Women**. When you're finished typing, click the check mark on the Options bar. This will create a new Type layer named Amazing Flying Women. Your text should resemble Figure H2.17.

Entering Type On a Path

Now you'll place the subheading on a vector path:

1. Select the Pen tool . Click about 2 inches below the *F* in the word *Flying*. Click and hold the mouse while you drag up at about a 45-degree angle and about 1 inch to the right. Release the mouse. Click 2 inches below the space between the *g* and the *W*, and drag to the right and down. Release the mouse. Click 2 inches below the *n*. Drag to the right and up at a 45-degree angle for about an inch to finish the path. The path should look like Figure H2.18 (see Chapter 9, "Drawing Paths" for more information on that topic).

2. Click the Text tool. Change the settings on the Options bar to the following:

Font	Helvetica Medium
Size	45
Color	Yellow
Alignment	Flush Left

3. From the Character Palette pull-down menu, choose All Caps.

4. Click on the leftmost point on the path; you'll see a blinking insertion point. Type the words **FROM OUTER SPACE**. Click the check mark in the Options bar to create the new Type layer. Your text should resemble Figure H2.18.

Warping Text

You can bend and twist type to a variety of shapes as you will do with the headline text. :

1. Target the Amazing Flying Women layer and select the Text tool.

Figure H2.16
The Red Woman flying through the rings, and the drop shadow cast on the planet

Figure H2.17
The basic headline for the poster

Figure H2.18
The subheading type placed on a curved path

2. Click the Create Warped Text button ▣ in the Options bar.

3. Choose Style → Arc (see Figure H2.19).

4. Enter the following values and click OK:

Bend	30%
Horizontal Distortion	0%
Vertical Distortion	0%

5. After you've warped the text, you might find that you'll want to move it down a little. Select the Move tool and drag the text into position. The text should look like Figure H2.20.

Applying Multiple Effects to a Layer

You've seen how you can apply a drop shadow to a layer. You'll now apply several other effects to a Type layer:

1. Target the Amazing Flying Women layer.

2. Opt/Alt-double-click the layer to display the Layer Style dialog box.

> When working in the Layer Style dialog, you must click the name of the style in order to display the individual layer style controls. Selecting the check box next to the name doesn't display the controls; it's an indicator that the effect has been applied to the current layer.

3. From the Style list on the left, click the name Inner Shadow. The check box is automatically selected, and the Inner Shadow controls are displayed.

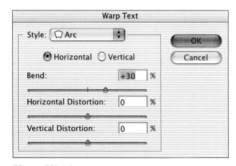

Figure H2.19

Setting values for the warped text

Figure H2.20

The text warped into an arc

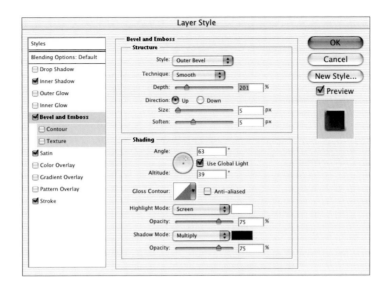

Figure H2.21

The Layer Style dialog box with Bevel and Emboss controls displayed

4. Set the following specifications (use the default values for settings that aren't listed here):

Angle	63º
Distance	8 px
Choke	0%
Size	5 px

5. Click the Bevel and Emboss style. Set the following specifications (use the defaults for the remaining options, as shown in Figure H2.21.):

Style	Outer Bevel
Technique	Smooth
Depth	201%
Direction	Up
Size	5 px
Soften	5 px

6. Click the Satin style.

7. Click the Color Overlay style.

8. Click the Stroke style. Click on the color swatch, and from the Color Picker set the color to gold, and the size to 3 px. Use the defaults for the other settings.

   Your text should now look like Figure H2.22.

Figure H2.22

The styles applied to the type

It makes no difference in what order you apply the multiple layer styles.

As I said earlier in this exercise, type is more than just words. By applying the type-twisting techniques and multiple effects that you have learned, you transform your type into a strong visual element that resonates with form, texture, and color. With such a multitude of controls, the choices are infinite.

Merging Layers and Flattening the Image

To reduce the file size and to more efficiently manage your document, you can merge layers or flatten the image:

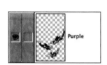

Figure H2.23

You can merge the contents of all three layer sets into one layer.

1. Click to deselect the visibility icons next to all the layers except for the Blue, Purple, and Yellow layer sets. Target the Purple layer set.

2. Choose Merge Visible from the Layers palette menu. The content of all three of the layer sets is merged into a single layer (see Figure H2.23). Notice the reduction in the file size in the information field in the lower-left corner of the image window.

   To finish the image, you will flatten it.

3. Choose Image → Duplicate. Name the new image `Flying_Women_flat.psd`.

4. Be sure all the layers and layer styles are visible. From the Layers Palette pull-down menu, choose Flatten Image.

5. Save the image.

CHAPTER 9

Drawing Paths

Photoshop provides several methods for isolating areas of an image, as you saw in Chapter 6, "Making Selections." Still, making accurate selections can be difficult or time-consuming, because each image presents different problems. The Pen tool and the Paths palette add more capabilities to further enhance the accuracy and speed of making selections and defining the smooth edges. After you've learned to draw with the Pen tool, you'll probably find it indispensable, because it can often be the easiest and fastest way to select areas that are defined by long, smooth curves.

Photoshop also offers several other vector-generating tools that are used for making lines and shapes.

This chapter will cover topics including:

- **Using the Path tools and the Paths palette**

- **Drawing and editing paths**

- **Using paths to apply color**

- **Converting, importing, and exporting paths**

- **Using vector masks and clipping paths**

- **Using the Shape tools**

What Is a Path?

If you have used any vector illustration software, then the Paths function in Photoshop should be familiar to you. Paths represent *vector objects* that mathematically define specific areas on an image by virtue of their shape and position. Vector objects are composed of anchor points and line segments, known as *Bezier curves,* like the ones shown in Figure 9.1 (see Chapter 3, "The Nature of the Beast," for more information on these terms).

The Path tools enable you to create straight lines and curves with much greater clarity and precision than the selection tools. If you create an open-ended path, you can then stroke it with a color to form a curved line (using the path as a drawing tool). If its two end points have joined, the path encloses a *shape.* You can then fill the shape with color, stroke it with an outline, or store it in the Paths palette (or the Shape library) for later use. It can also be converted into a selection, to which you can then apply some other Photoshop operation.

The Path Tools

The primary Path tool is the Pen tool, located in the Tool palette. To choose the Pen tool, click its icon or press P. If you hold down the mouse button, you can expand the Tool palette to display the other Path tools. Photoshop has tools for drawing paths (Shift-P

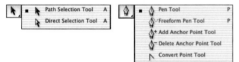

cycles through these) and tools for editing paths (Shift-A cycles through these tools). There are also two tools designed specifically to select and move a path or a portion of a path. You'll explore these tools throughout the chapter, but here is a quick preview.

Path-Drawing Tools

This set of tools includes the following:

The Pen tool draws paths by clicking and dragging.

Figure 9.1

Components of Bezier curves

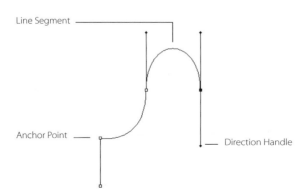

Figure 9.1

Components of Bezier curves

[icon] **The Freeform Pen tool** draws a freeform line that converts itself into a path when the mouse is released.

[icon] ☑ Magnetic **The Freeform Pen tool with the Magnetic option**, sometimes simply called the Magnetic Pen, intuitively defines edges based upon contrasting colors.

Path-Editing Tools

This set of tools includes the following:

[icon] **The Add Anchor Point tool** adds anchor points to existing paths.

[icon] **The Delete Anchor Point Tool** removes anchor points from existing paths.

[icon] **The Convert Point tool** changes a corner point to a curve, or a curve to a corner point.

[icon] **The Path Selection tool** selects and moves the path as a unit.

[icon] **The Direct Selection tool** selects and moves individual anchor points and segments.

Drawing Paths

Each path-drawing tool employs a slightly different method for creating a path outline. Learning to draw accurately with the Pen tools can be challenging at first, because drawing with Bezier curves is unlike any form of traditional drawing. With a little practice, however, as you become familiar with the process, your speed and accuracy will improve considerably.

The Pen Tool

The Pen tool enables you to draw straight lines and smooth curves with a high degree of control and precision. The basic techniques and concepts used for drawing paths in Adobe Photoshop closely parallel those used in Adobe Illustrator. Usually, a path is drawn to follow the form of the area to be isolated, and then the path is edited and refined to a considerable degree of accuracy.

The Pen Tool Options bar displays options that enable you to modify the tool's behavior (see Figure 9.2). Before you draw a path or a shape, specify in the Options bar whether to make a new Shape layer or a new work path. This choice will affect how the shape can later be edited. If you choose the Shape Layer icon, Photoshop generates an independent Shape layer (see "Creating Lines and Shapes" near the end of this chapter). If you choose the Work Path icon, Photoshop draws an independent path and creates a work path in the Paths palette. For now we'll be working with work paths. Select the Auto Add/Delete check box to automatically add anchor points when one of the Pen tools is placed on a segment or to delete a point when a Pen tool is placed over an anchor point.

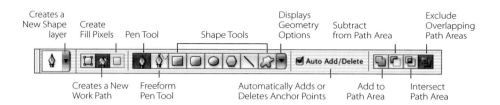

Figure 9.2

**The Pen tool
Options bar**

When you choose the Pen tool, you have a choice of four behaviors represented by the four icons on the right side of the Options bar. Use them to add to an existing path, subtract from an existing path, intersect with an existing path or exclude overlapping path areas. The results of these operations can be seen when a fill is applied to the path.

> Using the Zoom tool or the Navigator to view the image more closely greatly enhances your ability to draw with precision.

Straight Paths

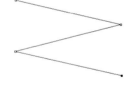

The simplest of all paths consists of two anchor points joined by a straight line segment (anchor points that connect straight line segments are called *corner anchor points*). You add additional segments to the straight path by moving the cursor and clicking the mouse. The segments can abruptly change direction as the corners zigzag their way across the image.

Take these steps to draw a straight path:

1. Select the Pen tool and click the image where you want to begin the path. An anchor point appears; release the mouse button.

2. Click (and release) your mouse at the next point on the image. A line segment with another anchor point appears between the two points.

3. Continue to move and click your mouse to produce a series of straight-line segments connected to each other by corner anchor points.

Curved Paths

A curved path consists of two anchor points connected by a curved segment. *Direction handles* determine the position and shape of the line segment.

Take these steps to draw a curved path:

1. Select the Pen tool and place the cursor over the image where you want the path to begin.

2. Click your mouse *and drag*. An anchor point with a direction handle appears. Without releasing the mouse button, drag the handle in the general direction you want the curve to travel.

3. Release the mouse and move the cursor to the next point on the image.

4. Click your mouse *and drag.* A curved segment with another anchor point and direction handle appears. Drag in the opposite general direction of the curve.

5. With the mouse button still depressed, adjust the direction handle until the curved line segment is in the desired position, and then release the mouse.

Tips for Drawing Curved Paths

Keep the following suggestions in mind as you practice drawing curved paths:

- Drag the first point in the direction of the peak of the curve and drag the second point in the opposite direction. Dragging the first and second point in the same direction produces an S curve, which is undesirable because its shape is difficult to control.

- Use as few anchor points as possible to assure a smooth path.

- Place the anchor points on the sides of the curve, not on the peaks or valleys, to maintain better control and smooth transitions.

- A path is a continuous series of segments connected by anchor points. You can add anchor points to the middle of a segment, but you can add segments only to the end points of an open path.

- An anchor point can connect only two segments.

- If you stop drawing and want to add a new segment to a path, resume drawing by first clicking one of the end points with a Pen tool.

- If you are drawing an open path and want to begin a second path that is not connected to the first, press ⌘ (Macintosh) or Ctrl (Windows) to get the Direct Selection tool. Click off the path and release the keys. Resume drawing the new path.

Changing the Direction of a Curved Path

You can draw a scalloped path by changing the direction of the curve. When performing this operation, it helps to think of the Option/Alt key as a turn signal. In the following example, the segments will curve upward. Follow these steps:

1. Select the Pen tool. Click the image where you want to begin the path and drag up. An anchor point with a direction handle appears. Without releasing the mouse button, drag to adjust the direction handle; then release.

2. Click where you want the next part of the curve. Click your mouse and drag down. A curved segment with another anchor point and direction line appears, as in Figure 9.3; release the mouse.

Figure 9.3

A curved segment with another anchor point and direction line

Figure 9.4

Placing the cursor on the last anchor point and pressing Option/Alt

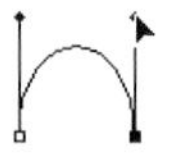

Figure 9.5

Dragging the direction handle up

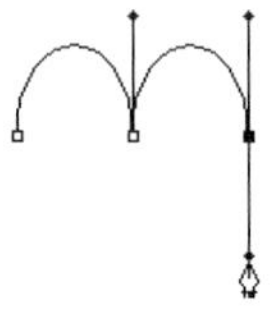

Figure 9.6

Drag and adjust to the desired position.

3. Place your cursor on the last anchor point and press Option/Alt (the turn signal!). See Figure 9.4.

4. Click and drag the direction handle up and release the mouse (see Figure 9.5).

5. Move your cursor to the next location, click your mouse, and drag down. Adjust the segment so that the curve is the desired length and position (see Figure 9.6).

6. Repeat steps 3 and 4.

7. Repeat steps 2 through 5 until the desired number of curves are drawn (see Figure 9.7).

Adding a Curved Path to a Straight Path

Usually, the paths you draw are combinations of straight and curved paths. These techniques combine the two into one continuous path:

1. Select the Pen tool and click the image where you want to path to begin. An anchor point appears; release the mouse button.

2. Click the next point on the image. A straight segment with another anchor point appears.

3. To add a curved segment, place your cursor on the last anchor point, and press Option/Alt while holding down the mouse button and dragging up.

4. Release your mouse button and move your cursor to the next location.

5. Click your mouse and drag down to finish the curve. Release the mouse when the size and position of the curve are achieved (see Figure 9.8).

Adding a Straight Path to a Curved Path

You can also begin with a curve and add a straight line to it:

1. Select the Pen tool, click the image where you want to begin the path, and drag up. An anchor point with a direction handle appears. Without releasing the mouse button, drag the direction handle in the direction of the curve.

2. Release the mouse and move the cursor to the next point.

3. Click your mouse and drag down. A curved segment with another anchor point and direction line appears. Release the mouse.

4. Place your cursor on the last anchor point, press Option/Alt, and click your mouse once.

5. Move your cursor to the next location and click your mouse to complete the segment.

Figure 9.7

Repeat to draw more curves.

Figure 9.8

Adding a curved segment to a straight segment

Closing a Path

By closing a path, you create a *shape.* To close a series of straight paths, draw at least two paths, and then place your cursor directly over the first anchor point. A little circle appears beside the pen cursor to indicate that the path is ready to be closed. Click the mouse. To close one or more curved paths, draw at least *one* path and click the first anchor point.

The Freeform Pen Tool

Drawing with the Freeform Pen tool is very similar to drawing with the Lasso tool, introduced in Chapter 6. If you place your cursor on the image, click, and drag your mouse, the Freeform Pen will be followed by a trail that produces a path when the mouse is released (see Figure 9.9).

The Freeform Pen tool provides a quick way to draw a curve, but it doesn't offer the same level of control and precision as the Pen tool. You can't control the number or placement of anchor points. Paths created by the Freeform Pen usually require editing or removal of excess anchor points after the path has been completed.

When you select the Freeform Pen tool, the Options bar provides new settings in the Freeform Pen Options drop-down menu: Curve Fit and Magnetic. You can specify the Curve Fit between 0.5 and 10.0 pixels, to determine the sensitivity of the tool to the movement of your mouse. A lower tolerance produces a finer curve with more anchor points. A higher tolerance produces a simpler path with fewer anchor points, and fewer anchor points produce a smoother curve.

The Magnetic Pen Option

The performance of the Freeform Pen tool with the Magnetic check box selected (also called "the Magnetic Pen tool") is similar to the Magnetic Lasso (see Chapter 6). It automatically snaps to areas of high color contrast within an image as you drag. You define the area within which snapping will occur and the degree of contrast needed to trigger snapping. Whereas the Magnetic Lasso converts to a selection, the Magnetic Pen converts to a path. Thus, whereas the Magnetic Lasso is a good tool for cropping, say, a face out of a contrasting background, the Magnetic Pen is useful for defining its edges based on contrasting colors.

To access the Magnetic Pen, select the Freeform Pen tool (click and hold the cursor on the Pen tool in the Tool palette, and choose the Freeform Pen from the fly-out; or press Shift-P once or twice to select the tool) and select the Magnetic check box in the Options bar. Then use the Freeform Pen Options menu to display the Magnetic options:

Width Enter a distance in pixels from the edge that the tool will be active. Higher values mean the tool is "attracted" to the edge from a greater distance.

Contrast Enter a value between 1% and 100% to determine the tool's sensitivity in detecting contrasting borders. Higher values detect edges of greater contrast, and lower values increase the tool's sensitivity to low-contrast edges.

Figure 9.9

The Freeform Pen tool draws an unrestricted path.

You can increase the detection width in one-pixel increments *while drawing* by pressing the] key. You can decrease the width by pressing the [key.

Frequency Enter a value between 1 and 100 to establish the rate at which the Magnetic Pen places anchor points. Higher values place more anchor points over a shorter distance.

Pen Pressure If you are working with a stylus tablet, check Pen Pressure. As you drag, the pressure of the stylus will correspond to the Width setting. An increase of pressure on the stylus will thicken the pen width.

Open the file `el_jefe.psd` in the Chapter 9 folder on the *Photoshop CS Savvy* CD. You can use this image to practice the Path and Shape tool techniques described in this chapter.

Take the following steps to draw with the Magnetic Pen:

1. Click the image to set the first point, near an edge of relatively high contrast.

2. Release the mouse button and drag slowly. A path will follow along the most distinct edge within the Pen width. Periodically, the Pen places anchor points along the specified border, while the most recent segment remains active (see Figure 9.10).

3. Press Return/Enter to end an open path. You can resume drawing the open path by clicking the last anchor point and dragging.

4. If you stop dragging and double-click, you create a segment that connects the last anchor point with the first one and closes the path. You can also close the path by hovering over the first anchor point until the little circle appears. Click once.

Figure 9.10

A path made with the Magnetic Pen "snaps" to a line of contrasting pixels.

Figure 9.11

Option/Alt-drag with the Path Selection tool to duplicate a path.

You can temporarily turn off the Magnetic option by holding down the Option/Alt key with the mouse button depressed to draw a straight path, or with the mouse button released to draw a freeform path.

Editing Paths

After a path has been drawn, all or part of it can be moved or reshaped. Anchor points can be added or omitted, and corners can be converted into curves or curves into corners. Paths can also be transformed and combined.

The path-editing tools include the Path Selection tool, the Direct Selection tool, the Add Anchor Point tool, the Delete Anchor Point tool, and the Convert Point tool.

Using the Path Selection Tool

The black arrow, the Path Selection tool, selects all the anchor points and segments of a path. You can then reposition the path anywhere on the image by dragging it with this tool.

Another method of selecting a path is to use the Path Selection tool to click and drag a marquee that touches any part of the path. All the anchor points will appear solid, indicating that the entire path is selected.

You can duplicate a path by dragging and dropping it with the Path Selection tool and the Option/Alt key depressed (see Figure 9.11).

Aligning Paths

By using the Path Selection tool, you can automatically align and distribute multiple paths and vector objects such as lines and shapes. You cannot, however, align or distribute shapes that are on separate layers. To align multiple paths, select two or more paths with the Path Selection tool by dragging a marquee that touches the objects, or by Shift-clicking the paths. From the Options bar, choose one of the alignment options shown in Figure 9.12.

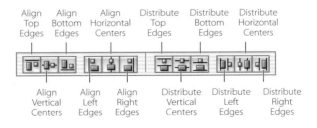

Align Top Edges Align Bottom Edges Align Horizontal Centers Distribute Top Edges Distribute Bottom Edges Distribute Horizontal Centers

Align Vertical Centers Align Left Edges Align Right Edges Distribute Vertical Centers Distribute Left Edges Distribute Right Edges

Figure 9.12

Alignment features of the Path Selection tool

The Align choices match up the edges or centers of paths and objects, as follows:

Top Edges	Aligns the top edges of the path or vector object
Vertical Centers	Aligns the vertical midpoints
Bottom Edges	Aligns the bottom edges
Left Edges	Aligns the left edges
Horizontal Centers	Aligns the horizontal midpoints
Right Edges	Aligns the right edges

The Distribute choices position the edges or centers of paths and objects over equal distances, in these ways:

Figure 9.13

In the first row, the top edges are aligned. In the second row, the top edges are distributed.

Top	Distributes the top edges of the path or vector object
Vertical Centers	Distributes the vertical midpoints
Bottom Edges	Distributes the bottom edges
Left Edges	Distributes the left edges
Horizontal Centers	Distributes the horizontal midpoints
Right Edges	Distributes the right edges

Figure 9.13 illustrates the difference between aligning and distributing.

Using the Direct Selection Tool

The Direct Selection tool selects or modifies a segment, or the position of an anchor point, on a path. It is an essential tool for revising and reshaping a path after it has already been drawn.

To select, move, or edit a segment or anchor point, choose the Direct Selection tool. Click on a segment or anchor point to select it. Click and drag an anchor point to reposition it or a segment to reshape it. To deselect a path, click anywhere on the image.

> You can toggle from any of the Pen tools or path-editing tools to the Direct Selection tool by pressing the ⌘/Ctrl key.

Reshaping Paths

To alter the shape of a path after it has been drawn, follow these steps:

1. Choose the Direct Selection tool.

2. Click an anchor point to select it.

3. Click and drag one of the anchor point's *direction handles* until the desired shape of the curve is achieved (see Figure 9.14).

Figure 9.14

Reshaping a path

Editing Anchor Points

After you have drawn a path around an area on the image, you might need to refine it by adding or deleting anchor points. When you do so, you increase your ability to edit the path.

It might be tempting to add dozens of anchor points, to facilitate the drawing of a path. That's not always a good idea, because too many extra points increase the path's complexity and compromise the smoothness of the shape.

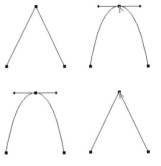

Adding and Deleting Anchor Points

To add an anchor point, select the Add Anchor Point tool and click the path. A new anchor point will appear where you've clicked. To delete an anchor point, select the Delete Anchor Point tool and click an anchor point. The two segments connected by the point will join into one.

Figure 9.15

Converting (top) a corner to a smooth point and (bottom) a smooth to a corner point

Converting Anchor Points

There are two types of anchor points. *Smooth points* connect curved or straight lines that "flow into" each other. *Corner points* connect lines that change direction abruptly. An anchor point can be converted from corner to smooth or from smooth to corner by clicking the point with the Convert Point tool (see Figure 9.15). Click a smooth point, and it converts to a corner point; to convert a corner point, click it and drag out the direction handles until the desired curve is achieved, and release the mouse.

Transforming Paths

Like selection outlines and selection contents, paths can also be modified with the transformation tools. After a path has been drawn, you must select it with one of the arrow tools. If you select it with the Path Selection tool, you can employ any of the transformation operations in the Edit menu (including Free Transform, Scale, Rotate, Skew, Distort, Perspective, or Flip) to edit the entire path. If you select one or more points or segments with the Direct Selection tool, you can apply any of the transformation operations to the selected part of the path.

> To learn how to use Photoshop's transformation features, see Chapter 13, "Sizing and Transforming Images."

Combining Paths

If you have drawn two or more paths that intersect, you can combine them into one path. Select both paths with the Path Selection tool by pressing your mouse button and dragging a marquee that touches both of them or by clicking them in sequence while pressing the Shift key. On the Options bar, click the Combine button. The elements of both paths combine into a group of paths. If you click any member of the group with the Path Selection tool, then all will be selected.

The Paths Palette

The Paths palette is the central control for all path operations. Like a layer or a channel, a path can be stored into a palette so it can later be edited or converted into a selection. You can access the Paths palette by choosing Window → Paths (see Figure 9.16). If you still have the Paths palette in the default cluster—grouped with the Layers palette—pressing the F7 function key will also bring it up.

Work Paths

When you begin drawing a path with the Pen tool, it appears in the Paths palette as a thumbnail named Work Path. The *work path* is a temporary element that records changes as you draw new sections of the path. If you complete a path on an image, click the Pen tool, and draw another path, it will appear on the same Work Path thumbnail as the first path. To create separate additional paths, you must save the work path to the Paths palette.

You can increase or decrease the size of the Paths palette thumbnails, or turn them off, by choosing Palette Options from the palette pull-down menu and clicking the radio button next to the desired thumbnail size.

Figure 9.16

The Paths palette and its menu

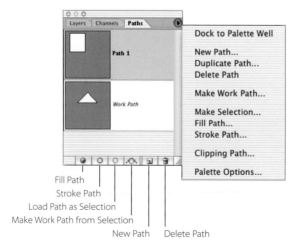

Saving Paths

Saving a path to the Paths palette has a distinct advantage over saving selections as alpha channels (which are described in Chapter 12, "Using Channels and Quick Mask"): the file size of a document does not substantially increase with each saved path.

After your path has been drawn and appears as a Work Path thumbnail, you can save it by choosing Save Path from the palette menu. A dialog box appears where you can name the path; if no name is entered, the path name defaults to Path 1. You can also save a path by dragging the Work Path thumbnail to the New Path icon at the bottom of the palette.

The Paths palette lists saved paths from top to bottom in the order in which they were created. The paths can be reorganized within the list by clicking the path's name or thumbnail and dragging it to the desired location.

Displaying Paths

To display a path, click the path's name or thumbnail image in the Paths palette. Photoshop allows only one path to be displayed at a time. When displayed, it will appear on the image. You can edit it, move it, add other paths to it, or delete portions of the path. To conceal a work path or saved path from view in the image window, click the empty portion of the Paths palette.

Deleting Paths from the Image Window

To delete a path from the image, do one of the following:

- Select an entire path with the Path Selection tool. Press the Delete/ Backspace key. If it's a work path, the path and its icon are deleted. If it's a saved path, the path is deleted from the image window, but its empty thumbnail remains in the Paths palette.

- Select a part of the path with the Direct Selection tool. Press the Delete or Backspace key once to delete the selected part of the path or twice to delete the entire path.

Deleting Paths from the Palette

You might want to discard a path from the Paths palette after you are sure you will have no further use for it. To do so, target the path's name in the palette and perform one of the following operations:

- Drag the path thumbnail to the trash icon at the bottom of the palette.

- Choose Delete Path from the Paths Palette menu.

- Click the trash icon in the Paths palette. In the dialog box that appears, click Yes.

- Target the path in the Paths palette. Press the Delete or Backspace key.

Using Paths to Apply Color

You can apply color to an area of an image within a closed path or to the edge of a path.

Filling a Path

To fill the area within a path follow these steps:

1. Draw an open or closed path or display an existing path from the Paths palette by clicking its thumbnail.

2. Choose a foreground color and then choose Fill Path from the Paths Palette pull-down menu. The Fill Path dialog box appears (see Figure 9.17). Its Contents and Blending areas are identical to the Fill dialog box accessed from the Edit menu and are discussed in Chapter 10, "Creating and Applying Color."

3. In the additional Rendering field, you can enter a feather radius for the edges of the path and select the Anti-Aliased check box. Click OK when you have the settings you want.

You can fill a path with the current Fill Path dialog box settings by clicking the Fill Path icon at the bottom of the Paths palette.

Stroking a Path

A path can be stroked with a line of a specific color and width. This is an important operation in Photoshop because it is really the only way to create smooth, curved lines precisely. Try drawing one with the Paintbrush or Pencil; you'll see that it's quite difficult to achieve satisfactory results. Drawing an open path, editing it to your exact specifications, and then stroking it with a color produces perfect results every time.

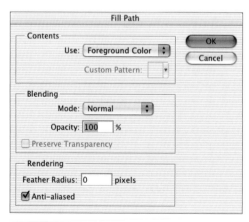

Figure 9.17

The Fill Path dialog box

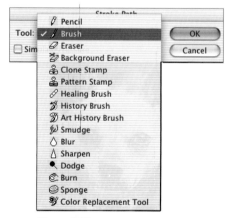

Figure 9.18

The Stroke Path dialog box

To color the line of a path, first

1. Draw a path or load one from the Paths palette.

2. Choose a foreground color from the Color Picker, Swatches palette or Color palette.

3. From the Paths Palette menu, choose Stroke Path. The Stroke Path dialog box appears (see Figure 9.18).

4. Pick a tool from the Tool list.

5. After you click OK, the stroke is painted with the current characteristics of the chosen tool as defined in the Options bar.

Figure 9.19

A stroked path

You can quickly stroke a path with the current tool characteristics set in the Stroke Path dialog box by clicking the Stroke Path icon ⬚ at the bottom of the Paths palette. Figure 9.19 shows an example.

Converting Paths

The primary reason for using paths is the ease and facility with which you can precisely define regions of an image. Although some of the selection tools offer unique selection techniques, there is nothing quite like the path operations to quickly and precisely surround an area.

Paths are easy to edit and require less real estate on your disk than selections saved as alpha channels. Eventually, though, you will need to convert your path into a selection before you can apply a Photoshop operation to the area it surrounds.

Converting a Path into a Selection

When you convert a path to a selection by using the Make Selection dialog box, you can specify the characteristics of your new selection and its relation to active selections on the image. To do this, target the path in the Paths palette and choose Make Selection from the Paths Palette pull-down menu. The Make Selection dialog box is displayed, enabling you to choose the characteristics of the new selection:

Feather Radius	Sets a distance in pixels for feathering of the selection outline
Anti-Aliased	Determines whether the selection will possess an anti-aliased edge
New Selection	Makes a selection from the path
Add To Selection	Adds the area defined by the path to the active selection
Subtract From Selection	Omits the area defined by the path from the active selection
Intersect With Selection	Makes a selection from the overlap of the path and the active selection

Click OK to convert the path into a selection.

Another way to convert a path into a new selection is by clicking the Load Path As Selection icon ⬚ at the bottom of the Paths palette.

Converting a Selection into a Path

To convert a selection into a path, draw a marquee with one of the selection tools. Choose Make Work Path from the Paths Palette menu. A dialog box is displayed that enables you to set the tolerance of the path in pixels. Tolerances with low values produce more-complex paths with greater numbers of anchor points, whereas tolerances with higher values produce simpler paths. Click OK to convert the selection into a path.

You can also convert a selection into a path by clicking the Make Work Path From Selection icon ▨ at the bottom of the Paths palette.

Importing and Exporting Paths

Photoshop paths can be used by other programs, where they can be modified. You can transfer a path directly from Photoshop to popular vector-based drawing programs such as Illustrator or FreeHand, or vice versa, to take advantage of either program's unique path-editing features.

Copying and Pasting

Figure 9.20

The Paste dialog box

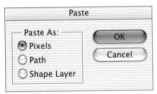

If you're moving the path from Photoshop to a vector-based drawing program, you can select the entire path with the Path Selection tool and copy it to the Clipboard (by choosing Edit → Copy or pressing ⌘/Ctrl-C). Open a document in the other program and paste the path into it. The paths remain fully editable in either program.

When you paste a path from a drawing program into Photoshop, a dialog box appears that asks you to choose to place the path as a rasterized image (pixels), a vector path, or a Shape layer (see Figure 9.21).

Dragging and Dropping

You can drag and drop a path from Photoshop to Illustrator. With both programs running, select the path with the Path Selection tool. Drag the path onto the Illustrator pasteboard. The new Illustrator path is fully editable.

Exporting Paths to Illustrator

If you can't run Photoshop and Illustrator simultaneously, you can export the file as a native Illustrator format (.ai) file by choosing File → Export → Paths To Illustrator. In the dialog box that appears, choose Work Path from the Write menu. After you quit Photoshop, launch Illustrator, and open the document, the exported path will be fully editable in Illustrator.

Paths exported from Photoshop to Illustrator do not contain fill or stroke information.

Using Vector Masks

When working with Photoshop graphical elements, it is sometimes necessary to "knock out" portions of an image—that is, make those areas invisible so that elements in layers below can show through. This can be done by using a *vector mask.* When you use a vector mask, the interior portion of the path will be displayed, and the area outside the path will be completely transparent (for more about layer masking, see Chapter 22, "Advanced Layer Techniques"). Vector masks are best used when you want a clean, crisp edge to your element—not always easy to create with regular selection methods!

To create a vector mask:

1. Open el jefe.psd in the Chapter 9 folder on the CD

2. In the layers palette, double click the Background to make it into a layer. Name the layer *Head.*

3. Choose the Freeform Pen Tool. In the Options bar check the Magnetic option. and click the Paths icon. Draw a path around El Jefe's head with the pen tool to isolate it (see Figure 9.21). Use the Direct Selection tool to tweak it for accuracy.

4. From the Paths Palette pull-down menu, choose Save Path, and name it Vector Head.

5. With the path selected in the Paths palette, choose Layer → Add Vector Mask → Current Path from the Palette menu.

6. The path outline will clip out anything outside the path, making it invisible and letting any layer beneath show through. The vector mask is also represented in the Layers palette, to the right of your active layer. At this point you can refine the path even further with the Path selection tool to produce an even more accurate mask. Notice also that you can apply a layer style such as the drop shadow (shown in Figure 9.22) with vector masks.

7. Click on the New Layer icon at the bottom of the Layers palette. Choose a foreground color and press Opt/Alt-Delete/Backspace to fill the new layer with the color. Drag the new layer under the Head layer.

8. To add the star draw it with the pen tool and repeat steps 2, 3 and 4. You can add the text or any other graphic elements, the choice only being limited by your imagination! Figure 9.23 shows the completed image.

Figure 9.21

Selecting the area with the free form Pen tool with the Magnetic option

Using Clipping Paths

The Clipping Path option has essentially the same effect as the Vector Mask option, except that clipping paths are designed to be exported with your image into a vector illustration program (such as Adobe Illustrator) or a page layout program (such as Adobe InDesign) instead of embedded within a Photoshop layer.

To create a clipping path:

1. Create a path around an area of your image as before by using the Path tools.

   Check the Options bar to be sure the Path option is chosen (not shape layers or fill pixels) and the Exclude Overlapping Path Areas option is also chosen (not the add/subtract/intersect options). If these two settings are inactive it often confuses users wishing to create simple compound clipping paths.

2. From the Paths Palette pull-down menu, choose Save Path, and give it a name.

3. Choose Clipping Path from the palette menu, and the Clipping Path dialog box appears (see Figure 9.24).

4. Select the name of the path you want to convert to a clipping path from the Path list. Click OK.

Figure 9.22

Applying a drop shadow layer style

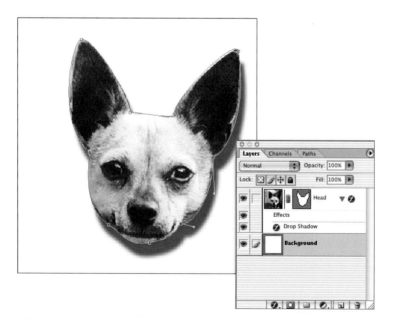

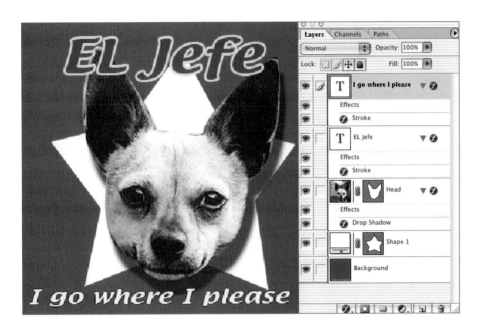

Figure 9.23

The finished image with the vector mask's thumbnails in the layers palette.

5. For most paths, leave the Flatness setting blank. When you print the image, the printer's default flatness setting will be used to define the shape. However, if you experience printing problems, try saving the path with new settings (see the "Troubleshooting" sidebar).

The path name is boldfaced in the Paths palette, indicating that it is a clipping path.

Images containing clipping paths must be saved in either EPS or TIFF format, depending on the program, and therefore can be imported only into programs that support these images. It's best to save a *copy* of the image so that the original image retains Photoshop's attributes.

To save an image with a clipping path as an EPS:

1. Choose File → Save As. Check the As A Copy box.

2. From the Format list, choose Photoshop EPS to display the EPS Options dialog box (see Figure 9.25).

Figure 9.24

The Clipping Path dialog box

Figure 9.25

EPS file options

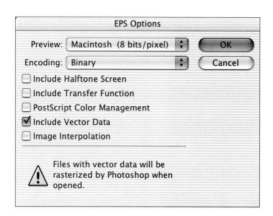

3. Choose a Preview option, depending on the type of computer and the platform you are using: Macintosh or Windows, 1 bit or 8 bit (see Appendix B, "File Formats," for a detailed explanation of the EPS Options dialog box).

4. For the Encoding type, choose Binary.

5. Click OK.

6. Open a document in a desktop-publishing program or vector-drawing program, and place the EPS image. The clipping path will mask out everything outside the path, much the same as the vector mask does within Photoshop.

Creating Lines and Shapes

Photoshop handles lines and shapes in a manner much like Illustrator. Like type, lines and shapes are vector objects (drawn and defined by paths). You draw a predefined shape by using one of the Shape tools, or a custom shape by using the Pen tool. Once drawn, shapes can be edited by adjusting their anchor points with the path-editing tools. When you create a shape on a Shape layer, it appears on an independent layer with a Vector Mask thumbnail next to a Color Fill Layer thumbnail.

The shape also appears as a separate path in the Paths palette. To apply any filter to a shape, it must first be *rasterized,* or turned into pixels. If you flatten the image, shapes are automatically converted to pixels.

The Shape tool can instantly create precise shapes, such as rectangles, rounded rectangles, ellipses, polygons, lines, and custom shapes that you can edit with the path-editing tools. When you click the Shape tool icon in the Tool palette, it expands to reveal all of the available tools. After you've chosen a shape from this fly-out, click in the image and drag to size the shape.

The Shape Tool Options Bar

As you choose a different shape from the Tool palette or from the Shape list in the Options bar, the Options bar changes to accommodate specific characteristics of the shape. Figure 9.26 illustrates the differences in the Options bar when the three different drawing options are selected.

TROUBLESHOOTING CLIPPING PATH POSTSCRIPT ERRORS

A raster image processor (RIP) is software on a computer, or a device inside an imagesetter or PostScript printer, that interprets a vector curve by connecting a series of straight line segments together. The *flatness* of a clipping path determines the fidelity of the lines to the curve. The lower the setting, the more lines are produced, and the more accurate the curve.

But if a clipping path is too complex for the printer's capabilities, it cannot print the path and will produce a limit check or PostScript error. Any printer can be jammed up with a complex clipping path, although you might find that a clipping path will print perfectly well on a low-resolution printer (300–600 dpi) because that device uses a higher flatness value to define the curve. The same clipping path might not print on a high-resolution imagesetter (1200–2400 dpi). If you run into printing problems on an image with a clipping path, troubleshoot them in the following ways:

- Increase the Flatness settings and resave the file. Flatness values range from 0.2 to 100. Enter a flatness setting from 1 to 3 for low-resolution printers and from 8 to 10 for high-resolution printers.

- Reduce the number of anchor points in the curve by manually eliminating them with the Delete Anchor Point tool.

You can also re-create the path with lower Tolerance settings:

1. Target the path in the Paths palette.

2. Click the Load Path As Selection icon at the bottom of the palette.

3. Click the trash icon to delete the path but leave the selection.

4. Choose Make Work Path from the palette menu. In the dialog box, decrease the Tolerance to 5 pixels (a good place to start).

5. Name and save the new work path.

6. Choose Clipping Path from the palette menu.

7. Save the file in EPS format.

The Options bar features are as follows:

Options Bar Feature	Function
Shape layers	Makes a shape and a path on a new layer
Paths	Makes the path outline of the shape on an existing layer or Background
Fill pixels	Fills an area with the foreground color in the form of the shape
Shape list	Lets you choose a shape
Custom Shape Options	Lets you enter specifications for the size and proportion of the shape
Style	Attaches a layer style to the Shape layer (available with New Shape Layer)
Shape characteristics	Assigns values for the characteristics of a particular shape or chooses a custom shape
Mode	Lets you select a blending mode for the shape (available only with Create Fill Pixels)
Opacity	Sets the Opacity for the shape by moving the slider (available only with Create Fill Pixels)
Anti-Aliased	Applies an anti-alias to the shape (available only with Create Fill Pixels)

Drawing Shapes

To draw a shape, first choose a foreground color. Click the Shape tool in the Tool palette and choose a tool type from the expanded palette or from the Options bar. Click in the image and drag to form the shape.

Because shapes are vector objects, you can use the Path Selection tool, the Direct Selection tool, or the path-editing tools to move or edit a shape or to add and delete anchor points.

Each shape performs slightly differently. The Options bar of each shape lets you adjust its individual characteristics. For example, you can enter a value for the radius of the corners on the Rounded Rectangle tool, or for the number of sides on the Polygon tool.

Figure 9.26

The Options bar of the Shape tools

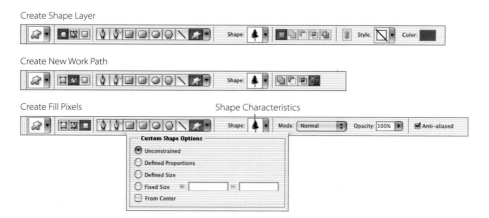

The Rectangle Tools and Ellipse Tool

As with the marquee tools, icons on the Shape tool Options bar let you add, subtract, intersect, or exclude areas from a shape as you draw. Clicking the arrow to the right of the Shape tool icons on the Options bar offers additional controls on a pop up list. When you choose the Rectangle, Rounded Rectangle, or Ellipse tool, the down-arrow button on the Options bar offers you these choices:

Unconstrained	Sizes and proportions the shape as you draw
Square (or Circle)	Constrains the shape
Fixed Size	Lets you sets values for the shape's width and height
Proportional	Uses Width and Height fields to define the shape's proportion
From Center	Radiates the shape from a center point
Snap To Pixels	Aligns the shape to the on-screen pixels (Rectangle and Round Rectangle only)

To constrain the Rectangle or Round Rectangle to a square, or the Ellipse to a circle, hold down the Shift key as you drag.

The Polygon Tool

When the Polygon tool is selected, a Size field in the Options bar enables you to set the shape's number of sides. The Polygon Options panel choices differ from those of the other shapes. Figure 9.27 illustrates the wide variety of shapes you can create by adjusting these settings:

Radius	Enables you to enter a corner radius for a round-cornered polygon
Smooth Corners	Rounds the corners of the polygon
Indent Sides By	Enables you to enter a percentage value to curve the sides inward
Smooth Indents	Rounds the indents

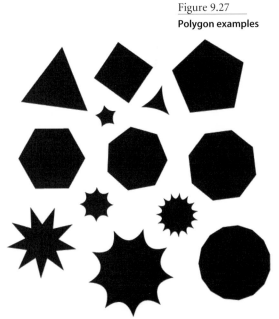

Figure 9.27

Polygon examples

The Line Tool

When the Line tool is selected, you can enter a value in the Options bar for the weight of the line in pixels. Choices in the Line Options panel determine the type of arrow that will appear at either end of the line. Select the Start or End check boxes, or both, to produce an arrowhead at the beginning and/or end of the line (see Figure 9.28). Enter values in Width, Length, and Concavity for these characteristics of the arrowhead. Figure 9.29 demonstrates the wide variety of possibilities in these settings.

Figure 9.28

**Arrowhead
characteristics**

The Custom Shape Tool

You can generate custom shapes with the Shape tool . With the Custom Shape tool
selected, the Options panel displays these options:

Unconstrained	Manually determines the proportion of the shape as you draw
Defined Proportions	Enables you to drag to constrain the proportion of the shape.
Defined Size	Draws the shape at the size it was created
Fixed Size	Enables you to enter values for the shape in the height and width fields
From Center	Radiates the shape from a center point

The Options bar Shape list lets you choose from many predefined custom shapes. You
can create additional shapes with the Pen tool and save them to this list (see Figure 9.30).

The pop up list provides a list of commands that let you Delete, Reset, Load, Save, and
Replace custom shapes, plus several palette-viewing options. The options at the bottom
rung of the list replace the default list with additional shapes. With the All option, you can
view a comprehensive list of all available shapes.

PLACING CUSTOM SHAPES ON AN IMAGE

Applying predefined custom shapes is a snap. First, open an image or create one; then take
the following steps:

1. Choose a foreground color.

2. Make a new empty layer by clicking the New Layer icon in the Layers palette.

3. Click the Shape tool in the Tool palette.

4. In the Options bar, click the Custom Shape icon to display the Shape Options panel.
   Click the Unconstrained radio button.

5. In the Options bar, click the Shape list arrow to display the default custom shapes.
   Click the arrow on the panel to display the list of commands in the pull-down submenu; choose All to load all the additional shapes.

Figure 9.29

**Examples of lines,
with and without
arrowheads**

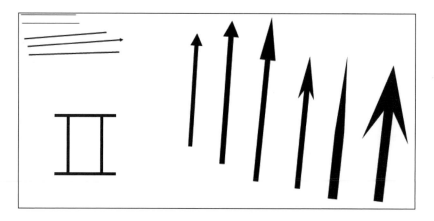

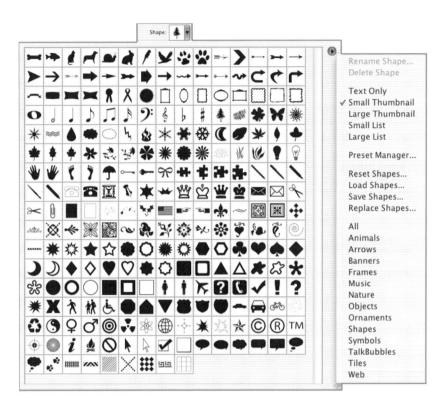

Figure 9.30

The Shape list

6. Click a shape in the Shape list. Place your cursor on the image, click, and drag until the shape is the size and proportion you want. To reposition the shape, press the spacebar while dragging. Then release the mouse.

7. Optionally choose additional shapes from the Shape list and repeat for all the shapes you want on your image layer. Your result might look like Figure 9.31.

DEFINING CUSTOM SHAPES

To create your own custom shape:

1. Use one of the Pen tools and draw a shape outline.

2. Choose Edit → Define Custom Shape.

3. Select the Custom Shape tool. The new shape appears in the Shape list in the Shape tool Options bar.

Figure 9.31

El Jefe adorned with custom shapes

CHAPTER 10

Creating and Applying Color

The methods used by painters and computer artists differ in their physical application. Painters, of course, paint with pigment, whereas computer artists paint with light. The similarity, however, is that Photoshop's painting functions are designed to simulate the real-life studio environment with a variety of virtual tools for applying color. Photoshop draws and paints with light, yet has the ability to simulate almost any effect that can be created on paper or canvas. These same capabilities can be greatly extended by applying artistic, textural, and brush stroke filters that can convert a photograph into anything—from a Rembrandt to a Picasso—instantaneously.

In this chapter, you'll learn about:

- **Understanding digital color**

- **Choosing colors, color modes, and color models**

- **Creating and modifying brushes**

- **Using the painting and editing tools**

- **Making and applying gradients and patterns**

- **Filling and stroking**

Painting with Paint and Pixels

Applying color to a surface is one of the oldest and most common forms of self-expression. From the meticulous application of thinned glazes used to render exacting detail on photo-realistic paintings to pigment splashed by the gallon on Abstract Expressionist canvases, the application of color is the artist's way of whispering, speaking, or shouting.

Paint is indeed a versatile medium. Colors are made from minerals or organic substances, ground, and then mixed with either an oil- or water-based vehicle that forms a liquid or paste to make them fluid enough to apply. It can be brushed, troweled, rolled, sprayed, poured, spattered, or thrown onto a surface. It can be mixed, blended, glazed, or smeared, thin or thick, to produce an infinite variety of colors and surface effects.

Photoshop's drawing and painting features enable you to use light instead of physical compounds on paper or canvas. Specifying digital color and applying it with one of the painting tools is fundamental to digital imaging. The painting tools go far beyond just the ability to apply color in an artistic capacity, however. They are essential for spot editing and photo retouching, creating textural surfaces, and image compositing.

Understanding Digital Color

Every pixel in each color channel of your image is assigned a numeric value. These values can be translated into specific color systems that distribute the information depending on your needs. For example, the three-channel RGB system is used to display images on-screen, but the four-channel CMYK color system is designed to organize the information into color separations so that it can be printed on paper.

In Photoshop, you can choose a specific color system. Some of these systems—such as RGB, CMYK, Lab, and Grayscale—are called color *modes*, in which the information is organized into color *channels* with specific characteristics. Others, such as HSB, are called color *models* and are supported for your convenience, so that you can easily pick the exact color you want by determining its basic characteristics.

Color Models and Modes

A color mode or model is a system of displaying or printing color. Photoshop supports the HSB color model and RGB, CMYK, Lab, Grayscale, Bitmap, Indexed, Duotone, and Multichannel color modes. To convert an image from one color mode to another, choose Image → Mode and select a color mode.

Because the *gamut*, or range of possible colors, of one color mode might be different from that of another, converting your image can sometimes present problems in the form of color shifts. See Chapter 15, "Color Management and Printing," for more information.

DIGITAL IMAGING AND FINE ART

Since the introduction of painting and imaging software such as Adobe Photoshop, there has been an ongoing debate in art circles about whether painting will be replaced by its digital counterpart. The controversy embraces many aspects of the meaning and purpose of art and especially its commercial value to collectors, museums, and galleries.

When it was first introduced, graphic designers and commercial illustrators immediately gravitated to photo manipulation and desktop-publishing software to replace traditional graphic arts techniques performed with paste-up, technical pens, and process cameras. It took almost a decade, however, for digital art to be taken seriously as a "real" art form by the art establishment of universities, galleries, and museums. This was due, in part, to reluctance by the institutions to accept a new medium, and to the limitations of hardware to produce archival-quality output. (*Archival* simply means that the ink won't fade and paper won't deteriorate over time.)

These days, however, many images that we see hanging on the walls of museums and galleries are produced by computers. In March 2001, the Whitney Museum of American Art in New York City presented an exhibition of digital prints that emphasized the importance of digital printing technology to American art. The introduction of direct, high-end printing to archival-quality paper with archival ink, as with *giclée* (this term literally means *squirt from nozzle*) printers, or photographic output devices such as the Chromera RG4 digital Photo Imager, has made museum-quality computer art possible. Some of these direct-to-print digital images are photographic, and some are painterly. Because they can be systematically reproduced, they acquire the status of limited-edition prints or photographs.

Owing to the unique differences of the processes of painting and computer art, one can hardly replace the other. Painting is a much more physical process than computer art. It requires broader movement of the body and direct contact with wet media, which intrinsically presents entirely different visual, tactile, and olfactory sensations. On a computer, most operations can be performed using the fingers, hand, and wrist in an environment that is free of the odors of solvents and the feel of the brush against a surface.

Just as the traditional visual arts have continued to thrive in our society as a means of self-expression, the computer has emerged as another dynamic art form. In addition, the computer has become an aid to the artist. With the capability of quickly creating multiple versions, it helps some artists visualize and refine the style, composition, and color relationships of their work.

HSB Color Model

The HSB model uses the basic characteristics of color to define each color; HSB is the Color Picker's default model, as it is usually the easiest model by which to locate any given color quickly. Each possible color consists of the following characteristics:

Hue This is the *color* of light that is reflected from an opaque object or transmitted through a transparent one. Hue in Photoshop is measured by its position on a color wheel, from 0 to 360 degrees.

Saturation Also called *chroma,* this is the intensity of a color as determined by the percentage of the hue in proportion to gray, from 0% to 100%. A saturation of 0% means that the color is entirely gray.

Brightness Also called *value,* this is the relative lightness or darkness of a color, measured from 0% to 100%.

RGB Color Mode

The RGB mode represents the three colors—red, green, and blue—used by devices such as scanners or monitors to acquire or display color. Each range of color is separated into three separate entities called *color channels.* Each color channel can produce 256 values, for a total of 256^3, or 16,777,216, possible colors in the entire RGB gamut. Photoshop can display all these colors, providing you have a monitor and video card capable of supporting 24-bit color.

Because RGB produces color with light, the more light that is added, the brighter the color becomes; hence, RGB is referred to as an *additive* color model (see Figure C10, left image, in the color section). Each pixel contains three brightness values—a red, a green, and a blue—ranging from 0 (black) to 255. When all three values are at their maximum, the color is pure white. Colors with low brightness values are dark, and colors with high brightness values are light.

CMYK Color Mode

The CMYK (cyan, magenta, yellow, and black) color mode produces a full range of color by printing tiny dots of cyan, magenta, yellow, and black ink. Because the colored dots are so small, the eye mixes them together. The relative densities of groups of colored dots produce variations in color and tonality. The more ink you add to a CMYK image, the darker it becomes; conversely, less ink produces lighter colors, and the absence of ink produces white. For this reason, CMYK is referred to as a *subtractive* color system (see Figure C10, right image, in the color section). You specify CMYK colors to ultimately segregate colors into color separations for use in the offset lithography printing process.

Lab Color Mode

The CIE Lab color mode is an international color measurement system, developed in 1931 by the International Commission on Illumination (Commission Internationale de l'Éclairage, or CIE). Lab color is *device independent*, meaning that the color model is based on the perception of the human eye rather than a mechanical ink or light system. Lab color consists of three channels: a luminance or lightness channel (L), a green–red component (a), and a blue–yellow component (b) (see Figure C8 in the color section). In the Color Picker, entering a value from 0 to 100 in the L channel controls the lightness, or *luminosity*, information; values from +120 to –120 in the a and b channels control the color information.

As a color model, Lab can be used to independently adjust luminosity and color… Photoshop uses Lab as an interim color space when converting files from one color mode to another.

Grayscale Mode

Grayscale is a mode that displays what we traditionally think of as a black-and-white image. A grayscale image is composed of one channel with 256 possible shades of gray. Each pixel has a brightness value from 0 (black) to 255 (white). Sometimes Grayscale pixels are measured in percentages of black ink, from 0% (white) to 100% (black). When color images are converted to grayscale, their hue and saturation information is discarded, while their lightness, or luminosity, values remain intact.

Bitmap Mode

Bitmap mode images (not to be confused with the bitmap file format) are the simplest form of true black-and-white graphic image. They contain two types of pixels, literally black or white, and are used to create line art and digital halftones. Bitmap images contain only 1 bit of information per pixel, so their file sizes are much smaller than grayscale images, which contain 8 bits per pixel, or color images, which contain 24 bits per pixel. Figure 10.1 compares an 8-bit, 256-level grayscale image with a 1-bit, 2-color (black or white) bitmap image.

Indexed Color Mode

Indexed color mode uses a maximum of 256 colors to display full-color images. When you convert an image color to the Indexed mode, Photoshop stores the color information as a color look-up table (CLUT). You can then use a specific palette to display the image to match the colors as closely as possible to the original. Because it contains fewer colors, Indexed color creates smaller file sizes, which is why it is often used when publishing files to the Web or to multimedia applications.

Figure 10.1

A grayscale and a bitmap image

Duotone Mode

Duotones are images that have been separated into two spot colors. Duotone modes support Monotone, Duotones, Tritones (images with three colors), and Quadtones (four colors). The Duotone color information is contained on one color channel. Photoshop displays a preview that is an RGB simulation of the ink combinations. Duotones and spot color are covered in more depth in Chapter 18, "Duotones and Spot Color."

Multichannel Mode

The number of channels in a Multichannel document depends on the number of channels in the source image before it was converted. Each channel in a Multichannel document contains 256 levels of gray. This mode is useful for converting a Duotone image into separate color channels for the purpose of analyzing the color information. Multichannel will convert RGB to cyan, magenta, and yellow spot color channels and CMYK into CMYK spot color channels.

> Although RGB will convert to spot CMY, these are not true CMY separations that are press-ready; they are simply the theoretical subtractive opposites of the additive original.

You cannot print a color composite from Multichannel mode. Most export file formats do not support Multichannel. However you can save a Multichannel file in DCS 2.0 file format. See the Bonus chapter "File Formats" on the companion CD.

Choosing Colors

Picking a color in Photoshop is as simple as squeezing paint from a tube. It is a matter of choosing a color from one of Photoshop's three color interfaces or sampling colors directly from any open image.

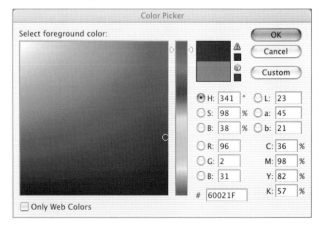

There are two color swatches near the bottom of the Tool palette, representing the current *foreground* and *background* colors. The swatch on the left is the foreground color, which is applied directly by any of the painting tools. The default foreground color is black. The background color on the right is applied with the Eraser tool or by cutting a selected portion of an image on the Background. The default background color is white.

You can reverse the foreground and background colors by clicking the curved arrow to the upper-right of the swatches. To restore the colors to the default black and white, click the icon at the lower-left of the swatches.

> When you cut a portion from an image on a layer, the area becomes transparent.

The Color Picker

To choose a foreground or background color, click its swatch; the Color Picker appears (see Figure 10.2; for a color version of this dialog box, see Figure C7 in the color section). The Color Picker lets you choose from four methods of defining your colors: HSB, RGB, Lab, and CMYK. Your main tools in the Color Picker are a vertical slider and a large color field.

You can also set values for the following characteristics in the Color Picker:

Hue A color's hue is its position on a color wheel measured in degrees. When the H radio button is selected in the Color Picker, the vertical slider displays the spectrum of all of the available hues, and the color field presents that hue's saturation and brightness variations.

Figure 10.2
The Color Picker

Notice that the top and bottom of the spectrum slider are both red. If you drag the slider to the top or bottom of the color bar, the values in the Hue box are the same: 0 degrees. No, you are not taking the hue's temperature; you're determining its position on a color wheel. The vertical bar is actually a color wheel that has been cut at the 0-degree, or red, position and straightened. Drag the slider anywhere on the bar, and notice that the hue value changes to a number between 0 and 360 degrees. As you move the slider, the field to the left changes color.

Saturation The color field on the left determines the saturation and brightness of the hue. Saturation is the intensity of a particular hue and is represented by the *x*, or horizontal axis in the color field. There are two ways to determine the saturation of a color in the Color Picker: enter a value in the Saturation box or click within the color field. If the value in the Saturation box is 100%, or if the circle on the color field is to the far right, the color will be at its maximum intensity. If a 0 is entered in the Saturation box, or if the circle is placed at the far left of the field, the color will be gray.

Brightness The value of a color is controlled in a similar manner. The *y*, or vertical axis in the color field represents brightness. Brightness, sometimes called luminosity, is the lightness or darkness of a color. Lower values produce darker colors, with 0% equaling black. Higher values produce lighter colors, with 100% equaling white when there is no color saturation or the lightest possible combination of hue and saturation. Click toward the bottom of the color field to darken the color or toward the top to lighten it.

Active Parameters of Color

By default, the Color Picker opens in HSB mode with Hue as the active parameter. The slider represents the colors (hues) on the color wheel, and the field represents the saturation and brightness of the selected hue. The Color Picker can be changed to display several other configurations.

The Color Picker can be configured for HSB, RGB, Lab, and CMYK active parameters by clicking a radio button next to the desired model. The vertical bar then represents the selected characteristic in the selected model. When the S radio button is active, for instance, the active parameter of the Color Picker shifts to Saturation mode and the vertical bar becomes a Saturation slider. The color field now displays hue and brightness variations. If you click or drag in the field, to the left or right, you affect the hue; if you click or drag up or down, you affect the brightness.

When the B radio button is checked, the active parameter of the Color Picker shifts to Brightness, and the vertical bar becomes a Brightness slider. The color field now displays hue and saturation variations; clicking in the field or dragging the circle to the left or right affects the hue, and dragging it up or down affects the saturation.

In the case of RGB and Lab, when a color channel's radio button is selected, the vertical slider displays the variations of color within that channel, and the color field becomes the other two color channels, one represented horizontally and the other represented vertically.

The color swatch at the top of the Color Picker has two parts. The bottom of the swatch shows the current color setting; the top shows the color you've selected in the Color Picker.

Specifying CMYK Colors

Let's say a client wants you to add a logo to an image with specific CMYK color values to correspond to the official corporate colors of the business. After you've scanned the logo, you can define the colors in the Color Picker and fill the logo with the exact tint values of cyan, magenta, yellow, and black needed to produce the corporate color.

To define and apply CMYK colors:

1. Click the foreground swatch to display the Color Picker.

2. Enter the CMYK percentage values in their boxes.

3. Click OK. The color appears as the foreground color.

4. Select the area to be filled.

5. Press Option-Delete (Mac) or Alt-Backspace (Win) to fill the selected area.

The CMYK Gamut Warning

You would think that, because CMYK is represented by four color channels instead of three, more colors would be available in this color mode. But in fact, a high percentage of black plus any combination of cyan, yellow, and magenta usually yields black, and this greatly limits the possibilities of CMYK. The CMYK gamut is so small that some colors, especially highly saturated ones, cannot be produced at all. (For a schematic comparison of the gamut of visible, RGB, and CMYK colors, see Figure C9 in the color section.)

If you choose a color in HSB, Lab, or RGB that is outside the printable range or gamut of CMYK, you will see the percentage values in the CMYK boxes. You will also see a CMYK Gamut Warning next to the color swatch in the Color Picker. The small swatch below the warning represents how the color will print. Some CMYK colors, especially highly saturated colors, can vary significantly from their RGB counterparts. If you get a warning, you might want to specify a different color for a closer match, or be prepared to accept considerable variation of the color on the printed piece.

Specifying Web Colors

In HTML, colors are coded with a combination of six hexadecimal characters so that World Wide Web browsers can read and display them. Not all browsers can display all colors. You can use the Color Picker to ensure that the colors you use are browser-safe.

To specify a Web color, check the Only Web Colors box at the bottom of the Color Picker. The color bar and color field then limit themselves to 216 Web-compatible colors; note the banding in Figure 10.3, indicating that the color field no longer has a continuous, nearly infinite color set. When you click any variation, the color's six-character hexadecimal number appears in the # box (each character pair represents the channels R, G, and B, respectively). If you know the Web color's number, you can select that color simply by entering the number in the # box.

Like CMYK colors, Web colors have a very limited gamut compared to RGB. When the Only Web Colors check box is cleared, the Color Picker displays a Web Color Gamut Warning next to the large swatch in the Color Picker. The small swatch below the warning shows how the color will be seen on Web browsers.

It is very hard to control exactly how even Web-safe colors are seen on browsers. A lot depends on the quality and age of the viewer's monitor, what system palette they are using, and how the brightness and contrast controls are set. The Web-safe colors feature lets you choose colors that will not radically change when viewed on other monitors of the same quality and calibration as the one you are working on. They also produce dither-free solids.

It is not absolutely necessary to use the Web-safe palette when creating graphics for the Web because the limited gamut can reduce color options and overall image quality. The option is there in case some viewers might not be able to view more than 8-bit color with older video cards/monitors. However, though the image might look slightly better to these users, overall it would appear less than marvelous to the majority of users capable of viewing 24-bit color. As the curve of technology improves with time, and older equipment declines in use, this becomes less and less of an issue.

Specifying Custom Colors

Photoshop supports the PANTONE Matching System, which is a group of inks used to print spot colors. Whereas CMYK mixes only four colors to produce a full-color spectrum, PANTONE inks are solid colors used to print rich solid or tinted areas. The PANTONE system is recognized all over the world; a PANTONE ink can be specified in the U.S. and printed in Singapore, for example, simply by telling the printer its number. Photoshop also supports other matching systems, such as ANPA, DIC, Toyo, Focoltone, HKS, and TRUMATCH (a CMYK computer color-matching system).

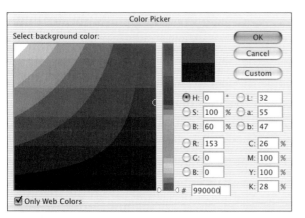

Figure 10.3

When the Only Web Colors option is selected, the Color Picker restricts itself to browser-safe possibilities.

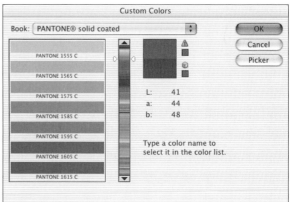

Figure 10.4

Choosing custom colors

To specify a custom color:

1. Click a color swatch to display the Color Picker.

2. Click the Custom button to display the Custom Colors dialog box (see Figure 10.4).

3. From the Book list, choose the desired matching system.

4. Enter the color's number by using the keypad. You can, instead, scroll through the color list by using the slider; when you find the color you want, click it.

5. Click OK.

The PANTONE library specifications match the latest PANTONE ink guides. This could cause problems if older versions of desktop-publishing or illustration software use outdated PANTONE library definitions. Check your application to be sure it is consistant with the latest published versions of the guides before importing Photoshop documents in which custom colors or spot colors are specified. The color library files are not built into the Photoshop CS application, as they were prior to version 7, but are now contained in preset files known as Color Books. You can remove unwanted library color choices to streamline the menu by removing them from the Photoshop folder.

Using Color Palettes

Although the Color Picker displays all the color characteristics and models in one integrated field, it is sometimes cumbersome to use because it is not *context sensitive*. A context-sensitive palette will respond immediately to your commands without having to click an OK button. You must display the Color Picker by clicking the foreground or background swatch, then choose a color model and a color, and, finally, you must click OK. This process can be time-consuming because of the many steps required. Instead, you might want to use the context-sensitive Color and Swatches palettes that conveniently float on the desktop.

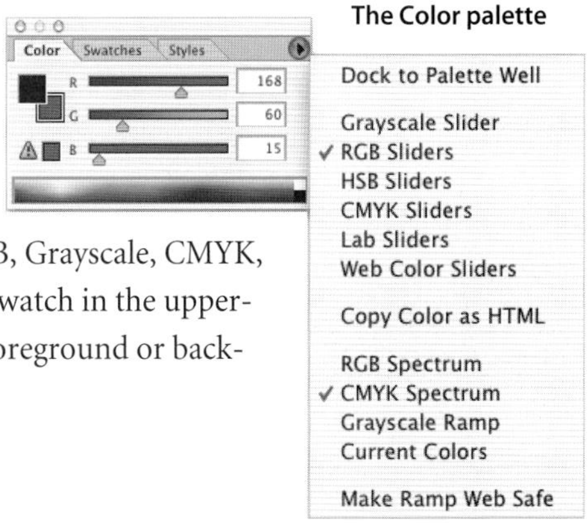

Figure 10.5

The Color palette

The Color Palette

The Color palette (see Figure 10.5) is in the same default palette cluster as the Swatches and Styles palettes. You can access it by choosing Window → Color (or by pressing the F6 function key). By default, the RGB color model is displayed, but you can choose HSB, Grayscale, CMYK, Lab, or Web Color sliders from the palette pull-down menu. Click a swatch in the upper-left corner of the palette to designate whether you want to affect the foreground or background color.

Dock to Palette Well

Grayscale Slider
✓ RGB Sliders
HSB Sliders
CMYK Sliders
Lab Sliders
Web Color Sliders

Copy Color as HTML

RGB Spectrum
✓ CMYK Spectrum
Grayscale Ramp
Current Colors

Make Ramp Web Safe

The position of the sliders determines the color. By default, the sliders are *dynamic*, meaning that a gradient bar displays the selected color that corresponds to the position of the sliders. The Tool and Color palette swatches simultaneously change to indicate the color as you drag the slider. You can also enter specific values for each component of any color model in boxes to the right of the sliders.

The fastest way to select a color is to click or drag in the spectrum bar at the bottom of the Color palette to designate an approximate color. Release the mouse, and the color will appear as the foreground color. Then move the sliders to tweak the color until you get exactly the color you want.

The Swatches Palette

To display individual swatches of color, choose Window → Swatches or click the Swatches tab on the Color palette cluster (see Figure 10.6). You can choose from predefined colors, or add and save new colors. See Table 10.1 for tips on swatch techniques.

Table 10.1 Swatch Techniques	TECHNIQUE	HOW TO DO IT
	Selecting a foreground color	Click the desired color; it will appear as the foreground swatch on the Tool palette.
	Selecting a background color	Press the F/Ctrl key while clicking the color.
	Adding a color	Place your cursor in the blank space below the color swatches. The cursor changes to a paint can. Click your mouse, name the color, and the foreground color will appear in the palette as a new swatch.
	Deleting a color	Press Option/Alt and click the swatch. Or, Control-click/right-click and select Delete Swatch from the shortcut menu.
	Saving a Swatch palette	After you've added colors to the swatches, you might want to save the palette for use in other documents. From the Swatches Palette menu, choose Save Swatches. Designate a folder in which to store your palette.
	Loading swatches	To access a saved palette, choose Load Swatches from the Swatches Palette menu. (New Swatches palettes can also be loaded from the Preset Manager found in the Edit menu.) You can then access the swatch from the folder in which you saved it, or choose a specific palette such as PANTONE, Focoltone, ANPA, or Web-Safe Colors from the list.
	Resetting swatches	The Reset Swatches command on the palette menu restores the swatches to the Photoshop default palette.
	Naming a swatch	Color swatches can be named for identification. To name a swatch, double-click it and enter the name in the Swatch Name dialog box. Or Control-click/right-click and select Rename Swatch.

Introduction to Brushes

Photoshop provides you with an abundant supply of built-in brushes that can be used to apply color to your image in a variety of ways with the painting and editing tools. In addition, you can create new brushes and control such characteristics as size, hardness, spacing, roundness, and angle. You can also make custom brushes in virtually any shape.

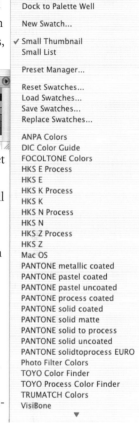

The preset brushes are displayed by means of a pop-up palette on the left side of the Options bar whenever a painting or editing tool is activated. Click the small arrow to the right of the Brush icon in the Options bar to open the pop-up palette called the Brush Preset Picker (see Figure 10.7). By default, the brushes will be displayed with a thumbnail view of each loaded brush tip, along with a brush stroke view. Clicking on the view will select the brush. You can modify the selected brush's size and softness on the fly by moving the Master Diameter and Hardness sliders. The thumbnail in the Options bar at the top of the pull-down menu will reflect the changes. If you wish to save the brush as a new preset, click the arrow at the upper-right of the Presets palette. Choose New Brush Preset. The resulting dialog box displays a descriptive name of the brush (see Figure 10.8). Or you can rename the brush and click OK.

You can change the display characteristics in the palette menu, which also has options for renaming and deleting brushes and for loading additional brush sets. The default brushes go in order from the smallest and hardest on the top to the largest and softest on the bottom. Each brush is displayed at actual size unless it is too big to fit in the thumbnail view, in which case it is displayed with a number that indicates its diameter in pixels.

Figure 10.6

The Swatches palette

> When a brush tip is selected by clicking it in the Brushes palette, the brush stroke view will display in the larger view window at the bottom of the palette. If you hold your mouse cursor over any brush tip in the Brushes palette long enough for the brush name to appear as a tool tip, you will then be able to merely hover the cursor over the other brush tips to quickly view the brush stroke displays in the view window.

You can also view, select, and load the brushes via the Brushes palette (Window → Brushes). It is located in the Palette Docking Well by default, but it can be moved out of the well or clustered with other palettes. The Brushes palette is also used to design customized brushes and to control various brush dynamics (see Figure 10.9). The palette can be toggled on and off by clicking the Brushes Palette icon in the Options bar or by pressing the shortcut key F5.

Creating a Custom Brush

A brush tip is a specific shape with several options pertaining to it that will affect the way it appears when applied with brush strokes. You can easily create custom brush tip shapes from selected areas of an image and use the editing options to achieve the desired look.

To create a custom brush, follow these steps:

1. Select an area of an image with a selection tool.

2. Choose Edit → Define Brush. The Brush Name dialog box appears, as seen in Figure 10.10.

3. Name the brush and click OK.

4. Choose a painting tool. The custom brush is now available as a choice in the Brushes palette.

Modifying Brushes

Brush tips have several basic characteristics that can be adjusted with options located in the Brush Tip Shape portion of the Brushes palette when a painting or editing tool is activated.

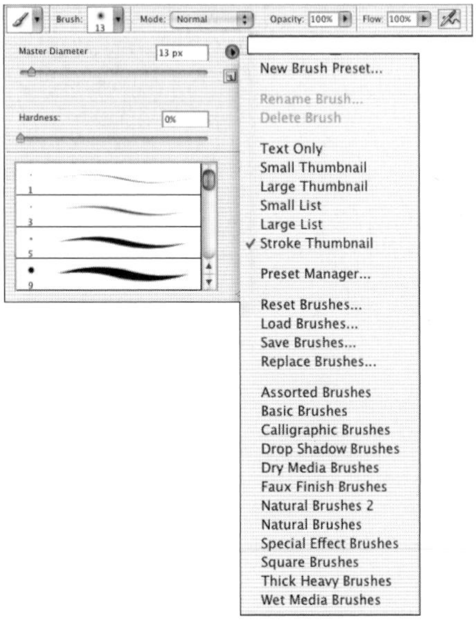

Figure 10.7

The Options bar Brush Preset Picker and menu

Open the Brushes palette. To the left of the brush display window, you'll see a list of choices. At the top of the list is Brush Presets, which has the same function as the Brush Preset Picker in the Options bar pop-up palette noted earlier. The second option is Brush Tip Shape—select it and notice the assortment of settings that appears in the right portion of the palette (see Figure 10.11).

Select a brush tip to experiment with the different settings while viewing the changes in the brush stroke display window at the bottom of the palette:

Diameter This setting determines the size of the brush, from 1 to 2500 pixels. Use the Diameter slider or enter a numerical value to change the size. The Use Sample Size button can be used to reset to the original diameter.

Flip X, Flip Y Select these check boxes to flip the brush across its horizontal and/or vertical axis.

Figure 10.8

Naming a new brush

Angle This setting rotates the angle of the brush tip by degrees from the horizontal axis. You can drag the horizontal axis (the line with an arrow at the end running through the circle) in the interactive display window or type in a numerical value.

Roundness Use this setting to adjust the roundness of the brush shape. Drag the dots along the vertical line running through the circle in the display window, or type in a numerical percentage value. A setting of 100% gives the full roundness of the brush, whereas 0% gives a linear shape.

Hardness This option adjusts the hardness of the edges of a brush by using a percentage of the brush diameter as a basis; for instance, if a brush is set to 50% hardness, the 50% consisting of the central core will be hard, and the remaining 50% consisting of the outer edges is gradually softened through a gradient transition.

Spacing Use this setting to affect how frequently color is deposited by the brush tip as you create a brush stroke, determined by percentages of the brush diameter, from 0% to 1000%.

Higher-resolution documents need larger brushes; for example, a 72-pixel brush on a 72 ppi document will paint a stroke 1 inch in diameter. The same brush will paint a half-inch stroke on a 144 ppi document.

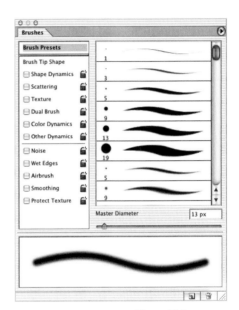

Figure 10.9

The Brushes palette

Saving Modified Brushes

When you modify a preset brush tip by using the Brush Tip Shape options in the Brushes palette, the modifications will apply only as long as you have the brush activated, but will revert to the default original settings when you change brush tips or brush tools. To save a modified version of a brush tip, first make the desired modifications, and then click the Create New Brush icon located at the bottom of the

Figure 10.10

Naming a custom brush

Brushes palette or choose New Brush Preset from the palette options menu. The Brush Name dialog box (shown back in Figure 10.8) will appear—name the modified brush, click OK, and it will be added to the currently open set of brushes. It will then be available for use with all the painting and editing tools.

A word of caution, however: if the brush set containing the new brush is later reset to the defaults, the new brush will be lost. Adding the modified brush permanently to a brush set requires saving the entire set through the palette menu's Save Brushes option, which is activated when you choose Brush Presets from the top of the Brushes palette list. Saving the set by using the original set name will replace the default set with the modified set, or if the set is renamed during the saving operation, the modified set will then be saved as a new set.

More Brush Dynamics

Photoshop includes many options for adding variable elements to the brushes. Two of the key variables you'll work with when manipulating these options are Jitter and Control, found under the Shape Dynamics tab:

Jitter This setting determines the randomness of the given effect, measured by percentage: 0% equals no change, whereas 100% brings about the maximum amount of change. You can choose to affect Jitter of the Size, Angle, and Roundness.

Figure 10.11

The Brush Tip Shape settings

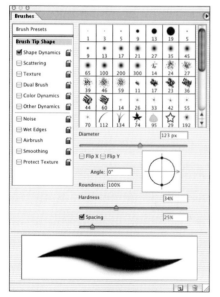

Control This setting contains drop-down menus of choices pertaining to the way in which you control the variation of the jitter; the Off setting indicates no control, whereas Fade enables you to input a specified number of steps with which to fade the effect. Pen Pressure, Pen Tilt, and Stylus Wheel enable you to vary the effect based on those properties of a pressure-sensitive pen/tablet if you use one instead of a mouse.

Setting Brush Dynamics

As with the Brush Tip Shape options, you access these options in the Brushes palette. Clicking the name of the option (rather than clicking the check box) will bring up its settings (for those that have extra settings) as well as select it. Combining Brush dynamics can produce infinite possibilities in the behavior and appearance of your brush strokes. Experimentation will yield the perfect brush for the job.

The new options include the following:

Shape Dynamics Use this option to establish the variation of shape in the brush marks along a brush stroke, according to size, minimum diameter, angle, roundness, and minimum roundness (see Figure 10.12).

Scattering Use this setting to regulate the number brush tip marks contained in a stroke, as well as how they are distributed (or *scattered,* if you will), according to randomness, direction, count, and count jitter (see Figure 10.13).

Texture This setting incorporates a chosen pattern into the brush tip, resulting in the appearance of painting with a texture, as shown in Figure 10.14.

Dual Brush This option combines properties of two brush tips. The primary brush tip is the tip selected by using the brush presets, and the secondary (dual) tip is then selected in the Dual Tip options. Extra settings of diameter, spacing, scatter, and count can be applied to the secondary tip (see Figure 10.15).

Figure 10.12

The star shape on the left is painted without shape dynamics, and the one on the right includes shape dynamics.

Figure 10.13

Examples of no scattering (left) and scattering (right)

Figure 10.14

Examples of a nontextured (left) and a textured (right) brush stroke

Figure 10.15

Examples of a single tip and a dual tip brush stroke

Color Dynamics Adjust how paint varies over the course of a stroke, according to foreground and background color, hue, saturation, brightness, and purity (see Figure 10.16).

Other Dynamics Adjust how paint varies over the course of a stroke, in regards to opacity and flow (see Figure 10.17).

Noise Add a noise effect to the outer edges of brush tips, resulting in a sort of frayed-edge appearance (see Figure 10.18), especially noticeable when used with soft brushes.

Wet Edges Permit color to build up along the edges of the brush strokes, simulating a watercolor style, as in Figure 10.19.

Airbrush Apply color similarly to the way a real airbrush operates, by spraying to build up the color gradually.

Smoothing Generate smoother curves in brush strokes by using this option.

Protect Texture Use this setting to lock the texture pattern and scale so that it will remain the same for all brushes.

Dynamic Locks New to Photoshop CS is the option of locking a brush dynamic. Click the lock icon next to the dynamic's name. This locked set of characteristics becomes the default and will apply to any brush you choose. Click the lock icon again to unlock the dynamic.

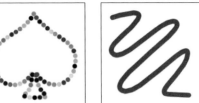

Figure 10.16

Examples of a brush stroke with (right) and without (left) color dynamics

Figure 10.17

Examples of a brush stroke with (right) and without (left) other dynamics

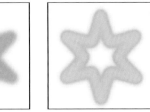

Figure 10.18

Brush stroke with (right) and without (left) noise

Figure 10.19

Brush stroke with (right) and without (left) the Wet Edges option

Using the Painting and Editing Tools

Use the painting and editing tools to manually apply color or to modify an area of the image. With the exception of the Gradient and Paint Bucket tools, the painting tools rely on the motion of your hand and choice of brush tip to distribute the color or apply an effect. Each tool has its own unique set of characteristics. You can access the painting and editing tools by clicking them in the Tool palette or by pressing the appropriate shortcut key on the keyboard. (The letter in parentheses after some of the tool names in the following sections indicates its keyboard shortcut.) The behavior of the painting and editing tools can be adjusted by setting certain characteristics in the Options bar.

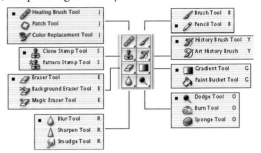

> If the option is checked in the General Preferences, you can toggle between most tools in an expandable tool cluster in the Tool palette by simultaneously pressing the Shift key and the tool's keyboard shortcut.

The Painting Tools

The painting tools include the Brush tool and the Pencil; these tools are designed to simulate real studio painting techniques by emulating their real-life counterparts.

Brush Tool (B)

You apply color to the image with the Brush tool by clicking your mouse and dragging. By default, the stroke is a solid color. You can adjust the characteristics of the tool to alter the quality of the paint stroke with the following options:

Color Blending Modes Blending modes control the relation of the color that is being applied to the existing colors on the image, and are available for most of the painting and editing tools. The Normal blending mode, at 100% opacity, applies the color as if it were painted straight out of a tube (subject to the settings of the particular brush being used, of course). Other blending modes produce less predictable results and require a bit of experimentation. For a complete list of blending mode characteristics, see the Bonus chapter "Blending Modes" on the companion CD.

Opacity The transparency of the stroke is controlled with the Opacity slider, going from 0% to 100%. When painted on a colored surface, the transparent or translucent stroke will reveal the pixels underneath it.

> When the Brush tool is active, you can type a number from 01 to 100 to set the opacity on the Options bar.

Flow The Flow control adjusts how quickly the paint flows by percentage; 100% results in complete coverage, whereas a lower flow percentage reduces the amount of virtual paint in the brush.

Airbrush Use the Airbrush option to spray color as if using an actual airbrush—that is, building up the color by dragging the cursor slowly or stopping while still spraying.

If the Airbrush option is activated in the Options bar, it will be selected in the Brushes palette as well, and vice versa.

> In previous versions of Photoshop, the Airbrush option was a separate tool. Although there is no longer an Airbrush tool, the airbrush capability is now incorporated as an option in many of the painting and editing tools.

Pencil (B)

The Pencil is the only tool that produces an aliased, or hard-edged, stroke. Use the Pencil to draw crisp horizontal or vertical lines or stair-stepped diagonals. Like the Brush tool, you can adjust the opacity or assign a color mode to the stroke.

You can use the Pencil as an eraser by selecting the Auto Erase check box. If you start painting on an area containing the foreground color, the Auto Erase function replaces it with background color. If you start painting on an area containing any color other than the foreground color, the Pencil paints with the foreground color.

The Editing Tools

The editing tools include the Clone Stamp, Pattern Stamp, Healing Brush, Patch, Color Replacement, History Brush, Art History Brush, Eraser, Background Eraser, Magic Eraser, Blur, Sharpen, Smudge, Dodge, Burn, and Sponge tools. Although the editing tools don't apply color directly to the image, they are essential for manipulating small regions within the image and modifying existing colors. Many of the editing tools have filter counterparts that produce the effect over larger areas, but the tools offer the dexterity and control of a smaller hands-on operation.

Clone Stamp (S)

Use the Clone Stamp ![icon] to copy an area of the image and paint it elsewhere with a brush. The Clone Stamp is perfect for cloning textures from one small area of the image to another.

To clone an area, you must first sample it:

1. Choose the Clone Stamp from the Tool palette.

2. Choose an appropriate brush from the Brush Preset Picker on the Options bar.

3. Press the Option/Alt key and click your mouse on the point that you want to copy.

4. Release your mouse and reposition the cursor where you want the sample to be painted.

5. Click your mouse and begin painting. As you paint, the tool will begin copying the point of the image that was sampled. A small cross will indicate the area that is being copied as you drag the brush across the image.

Check the Aligned option to maintain the alignment of the Clone Stamp brush with the original sampled area. Each time you release the mouse, move the brush, and resume cloning, the alignment will persist depending on where the brush is in relationship to the original sampled point (as seen in the middle image in Figure 10.20). If Aligned is not checked, each time you click, you restart cloning from the original sample point as the source of the image.

If the Use All Layers option is checked, the Clone Stamp image is sampled from all the visible layers. If it is cleared, the image is sampled from only the targeted layer.

Pattern Stamp (S)

Use the Pattern Stamp ![icon] to paint an area with a repeating pattern that you choose from the Pattern list on the Options bar. Photoshop provides you with several default patterns in the list, or you can define your own (see "Creating Patterns" later in this chapter.)

The Aligned option works in the same manner with the Pattern Stamp as it does with the Clone Stamp. By checking the Impressionist box, the pattern will be applied with an Impressionist-style painting effect.

Figure 10.20

An original image (top), with aligned (middle) and non-aligned (bottom) clones

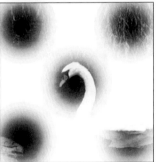

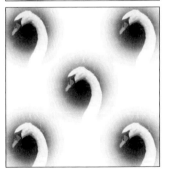

Healing Brush (J)

The Healing Brush functions in a manner very similar to the Clone Stamp, in that it enables you to sample a chosen area of an image by pressing Option/Alt as you click the desired area, and then paint the sample into another area. The difference with the Healing Brush is that when the sampled area is painted into the new area, it seemingly absorbs the texture, lighting, and shading of the surrounding pixels, creating a virtually seamless blend. This capability makes it an invaluable tool for tasks such as photo retouching, as shown in Figure 10.21.

Photoshop CS now enables you to sample a source area on a layer and heal to an area of transparency on a separate layer.

Patch Tool (J)

The Patch tool works in much the same way as the Healing Brush, except that it gives you the ability to heal a selected area with a sampled area, rather than using a brush. Unlike the healing brush, the Patch tool does not heal to all layers or transparency. This can come in handy when you have a large area that needs to be repaired. You can either make the initial selection with the Patch tool activated, or you can use any of the other selection tools to make the selection first, and then switch to the Patch tool. The Patch tool can then be used in either of the following two ways:

- Select the area that you wish to repair, choose Source from the Options bar, and then drag the selection marquee over the area from which you want to sample. An important new feature of the Patch tool is the ability to preview the pixels in the source marquee as you drag the selection marquee. To use this feature click the Source radio button in the Options bar.

- Select the area from which you want to sample, choose Destination from the Options bar, and then drag the selection marquee over the area you wish to patch.

You can also make a repair by using a pattern: first choose a pattern from the Pattern Picker in the Options bar and then click Use Pattern.

Color Replacement (J)

The Color Replacement tool replaces the existing color on an image with the foreground color. The default settings in the Options bar maintain the luminosity and saturation of a color while replacing its hue.

Mode Choose an alternative mode from the Mode pull-down menu, which will apply other characteristics of the foreground color to the image.

Sampling Use the following options to determine the method in which the colors to be changed will be chosen:

> **Continuous** samples colors continuously as you drag, coloring areas of different colors.
>
> **Once** samples a color when you first click and then continues to affect only that color. Use this option to affect areas of solid color.
>
> **Background Swatch** colors areas that are the current background color.

Limits Control what pixels will be colored by choosing from the following:

> **Discontiguous** colors all the pixels within the Tolerance range on the entire layer.
>
> **Contiguous** colors pixels of the sampled color that are adjacent to each other.
>
> **Find Edges** affects pixels of the sampled color that are adjacent to each other but better preserves the sharpness of the edge pixels of the remaining image.

Tolerance Use this setting to control the range of colors to be altered. Low Tolerance affects colors that are similar to the sampled colors; High Tolerance affects colors that are more diverse in range.

Anti-Aliased Select this check box if you want the deposited color to have anti-aliased edges.

Let's test some of the effects of the Color Replacement tool:

1. Open the file `Fannie.psd` in the Chapter 10 folder on the CD.
2. Choose the Color Replacement tool and use the default settings in the Options bar.
3. Specify a brush size and shape on the Options bar or the Brushes palette.
4. Choose a blue foreground color from the Color palette.
5. Drag over the red areas of the image. Notice the change in hue.
6. Change the specifications in the Options bar and drag over the red areas of the image again as you experiment with the various properties of the new tool.

For more about the Healing Brush, the Patch tool, and the Color Replacement tool, refer to Chapter 19, "Photo Retouching," and Hands On 7, "Restoring a Color Photograph."

Figure 10.21

After initially sampling a portion of smooth skin texture, it takes only a few dabs with the Healing Brush to miraculously eliminate the wrinkles from around the eye in this photo.

History Brush (Y)

The History Brush ![icon] restores a portion of the image to a former state, or a previous point in the image's history. Choose the History Brush. Target a state in the History palette. Choose a brush size, press the mouse, and drag across the image. For more information about the History Brush, see Chapter 11, "Altered States: History."

Art History Brush (Y)

This tool ![icon] is quite handy for creating instant Impressionist effects, as illustrated in Figure 10.22. Its behavior is really wild—like an industrial-strength Smudge tool, Paintbrush, and Blur tool all in one. It paints with stroke clusters that vary in color depending on the color of the area you are painting on. When you paint with the Art History Brush, color is deposited rapidly in several directions.

Choose from a list of characteristics in the Options bar that affect the style of the stroke and the rapidity in which it is deposited:

Style Determine the size and shape of the strokes that are deposited by choosing from a list of options including Tight, Loose, Short, Long, Dabs, and Curls.

Area Determine the width of the region in which the strokes will be deposited, from 0 to 500 pixels. Higher-resolution files need higher values.

Tolerance Use this setting to restrict the areas that can be painted. A low tolerance enables you to paint all image areas; a higher tolerance limits painting capabilities to areas that differ considerably in color from the source state or snapshot.

Figure 10.22

The version on the right has been altered with the Art History Brush, giving it an Impressionist look.

Eraser (E)

The Eraser 🖫 performs differently depending on whether you're working on the Background or a layer. When working on the Background, the Eraser replaces the area with the background color in the Tool palette. When erasing on a layer, it replaces the layer content with transparency. If the transparency option on the layer is locked, then the pixels are replaced with the background color.

The Eraser offers three modes in which to work: Brush, Pencil, or Block. The characteristics of each tool are inherent in the erasure.

You can erase the image back to a History state by clicking the first column in the History palette to set a source and choosing the Erase To History option from the Options bar.

Background Eraser (E)

The Background Eraser tool 🖫 functions like a combination of the Magic Wand tool and the Delete key command, in that it lets you sample and set a tolerance to determine the range of color that will be erased. You can also determine the sharpness of the remaining edges. The Background Eraser erases to transparency on a layer, or automatically converts the Background into a layer when applied there.

Use these options to control this tool:

Erasing Modes Control what pixels will be erased by choosing from the following:

> **Discontiguous** erases all the pixels within the Tolerance range on the entire layer.

> **Contiguous** erases pixels of the sampled color that are adjacent to each other.

> **Find Edges** erases pixels of the sampled color that are adjacent to each other but better preserves the sharpness of the edge pixels of the remaining image.

Tolerance Use this setting to control the range of colors to be erased. Low Tolerance erases colors that are similar to the sampled colors; High Tolerance erases to colors that are more diverse in range.

Sampling Option Determine the method in which the colors will be chosen by selecting from these options:

> **Continuous** samples colors continuously as you drag, erasing areas of different colors.

> **Once** samples a color when you first click and then continues to erase only that color. Use this option to erase areas of solid color.

> **Background Swatch** erases areas that are the current background color.

> **Protect Foreground Color** ensures that areas of the foreground color are not erased.

Magic Eraser (E)

The Magic Eraser ⬚ erases all pixels of similar color within the tolerance range when you click the color you want to erase. It enables you to isolate the erasure to specific colors.

These settings control the tool:

Tolerance Use this setting in the Options bar to control the range of colors to be erased. Low Tolerance erases colors that are similar to the sampled colors; High Tolerance erases to colors that are more diverse in range.

Anti-Aliased Use this option to create a smoother appearance along the edges of the erased areas.

Contiguous Determine what pixels will be erased. When this option is selected, you erase only *adjacent* pixels of the color; with Contiguous deselected, the Magic Eraser erases all pixels of the color on the layer.

Use All Layers Determine where the information will be erased. With this check box selected, the Magic Eraser erases through all the visible layers; without this option, it erases only the pixels on the target layer.

Opacity Use this option to determine the strength of the erasure.

Blur (R)

The Blur tool ⬚ softens the region it is applied to by decreasing the relative contrast of adjacent pixels. Use it to blend colors and soften edges, or to reduce the focus of a background. Increase the Strength setting in the Options bar to strengthen the effect.

Sharpen (R)

The Sharpen tool ⬚ increases the relative contrast values of adjacent pixels. As you drag over an area, the pixels randomly change color. The more you drag, the more diverse the colors of the adjacent pixels become. Increase the Pressure setting in the Options bar to increase the intensity of the effect.

Sharpening fools your eye into thinking an image is in focus. This tool can be used to enhance portions of an image that you want to emphasize or as a quick fix for photographs that are slightly out of focus.

> The Luminosity blending mode for the Sharpen tool reduces the randomness of the sharpened effect by replacing pixels with colors closer to the original image.

Smudge (R)

Use the Smudge tool 🖐 to simulate charcoal or pastel effects. As you drag with the Smudge tool, you move one area of color into another while blending and mixing the colors as you move them.

Selecting the Use All Layers check box smudges areas of colors on different layers (otherwise, the Smudge tool blends areas on only the targeted layer). If you select the Finger Painting check box, you mix the current foreground color into the smudged area.

Dodge (O)

Dodging is a technique used by photographers in the darkroom to overexpose or lighten specific areas of an image. In Photoshop, the Dodge tool 🔍 performs a similar function by increasing the brightness values of pixels as you paint with it. The Dodge tool's Options bar lets you concentrate the effect on a specific range of tonality by choosing Highlights, Midtones, or Shadows from the Range pull-down menu. Adjusting the exposure will weaken or strengthen the effect.

Burn (O)

Photographers burn an image in the darkroom to underexpose or darken areas of an image. Photoshop's Burn tool 🤚 darkens by lowering the brightness values of pixels as you move it over the image. As with the Dodge tool, the Options bar lets you pick a range of pixels to affect by choosing Highlights, Midtones, or Shadows from the list in the Options bar. Again, adjusting the exposure will weaken or strengthen the effect.

Sponge (O)

The Sponge tool 🧽 changes the intensity of a color as it touches pixels. From the Options bar, choose either Saturate to enhance a color or Desaturate to diminish the color and push it toward gray.

> Using the Dodge, Burn, or Sponge tool at full strength can often be overpowering. When you use these tools, try lowering the Exposure or Pressure setting to between 5% and 20% and making multiple passes to gradually build up the effect.

Painting Tool Shortcuts

Here are a couple of shortcuts that will increase your dexterity in handling the painting tools and performing tasks that could be otherwise difficult:

- For horizontal and vertical lines, press Shift as you drag up or down, left or right.
- For a straight line in any other direction, click and release your mouse, and then move the cursor to a new location and Shift-click.

Making and Applying Gradients

In nature, we see countless variations of color that subtly blend into one another as light and shadow intermingle into dimensional forms. The ability to gradually blend colors is essential to the credibility of any realistic image. Photoshop gradients blend multiple colors into each other, or into transparency, over a specified distance.

Choosing Gradients

Choose the Gradient tool 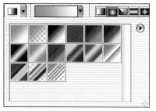 from the Tool palette and notice how the Options bar configures itself. At the far left is a preview bar, or *gradient swatch,* with a down arrow. Clicking in this swatch calls up the Gradient Editor, and clicking the arrow pops up a simpler Gradient Picker. Both display all saved gradients, beginning with the several preinstalled gradients. The default gradient creates a fill that blends from the foreground color to the background color. Another gradient, called Foreground To Transparent, fills from the current foreground color to transparency. Use it to gradually fade a single color or multiple colors. You can choose from the gradients on the default list that comes with Photoshop, and you can create new ones.

If you click the arrow at the upper-right of the Gradient Picker pop-up panel, you will display the Gradient Options pull-down menu. The first group of commands on this menu lets you reset, load, save, or replace gradients. The second group displays different ways of viewing the gradients in the menu, either by thumbnail or by name. At the bottom of the menu is a list of additional premade Photoshop gradients.

On the Options bar, to the right of the gradient swatch, are icons for the five gradient types, which blend the color in unique ways (as demonstrated in Figure 10.23). Choose one to indicate the direction in which you want your gradient built:

Linear	Applies a continual gradient over a specified distance from beginning point to end point
Radial	Radiates around a center point to its end point
Angle	Radiates clockwise around a center point
Reflected	Creates two linear gradients on each side of a center point
Diamond	Radiates from a center point into a diamond blend

Making Custom Gradients

The Gradient Editor is used to edit existing gradients, or to make new custom gradients and add them to the list. You can also save and load entire gradient palettes from the Gradient Editor or from the Preset Manager.

You can call up the Gradient Editor by clicking the gradient swatch in the Options bar (see Figure 10.24). Click a gradient in the Presets list to select it. The gradient preview bar shows the gradient's colors, their proportional distribution, and the position of any transparency. These characteristics can be edited.

Editing Gradient Color

The house-shaped markers along the *bottom* of the color bar are *color stops,* which determine where a solid color ends and where a gradient begins. You can assign a color to a color stop by clicking it to highlight it. Move the cursor off the Gradient Editor and onto the image, the Color palette, or the Swatches palette to sample a color. Another method of choosing a color is to double-click the color swatch in the Stops area to display the Color Picker. To redefine a stop's location, drag it left or right, or set a value in the Location field as a percentage of the gradient's length.

The small diamond under the preview bar marks the *midpoint* of the transition between the two colors that are being blended. Move it to redistribute the relative color proportions of the gradient.

To add a color to a gradient, click underneath the preview bar and a new color stop will appear. Determine a color for the color stop, drag the stop into position, and adjust the color's midpoint. To delete a color, drag its color stop off the Gradient Editor.

Editing Gradient Transparency

The house-shaped markers along the *top* of the gradient preview bar determine where transparency ends and where it begins. To blend transparency into the gradient, click a transparency stop and enter a percentage value in the Opacity field. Drag a stop to determine its location, or enter a number in the Stops area.

If transparency is set anywhere along the gradient, a diamond on top of the preview bar marks the center point of the transparency range. Move the midpoint to redistribute the proportion of transparency in the gradient.

To add a transparent area to a gradient, click above the color bar. Determine an opacity value in the Opacity field, move the stop into position, and adjust its midpoint. To delete a transparency, drag the transparency stop off the Gradient Editor.

Editing an Existing Gradient

You can edit existing gradients by adding, subtracting, or redistributing their colors:

1. Choose the Gradient tool and click the gradient swatch on the Options bar to display the Gradient Editor.

2. At the top of the Editor is a list of presets—the gradients that have already been saved. Double-click the gradient you want to edit. The Gradient Name dialog box appears. If desired, enter a new name and click OK.

Figure 10.23

The gradient types

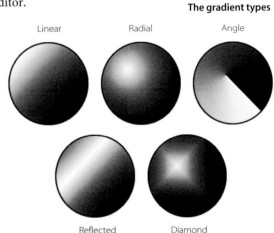

Linear   Radial   Angle

Reflected   Diamond

Figure 10.24

The Gradient Editor

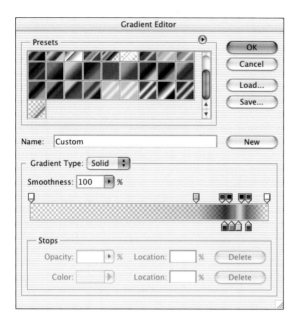

3. On the preview bar in the Gradient Editor, you see the configuration of color and transparency of the selected gradient as determined by the number and position of the color and transparency stops and the midpoint diamonds. Slide the stops to the left or right to adjust the color or transparency proportions. Slide the midpoint diamonds to adjust the centers of the blend.

4. Add a color by clicking under the preview bar to create a new stop.

5. Double-click the stop to display the Color Picker. Choose a color for the stop and click OK.

6. When satisfied with the edited gradient, click OK to leave the Gradient Editor. The edited gradient now appears in the Options bar.

7. Choose a Gradient tool, click in the image, and drag. Release the mouse to apply the gradient.

Making a Noise Gradient

The Noise option under Gradient Type in the Gradient Editor adds random colors to a gradient depending on the predefined colors you choose. The results can be somewhat unpredictable, so experiment to achieve the best results.

To create a noise gradient:

1. In the Gradient Editor, under Gradient Type, choose Noise, as shown in Figure 10.25.

2. For Roughness, choose or enter a percentage. This will determine the strength of the noise.

3. Choose a color mode or model—RGB, HSB, or Lab. The effect will vary significantly with each system.

4. Select the Restrict Colors check box to prevent oversaturation.

5. Select the Add Transparency check box to create a transparent gradient.

6. Click the Randomize button to preview variations of the effect.

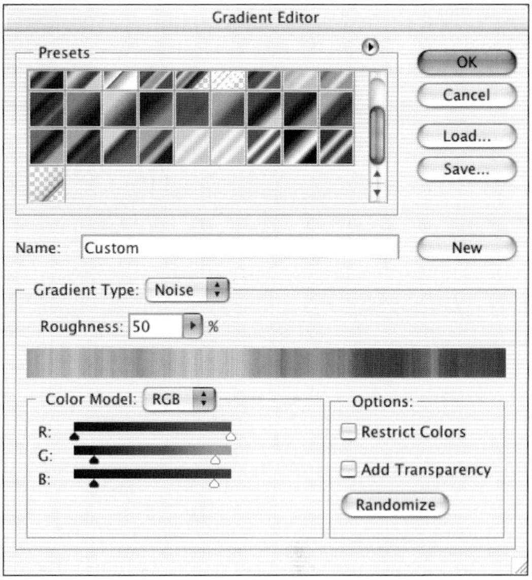

Creating a New Gradient

Follow these steps to make your own gradient:

1. Click the gradient swatch on the Options bar to display the Gradient Editor.

2. Click the New button. The Name field displays the name of the currently selected gradient, and the preview bar displays its properties.

3. Enter a name for the new gradient. It's easy to be thrown by the fact that the name and properties of the new gradient are the same as the current gradient. It's important to change the name immediately to avoid confusion.

4. Target each of the color or transparency stops and change their colors and locations as described under "Editing an Existing Gradient," earlier in this chapter.

5. Click below the color bar to add color, or above to add transparency.

6. Click OK to finalize the gradient and to select it into the gradient swatch.

Applying Gradients

All gradients are applied over a specified distance (see Figure 10.26). You choose the Gradient tool, click the image where you want the gradient to start, and drag in the desired direction. Release the mouse where you want the gradient to end. You will fill a selection if one is active, or the entire Background or layer if no selection is active. The distribution of the gradient depends on its color content and the positions of the stops, but just as important are the placement of the cursor and the length and direction you drag on the image.

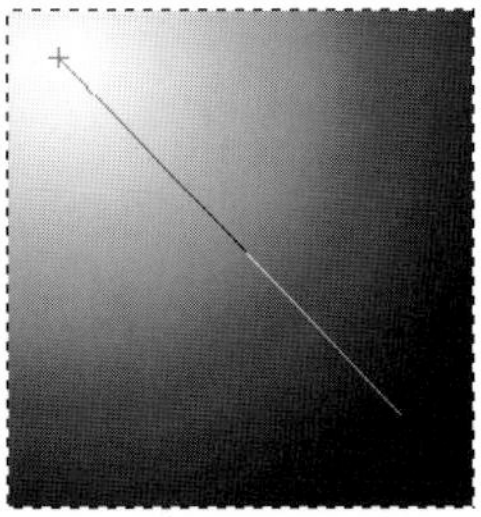

Figure 10.25

Choosing the Noise type in the Gradient Editor

Figure 10.26

Applying a gradient includes choosing its direction.

Press Shift while dragging to constrain the gradient to a vertical, horizontal, or 45-degree angle.

Creating Patterns

You can fill a selection with a repeating pattern. A pattern can be any image contained within a rectangle, or *tile,* that defines its top, bottom, left, and right edges.

To create a pattern in Photoshop:

1. Select an area on an image by using the rectangular marquee.

2. Choose Edit → Define Pattern.

   The rectangular marquee must have a feather radius of 0 pixels. In other words, it cannot have a feathered edge. It can, however, have an anti-aliased edge. If you select an area on the image and you find that the Define Pattern command is grayed out in the Edit menu, check the rectangular marquee's Options bar to be sure that the Feather Radius reads 0 px.

3. If you look in Edit → Preset Manager → Preset Type → Patterns, you'll see that the pattern has been added to the list.

You apply patterns to the image with the Pattern Stamp, the Fill command, the Paint Bucket, the Healing Brush, and the Patch tool, or as a Pattern Fill layer (see the sections on these features elsewhere in this chapter).

Filling and Outlining

You might find it difficult or time-consuming to paint large areas of the image and impossible to paint the outline of a shape. Photoshop provides several alternatives that automatically perform these tasks.

The Fill Command

Filling an area changes its pixels to a designated color:

1. Before an area can be filled, it must first be selected. Make an accurate selection with any of the selection tools to define the area. If the selection is feathered, the area that is filled will have a soft edge.

2. Choose Edit → Fill. The Fill dialog box is displayed (Figure 10.27).

3. From the Use pop-up list, choose a color or method to fill your selection:

Foreground Color Fill the selected area with 100% of the current foreground color.

Background Color Fill the selected area with 100% of the current background color.

Color The Color option will display the Color Picker for the user to select a new color.

Pattern Fill the selected area with a pattern chosen from the Pattern menu.

History Fill the selected area with a selected state in the History palette (see Chapter 11).

Black Fill the selected area with 100% black or an RGB value of 0 red, 0 green, 0 blue.

50% Gray Fill the selected area with 50% black; an RGB value of 128 red, 128 green, 128 blue; or HSB values of 0 h, 0 s, 50 b.

White Fill the selected area with 0% black or an RGB value of 255 red, 255 green, 255 blue.

4. Choose a blending mode and opacity. (See the appendix on the CD for details on blending modes.)

5. If you are filling a layer, you can choose to preserve the transparent areas and fill only the areas that contain pixels by selecting the Preserve Transparency check box.

6. Click OK.

> A fast method of filling an area with 100% of the foreground color is to press Option-Delete/Alt-Backspace. To fill an area selected on the Background with 100% of the background color, press Delete/ Backspace.

The Paint Bucket (G)

The Paint Bucket tool works like a combination of the Magic Wand tool and the Fill command, in that it will fill an area with color based on the tolerance, or range of color, of the target pixels.

To fill with the Paint Bucket:

1. Expand the Gradient tool in the Tool palette and choose the Paint Bucket.

2. In the Options bar, choose the type of fill—either the foreground color or a pattern. If filling with a color, choose a foreground color from the Color palette, Swatches palette, or Color Picker.

3. Set the blending mode and opacity for the fill.

4. Set the tolerance to determine the range of adjacent pixels to be colored. Higher tolerances color a wider range of pixels.

5. If you want only adjacent pixels to be colored, select the Contiguous check box. If the box is not selected, all the pixels within the tolerance on a targeted layer will be affected.

6. Select the Anti-Aliased check box if you want the fill to extend into the edge pixels of the selection or image.

Figure 10.27

The Fill dialog box

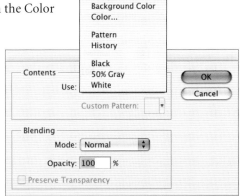

7. Select the All Layers check box if you want the tolerance measured and the fill applied through multiple layers.

8. Place your cursor on the area you want to affect, and click your mouse.

Using Fill Layers

Another unique method for filling an area is using a Fill layer. Fill layers are more dynamic than the traditional methods of filling large areas of color, because they combine the potential of the Fill command with the flexibility of layers. You can create Fill layers with solid colors, gradients, or patterns (see Figure 10.28).

See Chapter 7, "Layering Your Image," and Chapter 22, "Advanced Layer Techniques," for more on how to manipulate Fill layers.

Creating a Solid Color Fill Layer

Follow these steps to create a Solid Color Fill layer:

1. Choose Layer → New Fill Layer → Solid Color.

2. The New Layer dialog box appears, with the layer named Color Fill 1 by default. Enter a name for the layer to better identify it and click OK.

    As with any layer, you can group the Fill layer with the one immediately above it, forming a clipping group. Choose a color from the list if you want to color-code it; then choose an opacity setting and a blending mode.

3. The Color Picker is displayed. Choose a color and click OK.

4. The new layer that appears in the Layers palette has a layer mask linked to it and is represented by the thumbnail to the left of the layer name. A layer mask enables you to conceal portions of the image by painting on it. See Chapter 22 for more on layer masks.

If you make a selection prior to creating a Fill layer, the new Fill layer will fill only the selected area and create a layer mask that conceals the unselected areas. The layer mask thumbnail that appears in the Layers palette displays the revealed area as a white shape and the masked area as a black border.

Creating a Gradient Fill Layer

To create a Gradient Fill layer:

1. Choose Layer → New Fill Layer → Gradient.

2. The New Layer dialog box appears. The name of the new layer defaults to Gradient Fill 1. Enter a different name for the layer to better identify it. Click OK; the Gradient Fill dialog box appears (see Figure 10.29).

3. The colors of the gradient default to the last gradient chosen. If you want a gradient other than the one presented, click the down arrow to the right of the gradient swatch to choose a saved gradient, or click the swatch itself to display the Gradient Editor and create a new one. In the Gradient Fill dialog box, set the following specifications:

   Style Choose a gradient type from the Style pop-up list.

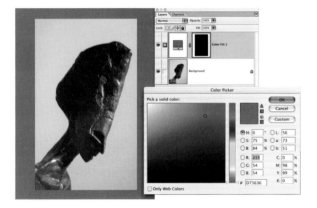

Figure 10.28

Solid Color, Gradient, and Pattern Fill layers (top to bottom-left to bottom-right)

Angle Enter a number or click the diagram to choose an angle to control the direction of the gradient.

Scale Choose a scale, by clicking on the arrow and moving the slider or by entering a value, to control the gradient's relative distribution over an area.

Reverse Select the Reverse check box to flip the gradient's direction over the entire layer.

Dither Select the Dither check box to soften the blending of the gradient. Dithering can help prevent banding that sometimes occurs when the Gradient is printed.

Align with Layer If the gradient is contained within a selection, select Align With Layer to distribute the gradient within the selection; not selecting this check box distributes the gradient over the entire layer but reveals only the selected portion.

4. Click OK to fill the layer.

Creating a Pattern Fill Layer

A pattern chosen from the Pattern presets can be applied to a layer in the same way a Solid Color Fill or a Gradient Fill can:

1. Choose Layer → New Fill Layer → Pattern.

2. The New Layer dialog box appears, with the layer named Pattern Fill 1 by default. Enter a name for the layer to better identify it and click OK; the Pattern Fill dialog box appears (see Figure 10.30).

3. Click the down arrow to choose a pattern, and set the following options:

    Scale Choose a percentage to determine the size of the pattern.

    Snap to Origin You can move the pattern by placing your cursor on it in the image window, or you can snap it back to its origin by clicking the Snap To Origin button.

    Link with Layer Selecting this check box aligns the pattern's layer mask to the layer.

    Create a New Preset from This Pattern Click the small document icon to save the pattern to the Presets.

Figure 10.29

The Gradient Fill dialog box

After they have been created, Solid Color Fill, Gradient Fill, and Pattern Fill layers can be edited by double-clicking their thumbnails in the Layers palette to reveal the Color Picker, the Gradient Fill dialog, or the Pattern Fill dialog, respectively. Unlike regular layers filled with pixels, these dynamic effects will resize if the canvas is resized.

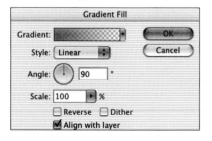

Outlining with the Stroke Command

The Stroke command in Photoshop outlines a selection border with a color. Strokes can vary in width and relative position on the selection border, as you can see in Figure 10.31. A feathered selection will soften the edge of the stroke.

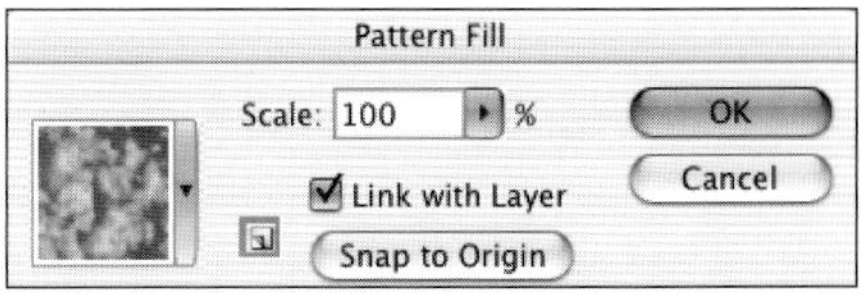

To apply a stroke to a selection:

1. Make a selection with any of the selection tools.

2. Choose a foreground color.

3. Choose Edit → Stroke. The Stroke dialog box appears (Figure 10.32).

4. Set the following attributes:

   Width Enter a value in pixels, between 1 and 250, for the stroke width.

   Color Click the swatch to reveal the Color Picker. Choose a stroke color and click OK.

   Location The Inside option places the stroke on the inside of the selection outline; Center centers the stroke between the inside and the outside of the selection outline; and Outside places the stroke on the outside of the selection outline.

   Blending Mode Choose a blending mode from the pop-up list to affect the relationship of the color that is being applied to the existing colors on the image.

Figure 10.30

The Pattern Fill dialog

Figure 10.31

You can position your stroke in different places relative to the selection.

Stroke Inside

Stroke Center

Stroke Outside

Feathered

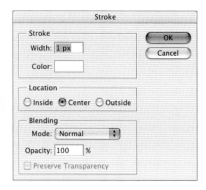

Figure 10.32

**The Stroke
dialog box**

Opacity Set the opacity from 1% to 100%.

Preserve Transparency If the image is on a layer surrounded by transparency, selecting the Preserve Transparency check box will prevent the transparent area from being stroked. Depending on selection and stroke location, if you place the stroke on the outside of a selection on a transparent layer, and you choose this option, you might not see any results.

5. Click OK to apply the stroke.

CHAPTER 11

Altered States: History

As you've seen in previous chapters, the application of such fundamental procedures as using layers during the editing process helps to keep an image dynamic. As you work, you can make changes to the image, or even just a portion of the image, one step at a time, until the results are satisfactory. In this chapter, you'll examine Photoshop's capability to take a step backward as well as forward. In this respect, I like to think of Photoshop as the "bachelor's software": you *never have to make a commitment*—that is, until you finally settle down and publish your work.

Photoshop takes the concept of bachelor's software to the max with the extreme flexibility of its History palette. The History palette is Photoshop's answer to the concept of multiple undos. Whereas some programs provide a system of undoing operations backward in sequence, Photoshop's interactive History palette features both sequential and nonlinear editing.

This chapter will explore Photoshop's undo and History features. In addition, Hands On 3, "Painting, Paths, and History," immediately following this chapter, will put you through the moves using the information covered in Chapter 9, "Drawing Paths," Chapter 10, "Creating and Applying Color, and this chapter.

In this chapter, you'll learn about:

- **Undoing what you've done**

- **Using Photoshop's Time Machine**

- **Working with snapshots**

- **Editing history**

Undoing What You've Done

Even the most accident-prone among us will find that it's almost impossible to do any *permanent* damage while working in Photoshop, because Photoshop can instantly undo errors. You never have to compromise, because you can reverse any operation. With this in mind, you can feel secure while experimenting freely with your images.

The Undo Commands

There are several techniques that reverse unwanted edits. Let's say you are carefully cloning out the blemishes on Uncle Herman's portrait. You've had one too many double espressos, and your hand is a bit jittery. You slip, you drag a little too far, and you place a rather unsightly blotch on the tip of his nose.

An easily corrected mistake? Yes! The first course of action is to head straight to the top of the Edit menu and choose Undo, which will instantly revert the image to the moment before you made the ill-fated clone stroke. When you choose Undo, you get a new command on the Edit menu—Redo—which restores the undone action. You can toggle back and forth between the previous artwork (Undo) and the later look (Redo) by selecting the command again, or better yet, use the key commands in the upcoming list.

There are two additional commands in the Edit menu that apply to the Undo operations:

Step Backward This undoes the last command and then continues backward through the operations you've performed, undoing them one at a time. As the operations are undone, you see them disappear one by one in the image window.

Step Forward If you've applied the Step Backward command more than once, you can restore the undone operations by choosing Edit → Step Forward. As the operations are redone, you see them appear one by one in the image window.

> As you apply them, the Step Backward and Step Forward commands move one by one through the state list in the History palette. See "Working with the History Palette" section later in this chapter.

You'll use these operations so frequently that it's worth remembering their corresponding key commands:

Command	Windows	Macintosh
Undo	Ctrl-Z	⌘-Z
Step Backward	Ctrl-Alt-Z	⌘-Option-Z
Step Forward	Shift-Ctrl-Z	Shift-⌘-Z

By default, Ctrl/⌘-Z will toggle between Undo and Redo in Photoshop, although in ImageReady, the default command for Redo is Ctrl/⌘-Shift-Z (see Chapter 25, "Web Design with Photoshop and ImageReady"). In Chapter 23, "Automating the Process," I'll show you how to make custom key commands.

New Beginnings

Another lifesaving operation reverts the image to the last time you saved it. Suppose you've been working on an image for 10 minutes since your last save, and you decide that somewhere along the line you went astray and the image is not going in the direction you want it to. You have gone too far to make corrections, so you decide you want to begin again. Choose File → Revert, and the image will be reopened to the last saved version.

If you are working on a newly formed image that has not yet been saved, the Revert command will be grayed out in the File menu.

Using Photoshop's Time Machine

The *history* of a Photoshop image is simply a record of work that has been performed on it. Photoshop automatically records every edit, operation, or technique that you apply to an image. As you work, each event, called a *state*—whether it's a paint stroke, filter, color correction, or any other operation—is listed in the History palette (see Figure 11.1). You can target a specific state on the list and display its contents in the image window. Like riding in an H.G. Wells time machine, you can freely move through the history of the document, alter states, and in so doing affect the outcome of the final image.

The History states are not layers. They do not contain isolated parts of the image per se. Rather, each state is a record of how the image looked after a specific tool or operation was applied to it. The history is exclusively a record of the changes to the image during the current work session. After the image is closed, the history is wiped clean, and when you reopen the document, the history begins again. The history cannot be saved or transferred

to another image. However, Photoshop CS has a new feature that enables you to record your history as metadata (information embedded in the file) or as a text file (see the "General Preferences" section in Chapter 5, "Setting Up Photoshop," for more on the History log). Program changes to preferences, palettes, color settings, and Actions are not recorded.

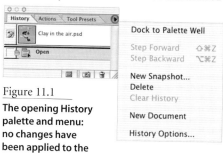

Figure 11.1

The opening History palette and menu: no changes have been applied to the image yet.

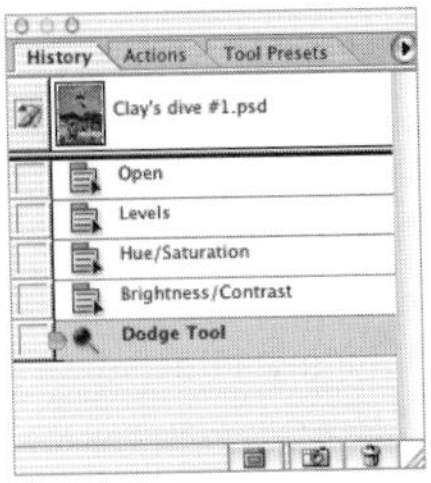

Figure 11.2

The History palette after a few operations

Working with the History Palette

The recorder for all the states is the History palette, which you access by choosing Window → History. By default, when the image is opened, the History palette displays a snapshot of the image as it appeared when it was last saved. It is from this point on where you will make changes to the image. Each time you perform an operation, the History palette produces a state with the name of the operation or tool that was used—for example, Brush Tool, Levels, Smudge Tool, and so forth. The most recent state is at the bottom of the History stack; note that in Figure 11.2, the act of opening the document appears at the top. The higher the state appears in the stack, the earlier in the process the state was created.

Changing History

They say you can't change history, but in Photoshop you can. If you want to move backward in time and see a previous state, click it in the History palette. The image window will display the image as it was during the targeted state. All states below it in the History palette are grayed out.

> Be careful! If you work on the image with a state targeted earlier than the most recent, all states below it will be deleted. You can still use the Undo and Step Backward features to get back to where you were, but you would lose all your new work.

For example, if you paint a brush stroke with the Brush tool while an earlier state is targeted, all states below it will be replaced by the state called Brush Tool. Later I'll show you how to avoid this by using the Allow Non-Linear History option.

Increasing History States

What enables Photoshop to remember all the History states is, of course, memory. Each state is stored in your computer's RAM or on the scratch disk. When you exceed the current limit on states, the oldest state is deleted to make room for the most recent state. The number of History states is limited to 20 by default. You can increase or decrease the default number of History states by choosing Edit → Preferences → General → History States and entering a number from 1 to 1000.

Specifying an excessive number of History states earmarks memory for the History cache and takes the allocation away from Photoshop's other operations. This could compromise Photoshop's performance. Whenever possible, keep the number of states at the default.

Looking at History Options

You can change the behavior of the history by selecting options in the History Options dialog box. In the History Palette pull-down menu, choose History Options to view or change these settings (see Figure 11.3):

Figure 11.3

Use this dialog box to change the behavior of the history.

Automatically Create First Snapshot produces a snapshot of the original image upon opening it and places its thumbnail at the top of the History palette (see the next section, "Working with Snapshots").

Automatically Create New Snapshot When Saving generates a snapshot of the current state when saving and adds its thumbnail to the top of the History palette.

Allow Non-Linear History enables you to discard or edit a previous History state without deleting more recent states.

Show New Snapshot Dialog By Default automatically displays the Snapshot dialog box when a new snapshot is created, prompting you to name the snapshots as they are made.

Working with Snapshots

At any time, you can save the current image to a snapshot (see Figure 11.4). By saving a snapshot, you can explicitly preserve various states of the image. Snapshots don't count toward the History state limit; they're saved—period—and you don't have to worry about that state being discarded when the limit is exceeded. But of course, they use up memory and, like the rest of the history, are discarded when the file is closed.

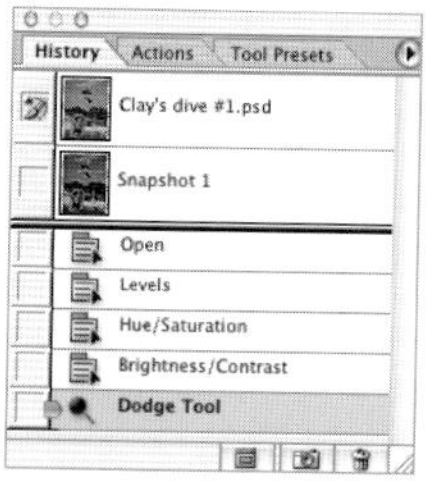

Figure 11.4

The History palette with a snapshot

Saving Snapshots

Click the History Palette pull-down menu and choose New Snapshot. The dialog box that appears enables you to name the snapshot and determine which combination of layers the snapshot will be made from.

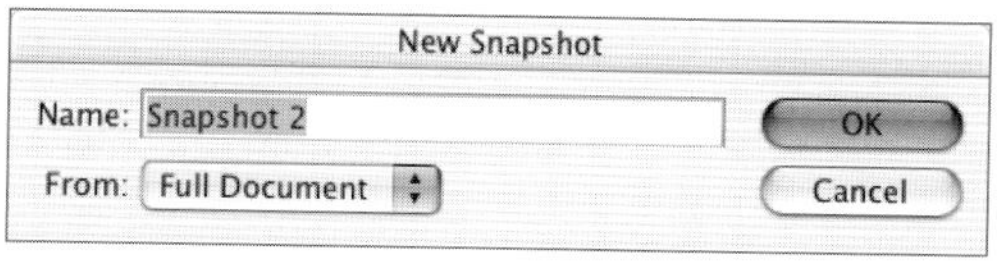

Full Document makes a snapshot of all the visible layers and the Background.

Merged Layers makes a snapshot of all the layers and merges them into one layer.

Current Layer makes a snapshot of the currently targeted layer.

A fast way to make a snapshot is to target a History state and click the Create New Snapshot icon  at the bottom of the History palette. By default, it will be given a name based on the snapshot number (Snapshot 1, Snapshot 2, and so forth). To rename it, simply double-click the name in the palette and type in a new one.

Saving a Snapshot As a New Document

If you want to work on multiple versions of an image or preserve the image in a particular state, you can save a snapshot as a new document. Follow these steps:

1. Save the History state as a snapshot.

2. Target the snapshot in the History palette and choose New Document from the pull-down menu.

3. Choose File → Save As and save the document to a location on your disk.

You can quickly make a new document from a snapshot by dragging the state to the Create New Document From Current State icon ▣ .

> Photoshop CS has a new feature called Layer Comps that gives you even more control over multiple versions of an image. See Chapter 22, "Advanced Layer Techniques" to find out how to use Layer Comps.

Deleting Snapshots

When you no longer need your snapshots, you can discard them. Here are several ways to do it:

- Drag the snapshot to the trash icon in the lower-right corner of the History palette.

- Click the snapshot and choose Delete from the History Palette pull-down menu.

- Click the snapshot and then click the trash icon.

Editing History States

The primary purpose of Photoshop's history is to keep the editing process dynamic. There are several ways to use the History palette to keep the workflow flexible so that you can experiment freely and confidently.

For all history operations, to target a state, click it in the History palette.

Deleting History States

Sometimes you'll want to delete a state. Try any of these methods:

- Drag the state to the trash icon at the bottom of the History palette.

- Target the state, and then choose Delete from the palette's pull-down menu or click the trash icon.

- Target a state. All states beneath it will be grayed out. Perform an edit to the state, and the grayed-out states will be purged.

- Choose Clear History from the palette's menu to clear all the states except the last state. Clearing the history retains the snapshots.

- Choose Edit → Purge → Histories. All the states but the one at the bottom of the list will be deleted. This option cannot be undone. The snapshots are retained.

Working with a Nonlinear History

If you delete a state, then by default, you'll also eliminate all of the more recent states (those underneath it in the palette). You can, however, change this default. From the History Palette pull-down menu, choose History Options and check Allow Non-Linear History box.

The Allow Non-Linear History option gives you the ability to eliminate or edit a state in the History palette and still preserve all the states below it in the stack. For example, you can target a state, make changes to it, save the altered state as a snapshot, target the most recent state, and continue working on the image. Experiment carefully with this option, because you can produce strange and unexpected results.

Using the History Brush

The History Brush tool ⟋ enables you to paint with a chosen state. You can use the History Brush to reestablish portions of a state even if you've edited them later. The Source column at the far left of the History palette tells Photoshop which state you want to paint with.

For example, suppose you paint a brush stroke on an image. As you continue to work, each time you perform an operation, a new state is added. If you later decide that you want to retain only half of that original brush stroke, here's how to do it:

1. Open the History palette.

2. Look through the states from bottom to top in sequence, until you find the state where you made the brush stroke.

3. Click the Source column to the left of the previous state, just above the state with the brush stroke. A History Brush icon appears in that column.

   By choosing the state previous to the brush stroke as the Source, you are telling the History palette that this is what you want the corrected portions of the image to look like. You are actually painting with the previous state in order to eliminate a portion of the brush stroke.

4. Choose the History Brush from the Tool palette and retarget the most recent state.

   If the Allow Non-Linear History option is not selected, you must target the last state in the history if you want to avoid losing the intervening states.

5. Paint over the portion of the brush stroke you want to cover up with the chosen previous state.

Painting with a Snapshot

You can use a snapshot in a similar manner when using the History Brush. Suppose you take a snapshot of an edit you made with a filter. After undoing the filter or eliminating its state, you can selectively apply the snapshot to specific portions of the image. If you save the snapshot as the full document or a single layer, the History Brush will paint from one layer to the corresponding layer on the targeted state. (The color section of this book includes a demonstration of painting with the History Brush. See Figures C11a–c.)

To paint with a snapshot:

1. Apply a filter, brush stroke, color adjustment, or any other effect to an image.

2. Choose Make Snapshot from the History Palette pull-down menu.

3. Choose Edit → Undo to undo the effect.

4. Click the Source column next to the new snapshot.

5. Choose the History Brush from the Tool palette. Choose a brush size and specify opacity and other brush characteristics in the Options bar.

6. Paint on the areas of the image that you want to affect.

Working with Other History-Editing Features

There are a couple of history-editing features scattered throughout the program that you should be aware of:

The Eraser Tool With the Erase To History option selected, the Eraser tool erases to a designated History state. You must designate the History state by clicking the Source column in the History palette next to the state you wish to erase to.

Fill from History Choose Edit → Fill → Use History to fill a selected area with a designated state. You must designate the History state by clicking the Source column in the History palette next to the state you wish to fill with.

Using the Art History Brush

This tool is called the Art History Brush because it's quite handy for creating instant Impressionist effects (Impressionism being an important movement in the history of art). And I mention it here only because it is in the History Brush fly-out on the Tool palette. But it does not use the history to alter the image as the History Brush does, except, like any other tool or operation, its effects are recorded as a state each time you apply it. (See Chapter 10 for a complete description of the Art History Brush tool and a demonstration of what it can do.)

Painting, Paths, and History

When working on an image in Photoshop, you will almost never use just one particular tool. In nearly every real-world project, you will draw upon the many features that Photoshop has to offer. In this lesson, you'll combine many of the basic tools and techniques introduced in Chapters 9, 10, and 11—painting colors, working with paths, and using the History palette—to create a virtual painting from a line-art image.

Getting Started

To ensure that your settings match the settings shown in this Hands On exercise, discard your preferences before beginning. The section titled "Modifying Photoshop's Settings" in Chapter 5, "Setting Up Photoshop," details how to reset your preferences to Photoshop's defaults. After you've launched Photoshop with default preferences, you'll create a written record of the image's history with Photoshop's new History Log feature. From the Photoshop menu (on a Mac) or the Edit menu (in Windows), choose Preferences → General. Select the History Log check box and the Text File radio button. Choose Detailed from the Edit Log Items list. Then click Choose. Pick a folder on your disk in which to save the text log (see Figure H3.1).

You are now ready to begin the Hands On project. Figure H3.2 shows the drawing you'll start with, and Figure H3.3 shows the finished version. (You can get a better preview of it by opening the Seahorse_end.tif file in the H03 folder on the CD.) See also Figures C44 and C45 in the color section for the beginning and completed seahorse images.

Take these steps to begin:

1. Insert the *Photoshop CS Savvy* CD into your CD-ROM drive.

2. From the H03 folder on the CD, open the file Seahorse_begin.psd (see Figure H3.2).

3. Choose File → Save and save the file to your disk.

You'll notice by looking in the Layers palette of the Seahorse_begin.psd file that there is a Background with four layers above it. The layers labeled Plantlife, Painting, and Extras are empty, and the Outline layer contains a black outline of the seahorse.

You will work on each of the layers during the exercise, but it is important to keep them in their original stacking order throughout the editing process.

Painting the Main Character

You'll start this lesson by selecting the central character—the seahorse—and then you'll use several of the painting tools to color, shade, highlight, and texturize the skin within the selected area.

Selecting the Painting Area

To begin the project, you'll use a selection tool to select the outer areas of the layer, and then inverse it to select the seahorse:

1. Target the Outline layer.

2. Click the Magic Wand tool 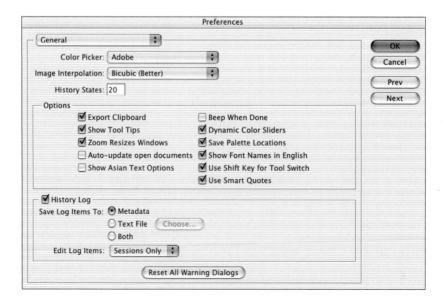. In the Options bar, check to make sure the tolerance is set to 32, with the Anti-Aliased and Contiguous check boxes both selected.

3. In the image window, click once in the white area outside the seahorse outline.

4. Hold down the Shift key to add to the selection (or click the Add To Selection icon in the Options bar), and click inside the small circular area created by the curl of the seahorse's tail. All image areas outside the outline are now selected, as evidenced by the "marching ants" of the selection marquee.

5. Inverse the selection via Select → Inverse (use Shift-⌘-I for Macintosh or Shift-Ctrl-I for Windows) so that the seahorse, rather than the outer area, is now selected.

6. The marching ants could prove to be a bit distracting. You can hide them from view by choosing View → Show → Selection Edges, or press ⌘/Ctrl-H while clicking to clear the option.

Figure H3.1

The Text File option in the General Preferences dialog box

Preferences

General

Color Picker: Adobe

Image Interpolation: Bicubic (Better)

History States: 20

OK

Cancel

Prev

Next

Options

☑ Export Clipboard
☑ Show Tool Tips
☑ Zoom Resizes Windows
☐ Auto-update open documents
☐ Show Asian Text Options

☐ Beep When Done
☑ Dynamic Color Sliders
☑ Save Palette Locations
☑ Show Font Names in English
☑ Use Shift Key for Tool Switch
☑ Use Smart Quotes

☑ History Log
Save Log Items To: ⦿ Metadata
                   ○ Text File   Choose...
                   ○ Both
Edit Log Items: Sessions Only

Reset All Warning Dialogs

Figure H3.2

The project begins with a simple line-art image.

Figure H3.3

Our line-art character will develop a bit more personality after a Photoshop paint job.

Hiding the edges of a selection keeps the selection active but conceals the selection outline. Sometimes it's possible to forget that you have a selection active, which can result in you performing a task to another area and getting no results. If that is the case, simply press ⌘/Ctrl-H again to reveal the marquee and then ⌘/Ctrl-D to deselect.

Painting the Base Color

Now that the area is selected, choose a base color and the right tool in which to apply it:

1. Target the Painting layer.

2. Choose Window → Swatches, and click the Pastel Green Cyan color in the Swatches palette to set it as the foreground color. (This was my color choice, but feel free to make your seahorse any color you like.)

3. Click the Paint Bucket tool ![icon] in the Gradient tool fly-out on the Tool palette or press Shift-G. Make sure the Fill choice in the Options bar is set to Foreground, and click inside the seahorse to fill it with color (see Figure H3.4). Even though the marching ants are hidden from view, the selection is still active, so you don't have to worry about staying within the lines.

4. Press ⌘/Ctrl-S to save your work.

Figure H3.4

The coloring process begins by filling the selected area in the Painting layer with a base color.

Shading and Highlighting

To add shading and highlights, you could use darker and lighter shades of the same color, but instead you'll take a shortcut and simply utilize some of Photoshop's specialty painting tools to achieve the desired look:

1. In the Tool palette, click the Burn tool ⬚ in the Dodge tool fly-out, or press Shift-O. Choose a medium size, soft brush such as a 17-pixel Soft Round. While still on the Painting layer, paint along the seahorse outline, and then along and just below each body ridgeline to give those ridges a bit of depth by shading. Switch to a smaller soft brush to shade the smaller areas, such as the ridges along the tip of the tail. See the first part of Figure H3.5 for an example of the shading process.

2. Activate the Dodge tool ⬚ by pressing Shift-O twice. Once again choosing the 17-pixel Soft Round brush, paint just above the body ridges and inside the larger areas to add highlighting (see the second part of Figure H3.5). Paint inside the inner part of the eye area until it becomes very light, almost white. Just as before, switch to a smaller soft brush to perform the more detailed work in the smaller areas.

To strengthen the effect, you can make multiple passes or you can increase the exposure percentage in the Options bar.

3. Select the Sponge tool  by pressing Shift-O twice. In the Options bar, set the mode to Saturate and the flow rate to 15%; then click the Airbrush icon ✐ to enable the airbrush capabilities. As you learned in Chapter 10, "Creating and Applying Color," the Airbrush option provides the ability to build up an effect just as a real airbrush would do. Choose a 27-pixel Soft Round brush, and then sweep the Sponge tool over any of the lighter areas that you wish to brighten with more saturated color, holding it in place longer in areas you wish to make more colorful, such as the fins and "mane" of the seahorse.

4. To blend the shaded and highlighted areas, select the Blur tool ◖ from the Tool palette or press the R key. Choose a medium size, soft brush. Make a quick pass over the entire seahorse. The Blur tool's effect can be very subtle, but you'll notice that it does help to achieve a smoother transition between the different shades.

5. Press ⌘/Ctrl-S to save your work.

Any time you make a mistake or simply don't like the result of an operation, click a step back in the History palette to restore the image to a previous state.

Figure H3.5

The Burn (left) and Dodge (right) tools make easy work of shading and highlighting.

Adding a Texture with the History Brush

The seahorse now has the base coloring and shading in place, along with flawlessly smooth skin. But because smooth skin is generally not characteristic of seahorses, you'll remedy the situation by using a combination of snapshots, a pattern fill, and the History Brush tool to give the skin a textured appearance:

1. In the History palette, click the Create New Snapshot button 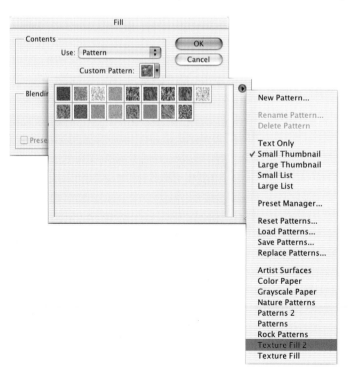. A snapshot of the image in the current state is generated. The new snapshot is located in the History palette just below the original image's opening shot (`Seahorse_begin.psd`). By default, the new snapshot will be labeled Snapshot 1. Double-click the name of the new snapshot and type **Smooth Skin** so you will remember what this snapshot contains and can find it later.

2. Choose Edit → Fill and, from the list under Contents Use, choose Pattern. Click the Custom Pattern Picker to open the pattern window. Click the arrow to bring up the menu list (see Figure H3.6). Click Texture Fill 2 to load the texture patterns. You'll see a dialog box asking if you want to replace the current patterns with the Texture Fill 2 patterns; click OK.

3. After the Texture Fill 2 patterns are loaded, they will appear in the Pattern Picker window. Choose the pattern called Shingles (which happens to be the first one), and click OK. Your seahorse will be entirely filled with the texture, as in Figure H3.7.

Figure H3.6

The Custom Pattern Picker menu contains several categories of useful patterns.

4. In the History palette, click the Create New Snapshot button to create a snapshot of the image now filled with texture, and name it **Skin Texture**.

5. Click in the Source column next to the Skin Texture snapshot to set it as the source for the History Brush tool. The History Brush icon then appears in the column.

6. Target the Smooth Skin snapshot (see Figure H3.8). After you do, you will no longer be able to see the texture in the actual image.

7. Activate the History Brush in the Tool palette. Choose a medium size, soft brush. In the Options bar, set the mode to Overlay so that when the texture is applied with the brush, it will overlay the color of the seahorse, blending it rather than just painting in the grayscale texture. Set the opacity to 50%.

8. Paint the texture into the body of the seahorse, as in Figure H3.9. Switch to a smaller brush size to paint the more detailed areas, such as the face, tail, and fin.

9. Save your work.

Figure H3.8

Targeting the Smooth Skin snapshot

Even when you're painting from a snapshot with the History Brush, you can still use the History palette as usual to go back a step if you make a mistake.

Figure H3.7

The skin-texturing procedure begins by filling with a texture pattern.

Figure H3.9

By using the History Brush to apply the texture from a snapshot, you can be choosy about which areas to texturize.

Softening the Outline

Now that you've completed the skin color and texture, you'll move on to the finer details, such as smudging the black outline to produce a softer appearance:

1. Target the Outline layer.

2. Select the Smudge tool 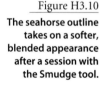 from the Blur tool fly-out, or press Shift-R twice. Choose the 9-pixel Soft Round brush, Normal Mode, and Strength at 50%.

3. Use your Zoom tool 🔍 to zero in on specific areas for the smudging process. Begin by following the perimeter of the seahorse outline with the Smudge tool. This will smudge the harshness of the drawn lines into a softer, more painted appearance, so that the lines become more like shading. Remember, you still have the selection around the seahorse (although you have the marching ants hidden from view), so you will stay within the lines while working on the Outline layer, just as you did on the Painting layer.

4. After you've made your way around the perimeter, begin smudging the lines inside the body area. If you feel the lines are a bit too smudgy, take a few steps back by way of the History palette, and then turn down the Strength in the Options bar, or switch to a smaller brush before continuing. Don't worry about keeping the lines perfect, though—this is the fun part where you can reshape, smear, and blend them to your heart's desire. See Figure H3.10.

5. After you've completed this step, choose Select → Deselect or ⌘/Ctrl-D to remove the selection.

6. Save your work.

Figure H3.10

The seahorse outline takes on a softer, blended appearance after a session with the Smudge tool.

If you've had to close and reopen your image at any time during the lesson, your selection will have been disabled, and you'll need to reselect the seahorse just as you did in the first part of the project. In Chapter 12, "Using Channels and Quick Mask," you'll learn to save selections in your image as alpha channels.

Using a Path to Shape the Eye

To complete the seahorse portion of your image, you'll employ the Path tools to create an unusually shaped, cartoon-style eye. (See Figure H3.11 for a visual step-by-step guide of the eye creation.)

1. Target the layer labeled Extras.

2. Zoom in on the eye area.

3. Activate the Ellipse tool ![icon] from the Shape tool fly-out, or press Shift-U three times. In the Options bar, click the Paths icon (see Figure H3.12).

4. Place an ellipse on your image, approximately as large as the white of the eye area (see Figure H3.11, square A).

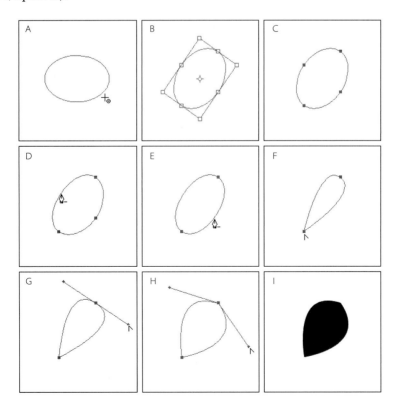

Figure H3.11

The eye is formed with the Ellipse tool in Path mode and then manipulated to the desired shape before filling with color.

Figure H3.12

Setting the Ellipse tool to Paths

Figure H3.13

Setting the rotation area

Figure H3.12

Setting the Ellipse tool to Paths

Figure H3.13

Setting the rotation area

5. Choose Edit → Transform Path → Rotate, type **125** into the Set Rotation area in the Options bar (see Figure H3.13), and click the check mark to commit the transformation (see Figure H3.11, square B).

6. Activate the Path Selection tool (type A on the keyboard). Click inside the path to select it (see Figure H3.11, square C), and then drag the path to the eye area, placing it directly over the white of the eye.

7. Activate the Delete Anchor Point tool in the Pen tool fly-out. Click on the point in the upper-left side of the path to delete it (see Figure H3.11, square D), and then click on the lower-right point to delete it as well, leaving a sort of egg shape (see Figure H3.11, square E).

8. Activate the Convert Point tool . Click the lower-left point to convert it to a corner point (see Figure H3.11, square F).

9. For the upper-right point, click and drag the handle toward the lower right to bring the shape into something like an upside-down teardrop (see Figure H3.11, square G). After that, use the handles one at a time to shape the path similarly to the line around the white of the eye (see Figure H3.11, square H).

10. If necessary, use the Path Selection tool again and drag the path to the proper position. You'll want the path to be just a tad smaller than the white part. If it is too large or small, choose Edit → Transform → Scale, and use the resulting bounding box to scale to the correct size.

11. Set the foreground and background colors to default black and white by either clicking the tiny black-and-white swatch in the Tool palette or using the keyboard shortcut D.

12. Choose Window → Paths, or press the F7 key on the extended keyboard and click the Path tab in the palette cluster, to bring the Paths palette into view. There you will see the work path you just created. Click the arrow in the upper-right corner to display the Paths Palette menu and choose Fill Path. Under Contents, choose Foreground Color, and click OK to fill the path with the black foreground color (see Figure H3.11, square I).

13. Click the palette's menu button again and choose Delete Path.

Adding Highlights to the Eye Shape

Now that you have the basic black eye shape in place, you'll add highlights to liven it up

1. Activate the Pen tool 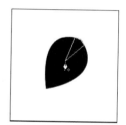. Click the Paths icon in the Options bar.

2. Zoom in very closely on the eye shape. With the next few steps, you will create a wedge-shaped path in the upper-right portion of the eye (see Figure H3.14).

3. Click to place your first point approximately in the center of the shape.

4. Move the Pen straight up and then slightly off to the right to place the second point at the upper-right outer edge of the eye.

5. Moving down, place two more points along the edge of the eye, each point falling just a bit below the last one.

6. Finally, close the path by clicking the point you first placed in the center of the eye.

7. If you feel the wedge is too large or small, choose Edit → Transform → Scale, and use the resulting bounding box to scale to the correct size. If necessary, use the Path Selection tool to drag the path to reposition it.

8. Choose Window → Paths to bring the Paths palette into view. Click the palette menu button and choose Fill Path. Choose White for the fill color and click OK.

9. Click the palette menu button again and choose Delete Path.

10. Activate the Brush tool (press B on the keyboard); set the Foreground color to White in the toolbox, and choose the 5-pixel Soft Round brush. Click once just to the left of the wedge highlight to create a specular highlight.

11. Save your work.

Figure H3.14

Highlighting the eye shape with the Pen and Brush tools

Creating the Background

Now that you have the basic character finished, you'll move on to adding a background environment.

Applying Color as a Diagonal Gradient

To begin creating the background setting, you'll use the Gradient tool to place the initial colors for the water:

1. In the Layers palette, target the Background.

2. Click the foreground color swatch in the toolbox to bring up the Color Picker, and choose a shade of light blue. Click the Background color swatch. Choose a medium blue, perhaps with a bit of purple tint, for the background color.

3. Choose the Gradient tool (press Shift-G) and click the Linear Gradient icon in the Options bar. Click the Gradient Picker in the Options bar and choose Foreground To Background, as in Figure H3.15.

4. Place your cursor in the upper-left corner of the image and press the Shift key to constrain the angle of the gradient to 45 degrees. Click and drag to the lower-right corner.

5. Save.

Using a Pattern Fill for the Water

A pattern fill will now be added to give the background a watery quality while still retaining the gradient effect:

1. From the H03 folder on the CD, open the file water.psd.

2. Choose Edit → Define Pattern. The Pattern Name dialog box will pop up for you to name the pattern—keep the default water.psd name and click OK.

3. Go back to the Seahorse image, and with the Background still targeted, choose Edit → Fill. Choose Pattern as the fill content, and then click the water.psd pattern in the list. Fill in 25% for the Opacity value and click OK.

    By choosing a reduced opacity for the pattern fill, you permit the gradient background color to partially show through the pattern, as seen in Figure H3.16.

4. Press ⌘/Ctrl-S to save your work.

Forming the Plant Life with Custom Shapes

With the Custom Shape tool, you'll add more details to the image by creating plant life from built-in custom shapes:

1. Target the Plantlife layer.

2. Use the Swatches palette to choose Dark Green as the foreground color.

Figure H3.15

Choosing the Foreground To Background option

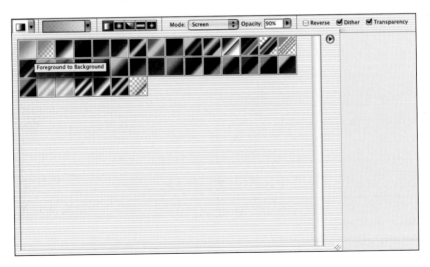

3. Activate the Custom Shape tool  (press Shift-U three times or until it appears in the Tool palette). Choose the Fill Pixels icon from the Options bar.

4. Open the Custom Shapes Picker in the Options bar, click the menu arrow in the upper-right of the picker, and choose Nature from the menu list to replace the current default shapes with the nature shapes.

5. Scroll to the last row of shapes now showing in the Custom Shapes Picker and choose Grass 3 (see Figure H3.17).

6. Click and drag a few of the grass shapes into your image, making them different heights and widths for variety.

7. Don't forget that if you are dissatisfied with the shapes you produce the first time, you can use the History palette to back up a few steps and try again.

8. Go back to the Custom Shapes Picker and choose Grass 2 this time. Click and drag a few of these grass shapes into your image, making them different heights and widths, as in Figure H3.18. To add variety, you can choose different green colors from the Swatches palette for the different grasses.

9. To quickly apply some shading to the grass, choose Layer → Layer Style → Satin. Move the sliders around to experiment with the effect and click OK.

10. Save.

Figure H3.16

The water pattern fill over the gradient

Using a Pattern Fill Layer to Build Up the Water

To add more of a motion effect to the water, you can utilize the Scale option in a Pattern Fill layer:

1. With the Plantlife layer still targeted, choose Layer → New Fill Layer → Pattern.

2. In the resulting dialog box, name the pattern **Water**, set the blending mode to Soft Light and the Opacity to 75, and click OK (see Figure H3.19).

3. In the Pattern Fill dialog box, choose the water pattern you used previously (water.psd). By using a Pattern Fill layer, you can scale the pattern to a different size—use the slider to scale it up to around 155% (see Figure H3.20).

4. Save your work.

Figure H3.17

Choosing from the nature shapes

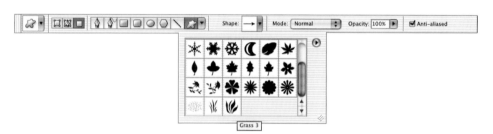

Figure H3.18

By using Photoshop's built-in custom shapes, you add plant life to the waterscape instantly.

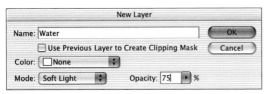

Figure H3.19

Use the New Layer dialog box to set the water's blending mode and opacity.

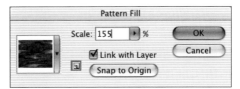

Figure H3.20

Use the Pattern Fill dialog box to scale the pattern to a different size.

The Pattern Fill layer enables the water pattern to not only blend with the water below it, but to give the impression of water flowing over the plants (see Figure H3.21).

Creating and Cloning the Bubbles

To complete the background environment, you'll use the Gradient tool in a selected area to form a few bubbles in the water:

1. Target the Extras layer.

2. Select the Elliptical marquee tool ⬭ (press Shift-M until it appears in the Tool palette). Drag a small circular selection in the upper-left corner of the image. Press the Shift key as you drag to constrain the marquee into a perfect circle.

3. Set the foreground color to black. Zoom in on the marquee with the Navigator or the Zoom tool.

Figure H3.21

A Pattern Fill layer intensifies the water effect.

4. Select the Gradient tool ■ from the Tool palette (press the G key). In the Options bar, click the Gradient Picker and choose Foreground To Transparent from the gradient list (Figure H3.22). Click the Radial Gradient icon in the Options bar and, select the Reverse check box.

5. Click in the lower-right portion of the selection just a short way from the edge, and move up toward the upper left until you've gone a bit past the outer edge of the selection marquee (see Figure H3.23) and release. This will produce a radial gradient with its center at the starting point. Deselect (⌘/Ctrl-D).

6. Activate the Brush tool (press the B key). Set the foreground color to white (press your X key or click the tiny arrows at the upper-right of the color swatches in the Tool palette). Choose a 5-pixel Soft brush and paint a specular highlight in the upper-left portion, similar to the highlight you painted in the eye earlier.

7. Repeat steps 2 through 6 to create another bubble of a different size than the first.

8. Zoom out. Activate the Clone Stamp tool ■ (press S on the keyboard).

9. Option/Alt-click on a bubble you wish to reproduce.

10. Choose another location and clone in the new bubble.

11. Repeat steps 9 and 10 until you have as many bubbles as you wish.

12. Save your work.

Figure H3.22

Choosing the Foreground To Transparent option

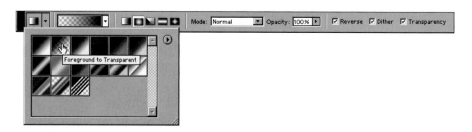

Figure H3.23

The bubble creation procedure adds the finishing touches to the project.

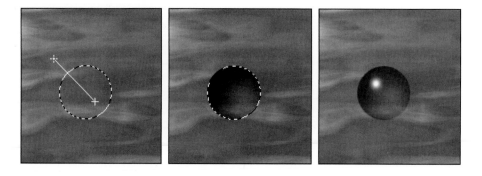

Viewing the History Log

At this point, you've performed quite a few steps to produce the seahorse image. By default, the last 20 steps appear in the current History palette. If you close the file, its History will be lost. When you reopen the image, a new History will begin.

At the beginning of this exercise, you set the preferences to save a detailed record of the history as a text file for future reference. You can open and view the History log in TextEdit (Mac) or Notepad (Win) or any other text editor or word processor that reads text (.txt) documents. The log has recorded the editing operation performed in each History state and its date and time. Figure H3.24 shows a portion of the history in the History log.

Be sure to turn off the History log feature in the General Preferences to avoid the continuation of the recording of data in the current text file. If you plan on working on additional images, you can turn it on again when you open them.

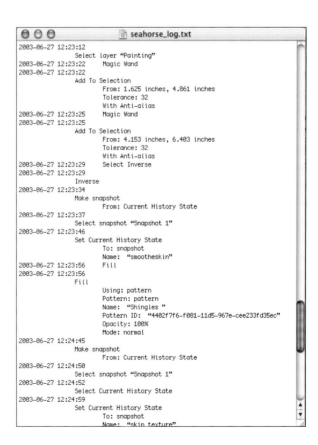

Figure H3.24

A portion of the History log as a text document generated with Photoshop's new History Log preference

CHAPTER 12

Using Channels and Quick Mask

It's raining outside. You're quite comfy in front of your computer, working on an assignment to colorize a black-and-white group photograph of 34 mariachis. You've spent the last half-hour carefully outlining each one of their pants, tunics, and sombreros with the selection tools. You're about to apply the Hue and Saturation command to simultaneously color all of their costumes a brilliant turquoise. You hear thunder in the distance. The lights flicker. Your screen goes dead!

You're not worried; you've been regularly saving your work. You restart your computer, launch Photoshop, and open the image. The 34 mariachis are there, but without the precious selection marquees over which you labored for so long.

More than a half hour of work has just vaporized into pixel dust. Before you utter a stream of unprintable obscenities, however, remember that you've learned a valuable lesson: Save your selections! In this chapter, you'll explore some great methods of making and saving selections. This chapter will cover:

- Creating alpha channels
- Looking at the Channels palette
- Editing alpha channels
- Performing channel operations
- Using Quick Mask

Understanding Photoshop Channels

There are two types of channels in a Photoshop document. *Color channels* are graphic representations of color information. They are an integral part of the image. Having access to this information enables you to perform powerful modifications and corrections to the image's appearance and color relationships. *Alpha channels* are graphic representations of selections that have been stored for later use.

Color channels are composed of information segregated by color. Each color channel is actually a separate grayscale image. When you view the color channels superimposed on each other in an image, you see the full-color composite image. For a detailed description of color channels, see Chapter 3, "The Nature of the Beast."

An alpha channel is also a grayscale image. Like a color channel, it can support 256 shades of gray. Unlike a color channel, however, an alpha channel does not contain information that contributes to the image's appearance. And instead of the values of gray representing tonality or color, they represent the areas of opacity, semitransparency, or transparency of a mask.

Photoshop provides many features that isolate areas of an image so that you can perform edits and adjustments to a specific region. It's helpful to think of an alpha channel as a tool that you create, store, and later use to isolate an area so that a tool or command can ultimately be applied to it.

Bear in mind that although alpha channels are stored selections and do not affect the way the image appears, they are perceived by Photoshop as part of the image, and therefore increase the file size of the image proportionally each time you save a selection. Photoshop supports a maximum of 56 channels in a document (except in bitmap images which don't support alpha channels). Images with alpha channels can become quite large and consume a great deal of disk space, so it is best to delete your alpha channels when you are sure you are done with them.

Looking at the Channels Palette

Channels are displayed in the Channels palette (see Figure 12.1). To access the Channels palette, choose Window → Channels, or you can press F7 to display the Layers/Channels/Paths cluster.

The composite channel appears at the top of the palette. The individual color channels appear underneath, each labeled with the name of the color that it represents and a key command that displays it in the image window. As in the Layers and History palettes, the first column, to the left of the thumbnail, displays or conceals an eye icon (a visibility indicator) that tells you what you can see—in this case, it indicates what channels are displayed. Clicking to turn off the visibility indicator next to the red channel, for example, reveals the content of the green and the blue channels. Clicking the composite channel visibility indicator reveals the full-color image.

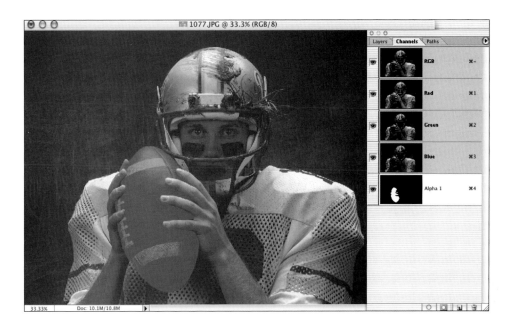

Figure 12.1
The Channels palette with the alpha channel visible on the image

If you save a selection to an alpha channel, it is placed underneath the color channels in the stack in the order in which it was created.

Saving Selections as Alpha Channels

Because making an intricate selection can sometimes be difficult or time-consuming, Photoshop enables you to store selections to the Channels palette so that they can be used when you need them. It is wise to save a selection as an alpha channel if the selection is complex, if you need to refine it, or if you are going to use it more than once.

To save a selection:

1. Make a selection with one of the selection tools.

2. Choose Select → Save Selection.

3. In the dialog box that appears (see Figure 12.2), designate the document where the selection will be saved and determine the following settings:

   Document You can save a selection as an alpha channel to the document where the selection was made or to any open document that is the exact same height, width, and resolution. The names of

Figure 12.2

The Save Selection dialog box

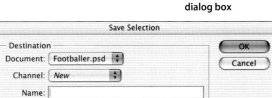

the documents that conform will appear in the Document pop-up list. Choosing New creates a new document with no color channels and one alpha channel in the Channels palette.

Channel Choosing New here makes a new channel. You can name the new channel in the Name field. If you don't name it, the saved selection will appear on the Channels palette titled as Alpha 1, 2, and so on. Selecting a channel name in the Channel pop-up list writes over an existing channel.

Choosing Layer 0 Mask saves a selection to a layer mask, if you created a layer mask on the image. The name of the layer mask defaults to Layer 0 Mask (see Figure 12.3). It appears in both the Layers palette and the Channels palette. (See Chapter 22, "Advanced Layer Techniques," for more information on layer masks.)

4. If you have an active selection on the image and you choose a channel name to write over, the Operation area presents you with the following four options. To choose, click the radio button next to the operation.

> **New Channel** discards the original mask channel and replaces it with an entirely new alpha channel.
>
> **Add To Channel** adds the new selected area to the alpha channel.
>
> **Subtract From Channel** removes the new selected area from the alpha channel.
>
> **Intersect With Channel** creates an alpha channel of the area where the original channel and the new selection overlap.

5. Click OK to save the selection.

You can quickly save a selection as a new alpha channel by clicking the Save Selection As Channel icon at the bottom of the Channels palette.

Figure 12.3
Saving a selection

Viewing Channels

It is often necessary to examine a color channel in black-and-white to better observe the brightness relationships of its pixels. By default, color channels are displayed in the Channels palette as black-and-white thumbnails and in the image window as grayscale images. You can display color channels in their native color by choosing (from the Photoshop menu on a Mac or the Edit menu in Windows) Preferences → Display & Cursors → Color Channels In Color.

To display or conceal a color or alpha channel, click the visibility indicator in the first column to the left of its thumbnail, or press one of the keyboard commands displayed in Table 12.1.

After a selection has been saved as an alpha channel, it can be viewed independently in the image window (see Figure 12.4). To view a channel in the image window, first click in the box to the right of the channel's thumbnail to make it visible. Then do one of the following:

- Click the eye icon next to the composite channel at the top of the palette to conceal it.

- Press Option (Macintosh) or Alt (Windows) and click its thumbnail or name.

- Press ⌘/Ctrl and the appropriate number key (see Table 12.1).

By default, black represents masked areas, white represents selected areas, and gray represents semitransparent areas.

When both color channels and alpha channels are visible, you see the alpha channels as superimposed translucent color overlays. By default, the overlays are 50% red, which is designed to resemble Rubylith, a traditional masking film used in the graphic arts industry (see Figure C12 in the color section).

Figure 12.4

An alpha channel displayed in the image window

KEYBOARD COMMAND	RGB	CMYK	LAB	GRAYSCALE & INDEXED	MULTICHANNEL
⌘/Ctrl-~	Composite RGB Channel	Composite CMYK Channel	Composite Lab Channel	Gray Channel	Cyan
⌘/Ctrl-1	Red	Cyan	Lightness	Gray Channel	Cyan
⌘/Ctrl-2	Green	Magenta	a	Alpha 1	Magenta
⌘/Ctrl-3	Blue	Yellow	b	Alpha 2	Yellow
⌘/Ctrl-4	Alpha 1	Black	Alpha 1	Alpha 3	Black
⌘/Ctrl-5	Alpha 2	Alpha 1	Alpha 2	Alpha 4	Alpha 1

Table 12.1

Color Channel Modes

Using the Channel Options

You might need to change the color of an alpha channel overlay if you are looking at more than one channel at a time or if the content of the image closely resembles the color of the overlay. If you double-click the thumbnail of the alpha channel, the Channel Options dialog box appears (see Figure 12.5). You can then set display options for that channel. The radio buttons in the Color Indicates area let you choose masked areas or selected areas to be displayed as color overlays, or if you are working with spot colors, you can designate a spot color channel (described in Chapter 18, "Duotones and Spot Color").

Always check the Channel Options dialog box to see if masked areas or selected areas are represented by color. Prior to Photoshop CS, the default was Masked Areas, but it has been changed in this new version to Selected Areas. Look at the alpha channel in the image window by its thumbnail. When color represents masked areas, the masked area will appear black and the selected area will appear white. The reverse is true when color represents selected areas.

To change the color of a mask:

1. Double-click the channel thumbnail to display the Channel Options dialog box.

2. Click the swatch to bring up the Color Picker.

3. Choose a color and click OK.

You can specify the opacity of the mask from 0% to 100%, which affects only the way you see the mask and not its masking characteristics. Reducing the opacity helps you see the image more clearly through the mask.

Loading Selections

Once saved to the Channels palette, the alpha channel can be loaded as a selection. Loading a selection surrounds the area with a selection marquee just as if you outlined it with a selection tool.

Figure 12.5

The Channel Options dialog box

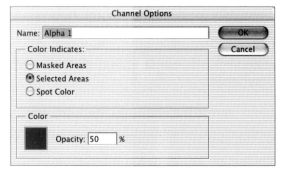

To load a selection:

1. Choose Select → Load Selection.

2. In the Load Selection dialog box, the options are similar to the Save Selection dialog. From the Document pop-up list, choose the name of the document where the channel was made. This list will display all alpha channels from all open documents that are the same height, width, and resolution.

3. From the Channel pop-up list, choose the source channel to be loaded. This list displays all alpha channels and layer masks from the current document. The Invert box loads an inversed selection of the mask.

4. If you have an active selection on the image, the Operation area presents four options:

   New Selection loads a new selection on the image, replacing any currently selected area (if there is one) with the selection derived from the alpha channel.

   Add To Selection adds the loaded selection area to an active selection marquee.

   Subtract From Selection omits the loaded selection area from an active selection marquee.

   Intersect With Selection loads the area where the loaded selection and an active selection marquee intersect.

5. Click OK to load the selection.

   A faster method is to load a selection by dragging its icon to the Load Channel As Selection icon [ ] at the bottom of the Channels palette. You can rename the channel by double-clicking its name and then typing the new name.

Editing Channels

It is sometimes desirable to change portions of the channel by using the painting or editing functions. If, for example, you missed a small part of the selection while using the Lasso tool, you can alter the contents of the mask channel with the Brush tool to include the areas that were excluded from the original selection. Any painting or editing function that can be applied to a grayscale image can be applied to an alpha channel.

Fine-Tuning Alpha Channels by Painting

Suppose that after having saved a selection, inaccuracies are visible on the mask that weren't visible on the selection marquee. You can fine-tune these and other flaws by painting directly on the alpha channel.

Here's a practice exercise on how to save and alter the contents of an alpha channel:

1. Open the file titled `big_bug.psd` from the `Ch12` folder on the *Photoshop CS Savvy* CD.

2. Select the Magic Wand tool. In the Options bar, be sure the tolerance is set to 32, and deselect the Contiguous check box. Click the white background.

3. Choose Select → Inverse (Shift+⌘+I/Shift+Ctrl+I) to deselect the white background and select the bug.

4. Click the Save Selection As Alpha Channel icon in the Channels palette. The channel will be named Alpha 1. Double-click the name and type the word **Wings.**

5. View the alpha channel in the image window by pressing Option/Alt and clicking its name or thumbnail. The black-and-white channel will appear in the image window.

6. The foreground and background color swatches in the Tool palette have changed to white and black. By default white is the foreground color. This is because a channel is a grayscale image and does not support color. Choose the Brush tool, Airbrush, Pencil, or any tool that deposits foreground color.

7. Display the composite channel by clicking its visibility icon, but be sure that the Alpha 1 channel is targeted and visible. You'll see a red color where the channel masks the bug. Paint the body, legs, and antenna of the bug with white, leaving only the wings covered with red, as shown in Figure C13 in the color section (see also Figure 12.6). The resulting painting will, by default, alter the marquee to select the newly painted areas when the selection is loaded.

Figure 12.6

Painting on the alpha channel (left) alters the selection when the channel is loaded (right).

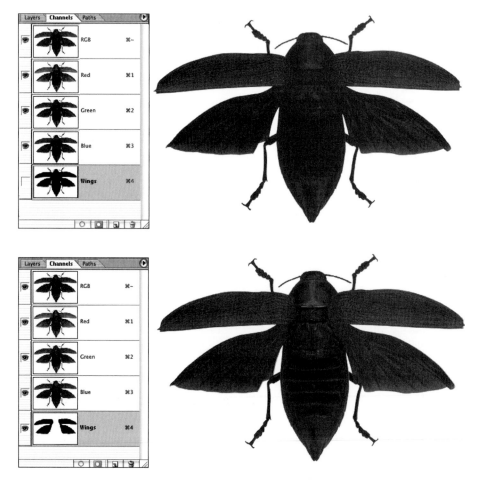

8. To see the result, choose Select → Load Selection, and choose Alpha 1 from the Channel pop-up list.

> Painting with a shade of gray creates a partially masked area; the degree of masking depends on how light or dark the gray is. The darker the shade of gray, the more an area will be masked; applying black will produce areas that are entirely protected, whereas painting with white will entirely erase the painted area.

Performing Channel Operations

You can perform several operations within the Channels palette that change the structure of the document. Some of these operations produce shifts in the color mode, and some disperse the channels into several documents.

> Because of the radical changes to the color information, it is always a good idea to make a copy of the document before implementing most of these channel operations. To duplicate the document, choose Image → Duplicate.

Duplicating Channels

When you duplicate a targeted channel, you get an exact copy of it in the Channels palette. You should duplicate the channel if you want to experiment with modifying it by painting, applying a filter effect, or using any other editing function. Also duplicate the channel if you want to invert it and save it for alterations, as seen in Hands On 4, "Channels." Click the arrow in the upper-right corner of the Channels palette and scroll down to the Duplicate Channel command.

Dock to Palette Well
New Channel…
Duplicate Channel…
Delete Channel
New Spot Channel…
Merge Spot Channel
Channel Options…
Split Channels
Merge Channels…
Palette Options…

> The Duplicate Channel option will be dimmed if the composite channel is targeted, because you can duplicate only one channel at a time.

A fast way to duplicate a channel is to drag it to the New Channel icon [icon] at the bottom of the Channels palette.

Deleting Channels

You can delete a targeted channel from the document by choosing Delete Channel from the palette pull-down menu. You can delete alpha channels and maintain the integrity of the image, but when you delete color channels, the color mode of the image will change to Multichannel (see the section titled "Using Multichannel" later in this chapter). If you delete the red channel of an RGB image, for example, the remaining color channels will convert to magenta and yellow. (Multichannel documents always default to CMYK descriptions.) You cannot delete the composite channel.

A fast way to delete a channel is to drag it to the Delete Current Channel icon (the trash icon) at the bottom of the Channels palette.

Splitting Channels

Photoshop can split a document's channels into independent grayscale documents. The title of each window is automatically appended to the channel's color name as a suffix in the image title bar at the top of the window. For example, a CMYK document named Box will be divided into four channels: Box_C, Box_M, Box_Y, and Box_K. Alpha channels will be converted to separate grayscale documents. This option is useful as a first step in redistributing channels or for making a single document out of the channels information. This is not a process you'll use every day, unless you're a printer who needs to isolate the color information to a single document or you have very specialized needs to analyze the channel information. The new documents are not automatically saved, so you should save them to your hard disk.

To split a channel, first flatten the image. Choose Split Channels from the Channels Palette menu. When you perform this operation, the original document is automatically closed.

Merging Channels

Separate channels can be merged into a single Multichannel document by choosing Merge Channels from the Channels Palette menu. The images must be open, grayscale, and the exact same height, width, and resolution. A dialog box appears that enables you to assign a color mode to the image, based on the number of images open. Three open images will produce an RGB, Lab, or Multichannel image; four open images will produce a CMYK or Multichannel image. Click OK and another dialog enables you to determine the distribution of the color channels. You can create some rather surprising color distortions by switching color information between channels.

One of the most common uses for the Merge Channels command is for recombining EPS DCS files. Prepress users have to recombine an EPS DCS 1 or 2 file that has lost the composite preview file, which links the separations. A new EPS DCS file can be created that includes the composite preview file and the high-resolution separations.

Using Multichannel

You can divide an image's channels into an individual series of channels. When you choose Image → Mode → Multichannel, the new channels lose their color relationships to each other and appear as individual grayscale channels within a single document. There is no composite channel. This can be useful if you want to separate the color information of a composite channel such as a Duotone, Tritone, or Quadtone and view the color information of each ink color separately. (Chapter 18 goes into more detail on image features such as Duotones and spot colors.) The Multichannel operation converts the red, green, and blue channels on RGB images into separate cyan, magenta, and yellow channels within the same document.

Mixing Channels

The Channel Mixer is a Photoshop feature that enables you to adjust the color information of each channel from one control window. You can establish color values on a specific channel as a mixture of any or all of the color channels' brightness values. The Channel Mixer can be used for a variety of purposes, including:

- Creating an optimal grayscale image from an RGB or CMYK file
- Making a high-quality sepia tone from a CMYK or RGB file
- Converting images into alternative color spaces
- Swapping color information from one channel to another
- Making creative color adjustments to images by altering the color information in a specific channel

To learn how to use the Channel Mixer, see Chapter 16, "Adjusting Tonality and Color."

Using Spot Color Channels

The spot channel features in the Channels Palette pull-down menu are used to create images that are output to film for printing on printing presses. They are most frequently applied to grayscale images for two- and three-color print jobs. They are also used on four-color process (CMYK) images when additional areas of solid rich color, varnishes, and special inks are specified. Spot colors are usually printed with PANTONE or other custom color inks. See Chapter 18 to learn how to work with spot colors.

Using Quick Mask Mode

As you become more proficient in Photoshop, the speed of performing tasks will become more crucial to your particular style of work. As you understand the mechanics of the tool functions and begin to recognize the logic and similarity of the various windows, palettes, and toolbars, you'll want to explore shortcuts that accelerate your work. Selecting areas on a Photoshop image can be the most time-consuming part of the image-editing process; Quick Mask mode can accelerate the selection-making process and enhance its precision.

Quick Mask mode is an efficient method of making a temporary mask by using the painting tools. Quick Masks can quickly be converted into selections or stored as mask channels in the Channels palette for later use. By default, the Quick Mask interface is similar to the channels interface in that Photoshop displays a colored overlay to represent the masked areas. You can toggle directly into Quick Mask mode on the Tool palette by pressing the letter Q or clicking the Quick Mask icon .

> Quick Mask provides a versatile way of making or editing selections by using many of Photoshop's painting tools, filters, and editing tools. You can even use the selection tools to define areas of the Quick Mask to edit.

When you choose Quick Mask mode from the Tool palette, a temporary thumbnail labeled Quick Mask, in italics, appears in the Channels palette. The thumbnail will change appearance as you apply color to the Quick Mask.

Quick Mask Options

The Quick Mask Options dialog box (see Figure 12.7) is almost identical to the Channels Options dialog, and can be accessed by double-clicking the Quick Mask icon.

To practice creating a mask in Quick Mask mode, follow these steps:

1. Open the file `big_bug.psd` from the `Ch12` folder on the CD.

2. Click the Quick Mask icon in the Tool palette. Notice that the foreground and background swatch colors in the Tool palette become white and black respectively. Press the X key on the keyboard or click the arrow next to the foreground and background colors on the Tool palette to invert the colors.

3. Choose the Brush tool from the Tool palette. Choose a brush from the Brush menu and paint over the body of the bug. I started with a 35-point Hard Round brush and chose smaller brushes to fill in the corners. Painting on a Quick Mask is similar to painting on an alpha channel with the composite channel visible. By default, as you paint, if the foreground color is black, the painting tool will deposit a red color. If the foreground color is white, the painting tool will erase the mask color.

4. Carefully paint around the edge of the bug's body. If you make a mistake, choose white as a foreground color and erase it.

5. When you have completed painting the bug, click the Edit In Standard Mode icon on the Tool palette. By default, the areas that were painted are now outlined by a selection outline as in Figure 12.8.

6. After all that work, you should save the selection as an alpha channel. Click the Save Selection As Alpha Channel icon at the bottom of the Channels palette.

Figure 12.7

Quick Mask Options dialog box

> If you want to be sure that the area is completely masked, set the Opacity slider in the Brush Options bar to 100%. Setting the opacity to 50%, for example, will paint with translucent color; the result will be that the painted area will be only partially masked.

After a Quick Mask has been made, I recommend that you carefully examine it for missed areas and pinholes. It is quite easy to make mistakes because it can be difficult to see omissions and errors on the image. The best way to examine the Quick Mask is to view it as a grayscale image. You can see the Quick Mask as a grayscale by turning off the visibility icon on all the channels in the Channels palette except for the one to the left of the Quick Mask. Examine it carefully to ensure that the masked areas are solid and opaque. If necessary, apply more paint to deficient areas. (See the Hands On 4 section that follows this chapter for a demonstration.)

Quick Mask is ideal for cleaning up selections that you have made with one of the selection or marquee tools. You can paint a few pixels at a time with a small brush or with the Pencil tool, greatly enhancing the precision of making selections.

Figure 12.8

The Quick Mask left) and the selection that results when you click on the Standard Mode icon (right).

▲**Figure C1** A photograph altered to look like a painting using Photoshop's brushes and filters [Chapter 1]
▼**Figure C2** A raster image composed of pixels (left) and a vector version of the same image (right), composed of shapes constructed from Bezier curves [Chapter 3]

▲**Figure C3** Paul Signac, *The Port at Sunset*
[Chapter 1]
▶**Figure C4** Detail of a four-color process
image. The Pointillist movement influenced
the development of the four-color process.
[Chapter 1]

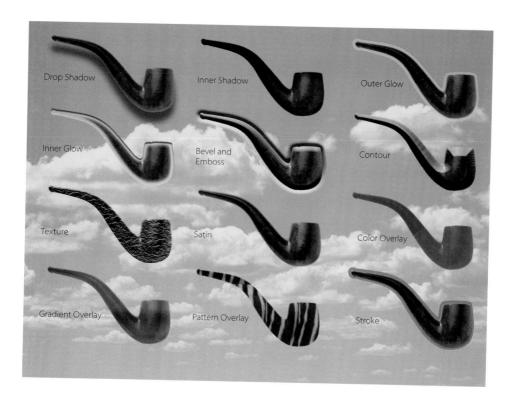

▲**Figure C5** Layer Styles applied to the pipe [Chapter 7]
▼**Figure C6** Examples of blending modes applied to an image [Chapter 7]

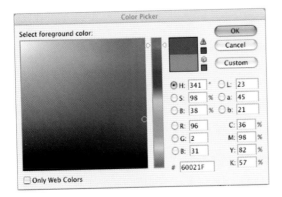

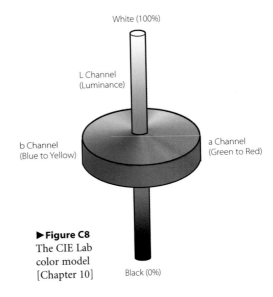

◀ **Figure C7** The Color Picker [Chapter 10]

▶ **Figure C8** The CIE Lab color model [Chapter 10]

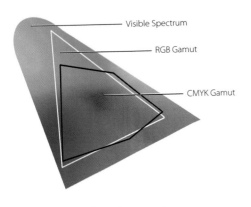

▲ **Figure C9** A schematic comparison of the gamut of visible, RGB, and CMYK colors [Chapter 10]

▶ **Figure C10** The RGB (left) and CMYK (right) color models [Chapter 10]

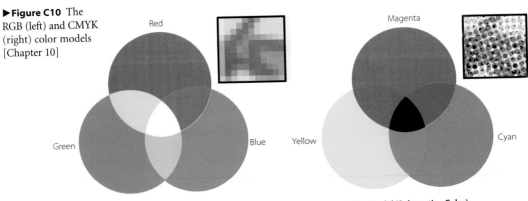

▲**Figure C11a** The original image from which a snapshot has been taken [Chapter 11]

▲**Figure C11b** The image after a Hue/Saturation adjustment

▲**Figure C11c** Portions of the image have been painted back to the original with the snapshot

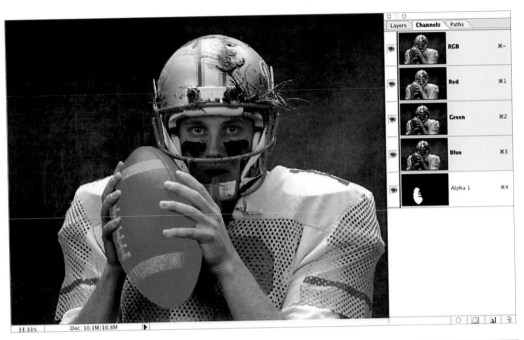

▲**Figure C12** An alpha channel can be displayed on the image as a mask by activating its visibility icon in the Channels palette. [Chapter 12]
▼**Figure C13** Painting on the alpha channel (left) alters the selection when the channel is loaded. [Chapter 12]

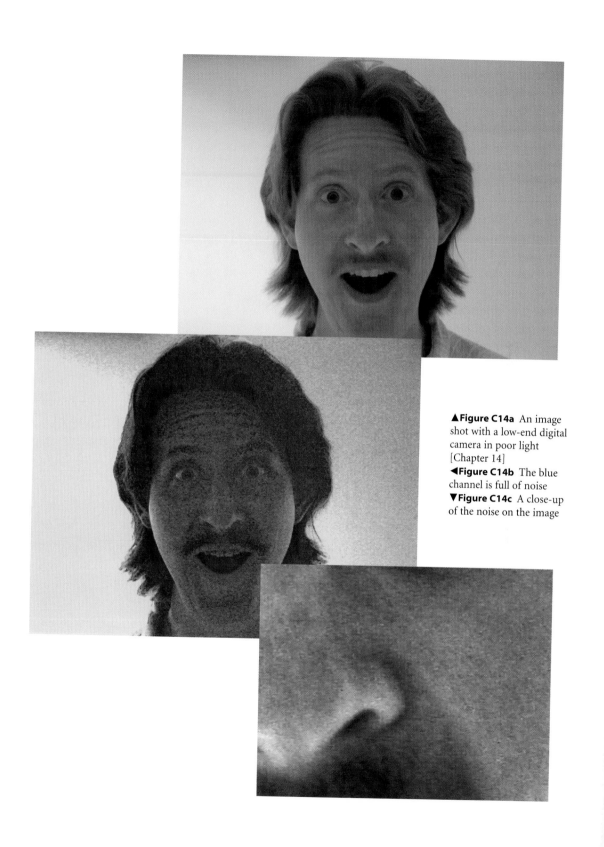

▲**Figure C14a** An image shot with a low-end digital camera in poor light [Chapter 14]
◀**Figure C14b** The blue channel is full of noise
▼**Figure C14c** A close-up of the noise on the image

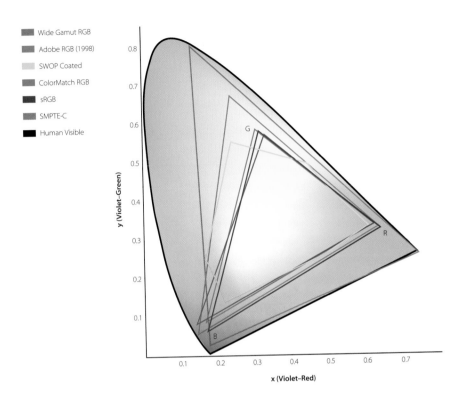

Wide Gamut RGB

Adobe RGB (1998)

SWOP Coated

ColorMatch RGB

sRGB

SMPTE-C

Human Visible

y (Violet–Green)

x (Violet–Red)

▲**Figure C15** The color gamuts of various working spaces [Chapter 15]
◄**Figure C16** This Learjet airplane needs more contrast. [Chapter 16]
▶**Figure C17** After Levels adjustment, the Learjet's contrast is significantly improved. [Chapter 16]

▲**Figure C18** The results of applying a Cooling Filter 80 to an image with a yellow color cast [Chapter 16]
▼**Figure C19** The Shadow/Highlight command applied to a backlit image produces more detail in the shadow areas. [Chapter 16]

▲**Figure C20** The color match workaround applies hue and saturation modifications to the yellow die, resulting in a perfect match. [Chapter 17]

▼**Figure C21** A grayscale image can be colorized by first changing its mode to RGB and then applying hue, saturation, and lightness adjustments. [Chapter 17]

▲**Figure C22** The new Match Color command enables you to sample color from one document, layer, or selection and to apply that color to another document, layer, or selection.[Chapter 17]

◀**Figure C23** Before and after applying the Equalize command [Chapter 17]

▲**Figure C24** The original image (top) remapped to threshold levels of 85, 128, and 200 (bottom, left to right) [Chapter 17]

▲**Figure C25** The original image [Chapter 17]
◄**Figure C26** The posterization workaround lets you control the number of colors in your posterized image. [Chapter 17]

▲**Figure C27a** The original image [Chapter 17]
▼**Figure C27b** The image with the gradient map applied [Chapter 17]

Figure C28 These four images illustrate how Duotones can affect the mood of a photograph. [Chapter 18]

▲**Figure C29a** The spot color applied
over a knockout [Chapter 18]
▶**Figure C29b** The spot color has been
applied directly over the image.
▼**Figure C29c** The spot color with tonal
variations applied over a knockout

▲**Figure C30a** The original image [Chapter 20]

▲**Figure C30b** Mezzotint, Grainy Dots

▲**Figure C30c** Pointillize

▲**Figure C30d** Crystallize

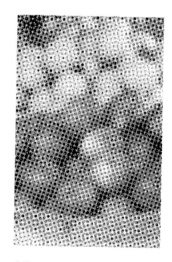

▲**Figure C30e** Color Halftone

▲**Figure C31a** The effect of the Trace Contour [Chapter 20]
▶**Figure C31b** Glowing Edges
▼**Figure C31c** Find Edges

▲**Figure C32** The final Electric Telephone image with the lightning clipped and modeled with the layer mask [Chapter 22]
◀**Figure C33** On the top is the original N.Y. poster image; on the bottom is the image after its colors have been edited using the Replace Color command [Chapter 17]

◀**Figure C34a** The original image [Chapter 20]

▲**Figure C34b** The Artistic → Watercolor effect

▲**Figure C34c** The Artistic → Palette Knife effect

▲**Figure C34d** The Sketch → Crosshatch effect

▲**Figure C34e** The Sketch → Ink outlines effect

◀**Figure C35** The shadowless cat [Chapter 22]
▶**Figure C36** The cat with the cast shadow set to 40% opacity [Chapter 22]

◀**Figure C37** The completed Uninvited Guest image [Chapter 22]

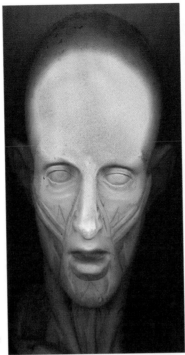

◀**Figure C38a** The original image [Chapter 20]
▶**Figure C38b** Light source from below

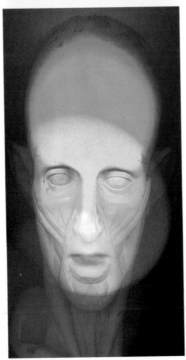

▶**Figure C38c** RGB lights

◄**Figure C39a** The original Apples image [Chapter 24]

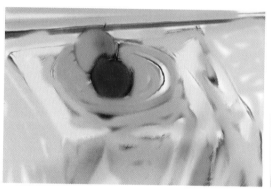

▲**Figure C39b** The broadly painted source

▲**Figure C39c** Subtract mode at 50% opacity

▲**Figure C39d** Multiply mode at 50% opacity

▲**Figure C39e** Exclusion mode at 100% opacity

▲**Figure C40** The beginning pieces for the Fred Photato Head project [Hands On 1]
▶**Figure C41** The completed Fred Photato Head [Hands On 1]

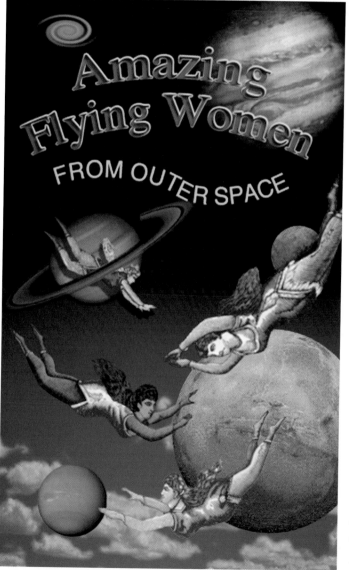

▲**Figure C42** The beginning Flying Women file showing the content of the poster [Hands On 2]

◀**Figure C43** The completed Flying Women poster [Hands On 2]

▲**Figure C44** The original seahorse starts with a piece of line art. [Hands On 3]

▲**Figure C45** Our line-art character will develop a bit more personality after a Photoshop paint job. [Hands On 3]

◄**Figure C46** The original chickens, standing around [Hands On 4]

▲**Figure C47** If an area is predominantly red, it helps to change the color of the mask. [Hands On 4]
◄**Figure C48** The chickens in motion [Hands On 4]

▲**Figure C49** The beginning Big City Night image is in need of cropping, rotating, and color correction. [Hands On 5]

▼**Figure C50** The completed Big City Night image shows remarkable improvement. [Hands On 5]

▲**Figure C51** The beginning Sun God image
[Hands On 6]
◄**Figure C52** The completed Sun God image
is a Tritone with a spot color graphic and type.
[Hands On 6]

▲**Figure C53** The original image lacks rich colors and appears flat. [Chapter 24]

▲**Figure C54** Stacking layers with similar content and applying a blending mode and opacity and fill adjustments can greatly enhance an image's contrast and color. [Chapter 24]

▲**Figure C55** The beginning image needs restoration. [Hands On 7]
▶**Figure C56** The completed image after restoration [Hands On 7]

▲**Figure C57** The beginning Flamingo Hotel image with its Layers palette [Hands On 8]

▲**Figure C58** The finished Flamingo Hotel showing all of its guests [Hands On 8]

▲**Figure C59** The finished Ballet Bleu homepage [Hands On 9]

Channels

The goal of this project is to learn important techniques that enable you to make, store, and edit selections as alpha channels. You'll begin by selecting a region of an image with the manual selection tools (you've had plenty of practice making selections in Hands On 1). Then, using Quick Mask, you'll refine the selection to a high degree of accuracy. Next, you'll save the selection as an alpha channel, duplicate it, and apply a fill that will greatly alter its capabilities. Finally, you'll apply a Photoshop filter through the new selection to give the image movement and life.

Getting Started

Discard your preferences file before beginning this Hands On exercise. The "Modifying Photoshop's Settings" section in Chapter 5, "Setting Up Photoshop," details how to reset your preferences to Photoshop's defaults. After you have launched Photoshop with default preferences, open the file Chickens_in_Motion_start.psd in the H04 folder on the *Photoshop CS Savvy* CD. Save the file to your disk. Figures H4.1 and H4.2 show the before and after images (for a color version, check Figures C46 and C48 in the color section).

Figure H4.1

The original chickens, motionless

Figure H4.2

The chickens in motion

Selecting the Chickens

You'll start by selecting the white surface of the chickens' bodies. Follow these steps to begin:

1. Choose the Magic Wand tool  from the Tool palette or press the W key. Set the tolerance to 32. Click on any white area on the chickens. In the Options bar, click the Add To Selection icon and click again. Continue this process until a portion of the background is selected.

2. Because the colors of the chickens are within the tolerance of the areas surrounding them, it is impossible to isolate them without also selecting the background. Deselect.

3. Again, click the lightest area of a chicken with the Magic Wand tool. Click the Add To Selection icon in the toolbar and continue to select the lightest areas. Select as much as you can, without selecting the background. When the selection marquee extends onto the background, press ⌘/Ctrl-Z to undo that step (see Figure H4.3).

4. Click the Quick Mask icon in the Tool palette or press Q. By default, what you've selected becomes the unmasked areas in the Quick Mask.

5. Select the Paintbrush. Click the Reverse Colors icon in the Tool palette, or press X, so that white is the foreground color. Choose a brush from the Brush Preset menu. I chose a 50-point Hard brush to erase the red transparent color on the chickens, and smaller brushes as I erased closer to the edges. If you make a mistake and paint outside the edge, reverse the colors so that black is the foreground color, and paint out the mistake.

Figure H4.3

Select the chicken parts by selecting the lightest areas of the chickens first.

Figure H4.4

Selecting the wall

6. When you get to the chickens' red combs, it becomes difficult to see where to erase the red color. Change the color of the mask by double-clicking the Quick Mask thumbnail in the Channels palette. In the Quick Mask Options dialog box, click the swatch, choose a green color from the Color Picker, and click OK. (See Figure C47 in the color section for a comparison of a red and a green mask.)

7. Reduce the opacity of the Quick Mask to 30% for a better view of the background.

8. Erase the mask from the chickens and their legs with the Paintbrush tool, using white as a foreground color.

9. After you've completed that selection, choose the Lasso tool and select the wall they are standing on (as in Figure H4.4) and the parts of their feet that extend upward slightly from the wall.

10. Be sure that white is the foreground color. Press Option-Delete (Mac) or Alt-Backspace (Win) to delete the green mask from the wall area. Press ⌘-D/Ctrl-D to deselect.

11. When the Quick Mask of the chickens is complete, click the Edit in Standard Mode icon, or press Q, to convert the mask into a selection.

12. Save the document.

Saving and Cleaning Up the Alpha Channel

Follow these steps to repair and save your selection as an alpha channel:

1. Click the Save Selection As Channel icon ![icon] in the Channels palette to quickly save the selection. A thumbnail labeled Alpha 1 appears in the palette. Deselect.

2. Click the thumbnail to display the alpha channel in the image window. Notice that there are some flaws—areas that you missed or edges that are not sharp (see Figure H4.5). Choose the Paintbrush, choose white as a foreground color, and paint out the flaws in the white area of the alpha channel.

3. While making repairs to the edges, you might want to see the image. Click the eye icon next to the RGB composite channel to reveal the image and the alpha channel at the same time.

4. When the alpha channel is complete, save the document (File → Save or ⌘/Ctrl-S).

Figure H4.5

The flaws in the alpha channel

Duplicating and Modifying the Channel

Follow these steps to copy and edit the alpha channel:

1. Drag the Alpha 1 channel to the New Channel icon at the bottom of the Channels palette to duplicate it. The new channel is named Alpha 1 Copy.

2. Choose Image → Adjustments → Invert to reverse the colors of the channel, making the black areas of the channel white and the white areas black (see Figure H4.6).

3. Double-click the channel thumbnail. Name it **Gradient Mask**.

Figure H4.6

The inverted alpha channel

Figure H4.7

Drag the gradient on the inverted alpha channel.

Figure H4.8

The completed Gradient Mask channel

4. The Gradient Mask channel should be targeted. Click and drag the Gradient Mask channel to the Load Selection icon  at the bottom of the Channels palette to select the white area of the alpha channel. You can also select the white area by clicking it with the Magic Wand tool.

5. Press the D and then the X key to make the foreground color black and the background color white (or click the Switch Colors double-arrow icon on the Tool palette swatches). Choose the Gradient tool and click the Radial option in the Options bar. Click and drag from the center out toward the edge of the document to modify the areas surrounding the chickens with a gradient, as in Figure H4.7. Your alpha channel should then look like Figure H4.8. Deselect.

Filtering and Adjusting the Selection

Now you'll apply a filter and an adjustment through the selection to affect the image. To filter and adjust your selection:

1. Click the RGB composite channel to target it.

2. Load the Gradient Mask channel by dragging it to the Load Selection icon at the bottom of the Channels palette. Your image should look like Figure H4.9.

3. Choose Filter → Blur → Radial Blur, set these options, and then click OK:

Amount	100
Blur Method	Zoom
Quality	Best

4. For added movement apply the filter again with the same specifications by pressing ⌘/Ctrl-F.

5. You'll want to further enhance the image by adjusting its brightness through the Gradient Mask channel. Target the RGB composite channel. With the Gradient Mask channel still loaded, choose Image → Adjustments → Auto Levels. Apply this operation a second time. Then choose Edit → Fade Auto Levels. Move the slider to mitigate the second application of the effect.

6. Deselect (⌘/Ctrl-D) and save (⌘/Ctrl-S).

Figure H4.9

The loaded selection

CHAPTER 13

Sizing and Transforming Images

Photoshop documents can be resized and transformed in several ways. An image can be enlarged by adding new solid-colored pixels or reduced by cropping out unwanted areas from its edges. An image can also be made smaller or larger by resampling. When you reduce the size of an image in this way, you discard pixels from the image content. When you resample to enlarge an image, you add new pixels. All of these operations can significantly affect the look of the final published work. This chapter will examine issues related to image size and will help you best determine the methods to choose when capturing, sizing, and transforming an image to achieve optimal results.

This chapter will help you understand:

- **Resolution and image size**
- **The Crop tool**
- **Canvas size**
- **The Resize Image Assistant/Wizard**
- **Transformation operations**

What Is Resolution?

Resolution determines the quality of an image and the amount of detail that can be displayed or printed. There are several important terms relating to resolution that you should know:

Image resolution The number of pixels that occupy a linear inch of a digital image, usually measured in pixels per inch (ppi).

Monitor resolution The number of pixels that occupy a linear inch of a monitor screen (72 ppi for most Macintosh RGB monitors, 96 ppi for Windows VGA monitors). This resolution never changes, as it represents the physical matrix of the monitor.

Image size The height, width, and resolution of an image.

Printer resolution The number of dots that can be printed per linear inch, measured in dots per inch (dpi). These dots compose larger halftone dots on a halftone screen or stochastic (random pattern) dots on an ink-jet printer.

Halftone screen The dot density of a printed image, measured in lines per inch (lpi) or, in rare instances, lines per centimeter (lpc). A halftone screen is a grid of dots. The tonality of a printed image is determined by the size of the dot within the specific matrix. Table 13.1, later in the chapter, lists some standard values.

Optical systems enable us to capture and organize visible light. Each type of optical system breaks up light in its own unique system of units. Though each system determines resolution differently, the more information that can be collected or printed, the better the quality of the image. Let's take a look at reality through several optical systems and see how they work.

The Human Eye

Probably the most perfect optical device is the human eye. Our eyes collect light through a lens called the *cornea* and focus it on a light-sensitive field called the *retina*. Color and tonal information are transmitted through the optic nerve and interpreted by the brain into a completely continuous-tone reality. When an image is *continuous-tone,* there are no visible divisions between colors and shades. Our eyes enable us to see reality as a seamless fabric of color and form. The closer we look at something, the more detail we perceive.

DPI VS. PPI VS. LPI

The terms *dots per inch (dpi)*, *pixels per inch (ppi)* and *lines per inch (lpi)* are often confused. Manufacturers often refer to the resolution capabilities of their scanners in dpi, but a scanner creates pixels and a printer prints dots. In this book, I use *ppi* when referring to pixel resolution from a scanned image or digital camera, or on a monitor. I use *dpi* when I refer to the output of a printer, and *lines per inch (lpi)* for the screen frequency of a halftone screen.

The Traditional Camera

The traditional camera is a mechanical replica of the human eye. It, too, collects light through a lens and focuses it on a light-sensitive field—but this field is made of film or paper coated with chemicals called *emulsions* that, when developed, respond to light. The grain of the emulsion determines the maximum visual depth of the image. Photographic grains are microscopic, which enables photographic images to be produced at exceptionally high quality. Even though photographs are described as continuous-tone in the industry, when a photograph is enlarged too much, its grains become visible, which can diminish its quality.

Scanners and Digital Cameras

The scanner and digital camera are two other optical devices that "see" tonality and color. In Chapter 14, "Image Capture and Digital Photography," I discuss how these devices work in more detail. Suffice it to say that scanners and digital cameras collect red, green, and blue color information and interpret it into pixels. Like all digital information, these pixels are assigned numbers that identify their color content. A computer is needed to decipher these values. A video card and monitor are necessary to display them. Because the image is constructed of individual units of color, it is a mosaic of colored squares. Each pixel is like an individual building block. The more pixels contained within the image, the more information there is, and hence, the more detail that can be displayed (see Figure 13.1).

Should a pixel-based digital image be considered continuous-tone or not? That's a matter of ongoing debate in the industry. One of the best discussions of this issue can be found at www.deluxacademy.com/articles/digitalphoto/contone.html.

Figure 13.1

Identical images at different resolutions: the image at 30 ppi (left) and the image at 300 ppi (right)

	VALUE	DEFINITION
Table 13.1 **Typical Halftone Screen Frequencies**	60 lpi	This value produces a coarse halftone screen, suggested for screen printing.
	85 lpi	This value works well for newsprint and porous paper stock.
	133 lpi	This value produces finer detail. It's used on web presses for printing medium-quality weekly magazines, books, and other jobs on uncoated paper.
	150–175 lpi	These frequencies are suitable for brochures, pamphlets, and commercial printing on coated stock.
	200–300 lpi	These values produce the finest images with lots of detail and color depth. You might use this option when creating annual reports or fine art prints.

Halftone Screens

Printing an image with ink on paper presents a unique set of problems. How does a mechanical device such as a printer communicate tonality to a flat piece of paper? Because the printer must distribute ink, it needs a method that will portray the tonal range without smearing the ink. To accomplish this task, printing technologies divide the ink into individual dots on a grid called a *halftone screen*. On traditional halftone screens used for black-and-white images, the size of the dots determines the darkness or lightness of an area (see Figure 13.2). Areas on the screen that contain larger dots are darker than areas with smaller dots (which enable more of the paper to show through, providing a lighter perceived tone).

Figure 13.2

A halftone screen, enlarged to show tonal density

With full-color images, four different-colored halftone screens called *color separations*—one each of cyan, magenta, yellow, and black—are used. These colors combined in varying densities on the screens can produce a full range of color. The finer the halftone screen, the more detail can be displayed. The line frequency of the halftone screen is determined by the type of printing that is being performed. Table 13.1 lists common line frequencies used in various types of printing.

> Screen frequencies higher than 200 lpi are not as common as 175 lpi or less. The physical demands of printing finer screen rulings often prohibit their successful use. To avoid difficulties, ask your print shop early in the process about stock requirements and other details related to the choice of screen frequency.

Ink-Jet Printers

Some ink-jet printers produce colored dots similar to a halftone screen when viewed from a distance. These ink-jet printers, however, use a *stochastic*, or *frequency modulated*, screen to produce tonality. A traditional halftone screen is a grid with a fixed number of lines. The size of the dots within the grid varies, which produces variations in color and tone. A stochastic screen, however, deposits dots of a uniform size. Instead of the size of the dot, it is the number and distribution of dots that determine tonal value and color density (see Figure 13.3).

Figure 13.3

A stochastic screen, enlarged to show tonal density

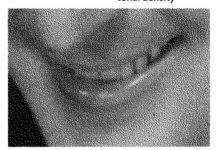

Image Resolution vs. Monitor Resolution

Image resolution refers to the number of pixels per linear inch collected at the scanner or digital camera. The *monitor resolution* is a fixed matrix of pixels. When an image with the same resolution as the monitor is displayed at actual size, it appears at its actual physical size, because at 100%, one image pixel equals one monitor pixel. If the image has a higher resolution, it will appear larger than its physical size. For example, a $4' \times 5'$ image that is 288 ppi will appear four times larger at 100% than an image that is $4' \times 5'$ at 72 ppi ($288 = 4 \times 72$). If you copy and paste (or drag and drop) an image that is the same physical size but a lower resolution to a document of higher resolution, the pasted image will reduce in physical size (see Figure 13.4).

To see a preview of the printed size of an image, choose Print Size from Photoshop's View menu. The image displays at the size at which it will print, no matter what its resolution.

Determining Resolution

As noted earlier the physical *size* of an image is its height and width when printed. Its *resolution* is the number of pixels that occupy a linear inch of a digital image, measured in pixels per inch (ppi). You determine this resolution when you scan an image or shoot a digital photo at a given setting.

To acquire sufficient information to produce good-quality images from your high-resolution imagesetter or laser printer, scan your images at 1.5 to 2 times the screen frequency of the halftone screen you will use for printing (again, see Table 13.1 for common halftone screen frequencies). That means if your image is going to be printed in a newspaper or in a newsletter, scan it anywhere from 128 to 170 pixels per inch (1.5 or 2 × 85 lines per inch). If your image will be printed in a glossy magazine, scan your image at 225 to 300 ppi (1.5 or 2 × 150 lpi). The image size should be scanned at 100% of the size it will be printed.

Figure 13.4

The small monkey was dragged and dropped from a 72 ppi file that was 6' wide by 7.2' high onto a file that was the same physical size but with a resolution four times greater, or 288 ppi.

Should you use 1.5 or 2? Whether to use the higher or lower setting depends on the content of the image. If you are scanning images of big puffy clouds, for example, where the content is intrinsically soft, use the lower setting to decrease file size. If sharpness is critical to your image, then scan at the higher setting.

If you're going to print only to desktop ink-jet printers,, I recommend that you scan your images at a minimum of one-third the desired print resolution. For example, for a print resolution of 720 dpi, set the scan resolution to 240 ppi or higher. If you are going to increase the size of the printed image, then you should scan at a higher resolution. This equates to common scan resolutions of 120 ppi, 240 ppi, and 480 ppi—although anything over 360 ppi is probably overkill. If you scan a picture at 600 ppi and print it at 300 dpi, you can increase its physical size by a factor of two without compromising its quality.

When scanning for output to high resolution inkjet, large format giclée or RGB printers, always consult the documentation or the service provider for the desired resolution.

Line art or bitmap content is different. Ideally, scan at the same resolution as the printer's dpi resolution or in evenly divisible units of the printer's resolution. For example, you would scan at 360 ppi for a 1440 dpi print.

Exceeding the optical resolution of a scanner is essentially the same as resampling up in Photoshop. It will produce less than desirable results. For best results, don't exceed the scanner's optical resolution.

Resampling Image Resolution

The image resolution and the physical size of an image are interchangeable values. For example, an image that is 4′ × 5′ at 72 ppi has the same amount of information as an image that is 2′ × 2.5′ at 144 ppi. Therefore, you can enlarge the physical size of an image with no loss of quality if you reduce its resolution. To perform this operation, follow these steps:

Figure 13.5

The Image Size dialog box

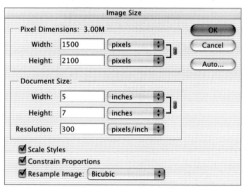

1. Open the file little_monkey.psd in the Chapter 13 folder on the CD.

2. Choose Image → Image Size. The Image Size dialog box appears (see Figure 13.5). The image is 3′ wide and 4.18′ high, and has a resolution of 300 ppi.

3. Clear the Resample Image check box, which also clears the Constrain Proportions check box and grays out the option.

4. Enter a new value into the Resolution field. In this example, change the resolution from 300 ppi to 150 ppi, decreasing the resolution of the image by half but doubling its physical size to 6′ × 8.36′.

5. Click OK to apply the changes.

When you clear the Resample Image option and change the resolution, your image retains the same quantity of pixels and its height and width change proportionally to accommodate the new resolution.

In contrast, resampling changes the image resolution and/or physical size by adding or deleting pixels. When you resample down, you discard pixels. When you resample up, you create new pixels.

To use this feature, check the Resample Image box in the Image → Image Size dialog and pick from one of the five predefined interpolation sizing algorithms. In previous versions of Photoshop, the first three algorithms—Nearest Neighbor, Bilinear, or Bicubic—produced a loss of sharpness and dulling of color when an image was resampled up (that is, enlarged; see Figure 13.6). Although it is always better to scan an image at the size and resolution that the image will be output, two new interpolation algorithms—Bicubic Smoother and Bicubic Sharper—have been added to the Image Size dialog that help reduce the diminished quality of enlargements (see Figure 13.7). Each of these choices determines how Photoshop adds or removes pixels from your image:

Nearest Neighbor evaluates an adjacent pixel. Use this option for line art, desktop icons, software interface screen captures, or any time that anti-aliasing creates artifacts.

Bilinear averages the four surrounding pixels, immediately above, below, and on either side for smoother transitions.

Bicubic averages the eight closest neighbors and adds a sharpening effect to increase the contrast.

Figure 13.6
A comparison of an image scanned at 288 ppi (left) and one scanned at 72 ppi and resampled up to 288 ppi (right) by using the standard Bilinear interpolation algorithm. Note the loss of detail and the softening of edges.

Figure 13.7

A close-up of the same image scanned at 72 ppi and resampled up to 288 ppi by using the Bilinear Smoother (left) and Bilinear Sharper (right) algorithms

Bicubic Smoother slightly blurs the edges of areas to produce the most contrast when it adds pixels for a more sublimated continuous-tone look.

Bicubic Sharper Does a better job of increasing the size and enhances edge contrast. Both of these new methods require much less time than third-party plug-ins, but for best results, you should experiment and compare.

A third-party plug-in called Genuine Fractals also does a decent job of resampling images up with a minimum loss of quality. Developed by Altamira and now available through LizardTech, www.lizardtech.com/products, it comes in several versions for different purposes.

The default interpolation settings are found under Edit → Preferences → General. The default interpolation is also active when using transformation commands such as Edit → Free Transform or Edit → Transform → Distort And Perspective, several of the distortion filters such as Spherize or Pinch, and the Crop tool when cropping to size.

Constraining Proportions

When you enable the Resample Image feature, you have the option to constrain the image's proportions. When selected, the Constrain Proportions check box ensures that image height will vary proportionately with the width. If you change one dimension, the other will automatically update to preserve the dimensional relationship. When you deselect this option, the link between height and width disappears, and you can increase the height or width independently. Your image, in this case, will stretch disproportionately vertically or horizontally.

You can turn off Constrain Proportions only when the Resample Image box is checked. Without resampling, proportions remain automatically constrained, as shown by the link icon.

Scaling Styles

This new feature enables you to choose whether or not to scale layer styles. When you have the Scale Styles option checked, layer styles that are assigned to the image will be resized proportionately. Unchecking this box results in the layer styles maintaining their original dimensions.

Applying Auto Resolution

You can automatically size an image for output to a specific halftone screen. Click the Auto button in the Image Size dialog box to display the Auto Resolution dialog box (Figure 13.8). Type a screen value. (see Table 13.1 to determine which halftone screen is most suitable). Choose a quality. Draft resamples an image at the same resolution as the halftone screen. Good resamples at 1.5 times the halftone screen and Best resamples at 2 times the halftone screen. This feature does not affect the height and width of the image.

Figure 13.8
The Auto Resolution dialog box

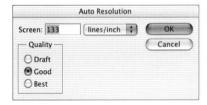

Getting Help with Resizing Images

Photoshop provides the Resize Image Assistant (Macintosh) or Wizard (Windows) to help you determine the best possible options for size and resolution. When you use the Resize Image Assistant/Wizard, Photoshop duplicates your document. The operation has no effect on the original.

This interactive tool, seen in Figure 13.9, guides you through the entire process of resizing your image:

Figure 13.9
Resize Image Assistant

1. Choose Help → Resize Image and wait for the Resize Image Assistant/Wizard window to appear.

2. Choose Print or Online, depending on how you will use the image. Then click Next.

   When preparing an image for online use, you need only enter specifications for the height or width in pixels because the proportions are constrained. Photoshop will automatically resize the image to these specifications, which completes the Online process.

3. If you're resizing an image for print, set the new image height or width in the desired units. You can choose from inches, centimeters, points, picas, and columns. These values are proportionately constrained. Click Next.

4. Choose a halftone screen frequency. You can choose from common line screen (lpi) values for standard applications or you can enter a custom value. The Description field explains the purpose of each value. Click Next.

5. Set the image quality level for the image by moving the slider between 1× and 2×. *Image quality level* refers to the proportion between the final image resolution and the screen frequency you picked in the previous step. The higher the number, the better the image quality and the larger the file size. When you pick a value between 1.5 and 2 times the screen frequency, you're assured of creating images at the highest quality the printer can produce. Because you include more information, the printer can create smoother and more natural transitions. The Results area below the slider displays the file size of the original image, the file size of the new image, and the pixels per inch that will be produced. Click Next.

6. Wait for Photoshop to complete the transformation. When the confirmation dialog box appears, click Finish.

Using the Crop Tool

Sometimes the best way to resize your image is to eliminate part of it. The Crop tool  enables you to trim your images precisely. (You can also select an area with the Rectangular Marquee or Elliptical Marquee tool and then choose Image → Crop, but with the marquees, you sacrifice the flexibility and control of the Crop tool's features.) The Crop tool is found in the default Tool palette, on the left column in the third row.

To perform a basic crop with the Crop tool, open the `mandrill.psd` file from the `Ch13` folder on the CD and follow these steps:

1. Choose Image Duplicate to make a copy of the image.

2. Choose the Crop tool from the Tool palette.

3. You'll crop the black border out of the picture. Drag the mouse to define the bounding box. As you can see in Figure 13.10, the area outside the crop will darken, highlighting your selection.

4. Fine-tune the bounding box interactively. Use the handles to encompass more or less of the image, and move the bounding box by placing the cursor inside its boundaries and dragging.

> Pressing the Shift key will constrain the crop bounding box proportions. As you drag from a corner point, the opposite corner point will retain its position on the image. Pressing the Option/Alt key will constrain the crop bounding box proportions as you drag from a corner point, but the point of origin in the center of the box will retain its position. You can reposition the point of origin by clicking and dragging it.

5. To implement the crop, click the Commit (check mark) button 🚫 ✔ in the Options bar or press Return (Mac) or Enter (Win). You can also double-click inside the cropping area to commit your crop. Figure 13.11 shows the result of applying the crop. If you decide to cancel the crop, press the Esc key or click the Cancel button.

> You can turn the crop shield on and off by checking or clearing the Shield Color box in the Crop tool Options bar. Choose a color for the shield by clicking the swatch to display the Color Picker. Click the arrow in the Opacity box, and drag the slider or type a numerical value for the opacity of the shield.

Rotating a Crop

One of the Crop tool's most useful features enables you to crop down to a *rotated* area. To practice simultaneously cropping and rotating an image, start, as earlier, by opening the `mandrill.psd` file from your CD. Then follow these steps:

1. Choose Image Duplicate to make a copy of the image.

2. Choose the Crop tool from the Tool palette, and define your initial crop area, just as in Figure 13.10 in the previous procedure.

3. Move your mouse just outside any of the corner selection handles until the cursor changes to the curved rotation icon.

   The Crop Rotation option becomes active when the cursor is anywhere outside the crop selection; when the cursor is too close to the bounding box, a Crop Bounding Box Resize icon will appear.

4. Drag the mouse to rotate the bounding box (see Figure 13.12). Make further adjustments by dragging any of the handles until you're satisfied with the new, rotated crop.

5. As before, click the Commit (check mark) icon in the Options bar. Photoshop crops the image and rotates it (see Figure 13.13).

Cropping to Size

With the Crop tool, you can trim your image to a fixed size and new interpolated resolution by entering values for the height, width, and resolution. The Crop bounding box automatically constrains to your specified image size. Here are the steps:

1. Duplicate the mandrill.psd file again. Choose the Crop tool from the Tool palette.

2. Locate the Width and Height fields in the Options bar. Enter **6** inches for the width, **4** inches for the height, and **72** (ppi) for the resolution (see Figure 13.14).

Figure 13.10

After you define the initial cropped area, the borders outside the Crop bounding box will darken. Use the handles to fine-tune the bounding box.

Figure 13.11

Applying a crop removes all areas outside the bounding box.

3. Click the arrows between the width and height fields to reverse the width and height values. The height is now 6 inches and the width is 4 inches.

3. Drag the bounding box. It will automatically be constrained within the proportions that you entered in the Width and Height fields. No matter what part of the mandrill the bounding box encompasses, its contents will be 4′ wide by 6′ high and 72 ppi when the crop is applied. You can still rotate the bounding box as described previously.

4. Commit your change (click the check mark icon in the Options bar or press Return/Enter) to finish cropping your image.

Most cropping is usually performed with the Width, Height, and Resolution fields left blank. The Clear button on the Options bar will clear the number fields so that no resampling takes place. The Front Image button on the Options bar fills the current active document's width/height/resolution into the number fields.

The Crop tool can be used to increase the size of a cropped area if the height and width values entered are greater than the original size.

Figure 13.12

With the Crop tool, you can rotate the bounding box to encompass a diagonal area.

Figure 13.13

The resulting crop, after rotation and cropping

Figure 13.14

The Crop Options bar

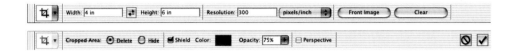

Using Perspective Cropping

After you've drawn a Crop marquee, the Options bar presents several additional options. The Perspective option enables you to adjust the corner anchor points of the bounding box independently. This feature is useful if you want to distort an image as you crop it or to fit an image's content into a rectangular document of a specific size. When you implement the crop, the image area will distort to conform to the new document's height and width (see the examples in Figures 13.15 and 13.16).

Trimming an Image

The Trim command automatically eliminates edge pixels of a specific color to quickly refine the edges of an image. To trim an image, follow these steps:

Figure 13.15

The Perspective crop option lets you crop an irregular shape into a rectangle.

1. Duplicate the mandrill.psd image again.

2. Choose Image → Trim. The Trim dialog box appears (see Figure 13.17).

3. In the Based on field, click the Top Left or Bottom Right Pixel Color radio button. If the image has a transparent edge that you want trimmed, click the Transparent edge radio button. In the Trim Away field, check all four boxes to trim the entire black rectangular border from all four sides.

4. Click OK. The entire border is removed, and the image is cropped to a new size.

Sizing the Canvas

The Canvas Size command produces more space around the image and more pixels to work with. When you apply this feature to an image that has a Background, by default, the new canvas is filled with the background color specified in the Tool palette. If there is no Background, the new canvas extension will be transparent.

Figure 13.16

The image after perspective cropping

Choose Image → Canvas Size to access the dialog box that enables you to expand or shrink your canvas (see Figure 13.18).

The Current Size area displays the file size and the width and height of the image. Type a new width and/or height value in the New Size area. Check the Relative box and type the width and height amounts you want to add to an existing canvas. You can work in any of eight units: percent, pixels, inches, centimeters, millimeters, points, picas, or columns.

The anchor grid controls where the new canvas will be added. Click the center cell, and the canvas will grow on all sides. Click any of the cells on the edges of the grid to anchor the existing image. The arrows point to where the new canvas will be added.

New to Photoshop CS (finally!) is the capability to choose a Canvas Extension color from within the dialog box. Choose Foreground or Background color to apply either color specified in the tool palette, or White, Black, or Gray from the predefined color menu. You can choose a color from the Color Picker by clicking on the swatch to the right of the menu or by choosing Other from the list. When the Color Picker is displayed, you can sample colors from the image by dragging over it.

In the following example, you will expand your canvas a couple of different ways. Open `rhinoroom` `.psd` from the `Ch13` folder on the CD. First, let's add some canvas to the image, which will produce an even, white border around the image and more space on which to work.

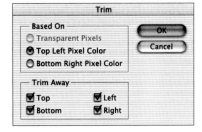

Figure 13.17
The Trim dialog box

1. Choose Image → Canvas Size.

2. Check the Relative box and enter **2** in the Height and Width fields. Click on the center box to anchor the image to the center.

3. Click the swatch next to the Canvas extension color menu, and choose a color from the Color Picker or choose a predefined color from the list.

4. As an alternative, anchor the image to the bottom-left corner. Enter the same Relative values and click the lower-left box. The results are shown in Figure 13.19.

Figure 13.18
The Canvas Size dialog box

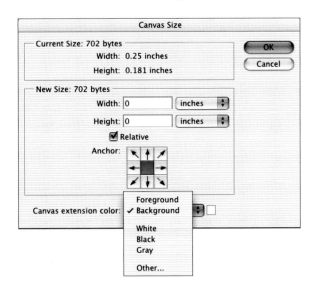

Figure 13.19

Expanding the canvas produces new areas around the image. On the left is the original image. The middle image was anchored in the center and canvas added evenly around it. On the right, the image was anchored at the bottom-left corner.

Rotating the Canvas

To rotate the entire image rather than a single layer or selection, use the Rotate Canvas commands. These menu options, which are found under Image → Rotate Canvas, will reorient your entire document:

180° rotates the image so that it appears upside-down. The image retains its left-to-right orientation.

90° CW rotates the canvas by 90 degrees in a clockwise direction.

90° CCW rotates the canvas by 90 degrees in a counterclockwise direction.

Arbitrary displays the Rotate Canvas dialog box (see Figure 13.20). Specify a precise angle by entering a number in the Angle field, choose CW or CCW (clockwise or counterclockwise), and click OK.

Flip Canvas Horizontal mirrors the image across the vertical axis. Each pixel will mirror horizontally, so items from the right will appear on the left and vice versa. Writing and other features will appear reversed.

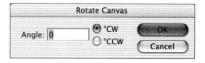

Figure 13.20

The Rotate Canvas dialog box

Flip Canvas Vertical mirrors your image across the horizontal axis with vertical mirroring. Do not confuse this menu option with 180-degree rotation. This command will alter picture elements through mirroring, whereas the standard rotation will not.

Transforming Your Image

Images can be stretched, squeezed, rotated, and otherwise altered. These operations can be found in the Edit → Transform submenu (see Figure 13.21). You can apply any of them to a selection or to an independent layer. Many of these transformations act very much like the cropping operations discussed earlier in this chapter. They differ in that they affect only your current selection or the active layer (and any layers linked to it), and they simultaneously affect all of the layers in a layer set.

You'll save time and effort if you copy or cut the item to be transformed to its own layer before performing a transformation. The advantage is that you can apply the transformation to the entire contents of a layer without having to make a selection.

When you choose any of the manual transformation operations, the Options bar displays numerical data of the transformation (see Figure 13.22). You can choose to manually transform or you can enter values in the fields to numerically transform the contents of a layer or selection.

Figure 13.21

The Transform submenu

Scaling Image Content

Scaling changes the size of an area within the image by stretching or squeezing it along the horizontal and/or vertical dimensions. For example, you might stretch the contents of a layer or selection along the vertical axis to create an excessively tall, fun-house-mirror look. Similarly, you might shrink your selection symmetrically along both axes to reduce its size proportionately. To use this feature, choose Edit → Transform → Scale. This menu command displays an interactive bounding box (like the one in Figure 13.23) that enables you to apply a variety of scaling operations to your selection:

Resize along Both Axes Drag one of the bounding box corners. The new bounding box will expand or contract following your mouse movement. Release the mouse, and the contents of the bounding box will resize.

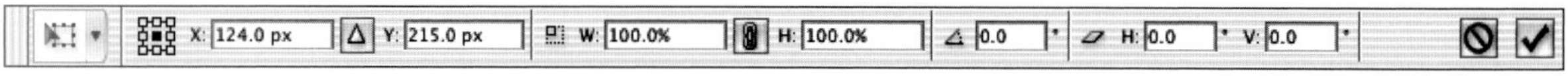

| ⬚ ▾ | ⬚ | X: 124.0 px | △ Y: 215.0 px | ▦ W: 100.0% | ⬚ H: 100.0% | ◿ 0.0 | ▪ | ⬚ H: 0.0 | ▪ V: 0.0 | ▪ | ⊘ ✓ |

Figure 13.22

When you choose a transformation function from the Edit → Transform submenu, the Options bar enables you to specify numerical values.

Resize Proportionately along Both Axes Press the Shift key while dragging a bounding box corner. The new bounding box will increase or decrease in size as you move the mouse, but it will retain the proportions of the original bounding box. Release the mouse to finish the resize task. The step-by-step example that follows demonstrates this operation.

Resize along One Axis Drag one of the four midpoint handles on the bounding box to stretch a selection or the contents of a layer along one axis while retaining the dimension of the other axis. The bounding box will stretch or shrink as you move the mouse. Release the mouse, and the contents of the bounding box resize to the new dimension.

To practice resizing, follow these steps:

1. Open the ge_radio.psd file, found in the Ch13 folder on your CD.

2. The image is separated into two layers and the Background. The radio is covering some of the ad text, and you need to fix that. Target the Radio layer and choose Edit → Transform → Scale.

3. Hold down the Shift key while dragging a corner handle to reduce the size of the radio proportionately (see Figure 13.24).

4. After scaling, reposition the image by placing the cursor inside the bounding box and dragging.

5. Click the check mark in the Options bar to implement the transformation and the move.

Rotating Image Content

Rotation enables you to change the diagonal orientation of a selection or the content of a layer. To rotate an image, choose Edit → Transform → Rotate.

When you rotate a selection or layer, it's important to understand the concept of the *point of origin*. The point of origin is initially in the exact center of the bounding box. It looks like a tiny compass rose.

Figure 13.23

You can apply a variety of scaling operations in an interactive bounding box.

The center point defines the fulcrum around which the rotation turns. In the left image in Figure 13.25, the center point remains in the middle as the radio is manually rotated counterclockwise. In the right image, the center point has been moved to the lower left, outside the box, and the radio has been rotated around it.

To move the point of origin, drag it to its new location. Here are several tips that will help you position it:

- The location of the point of origin need not lie within the bounding box. Choose any place on the image to place the point or you can even place it outside the edges of the image. You can use this feature to rotate around your picture's corners or around an important design feature.

- If you drag the point of origin near the original central location of the bounding box, the point will automatically snap back to the default. This enables you to return it to its original position after you experimented with moving it.

- Hold down the Shift key when moving the point of origin to constrain it to horizontal, vertical, or 45-degree axes.

- The point of origin's location is shown in the first fields of the Options bar, *x* and *y*.

Figure 13.24

The result of dragging the Scaling bounding box inward while pressing the Shift key to constrain proportions

Performing the Rotation

After you set the point of origin, you're ready to rotate the selection. Move the mouse to just outside of the bounding box. The cursor will change, becoming a small arc with arrows at each end. Drag the mouse and the bounding box will rotate, following the movement of the mouse. Release the mouse to complete the rotation. The following tips might help you while rotating:

- Hold down Shift while rotating to limit your rotation to increments of 15 degrees. This allows you easy access to such important and common angles as 30, 45, and 60 degrees.

- Sometimes your hand might slip when making an important rotation. Choose Edit → Undo (or ⌘/Ctrl-Z) to reverse any rotation by one manipulation. This option leaves you within the rotation but undoes your last movement.

Figure 13.25

The image rotated manually around a center point within the box (left), and the point of origin moved to the lower left outside the box and the image rotated (right)

- Press the Esc key to cancel all rotation operations or click the Cancel button in the Options bar.

- To commit your rotation, press Return/Enter, double-click inside the boundary, or click the Commit button (the check mark) in the Options bar.

- The Options bar will show you the exact degree of rotation you selected in the fifth field, the one marked by an angle symbol. To specify an exact angle of rotation, type the value into this field. Use negative numbers for counterclockwise rotation, and positive numbers for clockwise rotation.

Other Rotations and Flipping

The Edit → Transform submenu offers five standardized transformations. These options work the same as their Image → Rotate Canvas counterparts, but they affect only the active selection or layer, and offer you one-click access to some of the most common image modifications:

Command	Action
Rotate 180°	Rotates your selection by 180 degrees, turning it upside down
Rotate 90° CW	Rotates your selection clockwise by 90 degrees
Rotate 90° CCW	Rotates your selection counterclockwise by 90 degrees
Flip Horizontal	Mirrors your selection across the vertical axis, creating a horizontal reflection
Flip Vertical	Mirrors your selection across the horizontal axis, creating a vertical reflection

Skewing, Distorting, and Applying Perspective

These three functions—skewing, distorting, and applying perspective—all share a common basis: each alters the layer or selection by slanting image elements. Open the ge_radio.psd image on the CD and try them out. They work as follows:

Skew This function slants your selection along one axis, either vertical or horizontal. The degree of slant affects how pitched your final image will become. To skew, drag one of the handles of the bounding box. The border will update after each drag. When skewing, you can move each corner independently (affecting only one border side), as shown in Figure 13.26, or you can drag the handle at the center of an edge to skew parallel borders symmetrically.

Distort When you distort a selection, you can stretch either of its axes. Unlike skewing, slanting is not restricted to a single border at a time. Drag a corner, and both adjacent edges will stretch along that corner (see Figure 13.27). If you drag a border midpoint, you will stretch or shrink your selection along that edge. You can also drag the selection from any point in the middle to relocate it.

Figure 13.26

Slant an image with the Skew command.

Figure 13.27

Distort the image by adjusting the handles on the bounding box.

Perspective The Perspective transformation squeezes or stretches one edge of a layer or a selection, slanting the two adjacent sides either inward or outward (see Figure 13.28). This produces converging edges used in a one-point perspective. To create perspective, you drag a corner in only one direction, either horizontally or vertically. As you drag, you will pinch or expand the two opposite corners of the bounding box.

To create skewed perspectives, drag any border midpoint to skew the bounding box and then drag the corner point to apply the perspective effect.

Skew, Distort, and Perspective share some common traits. Here are some tips that apply to all three operations:

- You can enter an angle into the Angle field in the Options bar to rotate your selection at the same time that you skew, distort, or change perspective.

- Choose Edit → Undo to reverse your last manipulation without leaving the interactive mode that enables you to skew, distort, or change perspective.

- To finish your transformations, click the check mark in the Options bar or press Return/Enter. You can also double-click inside the bounding box to implement the transformation.

- To cancel your transformation, press Esc or click the Cancel button in the Options bar.

- Because each image transformation resamples the image data, multiple transformations should be applied to the image before implementation.

Figure 13.28

Applying perspective to the image creates diagonal lines that intersect at a horizon point.

Using the Free Transform Command

Photoshop provides an interactive bounding box that you can use to scale, rotate, or move a selection or the contents of a layer. This combines the features of several of the tools described in the previous sections in a handy, Swiss-Army-knife sort of transformation. You can access this command either by choosing Edit → Free Transform or by pressing ⌘/Ctrl-T.

After you've activated a free transformation, you can directly access its features from the bounding box:

- Drag the center point as needed. It works exactly as described in "Rotating Image Content earlier.

- Move your mouse just outside any of the eight squares on the bounding box, and your cursor will change to a quarter-circle with arrows on each end. You are now in Rotate mode and can use all the rotation techniques described earlier.

- Click the mouse on any of the borders, and you can scale them horizontally or vertically.

- Click the mouse on any of the corners to scale them by dragging. You can use all the scaling techniques described previously.

- Hold the ⌘/Ctrl key while dragging a corner to enter Distort mode. The corner will drag independently of the rest of the selection.

- To duplicate the selection you wish to transform, hold down Option/Alt while you transform it.

- If the cursor is inside the bounding box but not on the center point, you can move the bounding box.

Transforming with the Move Tool

The Move tool ⊹ has become the transformation shortcut in Photoshop that transforms images on-the-fly. No more fishing around in the Edit menu for transformation features—you simply choose it and use it. When you choose the Move tool, the Options bar displays the Show Bounding Box check box. When you check the box, a bounding box surrounds the selection or the contents of a layer. You can move, rotate, or scale the bounding box as you would with the Free Transform feature, or use the input fields to alter the layer contents numerically. The Options bar displays alignment options for the bounding box. When you perform a transformation, the Options bar changes to enable you to specify numerical transformations (see Figure 13.29).

CHAPTER 14

Image Capture and Digital Photography

The process of digital imaging begins when an image is captured. Two broad types of devices can be used to convert a real-world scene into digital information: the scanner and the digital camera. These devices "see" light and color and convert what they see into numerical information that Photoshop can use. Learning to use a digital camera or a scanner properly is an important skill, and many variables enter into producing a quality image. In addition to image size, factors such as resolution, contrast adjustments, and hardware limitations must be taken into consideration. This chapter will introduce you to the best methods for inputting your image so that you can be assured of producing the best possible results in Photoshop.

In this chapter, you'll learn about:

- ■ Scanners and digital cameras

- ■ Scanning images

- ■ Attributes of digital photographs, including 16-bit images

- ■ Digital panoramic photography

Scanners and Digital Cameras

A variety of hardware is available that captures image data in a form that your computer—and particularly Photoshop—can understand. These technologies transform visual information into digital data. They work by translating light striking the sensors in the device into digital values that you can store and manipulate on your computer. As a preview of the issues this chapter will explore, Table 14.1 summarizes the factors that determine the quality of a scanner or digital camera.

Scanners

Scanners convert reflective images (photographic prints, drawings), film negatives, or color transparencies into digital data. A scanner measures the color content and tonal variations and converts the data it collects into numerical values. Each value sampled is assigned a value for its red, green, and blue components or, if the image is black-and-white, a grayscale value. The values are transferred to Photoshop, where they are displayed as color (or monochrome) pixels on the computer display.

Table 14.1

Factors That Determine the Quality of an Image-Capture Device

FACTOR	MEANING
Optical resolution	The maximum number of pixels per linear inch the device can create from information it gathers from a reflective or transparent image. (See the upcoming section "Flatbed Scanners" for a warning about optical vs. "effective" resolution.)
Scanning sensor	Charge-coupled device (CCD) or complementary metal-oxide semiconductor (CMOS). Some of the latest digital cameras feature CMOS sensors that are of very high quality.
Interface or driver	The computer program that controls the device's behavior.
Scanning modes	RGB, CMYK, Grayscale, CIE Lab. Scanners *always* scan in red, green, and blue, but the resulting file can be converted to and saved in these modes.
Document dimensions	The maximum physical size of the image to be captured in one piece. In the case of a flatbed scanner, that would be limited to the size of the bed.
Dynamic range	How extensively the device can sense render density in an image. The higher the dynamic range, the more tonal information the scanner can discern and gather. Dynamic range is measured in Density units (0–4.0 Dmax), a logarithmic scale of light intensity.
Speed	The length of time it takes the device to capture an image.
Bit depth	The amount of tonal information the device attributes to each pixel. This is a reflection of the number of steps the tonal scale is divided into for each color scanned. Most devices are 8-bit, enabling a grayscale image to be recorded in 256 steps, whereas a 16-bit device will record 65,792 tonal steps for each color it scans.
Passes	The number of times the device must "look" at the image. Some older scanners require three passes to collect the data—one each for red, green, and blue. Single-pass scanners are usually faster and more precise. Some modern scanners offer multiple "samples" in which the scanner makes multiple scans of the same area and averages them (or takes the "cleanest" sample) to create a pixel value for the scanned area.

Flatbed Scanners

A *flatbed scanner* bounces light off reflective art and directs the bounced light through a system of lenses to a sensor that converts color and tonal variations into digital values. Flatbed scanners produce images composed of numerical values that are later translated into image pixels. Compare flatbed scanners by evaluating the number of pixels produced per inch—the more pixels the scanner can produce, the more detail the image can have.

When choosing a scanner, be aware of the difference between its optical resolution and its interpolated resolution (sometimes called effective resolution). *Optical* resolution is the amount of data that the scanner can collect optically. *Interpolated* resolution uses software to increase the resolution by generating image pixels with a mathematical algorithm. This can produce the undesirable softening of an image. Dynamic range is also a critical factor. A flatbed scanner can currently be purchased for less than $100 to more than $3,000 for professional-quality units. Usually the difference in price is in the actual resolution of the scanner.

Film Scanners

Instead of reflecting light off of a reflective image, a *film scanner* passes light through the emulsion layers of a film negative or a color transparency. The quality of film scanners is typically better than flat-bed scanners because they are of higher resolution and greater dynamic range. A film scanner's *dynamic range* determines its ability to distinguish variations of highlight and shadow detail.

If you're going to purchase a film scanner, look for one with a high dynamic range (3.4–3.8 Dmax) and a high optical (actual) resolution (3,000–8,000 dpi). Good film scanners for 35mm films range in price from $1,000 to $3,000. Film scanners are also available for 2.25″ × 2.25″ and 4″ × 5″ film, but these are significantly more expensive, typically $7,500 or more.

Although film adapters are available for some flatbed scanners, these devices don't produce the quality of scan that a dedicated film scanner can produce.

Drum Scanners

Drum scanners are analog/digital devices that have been used in the graphic arts industry for decades. Reflective art or transparent film is mounted on a drum that spins while the scanner's sensors record a small, tightly-focused area of image information. Older drum scanners output to process color separations, converting the information directly into halftone-screened film. Newer drum scanners convert the scanned information to pixel data and store it as a file.

The greatest advantage of a drum scanner is the fine detail it allows, producing images that are free of the optical flare that is common on most CCD sensor scanners. Drum scanners can produce extraordinary color separations, but they are quickly being replaced by high-end flatbed and film scanners whose greater productivity makes them more cost-effective in production. Only a few manufacturers are still making drum scanners. Another factor in the sunset of the drum scanner is the emergence of professional digital cameras.

Digital Cameras

Every digital camera contains a two-dimensional array of sensors that convert light from an entire image into pixels, and then into digital values. Light enters the camera through a lens and is focused onto the sensor array. Two types of sensors dominate the digital camera market: charge-coupled devices (CCD) and the newer complementary metal-oxide semiconductor (CMOS) chips.

CMOS sensors are becoming more popular, and will likely take over the digital camera market in the long run because of their lower cost of manufacture. Early CMOS sensors suffered from excessive noise, but the latest chips are successfully challenging CCDs common in most digital cameras. The most sophisticated CMOS chips have the advantage of having a discrete sensor layer for each color, eliminating the need to extrapolate color values from a grid of dispersed red, green, and blue sensors on a single plane.

The size (dimensions in pixels) and quality (dynamic range) of the sensor determine the amount of data that a digital camera can collect and the tonal range that the sensor is able to record without overexposure. Consumer digital cameras have become so sophisticated and inexpensive that they are now outselling consumer film cameras.

The appeal of digital cameras is obvious—immediacy and quality are compelling factors that make these cameras so successful. Amateurs and professionals alike enjoy the ability to determine immediately whether their image is successful (Is it properly exposed? Did the subject blink?). After the image is recorded, it is ready for print or for another destination without processing and printing. The appeal of digital cameras to professional photographers is also knowing that the quality of the image is now superior to that of scanned film. The latest professional digital cameras have at least two f-stops of shadow information more than film, resulting in a better image.

Enter the *megapixel*. Cameras are now touted as having a certain number of megapixels, a measure of the count—in millions—of image sensors on the array in the camera. A 1500 × 2000 pixel sensor is a 3-megapixel sensor, and it will yield an image of approximately 9 MB when uncompressed (most digital cameras compress their images by using the JPEG method in order to save space on the internal storage card).

Consumer-quality 3-megapixel digital cameras now cost less than $300. (There is even a *disposable* digital camera available!) Semiprofessional ("prosumer") digital cameras are moderately high-resolution—up to about 6 megapixels—that have a built-in optical zoom lens (2x to 3x zoom range). These cameras cost between $500 and $1,500.

Professional single-lens reflex (SLR) 35mm-style digital cameras with interchangeable lenses can produce digital images that are comparable to any 35mm slide (usually better). These are significantly more expensive than prosumer cameras, ranging from $2,000 to more than $30,000. Digital camera backs that attach to medium-format and 4′×5′ film cameras are also available. The return on investment for a professional studio photographer is tremendous; payback of the initial investment can take as few as eight months based on the savings of film and processing not purchased. Add to the cash savings the ability to *know* that the photographer got the shot, and these seemingly expensive cameras are a bargain for those who make their living with a camera.

Professional SLR digital cameras (such as the Canon 1D, the Fuji S2, and the Nikon D1X) all use interchangeable lenses. These lenses are compatible with their film counterparts but some have a different *effective* focal length when used on a digital camera because the image sensors in most of these cameras are smaller than the frame of 35mm film in a conventional camera. The Canon EOS 1D uses a full-size (24 × 36mm) sensor, whereas the Fuji and the Nikon cameras require a conversion factor of 1.5 (both use Nikkor lenses). For the current Nikon and Fuji offerings (and some of the Canon digital cameras), a 50mm lens for a film camera will produce a 75mm equivalent image on a digital camera, and a 105mm telephoto portrait lens will produce the equivalent of a 152mm lens image.

The real effect of these slightly smaller sensors is that true wide-angle photography requires a lens that is exceptionally wide. Nikon announced in early 2003 a 12–24mm zoom lens to answer the demand for a genuinely wide lens for their popular D1X professional digital camera.

> Many photo processors will digitize your traditional photographs. For a few dollars per roll, they will digitize your film and either ship the resulting files to you on a CD, upload them to a website, or both.

Digitizer Boards and Software

These special-purpose computer cards transform analog video signals into digital image data. Image sources for this technology include television signals and the output from VCRs and traditional (nondigital) video cameras. Such sources produce a picture screen (or *frame*) by sending out a stream of image information. Digitizer video boards, sometimes called *frame grabbers,* wait until an entire screen has been received and then display it. Select the Capture function for your board, and you can grab one screen at a time.

This method of image capture produces the noisiest and poorest-quality pictures. Most video systems depend on motion to enable your brain to fill the gaps between successive frames, providing the illusion of greater image quality. As I'm sure you've seen, when you hit the Pause button on your VCR, the actual images are quite poor.

It is also quite easy to capture still images from video by using video-editing software. The latest digital video products—Adobe Premiere and Apple Final Cut Pro and Final Cut Express—enable still images to be captured from digital sources. Final Cut Pro's Freeze Frame function will capture a single frame (actually two interlaced frame cycles) and allow the export of the image in a variety of still photo formats. The results are slightly better than those captured through digitizer boards. Application of the Photoshop Video → De-interlace filter will usually improve captured video frames significantly by removing the obvious horizontal scan lines that are common in video frames (see Figure 14.1).

Challenges in Digitizing

No matter which technology you use to capture your images, you should bear in mind the kinds of problems you might encounter when capturing digital images. Some of these problems are unavoidable. With others, preemptive measures can ensure that you create the highest-quality image possible.

Some scanners, including Nikon's line of Super Coolscan film scanners, can automatically repair many flaws found in film, such as fingerprints, film base scratches, and many emulsion defects (though not emulsion scratches). These scanners can also feature grain improvements and restoration of faded color in films scanned. Combined, these features will repair old film, remove harmful defects, and restore color to an image that has long been forgotten.

Figure 14.1

The picture on the left shows a still image captured from digital video over a FireWire connection. The one on the right shows the same image after applying the De-interlace filter in Photoshop.

Figure 14.2 presents one example of this kind of capability. A scan from a 35mm transparency shows serious dust and fingerprints; this image is clearly unacceptable. But the same transparency scanned with Digital ICE enabled on the Nikon Super Coolscan LS4000 scanner removes most of the dust and makes the image better. (Cleaning the film would help a lot, too.)

Figure 14.3 shows a photograph of a United Airlines DC3 airliner that was taken in 1941 on early Kodachrome film; over time it has faded to a nearly unintelligible condition. But applying Digital Grain Enhancement and Management (GEM) and Restoration Of Color (ROM) on the Super Coolscan improves the image immensely. Almost astonishing results are possible with these extended capabilities, now available on several quality film scanners.

What follows are some of the problems you'll face in digitizing your images and some of the techniques you can use to solve them:

Noise Random digital values—*noise*—can inadvertently be added to and distributed across a digital picture. Noise is primarily a result of digitizing technology. Video capture boards create the most noise, scanners the least. To help limit noise, shoot digital photos or video with as much ambient light as possible. Image noise appears most in the shadows, and is often more pronounced in the blue channel than the other two channels. (See Figures C14a–c in the color section.) You can correct noise to a certain extent by applying the Despeckle or Gaussian Blur filters to the blue channel (see the "Removing Image Noise and Artifacts" sidebar).

Artifacts Unintentional image elements, or *artifacts*, are sometimes produced by an imaging device or a compression scheme such as low-quality JPEG compression. Make sure to clean your scanner glass, and dust your scanner bed and lid—and the original photo—to help prevent artifacts in your scans. Also be sure originals are free of dust, fingerprints, and other surface marks if possible.

Figure 14.2

(left) A scan from a 35mm transparency shows many flaws. (right) The same transparency scanned with Digital ICE enabled removes most of the problems.

REMOVING IMAGE NOISE AND ARTIFACTS

An image's blue channel often contains the most noise and artifacts. The blue channel is the least critical to the human visual system—but it is still necessary for producing full-color images. Instead of blurring the blue channel directly, a better technique is to duplicate the Background of a flattened image. On the new layer that is created, change the blending mode to Color (from the pull-out menu on the Layers palette) so that detail is not affected and then apply the Despeckle or Blur filter conservatively on this layer. Merge or flatten the two layers into one. Indirect filtering in this case leads to superior results, while remaining artifacts can be removed directly in their respective channels with the Blur tool, instead of being globally filtered.

Resolution The *resolution* of a digitizing device is measured by the pixel count per unit of measure it produces: the higher the pixel count, the better the potential image quality. Keep this in mind when purchasing a scanner or digital camera. In general, when capturing an image, use a higher resolution than you will ultimately need. You can always use Photoshop's Image Size command to reduce the resolution to a more manageable final size. Be cautious about increasing resolution or interpolating (up-sampling). When Photoshop adds pixels by interpolation, the image might lose its contrast and sharpness.

Chapter 13, "Sizing and Transforming Images," shows how to determine scan resolution.

Bit Depth *Bit depth* refers to the capability of your scanner or digital camera to capture tonal information. The more bits a capture device allocates to each pixel, the more *shades of colors* can be identified in the original and captured with the scan. The most common color depth, 8 bits per channel (or 24-bit RGB color), can produce 256 shades of red, green, or blue each for a total of 16,777,216 digital values or colors.

Figure 14.3

(left) This photograph has faded to a nearly unintelligible condition. (right) Applying Digital GEM and ROC improves the image immensely.

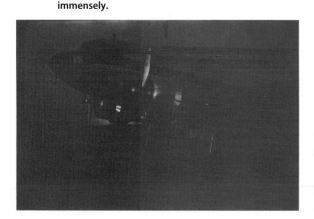

High bit images consisting of 36-bit color (three channels with 12 bits per pixel) and 48-bit color (three 16-bit channels) can produce billions of color combinations at the cost of much larger file sizes. In Photoshop CS, these high-bit files can enjoy more of the image adjustments than in the past, so it is possible now to open or acquire, save and manipulate high-bit images in Photoshop without converting to 8-bit data.

> High-bit files need to be duplicated and reduced to 8-bit depth for output to print. This process will average out the larger amount of possible channel values in higher-bit data into regular 8-bit data, which will theoretically be superior to a file that has been scanned in 24-bit image mode. Some photographers swear by this process. Chapter 3, "The Nature of the Beast," discusses bit depth in more detail.

Moiré Patterns in Scanned Images *Moiré patterns* are optical anomalies produced when one pattern is superimposed over another. They are usually created by scanning already-printed halftone images or repeating patterns in an original (this occurs, for example, when scanning photos of patterned fabrics or rattan furniture) that produce interference with the scanner's matrix of image sensors, as seen in Figure 14.4. Editing moiré patterns can be problematic because they can vary significantly from image to image, depending on the scan and halftone resolution and the screen angles. You can avoid them by scanning only continuous-tone images or by using the scanner's descreening function (if available), described in the next section, "Scanning Images." You can sometimes reduce moiré patterns by changing the angle of the art on the scanner bed. After the image has been scanned, rotate it back with the Crop or Rotate Canvas tools. This technique requires some experimentation. Also note that eliminating the moiré pattern from the most pronounced channel (usually the blue) can reduce or eliminate moiré patterns.

Figure 14.4

Scanned directly from a printed magazine page, this image contains heavy moiré patterns caused by the interference of the original halftone screens and the scanner's sensor.

Scanning Images

Photoshop provides direct integration with most scanner control software. And although you can open a previously scanned image, you can also scan images directly into Photoshop. The File → Import submenu offers direct access to any installed scanners. This menu will vary with the scanning software currently installed. The TWAIN software is designed to provide universal controls for scanners and other image-capture devices.

After you select a scanner from the submenu, its controlling dialog box will appear. The software for every scanner will vary, but most scanner control software enables you to control attributes such as these:

Type Most interfaces offer you the opportunity to choose among multiple scanners.

Beginner/Advanced Typically you can choose between a Beginner mode that offers limited control using everyday terminology and an Advanced mode that offers precision scanning options.

Resolution Enter a value to determine the pixel count. Be aware that some scanner software refers to resolution in DPI (dots per inch) instead of the PPI (pixels per inch) used by Photoshop. In this case, the terms are synonymous.

B & W or Color Most scanners enable you to select between a grayscale or color scan. Grayscale images are typically one-third of the size of color images of the same dimensions because only one channel of information is being recorded.

Descreen/No Descreen The function will attempt to remove rhythmic interference patterns produced by scanning already-printed images from newspapers or magazines. Use it to reduce or eliminate moiré patterns produced by the interference of the image's halftone screen with the sensors of the scanner. The scan can take considerably more time, and when effective, will seem slightly less sharp because moiré removal often creates a slight blur in images.

Preview The Preview (often called Overview) feature performs a quick, low-resolution scan that you can use to crop the image to eliminate unwanted areas.

Filter This option applies a sharpening operation to the image after the data has been collected. It's better to use Photoshop's Unsharp Mask filter after the image has been scanned, because it affords more control, and enables you to Undo the effect to compare before and after images on-screen. Sharpening is dependent on image size, printing process, intended use, viewing distance, and subject matter of the photo. It's a mistake to allow a scanner to sharpen images while scanning.

Auto Adjustment Check this box to perform automatic contrast adjustments to the image. In most cases, it's better to scan the image and perform a Levels or Curves adjustment in Photoshop.

Scan Every scanner provides a Scan button to initiate the scanning process. As the scan proceeds, you will usually see a progress bar indicating what percentage of the document has been scanned.

Transparency/Reflective Those scanners that can handle both reflective art (prints) and film (negatives and transparencies) will have a control for this setting.

Other Uses for Scanners

Flatbed scanners are designed to scan images that are drawn, painted, or printed on flat sheets of film or paper. They can also be used to scan text if optical character recognition (OCR) software is installed on the computer. OCR software can convert a scanned image of text, usually saved as a TIFF, to an editable text document. OCR software does this by recognizing the shapes of characters and applying conversion algorithms to produce an editable text document of significantly smaller file size. The quality of this process is highly variable. If the text is very clear and in a font that the software can easily discern, the translation into text will be excellent. With some pages, however, the fonts and the print quality will reduce the efficacy of the text conversion.

There are also nontraditional uses for scanners that you might want to try for fun. A scanner can be used to scan three-dimensional objects. Place the object on the bed of the scanner and position the cover over the object (be careful not to break the glass!). Cover the entire scanner with a piece of black cloth to prevent light leaks. You can scan any object that fits on the bed with surprising quality. The depth of field of some flatbed scanners is more than 0.5 inch.

Just for fun, you might also try scanning your hand or even your head. Remain very still during the process of the scan. Or try moving a little to produce some really weird results. Don't stare directly into the light or you'll be seeing stars for a while, and make sure you clean the glass after this twisted little adventure.

Digital Photographs vs. Scanned Images

Digital photographs share traits with scanned images but also have some unique attributes of their own. Here are some of the ways in which they differ:

Size Consumer- and prosumer-quality digital cameras usually produce smaller images than scanners do. Their image size is limited to the capacity of their CMOS or CCD sensor chip. Their resolutions and file sizes depend on the amount of data their detectors can collect and process. Advertising materials often describe the resolution of a digital camera measured in megapixels. For example, a 2.5-megapixel camera will have a sensor that converts the image into approximately 7,500,000 pixels (2.5 million × 3 channels—red, green and blue).

Functionality Digital cameras work best when used in the same way you'd use a traditional camera. Many do not capture pages or printed photographs particularly well, although they can be used in a pinch to create relatively low-resolution copies of printed material.

Blue Channel In many CCD-based digital cameras, the blue channel displays more noise than the red or green channels. This can be quite pronounced in some digital photographs. To correct this problem, the blue channel can be blurred slightly with the Gaussian Blur or Despeckle filter in Photoshop. As camera sensors improve, this noise is being reduced.

Noise Noise in digital photographs tends to be the product of low lighting conditions. As I said earlier, one of the best ways to avoid noise in digital snapshots is to increase ambient light. Of course, an even better method is to purchase better-quality equipment with better sensors—and also use more light.

Editing 16-Bit Images

In all versions of Photoshop prior to CS, the manipulation of high-bit-depth images (more than 8 bits per channel) was problematic. Although the acquisition and handling of images from devices capable of capturing 16-bit images was simple, the variety of controls available was extremely limited.

In Photoshop CS, the list of image adjustments has been expanded to include more than Levels and Curves. Image filters, like the artistic functions of Watercolor, Chalk, Pastels, and others, are still not available for these high-bit images.

Some scanners will generate 16-bit images, and several professional digital cameras will also generate these images on capture, ensuring a smooth tonality and tremendous gradation quality from these devices.

In general, the tools used to manage high-bit-depth images are Levels, Curves, and Unsharp Mask, each of which can be applied to original images without requiring a conversion to the coarser 8-bit mode (see Figure 14.5). Each of these functions behaves the same with 16-bit images as it does with 8-bit images. And today's fast computers enable Photoshop to process 16-bit images without significant delays. (Remember when it took 10 minutes to perform Unsharp Mask on a 50 MB file?)

Changing between 16-Bit and 8-Bit

After you have made necessary adjustments to your 16-bit image, you must convert to 8-bit to print to most printers and output devices. The change is made by choosing Image → Mode → 8-bits/Channel control. Be sure to save the resulting file *as a copy of the original* to prevent permanent harm to your 16-bit files.

Although no obvious benefit exists in converting 8-bit images into 16-bit, there are a few good reasons to do so. One practical reason is to expand the tonality of an image in the process of restoring the image—useful when working with old or faded images. If you convert to 16-bit *before* making severe tonal changes (Levels, Curves, Shadow/Highlight), there will be more tonal steps in the image to redistribute, and thus more available to the image *after* the adjustment (see Figures 14.6 through 14.8). Converting back to 8-bit after this procedure will result in an image with a more complete histogram (more complete tone scale), and thus fewer or no missing tonal steps.

If you are serious about image restoration, this procedure will result in the best-quality conversion after tonal adjustment. Prints from these files on high-quality ink-jet printers and photographic printers will show no posterization, and the faces of people in such images will generally be free of visible tonal steps.

Taking Better Pictures with Digital Cameras

Digital cameras are all the rage—everyone has one or wants one. They can take great photographs, and they can make the images available to us in seconds, eliminating even the one-hour photo kiosk. They have also spawned a new generation of digital darkroom specialists, people who can make images look great, and make beautiful prints without enlargers or chemistry. In a word, digital cameras are miraculous.

But, digital cameras are still just cameras, and in the hands of a thoughtless photographer, they can produce bad images (although sometimes even thoughtless photographers get lucky!). The conventions of good composition, correct exposure, a level horizon, and other considerations apply equally to digital and film cameras. Just because you can fix a digital image easily does not excuse making a digital image badly.

Here are seven tips for better digital photography:

Look—*really look*—through the viewfinder (or at the little LCD screen) of the camera. Ask yourself whether the composition is interesting. Does everything in the shot look good? Are people positioned nicely, and are extraneous objects properly omitted?

Think about the use of the photograph. Should it be vertical? Do you need to establish the scene better to tell a better story?

Double-check white balance and autofocus; make sure you have the white balance set correctly, and that autofocus is either on or off, depending on how you prefer to shoot. Digital cameras are unforgiving of images made with the wrong white balance setting.

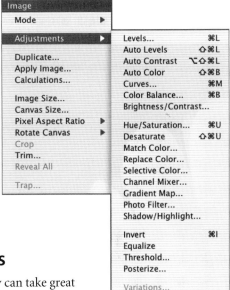

Figure 14.5

In Photoshop CS, the available Image Adjustments have been expanded to include all of those available to 8-bit images, allowing color correction, selective color, and others to be applied to these high-bit-depth images.

Figure 14.6

This old photo has faded over time; its histogram shows it needs some work in the shadows.

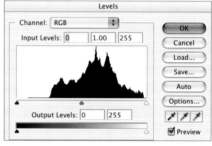

Figure 14.7

The same photo, after tonal adjustments—the histogram shows that gaps now exist in the tone scale of the image.

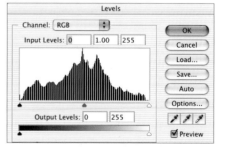

Use fill-flash whenever possible. Even in broad daylight, fill-flash can add tremendously to an image. When photographing people, light up their faces and make them the subject of the photo.

Underexpose rather than overexpose. If you have the option to over- or under-expose a digital photograph, always choose to underexpose, because there are many ways to enhance slightly underexposed images. Overexposed digital images cannot be fixed, because there is no data whatsoever in the overexposed areas (see Figures 14.9 through 14.11).

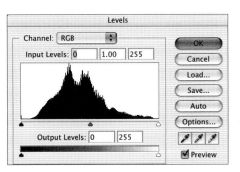

Zoom. If your camera has a zoom lens, zoom to its widest position and tell the greatest story with that perspective. Get in close and don't be shy about making the image interesting.

Practice makes perfect. Share your photos with your friends and family. Use them to illustrate lectures, newsletters, ads, booklets, and brochures. A lot of photography is practice, and as you practice you'll get better and better. Professional photographers shoot lots of photos (some joke that it helps them beat the law of averages!). Digital photos cost nothing, so if you don't like a photo, delete it and move on.

Figure 14.8

By converting the image from 8-bit to 16-bit in advance of tonal correction, the resulting histogram shows no gaps in the tone scale of the photograph. This image will be slightly better looking than its 8-bit counterpart.

Digital Panoramic Photography

At the turn of the nineteenth century, an amazing photographic technique was developed for taking photographs in a complete circle. Using a rotating camera and long rolls of film, images were created that showed a scene that was impossible to capture with any lens on any conventional camera. The popularity of these photos was great, and it lasted well into the 1940s. Visit any county museum in any part of the country and you're almost certain to see these photos—rows of high school students standing in front of the camera or soldiers in uniform at attention on the parade grounds. And, bulky as these cameras were, panoramic photography was used to record historic events (see Figure 14.12) as well as high school graduating classes.

Panoramic photography faded (if you'll excuse the expression) into the realm of collectors and photo historians as we entered the era of 35mm photography and the explosion of consumer cameras that brought quality photography to the masses. The panoramic cameras still exist, but most of them are inoperable. It is a bygone era.

In 1995, Apple Computer reintroduced panoramic photography to the world with clever new software that can *stitch* a series of still photographs together to make a complete panoramic image that looks like those made with rotating cameras a century ago. Quick-Time Virtual Reality puts the viewer in the center of a scene that surrounds them. Today several computer applications on the market will produce panoramic photos from a series of overlapping individual images (see Figure 14.13).

Figure 14.9

An underexposed digital photograph can be adjusted to open up the shadows without harm to the highlights in the image.

Figure 14.10

After applying a gradient mask (left to right), the shadows are improved to make the photo look normally exposed. The highlights in the image are left untouched.

Figure 14.11

An overexposed digital image has absolutely no data in the highlights (255-255-255 values), which cannot be repaired.

Photoshop CS has the ability to stitch a series of images together with its new Photomerge tool (File → Automate → Photomerge). With this tool, derived from the panoramic stitching tool in Adobe Photoshop Elements, you can blend multiple images together with reasonable success. The Photomerge tool works best with files in the 1–5 MB range; large images (I tested it with a series of 34 MB files) are much harder for the program to digest, but do create acceptable images.

> A set of panoramic images for the following Photomerge practice is supplied on the companion CD. Named Merced1.jpg through Merced4.jpg, they provide an opportunity to test this new feature of the application.

To build a panoramic image from a series of individual digital images, follow these steps:

1. Begin with the Photomerge control (see Figure 14.14). A browse dialog opens, enabling you to select images from existing files or a folder of files.

2. Select the images you want to compose into a panorama (see Figure 14.15). If you check Attempt To Automatically Arrange Source Images, the Photomerge tool will attempt to stitch them together, so you must load them in order. If you want to position them manually, uncheck that box, and it will free you to be at the controls. Click OK.

Figure 14.12
A panoramic photo taken during the San Francisco earthquake and fire, April 18, 1906. This image was made with a rotating Kodak Cirkut camera; the film was 10 inches tall by more than 40 inches long.

Figure 14.13
A modern panoramic photo, taken with a Nikon professional digital camera as 12 vertical frames on a special camera bracket, then stitched with Apple QuickTime VR Authoring Studio.

Figure 14.14

The Photomerge command calls up a dialog box where you identify the pieces of the panorama, in the order they need to be included.

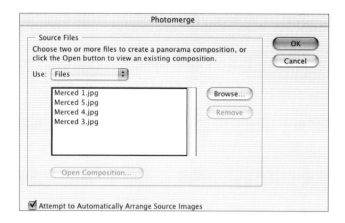

3. If you unchecked the Attempt To… feature, a palette opens that enables you to drag images, optionally rotate them, and then stitch the panorama into a single image (see Figure 14.16).

4. Photomerge will stitch images together by a combination of reverse-distortion and blending techniques. When it is finished, you have an image that will require considerable retouching and correction in Photoshop. Notice the gaps in the sky, and subtle discoloration between the frames. When Photomerge is finished, it delivers its composite image in a new window in Photoshop (see Figure 14.17).

Compared to dedicated stitching programs such as Apple's QuickTime VR Authoring Studio, Photomerge does not blend the image intersections perfectly. In each attempt, I was left with visible errors between the images. These were easy to repair with the Rubber Stamp tool, but still required much work to make a satisfactory finished image. Photomerge is a good tool, but not a great tool, for putting multiple images together.

Figure 14.15

The contributing images of a merged panoramic image. Each has an overlap of about 20 percent.

Some photographers prefer to stitch images manually by using the Layers functions in Photoshop and then selectively erasing parts of the overlapping images. This works fairly well when you are stitching several images that were made with a moderately long focal length lens. Wide-angle lenses exhibit too much distortion, which stitching programs remove by adding barrel distortion to compensate and make the adjacent images fit.

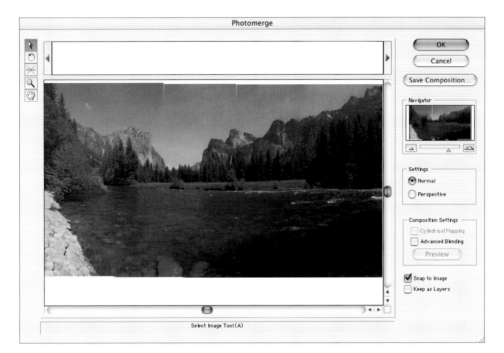

Figure 14.16

The Photomerge control palette, showing the overlaps in images it stitches together. Notice the visible demarcation between the frame edges, each of which need to be retouched.

Figure 14.17

The final file, after retouching, is quite handsome and represents the combined image area of four frames.

Opening Camera Raw Images from Digital Cameras

Offered as an extra-cost plug-in option for Photoshop 7, the CS version will open Camera Raw files from most professional digital cameras directly. Photoshop's File Browser will also preview images in Camera Raw format. Camera Raw images are those that have not been compressed by the digital camera into JPEG files, a process that is usually called *lossy*. JPEG is known for making compact files, but is also famous for delivering visible tonal artifacts while making the compression. Some cameras also allow images to be stored internally as RGB TIFF files that are not compressed by the camera.

The function supports the proprietary file formats of the following cameras:

Make	Models
Canon	EOS-1D, EOS-1Ds, EOS-D30, Eos 10D, EOS-D60; PowerShot models 600, A5, A50, S30, S40, S45, S50, G1, G2, G3, G5, Pro70, and Pro90 IS
Fujifilm	FinePix S2 Pro
Kodak	720X, 760
Leaf (Creo)	Valeo 6, Valeo 11
Minolta	DiMAGE 5, 7, 7i, 7Hi
Nikon	D1, D1H, D1X, D100, Coolpix 5700, and Coolpix 5000 with firmware version 1.7
Olympus	E-10, E-20, C-5050 Zoom

A Camera Raw file (DSC_0095.NEF) is supplied on the accompanying CD. It is a NEF file, a proprietary format found on Nikon professional digital cameras. Practice opening it with both 8-bit settings and 16-bit settings to see whether you can spot any differences.

1. To open the images, choose File → Open and select Camera Raw from the Format pop-up list (see Figure 14.18). Those file formats known to Photoshop will be opened in RGB mode in a new Photoshop window.

2. Photoshop CS will open Camera Raw files as either 8- or 16-bit RGB files, and can make a number of modifications to images as they are opened, including interpolation to make the image larger or smaller (see Figure 14.19). Color correction, rotation, image "exposure," and other settings are also available. Users who demand the best quality will be wise to open Camera Raw images at default size, and then use Photoshop's Image Size controls to modify the resulting files.

Size specifies the pixel size at which to open the image. The default for this setting is the pixel size you used to photograph the image. Use the Size menu if you want to resample the image to a larger or smaller size.

- For square-pixel cameras, the Size menu is mostly a convenience for the user. However, choosing a smaller-than-native size is useful to speed processing when you are planning a smaller final image anyway. Picking a larger size is similar to up-sampling in Photoshop.

- For non-square pixel cameras, the native size is the one that most closely preserves the total pixel count. This means the pixels in one dimension will be up-sampled, while in the other dimension they will be down-sampled. Choosing the next size larger than the native size keeps the pixel count along the high-resolution dimension constant, while up-sampling the lower-resolution dimension to create square pixels. This larger size preserves maximum detail for non-square pixel cameras, since neither dimension is down-sampled.

3. To introduce or remove a color cast in the image, various adjustment sliders are available to apply these changes as the file is opened (see Figure 14.20).

After the image is open in Photoshop, it will exhibit the characteristics of an 8-bit or 16-bit image, depending on how the file was opened.

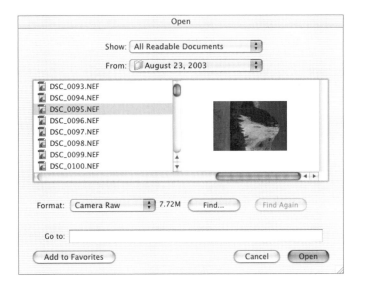

Figure 14.18

The Camera Raw image function enables images in proprietary and high-bit-depth formats to be opened directly from Photoshop.

Figure 14.19

Check to see a preview of the selected image.

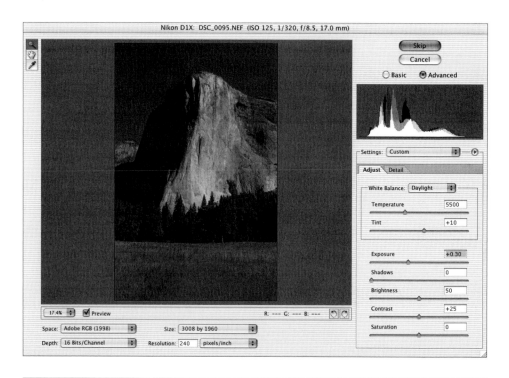

Figure 14.20

You can define the size, color space, and other characteristics of the Camera Raw image as it is opened.

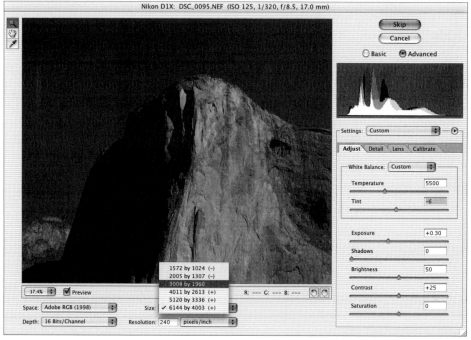

PART II

Photoshop Color

Photoshop is all about color! *When you select an area of an image with a selection tool and make any modifications to it, you are changing the color values of the selected pixels. There are many ways to perform color changes in Photoshop, (contrast, sharpness, lightness, and so forth) and therein lies its power.*

Color can present itself on your computer display in a variety of ways. Color working spaces affect how you see color. Much of your editing depends on your perceptions of the on-screen image. Color management and color correction are critical factors in the quality of the image. This section of Photoshop CS Savvy looks at using color settings, managing and correcting color, and preparing files for their ultimate destination—whether it's print, the Web, or even video.

CHAPTER 15

Color Management and Printing

You've labored long and hard to get the color exactly right. You've used all the tricks—Levels, Curves, Selective Color, Color Balance, Adjustment Layers, the Unsharp Mask filter (covered in Chapter 16, "Adjusting Tonality and Color")—and the image looks perfect on your computer display. Unfortunately, what your printer just spit out looks quite different. Those beautiful sky blues have turned to gloomy blue-gray. Furthermore, the image looks quite different from one display to another.

If you're a digital artist or graphic designer using Photoshop to print color images, you probably frequently ask yourself two important questions: How can I be confident that the color on my display will be matched by the color of the printer? And, how can I trust that the color on *my* display will look like the color on *your* display? These questions are about how you *manage* color from one device to another, and that's what this chapter is about.

In this chapter, you'll read about:

- Why you need to manage color

- Photoshop's color working space

- Managing color between displays

- Converting colors

- Printing images

Color Management—A Brief History

In the years before the desktop publishing revolution, professional color systems were used in the creation and modification of high-quality printing and publishing. These methods for processing color relied on what is called a *closed-loop* system, the idea being that nothing ever escaped the system. No outside files were accepted, and no files were ever allowed to leave the system except in the form of separated film, ready for printing. Looking back, those were the "good ol' days" when the reliability of color was—mostly—under control. These closed-loop systems were expensive, and compared to today's computers, very slow. But they worked, and the people who used them learned to trust them.

Desktop technologies created a *distributed* model for color production. Some of the work was done on a computer that wasn't connected to a prepress color system. It was the differences between systems—different displays, different viewing conditions, and different software applications—that created the need for color management.

Scientists went to work on the problem in the late 1980s, developing a model for color management that would eventually provide software tools to ensure that color would match, location-to-location and device-to-device. The first practical color management system, Apple ColorSync, arrived in 1991 and has undergone several significant improvements since. Over the years, Apple's ColorSync technology became the core of an industry-accepted method for managing color for computer displays, scanners, and various printing technologies. This method has been adopted by most professional software applications—including Adobe Photoshop. Today most computers and operating systems have a facility for color management, and most applications support color management. The challenge is setting it up correctly and getting it to work.

In the fall of 1998, the Adobe Photoshop development team rocked the design and printing community with a completely new outlook on color. The release of Photoshop 5 got the attention of all color practitioners in the digital imaging world. Prior to Photoshop 5, the color in an image was limited to the color available on the display, which proved to be a severely limiting factor in imaging.

Photoshop 5 removed that limitation, and created a new component to images handled by Photoshop.

The Color Working Space

What revolutionized digital color was the introduction of the concept of a specific environment for handling color. This environment, called a *color working space*, is independent of the display and can be chosen by the user. Under this model, it is possible to scan, save, edit, and store an image with a color working space embedded in it. When the image is saved and then opened again, its appearance will display the characteristics of the color working space. The image is embedded with an ICC (International Color Consortium) profile, information that describes the color characteristics of the color working space. The image can then move from one computer to another with its profile embedded, and will appear similarly on different computer displays.

The color working space concept created the opportunity for Photoshop to accommodate images from scanners and other sources whose colors exceed the available colors of the display. The color working space allows for color to be captured, modified, stored, and output without limiting or compressing the gamut of color of the original.

The color working space also creates something like a pedigree for images, describing their color characteristics so that downstream processing is more reliable, and the resulting images are more pleasing to the creator of the image.

A Window into a Window

To grasp the concept of a color working space, imagine that the image you see on your display exists on a separate, parallel plane, just behind your display, and that your display acts like *a window into the image.* The image you see might be the entire image, but it might not be. It might be distorted by the window's characteristics or size. Perhaps the window is not perfectly transparent, perhaps it is slightly tinted, or perhaps light is reflecting off its surface, causing the colors to appear slightly muted.

In fact, computer displays really behave like windows into your images, modifying the "reality" of the actual image and showing you something that is appropriate to the display's abilities, but not always the qualities of the image itself.

For professional graphic artists, the computer display is an excellent window into the image. This is true because we spend considerable sums of money on quality displays that have good color and a range of brightness that will enable us to see *almost* all the qualities of the image in Photoshop. But lesser displays don't provide such an undistorted view.

Display Quality

To better understand this, consider the display. Displays are light-emitting devices; they create light from electrical energy. A cathode ray tube (CRT) monitor, like the one on many computers, is similar to a television picture tube. As illustrated in Figure 15.1, it uses electrons beamed at the monitor's face from the back of the picture tube to stimulate mineral phosphors that are coated on the inside of the face of the tube, creating

Figure 15.1

A cross-section of a cathode ray tube showing the separate high-voltage amplifiers for the red, green, and blue signals.

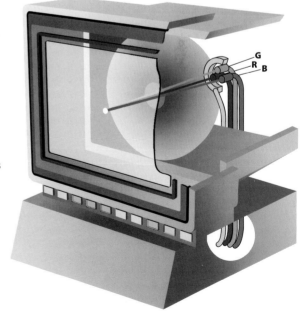

light of a single color on the face. The electrons are invisible to the human eye, but when they strike the coating, the phosphors react, emitting visible light in a spectrum that is within the color gamut of human vision. Activating those phosphors in combination with others causes "color" to be created on the face of the picture tube.

The latest computer displays are the flat-panel liquid crystal display (LCD) type, which use a fixed light source (usually a form of fluorescent illumination), and an array of liquid crystal transistors that modify the color of that light as it passes through the array, creating the colors on the display. Highly stable, with very high resolution available, these displays will likely supplant the cathode ray tube variety in the coming years.

Concerns about LCD image quality and viewing angle have largely been overcome by advances in technology. The best models available are huge, enabling two-page layouts to be viewed, and displaying stunning color with a gamut that rivals the best CRT monitors.

CRT Variability

As with many electromechanical devices, there is considerable variability in the manufacture of picture tubes and in the quality of minerals used to coat the inside of the tube. Some computer displays sell for less than $100, while others sell for more than $1,500. In addition to the size of the display, there are quality issues to take into account when evaluating a display's color. Is the color quality of a sub-$100 display likely to be very good? How will it compare to the color quality of a graphic-arts–quality display designed for critical color decisions?

Cost-cutting measures taken by the makers of low-end CRT monitors include coating the monitor with phosphors of inconsistent quality or low purity. It might also be possible to reduce manufacturing costs by reducing manufacturing quality-control checks. By contrast, a graphic-arts–quality display will be made from components that cost more to make, more to test, and more to deliver to the end user.

> CRT monitor characteristics change over time. You should calibrate your CRT at least once per month; LCD displays are very stable, and should be profiled every few months.

Display Profiles

A display's characteristics are described by its capability to display pure red, green, and blue colors as bright, clear components of the colors it can produce. In the visual arts, we use such colors and the millions of color permutations possible when mixing them together. To display an image correctly, Photoshop must know the characteristics of the display you are using. To do this, you provide Photoshop and other applications with a software *display profile*.

There are several ways to create a display profile. The easiest method is to make a visual calibration of your display by using version 5 or later of Adobe Gamma to test and adjust the appearance of the display, and then save the resulting information as a *color profile* (see Chapter 5, "Setting Up Photoshop").

> Some CRT displays are self-calibrating. The software that drives them can automatically readjust their output characteristics based on a preprogrammed profile as they change over time. These displays should be calibrated periodically to ensure that the designated white point and gamma are consistent with your preferred working environment.

Installed on your Windows system along with Photoshop, Adobe Gamma is a software display calibrator. To use it, follow the on-screen instructions, which provide a simple method for making a visual calibration and profile of your display. Mac OS 8.5 through OS X also offer calibration software bundled with their operating systems and accessible from their monitor or display settings. These programs are similar to Adobe Gamma.

CRT VS. LCD

Liquid crystal displays contain a viscous liquid crystal membrane sandwiched between two grids of transparent transistor-and-capacitor circuits and two opposed polarizing filters (90 degrees off-axis). These circuits can selectively turn the intersections (pixels) in the grid on and off to create the image you see on-screen. They can also modify the voltage applied, causing 256 variations to the "twist" of the liquid crystals, and in the process, creating tonality in the individual colors.

LCD displays are growing in popularity—and in size. Apple Computer has stopped making CRT monitors (except in their eMac entry-level machine) and now makes only LCD displays. These are integrated into the latest iMacs and available for their desktop machines in sizes from 19 to 23 inches horizontal (with 1920 horizontal pixels) in the Cinema HD Display model, a unit that carries the distinction of being certified by the SWOP organization, a standards group for publication-quality printing.

Numerous manufacturers have joined the graphic-arts–quality LCD supply chain, including Formac Electronic, LaCie, and Sony, all of which are offering displays that rival the CRT units they are designed to replace.

Benefits of LCD displays are their apparent sharpness, which is a result of their constant color state (as opposed to the rapid flicker of the CRT), their flat screen, which eliminates distortion common to CRT displays, and their weight. Apple's Cinema HD Display can be carried under one arm—it's about 8 kilos (18 lbs.), as compared to more than 40 kilos (90 lbs.) for a CRT with similar resolution.

LCD displays also do not decay slowly over time. Their color and brightness will remain constant for years. When the light source eventually fails—which will happen suddenly—it can be replaced with a new unit in a repair shop (not a consumer replacement).

Adobe Gamma for Windows, and its Macintosh counterpart display-calibration software, are visual calibration systems. Their settings are based on the perceptions of the viewer and are subjective. A visual calibration system can create only a generalized profile, and cannot be repeated or duplicated exactly.

Precision calibration of a display can be achieved by employing a device called a *colorimeter*. A colorimeter is a worthwhile investment if accurate color is critical to your work. For example, if you are doing a significant amount of color correction for output to color separations or high-end RGB or ink-jet prints, it's essential to work in a predictable color environment from session to session.

Never attach a suction cup device to an LCD display; the delicate glass and circuitry can be broken easily by the removal of the suction cup. Instead, tip the display on its back and place the instrument on the surface, or use a device that is specifically designed for LCD displays.

The Viewing Environment

Professionals in the printing and publishing industries have known for years that to achieve good color on a computer display you need (among other things) to put the display into a "proper" viewing environment. The International Organization for Standardization (ISO) and its partner national organizations adopted in 2001 a new color standard for viewing color for the photographic and graphic arts industries worldwide. Called ISO 3664, the standard dictates, among other things, that a proper viewing environment is a workspace without windows or skylights—no natural light at all. They also specify that the color of the walls should be neutral gray (the ISO committee specifies the colors Munsell N5 through N7). The walls should be absent of colorful artwork, and the artist in front of the computer should be wearing neutral clothing, preferably gray or black. Room lighting recommendations in the ISO standard are for very low, preferably diffuse lighting of the proper 5000 K temperature. The committee also ratified a 6500 K color white point for computer displays.

Is this a pleasant place to work? No; it's pretty dull, but it's a workplace where color can be viewed most accurately. Some design studios and professional prepress operations have such a workplace but reserve it for "soft proofing" visits, which provide an opportunity for workers to go into "the cave" only long enough to approve color on-screen. They then return to their own workstations to do production work.

Designating a Display Profile

Having a calibrated display and a proper viewing environment are not enough. You must tell your operating system about the profile, setting it as the system profile. Then, when you launch Photoshop, it will use your display profile for some of its color display calculations.

ACCURATE CALIBRATION WITH A COLORIMETER

A colorimeter attaches to the screen with suction cups (for CRTs) or a pressure pad (for LCD displays). It measures the color temperature, gamma, and white point of the display (see "The Yin/Yang of Color" later in this chapter if you aren't already familiar with those basic characteristics of any display). For this discussion, I've chosen to use a GretagMacbeth Eye-One Display, which currently costs about $250. The device is bundled with software that analyzes the color and creates an ICC profile based on the measured output of the display. The software provides instructions to take you through the calibration process.

Here's a step-by-step overview of display calibration with the Eye-One Display:

1. Be sure that the CRT display has been on for at least one half hour before calibrating (LCDs require about five minutes). Plug the Eye-One Display into any available USB port on your computer.

2. Next, launch the software. After the initial splash screen, you'll see the Eye-One application.

3. In the Gamma field, choose the correct Gamma (contrast and saturation). Choose either Gamma 1.8 for print or Gamma 2.2 for Web or video projects (these are often labeled Macintosh and PC standards, but they have more to do with the purpose of your work than the computer you use).

4. Choose a White Point. For printing applications, 6500 K (Kelvin) is the white point that is recommended by the ISO 3664 industry standard.

5. Click the right arrow. You are instructed to place the Eye-One on your display. The instrument has dozens of tiny, soft suction cups, and is safe to put on both CRT and LCD displays. By hanging the instrument over the top of the display, with the cord over the top of the display, it will usually stay in place. If not, you can hold it in place with gentle pressure. Click the Next button.

Continued on next page

ACCURATE CALIBRATION WITH A COLORIMETER

6. The software displays a series of black-and-white fields to determine the location of the instrument, and then displays a number of color fields—pure red, green, and blue, and a variety of grays. The Eye-One Display measures the colors and sends the readings to the software, which uses the measurements to calculate the profile.

7. After the calibration is complete, Eye-One Display asks you to name your profile. Typically the profile is automatically set as the default display profile.

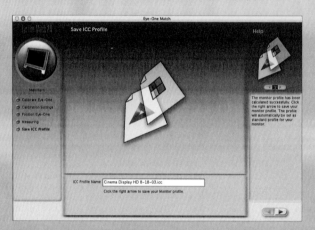

8. To repeat the procedure for a second display, change your default display in the control panels within your operating system and then repeat the process.

Instruments such as the Eye-One Display have the advantage of producing a consistent display environment from session to session (or display to display), ensuring the consistency of the color you see on-screen during the editing process over an extended period of time.

In Mac OS X, to tell your system about the display profile you have created, open the Apple menu → System Preferences → Displays → Color. Then, from the resulting menu, choose a display profile. (Running the Calibrate function in this menu, or running a calibration software application such as Eye-One Display, will automatically assign the profile.)

In Windows 2000 and XP, choose Start → Settings → Control Panel → Display → Settings → Advanced → Color Management.

Choose the system profile or the profile you created with Adobe Gamma or with the colorimeter. The computer will know how to correct the color displayed on your display through the profile, making adjustments on the fly to all images displayed on-screen.

Photoshop automatically looks to the operating system to get the current display profile, and you cannot change that setting from within Photoshop. But it is possible to "turn color management off" in the Color Settings control panel. This has the effect of returning Photoshop to the functionality of Photoshop 4, limiting the color gamut to that of the display and disabling all color-space conversions (this is *not* a good idea).

The Yin/Yang of Color

As I discuss the gamuts of color working spaces, you must understand that the gamut of a display is a pyramidal space with its lower corners in the red, green, and blue areas of an industry-standard color chart (the top of the pyramid is "white"). The gamut chart in Figure C15 in the color section plots the available colors of a device (a display, for example) compared to the gamut of colors humans can see—and the differences are extreme.

All the color spaces of the world of graphic arts and photography converge inside a large space that falls well within the colors of human vision. With Photoshop's support for the color working space, you want to choose a space that is adequate to accommodate all the colors of your output device, while providing a reasonable view of that color on your computer display.

The color system used for printing color on paper is the physical opposite of the color system used to emit light on the face of a display. With light-emitting devices, the unit creates, and mixes, colors from the three additive color primaries—red, green, and blue. When you add equal parts of full intensity red, green, and blue light on a display, you get white. The process is called *additive color* because you add colors together to get white.

The vibrancy and brightness of these primary colors on a computer display are usually very different than they will be on the printed page, because the printing process begins with the available white light in the viewing environment, and then filters out components of that light to create a visible color. The printing process is considered *subtractive color* because colors are created by subtracting color components from white light with filters (layers of ink).

When you put pigment on a sheet of paper, superimposing the primary colors of ink (cyan, yellow, magenta) on top of each other (in an ideal world) you should get pure black. In reality, because of impurities in the pigments, you get something that approximates deep, yucky brown (a highly technical term!). Because pigments subtract light components from the white light in the environment, they reduce its intensity, making it less bright than the original light. Subtractive colorants always reduce the amount of light reflected back at the viewer, and thus it's difficult for the printed page to compete with the beautiful color on a good computer display. And there we have the classic yin/yang of color—the conflict between the two physical principles of color reproduction—and another reason we need color management in our lives. The strengths of emitted light on a display are the weaknesses of colors on the printed page.

If you want to reproduce the best color possible on the printed page, while still displaying the color in the same images, you must acknowledge and accept the weakness of the display relative to the printed page, and vice versa. The compromise you must learn to accept is that there are colors at the blue, red, and brilliant green points of the triangle that you can show on a display, but cannot print with the standard four-color ink sets used on four-color ink-jet printers and printing presses.

Similarly there are colors on the printed page—specifically light green through cyan—that cannot be shown on a computer display accurately. This is not an issue of quality as much as it is an issue of exclusivity. The primary colors on computer displays are the opposites of the primaries for print; thus each is unable to show the strongest colors of its complementary process.

Making a Colorful Match

Choosing a color working space that is appropriate to the printed page is critically important so that you don't force Photoshop to remap the colors in an image inappropriately. You want to pick a working space that is not too big (so you don't add colors that are out of the printable range) and not too small (so you don't omit colors needed to accurately represent the image).

The gamut chart in the color section (Figure C15) shows the comparative gamuts of several of Photoshop's color working spaces. Superimposed in yellow is the gamut of standard printing inks on gloss paper (called the SWOP Coated gamut).

Gamma

Gamma is a measurement of the display's contrast and saturation. It is expressed as a number, from 1.0 to about 2.5, that describes the curvature of a contrast curve. The Macintosh has traditionally used a gamma of 1.8, which is relatively flat compared to television. Windows PCs use a 2.2 gamma value, which provides more contrast and saturation. The gamma of Windows is closer to the appearance of television images, and the 1.8 gamma adopted by the Macintosh is more like the contrast and saturation achieved by printing on good paper. If you are working on images destined for television, the World Wide Web, or multimedia, it's better to use a gamma of 2.2. If your destination is the printed page, a gamma of 1.8 to 2.0 is more appropriate.

Getting to Know RGB Color Working Space

The color working space is, as already mentioned, a plane for holding and handling images in Photoshop that is independent of the display and other devices. The RGB color working spaces of Photoshop CS include four popular color spaces, your default display profile, and a variety of others (all RGB profiles are listed). Photoshop gives you the ability to choose others that are designed for other working environments. Each has a combination of characteristics, including its color temperature, gamma, and white point (the settings for "white"). White is a variable thing in the world of computer-generated color, because the effective "whiteness" of the non-image areas is a key component in getting the color on the screen to match the color that is produced by a printer or a commercial printing press.

sRGB IEC61966-2.1

Of the color spaces available, sRGB (the *s* stands for *standardized*) is the smallest. This means that it puts serious limitations on the colors available in your color palette in Photoshop. The sRGB space, designed by Microsoft and Hewlett-Packard, is well suited to corporate computer displays and images destined for viewing on the World Wide Web. It is also suitable for output to low-end desktop printers. sRGB has taken a lot of flack for being destructive to images with large color gamuts, and indeed it is. But, if you look at the purpose of sRGB—making images look good on corporate computers—the color space makes more sense and is useful for its intended purpose.

It is set as the default color working space in Photoshop CS (as it was in the past few versions), and that is the root of the controversy surrounding it. Adobe allows you to change this setting—but most people don't realize that it is important to do so. Use sRGB as your color working space, or convert images to this space, when developing images for display on the Web or output to office printers. For photographic and graphic arts uses, it's better to use one of the following.

> The Japan Electronic Industry Development Association (JEIDA), a group of manufacturers that make consumer digital cameras, standardized sRGB as the default color space for *all* consumer digital cameras. Thus, opening an image from virtually any of the many consumer digital cameras is best done into the sRGB space. In 2001, Epson developed a special software tool that expands the color gamut of consumer cameras. Called Print Image Matching (PIM), it is available on consumer digital cameras from many manufacturers. PIM allows a much better color gamut in images without breaking any of the standards agreed to by the JEIDA group (Epson offers a free Photoshop plug-in that will unlock the larger gamut in images taken on PIM-enabled consumer cameras). Professional digital cameras do not suffer from the sRGB limitations, usually supporting one or more of the larger color gamuts.

Adobe RGB (1998)

The Adobe RGB (1998) color working space is large enough to accommodate graphic arts images and most scanned images, and allows for good representation on most high-quality displays. Adobe RGB (1998) has a white point of 6500 K, which is in line with the latest

ISO standard (ISO 3664) for color viewing in critical color conditions. Its gamma is 2.2. Adobe RGB (1998) is also able to accommodate conversions to CMYK for printing with good results; very little of the CMYK color is clipped or remapped in the process.

> Don't confuse the *K* that crops up in color discussions about white point with *K* for kilobytes or black (as in CMYK). Here it stands for degrees Kelvin; 6500 K is approximately the color temperature of outdoor ambient light in the middle of a clear day.

Apple RGB

The original desktop "graphic arts" CRT display was the Apple 13-inch RGB monitor. It created an industry, providing color previews to millions of users from 1988 to about 1995, when it was replaced by larger and much better displays. Based on a Sony Trinitron picture tube, the Apple monitor had good color saturation and a small but reasonable color gamut. The Apple RGB color working space is a good choice for converting images from unknown sources. Almost all the stock photos made between 1988 and 1995 were made with computers and scanners connected to an Apple 13-inch monitor; and although the quality of displays has improved substantially since then, that monitor still represents the colors of the era. This Apple RGB working space uses 6500 K color temperature for white and a 1.8 gamma, which is relatively flat in appearance, appropriate to print applications.

ColorMatch RGB

The Radius PressView monitor was, for years, the viewing standard of the graphic and visual arts. Almost all professional color work was created on monitors in this class. Now discontinued, the PressView will live on in the form of a color working space that matches its characteristics.

ColorMatch RGB represents a good gamut of colors, a 1.8 gamma, and a 5000 K white point, which causes some images to turn a sickly yellow color. Use this one if it causes the colors on your screen to look good while maintaining a pleasant white. If your images turn yellowish on-screen, switch to Adobe RGB (1998), which has characteristics that will deliver a cooler white and a more attractive appearance on most displays. If you have a PressView, this is an excellent working space for you. (If you have a PressView, it's too old to be a critical-color monitor; replace it this year.)

ColorSync RGB—Generic RGB Profile

This Mac-specific option loads the color profile currently set in the Displays control panel, as shown in Figure 15.2. From this control panel, you can choose from a list of ICC display profiles that are found in the ICC profiles list in the System folder. The list includes both display profiles and the Color Working Space profiles provided with Adobe Photoshop.

Display RGB

This profile sets the color working space to the current display profile. Use this working space if other programs that you will use to view the image do not support color management.

Other Color Working Spaces

You can choose or load other RGB color working spaces that were the primary spaces in Photoshop 5.0 and 5.5. These appear, along with several dozen others, in the Edit → Color Settings (Windows) and Photoshop → Color Settings (Mac) dialog box under Working Spaces RGB. They include:

CIE RGB The International Commission on Illumination (CIE, after its French name) is an organization of scientists who work with color. CIE standards define how we measure and describe color in every field of human endeavor. This working space is based on the CIE standard RGB color space, a 2.2 gamma, and Standard Illuminant E white point. Its gamut of colors is slightly larger than that of the Apple monitor, and it works almost identically when opening or converting images from older files, those that were created and saved from early versions of Photoshop.

NTSC (1953) The National Television System Committee established a color gamut and a white point for television in the U.S. that is maintained to this day. Use this color space if you are working on images that will be displayed on television. The gamma is 2.2, and the white point is a very cool Standard Illuminant C.

PAL/SECAM PAL and SECAM are European and Asian standards for television color and contrast. If your work is destined for television outside North America, this setting is appropriate. The gamma is 2.2, and the white point is 6500 K.

SMPTE-C A movie industry standard, SMPTE-C is compliant with the Society of Motion Picture and Television Engineers standards for motion picture illuminants. It has the same white point as the two television standards, above, and its color temperature is 6500 K.

Wide Gamut RGB Adobe created this color working space to accommodate images created on the computer, where vibrant greens, bright reds, and deep blues are created and must be maintained. This color space is particularly well suited to work that is destined for an RGB film recorder. The gamma is 2.2, and the white point is a yellowish 5000 K, especially useful to those recording onto "electronic" color transparency films. Wide Gamut might sound attractive to those who believe that more is better, but in fact, too large a color gamut can be damaging to many images. Wide Gamut color remapping will result in strange color shifts in images. Know what you are doing before using this space.

Figure 15.2

The ColorSync RGB option

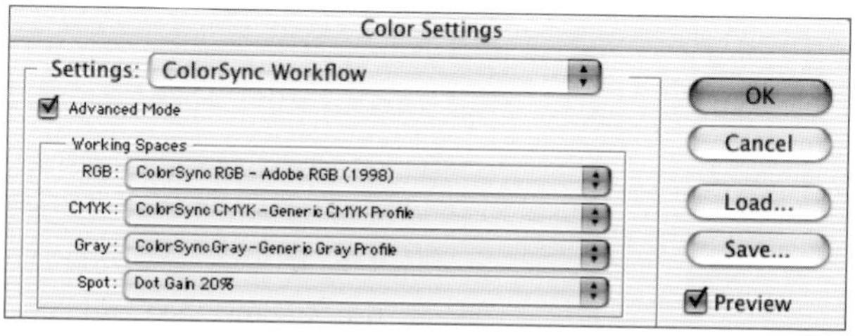

There are numerous RGB spaces available for profiles of specific displays, laptop computers, printers, or working conditions. You can save and load specific profiles from other sources, or you can make your own by using Adobe Gamma or a colorimeter and associated software.

Color Settings

Photoshop 5 made significant changes to the color settings, which remain intact through this latest version. Photoshop uses ICC color management at all times (even when color management is technically "off"). The settings you select for color handling can make a huge difference in the appearance and reproduction of color.

Choose Edit → Color Settings (Win) or Photoshop → Color Settings (Mac) to access the Color Settings dialog box (see Figure 15.3). It has two modes: Standard and Advanced. (The Conversion Options and Advanced Controls areas shown in the figure are hidden if you clear the Advanced box.)

You should configure color settings prior to opening a document or creating a new document. The Color Settings dialog box controls your color working spaces, your color management policies, and your settings for what should happen when Photoshop opens an image that either has no embedded profile or has one that is different from the current color working space.

First, set your Color Settings defaults according to the kind of work you do. Choose a setting from the Settings pull-down menu at the top of the window, as shown in Figure 15.4. If you are unsure, a good place to start is with U.S. Prepress Defaults, which includes the Adobe RGB (1998) color space and typical North American standards for printing color, U.S. Web Coated (SWOP) v2. This is a good space for both RGB and CMYK colors, and will cause little, if any, harm to images handled by the program (see the following section for more on this).

> Any change to the defaults will create a custom setting. You can save your custom settings with a new name by clicking the Save button. Your settings will remain intact until you change to another setting.

CMYK Working Space

If you plan to convert your image from RGB mode to CMYK, you can choose a color working space for CMYK. If you have a four-color (CMYK) profile for a printer, for example, or a printing press that you normally use, you can set it if it's on the list.

If you don't have a custom profile to use, there are several "generic" CMYK profiles you can load. For North America, you can use the U.S. Sheetfed Coated v.2 or U.S. Sheetfed Uncoated v.2 profiles provided by Adobe. If you are outside North America, choose either

Eurostandard (coated or uncoated) or the Japan Standard profiles as appropriate to your location. These CMYK profiles will be used when you convert to CMYK with the Mode → CMYK or Mode → Convert To Profile commands, and the results will be acceptable.

Creating and Using Custom Profiles

A custom profile, made with color management software, will often provide more precise color than any of the more generic profiles available in Photoshop. Custom profiles can often be obtained from your printer or from the manufacturers of the better quality ink-jet printers. Custom profiles can also be made with profiling software such as GretagMacbeth's ProfileMaker Pro, and Monaco Systems' MonacoCOLOR, among others.

If you are printing to a CMYK device that provides a custom profile, or if you've created a custom profile by using a spectrophotometer or a profile-writing program, you can load it as your CMYK workspace in the Color Settings palette. Simply load the profile in the appropriate directory on your computer (Windows requires the .icc suffix on profile names), and it will show up next time you restart Photoshop. Change the CMYK profile to the custom profile, and all CMYK conversions will be made with that profile when you change an image to CMYK by choosing Image → Mode → CMYK and apply the Convert To Profile and Assign Profile selections.

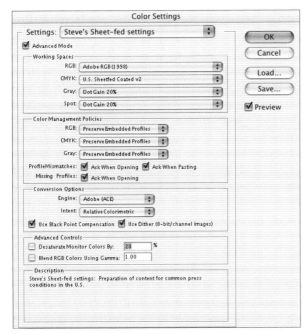

Figure 15.3

The Color Settings dialog box, where color profiles and color management policies are set. These settings are a critical part of getting color right in Photoshop.

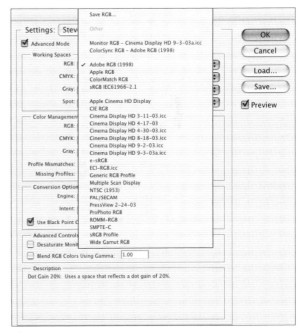

Figure 15.4

The pull-down options show most profiles available on your computer, allowing for custom configurations of the color settings.

Color Management Policies

Color management policies determine how Photoshop manages color as it opens an image. You can specify how Photoshop will manage the color of documents that have no embedded profile, or whose profile differs from that specified in the Color Settings dialog box.

If you simply reopen a file on the same machine, using the same color working space specified in the Color Settings dialog box, the file will open without interruption. But if you move the file to another machine with different color settings, or you open an image that came from a computer using different color settings, Photoshop puts on the brakes, asking, in effect, "Wait. This file is not from around these parts! What should I do with it?"

Putting the responsibility for controlling how files are opened on the user, Photoshop asks you to set one of the policies for each type of file you might be opening—RGB, CMYK, and Grayscale. The choices for these policies are as follows:

Off When a file type's Color Management Policies option is set to Off, files with unknown profiles will be opened with color management turned off. This causes Photoshop to behave more like Photoshop 4 (Adobe calls it *pre–color management*), where the display's color working space gamut limits the color available in any image (this is a bad idea).

Preserve Embedded Profiles Opening images that already have a color working space profile embedded will retain that space. Any new documents will be created within the current color working space. This is a safe approach to opening files with embedded profiles, because it will enable these images to be opened without making any modification to the color working space of the image. After working on the file, you can save the document and retain the embedded profile. When importing color to an RGB or grayscale document—cutting and pasting an image from another with a different profile document, for example—appearance takes priority over numeric values. When importing color to a CMYK document, numeric values take priority over appearance.

Convert To Working RGB/CMYK/Grayscale (This option changes according to the image type.) This will cause mathematic conversion, remapping all the color values in the image to the current color working space. This conversion can cause drastic changes in the color of an image from a color space much smaller or much larger than the current space; however, it is the preferred method for converting from other color spaces to the CWS and does not usually cause problems.

> Whenever Photoshop opens an image in a working space other than the default, it will mark the title bar with an asterisk to indicate that it is not using the default working space. The asterisk will also show when you are in the Proofing mode (⌘-Y). An image that has been opened with "Leave as is (don't color manage)" will display the color space in the title bar followed by a # symbol to indicate that the file has not been modified by a color profile.

The Embedded Profile Mismatch Dialog Box

In the Color Settings dialog box, there are two Ask When Opening and one Ask When Pasting check boxes. These determine the behavior of Photoshop when opening an image with no profile or a mismatched profile, or when pasting an image into a Photoshop document. It is a good idea to check each of these boxes so that you can decide, on a case-by-case basis, how to deal with these variables as they arrive. When you open or paste from a mismatched image, the Embedded Profile Mismatch dialog box (see Figure 15.5) will appear, displaying the name of the embedded profile. (If the file has no profile at all, the Missing Profile dialog comes up instead; that's described in the following section.)

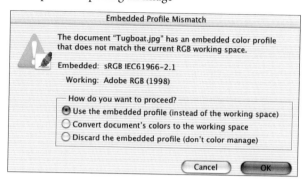

Figure 15.5

Photoshop can alert you that the image you're opening or pasting from doesn't use your current color profile.

Making color management decisions for each image may seem time-consuming, but it's important to handle each image according to its source and purpose. Assigning an incorrect color profile to an image is damaging to the color in the image. It's worth the time to assign the correct color profile as an image is opened.

Of course, in some circumstances you might want all CMYK images with mismatched profiles to be mapped to your current CMYK working space. If this is the case, you can set that CMYK working space in the menu in the Color Settings dialog box, and then clear the Profile Mismatches check box to cause this to occur every time an image is opened. (However, doing that will also cause RGB images to open into your RGB working space without notice.) If you change this setting for processing a batch of images, be sure to put it back to Ask When Opening after you have finished. This will prevent Photoshop from making unwanted color changes as you open files with missing or mismatched profiles.

Opening Images with Missing Profiles

When you open an image with no profile or with a mismatched profile, Photoshop displays the Missing Profile dialog box, where you can choose from several options (see Figure 15.6).

Option	Effect
Leave As Is	The image will not be color-managed and will display in the CWS.
Assign Working RGB	The current RGB working space is assigned to the image.
Assign Profile	The image will be assigned a profile selected from the pop-up menu.

The Assign Profile setting has a secondary check box that will subsequently convert the document to the current working space. This will result in the image taking on the embedded profile of the current working space when it is saved. The net effect of this is to assign the colors to a working space that you think is the correct one for the original image, and then convert it to the current working space so its embedded profile will be adequate for the reproduction plans you have. It is possible to harm an image by assigning a profile, and then converting to a smaller color working space, so be careful when making this selection.

Passing images through this dialog box requires some thought. If you know (or can guess) the source of the image, it is best to assign a profile appropriate to that source. For example, if the image comes from a source for which you have a profile, assign that profile. Converting to the working space after the assignment will cause the current working space profile to be embedded when the image is saved. It does not otherwise change the color in the image.

For example, say you open an image from a *Digital Stock* disc that was created prior to the common use of ICC profiles (about 1995). Although Digital Stock scanned everything with a calibrated display, the images themselves were not embedded with a scanner profile. Later, when ICC profiles became common, Digital Stock (later acquired by Corbis) made the profile available; applying that profile to the image results in the image being adjusted correctly for display.

But what if you don't have the right source profile? It's easy enough to try a few profiles to find a solution to your problem. If you assume that the image was scanned and saved on a Macintosh computer using an Apple 13-inch RGB monitor, you can assign the Apple RGB working space to the image.

If you think that the image came from a Windows PC with a "standard" monitor, try sRGB and the result will probably be good enough. There is not much difference between the Apple 13 and sRGB color spaces, and images processed into those spaces will look almost identical (apart from overall brightness differences between the 1.8 Macintosh gamma and the 2.2 Windows gamma).

But if the processed image seems flat and lacking in color, it is likely that it came from a larger color space such as Adobe RGB (1998). Choose Image → Mode → Assign Profile. Assign the Adobe RGB (1998) profile. The image will probably look much better. Remember that for this technique to work, your display must be calibrated. If not, the image you see on-screen might not be the image you'll see in print.

The theme here is to find a matching color space—one that is complimentary to the image you are opening. If you open into a color space that is too small, the color will be dulled, often shifted slightly toward green. If you open into too large a color space, the colors in the image will shift—often unpleasantly—resulting in an image that is too rosy or strangely green. If this happens, close the image without saving it and reopen it with another profile.

_____
Figure 15.6
The Missing Profile dialog box

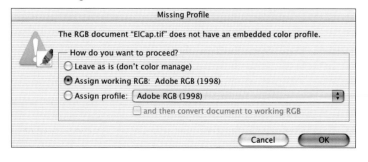

Advanced Color Settings

Checking the Advanced Mode check box at the top of the Color Settings dialog box displays two sets of additional settings shown at the bottom of Figure 15.3, Conversion Options and Advanced Controls.

Engine

In the Conversion Options area, the Engine setting enables you to set or change the color management "engine" that is used for color conversions (see Figure 15.7). Depending on the options available on your computer, those options range from a selection of two to six or more.

Adobe has its own color management engine (in the parlance of the industry this is called a CMM, or color management method): Adobe Color Engine (ACE). Other CMMs you might encounter include Apple ColorSync, Heidelberg, Kodak, Imation, or Agfa.

Which engine should you choose? Each company suggests that its CMM uses a superior method of polynomial voodoo to convert color. Adobe similarly claims that theirs is superior. A good suggestion is to use a CMM that is available in all of the applications you use to manage color. This will ensure that color is being converted similarly between applications. For example, if you use Adobe Photoshop to make some conversions and QuarkXPress (through Apple ColorSync) to make others, then it would be a good idea to set Photoshop to use Apple ColorSync, so that all your conversions are done with the same mathematical "engine."

In reality (and with apologies to the various authors of these CMMs), the net effect of a color management engine is essentially the same. Even experts can discern only subtle differences, so it's not worth a lot of worry. You are certainly welcome to try various combinations of engines and rendering intents and decide for yourself.

Conversions through Rendering Intent

The next item under Conversion Options is cryptically named Intent (see Figure 15.8). The ICC has established a set of four "rendering intent" settings under which color conversions can be made. Each has a purpose, and each can be used to maximize the quality of your images for a particular task. Rendering intents cause the color of an image to be modified while it is being moved into a new color space. These modifications can appear as subtle changes or glow-in-the-dark shifts that make color images look odd. Here you will examine them and learn about their purposes.

Figure 15.7

The Engine conversion options

Figure 15.8

The Intent conversion options

Perceptual

Perceptual is a rendering intent designed to make photos of generalized subjects look "good" when converted to a new color space. The Perceptual rendering intent uses a method of remapping colors that preserves the relationships between colors to maintain a "pleasant" appearance. Although color accuracy will often suffer, the appearance of the image will generally follow the appearance of the original scene. Most photo applications default to Perceptual rendering, and Photoshop does this in many of its default color settings (U.S. Prepress Defaults sets it to Relative Colorimetric, which is correct). Most people find Perceptual rendering pleasing—but read on before making a decision about your imaging policies.

Saturation

Saturation is for business graphics and illustrations made with solid colors. Of the four intents, it is the easiest to understand and the easiest to use. Saturation rendering will result in bright, fully saturated colors in solid areas, and fairly strong contrast applied to differences in color. Saturation rendering sacrifices color accuracy for sharp contrast and saturation. It simply lives up to its name.

If you convert RGB images from EPS illustration programs such as Adobe Illustrator, the Saturation rendering intent will result in a better-looking image after conversion than the other intents. Saturation is best used when converting graphs, charts, and other business presentations.

Relative Colorimetric

Relative Colorimetric rendering is a method in which color precision is preferred over saturation, resulting in a more accurate conversion of colors into a new color space. Adobe's experts and many prepress professionals recommend that Relative Colorimetric rendering be used for most color conversions. One of the key components of this rendering intent is its handling of white. Relative Colorimetric rendering uses the white of the color working space rather than the measured white of the paper, which may lighten the specular highlights in an image. Otherwise colors are mapped to their most accurate positions to prevent radical color shifts.

> Relative Colorimetric should always be used with Black Point Compensation. Otherwise, shadow detail will plug up, because the black points in the conversion might not be mapped correctly.

Absolute Colorimetric

This rendering intent is much like the Relative Colorimetric intent, except that it renders the whites differently. Whites in the source will remain the same in the resulting file. Although this sounds obscure, it produces an image that can be used effectively for proofing files that will print on nonwhite or off-white papers (such as newsprint). Absolute Colorimetric is a rendering intent that is designed for those who have a specific reason for using it; otherwise, avoid it.

Black Point Compensation/Dither

There are two additional settings in the Color Settings dialog box under Conversion Options: Use Black Point Compensation and Use Dither (8-Bit/Channel Images). Black Point Compensation is generally set, because it maintains saturation of solid black in conversions that would normally desaturate blacks.

An example of this can be seen when converting RGB images to CMYK for print. If you leave this box unchecked and make a conversion (Image → Mode → CMYK), the darkest blacks will often be remapped to the closest color that is within the gamut of the destination profile, which might include an adjustment for dot gain. This adjustment will desaturate the solids in order to keep their value below the total ink coverage number, but will result in some washed-out colors where a solid would be better. Black Point Compensation corrects this problem.

> See the sidebar on Dot Gain later in this chapter

The Use Dither check box causes 8-bit images to be dithered when converted to 8-bit images of another color mode. Dithering is a method of alternating tonal values in tiny steps to smooth out tonal shifts. Checking this setting will result in smoother gradations in the converted file.

Advanced Controls

The settings Desaturate Monitor Colors By and Blend RGB Colors Using Gamma, though recommended for "advanced users only," can improve the accuracy of the preview of images on your display.

Desaturating Monitor Colors

The Desaturate Monitor Colors By option instructs Photoshop to desaturate colors by a specified amount when displayed on-screen. This option can be helpful when attempting to view the full range of colors in images with color gamuts larger than that of your display.

An example of this might be viewing on any display an image whose color working space is Wide Gamut RGB. Because the gamut in Wide Gamut is larger than any production display, this function will simulate the tonality of the image—even though the monitor can't display the actual color beyond the range of its phosphors. Be careful, though—using this feature can cause errors between the displayed color and final output color.

Blending RGB Colors

The Blend RGB Colors Using Gamma setting controls the blending of RGB colors on-screen. When the option is selected, RGB colors are blended by using a selected curve. The range of values available here is between 1.0, which is linear (it has no effect), and 2.2, which creates slightly higher-contrast edge transitions. This option will also affect the blending of tones too (different values than in a gamma compensated edit), as in overlapping content in two layers at reduced opacity. This option should probably remain unchecked by most common users.

When the option is not selected, RGB colors are blended in the document's color space, matching the color display behavior of other applications.

Previewing in CMYK

The world of graphic arts reproduction is changing, and many printing firms are now using a fully color-managed work flow in preparation for printing. Those who do so want you to provide your images to them in RGB color, with embedded working space profiles.

Printers request these files because there is no "generic" CMYK separation that is correct for all types of paper and ink sets. The separation made for sheet-fed offset on uncoated paper is drastically different from the separation made for web-fed glossy paper. Printers want control over this conversion.

When an image is destined for the printed page, it is necessary to preview the image before sending the file to the printer. You also need the ability to preview an image in CMYK *without making the conversion* to CMYK. Photoshop provides the Proof Colors control, which enables the on-screen preview to simulate a variety of reproduction processes without converting the file to the final color space.

To prepare for and carry out an on-screen proof, first tell Photoshop what kind of proof you want to see. Choose View → Proof Setup to select the type of proof to preview (see Figures 15.9 and 15.10). The first option is for Custom setups, which enable essentially any profile to be applied for the proof.

After the setup has been completed, you can view a "soft proof" of the image on-screen by choosing View → Proof Colors or pressing ⌘/Ctrl-Y. The image will change to preview in the color space you've chosen in the Setup window. Options include proofing CMYK, each channel individually, or the CMY colors without black. Three RGB display profiles are also available, one for a generic Macintosh monitor, one for a generic Windows monitor, and one for the monitor set as Monitor RGB. Photoshop will look to the operating system to get the assigned profile for the display for this proofing simulation.

Simulating Paper White and Ink Black

One of Photoshop's proofing capabilities is to show the white point of the converted image as either *bright white*, using the display's white as the target, or *paper white*, as measured and calculated in the ICC profile. When working with papers such as newsprint and other nonwhite substrates, you can get a better simulation of the actual product if you check the option for Paper White in the View → Proof Setup → Custom menu. The display will show an image that more accurately represents the appearance of the image on the nonwhite substrate.

Simulating Ink Black in the proof setup will cause the proof to represent the actual measured black of the profile rather than a solid black as dark as the display might make it. When this happens, you will see the darkest black from the measured profile, and the image will usually shift away from deep, solid black to a slightly lighter charcoal image. On most images, the differences are hard to see. Some profiles are able to represent the dark blacks and the paper white with tremendous range, and these will cause less of a shift on the screen during a proof event.

Showing Out-of-Gamut Colors

There are usually colors in an original image (RGB as opposed to CMYK) that exceed the color gamut of the reproducing device. These colors are not going to print correctly when converted to CMYK and put on a press. To preview the colors that will not print accurately, you can ask Photoshop to highlight the out-of-gamut areas on-screen with a special color by choosing View → Gamut Warning. Usually these colors are small amounts of relatively unimportant information in an image, but checking is a good idea because the out-of-gamut color might be *the most important* color in the image.

In the Ch15 folder of the CD, I've included a photo of a yellow truck (gamwarn1.tif) that shows color and tonality nicely on-screen.

Figure 15.9

The Proof Setup menu enables you to preview any profile and rendering intent as the proof destination.

Figure 15.10

The Custom Proof Setup dialog box enables you to select an ICC profile, rendering intent, and whether to simulate Paper White or Ink Black.

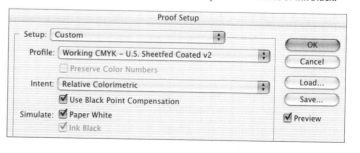

But when Gamut Warning is turned on, the colors that exceed the currently selected CMYK profile are shown in the color selected to show out-of-gamut values in Photoshop's Preferences palette—the default is gray (see Figure 15.11). These areas, some of them crucial to this particular image, indicate that the colors on the printed sheet will not look as vibrant as the colors in the original. For more on viewing and selecting out-of-gamut colors, see Chapter 21, "Making Difficult Selections."

If the image contains a great deal of gray, so as to make the gamut warning less distinct, you can change the warning color in the Transparency & Gamut preferences (see Chapter 5).

Converting Files

In spite of the color-managed work flow options, many Photoshop practitioners prefer to make their own CMYK conversions. Some printers insist that all files arriving for output be CMYK. To make such conversions, you must set the proper ICC color profile in the Color Settings dialog box, and then make a change of Mode to CMYK. Remember that the quality of a color separation made in Photoshop depends on the quality of the CMYK profile.

Converting Profiles

You can convert your color mode and profile by choosing Image → Mode → Convert To Profile. This dialog box enables you to select from RGB, CMYK, and other profile types, and also to select the rendering intent for the image you're making (see Figure 15.12). If you choose a profile that requires a change in color mode, Photoshop makes the switch; for example, if you're in an RGB file and select a CMYK profile, your file ends up in CMYK mode.

Figure 15.11

An image with considerable out-of-gamut color will surprise you. Choose Gamut Warning to show those colors that are in the original image but that cannot be reproduced by the current CMYK working space profile or Proof Setup profile. The out-of-gamut color is set in Photoshop's Preferences palette.

Assigning Profiles

To reassign an image from one profile to another *without changing color mode,* choose Image → Mode → Assign Profile to display the dialog box shown in Figure 15.13. This is helpful if an image was opened with color management turned off, and you want to assign a profile to the image so it can be processed in an ICC-compliant work flow. When working in RGB, only RGB profiles are available in this menu, and only CMYK are available profiles for those images.

> Assign does not change the current numerical values in the file, whereas Convert will alter the values of the file.

Grayscale Profiles

Converting from color to black-and-white (also called monochrome or grayscale) in early versions of Photoshop was less than ideal. Photoshop's luminance-only conversion was seldom optimal. Converting with the Channel Mixer improved the process, but the ability to use proper grayscale ICC profiles for grayscale conversions makes it even better.

Conversions using Image → Mode → Grayscale were often "too mechanical" to have much artistic value, and the methods using the Color Mixer and calculations were too tedious to be effective in production. When using an ICC grayscale profile, the conversion not only is correct for the reproduction process, but results in a more pleasing image than in past versions. Assigning a Grayscale profile in the Color Settings palette causes the Image → Mode → Grayscale process to use the profile to make the conversion rather than relying solely on the luminance value of the image. Some images will benefit from the use of the Channel Mixer, which allows conversions with an editorial bias, allowing the operator to change a color image into monochrome while asserting tonal changes that improve specific colors in an image.

Figure 15.12

The Convert To Profile dialog box

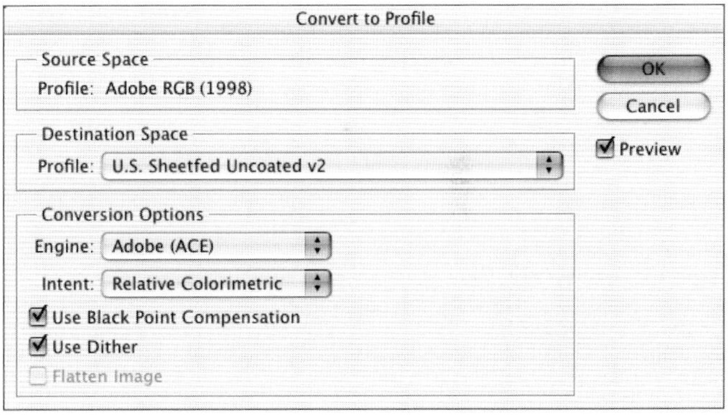

Figure 15.13

The Assign Profile dialog box

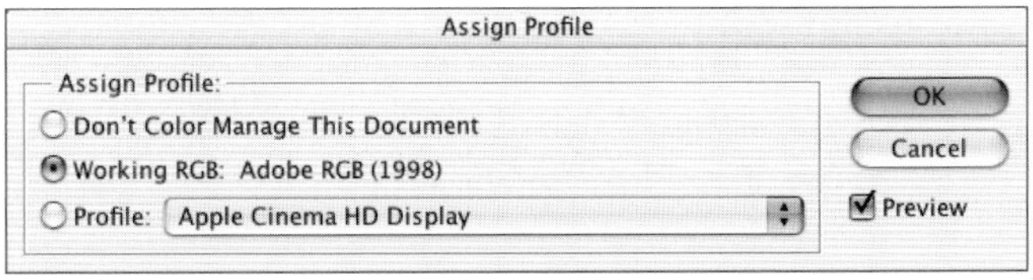

Spot Color Profiles

Photoshop treats spot color profiles like grayscale profiles and applies them in the same way. There are standard profiles loaded by the program, which are based on various dot-gain values. If

Figure 15.14

The Custom Dot Gain menu item is located in the pull-down menu for assigning a profile to grayscale and spot colors in the Color Settings dialog box.

you are inclined to make your own profiles, it's a process of printing a gray ramp scale (it is printed automatically by Photoshop if you choose Calibration Bars when printing) and then measuring the resulting target patches with a reflective densitometer.

What you are measuring is *dot area,* the ratio of ink to paper for a selected spot on the printed page. If you read the 50% patch, for example, you will get a value of 73% in typical gloss offset environments. To build a profile, you enter the actual measured values of dot area into a custom dot gain table, accessible from the Color Settings dialog box by choosing Custom Dot Gain from either the Gray or Spot pop-up lists in the Working Spaces area

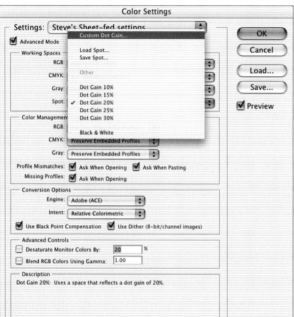

(see Figure 15.14). Saving the resulting curve creates an ICC profile.

A custom dot gain table (see Figure 15.15) enables you to enter actual grayscale performance curves, which are then used to compensate for the gain you experience. These curves are translated into grayscale and spot color profiles by Photoshop.

After you create these profiles in Photoshop, they are available to any application that supports ICC profiles. To save a custom profile, use the Gray or Spot pop-up list in the Working Spaces area of Color Settings and choose Save Gray or Save Spot. By using ICC grayscale profiles on images to be converted for monochrome printing, you create a file that is optimized for reproduction on the measured paper and ink used to make the dot area measurements. It is, in essence, a method for matching the image to the printing capabilities of the chosen process.

DOT GAIN

When a liquid comes in contact with a piece of paper, the capillary action of the paper's fibers spreads the liquid as it's absorbed. You can easily see this by placing a droplet of water on a piece of tissue.

Ink applied to paper on a printing press produces the same result. The size of the ink dot increases, spread by capillary action, pressure, and several other factors. This phenomenon is known as *dot gain*. Porous papers such as newsprint absorb more ink than coated stocks, producing greater dot gain (news ink is more fluid, also). Some lower-grade papers will spread an ink dot as much as 40%, whereas glossy coated stocks generally gain 20% or more (measured as the change in dot-area to the 50% dot). The profiles for CMYK, grayscale, and spot color in Photoshop attempt to predict the dot gain based on the qualities of specific paper types. With these profiles, the halftone dots on film output will be made smaller to compensate for the spreading ink when it is applied to paper.

Printing from Ink-Jet Printers

After you've completed your image, assigned RGB profiles to it, and converted it (or not converted it, depending on the circumstances), you can print it. The majority of desktop ink-jet printers use the RGB information to convert the image to CMYK (or CcMmYK) on the fly, so you should not convert to CMYK for those printers that handle this conversion internally.

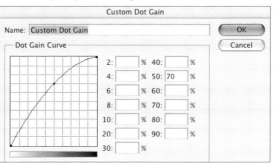

Ink-jet printing results can vary dramatically from model to model because of their different color gamuts. If you have the printer's profile, the results will be more predictable. If you don't have the profile of a specific printer, you can improve the results on ink-jet printers by printing the image in RGB and letting the printer software do the conversion on the fly. You can then use the print as a proof to recalibrate your display (using Adobe Gamma or other visual calibration software) to display the image as close to the proof as possible. Save the Adobe Gamma settings to be used specifically for editing images printed on the target printer. Make your adjustments to the image based on the on-screen display and save the image as a separate file, identifying it for the specific printer. This is a funky, trial-and-error way to match the printed image to the display, but it works if you're willing to pull a number of prints and tweak adjustments to get as close a match as possible.

A far more accurate and reliable method is to invest in a spectrophotometer (an instrument that makes spectral readings of color) and take a reading from the print, and then plug the information into the spectrophotometer's software and load the resulting profile into the Color Settings dialog box. Unfortunately a system like this can be quite costly, with prices starting at more than $1,000 for the instrument and up to $3,500 for the software.

Figure 15.15

The secondary palette in Custom Dot Gain allows the creation of curves that control how the image appears on the computer display.

USING A SPECTROPHOTOMETER

Reading color patches and creating a color profile requires a spectrophotometer and color profiling software. Several instruments are available, as are several profiling software products, each of them producing excellent color profiles for printers and printing press output.

Shown here is the GretagMacbeth Eye-One Pro, a hand-held spectrophotometer that is useful for making printer (called Output) profiles. The software that drives the unit includes special color patch targets that are printed on the device being measured. Once printed, the resulting colors are measured by the instrument, and the data is provided to the profiling software. Profiling software compares the measurement data (the actual printed output) to the original color values of the target, then creates an ICC profile that will produce more correct color on the application of that profile.

A cheaper option is to use the profile creation services of a consultant. You print and mail the print target; they read it and e-mail you the profile. This way, no hardware investment is needed by the end user.

The Printing Dialogs

Several dialog boxes offer similar functions for ultimately printing your image. They are Page Setup, Print With Preview, Print, and Print One Copy.

Page Setup

Choose File → Page Setup to determine the paper size, orientation, and scale of the image. The dialog box will include different options depending on your installed printer, sometimes including some of the same options found in the Print With Preview dialog box.

Print With Preview

Choose File → Print With Preview to display a printing dialog box with a preview on the left side of the screen. Set up your printing specifications (see Figure 15.16). The preview image on the left side of the screen displays the image's size in relation to the paper.

Figure 15.16

The Print With Preview dialog box

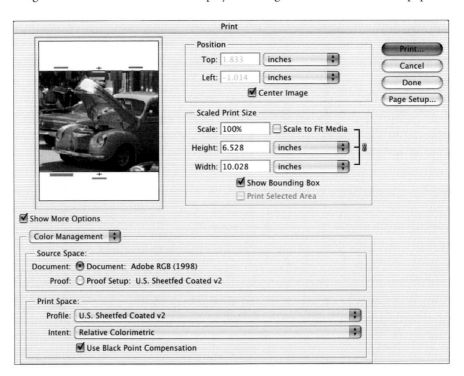

The Position settings specify the location of the printed image on the current paper size. Scaled Print Size lets you increase or decrease the image size while maintaining the image's constrained proportions. Check the Scale To Fit Media box to size the image to fit the paper. Check Show Bounding Box to manually scale and reposition the image by dragging. If you have an active selection, you can then choose to print only that part of the image with the Print Selected Area option.

Check the Show More Options box to expand the dialog box. In the expanded area, a pop-up list offers two groups of settings, Output and Color Management.

Output Options

Some of these options are demonstrated in Figure 15.17.

Background Choose a color from the Color Picker for the area surrounding the image.

Border Enter a value from 0.00 to 10.00 in points, inches, or millimeters to produce a black border around the image.

Bleed Enter a value from 0.00 to 0.125 inches to specify the width of the bleed. When printed, crop marks will appear inside rather than outside the image.

Figure 15.17

A printed image showing various Output options selected

Screen   Enter values for screen frequency, angle, and shape for the halftone screens or individual color separations.

Transfer   This function is designed to compensate for poorly calibrated printers. If a printer is printing too dark, for example, adjust the curve to lighten the image to achieve better results.

Interpolation   Check this box to automatically reduce the jagged edges that would be created when a low-resolution image is resampled up for printing.

Calibration Bars   Selecting this option produces an 11-step grayscale wedge for measuring dot densities with a densitometer. On CMYK images, a gradient tint bar is printed on each separation.

Registration Marks   These marks, including bull's-eyes and star targets, are used to register color separations.

Crop Marks   These marks show where the page is to be trimmed.

Captions   When checked, Photoshop will print the text of the Description area of File Info dialog box on the edge of the image.

Labels   When checked, Photoshop prints the filename on the image.

Emulsion Down   When checked, Photoshop prints the image with emulsion side of the image down. Film negatives are usually made emulsion-down so that the emulsion comes in contact with the printing plate when exposed, generating the best quality possible.

Negative   When selected, Photoshop will prints a negative image. Most printers in North America use negative film—emulsion-down—to expose printing plates.

Color Management Options

You can color-manage the image while printing. Let's say that your image is set up with profiles for prepress output to an imagesetter to make color separations, but you're going to print to an ink-jet printer to proof the image. You can temporarily convert the document to a more appropriate profile, such as U.S. Sheetfed Coated v.2, as you print. If you're printing to a PostScript printer such as a laser printer or imagesetter, you can designate PostScript color management, though most experts recommend using color management in the applications rather than in the RIP.

Choose a source space: Document uses the current *color* settings as a profile for the printed image, and Proof uses the current *proof* settings. Under Print Space, choose a working space from the Profile list. You can also choose a rendering intent.

And of course, click the Print button to print the image.

Print

You can also choose File → Print to display the Print dialog box (see Figure 15.18). The options here will depend on the printer you have selected. Some of the functions found in the Print dialog box might be redundant or irrelevant, such as specifying multiple pages and collation. (Photoshop does not support multiple-page documents.)

Clicking the Print button from the Print With Preview dialog box brings up the Print dialog, enabling printer-specific controls (page size, orientation, paper feed, and so forth) to be accessed. A small change in Photoshop CS brings up the Print dialog box when you type ⌘-P. To get the Print With Preview, choose the menu item File → Print With Preview or type ⌘-Option-P.

Print One Copy

This quick print option (File → Print One Copy) prints the image with the current defaults. No dialog box appears.

Preflight Checklist

As a final note, I've provided a general checklist of operations that you should perform to ensure accuracy on the printing press. These operations are covered in this chapter and throughout *Photoshop CS Savvy*.

1. Calibrate your display.

2. Scan the image at the proper resolution or open a digital camera file with the appropriate color settings applied

3. In the Color Settings dialog box, choose the appropriate RGB color profiles for display and printing.

4. Open the image. Crop it, rotate it and adjust its Image Size to suit the requirements of the project

5. Check the image in the Levels palette (⌘-L). I look for problems with highlights and shadows there first. Not all images need to be corrected here, but some are improved by resetting the end-points to establish black and white points.

6. Edit the image by using any combination of Photoshop's tools. I usually make color corrections first (⌘-B) and then make editorial and creative changes.

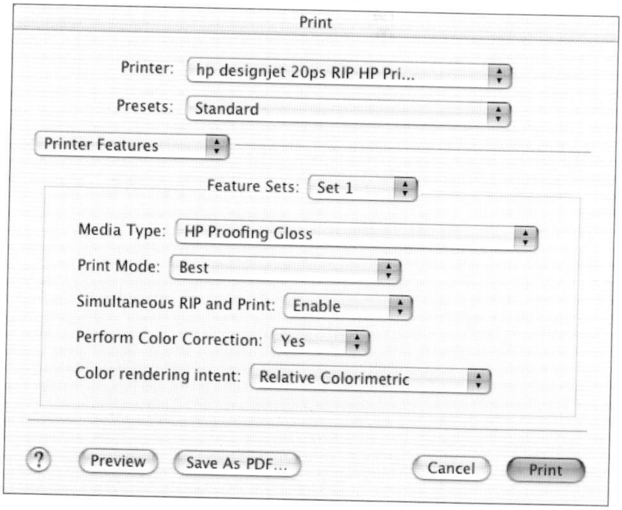

Figure 15.18

The Print dialog box

7. Flatten the image layers if necessary.

8. Apply the Unsharp Mask filter according to file size and printing requirements.

9. Under File → Page Setup, choose an orientation (portrait or landscape).

10. In the Print With Preview dialog box, set up the image for printing, choosing print size and position on the page, and, if necessary, attach crop marks, labels, and so forth.

11. Print the image. This will be a proof.

12. Depending on your relationship with the printer and their requirements for image color, prepare the file as RGB with an embedded ICC profile, or convert the file to CMYK using the correct CMYK profile, and Save As a new image to deliver the file to the printer.

CHAPTER 16

Adjusting Tonality and Color

Almost every photograph that finds its way onto your computer—whether it is scanned, copied from a Photo CD, transferred from a digital camera, or downloaded from the Web—will need some color adjustment, from minor tweaking to major surgery. Inferior photographic techniques, such as bad lighting, poor focus, and under- or overexposure, are a major cause of color problems in images; however, other variables can significantly degrade color and tonality. The type and quality of the equipment that is used to digitize the image is a factor—an expensive film scanner with a high dynamic range can "see" many more variations of tone than an inexpensive digital camera.

Inevitably, you will use Photoshop's color adjustment features to enhance contrast and remove color casts in order to compensate for the multitude of variables that can occur during input.

In this chapter, you will learn about:

- ■ **Measuring tonality and color**
- ■ **Making quick adjustments**
- ■ **Working with levels and curves**
- ■ **Adjusting Shadow and highlights**
- ■ **Balancing color and mixing channels**
- ■ **Using Adjustment layers**
- ■ **Working with color enhancement filters**

Measuring Tonality and Color

When you first open an image, scrutinize it carefully to determine what the colors on your monitor represent. Be aware that sometimes the on-screen image doesn't accurately represent the image's actual colors. First, be sure to calibrate your monitor by using Adobe Gamma, the operating system's calibration software, or a hardware device to create an accurate on-screen image before performing any color adjustments (see Chapter 5, "Setting Up Photoshop," and Chapter 15, "Color Management and Printing").

Next, look at the image's histogram to determine the distribution of tonal values within the image and whether the image has sufficient detail. To view the histogram, choose Window → Histogram.

> To accurately display the actual tonal values within an image, you should avoid using the Image Cache to generate the histogram. Instead, click the cache warning icon in the Histogram palette.

Histograms

A *histogram* is a graph composed of lines that show the relative distribution of tonal values within an image. The more lines the graph has, the more tonal values are present within the image. The height of a line represents the relative quantity of pixels of a particular brightness. The taller the line, the more pixels of a particular brightness the image contains (see the example in Figure 16.1). The histogram looks like a mountain range on some images, because a total of 256 tonal values can be represented at one time, and the lines are so close together that they create a shape. The dark pixels, or shadows, are represented on the left side of the graph; the light pixels, or highlights, are on the right. The midtone ranges are therefore shown in the central areas of the graph.

Photoshop CS's new Histogram palette has several features that enhance the way the brightness information is displayed and analyzed. When you choose Window → Histogram,

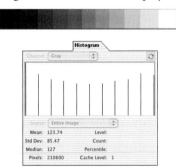

Figure 16.1

The new Histogram palette representing an 11-step grayscale image. Notice that there are 11 lines. Their position on the graph indicates their relative brightness. Their length represents the relative quantity of pixels.

the compact view of the histogram is displayed on the palette by default. Click the Histogram palette menu and choose Expanded View to display numerical data about the image. Click the cache warning triangle icon ![icon] to display uncached data. To refresh the uncached data after you've edited the image, click the Refresh arrows ![icon]. This will give you a more accurate reading. Choose All Channels

View from the palette menu to expand the palette and view the histogram of each channel individually (see Figure 16.2). Choose Show Channels In Color to display the histogram of each channel in its corresponding color. If the Image has multiple layers, you can choose to view the histogram of the entire image, a specific content layer, or the data on an adjustment layer by clicking the desired option from the source list.

The new Histogram palette is context sensitive. When you edit the image, it instantaneously displays an updated histogram, superimposed over the previous histogram for comparison.

The numbers below the graph to the left represent statistical data about the image's tonality. The numbers in the right column indicate values about a specific level or range. To view data about a specific level, place your cursor on the graph and click your mouse. To display data about a range of pixels, click the graph and drag to the left or right to define the range (see Figure 16.3). The data is organized in the following way:

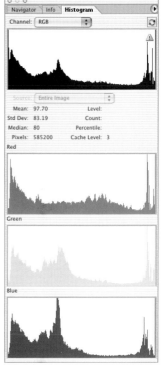

Figure 16.2

The Histogram palette with the All Channels View displayed

Value	Definition
Mean	Average brightness value of all the pixels in the image (0–255.00)
Std Dev	The standard deviation, or how widely brightness values vary
Median	The middle value in the range of brightness values
Pixels	Total number of pixels in the image or in a selected portion of the image
Level	The specific pixel value, between 0 and 255, of the position of the cursor if you place it on the graph
Count	Total number of pixels in the level
Percentile	Percentage of pixels equal to and darker than the level
Cache Level	The current image cache setting

A histogram can tell us about tonal characteristics of an image. For example, a histogram in which the majority of tall lines are clustered on the left side of the graph and short lines are on the right side indicates that the image is dark, or *low key*. A histogram in which the tall lines cluster on the right side of the graph indicates that the image is light, or *high key*. Compare Figures 16.4 and 16.5.

Histograms can also indicate deficiencies in the image. For example, a histogram devoid of lines on both the left and right ends of the graph indicates that most of the pixels are in the midtone range; therefore, the image lacks highlights and shadows and is of poor contrast (see Figure 16.6). A histogram that has gaps in the graph could indicate that there is insufficient color detail in the image (see Figure 16.7).

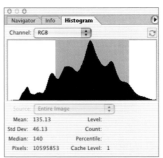

Figure 16.3

Selecting a range of tonal values within the Histogram window. Note the data now listed in the left column.

Figure 16.4

A histogram representing a dark, or *low key,* image

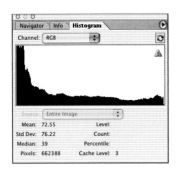

The Info Palette

The Info palette enables you to accurately measure the color of a single pixel and to determine the average color of a group of pixels. You can use these areas as markers when you make adjustments to the image. To access the Info palette, choose Window → Show Info. By default, the Info palette displays Actual Color (current color model) and CMYK fields, the *x* and *y* coordinates of the position of the cursor, and the height and width of the selection (see Figure 16.8). Place your cursor on the image to sample a pixel. As you drag over the image, the numeric values for the exact pixel under the cursor are displayed.

Click one of the eyedroppers in the palette to display an options menu. You can configure the options to display CMYK, RGB, Web, HSB, Grayscale, Lab, Total Ink, Proof Color, or Opacity information. The two options at the top of the menu display the values for the actual color or for the potential proof colors when previewing an image prior to CMYK conversion. The proof color numbers are displayed in italics to distinguish them from actual color numbers.

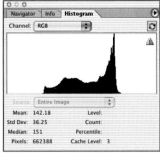

Figure 16.5

A histogram representing a light, or *high key,* image

Figure 16.6

A histogram representing an image with poor contrast

Figure 16.7

A histogram representing an image with insufficient detail

Choosing Palette Options from the Info Palette menu lets you pick from other color spaces for each of the information fields (see Figure 16.9).

The modes in the Info Options pop-up lists are the following:

Figure 16.8

The Info palette displaying the RGB values of the sample pixel

Setting	Explanation
Actual Color	Color values of the current mode of the image
Proof Color	Color after conversion to the ICC CMYK profile designated in the View → Proof Setup dialog box
Grayscale	Density of black ink that would be deposited if the image were printed in black-and-white
RGB	Color of the numeric brightness values, from 0 (black) to 255 (white) of each of the red, green, and blue channels
Web Color	RGB hexadecimal equivalents of the sampled color
HSB	Hue, saturation, and brightness values of the sampled color
CMYK	Percentages of cyan, magenta, yellow, and black that would be output to process color separations
Lab	Lightness (L), green–red (a), and blue–yellow (b) values of a CIE Lab color image
Total Ink	Cumulative percentage of ink densities of the combined CMYK separations in a four-color process print
Opacity	Cumulative level of opacity on all the visible layers of an image

The Show 16 Bit Values check box enables you to see the pixel values of high-bit images. You can read more about 16-bit images in Chapter 14, "Image Capture and Digital Photography."

The Eyedropper Tool

When using the Info palette, it is often more accurate to measure a group of pixels than just one, in order to get a better idea of the general tonality of a specific area. When you configure the Eyedropper tool ✐ to sample an average, the readings in the Info palette, or in any other operation that uses the Eyedropper to sample color, will reflect the new configuration.

In the Eyedropper Options bar, choose Point Sample to sample a single pixel. Choose 3 By 3 Average to sample the average color of a 9-pixel square, or 5 By 5 Average to sample the average color of a 25-pixel square. You will usually get the best results by averaging a 3 × 3 square; however, on high-resolution images greater than 400 pixels per inch, you might want to try the 5 × 5 option. See both options in Figure 16.10.

You can select colors from outside the image window—even outside of the Photoshop application itself! If you need to select a certain hue from another application, a Web browser window, or the desktop wallpaper, you can do so by simply clicking *and holding* the Eyedropper tool inside the image window, and then *dragging* the tool to any point outside the active image window. The color of any on-screen pixel that your cursor hovers over will appear as the current foreground color swatch—releasing the mouse will select that particular color.

The Color Sampler Tool

The Color Sampler tool ✐ marks areas of the image for before-and-after comparisons of color adjustments. Prepress professionals, for example, often find this tool useful to adjust areas to target CMYK values.

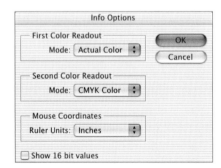

Figure 16.9

The Info Options dialog box

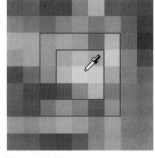

Figure 16.10

The Eyedropper tool can sample the average color value of a 3 × 3 or a 5 × 5 pixel area.

To place a color marker, expand the Eyedropper tool in the Tool palette and choose the Color Sampler. Place the cursor on the image and click your mouse. The cursor leaves a marker, and the Info palette expands to display the data for that particular marker, as in Figure 16.11.

Using the Shift key with the regular Eyedropper tool also invokes the Color Sampler.

You can sample up to four colors and record the information in the Info palette. To change the color model of a marker, click the arrow next to the Eyedropper icon in the Info palette and drag to the desired color model in the pull-down list shown previously in Figure 16.9.

To move a marker you've already placed, choose the Color Sampler tool and drag the marker to a new location. To delete it, choose the Color Sampler tool and drag the marker off the image window, or press Option/Alt and click the marker. The Clear button on the Options bar can also delete all placed Color Samplers with one click.

While a color adjustment is being made to the image, the Info palette displays two numbers for each value, divided by a slash, as seen in Figure 16.12. The number on the left is the numeric value of the sampled color prior to the adjustment, and the number on the right represents the new value of the color after the adjustment. You can compare these values and, with a bit of experience reading these numeric color relations, determine the effect the adjustment will have on the targeted area.

Figure 16.11

An image with Color Sampler markers and the expanded Info palette

Making Quick Adjustments

They say "never sacrifice accuracy for speed." Sometimes, however, expedience is a virtue, and you can therefore use one of Photoshop's semiautomatic operations to perform fast adjustments and correct simple, common problems. These commands can change tonal values in an image quickly, but they also lack the precision and control of the high-end adjustment features.

Figure 16.12

The number to the left of the slash is the value before the adjustment, and number to the right is the value after.

Using the semiautomatic adjustment features hands over the control of how your image looks to the software. Photoshop is not always the best judge of the aesthetic qualities of your image, so use common sense when applying these commands. Occasionally, you will luck out and they'll work just fine. But more often than not, they likely won't achieve the same quality of results you could achieve with a more hands-on approach.

Brightness/Contrast

Choose Image → Adjustments → Brightness/Contrast to perform a global adjustment of brightness or contrast to a selected area or to the entire image. The top slider (see Figure 16.13) controls how dark or light the image appears, by pushing the pixel values lower when you move the slider to the left or higher when you move the slider to the right. The slider on the bottom increases or decreases the contrast by changing the pixel values toward the midtone range when you move the slider to the left, or toward the highlight and shadow ranges when you move the slider to the right. Check the Preview box to see the results.

> It's a good idea to make sure the Preview check box, found in all of the adjustment operations, is always checked in order to see the changes to the image before OK'ing them.

Auto Levels

If you choose Image → Adjustments → Auto Levels, Photoshop makes the lightest pixel in each color channel white and the darkest pixel black. It then distributes all the other pixels in between proportionately. By default, the Auto Levels command ignores the lightest and darkest 0.5% extremes when choosing the lightest and darkest colors so as to choose more representative colors. If you use Auto Levels, watch the image carefully, because it can potentially introduce or remove color casts.

Figure 16.13

The Brightness/ Contrast dialog box

You can change the default 0.5% white-point and black-point percentage by choosing Image → Adjustments → Levels or Curves. Click the Options button and enter a value from 0% to 9.99% in the Black Clip or White Clip box. Adobe recommends a number between 0.5% and 1% for the least color distortion.

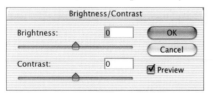

Auto Contrast

Choose Image → Adjustments → Auto Contrast to adjust the overall contrast relationships in an image. Like Auto Levels, Auto Contrast maps the lightest highlight to white and the darkest shadow pixel to black. Unlike Auto Levels, Auto Contrast maintains the color balance. By default, the Auto Contrast command clips the lightest and darkest 0.5% of the light and dark extremes so as to choose more representative colors.

Auto Color

Auto Color attempts to correct the image's contrast by first mapping the brightest highlight to white and the darkest shadow to black, and then neutralizing the midtones. (It attempts to map any grays in the image to the most neutral shade of gray, thereby removing any aberrant color casts in the image.) Auto Color, for an automated tool, is actually pretty effective much of the time. Your mileage may vary, of course.

> Often I find that the semiautomatic tools do actually perform alterations needed within the image, but might perform them *too well,* creating an overadjustment. You can correct this by using Edit → Fade to fade the last applied color adjustment and to tone it down to a level between the original and the auto-adjusted result. This will often result in a more subtle, natural finish.

Variations

If you need a little help visualizing what a color adjustment might look like, choose Image → Adjustments → Variations. The Variations command displays thumbnails of potential adjustments (such as the ones in Figure 16.14) in the color saturation and value of the image, enabling you to visually choose the most appropriate alternative. The two thumbnails at the top of the window display the original image, labeled Original, and the current image with adjustments, labeled Current Pick. The circle of thumbnails below shows what the image will look like if you add more of a specific color. The Current Pick thumbnail, which is in the center of the circle, changes as you click any one of the color thumbnails. To undo the addition of a color, click the thumbnail opposite it to introduce its complementary color and neutralize the effect.

You can increase or decrease the amount of color to be added, by moving the Fine/Coarse slider: Fine produces small adjustments, and Coarse produces large ones. You can choose to focus the adjustments on specific areas of tonality by clicking the Shadows, Midtones, and Highlights radio buttons.

Figure 16.14

**The Variations
dialog box**

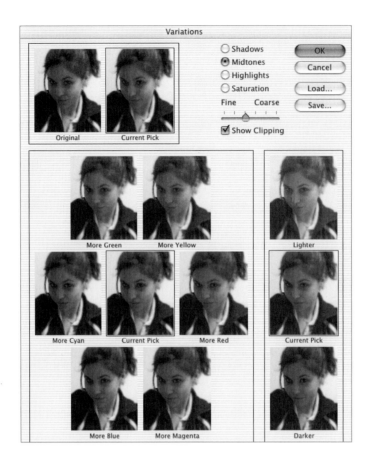

Clicking the Saturation radio button transforms the color circle into three thumbnails. Click the left thumbnail to desaturate, or the right thumbnail to saturate, the image.

The field at the right controls the brightness of the image. Click the top thumbnail to lighten the image and the bottom to darken the image.

As you use the Variations command, you might notice the proliferation of highly saturated color in the thumbnails. These are gamut warnings, and they're there to alert you that some of the colors might be outside of the range of the current color space, which could result in areas of flat or dithered color. To turn off the gamut warning, clear the Show Clipping check box.

Working with Levels

The Levels command displays an image histogram, which you can use as a visual guide to adjust the image's tonal range. Levels initially gives you three points of adjustment. The black slider on the left of the graph determines the darkest pixel in the shadow areas, which is called the *black point.* The white slider on the right determines the lightest pixel in the highlight area, called the *white point.* Move the black and white sliders to adjust the shadow and highlight extremes, respectively, of the image. The middle, or gamma, slider determines the median value between the black and white points. Move the slider to the right to decrease the median value, thereby making all values lower than the median darker, or to the left to increase it, making all values higher than the median lighter.

> Before using the Levels command, choose Photoshop → Preferences → Memory & Image Cache. Be sure that the Use Cache For Histograms check box is cleared. Quit the program and then relaunch it. (See Chapter 5 for more on setting memory preferences.)

Whereas Input Levels increase contrast, Output Levels decrease contrast. Move the white slider to the left and the black slider to the right to reduce the range of contrast in an image. You can eliminate the extremes of the highlight and shadow in an image. Printers frequently do this to control ink coverage in preparing files for the press. For example, if the black arrow is moved from 0 to 12, values below 5% (equivalent to a 95% dot value) won't print.

When you perform a Levels adjustment, you are actually reassigning pixel values. As an example, suppose you have a low-contrast image such as the photograph in Figure 16.15.

> To best assess the results of a Levels adjustment, open the Histogram palette (Window → Histogram) prior to applying the Levels command so that you can compare the before and after histograms.

Follow these basic steps to increase the contrast in this picture:

1. Open the image in the Ch16 folder on the *Photoshop CS Savvy* CD titled duckybar.psd.

2. Choose Window → Histogram to display the Histogram palette. From the Palette Options menu, choose Expanded View. Click the Refresh arrows to display the histogram of the uncached data.

3. Choose Image → Adjustments → Levels. The Levels dialog box displays an identical histogram. There is a deficiency in the highlight and shadow areas, where the absence of lines indicates there are no pixels of these brightness levels (see Figure 16.16.)

4. Move the white slider toward the center until it is aligned with the lines on the right of the graph, or until the Input Level box on the right reads about 207.

5. Move the black slider toward the center until it is aligned with the lines on the left of the graph, or until the Input Level value on the left reads about 60.

Figure 16.15

This picture definitely needs more contrast.

The context-sensitive Histogram palette displays the new histogram superimposed over the previous one. The range of pixel values in the histogram has been redistributed to encompass the length of the entire graph. The lines that had a value of 60 now have a value of 0 (black), and the lines that had a value of 207 now have a value of 255 (white).

Figure 16.17 shows the Levels dialog box, the Histogram palette and the image after the correction. Compare it to Figure 16.16.

Adjusting Channels

If you perform a Levels adjustment on the composite channel, you have only three points of adjustment. If you adjust the levels of each channel individually, you have nine points of adjustment in an RGB or Lab color image and twelve points of adjustment on a CMYK image. This triples or quadruples the power of the Levels command; it can also produce weird color combinations. To choose a specific channel in which to work, scroll down the Channel list in the Levels dialog box. (See Hands On 5, "Image Size, Transformation, and Color Adjustment," to try this operation.)

When adjusting individual channels, display the Histogram palette. Choose All Channels View from the Histogram palette menu to individually preview the result of each channel's histogram. Show Channels In Color will display the histogram of each channel in its corresponding color.

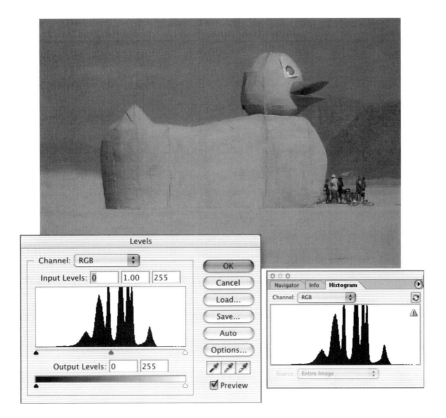

When adjusting the levels of individual channels, you might need to reset the Levels adjustment several times before producing the right combination of values. To do so, press the Option/Alt key. The Cancel button becomes the Reset button. Click it to begin again. Note that this cancels all the operations that you have performed in the dialog box, not just the individual channels. To cancel only the last operation, press ⌘/Ctrl-Z.

Determining the White Point and Black Point

You can use the Levels command in Threshold mode to locate the highlight and shadow areas of an image. You can then assign specific values to those points to redistribute all the other pixel values between those values.

Finding the Highlight and Shadow Points

Use this technique to determine the lightest and darkest areas of the image:

1. Be sure that the composite RGB channel is selected from the Channels palette.

2. Open the Levels dialog box (Image → Adjustments → Levels) and check the Preview box.

Figure 16.17

The image, the Levels dialog box, and the Histogram palette after the adjustment

3. Press Option/Alt and slowly drag the white Input Level slider to the left. A high-contrast preview appears. The visible areas of the image are the lightest part of the image.

4. Repeat the process with the black shadow slider, dragging it to the right to identify the darkest areas of the image.

You can assign specific values to the darkest shadow areas and the lightest highlight areas of an image and then redistribute the brightness information based on the light and dark extremes of the image. Prepress professionals frequently determine CMYK values for highlight and shadow areas based on the characteristics of their printing presses. When you determine the white point, it is often best to use the lightest printable area of the image that *contains detail,* not a specular white that when printed will contain no ink. The shadow area will be the darkest area that contains detail, not an absolute black.

Setting the White Point

You can determine a specific RGB value for the white point of the lightest highlight areas:

1. To set the target RGB values, open the image `learjet.psd` from the `Ch16` folder on the CD. Before (Figure C16) and after (Figure C17) versions of this image are included in the color section.

2. In the Eyedropper Options bar, set the Eyedropper tool to 3 By 3 Average.

3. Choose Image → Adjustments → Levels.

4. *Double-click* the white eyedropper. The Color Picker appears.

5. Enter values for the highlight to prepare the image for print. Enter these recommended RGB values if you are printing on white paper: 240R, 240G, 240B. The grayscale density is a 6% dot (you can determine the highlight density by subtracting the Brightness value, B, in the Color Picker from 100).

> The RGB values will vary depending on the RGB color space you are working in. I'm working in Adobe RGB (1998) as a color setting (see Chapter 15). The point is, you're going to shoot for about a 4% to 6% neutral gray mix.

6. Locate the lightest area on the image. Do not choose a specular highlight, which will be pure white; instead, choose the lightest area that will contain detail. In this case, click on the lightest area close to the nose cone of the jet to set the highlight.

Setting the Black Point

Determine a specific RGB value for the black point of darker shadows:

1. Double-click the black eyedropper. The Color Picker appears.

2. Enter RGB values for the shadow. Use these recommended values if you are printing on white paper and working in the Adobe RGB (1998) color space: 13R, 13G, 13B. The Grayscale density is a 95% dot. (As with the highlight value, you can determine the shadow density by the subtracting the Brightness value, B, in the Color Picker from 100.)

> If the image is to be converted to CMYK, the total ink coverage should not exceed 300% in the CMYK percentage fields for a common web-coated separation. You can input other values of ink in the CMYK fields—depending on the paper, printer, and press you are using—but it is important to maintain three equal RGB values to assure neutrality before converting to CMYK.

3. Locate the darkest area on the image that still contains detail. In this case, it's the dark circle of the left jet engine. Click your mouse there to set the shadow. Compare the results in Figure 16.18 (and in Figures C16 and C17 in the color section).

The process for determining the white point and the black point is the same for both the Levels and the Curves operations. I'll discuss curves in the next section.

Saving and Loading Levels Settings

After you've made a correction to the image, you might want to apply it to another image with the same color problems. Let's say you shot a roll of film at the wrong ASA and consequently underexposed all the images. You can adjust one image and apply those settings to the entire group by first saving and then loading the settings.

To save and load a setting:

1. Choose Save from the options on the right side of the Levels dialog box.

2. Choose a folder in which to save the settings, name them, and click OK. Click OK again to close the Levels dialog box. Now that you've saved the settings, you can reload them at any time.

Figure 16.18

The jet before (left) and after (right) determining the white and black points with the eyedroppers in the Levels dialog box.

3. To load the settings, choose Load from the options on the right side of the Levels dialog.

4. Locate the folder where the settings were saved, and click Open to open the settings.

Adjusting Curves

Curves are Photoshop's most powerful color adjustment tool. Whereas levels give you the ability to change three to nine points of adjustment, curves enable you to map many more. You can adjust an image's brightness curve to lighten or darken an image, improve its contrast, or even create wild solarization affects.

When you choose Image → Adjustments → Curves, Photoshop displays the Curves dialog box (see Figure 16.19). By default, the graph is divided into 16 squares, each representing 16 brightness levels. Press your Option/Alt key and click the graph to refine the grid into 100 squares, representing the total 256 brightness levels for finer adjustment.

You can expand the curves dialog box to make the graph bigger, which enables you to be more precise when you adjust the curve. Place your curser on the size icon in the lower right of the dialog box and drag down and to the right.

For more precision, click the Expand button in the lower-right corner to enlarge the dialog box.

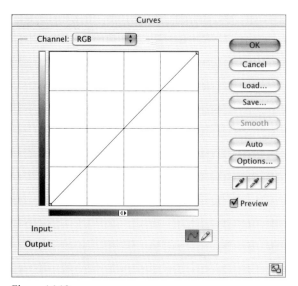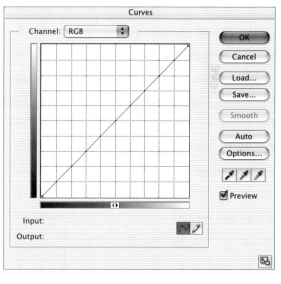

Figure 16.19

The default Curves dialog box shows a 16-cell graph (left); Option/Alt-clicking the grid changes it to a 100-cell graph (right).

The horizontal axis of the graph represents the *input* levels, or the colors of the image before the adjustment. The vertical axis represents the *output* levels, or the color of the image after it has been adjusted. By default, for RGB images, dark colors are represented by the lower-left corner of the graph, and light colors are represented by the upper-right corner. The diagonal line from bottom-left to top-right represents the brightness levels of the image. Adjustments are made to the image by changing the shape of this line.

Figure 16.20 illustrates the power of curves. The unaltered photograph (a) is perhaps slightly underexposed in the shadows. If you click the center of the diagonal line in the Curves dialog box and drag it toward the upper-left, you will lighten the image, as in (b). If you bend it toward the lower-right, you will darken it (c). If you perform either of these operations, you alter the position of the midtones.

A classic S curve, as shown in (d), will increase the contrast of the image by darkening the shadows and lightening the highlights. A roller-coaster curve (e) pushes the pixel values all over the graph and creates wild solarization effects.

Using the Brightness Bar

The horizontal brightness bar below the graph represents the direction of the values of the graph. By default, for RGB images, the light values are on the right and the dark values are on the left, but they can be switched easily by clicking the center arrows. If you reverse the graph, the light values will switch to the bottom and left, and the dark values to the top and right. If you are working on an RGB or Lab image and you switch the direction of the brightness bar, the numeric input and output values change from a measurement of channel information to ink coverage. This can be useful if you are planning to convert your image to CMYK.

The default Curves dialog box for a CMYK image is reversed from the RGB or Lab image. The brightness bars display dark values on the top and light values on the bottom. The input and output values are the percentage of ink coverage.

Choosing Graph Tools

Choose a graph tool from the Curves dialog box to edit the brightness curve. The Point tool ⬚ is selected by default. Click the curve to establish anchor points, which can then be moved by dragging them with your mouse. As you drag, you can see the changes to your image if the Preview box is checked.

Choose the Pencil tool ⬚ by clicking on its icon. Click and drag on the curve to draw freeform lines. It performs very much like the Pencil tool in the Tool palette. If you want to draw a straight line, click once, press Shift, and click elsewhere.

Changing Input and Output Values

When you move the cursor over the curve, the input and output values change to reflect its position relative to the horizontal and vertical axes of the graph. You can click a point on the curve and enter new values for that point in these boxes, which will result in the bending of the curve.

Figure 16.20

Examples of curve adjustments

(a) The unadjusted image

(b) Lighten

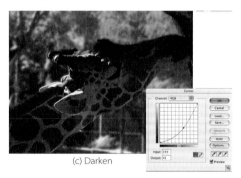

(c) Darken

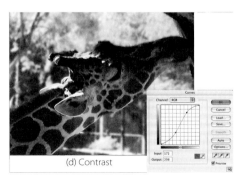

(d) Contrast

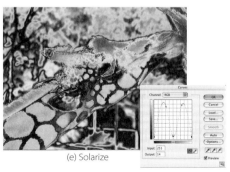

(e) Solarize

Adjusting Channels

If you perform a Curves adjustment on the composite channel, you affect all of its channels simultaneously. As with levels, you can work with more precision by adjusting the channels individually. To choose a specific channel in which to work, scroll through the Channel pop-up list in the Curves dialog box. You can also select a combination of channels by Shift-selecting them in the Channels palette before opening the Curves dialog box.

Making a Lock-Down Curve

It often helps to work with a *lock-down curve* so that other colors in the image are unaffected when you make an adjustment. A lock-down curve stabilizes the curve and prevents it from bending. The brightness values that are affected when manipulating the curve can then be better controlled. To make a lock-down curve, follow these steps:

1. Choose Image → Adjustments → Curves to open the Curves dialog box.

2. Press Option/Alt and click the grid to display the 100-cell grid.

3. Place your cursor on the diagonal line at the exact point where the horizontal and vertical grid lines intersect. Click your mouse.

4. Click each intersection point along the diagonal line (see Figure 16.21).

5. Choose Red from the Channel pop-up list. Repeat step 4.

6. Repeat step 4 for the Green and Blue curves. This way, if you need to lock down a specific channel, the curve will be contained within the file.

7. Choose Save, and designate a location for your curve. Name the curve `lockdown_curve` `.acv` and save the file. You can now load the curve on any RGB document in any channel at any time. A file of the same name is provided in the `Ch16` folder on your CD.

Determining the Position of a Color

You can pinpoint a color and determine its exact location on the curve. You can then place an anchor point and make a precise spot adjustment to that color only.

To determine the location of a color:

1. Open the file `giraffe.psd` in the `Ch16` folder on the CD.

2. Choose Image → Adjustments → Curves to display the Curves dialog box.

3. Choose Load from the options on the right side of the dialog. Load `lockdown_curve.acv` you made in the previous section.

Use caution when using a lock-down curve. You might cause posterization (hard edged transitions between colors) if a large adjustment is applied to a small range of tones. In cases like this, Selective color or Hue/Saturation may produce better results.

4. Place your cursor on the large brown patch on the lower part of the giraffe's neck. Press Option/Alt and click the mouse. Observe the circle on the graph as you move your cursor. Press your ⌘/Ctrl key and click the mouse to place an anchor point.

5. Place your cursor on the anchor point, click your mouse, and drag straight downward until the Output reads about 34 (see Figure 16.22). The targeted color on the giraffe intensifies because you've increased its brightness value. All the other colors in the image, such as the background, are left at their original values because you locked them down.

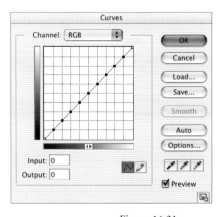

Figure 16.21

A lock-down curve

Saving and Loading Curve Settings

As with levels, after you've made a Curves adjustment to the image, you can save the settings and load them to another image:

1. Choose Save from the options on the right side of the Curves dialog box.

2. Choose a folder in which to save the setting, name it, and click OK.

3. To load the settings, choose Load from the options on the right side of the Curves dialog.

4. Locate the folder where the settings were saved and click Load to load the settings.

Figure 16.22

Adjusting the curve

Applying a Photo Filter

The new Photo Filter adjustment lets you apply the effects of traditional photographic filters to an image. These filters produce results that are commonly used by photographers to warm or cool the colors of an image, reduce glare, or simulate a specific atmospheric environment. Choose Image → Adjustments → Photo Filter to display the Photo Filter dialog box (see Figure 16.23).

Under Use, choose a specific filter from the menu. You can also choose a specific color by clicking the swatch to display the Color Picker. Control the amount of the application by moving the density slider between 1 and 100 percent. The Preserve Luminosity box, when checked, preserves the brightness values of the image.

Figure C18 in the color section shows the before and after results of applying one example of the Photo Filter: Cooling Filter 80.

Adjusting Shadow/Highlight

Another new addition to the Adjustments submenu is the Shadow/Highlight command. It enables you to quickly and precisely correct over- and underexposed areas of an image. Choose Image → Adjustments → Shadow/Highlight, and the dialog box appears (see Figure 16.24).

Shadow/Highlight corrects each pixel adaptively, according to the luminance of the neighboring pixels. This enables image contrast to be increased in the shadows or highlights without significantly sacrificing contrast in the other tonal regions. This can be essential for bringing out detail in overexposed or backlit images, as in Figure 16.25 (which is also shown in the color section as Figure C19).

You can adjust the following shadow and highlight characteristics in the dialog box:

Amount Determines how much the pixels will be affected. Larger values provide greater lightening of shadows or greater darkening of highlights. This slider controls the strength of the adjustment to each pixel.

Tonal Width Sets how much modification will be applied to the different tonal regions. For example, you might want to darken only the lightest highlights or to lighten only the deepest shadows. When correcting shadows, small values of Tonal Width put most of the emphasis on the darker regions of the image; larger values include more of the midtones and highlights.

Figure 16.23

The new Photo Filter dialog box

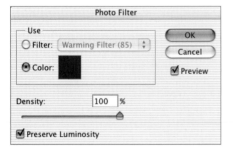

Radius Determines the neighborhood in which the pixels are affected. Every pixel is modified depending on how dark or light its neighbors are. The size of the neighborhood over which the luminance is averaged depends on the Radius setting. The larger the radius, the larger the extent over which the neighborhood luminance is averaged. As a starting point, I suggest that the radius be set to the approximate size of the subject being corrected.

After you've applied the Shadow/Highlight command, you might find that the image has acquired an undesirable color cast. Click the Show More Options check box at the bottom of the dialog box and move the Color Adjustment slider to the left to diminish the overadjustment. Moving the slider to the left decreases the saturation of the image. Moving it to the right increases the saturation.

You can also increase the midtone contrast by moving the slider to the right or diminish it by moving it to the left. The Black Clip and White Clip percentage fields enable you to enter a value for the amount that absolute black and specular white will be altered. By entering a value of 5%, for example, the value of 95% black will be increased to 100%, and all other colors will be remapped accordingly so the image will appear darker.

Balancing Color

After the tonal values have been corrected, you might want to make further adjustments to eliminate color casts, oversaturation, or undersaturation. Color in the image can be balanced by using several methods found in the Image → Adjustments menu:

Color Balance is used to change the overall color mix in an image.

Selective Color adjusts the quantities of cyan, magenta, yellow, or black in specific color components.

Levels and Curves adjust the brightness values of individual channels (see the previous sections in this chapter).

Hue/Saturation changes the basic color characteristics of the image (see Chapter 17, "Modifying and Mapping Color").

Replace Color replaces the hue, saturation, and brightness of specified areas (see Chapter 17).

Channel Mixer blends colors from individual channels (see the section titled "The Channel Mixer" later in this chapter).

Match Color enables you to select a color from the content of one selection, document, or layer and apply it to the content of another selection, document, or layer (see Chapter 17).

Figure 16.24

The Shadow/ Highlight dialog box

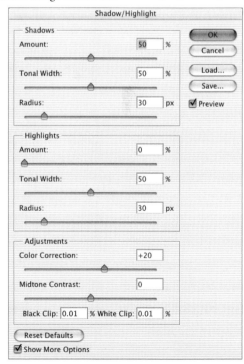

Figure 16.25

**The Shadow/
Highlight
command
applied to a
backlit image**

Color Balance

Color balance is used to adjust the overall mixture of colors in the image and especially to eliminate color casts. To use the Color Balance command, be sure that the composite channel is targeted in the Channels palette. Then follow these steps:

1. Choose Image → Adjustments → Color Balance to display the Color Balance dialog box (see Figure 16.26). You can also bring this up with the keyboard shortcut ⌘/Ctrl-B.

2. Click the Shadows, Midtones, or Highlights radio button to select the tonal range in which you would like to focus your adjustment.

3. Check the Preserve Luminosity box to maintain the tonal balance of the image and affect only the colors.

4. Each color slider represents two color opposites. By increasing the amount of a specific color (by moving the slider toward its name), you, in effect, decrease its opposite.

   To increase the amount of a color in an image, drag a slider toward it. To decrease the amount of a color, drag the slider away from it.

Selective Color

The Selective Color command is designed to adjust CMYK images; however, you can use it on RGB images, too. Selective color lets you determine the amount of cyan, magenta, yellow, and black that will be added to predefined color ranges. This is especially good for prepress professionals who need to control ink densities.

Follow these steps to use this command:

1. Target the composite channel in the Channels palette.

2. Choose Image → Adjustments → Selective Color; the Selective Color dialog box (see Figure 16.27) appears.

3. From the Colors pop-up list, choose the color range you want to affect. The list shows reds, yellows, greens, cyans, blues, magentas, whites, neutrals, and blacks. Adjust the CMYK sliders to determine how much of each process color the target color will contain. (Some colors might not contain any of the process color, so they will not be affected.)

4. Choose a method:

    Relative changes the existing quantity of process color by a percentage of the total. For example, if you start with a pixel that is 80% cyan and add 10%, then 8% is added to the pixel (10% of 80 = 8), for a total of 88% cyan. You cannot adjust specular white with this option, because it contains no color.

    Absolute adds color in absolute values. If, for example, you start with 30% cyan in the pixel and add 10%, you end up with a pixel that is 40% cyan.

5. Drag the sliders to the right to increase the amount of the process color component in the selected color, or to the left to decrease it.

Figure 16.26

The Color Balance dialog box

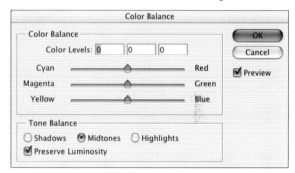

Figure 16.27

The Selective Color dialog box

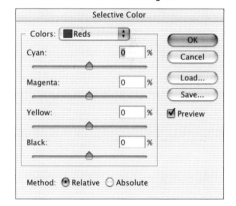

The Channel Mixer

The Channel Mixer enables you to adjust the color information of each channel from one control window. You can establish color values on a specific channel as a mixture of any or all of the color channels' brightness values.

The Channel Mixer can be used for a variety of purposes, including:

- Creating an optimal grayscale image from an RGB or CMYK file

- Making a high-quality sepia tone from a CMYK or RGB file

- Converting images into alternative color spaces

- Swapping color information from one channel to another

- Making color adjustments to images by altering the color information in a specific channel

- Creating weird-looking stuff

The Channel Mixer does not add or subtract colors per se; it combines values from each channel with those of the target channel. The effect is similar to copying the Red channel, for example, and pasting it on the Blue channel. The Channel Mixer, however, offers much greater control by enabling you to vary the degree of the effect.

To use the Channel Mixer:

1. Target the composite channel in the Channels palette.

2. Access the window by choosing Image → Adjustments → Channel Mixer.

3. Target the channel to be affected by choosing the Output Channel from the pop-up list.

4. Adjust the color sliders to modify the color relations between channels.

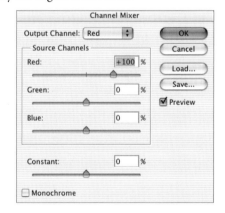

Swapping Colors within Channels

You can adjust color information globally on a particular channel or within a selection marquee, so that portions of the image can be quickly altered, corrected, or converted independently while previewing the results.

When you choose a channel by name from the Output Channel pop-up list, the value next to the corresponding Source Channel's color slider reads 100%, which represents the total amount of that color in the image. The values can be increased to 200% or decreased to −200%.

The performance of the Channel Mixer depends on the color mode of the image. When working in CMYK, increasing the numeric value of the color cyan or dragging its slider to the right increases the amount of cyan in the Cyan channel. Decreasing the numeric value or dragging to the left subtracts cyan from the channel. Adjusting the color slider of any other color, such as magenta, while the Cyan channel is targeted changes the amount of the cyan in the Cyan channel based on the relationship between the brightness values of magenta and cyan.

When working in RGB mode, the Channel Mixer performs differently. Increasing the numeric value shifts the selected color toward the color of the selected channel, while decreasing the value shifts the color toward its complement. (As with CMYK, the limits of these changes are 200% and –200%.) You can therefore decrease the value of red if you target the Red channel and move the Red slider to the left, which shifts the color toward cyan—the complement of red on the color wheel. Targeting the Green channel and moving the Green slider to the left shifts the color toward magenta. Targeting the Blue channel and moving the Blue slider to the left shifts the color toward yellow.

The Constant slider is like having an independent brightness, with an Opacity slider added to the targeted color channel to increase or decrease the channel's overall brightness values. Negative values darken the image, decreasing the brightness of the target channel. Positive values lighten the image, increasing the overall brightness of a channel.

Increasing the brightness of a color channel does not necessarily mean that the image will become lighter. It actually adds more of the channel's color to the image. You can demonstrate this by targeting the Blue channel, for example, and moving the Constant slider to the right. Any image becomes bluer. Drag it to the left, and it becomes more yellow (the complement of blue on the color wheel).

Making Optimal Grayscales

Converting a color image directly to a perfect grayscale was once a hit-or-miss process. With the Channel Mixer, you can easily make a perfect grayscale from an RGB or CMYK image by manual correction and previewing.

When you convert an RGB image to a grayscale, Photoshop uses an algorithm to convert the brightness values from the 16 million colors in its three color channels into 256 shades of gray. By applying the Channel Mixer to the unconverted RGB file, you can control how the image looks prior to the conversion. By moving the sliders, you can emphasize brightness and contrast within the image.

To convert an RGB image to grayscale:

1. Check the Monochrome box in the Channel Mixer.

2. Adjust each of the color sliders until optimal contrast is achieved.

3. Move the Constant slider to darken or lighten the image.

4. When you're satisfied with the results, click OK.

5. Choose Image → Mode → Grayscale to convert the image.

Using Adjustment Layers

When you apply an adjustment operation such as Levels, Curves, or the Channel Mixer to an image, you directly affect the information on a layer or on the Background. The only way to change these operations is to return to them in the History palette, which can have complicated and unexpected results if you've done a lot to the image. Photoshop's Adjustment layers segregate the mathematical data of the adjustment to a separate layer that can be re-edited at any time during the imaging process. Adjustment layers are very handy indeed, and another element in Photoshop's arsenal that keeps the process dynamic.

Creating an Adjustment Layer

Follow these steps to create an Adjustment layer:

1. Choose Layer → New Adjustment Layer and select the type of Adjustment layer you want from the submenu.

2. The New Layer dialog box appears. Name, color-code, and set the opacity and blending mode of the layer, if desired.

3. The Adjustment dialog appears. Make the adjustment and click OK. The new Adjustment layer appears on the Layers palette.

4. The Adjustment layer has an attached layer mask (see Figure 16.28), which lets you selectively conceal portions of the adjustment. (See Chapter 22, "Advanced Layer Techniques," for more on layer masks.)

By default, an Adjustment layer affects all the layers below it in the layer stack. You can, however, designate an Adjustment layer to affect *only* the layer immediately below it in the stack. Option/Alt-click the line that separates the Adjustment layer and the layer just below it. The grouped layer becomes indented and displays a clipping group icon, indicating that the two layers are now grouped. You ungroup an Adjustment layer in the same way.

You can also group a layer by clicking the Group With Previous Layer check box in the New Layer dialog box.

Masking Areas of an Adjustment Layer

The ultimate power of Adjustment layers is the ability to selectively apply an adjustment to the image and to interactively apply blending modes. An Adjustment layer can act as a mask so that you can conceal portions of the effect. To try out this process, display the Layers palette and follow these simple steps:

1. Open cactus.psd from the Chapter 16 folder on the CD.

2. Set the tolerance of the Magic Wand tool to 90. Click the center of the gray cloud on the right side of the image to select it. Click in the areas between the cactus' arms to select the additional areas of sky.

3. Choose Select → Inverse to inverse the selection.

4. Choose Layer → New Adjustment Layer → Levels. A new layer dialog appears. Name the layer and click OK. The Levels dialog box appears, and the Adjustment layer shows a Layer Mask thumbnail. The sky is masked, and the cactus is exposed.

Figure 16.28

An Adjustment layer, with thumbnails for a Levels adjustment and for a layer mask

5. Adjust the Levels control until the contrast of the cactus is increased. Move the white slider to the left until it reads 123, and the midtone slider to the right until it reads 0.77 (see Figure 16.29).

6. Click OK.

Using this masking method with Adjustment layers is an effective way to isolate an area of the image and to apply color manipulations to it without affecting the rest of the composition. As in the example, this method works well when you want to alter the color depth/contrast of the subject of an image without affecting the background.

Most filters work with the Adjustment layer masks. This can come in handy—for example, when you want to separate color adjustments between subject and background, but don't want an abrupt change, you can apply Filter → Blur → Gaussian Blur to soften the edges of the layer mask.

Applying the Unsharp Mask Filter

You might ask, "What is a filter description doing here in the color adjustment chapter?" The answer is that the Unsharp Mask (USM) filter is a contrast-adjustment tool that goes hand-in-hand with color correction, and if used properly, it can further enhance the color relationship and contrast of the image and make it really "pop."

Figure 16.29

The adjustment Layer, the Levels dialog box, and the image.

USM exaggerates the transition between areas of most contrast while leaving areas of minimum contrast unaffected. It can help increase the contrast of an image and fool the eye into thinking fuzzy areas of the image are in focus.

To apply the USM, choose Filter → Sharpen → Unsharp Mask (see Figure 16.30). The USM filter has a preview in which you see a thumbnail version of the image. You can reduce or enlarge the preview by clicking the – or + signs. This is helpful if you want to compare the affected preview to the original 100%-sized, unsharpened image. Check the Preview box to see the effect on the image itself.

You'll have a chance to practice unsharp-masking the image at the end of Hands On 5.

To apply the USM, move one of its three sliders:

Amount By moving this slider or entering a value from 1% to 500%, you determine how much sharpening will be applied. The higher the value, the more the image will be sharpened. Applying only an amount, however, will not sharpen the image. To see the effect, you must also specify a radius.

Radius By moving the Radius slider or entering a value, you control the thickness of the sharpened edge. Lower values produce thinner, sharper edges; higher values produce wider edges with more overall sharpening of the entire image.

Threshold To control the numeric value of adjacent, contrasting pixels, move the Threshold slider. This slider determines how different the pixels must be from the surrounding area before they are considered edge pixels and sharpened. It also restores smooth areas that acquire texture when the amount and radius are applied—the higher the value, the greater the restoration. Too much threshold will reverse the effect of the USM.

IF IT'S A SHARPEN FILTER, WHY IS IT CALLED *UNSHARP* MASK?

Many of the operations performed in Photoshop today were derived from traditional optical techniques performed in a process camera. Before computers, a special mask was cut to protect parts of images when they were being "bumped," or exposed to increase their contrast. This mask would leave important flesh tones and other critical areas unaffected while enhancing the contrast of the most prominent edges to produce the illusion of sharp focus. Because the area within the mask was being protected and the area outside the mask was being sharpened, the term for the process came to be known as *unsharp mask*. Photoshop essentially performs the same operation, only digitally and with more control and less labor.

Figure 16.30

**An image being
sharpened with the
Unsharp Mask filter
dialog box**

The goal in sharpening an image is to apply as much USM as possible without blowing out areas, shifting colors, creating dark or light halos, or amplifying noise and unwanted detail. These flaws can make the image appear garish or artificial. You can avoid most problems by applying one or more of the following methods.

Small-Dose Technique

USM works better in smaller doses. Apply USM several times with smaller settings, keeping the amount and radius lower and the threshold higher. Sharpen gently several times with the same low settings. Press ⌘/Ctrl-F to reapply the filter with the same values, or reduce the values slightly each time.

Keep a close watch on the image as you sharpen it. Sharpen the image until it appears a little too sharp. To see an overall comparison, toggle between the original thumbnail in the History palette (Window → Show History) and the last line of the History list where sharpening was applied.

Flesh-Tone Technique

This technique works particularly well on flesh tones. The problem presented by flesh tones when applying any sharpening filter is the tendency to increase the texture of the skin so that it appears rough or porous. To avoid this problem, apply a larger amount and a smaller radius. Keeping the radius low affects only the edge pixels while reducing the sharpening of noise and unwanted detail. Adjust the threshold to eliminate excess texture in the flesh tones and other areas of low contrast.

Lab-Mode Technique

This method is specially designed to avoid color shifts. In essence, you will be applying your sharpening to the brightness information only. Like RGB mode, Lab mode segregates the image data into three channels. In RGB, however, red, green, and blue channels each contain 256 brightness levels. In Lab mode, the information is divided into an *a* channel (red and green hues), a *b* channel (blue and yellow hues), and an *L*, or lightness, channel (the brightness information). The L channel is where the USM will be applied.

Follow these steps to use the Lab-mode technique:

1. Choose Image → Duplicate to make a copy of your image.

2. Choose Layer → Flatten Image.

3. Choose Image → Mode → Lab Color to convert to Lab mode. Don't worry, there is no appreciable loss of color information in this conversion as there is when you convert from RGB to CMYK.

4. Choose Window → Channels. Target the Lightness channel by clicking its thumbnail.

5. Click the visibility icon next to the composite Lab channel in the Channels palette so that the full-color image is visible in the image window.

6. Choose Filter → Sharpen → Unsharp Mask.

Move the Amount, Radius, and Threshold sliders to produce the desired effect.

Blending Mode Method

This method produces similar results to the Lab mode technique. It's used to avoid color shifts.

1. Choose Image → Duplicate to make a copy of the image.

2. Choose Layer → Flatten Image.

3. Duplicate the Background by dragging it to the New Layer icon. Target the new layer.

4. From the Blending mode list in the upper left of the Layers palette choose Luminosity.

5. Choose Filter → Sharpen → Unsharp Mask.

6. Move the Amount, Radius, and Threshold sliders to produce the desired effect and click OK.

7. You can mitigate the effect by dragging the Opacity slider in the Layers palette to the right to reduce the opacity.

CHAPTER 17

Modifying and Mapping Color

Color is one of the most significant factors in our visual experience of the world around us. Humans react to color emotionally. Cool, subdued colors can calm our senses, and hot, saturated colors can excite and motivate us. Color affects the decisions of our daily lives, such as whether we purchase a certain product or cross the street. It affects our physical and mental space and contributes to our sense of well-being.

Because color plays such an important role in our lives, how we use it to communicate ideas is essential to the success of our images. As you have seen, Adobe Photoshop provides numerous ways to apply and adjust color. In this chapter, you will explore features that can radically alter existing colors in an image—*color-mapping* operations that go beyond brightness and contrast adjustments and simple color fills. These operations provide the means to alter the basic characteristics of color while maintaining the image's detail. You can use these commands to change the entire color scheme of your image or to create eye-popping graphic effects, such as vibrant posterizations, high-contrast art, and textured halftones.

In this chapter, you will learn about:

- **Altering the hue and saturation**
- **Matching colors**
- **Replacing the colors in an image**
- **Limiting the number of colors in an image**
- **Producing graphic effects using halftones**

Altering Hue and Saturation

You find most of the color-mapping operations under the Image → Adjustments submenu. You use this same menu to access the brightness and contrast operations, such as Levels and Curves, and color-correction features, such as Color Balance, Selective Color, and Shadow/Highlight (see Chapter 16, "Adjusting Tonality and Color"). The Hue/Saturation command lets you alter the basic color characteristics of an image. When you choose Image → Adjustments → Hue/Saturation, you are presented with a dialog box with three sliders (see Figure 17.1). Each slider *remaps* a different color characteristic.

Changing Hue

If you drag the Hue slider to change relative color relationships of the image or selection, you can produce some really beautiful and unexpected color combinations. I encourage you to experiment with color images to get a feel for the Hue/Saturation command and to experience its potential. You'll find that changing the reality of an everyday landscape into a brilliant fauvist work of art is fun and easy. With these tools in hand, after all, who can resist the temptation to transform, with the click of a mouse, a humdrum blue sky to an electric fuchsia and the ordinary green leaves on the trees to bubble-gum pink?

The numeric values you see in the Hue/Saturation dialog box are based on the affected color's position on the color wheel and are expressed in degrees. Values in the box reflect the amount of rotation from the original color. Moving the slider to the right, or a positive value, indicates a clockwise rotation of the color wheel. Moving it to the left, to a negative value, indicates a counterclockwise rotation.

Figure 17.1

The Hue/Saturation dialog box

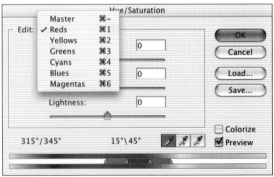

Figure 17.2

The ramps in the Hue/Saturation dialog box enable you to affect a targeted range of colors.

The color bars at the bottom of the dialog box are a graphic indicator of how the colors change as you move the Hue slider. By default, the color bars are aligned. The top color bar represents a color wheel that has been cut at the 180-degree point, or blue. As you move the Hue slider, the top color bar remains in place and represents the entire range of colors prior to the change. The bottom color bar is dynamic. It moves as you drag the Hue slider and realigns with the colors on the top bar to reflect the relative change of colors.

Adjusting Hue

The Edit pop-up list at the top of the dialog box enables you to target a specific range of colors to adjust. The colors are divided into basic color ranges of 90 degrees each, including the *overlap* (the amount that the colors adjacent to the target color on the color wheel are affected). The Master option (the default range) permits the entire spectrum of color to be affected when you move the Hue, Saturation, or Lightness sliders. The other options perform as follows:

Edit Option	Targets (on the Color Wheel)
Reds	Colors to be affected from 0 to 45 degrees clockwise and 360 to 315 degrees counterclockwise
Yellows	Colors to be affected from 15 to 105 degrees clockwise
Greens	Colors to be affected from 75 to 165 degrees clockwise
Cyans	Colors to be affected from 135 to 225 degrees clockwise
Blues	Colors to be affected from 195 to 285 degrees clockwise
Magentas	Colors to be affected from 255 to 345 degrees clockwise

When you choose a color from the Edit list, you can limit the changes to a specific range of hues. An adjustment slider appears between the two color bars, telling you which colors are being affected (see Figure 17.2) and letting you increase or decrease the range of hues to be affected, by dragging left or right in these ways:

- To change the range of color to be affected, drag the dark gray horizontal bar to move the entire adjustment slider.

- To extend the range of color and the amount of overlap, drag the light gray horizontal bars.

- To change the range while leaving the overlap unaffected, drag the white vertical bars.

- To adjust the overlap while leaving the range fixed, drag the white triangles.

Sampling with the Eyedroppers

The familiar eyedroppers that you saw in the Levels and Curves dialog boxes perform a slightly different function here. Once again, their performance is controlled by the presets made to the Eyedropper tool in the Options bar: Point Sample, 3 By 3 Average, or 5 By 5 Average. In the Hue/Saturation dialog box, they are used to pick specific colors to be adjusted. Choose the eyedropper that best suits your purposes:

The Eyedropper samples a pixel or set of pixels, depending on the options selected for the Eyedropper tool in the Options bar.

The Plus Eyedropper lets you add to the sample range by dragging over pixels in the image window.

The Minus Eyedropper lets you subtract from the range by dragging over pixels in the image window.

When you sample a color from an image with an eyedropper, the Edit pop-up list will at times produce an additional category, titled Reds 2 or Blues 2, for example. The new category includes the 90-degree range of default color categories with the specific, sampled hue at its center.

After you sample the color on the image with an eyedropper, drag the Hue, Saturation, or Lightness sliders to affect that color.

Adjusting Saturation

In a similar fashion, you can adjust the intensity of the colors in an image by dragging the Saturation slider. The default saturation value on the center of the slider is 0, which represents the relative saturation of the color. You can move the slider to the right—up to as much as +100%, where the affected colors will be fully saturated, producing intense neon colors—or to the left, to −100%, where the colors will be completely desaturated, or gray.

Most of the time your values will fall somewhere between the two extremes. You can enhance a color and make it "pop" by pushing the Saturation slider between +20% and +40%. On the other hand, if you're interested in muted pastel colors, drag the slider to the left, between −20% and −40%, to diminish the saturation.

> You can perform a quick, total desaturation of an RGB image or a selection by choosing Image → Adjustments → Desaturate. This operation accomplishes the same thing as moving the Saturation slider to −100 in the Hue/Saturation dialog box.

Adjusting Lightness

You can edit the brightness values of an image by moving the Lightness slider. Drag it toward the left to darken the image or selection, or to the right to lighten it. The 0 point marks the input lightness value of the image. The extremes are +100% lightness, which produces white, and −100% lightness, or black.

If an area of your image is very light and you find that adjusting the Hue and Saturation sliders has no effect on it, darken it a little by dragging the Lightness slider to the left. Then drag the Hue and Saturation sliders. The light areas will begin to change color.

> Don't like the results of your first try? At any time, you can reset the Hue/Saturation and other dialog boxes to the default by pressing Option/Alt and clicking the Reset button, or press ⌘/Ctrl-Z to undo just the last operation.

Colorizing

With this feature, you can create those cool effects that you see in movies such as *Schindler's List* or in magazine ads, in which the entire image is black-and-white except for one area that displays a brilliant spot of color. Before a black-and-white image can be colorized, you must change its mode from Grayscale to one that supports color, for example, RGB, CMYK, or Lab. The appearance of the grayscale image will be unaffected by this conversion.

When you colorize an image or selected area, you convert gray pixels to colored pixels. Gray pixels have RGB values that are equal. For example, the RGB values for black are red = 0, green = 0, and blue = 0. The RGB values for white are red = 255, green = 255, and blue = 255, and the RGB values for medium gray are red = 127, green = 127, and blue = 127. When you colorize a group of pixels, you shift the red, green, and blue components to disparate values.

When you check the Colorize box, the Hue and Saturation sliders change to represent absolute values instead of relative ones. The default hue that is produced when you check the Colorize box is the current foreground hue. The Hue slider now reads from 0 degrees on the left to 360 degrees on the right, and the current foreground color's position on the color wheel is displayed.

To change the hue, move the slider until you see the color you want, or, more precisely, enter its position on the color wheel (in degrees) in the Hue value field. The Saturation slider reads from 0% to 100% and defaults at 25%. Move the slider to the right to increase intensity or to the left to decrease intensity. The default lightness of the pixels remains unchanged, as does the Lightness slider. It continues to display relative values between –100 (black) and +100 (white). By colorizing, you apply color to the image without affecting the lightness relations of the individual pixels, thereby maintaining the image's detail.

Let's go through colorization step-by-step so you get the hang of how it operates. For this exercise and the one that follows, I've already selected pieces to be colorized onto separate layers. In later projects, you'll combine selecting or sampling with color adjustments. Here are the colorization steps:

1. Open the file `flowers.psd` (see Figure 17.3) in the `Ch17` folder on the *Photoshop CS Savvy* CD.

2. Notice that the file is in Grayscale mode. Choose Image → Mode → RGB. You'll be presented with a dialog box asking whether you want to flatten the layers before the mode change—choose Don't Merge.

3. When you initially apply colorization, the selection is colored with the foreground color. Click the Default Color icon, or press the D key, to restore the foreground color to black and the background color to white.

   Note that the default foreground color, black, is actually pure red hue, 0 degrees on the color wheel, with 0% saturation and 0% brightness.

4. Choose Window → Layers and target the layer named flowers.

5. Choose Image → Adjustments → Hue/Saturation.

6. Click the Colorize check box. The rose turns red (the foreground color). Move the hue slider to 44 degrees to color the flowers bright yellow.

7. Move the Saturation slider to 64% to increase its intensity. Click OK.

Figure 17.3

The Hue/Saturation adjustment will add a much needed splash of color to the grayscale flowers **image.**

8. Target the stamen layer and choose Image → Adjustments → Hue/Saturation again.

9. Click the Colorize check box. The stem turns red.

10. Set the Hue to 298; the stamen turns violet. Set the Saturation to 20 to decrease its intensity. Set the Lightness to -10. Click OK. (See the result in the color section, Figure C21.)

The Hue/Saturation command can be assigned to an Adjustment layer. You can then make changes to the colors of the image throughout the imaging process. For more about Adjustment layers, see Chapter 16.

Matching Colors

You can match colors within an image by using the Hue/Saturation command; you can also accurately match colors automatically by using Photoshop's new Match Color command.

Matching Colors by Using Hue Saturation

You can use the Hue/Saturation command to sample a color from one area of an image and apply it to another area, thereby perfectly matching the colors. Here's how:

1. Open the file dice.psd from your CD, in the Ch17 folder.

2. To make it easier to target specific areas of the image, I have separated it into two layers and a Background. Target the Background.

3. Choose the Eyedropper tool [icon]. In the Options bar, set the Sample Size to 3 By 3 Average.

4. Choose Window → Info. In the Info palette menu, choose Palette Options. For First Color Readout, select HSB Color in the Mode submenu. Click OK.

5. Place the cursor on a midtone region of the red die (I chose the area along the lower right of center of the die). Click your mouse to sample the color as a foreground color. Note the Hue and Saturation reading in the Info palette; in this case, it's 0 degrees for the Hue and 100 percent for the Saturation (see Figure 17.4).

6. Target the yellow die layer. Choose Image → Adjustments → Hue/Saturation. Be sure the Preview box is checked; check the Colorize box (see Figure 17.5).

7. If you sampled hue 100 as specified in step 5, then it is now the current foreground color. The Hue slider will read 0 when you click the Colorize box. If you did not sample the color, enter 0 in the Hue box and 100 in the Saturation box. (If necessary, you can also adjust the Lightness slider up or down a bit to best match the red die. I moved it to the left to –21 to darken the die.) Click OK, and the color of the two dice are perfectly matched.

The before and after images appear in the color section, as Figure C20.

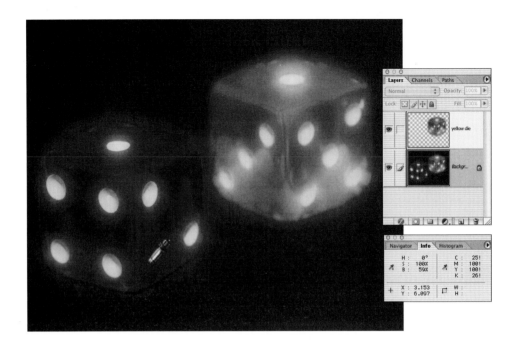

Figure 17.4

**Sampling the color
from the red die**

Matching Colors by Using the Match Color Command

Photoshop's new Match Color feature makes matching colors between documents, selections, or layers easy. When you choose Image → Adjustments → Match Color, a dialog box is displayed (see Figure 17.6).

The image that is active on the desktop is the Target image (the image that will be affected). If there is an active selection on the image, you can disregard it and match colors across the entire image by checking the Ignore Selection When Applying Adjustment box. The Image Options control the extent to which the color match will be applied. The Luminance slider affects the brightness of the image. The Color Intensity slider affects the saturation. You can control the strength of the color match by moving the Fade slider. Check the Neutralize box to eliminate color casts that might result from the color match.

The Image Statistics field is where you designate the source image from all images open on the desktop. They will appear in the source list. Choose the image whose

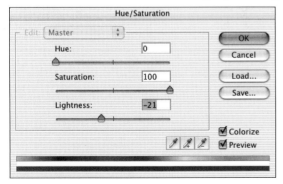

Figure 17.5

**The Hue/Saturation
dialog box**

colors you wish to match. A thumbnail of the image will appear in the box to the right of the menu. If a selection is active on the Target or the Source image, two check boxes will be active that enable you to designate the colors within the selection as the source colors.

> The check box Use Selection In Target To Calculate Adjustment enables you to apply color from a selection on a single image to an active layer on the same image.

After you've completed the match, you can save the statistics from the operation: click the Save Statistics button and then choose a location. You can load these statistics and apply them to another image.

To use the Match Color feature, follow these steps:

1. Open the images `colored_building.psd` and `drab_building.psd` from the Ch17 folder on the companion CD.

2. The colored building image has been divided into a layer and a Background. The drab building is flat. Activate `colored_building.psd` by clicking it. Be sure Layer 1 is targeted.

3. Press M on the keyboard to choose the Rectangular Marquee tool. Drag the tool in a small area of blue in the sky, as in Figure 17.7.

4. Activate `drab_building.psd`. Press the W key to choose the Magic Wand tool. Set the Tolerance to 32. Click on the sky above the building to select it.

5. Choose Image → Adjustments → Match Color. In the Source list, choose `colored_building.psd` as the source image. Check the Use Selection In Source To Calculate Colors box. In the Layer list, choose Background. The sky on the drab building will match the color of the sky selected from the colored building's Background. Click OK.

6. Activate the drab building and choose the Magic Wand tool; set the Tolerance to 80. Click on an area of brick to select it. (You might have to add small areas to the selection.)

Figure 17.6

The Match Color dialog box

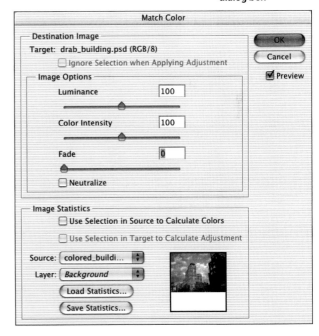

Figure 17.7

You'll match the sky of the target image (right) to contents of the selection on the source image (left).

7. Choose Image → Adjustments → Match Color. For the source image, choose colored_building.psd. For the layer, choose Layer 1. Uncheck the Use Selection In Source To Calculate Colors and the Use Selection In Target To Calculate Adjustment boxes.

> You might wish to experiment with the Use Selection in Target to Calculate Adjustment feature, which, in some instances, retains more detail.

8. Move the Luminance slider to the right until it reads 112, and the Color intensity slider to the right until it reads 109. Click OK. Figure C22 in the color section shows the results.

> By default Match Color uses the original target input image as the color source (source: none). You can now edit the luminance and saturation sometimes with better results than with the color correction commands.

Replacing Color

With Photoshop, you can do more than just alter the hue, saturation, and lightness of an image. You can sample a specific range of colors and automatically replace it with a different range of colors, without affecting the rest of the image. This is particularly useful if you need to change a similar color that is scattered throughout an image. The two features that are designed to replace colors effortlessly are Replace color command and the Color Replacement tool.

Using the Replace Color Command

When you choose Image → Adjustments → Replace Color (see Figure 17.8), you get a dialog box that is a combination of two powerful Photoshop operations: the Hue/Saturation command and the Color Range command. This dynamic duo can quickly perform miraculous color swapping. The Color Range command makes selections based on colors you sample in the image. (See Chapter 21, "Making Difficult Selections," for details on how to use Color Range.) The Replace Color dialog box combines this powerful feature with Hue, Saturation, and Lightness controls so that you can precisely sample colors and then instantly replace them. Once again, before you open the Replace Color dialog box, I recommend that you change the settings on the Eyedropper tool to 3 By 3 Average.

Figure 17.8

The Replace Color dialog box

The default Replace Color dialog box displays a black mask of the image. Be sure the Preview box is checked. Choose the eyedropper from the Replace Color dialog box, and click the color in the image window that you want to change. The mask reveals white portions that designate where the changes will be made. If you choose the Plus Eyedropper, you click and drag over areas to add colors. If you choose the Minus Eyedropper, and click and drag over colors, you delete them from the replacement. The mask reflects the changes you make.

> You can limit the areas that will be affected on an image by making a selection prior to opening the Replace Color dialog box.

After you've selected the colors to replace, the next step is to move the Hue, Saturation, and Lightness sliders to produce a new range of color. As you drag, the affected colors change in the image window. If you don't nail all the areas that you want to change when you sample with the Eyedropper, sample again with the Plus Eyedropper to extend the range. For a little more control, drag the Fuzziness slider to the right. If you click the Image radio button under the mask, you see the image before the change. You can then compare the "before" version in the Replace Color dialog box to the "after" version in the image window prior to committing to the alteration.

Let's take a crack at replacing colors:

1. From the Ch17 folder on the CD, open the image NYposters.psd.

2. Press the M key to choose the Rectangular Marquee. Drag a rectangular selection around the two images of the singer (see Figure 17.9).

3. Choose the Eyedropper tool. (In the Options bar, set the Sample Size to 3 By 3 Average.)

4. Choose Image → Adjustments → Replace Color. Make sure the Selection radio button under the preview window in the dialog box is checked.

5. Click on red areas in the selection to sample the color. Notice how the mask in the preview window changes to include the sampled red areas.

Figure 17.9

You can recolor all the red areas in the selection with the Replace Color command.

6. Now choose the Plus Eyedropper. Drag over any red areas of the image that did not get included in the first sampling. Be careful not to touch the surrounding colors.

7. Move the Hue/Saturation sliders to change the colors. I've specified Hue = –74, Saturation = +22, and Lightness = –2 to make the red areas a light shade of purple.

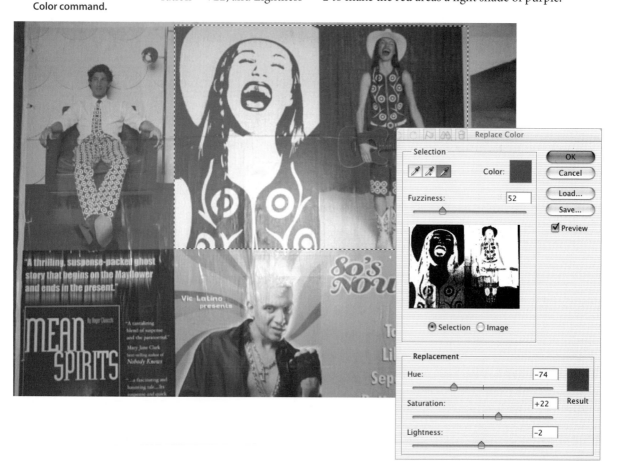

8. If significant portions of the image are still red, drag over them with the Plus Eyedropper. If you include too many of the colors in the selection, use the Minus Eyedropper to remove them. If you need to extend the color just a little bit, move the Fuzziness slider to the right. Or, if you want to decrease it, move the slider to the left.

9. Click the Image radio button to compare before and after versions. When satisfied with the replacement, click OK. Figure C33 in the color section compares the color change in this image.

Manually Replacing Colors

The new Replace Color tool in the Tool palette enables you to replace colors on-the-fly with the foreground color without affecting image detail. It is found in the Healing Brush fly-out. Press Shift-J to access it. In the Options bar, choose a brush size and set the tool's behavioral properties. You can choose from four blending modes: Hue, Saturation, Color, and Luminosity. (See Appendix C for blending mode descriptions.)

The Sampling menu determines how the tool chooses the color to be replaced. You have the following options to choose from:

Contiguous samples colors that are adjacent to each other, within the tolerance range.

Discontiguous samples all of the pixels within the tolerance range.

Once samples the color when you first click it and replaces only that color.

The Limits menu determines how the new pixels are distributed.

Contiguous spreads colors continuously as long as the mouse button is pressed.

Discontiguous spreads colors to all of the pixels on a layer.

Find Edges spreads color on the sampled pixels but detects areas of contrast to best preserve the sharpness of an edge.

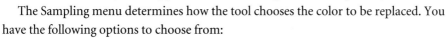

In Hands On 5 you'll have an opportunity to use the Color Replacement tool.

Rearranging Colors

Photoshop's color-mapping features enable you to limit the number and range of colors in your image. You can automatically produce higher levels of contrast, convert your images into line art, produce images that resemble serigraphs (silk-screen prints), and change your image from a positive to a negative. With so many choices for transforming your image, no doubt you'll never again be satisfied with just an ordinary photograph. Let's go through them one by one and determine what they do and how they work. You can find all of these features on the bottom rung of the Image → Adjustments submenu.

Equalizing the Contrast

You can use the Equalize command to alter the contrast of an image. It analyzes the color information in each channel, and maps the darkest pixel it can find to black and the lightest pixel to white. It then evenly distributes the color information between the two extremes. This doesn't mean that the image will contain black or white—only that, in at least one channel, there will be a pixel with a value of 0 and a pixel with a value of 255. Also, it doesn't mean that the image will be a higher contrast, only that the contrast values will be distributed over a larger range. The results can vary depending on the image. See Figure 17.10 for an example of this effect. You can also see a color version of the image, Figure C23, in the color section.

Inverting Color Values

Use the Invert feature to create negatives, because it expertly converts every color in the image to its exact opposite. If you're working on a 256-level grayscale image, black (0) will become white, and white (255) will become black. All other values will also switch; a light

Figure 17.10

Before and after applying the Equalize command

Figure 17.11

**Before and after
applying the Invert
command**

gray will become its dark gray counterpart if inverted. For example, if a pixel has a brightness value of 230 (that is, 255 − 25), it will have a value of 25 when converted (0 + 25), as in Figure 17.11.

Invert works the same way on RGB color images; they are converted channel-by-channel. Invert doesn't produce color film negatives very well, however, because it omits the colored tint, called an *orange mask,* that is part of the color negative's emulsion. You can use the Invert command and later make a color adjustment with the Color Balance or Variations commands to add an orange tint, but this will require some experimentation.

Because the operation converts the color values of each color channel, the results can vary substantially depending on the image's color mode.

If you invert an alpha channel, the selection it produces will be equal to an inverted selection. You can check the Invert feature in the Levels and Curves command to create negative effects as well; there is also an Invert Adjustment layer.

Adjusting the Threshold

When you choose Image → Adjustments → Threshold, you map all of your colors to either black or white. The Threshold dialog box displays a histogram of all the brightness values of your image. You drag the slider to the left or right to determine its midpoint. Values on the right side of the slider are white. As you drag to the left, more pixel values are included on the white side and the image gets increasingly lighter. As you drag to the right, more pixel values are included on the black side and the image gets increasingly darker. Figure 17.12 demonstrates several threshold midpoints. See Figure C24 in the color section for a color version of this image.

Figure 17.12

The original image (top) remapped to threshold levels of 85, 128, and 200

Threshold is useful for turning photographs into high-contrast line art, an effect formerly achieved by copying generations of images on a photocopier or by shooting extremely high-contrast film. Threshold has the advantage of being able to determine exactly how much of the image will be black and how much will be white, and therefore offers far more control than traditional techniques. Threshold is also quite handy for making alpha channels from color channels for use on those seemingly impossible selections, as you will see in Chapter 21.

Figure 17.13

The Posterize dialog box

Using the Posterize Feature

Whereas Threshold divides an image into two colors, Posterize lets you choose the number of colors in which to divide the image. The problem is, you have no direct way of controlling how the colors are mapped. Choose Image → Adjustments → Posterize to bring up the Posterize dialog box (see Figure 17.13). Input a Levels value from 2 to 255. Posterize applies the value to each channel of the image, so if you enter 2 while working in an RGB image, for example, you actually produce eight colors (2^3).

These effects can be interesting depending on how many colors you input into the Levels field. By breaking up the image into flat areas of color, with occasional dithering where the edges are ambiguous, you can achieve a much more graphic appearance to your image. Unfortunately, the results are also unpredictable.

You can, however, use Posterize to determine the number of colors and how they are distributed in your image. The following workaround will give you the ability to create flat areas of color with more precision and control. The results can vary, depending on your image and color choices. With this method, you can achieve an effect resembling a serigraph used on silk-screen posters with bright, vibrant colors, or tone down an image with pastel colors:

1. Open the RGB image `player.psd` in the `Ch17` folder on the CD (see Figure 17.14).

2. Choose Image → Mode → Grayscale to convert the image to a black-and-white version.

3. Choose Image → Adjustments → Posterize. Enter a Levels value of 4 (you can enter any amount from 2 to 255, but use 4 for this demo). Click OK. Notice that the image is now divided into four shades of gray: white, light gray, dark gray, and black (see Figure 17.15).

4. Choose Image → Mode → RGB to convert the image back to RGB so it can support the color that you are about to apply to it.

5. From the Tool palette, choose the Magic Wand tool . Set the Tolerance to 1 and clear the Anti-Aliased and Contiguous options. Click an area of white to select all of the white in the image.

6. Choose Window → Show Swatches. Pick a light color from the Swatches palette.

Figure 17.14

The original image

Figure 17.15

The posterization workaround lets you control the number of colors in your posterized image.

7. Use the Paint Bucket tool or press Option-Delete (Mac) or Alt-Backspace (Win) to fill the selected areas with color.

8. Repeat steps 5, 6, and 7 on the areas of light gray, dark gray, and black, choosing a darker color each time to replace the gray shades.

To see different color versions of this image created by using the effect described here, see Figures C25 and C26 in the color section.

Applying Gradient Maps

You can apply a Gradient Map to an image to adjust the equivalent grayscale range of an image to the colors of a specified gradient fill. An image mapped to a three-color gradient, for example, will change the highlights into gradations on the left end of the gradient, midtones to gradations in the middle of the gradient, and shadows to the gradation of the right endpoint.

To apply a Gradient Map, follow these steps:

1. Open the image `surf.psd` in the Chapter 17 folder on the CD. Choose Image → Adjustments → Gradient Map to bring up the dialog box in Figure 17.16.

2. To choose a gradient fill, click the down arrow to the right of the gradient fill displayed in the Gradient Map dialog box and then click a swatch.

   If you click the gradient fill, you can edit it or create a new gradient fill.

3. If desired, select one or both of the gradient options:

   Dither applies random noise to smooth the gradient and reduce banding effects.

   Reverse switches the direction of the gradient fill, reversing the Gradient Map.

See the color section for a comparison of the original image and the gradient mapped version, Figure C27a, and the image with the Gradient Map applied, Figure C27b.

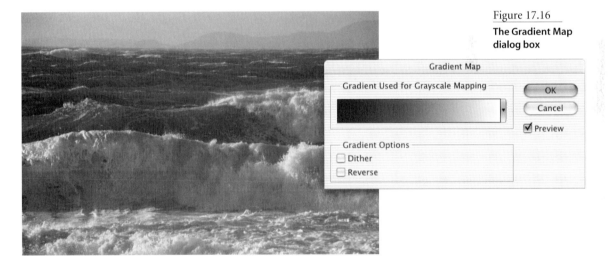

Figure 17.16

The Gradient Map dialog box

Creating Digital Halftones

A *halftone* is an image in which ink or toner is transferred to paper, and consists of dots on a grid. The resolution, or number of lines per inch (lpi), of a halftone depends on the printer's capabilities. The number of dots on a traditional halftone is finite and depends on the grid's lpi. The tonal densities of an image are determined by the size of the dots— the larger the dot, the more ink is deposited, and the darker the area appears.

Most low-end ink-jet printers, however, produce a *stochastic,* or frequency modulated, dot pattern, in which the tonal density is expressed not by the size, but by the number of dots deposited. That's why the resolution claimed by desktop ink-jets (commonly 720 × 1440) is usually higher, though not necessarily better, because the dots are smaller and distributed in a random pattern. When you send an image to a printer, Photoshop, in tandem with the printer driver software, automatically and transparently converts the tonal information contained in pixels into dot density information that the printer's "marking engine" uses to construct your image. Fortunately, you don't have to do any of the math!

Before you begin to create an image for print, you should be aware of the necessary ratio of pixels per inch (ppi) to line screen (lpi) to produce quality halftones. For more on this, see Chapter 13, "Sizing and Transforming Images."

Photoshop also has built-in tools that let you convert your images to bitmaps and take over the halftoning process before you send your image to the printer. The term *bitmap* describes images that are composed of pixels, each containing one bit of information. That means the pixels are either black or white. When you turn an image into a bitmap, Photoshop converts all of the tonal information into a series of black or white elements composed of—you guessed it—pixels. You can then print the bitmap on your laser printer as black-and-white line art or as a fully composited halftone. Even better, you can choose from a variety of bitmap types and patterns to produce specialized graphic effects.

You can't directly convert an RGB, CMYK, or Lab image into a halftone. You must first convert your image into Grayscale. Bitmapped images do not support layers, alpha channels, filters, or any operations involving color—in fact, about the only things you can do with them are invert them or paint on them with black or white. Because they contain only one bit of information per pixel, the file sizes of bitmaps are relatively small.

Choose Image → Mode → Bitmap to convert your Grayscale. In the Bitmap dialog box (see Figure 17.17), choose a resolution for the bitmap. The higher the resolution, the smoother the elements that define it will be. If you want a one-to-one ratio with your laser printer, set it to the printer's output resolution (commonly 300, 600, 800, or 1200 dpi).

Next, choose a method from the Use drop-down list:

50% Threshold converts the image to a black-and-white, line art bitmap with the midpoint at 128. The difference between this function and the Threshold command discussed earlier in this chapter is

Figure 17.17

The Bitmap dialog box

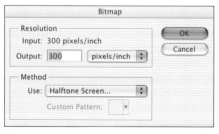

that the Threshold command works on color and grayscale images. It converts the image to black-and-white but retains the bit depth and, hence, the editability of the image. Plus, you can control the midpoint level, which lets you determine which pixels will be converted to white and which pixels will be converted to black. Bitmap images, on the other hand, are extremely limited as far as how they can be edited and what Photoshop operations they support. Another drawback is that 50% Threshold simply converts the image to black-and-white by using the mid-tone pixels of 127 and 128 as the dividing line. In the bigger scheme of things, you might be better off using the Threshold command.

Figure 17.18

The Halftone Screen dialog box

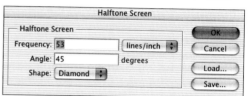

Pattern Dither applies a preprogrammed, geometric pattern to define the image's tonality. Unfortunately, it produces rather undesirable results, which have a tendency to close up when output to a laser printer.

Diffusion Dither applies a mezzotint pattern to the bitmap. The image is defined by a multitude of stray pixels peppered throughout the image. The effect can pleasantly soften the image but can also darken it. You might want to expose the image to a Levels adjustment to lighten it before you convert it to a bitmap by using the Diffusion Dither option.

Halftone Screen is by far the most useful option of the lot. When you choose Halftone Screen, the dialog box in Figure 17.18 appears. Enter a value for the frequency (lpi), angle of the screen, and dot shape.

Custom Pattern uses a pattern that you select from the Pattern list to define the tonality. The results can run from really interesting to incredibly ugly. Smaller patterns usually create effects that are more desirable.

To see variations of the potential results, open an image and apply each option in turn. See Figure 17.19 to get a quick idea of the possibilities. It might be difficult to see some differences at low monitor resolution or when printed to some printers.

When you view many of these bitmap effects on your monitor at certain sizes, you might see a strangely textured on-screen picture. This phenomenon is called a *moiré pattern* and is a result of the dot patterns of the image clashing with the matrix of the pixels on your monitor. Don't worry, the image will not print with these moiré patterns. There is not much you can do about this visual noise except to find a different size in which to view the image.

Figure 17.19

**The results of con-
verting an image to
Bitmap mode by
using different
methods**

Original

Halftone Screen

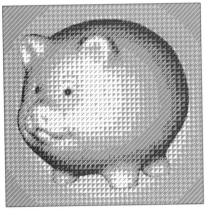

Pattern Dither

Diffusion Dither

Image Size, Transformation, and Color Adjustment

Often, an image needs more than minor color correction. This project covers techniques to improve the overall quality of an image. You will learn to manage color and to crop and size an image. You will apply color correction adjustments to enhance contrast, and eliminate color casts. You will also use some of Photoshop CS's newest adjustment features.

Figure H5.1
The original Big City Night image

Getting Started

Discard your preferences file before beginning this exercise. The "Modifying Photoshop's Settings" section in Chapter 5, "Setting Up Photoshop," details how to reset your preferences to Photoshop defaults. Then follow these steps:

1. Open the file named `big_city_night.psd` (see Figure H5.1) in the `H05` folder on the *Photoshop CS Savvy* CD. See Figure H5.2 for the completed image. (To see a color preview of the before and after versions of the image, look at Figures C49 and C50 in the color section.)

2. Save the file to your hard disk. Close the file.

Choosing a Color Space

Calibrate your monitor by using the operating system software or a colorimeter as described in Chapter 15, "Color Management and Printing." If you are a Windows user, you can calibrate with Adobe Gamma as described in Chapter 5. The image for this exercise is going to be used as an illustration for a story in a glossy magazine using four-color process printing. Before opening the document, choose an appropriate color space:

1. In Windows, choose Edit → Color Settings. In Mac OS X, choose Photoshop → Color Settings. The Color Settings dialog box is displayed.

Figure H5.2

The finished Big City Night image

2. From the Settings menu, choose U.S. Prepress Defaults, as shown in Figure H5.3. Note that the RGB working space for this setting is Adobe RGB.

3. Open the `big_city_night.psd` file you previously saved to your disk. Because you've changed the working color space to U.S. Prepress Defaults, and the image does not contain an embedded profile, you are now presented with the Missing Profile dialog box (see Figure H5.4). Choose to assign working RGB (which is now Adobe RGB) to the image, and click OK.

Cropping the Image

The image has a gray border around it and is at an angle. You'll need to crop it to eliminate the unwanted areas and adjust its angle relative to the page. Instead of using the Crop tool, try Photoshop's new automation. Choose File → Automate → Crop and Straighten Photos (Learn more about Crop and Straighten in Chapter 23, "Automating the Process"). A duplicate image will be generated with excess canvas. It will be trimmed and image rotated automatically to align with the edges of the page. Close the original file and save the new file as `big_city_ night.PSD`.

Sizing the Image

The final physical size of the image has to be 7′ wide to fit in the brochure. Resize the image by using the Image Size command (see Figure H5.5):

1. Choose Image → Image Size. Uncheck the Resample Image box. Change the width to 7′. The height automatically changes to 4.686′. The resolution has to be 300 ppi, which is the required resolution for printing to a high-quality printed publication. The image currently is 208 ppi at the current physical image size. Because you will have to increase the resolution of the image, you'll need to resample up. Check the Resample Image box to activate the interpolation options. The file size will more than double because you're adding pixels to the image. From the Resample Image menu, choose Bicubic Sharper. Click OK.

2. Click OK.

3. Press ⌘/Ctrl-S to save.

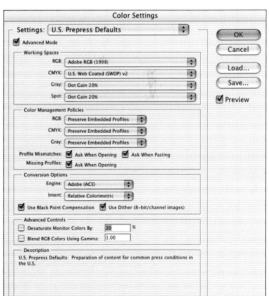

Figure H5.3

U.S. Prepress Defaults color setting

Adjusting Levels

Next you'll adjust the image's levels:

1. Choose Window → Histogram to display the Histogram palette.

2. From the Layers menu, choose New Adjustment Layer → Levels. The layer should name itself Levels 1; click OK.

    In the Histogram palette, and the Levels dialog box (see Figure H5.6), notice the histogram: The pixels are clumped into the center, which indicates that the image needs a contrast adjustment. The graph is also devoid of lines in the highlights and shadows. (The pixel cluster on the left indicates that most of the pixels are dark, which is consistent with the image being a night scene.) You can increase the overall contrast by moving the sliders to spread the highlights, midtones, and shadows over a broader range of values.

3. Move the White slider toward the center until the input level reads 198. Move the Black slider until it reads 36. Move the midtone slider until it reads 1.05 and click OK. You'll see a marked improvement in the contrast of the image.

4. Notice the histogram in the Histogram palette. The pixels are now spread over a much broader range.

5. Save.

Correcting Color with Curves

Now the image looks a lot brighter but has a reddish color cast. You'll use the Curves feature to eliminate the cast:

1. In the Layers palette, target the Background Layer.

2. Make a new Adjustment layer. This time, choose Layer → New Adjustment Layer → Curves. Click OK in the New Layer dialog box. The Layer will be named by default *Curves 1*.

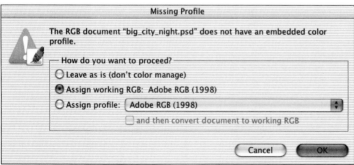

Figure H5.4

In the Missing Profile dialog box, you'll assign the Adobe RGB color working space to the image.

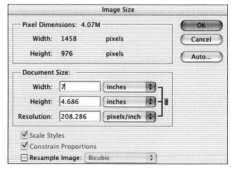

Figure H5.5

The Image Size dialog box

3. In the Curves dialog box, be sure the Preview box is checked to see the results as you work.

4. Press the Option/Alt key and click the grid to display a 100-cell grid. Choose the Red channel from the channels list. Click the point on the diagonal line where the grid intersects in the center of the graph. To reduce the amount of red in the image, drag the point downward until the Output value reads 96 as in Figure H5.7.

5. Choose the Blue channel. To cool down the midtones, drag the center point upward until the Output value reads 145 as in Figure H5.8.

6. Press ⌘/Ctrl-S to save the document.

> Be prudent in the amount you adjust the curve. Too great an adjustment will produce posterization and dithering. It's always a good idea to zoom in on a portion of the affected area and scrutinize it carefully after you've made the adjustment—but before you close the dialog box. Press ⌘/Ctrl-+ to zoom in, and - to zoom out.

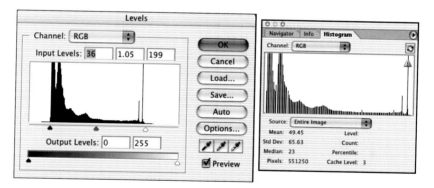

Figure H5.6

RGB levels

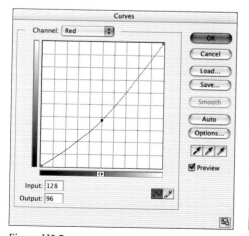

Figure H5.7

Adjusting the Red channel curve

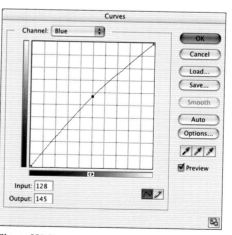

Figure H5.8

Adjusting the Blue channel curve

Adjusting Shadow and Highlight

The image is now looking good because you have adjusted its contrast and eliminated the color cast, but the highlights could be a little stronger and shadows could have more detail. Follow these steps:

1. In the Layers palette, target the Background. Choose Image/Adjustments ➜ Shadow/Highlight. A dialog box appears (see Figure H5.9).

2. Set the Shadows to the following settings—Amount: 54%, Tonal Width: 48%, Radius: 35 px. Set the Highlights to Amount: 0%, Tonal Width: 52%, and Radius: 30 px. Adjust the color correction slider to –25 and the Midtone Contrast slider to 0. Click OK.

Applying the Photo Filter

The image's contrast has improved, but there is still a slight pinkish cast in the neutral colors such as the white frame around the billboard. You can eliminate this stubborn cast by cooling the image down with the new Photo filter:

1. In the Layers palette, target the Curves Adjustment layer.

Figure H5.9

The Shadow/Highlight dialog box

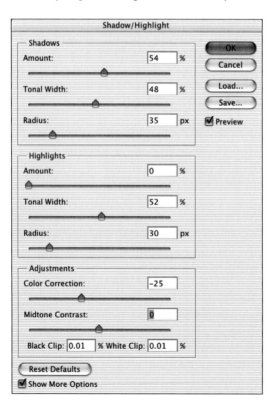

2. Choose Layer → New Adjustment Layer → Photo Filter. The Photo Filter dialog box appears. (see Figure H5.10).

3. Click the Color radio button and click on the swatch. You'll want a light blue so the effect will neutralize the pinks in the frame without discoloring the warmer colors. Enter the following values R: 148, G: 230, and B: 229, in the RGB fields. Click OK.

4. Check the Preserve Luminosity box and apply a density of 36%. Click OK.

5. Save.

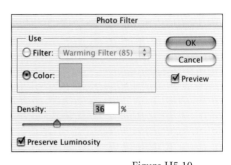

Figure H5.10

The Photo Filter dialog box

Removing Noise

The highlight and shadow operation revealed colored noise in the dark areas that were poorly lit when the photograph was taken. You'll diminish this by slightly blurring the Blue channel:

1. In the Layers palette, target the Background.

2. Click the Channels tab in the Layers/Channels/Palette cluster. Target the Blue channel but click the visibility icon next to the RGB composite channel.

3. Choose Filter → Gaussian Blur. Move the Radius slider to 2.8 (see Figure H5.11). Click OK and target the RGB composite channel.

4. There might still be a few areas of noise and dust in the darker regions of the image. Choose the Clone tool and spot clone them out.

Figure H5.11

The Gaussian Blur filter applied to the Blue channel to help diminish noise

Matching Color

To add counterpoint to the image, you'll match the color of the *8* on the billboard to a color from another image:

1. Choose the Elliptical Marquee tool from the Tool palette. Place the cursor in the center of the top circle of the 8. Click and drag to the right and down, and then press the Option/Alt key to constrain the marquee from the center point. Drag until you've selected the edge of the 8 (see Figure H5.12). If necessary, press the spacebar as you drag to position the ellipse.

2. Click the Add To Selection icon. Repeat the process for the bottom part of the 8.

3. Click the Subtract From Selection icon. Place the cursor in the center of the top part of the 8. Drag downward and to the right. Press the Option key as you drag to constrain the ellipse to the edge of the top inner circle of the 8. Repeat the process for the bottom part of the 8 (see Figure H5.12).

4. Choose the Rectangular Marquee tool. Click the Subtract From Selection icon. Position the curser next to the left side of the 8 and drag to the inner border of the frame, encompassing the left side of the 8 to deselect it.

5. Open the file city_street.psd. Choose the Rectangular Marquee tool and drag a selection in a pink area of the McDonalds awning.

6. Activate big_city_night.psd. Choose Image → Adjust → Match Color. The Match Color dialog box opens (see Figure H5.13). Be sure the Preview box is checked. Choose city_street.psd as the source document. Check the Use Selection In Source To Calculate Colors box. Uncheck the Use Selection In Target To Calculate Adjustment box. Set the Luminance slider to 73, the Color Intensity slider to 45, and the Fade slider to 23. Click OK and deselect. Close city_street.psd.

7. Save.

Replacing Color Manually

Let's enhance the color of the billboard image and change the color of the model's face from a jaundiced yellow to a soft flesh tone:

1. Click on the Foreground color in the Tool palette to display the Color Picker. Enter the following values in the appropriate fields—H: 12, S: 62, B: 84.

2. Choose the Color Replacement tool ![icon]. In the Options bar, set the Mode to Color, the Sampling to Contiguous, the Limits to Contiguous, and the Tolerance to 30.

3. Zoom in on the model's face. Choose a 55 px brush and carefully replace the color on the model's face. Choose red (H: 0, S: 100%, B: 100%) as the foreground color and a 14 px brush and paint the model's lips.

Figure H5.12

Selecting the 8 on the target image

4. Choose the Dodge tool ![dodge tool icon] and a 5 px brush. Set the exposure to 50%. Dodge over the whites of the model's eyes to lighten them. While you still have the Dodge tool selected, set the exposure to 10%. Dodge the two dark bottom windows in the building on the left.

5. Save.

Applying USM

The image is practically complete, but let's see if you can get a little more punch out of it. Because you are going to flatten the image, you should make a copy of it first:

1. To duplicate the image, choose Image → Duplicate. Name the image `big_city_night_flat.psd`. Check the Duplicate Merged Layers Only box to flatten the image.

2. Duplicate the Background by dragging it to the New Layer icon.

3. In the Layers palette blend mode menu choose Luminosity.

4. Choose Filter → Sharpen → Unsharp Mask. Set the amount to 81%, the radius to 4.2 pixels, and the threshold to 28 levels (see Figure H5.14).

5. Click OK.

6. Press ⌘/Ctrl-S to save the document.

Converting the Image to CMYK

If you are outputting the image to four-color process color separations, it's wise to convert it to CMYK first so that you can make any necessary adjustments and accurately predict how the image will print. First, preview the document; then follow these steps:

1. Duplicate the flattened, sharpened image. Name the file `big_city_night_cmyk.psd` and place it next to the original RGB image on-screen, making sure it's active.

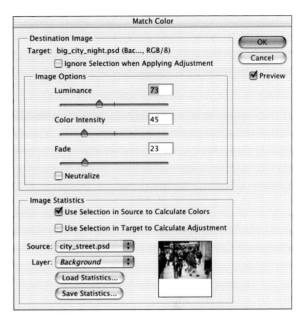

Figure H5.13

The Match Color dialog box

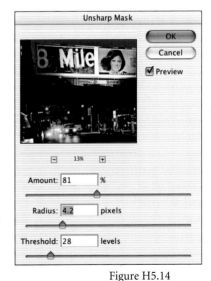

Figure H5.14

Applying the Unsharp Mask filter to the image is the final step in enhancing the contrast.

2. In the View menu, make sure that Proof Colors is checked, and then choose View → Proof Setup → Working CMYK to display the image in the CMYK setup that you selected in the color settings. In this case, it's U.S. Web Coated (SWOP) v2, which is part of the U.S. Prepress Defaults selected earlier in this project. By comparing the CMYK preview image to the RGB image, you'll notice minor color shifts in the sky of the CMYK preview file, but let's convert the file as is.

3. Choose Image → Mode → CMYK to convert the file.

4. Save the image.

> If there are radical color shifts, use the adjustment commands in the Image menu to restore the color, bearing in mind that there may be no possibility of exactly matching the colors in the RGB images.

CHAPTER 18

Duotones and Spot Color

Most images printed from Photoshop are printed in process colors. Printing presses use cyan, magenta, yellow, and black ink to print color images. Similarly, ink-jet printers deposit ink from cartridges containing CMYK colors. From time to time, however, the occasion arises when you need to create images by using custom color ink systems, either for a specific look or for reasons of economy. Photoshop has two functions that are designed to prepare images for printing by using custom colors: Duotones and spot colors. These systems depend on color information found in the Channels palette.

In this chapter, you'll discover:

- **The nature of Duotones**

- **How to make Duotones, Tritones, and Quadtones work**

- **How to create spot color channels**

- **How to print Duotones and spot color**

Why Use Duotones?

Duotones are a source of disagreement in the printing industry. Some press professionals call them a waste of two-color press time. Others claim they can turn otherwise lackluster halftones into subtle works of art. Duotones, and their siblings Tritones and Quadtones, print grayscale images by using two (or three or four) separate inks. Usually the inks are colored, but occasionally you'll see a Duotone created by using two black plates. Proponents claim that two blacks can attain a richness and depth out of reach of the simple halftone; critics say it's just one black plate too many. They might never reach an agreement.

No such controversy exists over the use of spot colors. Pressroom shelves are lined with tubs of premixed and mixable inks, and now with six- and eight-color presses becoming more and more common, combinations of four-color process, spot colors, and/or varnishes are being used with greater frequency. Photoshop's spot color channels provide a tool for creating and separating spot colors for printing.

Duotones and spot color differ from process color. Process color produces a complete color and tonal range by mixing cyan, magenta, yellow, and black ink in varying densities, while Duotones and spot color involve printing specific premixed ink colors on a substrate. Even though Photoshop deals with them in different ways, they appear together in this chapter and in the following Hands On project. You'll have a chance to try them out, and then you can decide for yourself where you come down on the Duotone question.

What Are Duotones?

When a grayscale digital image is converted to a halftone and printed with black ink on paper, the shades of gray that you created on your computer are represented by the size and concentration of dots. The black ink is still black, no matter what size you make the dot. It can't, however, represent all 256 levels of gray found in the grayscale image.

Duotones can help you achieve a wider tonal range in a grayscale image by using more than one shade of ink to fill in the gaps. You can enhance the detail and texture in an image. If you're printing a two-color book with halftones, adding the second color to the halftones can add an elegant touch. Duotones using a dark and a metallic ink can impart an opaque, antique quality, whereas lighter pastel shades might approximate a hand-tinted look or other variations, as you can see in Figure C28 in the color section.

Duotones do present one potential problem. Because two (or more) inks are being superimposed on one another, it is possible to generate too much ink. If the distribution of ink is not dealt with properly, it could saturate the paper and fill in the spaces between the fine halftone dots. That's why Photoshop's Duotone mode features a Curves palette in its dialog box, so that you can adjust each ink level individually—but I'll get to that in a minute.

Working with Duotone Mode

Suppose you start with a color photo you've scanned. Open your RGB image and then look in the Image → Mode submenu. You'll see that the Duotone mode is grayed out, unavailable as an option. To convert an image to Duotone mode, you first have to convert it to Grayscale mode. Wait! Before you do that, it's best to correct tonal and color values first, using Levels, Curves, or the other adjustment features discussed in Chapter 16, "Adjusting Tonality and Color." Get the image exactly where you want it before you reduce

it to a single channel. In fact, take a look at your color channels individually. You might find something there you like (the Green channel in an RGB image might contain a convincing microcosm of the whole, for example). Even better, use the Channel Mixer to get the perfect grayscale image. After you're happy with it, choose Image → Mode → Grayscale. If you want to do any further tweaking, do it while you're in Grayscale mode. *Then* choose Image → Mode → Duotone (see Figure 18.1). Now you're in Duotone country.

Figure 18.1

The Duotone Options dialog box

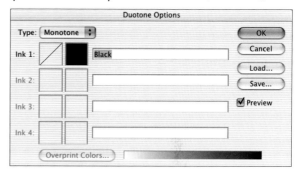

From the Duotone Options dialog box, choose a Type—that is, the number of inks you want to use, up to four. Monotones are just colored halftones, Duotones use two inks, Tritones three, and Quadtones…you guessed it. You can set curves and choose colors individually for each ink. Click an ink's color box to display the Color Picker. Because Duotones are usually printed in specific ink colors, you'll want to specify a custom ink. Click an ink swatch in the Duotone dialog box and then Custom in the Color Picker to display the Custom Color dialog box. Choose from a variety of ink swatch books and colors. Then click OK. (For more on custom colors, see Chapter 10, "Creating and Applying Color.") If you plan to import the Duotone into a page layout document, make a note of the names of your inks. Make sure the Duotone ink has exactly the same name as the other application's color dialog box. If necessary, reopen the Duotone Options dialog box and rename the ink so that the page layout program will recognize it. When you open the dialog box, Monotone is the default color Type. The designated Ink 1 color is Black, and Inks 2, 3, and 4 are grayed out.

To choose a second ink, choose Duotone from the Type list; Ink 1 will default to Black, and the Ink 2 swatch will be White. Click the swatch, and the Custom Colors dialog box is displayed. The default *book* (a term derived from the color swatch books produced by ink manufacturers to display their inks) is PANTONE solid coated (see Figure 18.2). Choose an ink color from the list and click OK. Define additional inks in the same way for Tritones and Quadtones. The color bar at the bottom of the Duotone dialog box displays the range, from light to dark, of the color mix you've specified. The image window also has a live preview. When you specify colors, the image displays the changes on-screen.

> When you define ink colors for Duotones, Tritones, and Quadtones, make sure the darkest ink is at the top and the lightest is at the bottom. When Duotone images print, the inks are applied in the order in which they appear in the dialog box. Allowing the darker inks to print first provides for a uniform color range from shadows to highlights.

Adjusting Duotone Curves

Duotone curves let you control the density of each ink in the highlights, midtones, and shadows. Click the curve thumbnail for any ink to display the corresponding Duotone Curve dialog box (see Figure 18.3). Here you can adjust the curve to define ink coverage for each color. Or enter values in one of the 13 percentage fields.

When you first convert a file to Duotone mode, the curves are straight by default. If you apply the straight curve, Photoshop will distribute the ink evenly across the entire tonal range of the image. If all the curves on a Duotone are straight, you'll end up with a dark, muddy mess. It's best to apply colors to suit the needs of the image in question; generally, you'll want dark inks densest in the shadows, somewhat lighter inks in the midtones, and light colors enhancing the highlights.

There are two ways of adjusting the curves in the Duotone Curve dialog box. Either type numeric settings for ink percentages in the boxes provided, or drag inside the curve's grid to adjust the curve directly. Like the Curves dialog box you encountered in Chapter 16, the grid's horizontal axis expresses the gradations in the image from white (highlights) on the left to black (shadows) on the right. The vertical axis maps ink density, increasing as you go up. Click anywhere on the line and drag up or down to add or subtract ink in that part of the curve. As you adjust the curve, the numbers change accordingly in the percentage boxes to reflect the changes you make. Likewise, when you type numbers in the percentage boxes, the curve adjusts itself to match. The first curve shown in Figure 18.4 retains the selected color in the shadow areas, while reducing the amount of ink to be printed in the highlights. The second curve concentrates its ink in the midtones and highlights, and the third enhances the highlights only. The final illustration is the Duotone Options box showing the curves for all three inks.

Figure 18.2

Choosing the color of Duotone ink

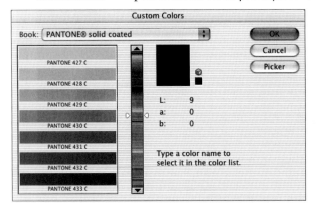

Save the curves you create in the Duotone Curve dialog by clicking the Save button; the program prompts you to choose where to save the curve file. Likewise, you can load curves you've already created by clicking Load and opening an earlier adjustment. The "master" Save and Load buttons in the Duotone Options dialog box will enable you to save or load a *complete* set of curves, inks, and overprint colors.

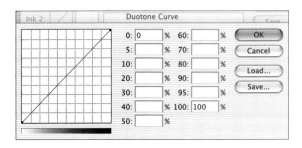

Figure 18.3

The Duotone Curve dialog box

Photoshop provides several sample settings for Duotones, Tritones, and Quadtones that you can use to see how these options work. Use them as a starting point for experimentation.

To load Photoshop's sample Duotone curves, follow these steps:

1. Open the `Rancho_Linda_Vista.psd` file in the `Ch18` folder on the *Photoshop CS Savvy* CD (see Figure 18.5).

2. Choose Image → Mode → Duotone. For the Type, choose Duotone. The Duotone Options dialog box is displayed.

3. Click Load to browse for the preset curves. These curves are located in the `PhotoshopCS\Presets\Duotones\Duotones\PANTONE Duotones` folder; choose one of the Duotone presets in that folder. Click Load to load the Duotone set and OK to apply the settings.

4. To make changes to your settings, to try different inks, or to tweak the curves, choose Image → Mode → Duotone, and your previous settings reappear with the Duotone Options dialog box. Make the changes you desire and click OK. See the images in Figure C28 in the color section for examples of the image with some of the Duotone curves applied.

Figure 18.4

Duotone curves for (a) shadow, (b) midtone, and (c) highlight inks. Figure (d) shows all the curves and color combinations.

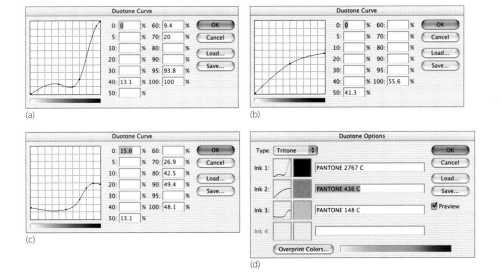

Figure 18.5

The Rancho Linda Vista image

Figure 18.5

The Rancho Linda Vista image

Multichannel Mode

If you look in the Channels palette of a Duotone image, you will see only one channel, labeled Duotone (or Tritone or Quadtone). Where are the channels representing the inks you've chosen? Photoshop creates Duotones by applying the various curves you've defined to a single channel.. To view the channels independently, you must convert the image to Multichannel mode (Image → Mode → Multichannel).

In Figure 18.6, you see the Channels palette with the Tritone channel. Next to it, the *same image's* palette has been split into three independent channels, listed separately, and

Figure 18.6

The Channels palette of the same Tritone image, in Duotone mode (left) and Multichannel mode (right)

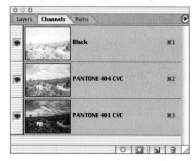

ordered according to the ink color names. If you make any changes or adjustments in this mode, you will not be able to return to Duotone mode. You can print directly from Multichannel, and you will get two, three, or four separated prints called color separations, one for each color. The advantage of using Multichannel is that the three channels can be edited independently.

Overprint Colors

Overprint colors are two or more unscreened inks that are printed one on top of the other. The order in which the inks are laid down can affect the final outcome. The Overprint Colors dialog box displays a chart that shows how different pairs of colors (or groups of three or four) will blend when printing. If you click any of the color swatches, the Color Picker comes up and enables you to replace the color. The new overprint colors will be applied to the image but affect only how the image appears on-screen. These settings do not affect how the image prints; use Overprint Colors to help you predict how colors will look when printed. You should use this feature only on a calibrated monitor.

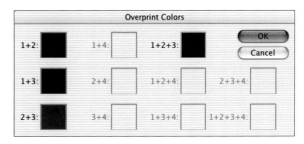

You can superimpose one ink over another in Duotone mode by using the same curve for each color. This is not a recommended practice because the results can look muddy from the application of excessive ink. The Overprint Colors feature can predict a color shift on two or more areas of semi-transparent spot color that are superimposed over each other.

Using Spot Color Channels

Spot colors are additional inks used in a print job other than black or process colors. The inks can be independently printed or overprinted on top of the grayscale or CMYK image. Each spot color requires a plate of its own. Spot colors are printed in the order in which they appear in the Channels palette, from top to bottom. Spot color channels are totally independent of the color mode of the image. They are not part of the composite channel in a grayscale, RGB, or CMYK or Lab image. Spot color channels are also independent of layers—you cannot apply spot colors to individual layers.

Here are some of the characteristics of spot color:

- Spot color channels are like layers in that they are independent of and separate from the Background image.

- Spot colors are unlike layers in that they cannot be merged with the image and continue to remain as spot colors.

- Spot color channels are like color channels in that they exist only in the Channels palette.

- Spot color channels are unlike color channels because, by default, they print separately from the rest of the image.

Creating Spot Colors

There are three ways to apply spot colors. You can overlay them on top of an image so that they mix with the underlying color and tint it. You can apply it as a solid color, or you can knock out the tonal image and replace it with the spot color. In this step-by-step exercise, you'll overlay the spot color over a grayscale image:

1. Open the grayscale image frying_panx.psd (see Figure 18.7) in the Ch18 folder on the CD. Save it to your disk.

2. Choose Window → Channels to display the Channels palette (see Figure 18.8). Load Alpha 1, which is a selection of the egg yolks, by dragging it to the Load Channel icon ▭.

3. From the Channels palette menu, choose New Spot Channel. The New Spot Channel dialog appears, and your selection fills with red (the default spot color).

4. Click the color swatch to bring up the Color Picker. Choose Custom Colors and choose a premixed ink, such as PANTONE 1225 C. The spot color channel will be named automatically with the name of the selected ink, as shown in Figure 18.9.

5. Choose a solidity percentage (see the "Solidity vs. Opacity" sidebar) and click OK.

After your new spot color channel has been created, it resides in the Channels palette just below the separate channels of the color mode you're working in. In a grayscale image, the first spot color channel is under Black; in an RGB image, it's under the Blue channel. You cannot move spot color channels above the color channels, unless you convert your image to Multichannel mode. Likewise, alpha channels are under the spot color channels in the stacking order. As with Duotone mode, spot color channels print in the order in which they're listed in the Channels palette.

Figure 18.7

The frying pan image

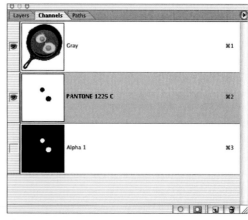

Figure 18.8

The frying pan with the spot color channel in the Channels palette

Viewing Spot Colors

If you're viewing the image in the composite view, and
your spot channel is active, the foreground color becomes
the channel's spot color, with white as the background
color. The foreground color swatch, however, will appear
black, white, or a shade of gray depending on the bright-
ness of the selected color. If you're viewing the spot color channel independently of the
composite, the foreground color is white and the background color is black. You can edit
a spot color channel exactly as you would an alpha channel: use painting tools, selection
tools, filters, type, placed artwork, and so forth, to impose the image you want to print.

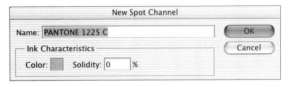

Figure 18.9

The New Spot
Channel dialog box
showing the name
of the selected ink

> Special rules apply to type in spot color channels. In fact, in Photoshop CS, type behaves in
> spot channels the way that type used to, before Adobe made it editable. In other words,
> when you apply type to a spot color channel, the text shows up as a selection outline on the
> channel; then you fill it. After you deselect it, it's no longer editable—except in the ways you
> would normally edit a selection.

Knocking Out Spot Colors

If you don't want your spot color to print over another spot color or a part of the underlying image, you can create a knockout. A *knockout* prevents ink from printing on part of the
image so the spot color can print directly on the paper. No blending of ink occurs in the
overlapping area. Activate the channel that you want to knock out. Choose Select → Load
Selection, and load the spot color channel in question. Choose Select → Modify → Contract
(or Expand) to adjust the fit of the knockout. (See Hands On 6, "Duotones and Spot Color"
following this chapter to try this.)

SOLIDITY VS. OPACITY

Entering a value in the Solidity box lets you control the viewing density of the spot color channel. The Solidity control is
for visual reference only. It's there to help you visualize what an ink might look like when printed in a tint value from 0%
to 100%.

Solidity is not to be confused with Opacity. Opacity affects the amount of color applied to an image with the painting tools,
or the transparency of an image on a layer. Solidity is a visual reference and does not affect the image unless you merge the
spot colors with the other color channels. It then applies the tint value of the color to the image and is no longer a spot color.

If you want the spot color ink to print as a tint, you have to create a gray (instead of black) selection in the spot color
channel. Spot color inks always print full intensity unless your selection mask in the spot color channel itself contains a
gradation or tint. Printing inks are usually transparent. When printed over the image, the spot color will mix with colors
underneath it.

You can create a trap by slightly reducing or enlarging the selection outline to enable a small outline of both inks to overprint. This way, no white space appears between two colors when the job is printed. After you have adjusted your selection to fit, press Delete (Mac) or Backspace (Win) to eliminate the underlying image. Now the spot color can imprint without mixing with an underlying color except at the edges of the trap.

Figure 18.10

Contract Selection dialog box

Lighter-colored inks are usually *spread,* meaning that the knockout hole stays the same size, while the original spot color shape that prints over the hole is expanded slightly. Darker inks *choke,* meaning that the spot color shape stays the same size, while the knockout hole is contracted slightly to form the trap.

You can also select a portion of the image, copy it, and then attribute a spot color to it by using its tonal qualities. You will use this technique on the Froggy image to create a different spot color effect.

To create a spot color from a tonal area on the image with a knockout:

1. Open the image froggy.psd in the Ch18 folder on the CD. Save it to your disk as froggy_knockout.psd.

2. Choose Window → Channels to display the Channels palette. Load Alpha 1 by dragging it to the Load Channel icon, to select the spots on the frog's back.

3. Choose Edit → Copy to copy the content of the selection to the Clipboard.

4. Choose Select → Modify Contract to create a 1-pixel choked trap, as seen in Figure 18.10.

5. Press D to set the default black-and-white foreground and background colors. Press your Delete key to create the knockout, as in Figure 18.11. Deselect.

6. Load Alpha 1 again. From the Channel Options pull-down menu, choose New Spot Channel. Choose a PANTONE color for the channel.

7. Press ⌘/Ctrl and click on the spot color channel to select it. When viewed close-up, the selection should slightly overlap the knockout, as in Figure 18.12.

8. With the spot color channel targeted, choose Edit → Paste Into to paste the tonal image of the frog's skin into the selection. The image should look like Figure C29c in the color section.

Figures C29a, C29b, and C29c in the color section show examples of the Froggy image with various applications of spot color.

Other Uses for Spot Color

Spot color can also be used to create varnish plates and dies. Varnishes are simply unpigmented inks. Apply them to highlight areas of an image or to coat the image with a glossy surface. Dies are shaped forms used to cut paper. Remember those birthday cards that have an oval hole cut to reveal George Washington's face on the dollar concealed within? That's die-cutting. Precise shapes can be created by using spot color channels; those shapes can then be printed as negatives, which are then used to create the die.

Printing Duotones and Spot Color

Printing Duotones and spot colors presents its own set of challenges. For example, in this book, the Duotones and Tritones were created by using two or three custom color inks. But the color section of the book is printed by using four-color process. So the Duotones and Tritones had to be converted to CMYK before printing, which can result in darker, less distinct colors than provided by premixed inks.

If you want to import your Duotone into another application, you'll have to save it in EPS format. Only EPS preserves Duotone mode's color information properly. If you save it in another format, the additional curves simply won't be recognized; only Ink 1 will end up printing. Spot color channels, however, are supported by PSD, TIF, EPS, PDF, and DCS 2.0 formats.

A special problem common to Duotone and spot color jobs is the difficulty in proofing. Most color proofers convert everything to CMYK when printing; custom ink colors simply aren't recognized. If you have Duotones composed of, say, black and magenta, things will work out fine. But a proofing device can't recognize those painstakingly chosen PANTONE colors unless it can read the color's CMYK equivalents. You have to fake it out by either renaming the colors (in which case you don't get a true color proof) or by converting it to CMYK (same result). This is part of the reason some printers are loath to work with Duotones; they feel as though they're working blind, because no real accurate proof is available to guide them.

The problem is similar but not quite as worrisome with spot colors. When you print a job with spot colors on your printer, a composite is printed, and the spot color channels print out separately only when you image film or plates. Once again, proofs can be created, but only by compromising the integrity of the color channels. When you choose

Figure 18.11

The frog with the knockout

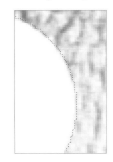

Figure 18.12

The selection showing the trap

Merge Spot Color Channels from the Channels palette menu, the spot color is converted to your image's color mode and blended in with the other channels. The spot color channels are eliminated at this point. You end up with a composite image incorporating your spot colors (now defined as RGB or CMYK colors). It's important to have the spot colors in the right order before taking this step. Different Solidity settings can produce different results when merging. Layered images flatten during this procedure. And once again, you run the risk of altering the color matching, because the CMYK inks reproduce colors differently than premixed inks. If you want a composite CMYK proof of the spot color image, always duplicate the file first. Print the duplicate image to your ink-jet or other proofing device and print the separations to an imagesetter or laser printer from the spot color original.

If you plan on importing an image with spot color channels into a layout or illustration program, you must save it in Photoshop's DCS 2.0 format. This is the only format that will enable other applications to recognize the individual spot color channels.

Hands On 6, which follows this chapter, will give you further practice applying these features.

Duotones and Spot Color

Here is a chance for you to work in Duotone mode and with spot color channels. In this Hands On project, you'll convert a grayscale image into a Tritone to enhance its tonal depth, create more drama in the image, and bring out its details. Then you'll apply a spot color to a prominent area on the image and to some type. Finally, you'll convert it to an entirely different mode to be able to observe the channels as separations.

Getting Started

Discard your preferences file before beginning this Hands On exercise. The "Modifying Photoshop's Settings" section in Chapter 5, "Setting Up Photoshop," shows how to reset your preferences to Photoshop's defaults. After you've launched Photoshop with default preferences, here's how to begin the Hands On project:

1. Insert the *Photoshop CS Savvy* CD in the CD-ROM drive.

2. Choose File → Open; select and open the sun_god.psd image in the H06 folder on the CD (see Figure H6.1).

   Full-color versions of the beginning and final stages of this project are included in the color section (see Figures C51 and C52).

3. Save the file to your disk.

4. Choose Image → Mode → Duotone. The Duotone Options dialog box appears.

5. From the Type list, choose Tritone.

6. Click the top color swatch. The Color Picker appears. Choose Custom. In the Book field, choose PANTONE Solid Coated. Enter **289** by using the keypad, or scroll down the list and find PANTONE 289 C (it's a dark blue). Click OK.

Figure H6.1

The beginning image

Figure H6.2

The Duotone Options dialog box after the colors have been chosen

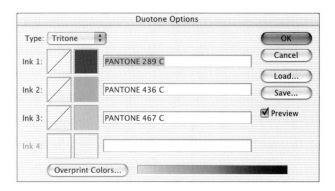

Figure H6.2

The Duotone Options dialog box after the colors have been chosen

7. Click the second color swatch. On your keypad, enter **436** to designate PANTONE 436 C, a medium-value warm gray. Click OK.

8. Click the third color swatch. On your keypad, enter **467** or click in the middle of the slider and move the slider until you find PANTONE 467. Click OK. The Duotone Options dialog box should look like Figure H6.2.

9. Save the image.

Adjusting Curves

Now you'll adjust the curves of each color for precise control over the distribution of ink in the highlights, midtones, and shadows:

1. Start with the shadows: In the Duotone Options dialog box, click the PANTONE 289 C curve thumbnail to display the Duotone Curve dialog box. The values you'll enter in the next few steps are shown in Figures H6.3 a, b, and c. Clear any presets from fields that aren't listed here.

2. In the percentage fields, enter the following values: For 0%, enter **15**. For 20%, enter **16.3** to reduce the amount of darker ink in the lower midtones. For 50%, enter **33.8** to slightly reduce the coverage in the midtones. For 80%, enter **90** to boost the coverage in the shadows. For 100%, enter **100**; you'll keep the darkest ink at full intensity in the deepest shadows.

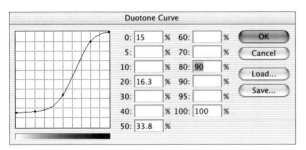

(a) PANTONE 289

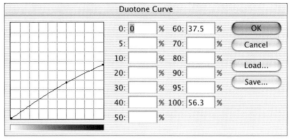

(b) PANTONE 436

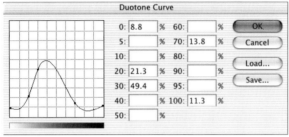

(c) PANTONE 467

Figure H6.3

Duotone curves for
(a) PANTONE 289,
(b) PANTONE 436,
and (c) PANTONE 467

3. For PANTONE 436 C, enter the following values to distribute the color in the midtone range: For the 0% field, enter **0**. For 60%, enter **37.5** to reduce the coverage of the medium ink in the darker midtones. For 100%, enter **56.3** to keep coverage light in the deep shadow areas. For PANTONE 467 C, enter the following values: For the 0% field, enter **8.8** to distribute this ink into the brightest highlights. For 20%, enter **21.3** to bend the curve and slightly increase the highlight in the face. For 30%, enter **49.4** to increase the coverage of light ink in the light midtones. In the 70% field, enter **13.8**. In the 100% field, enter **11.3** to almost eliminate ink coverage in the shadow areas and help prevent muddying from over-coverage. Click OK. After you're finished, your Duotone Options dialog box should look like Figure H6.4.

4. Save.

Figure H6.4

The Duotone
Options dialog box
after setting the
Duotone curves

Adding Color to the Sun

The sun can use a spot of color to give the image that extra sparkle. Follow these steps:

1. Choose the Magnetic Lasso tool 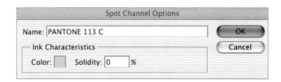. Drag it around the edge of the sun to make a selection, as in Figure H6.5.

2. Display the Channels palette (Window → Channels). From the Channels palette menu, choose New Spot Channel. The Spot Channel Options dialog box appears.

Figure H6.5

The sun selected

3. Click the color swatch. The Color Picker appears. Click the Custom button on the Color Picker. For Book, Choose PANTONE Solid Coated. Enter **113** on the keypad to choose PANTONE 113 C. Click OK. The new spot channel appears in the Channels palette (see Figure H6.6), and the sun turns a cheerful yellow.

4. Save the image.

Figure H6.6

The Channels palette showing the spot color channel

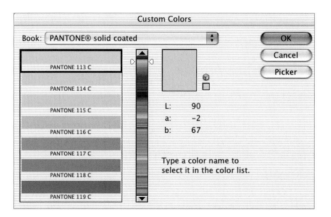

Adding Type

You'll add some type as a new spot color channel, using PANTONE 113 C:

1. Click the Channels palette to activate it.

2. Target the PANTONE 113 C spot color channel.

3. Choose the Type tool $\boxed{T}$. In the Options bar, I chose 72-point Hurculaneum, but you can choose any font you like. Center the cursor above the sun on the image and click your mouse. You'll notice that when you enter type on the spot color channel, a red mask is displayed, as in Figure H6.7.

4. Enter the words **SUN GOD**. In the Options bar, choose the Warp text feature $\boxed{\textit{1}}$ and warp the text into an arc by using the defaults (again, see Figure H6.7).

5. Commit the type by clicking the check mark in the Options bar. The type converts to a selection (see Figure H6.8) that you will use to create a trap and a knockout. Save.

6. Target the Tritone channel. Choose Select → Modify → Contract. Enter **1** pixel in the box and click OK. Making sure the background color is white, press Delete to fill the type selection with white. This knocks out the other colors from behind the yellow type. Figure H6.9 shows a close-up of the text knocked out of the background with the trap, and Figure H6.10 (which also appears in the color section as Figure C52) shows the final version of the Duotone with the spot color and knocked-out type.

Figure H6.7

The type entered on the spot color channel displays a type mask.

The spot color channel can be directly output only from Photoshop, as it will not be recognized from the Duotone mode EPS file when imported into layout or illustration software. The Duotone mode file can be duped, split into Multichannel, and then saved as EPS DCS 2, so that the imported image will contain the Tritone separations and the spot color.

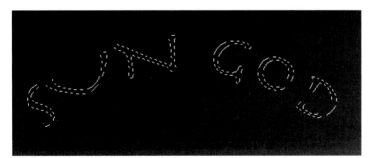

Figure H6.8

The type selection

Figure H6.9

A close-up of the text with the knockout and the trap

Converting to Multichannel

To see the content of the separated channels, it's a good idea to convert the image to Multichannel mode. You can look at the channels to get a better understanding of how Duotones and spot colors distribute ink when they are printed. Follow these steps:

1. Choose Image → Mode → Multichannel. In the Channels palette, the three Tritone channels are separated and named for their PANTONE colors, and the one spot color channel is at the bottom of the list, as in Figure H6.11.

2. Choose Photoshop (Macintosh) or Edit (Windows) → Preferences → Display And Cursors → Color Channels In Color.

3. Click the visibility icon of each channel, one at a time, to observe the densities of each color as it will be printed on paper.

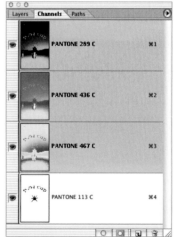

Figure H6.10

The final version of the image with the type

Figure H6.11

The Channels palette after conversion to Multichannel mode

PART III

Photoshop Savvy

Now that you've covered all the basics, you're ready to start combining techniques. The chapters in Part III cover advanced Photoshop techniques that will help you up the amperage of your images. In the following pages, you will learn about the art and science of image restoration and how Photoshop techniques can revive those old images. You'll look at the world of Photoshop filters and how they can produce everything from a minor correction to a complete transformation of your images.

Also covered are advanced selection, layer, and overlay techniques that help you better manage the image during the editing process. Finally, I'll show you automation operations that streamline your work flow.

CHAPTER 19

Photo Retouching

Since the introduction of the box camera by Kodak in the late nineteenth century, photography has become a popular pastime, practiced by countless people. If your attic is anything like mine, there are no doubt hundreds of photographs sitting in envelopes or boxes that haven't been looked at for years. We don't throw these images away because they are valuable to us and are part of our legacy. Many of these images are of relatives who have passed on and are the only living reminder we have of their lives.

Unfortunately, few of us have the time or money to create an environmentally safe archive for the original images, and so, with the passing of time, many of these photographs remain neglected and begin to fade or collect dust, scratches, and abrasions. This chapter is about restoring those long-neglected pictures.

You'll learn about:

- **Scanning old photographs**
- **Removing dust and scratches**
- **Adding missing pieces to a photograph**
- **Restoring contrast**
- **Making and browsing an archive**

Problems with Old Photographs

Several common problems can occur in old photographs that will determine the best strategy for their reconstruction. Here is a list of problems you are likely to encounter:

All or part of the photo is faded. This problem results from the deterioration of the emulsion on an image, caused by exposure to ultraviolet light, air, or fluctuating temperatures. (It could also result from an image that was overexposed to begin with.) Sometimes the photograph might be perfect on one side and fade gradually to the other.

The photo has a color cast. A color photograph might have washed-out colors or a yellow or red cast over its entire surface. This can be the result of the emulsion's chemical reaction with air or paper.

The image is wrinkled, torn, scratched, or covered with spots. Wrinkles and scratches are often a result of mistreatment of the photograph. Spots will develop from exposure to dust. Images stored in a damp environment can collect mold that appears as large or small splotches.

The surface is textured. Many old photographs were printed on textured paper. The removal of this surface can present problems during the retouching process.

Part of the photograph is missing. A vital portion of the image such as a hand or a face might have a severe scratch on it or might be missing entirely. A corner might be missing or an area of the photograph might have peeled or faded away.

Bad photography. The image might have superfluous elements such as phone lines or portions that are out of focus. The image might have been shot at the wrong moment, the composition might be unbalanced, or the image might be underexposed or overexposed.

Photo restoration can be extremely labor-intensive. Some images are simply beyond repair. Experience will show you which images are worth restoring and which ones, like the photo in Figure 19.1, would be a waste of a lot of time and effort.

Figure 19.1

This photograph is not worth the effort that it would take to restore it. Critical parts of the image are missing. There is hardly any detail in the highlight areas, and it is blurred, faded, stained, and covered with scratches and dust.

Scanning Old Photographs

If you've read Chapter 14, "Image Capture and Digital Photography," you are aware of the many types of input devices available to scan images. Before scanning an old photograph, you'll want to examine the image closely. Observe the darkest and lightest areas of the image and see whether there is detail within these areas that needs to be preserved. If so, you might want to adjust the contrast by using the scanner software's brightness and contrast features. Don't expect to correct the entire image. Adjust the image just enough to capture the details. You can later make more refined adjustments in Photoshop. Observe the digital image carefully. If you haven't captured the detail you want, rescan it at different settings. You can also make multiple scans of the same photo at different settings and composite the best parts of each image into a master image. This technique, though labor-intensive, will enable you to combine the enhanced detail of the highlight, midtone, and shadow areas into one optimal image.

Scanning at higher resolutions helps preserve detail. Scan the image at 300 pixels per inch or higher on a flatbed scanner. If the image is especially small, increase the scale and the resolution. Avoid exceeding the scanner's optical resolution if possible. For example, if the scanner's optical resolution is 600 dpi, you can scan it at 300 dpi and 200% size.

There is no advantage to scanning a black-and-white photograph in RGB mode; that will only produce an image with a larger file size. In most cases it will require desaturation to eliminate discoloration. If there are stains on the image, scanning it in RGB will exaggerate them. For best results, scan the photo as a 16-bit grayscale to maximize the tonal range. After repairing it, convert it to an 8-bit grayscale before printing. If you later decide to add color or a sepia tint to the image, you can convert it to RGB mode (Image → Mode → RGB Color), and adjust it by using the Image → Adjustments → Hue/Saturation command. (See Chapter 17, "Modifying and Mapping Color," and Hands On 7, "Restoring a Color Photograph," which follows this chapter.)

Removing Dust and Scratches

The Dust & Scratches filter (choose Filter → Noise → Dust & Scratches) was created for the purpose of removing those ugly artifacts that are unavoidable when scanning old photos. With its Radius and Threshold sliders to help define edges, the Dust & Scratches filter is a powerful tool for eliminating a good deal of the unwanted debris from an image. If you're scanning a batch of old pictures from your grandmother's scrapbook, or that old team shot from your high school yearbook, Dust & Scratches works wonders. It can also help a great deal in getting rid of moiré patterns that can appear when scanning printed halftones.

When using the Dust & Scratches filter, select small areas of similar texture in which to work. Each area of the image might require different settings. Applying it to the entire image all at once can result in a loss of detail. The Dust & Scratches filter has two controls, Radius and Threshold. Use the minimum Radius and Threshold you need to achieve the best results (as in Figure 19.2).

Radius blurs, and Threshold restores. When you move the Radius slider to the right, you effectively blur the areas of most contrast. Move the Radius slider until the specks or scratch lines disappear, but do not overblur the image. Next, move the Threshold slider just enough to restore the surrounding texture but not enough to restore the specks.

Be cautious when using the Dust & Scratches filter. If you go too far with it, you could end up losing detail along with the unwanted specks. Sometimes a little elbow grease and the Rubber Stamp tool will be necessary to finish the job. When used in tandem with the Unsharp Mask filter, Dust & Scratches can work wonders. (See Chapter 16, "Adjusting Tonality and Color," and Chapter 20, "Using Filters.")

For practice with the Dust & Scratches filter using the publicity photo that is partially shown in Figure 19.2, open `dust_and_scratches.psd` in the `Ch19` folder on the *Photoshop CS Savvy* CD.

Adding Missing Elements

Often in old photographs, large areas have been scratched beyond recognition or are missing completely. Based on the severity of the problem, you'll have to decide the best approach to restoration. In many cases, Photoshop's tools and commands can be combined to remedy these problems, but some parts of photographs might be too damaged to restore. If, for example, the face of a person is missing from an image, I recommend that you avoid trying to paint it back in, because this will prove to be a virtually impossible task to accomplish with any credibility. A better approach might be to composite the face from another photograph or, if that's not possible, fill the area with neutral gray.

Figure 19.2

The area selected (left), and the filter applied (right)

  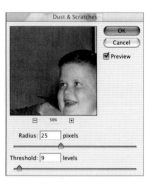

Cloning

Small areas that are missing can be repaired with the Clone Stamp tool . I recommend that you first make a rough selection around the area so as to avoid applying the clone to unwanted areas. To practice using the Clone Stamp tool, follow these steps:

Figure 19.3

Cloning a selected area

1. Open `clone_practice.psd` from the `Ch19` folder on the CD.

2. Choose the Magic Wand tool. Click inside the area to be repaired. Choose Select → Modify → Expand By: 4 Pixels.

3. Choose the Clone Stamp tool from the Tool palette. Place the cursor on the area of texture below and outside the selection outline. Press the Option (Mac) or Alt (Windows) key and click the mouse to sample the area. (Notice that the cursor turns into a target.) Release the mouse and the key.

4. Choose a soft brush. Place the cursor inside the selection. Click the mouse and drag. Notice that the area that is being cloned displays a small cross, and the area that is being repaired displays a circle as in Figure 19.3.

5. You might have to sample more than once. Place the cursor outside of the marquee, press the Option/Alt key, and click the mouse to sample another area.

6. After you're finished cloning within the selection marquee, deselect the area and clone any disparate edges that might have resulted. Carefully blend the edges of the region with the areas surrounding it.

7. Repeat the process for the other torn areas. Be sure to sample from areas of similar texture and value.

> You can perform this process on an empty layer with the Use All Layers option checked. This technique offers the advantage of sampling from the entire image and cloning to a new layer.

The Clone Stamp tool provides two options in the Options bar:

Aligned Checked The clone is aligned with the original sample. When you clone and release the mouse and clone again, the alignment on the original sample is maintained.

Aligned Unchecked Each time the mouse is released and the cloning is resumed, the original sample is repeated.

The Clone Stamp tool can also be used to remove unwanted elements or to add texture to the image. Careful observation of variations in color and texture of the image are crucial in determining the best place to sample for cloning.

Applying the Healing Brush

In many ways, the Healing Brush tool performs like the Clone Stamp. The process of sampling is similar, but the application of the sampled areas to the image differs. When the sampled area is painted onto the target area, it takes on the characteristics of the surrounding pixels, thus creating a seamless blend.

To try out the Healing Brush, follow these steps:

1. Open the `heal_me_patch_me.psd` file from the `Ch19` folder on the CD.

2. Zoom in on the scratch above the baby's head.

3. Choose the Healing Brush and a 19-pixel brush from the Brush menu. Press the Option/Alt key and click in the area about a half-inch above the scratch to sample it, as in Figure 19.4.

4. Release the Option/Alt key. Move the cursor onto the scratch. Drag the mouse to the left. As you drag, the scratch is replaced by the sample. When you release the mouse, the sample blends seamlessly into the surrounding pixels, as seen in Figure 19.5.

Using the Patch Tool

The Patch tool is similar to the Healing Brush, except that it gives you the ability to patch a selected area. This works well on large areas in need of repair. You can either make the initial selection with the Patch tool activated, or you can use any of the other selection

Figure 19.4

First sample the area to be copied.

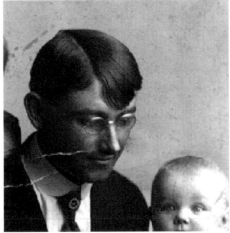

Figure 19.5

The healed image

tools to make the selection first and then switch to the Patch tool. The tool's performance has been improved in Photoshop CS. A new feature has been added so that as you drag the selection marquee over an area of the image, you see a live preview of the sample in the destination selection area.

The Patch tool can be used in any of the following ways, depending on the specifications in the Options bar:

Source Drag the selection marquee over the area from which you want to sample. It will sample the area and automatically copy it over to the area to be patched.

Destination Select the area from which you want to sample. Drag the selection marquee over the area you wish to patch.

Transparent Check this box to better blend the sampled area with the underlying area.

Use Pattern Choose a pattern from the list and click the Use Pattern button to blend the pattern with the initial selection.

To see how the Patch tool works, follow these steps:

1. Open the file heal_me_patch_me.psd on the CD.

2. Choose the Patch tool. Check Source in the Options bar.

3. Drag a marquee around the scratch on the man's face (see Figure 19.6).

4. Place your cursor within the marquee. Drag the marquee slightly to the left and up, as in Figure 19.7. You'll see two marquees; the source and the destination. The image of the source area appears in the destination marquee. Move the marquee until you are satisfied with the destination image. Release the mouse, and it automatically creates a patch from the area you choose, as seen in Figure 19.8.

Figure 19.6

Select the image first.

Figure 19.7

Move the selection to the area that you want to sample.

Figure 19.8

The sampled area is patched.

Duplicating and Manipulating Larger Areas

Sometimes the area you need to fix on the image is too big or too inconsistent to clone. Or you might find that it needs more precision than the Clone Stamp tool can offer. If there is a similar area on the image that can be duplicated, try this technique, using the image shown in Figure 19.9.

Follow these steps:

1. Open duplicate.psd in the Ch19 folder on the companion CD.

2. Choose the Lasso tool. In the Options bar, set the feather radius to 10. With the Lasso tool, encircle the missing right eye. The selection should be a little bit larger than the scratch, as shown in Figure 19.10.

3. Place the cursor inside the selection. Press the mouse button and drag the selection marquee without its contents to the "good" eye.

4. Choose Layer → New → Layer Via Copy to copy the contents of the selection to a new layer.

5. Choose Edit → Transform → Flip Horizontal to flip the eye.

6. Choose the Move tool. In the Options bar, check Show Bounding Box. Drag the eye and place it on the missing area. To rotate it into position, place the cursor outside the bounding box near any corner until you see the Rotate icon. Then click and drag (see Figure 19.11).

Figure 19.9

Areas of an image that are missing or damaged can be replaced.

7. When the eye is in position, merge the Background with the new layer. Choose Merge Visible from the Layer Options pull-down menu.

8. Clean up any unrepaired areas with the Clone Stamp tool or the Healing Brush tool.

9. Choose the Rectangular Marquee. Drag a rectangular selection around the baby's head. Choose Filter → Liquify. Warp the image slightly so that it is not quite symmetrical with the left eye.

10. Choose the Dodge tool ![icon]. Dodge the areas under the eye to better match the surrounding tones.

11. Using the Clone Stamp tool, eliminate the scratch on the woman's head.

12. You can eliminate additional debris with the Dust & Scratches filter. Figure 19.12 shows the final result.

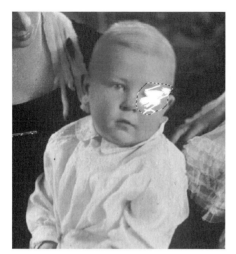

Figure 19.10

The selected area

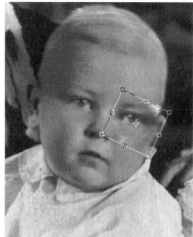

Figure 19.11

The eye, flipped and in position

Adjusting Contrast

The contrast of many old photographs diminishes over time because of the instability of the emulsion used to create the print. This emulsion might react chemically with nonarchival photo paper or it might have been exposed to sunlight; both of these can cause discoloring or fading. These problems can usually be remedied by adjusting levels or curves, as long as there is enough detail on the photograph to begin with. Areas of highlight that have washed out will be more difficult to restore, often requiring careful cloning, compositing, or passes with the Burn tool.

Frequently, however, contrast problems are more complex. When a photo has developed a gradual fade from one side to the other, as in Figure 19.13, the problem can be more difficult to fix. You might need to use special masks to apply precision contrast adjustments to the image.

Figure 19.12

The completed image

To get an idea of how these problems might be corrected, try this technique:

1. Open the file `gradual_fade.psd` from the `Ch19` folder.

2. Choose Layer → New Adjustment Layer → Levels. In the New Layer dialog box that appears, click OK. The Levels dialog box appears. Click OK again.

3. Target the Adjustment layer's layer mask by clicking on its thumbnail.

Figure 19.13

**An image whose
contrast fades
from right to left**

4. Press the D key or click the Foreground and Background icon ▨ in the Tool palette to choose black as a foreground color and white as a background color.

5. Choose the Gradient tool ▨. In the Options bar, choose the Linear Gradient icon. Make sure that the Foreground to Background gradient is selected from the Gradient Picker.

6. Click and drag the gradient from right to left. Press the Shift key while dragging to constrain the gradient horizontally.

7. Double-click the Levels 1 Adjustment Layer thumbnail. The Levels dialog box appears.

8. Move the Black Shadow slider to the right until the input level reads 69. Move the Gray Input slider to the right until the midtone input level reads 0.97, which will optimize the contrast on the left side of the image (see Figure 19.14). Click OK.

9. Repeat steps 2 through 5.

10. Target the layer mask of the Levels 2 layer. Click and drag the gradient from left to right.

11. Click on the Levels Adjustment layer thumbnail. The Levels dialog appears.

12. Move the Black Shadow slider to the right until the input level reads 45. Move the White Input slider to the right until the highlight input level reads 190, which will optimize the contrast on the right side of the image (see Figure 19.15). Click OK.

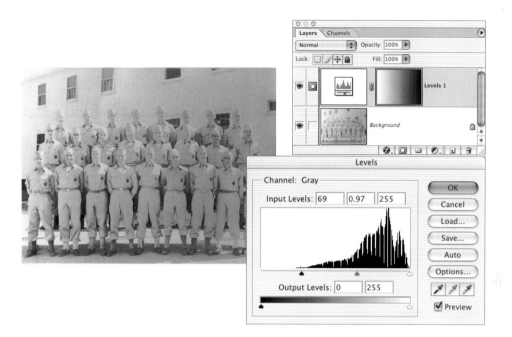

Figure 19.14

The same image with a levels adjustment applied through the gradient layer mask

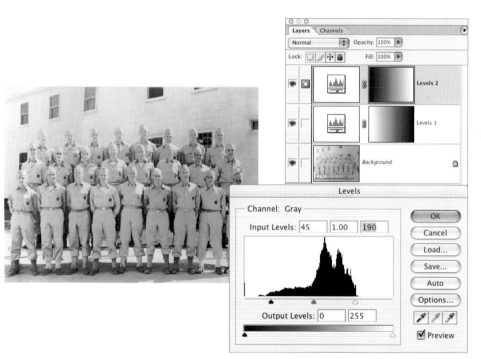

Figure 19.15

The same image with a levels adjustment applied through the reversed gradient layer mask.

Figure 19.16

The completed image with a global levels adjustment applied

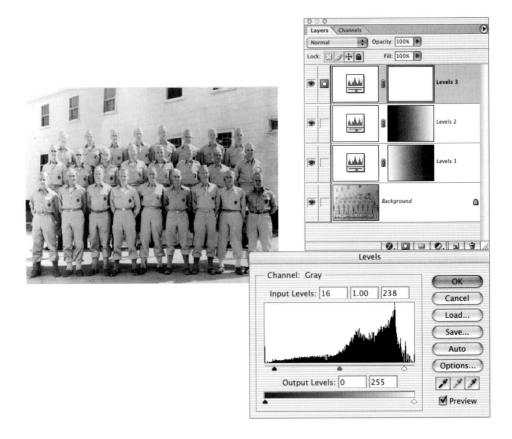

13. Now you'll perform a global contrast adjustment to optimize the contrast of the entire image. Once again, choose Layer → New Adjustment Layer → Levels. Click OK in the New Layer dialog box. The Layer will be named Layer 3 and will appear above Layer 2 in the stack. This time, move the Black slider to the right until the input level reads 16 and the White slider to the left until the input level reads 238. Click OK.

14. Save the image. Figure 19.16 shows the final result.

Making a Digital Archive

Having performed miracles on that old photograph, you should store your work in an archive, where it is readily accessible. Most commonly, images are stored in JPEG format to reduce file sizes, using the highest settings to reduce visible data loss. The disadvantage of saving to JPEG format—if you expect to do any further work with the image—is that you will end up discarding all of your layers and alpha channels in the process. You should save a version of the image in Photoshop format and another version in JPEG.

Archives are usually burned to a CD or a DVD; either provides an inexpensive storage medium with room for plenty of images. To review the content of the archive, you can use Photoshop's File Browser. You can quickly scan the contents of your archive in thumbnail form and open the desired image.

> Before burning the image directory to CD, choose from the File Browser's menu, File → Export Cache to pre-generate the File Browser cache data so that future browsing will be faster. Users can also use the File Browser to add custom Metadata and Keywords to images.

For efficient review of an archive's contents, you should place all the images in the same folder. Then choose File → Browse. The File Browser window appears, displaying the contents of the folder you last browsed (see Figure 19.17). Choose the desired folder from the topmost field. Click on an image in the image list to see a version of it in the Preview field. The preview area can be expanded or contracted by dragging its top and bottom borders. The field below the preview presents metadata (information about the image). Double-click or Ctrl/right-click an image to open it.

If you want further practice in photo restoration, try Hands On 7, immediately following this chapter. There you'll use some of the techniques introduced in earlier chapters, as well as what you've learned here.

Figure 19.17

The new File Browser window

Restoring a Color Photograph

The restoration of color photographs presents a unique set of problems. In addition to the usual dust and scratch repairs and contrast adjustments, the color emulsions can change with time, producing severe color casts. The best way to remove these color casts and restore natural color varies with each situation, but in general some specific tools are commonly used to make these adjustments. Usually, Levels, Curves, Color Balance, and the arsenal of color correction features covered in Chapter 16 work in combination with Adjustment layers and layer masks. In addition, you can use the new Replace Color tool and Match Color features to make the image look as though it were taken yesterday. In this Hands On exercise, you will restore a color photograph by employing some of these techniques. The before and after versions of the image can be seen in the color section (see Figures C55 and C56).

Cropping the Image

The scanned photograph you're going to work on is shown in Figure H7.1. As you can see, it has several problem areas. You will use a variety of commands, tools, and filters to restore this image to its former glory.

1. Open the file `violetta.psd` in the H07 folder on the *Photoshop CS Savvy* CD.

2. Choose the Crop tool. Click and drag from the top-left corner inside the yellow border to the bottom right.

3. Click the Commit (check mark) icon in the Options bar to commit the crop or the Cancel icon to cancel it.

Figure H7.1

The scanned photograph before restoration

Adjusting Contrast and Color

Adjusting levels by individual channels offers more control than a global adjustment to the RGB channel. You will use this technique on an Adjustment layer to improve the contrast and balance the color and monitor the changes in the new Histogram palette.

1. From the Histogram palette menu, choose All Channels View (see Figure H7.2).

2. Choose Layer → New Adjustment Layer → Levels. Click OK in the New Layer dialog box.

3. At the top of the dialog box, choose Red from the Channel pull-down menu. Move the Black slider to the right until the input field reads 36. Move the White slider to the right until the input reads 175 (see Figure H7.3a).

4. Choose Green from the Channel pull-down menu. Move the Black slider to the right until the input field reads 5. Move the White slider to the left until the input reads 145 (see Figure H7.3b).

5. Choose Blue from the Channel pull-down menu. Move the Black slider to the right until the input field reads 10. Move the White slider to the left until the input reads 93 (see Figure H7.3c).

Figure H7.2

The All Channels View of the Histogram palette before (left) and after (right) the adjustment

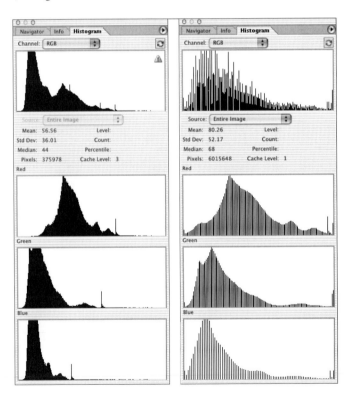

6. Notice the changes in the Histograms, The brightness values for each channel are spread across a wider range, which has improved the contrast and removed some of the color cast on the image.

7. You'll see a dramatic improvement in the color balance and contrast. Click OK and save the image.

Color Balancing

There is still a slight red cast on the image. You can eliminate that with the Color Balance feature, which was introduced in Chapter 16.

1. Choose Layer → New Adjustment Layer → Color Balance.

2. In the Color Balance dialog box, click the Highlights radio button (see Figure H7.4a).

3. Move the Cyan–Red slider toward Cyan until it reads –6. Move the Yellow–Blue slider toward Yellow until it reads –6.

4. Click the Midtones radio button (see Figure H7.4b).

5. Move the Cyan–Red slider toward Cyan until it reads –6. Move the Magenta–Green slider toward Green until it reads +4.

6. Click the Shadows radio button (see Figure H7.4c).

7. Move the Cyan–Red slider toward Cyan until it reads –7.

8. Click the Preview box twice to see the before-and-after changes, click OK, and save the image.

Cloning Out Artifacts

The color and contrast adjustments have enhanced surface artifacts in the image. They need to be removed. You will use the Clone Stamp tool to eliminate these imperfections:

1. From the Layers palette menu, choose Merge Visible to merge the two Adjustment layers with the Background.

2. With the Lasso tool, select the area adjacent to Violetta's hair to include the bluish surface artifacts (see Figure H7.5).

3. Choose the Clone Stamp tool and a 65-point Soft brush.

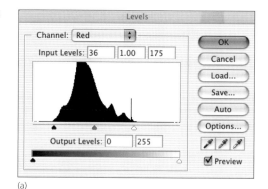

(a)

(b)

(c)

Figure H7.3

The Levels dialog boxes, showing red (a), green (b), and blue (c) levels

4. Place the cursor on the grass to the left of Violetta's head. Press Option (Mac) or Alt (Windows) and click the mouse to sample an area.

5. Place the cursor within the selection outline, and click and drag until the selection is filled and the artifacts have been eliminated.

6. Choose Select → Inverse to inverse the selection and clone the artifacts out of Violetta's hair, as in Figure H7.6.

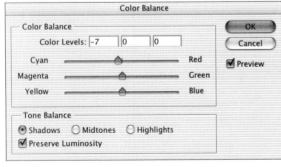

Figure H7.4

The Color Balance dialog boxes, showing highlights (a), midtones (b), and shadows (c)

(a)

(b)

(c)

Removing the Scratch

Now you will fix the scratch that runs diagonally across the grass and Violetta's ankle. You will need to sample both areas separately to repair them.

Follow these steps:

1. Choose the Healing Brush tool.

2. Select a suitable brush from the Options bar. Place the cursor on the grass. Press Option/Alt, and click the mouse to sample an area.

3. Drag over the scratch to heal it with your sample. You might want to sample more than once.

4. Sample the ankle and repair the scratch. (The result should look like Figure H7.7.)

5. Save the image.

Restoring a Scratched Area

Next you'll work on the scratched area in the upper-left corner, using the Patch tool:

1. Choose the Patch tool. In the Options bar be sure that Source is chosen. Drag a selection encircling the scratched area of the image in the upper-left corner, as in Figure H7.8.

2. Place your cursor in the center of the "marching ants." Click and drag the selection to an area of similar texture on the right side of the photo, near Violetta's head.

3. Release the mouse. The area is completely restored. Compare how the area looked before and after the repair in Figure H7.9.

Using a Filter to Remove Dirt

The contrast and color adjustments have amplified dirt on Violetta's skirt. Because it is in an area of consistent texture, you can easily remove it with the Dust & Scratches filter.

1. Choose the Lasso tool. Encircle the area as shown in Figure H7.10.

2. Choose Filter → Noise → Dust & Scratches (see Figure H7.11). Set the Radius to 14 and the Threshold to 20. Click OK and deselect.

3. Select the dirty area to the right of the original selection (in the shadow area of the skirt) and repeat the process with different settings. Experiment with the sliders to find the settings that work best.

4. Clone out additional smaller spots with the Clone Stamp tool, sampling areas of similar color and texture and painting out the flaws.

Figure H7.5

Selecting the area around the artifact

Figure H7.6

The artifacts cloned from Violetta's hair

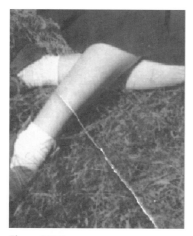

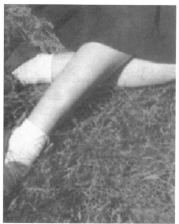

Figure H7.7

Selecting the area around the artifact

Figure H7.8

The area selected with the Patch tool

Figure H7.9

The scratched area before and after the repair made with the Patch tool

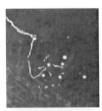

Replacing the Shoulder

A severely torn area like the right shoulder can be replaced and modified by using other parts of the image. To replace the shoulder, follow these steps:

1. Choose the Magic Wand tool ![icon]. In the Options bar, enter a Tolerance value of 80. Click inside the white tear to select it.

2. Choose Select → Modify → Expand → 6 pixels.

3. Choose Select → Feather → 4 pixels.

4. Choose Select → Transform Selection. Then choose Edit Transform → Flip Horizontal. Click the Commit icon to implement the transformation.

5. Drag the selection outline and place it on the opposite shoulder, as shown in Figure H7.12.

6. Choose Layer → New → Layer Via Copy. Double-click the layer name, name the layer **Shoulder**, and hit Return/Enter.

7. Choose Edit Transform → Flip Horizontal to flip the shoulder.

8. Choose the Move tool. Click and drag the shoulder and position it on the left shoulder, as shown in Figure H7.13. Deselect.

9. Target the Background. Choose the Clone Stamp tool. Clone the uncovered areas of the tear.

10. Check the Use All Layers box in the Options bar. Place the cursor on the forearm, press the Option/Alt key, and click the mouse to sample it. Clone out some of the folds near the shoulder to alter its appearance and make it look more natural, as in Figure H7.14.

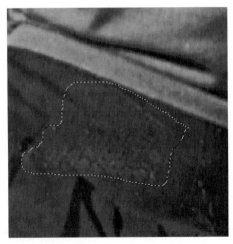

Figure H7.10

Select the area of similar texture first.

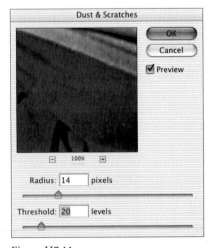

Figure H7.11

The Dust & Scratches dialog box

11. From the Layer Options palette, choose Merge Visible.

12. Save.

Coloring the Grass

The grass in our photo is quite brown, so next you'll color it. The best way to color the grass is to match it with the color of grass in another photo. Follow these steps:

1. Choose the Magnetic Lasso tool . Encircle Violetta as accurately as possible. You might need to use the Quick Mask (see Chapter 12, "Using Channels and Quick Mask") or another selection technique to tweak the results of the selection.

2. Inverse the selection so that the grass is now selected.

3. On the CD in the H07 folder, open the document grass.psd.

4. Activate the Violetta document. Choose Image → Adjustments → Match Color (see Figure H7.15). For the Source, choose grass.psd. Check the Use Selection in Target to Calculate Adjustment box.

Figure H7.12

Using the selection on the opposite shoulder

Figure H7.13

The replacement shoulder in place

Figure H7.14

The finished shoulder

5. The default results are too saturated. To correct them, move the Luminance slider to the left, to 77. Reduce the color intensity to 69. Drag the Fade slider to the right, to 24.

6. Save the image.

Coloring the Ribbon

At this point, most of the restoration is complete, but you'll make one final color alteration to add a sparkle to the image. Using the new Color Replacement tool ⬚ , you'll change the color of the ribbon in Violetta's hair:

1. Choose the Magnetic Lasso tool. Drag a selection around the ribbon.

2. Choose the Eyedropper tool and drag it over Violetta's sweater to sample its color. Notice the foreground color in the Tool palette. Stop dragging when you see a color you like. Choose the Color Replacement tool. Paint inside the selection outline to color the ribbon.

3. Deselect and save.

CHAPTER 20

Using Filters

When images created in Photoshop really make your eyes pop out, chances are good that *filters* were involved. Like many of Photoshop's other techniques, filters have their origin in the analog world of photography. A photographer uses a filter to correct or enhance lighting, and to create or adjust anomalies of perspective. Photoshop's filters take on these tasks and expand them far beyond the traditional tools.

You've applied filters in previous chapters to retouch images and enhance contrast. Here, you'll see further that with filters, you can adjust focus, eliminate unwanted artifacts, alter or create complex selection masks, breathe life into less-than-perfect scans, and apply a range of effects previously unavailable to the traditional photographer. Filters also have the capability to completely destroy anything recognizable in an image and turn it into a swirling vortex of pixels gone wild.

In this chapter, you'll look at the wonders filters can achieve. You'll learn about:

- **Filter basics**
- **Photoshop's new Filter Gallery**
- **Constructive and destructive filters**
- **Effects filters**
- **Render filters**
- **The amazing Liquify filter**
- **The Pattern Maker**

Filter Basics

Filters are nothing more than mathematical formulas that alter the features of pixels or groups of pixels in specified ways. What can be changed for any individual pixel are its brightness value, saturation, and hue, and its position in relation to other pixels. These changes are limited. What allows for the great variation among filter effects is the way they can alter groups of pixels over a specified range, following specific constraints. Some work subtly; others can be brash and flamboyant. Some effects gain strength when used gently and reapplied; sometimes a filter can be mitigated or softened by fading the effect. The Fade command extends the range and usefulness of filters by enabling you to use layer-like blending modes to blend the filter effect back into the original image.

It's beyond the limits of our space here to delineate every possible effect offered by Photoshop's filters. Rather, some of the most useful ones will be discussed in detail. I encourage you to play and experiment with filters to discover for yourself their vast potential. Keep in mind that when you're working with standard, automated special effects, they are available to every person who uses the software. Some of those effects, if applied generically, are immediately recognizable by anyone who's ever used them and can compromise the "magic" of the image. Be aware of what's available, but practice will indicate which techniques have more range of possibility and staying power; creativity will guide you to apply them in unusual or not-so-obvious ways. Sometimes the most effective special effect is the one that remains invisible.

Activating and Deactivating Filters

By choosing commands from the Filter menu, you can apply a filter to the entire image or confine it to a selected area. The Filter menu provides a long list of submenus, some of them long in turn. You can add or remove filters from these lists by placing items inside, or deleting them from, the Photoshop application's Plug-Ins folder. If you find there are large groups of filters you rarely use, you can save valuable memory space by removing those from the Plug-Ins folder. If a day comes when you can't get away without applying one, just slip it back into the Plug-Ins folder and it's available once again. Plenty of third-party plug-ins are available for special occasions; they can be treated the same way. See Appendix E for a list and descriptions of some of the more popular plug-ins.

> If you hold down ⌘-Shift (Macintosh) or Ctrl-Shift (Windows) when you launch Photoshop, you can specify which plug-ins folder you want to use for that session.

Filter Previews

When you're applying an effect as powerful and image-altering as some filters can be—and certain filters are among Photoshop's most memory-intensive functions—it's good to have some idea of what to expect. Most filters provide a preview inside the dialog box. You can zoom in or out by clicking the + and – buttons, and drag inside the preview box to scroll to the part of the image you wish to preview. Other filters, such as the majority of corrective filters, enable you to preview the effect in the image window itself; just click the Preview box or button. When the blinking bar below the Preview box disappears, the program has finished building the preview.

The Filter Gallery

Some of Photoshop's filters have been reorganized into a new, elegant interface called the Filter Gallery. Access the gallery from the top of the Filter menu. When you first open the gallery, you'll be presented with three fields, as in Figure 20.1. The left field displays a preview of the current image. Just below the preview field are plus and minus arrows and a view options list that enables you to preview the image in additional view ratios. The middle field displays a list of filter types neatly enclosed in category folders. The right field is inactive.

Figure 20.1

The initial Filter Gallery dialog box

Figure 20.2

The Filter Gallery dialog box after choosing a filter from the Filter list

The categories include Artistic, Brush Strokes, Distort, Sketch, Stylize, and Texture. Choose a folder by clicking its down arrow or name. You will then be presented with a list of filter names along with thumbnails that illustrate the filter's effect. Click a filter. The right field activates to display the filter's controls, as in Figure 20.2. The image display field on the left now shows the effect on the image of the filter with its current settings.

The bottom area of the control field displays the name of the filter that has been applied. If you want to apply a second pass of the same filter, click the New Filter icon at the bottom of the palette, and the filter is applied again and its name appears a second

Figure 20.3

You can preview a second pass of the same filter or multiple filters.

time in the list (see Figure 20.3). Click the visibility icon next to the filter name to reveal or conceal its effects. The preview will display the results of these applications. To try out the Filter Gallery, open the `tree.psd` file in the `Ch20` folder on the *Photoshop CS Savvy* CD.

Opt/Alt-click a filter name to add multiple filter entries to the filter list (this could be the same or different filters). Shift-click an entry on the filter list to update the current filter to the filter selected from the middle field.

Fading Filters

Don't like how strong that filter effect comes on? You can mitigate the effect by using the Edit → Fade command (see Figure 20.4). Fade blends the filter effect with the original image, just as you would with a separate layer. Fade offers a dialog box containing the same options you see in the Layers palette—that is, you can control Opacity from 1% to 100% and use any of the blending modes (with the exception of Behind and Clear). The Fade command is available immediately after a filter is applied. If you take any other action affecting the image, Fade becomes grayed out in the Edit menu.

Figure 20.4

The Fade dialog box

> To reapply a filter with the same parameters a second time, simply press ⌘/Ctrl-F. If you want to apply that same filter again but change the options, press ⌘-Opt-F or Ctrl-Alt-F. The last-used filter's dialog box appears, enabling you to make changes before reapplying.

Filter Types

Rather than go through the list filter by filter, let's divide them up by what they can do. First, we'll look at the *constructive* filters—those that are used to modify and enhance images for printing or screen display. *Destructive* filters are an entirely different animal. These equations can take your image and turn it inside out. Their entire purpose is to displace pixels, more or less radically redistributing image elements. Other filters provide *fine-art effects,* mainly textures and painterly techniques. In addition to these types, there are filters for preparing images for video, for creating a digital watermark, and custom filters that enable you to create your own effects.

Constructive Filters

Four groups of filters provide tools to help improve image quality by changing the focus, or by smoothing transitions within an image. These filters belong to the Filter → Blur, Noise, Sharpen, and Other submenus. These groups are the bread and butter of Photoshop filtering, the workhorses that are put to frequent, day-to-day use.

The constructive filters complement one another. For instance, Blur's effect is the opposite of Sharpen; Median acts on an image in exactly the opposite way from Add Noise. These complementary effects will be delineated in greater detail in this section.

Figure 20.5

The Average filter replaces pixels with a solid fill of their average color

Blur Filters

The Blur group contains eight individual filters: Average, Blur, Blur More, Gaussian Blur, Lens Blur, Motion Blur, Radial Blur, and Smart Blur. Like their Sharpen counterparts, Blur, Blur More and the new Average filter are fully automated. You click, the filter does its job, and that's that—no dialog box, no user input, no control. Blur and Blur More diminish contrast, resulting in softer, smoother edges and transitions. Average assesses the pixels in an image or selection and replaces them with a solid fill of the average color (see Figure 20.5).

Gaussian Blur

Gaussian Blur is named for 18th-century German mathematician Carl Friedrich Gauss. Gauss's work with number theory and distribution patterns made him a pioneer of modern mathematics. He is ultimately responsible for the distribution curves employed in the filter that bears his name (he'll crop up again in Photoshop when we get to the Add Noise filter), and he was one heck of a dancer.

Figure 20.6

The Gaussian Blur dialog box

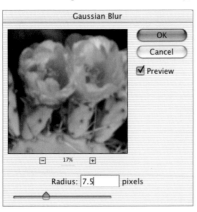

But seriously, if you learn to manipulate the niceties of the Gaussian Blur, you'll never need the Blur and Blur More filters. Even with only one variable in its dialog box (see Figure 20.6), Gaussian Blur offers much more control. By entering a number from 0.1 to 250 or by sliding along the Radius slider, you tell Gaussian Blur to apply its softening curve to a range of adjacent pixels. Lower values produce a slight, subtle blur effect, which can be used to smooth out rough transitions or blotchy areas; higher values can blur the image beyond recognition. You can create shadow effects by applying this filter to underlying layers. Figure 20.7 shows some of the Gaussian Blur filter's range.

 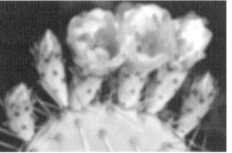

Figure 20.7

The original image (left), and the image with the Gaussian Blur filter applied (right)

With the Blur filters (as well as other filter types), the degree to which a given setting affects a particular image depends on the resolution of the image. The higher the resolution, the greater the settings have to be in order to achieve the effect.

Radically different effects can be achieved with Gaussian Blur, depending on whether you're applying it to a selection or freely to an image or layer as a whole. If Gaussian Blur is applied within a selection outline, its effect remains more or less constrained within the selected area. If you apply it to a layer or an entire image, the curve is allowed to carry its effect across the full range of the image. Compare the left image in Figure 20.8, where Gaussian Blur is applied within the confines of a selection, to the right image, where the same parameters were used on the entire layer.

Figure 20.8

Gaussian Blur applied (left) within a selection and (right) to the unselected image

Smart Blur

The Smart Blur filter (see Figure 20.9) is a kind of counterpart to Unsharp Mask in that it applies its blur to the open or continuous areas of an image while retaining edge definition. Like Unsharp Mask, Smart Blur offers the option of defining what it sees as an edge and how far the effect should extend. It's often used for retouching grainy or textured photographs and for creative effects on line drawings. The Radius and Threshold settings work the same as in Unsharp Mask.

Figure 20.9

The Mode option in the Smart Blur dialog box protects edges while blurring.

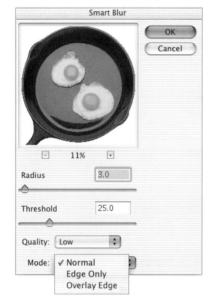

The options in the Quality pop-up list control the smoothness of the effect, with the High setting, logically enough, providing the smoothest transitions. The Mode control offers various methods of applying the blur. Normal mode applies the effect, well, normally, as seen in Figure 20.10. The Edge Only and Overlay Edge options trace the edges with white lines. Edge Only shows the edges as white lines against a black background, whereas Overlay Edge superimposes white edge lines over the visible image. The Normal mode is most likely the one you'll end up using 99% of the time with Smart Blur. Other edge-finding filters such as Filter → Stylize → Find Edges and Filter → Stylize → Trace Contour allow more control over your image and more interesting visual effects.

Figure 20.10

The original image (left), and the effect of the Smart Blur filter (right)

The Blur submenu contains two more filters that apply a blur along motion lines. Motion Blur (see Figure 20.11) enables you to specify a direction of movement, expressed as an angle in degrees and a distance in pixels. Your image spreads out along a path in a linear distribution in the direction and distance indicated.

Radial Blur

Radial Blur offers a different kind of directional movement in its dialog box. Two Blur Method options are available in this filter: Spin and Zoom. Spin distributes pixels by rotating them around a chosen center point, whereas Zoom's blur radiates pixels out from the center. The Radial Blur dialog box (see Figure 20.12) shows a Blur Center field containing a grid pattern. Click or drag the center point to reposition the starting point of the Spin or Zoom anywhere in your image. Enter an Amount to define how far the blur extends. (Why this slider is named Amount here but named Distance in the Motion Blur filter is a mystery. They both accomplish the same thing.)

Draft, Good, and Best are offered as options under Quality. If Draft is chosen, the effect takes less time to accomplish, but the blur is applied more roughly; Best provides a smoother blur but requires more time and memory capacity. Figure 20.13 compares the effects of the Motion Blur and Radial Blur filters.

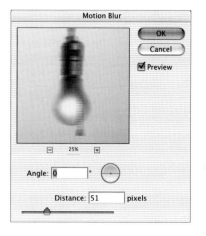

Figure 20.11

The Motion Blur dialog box

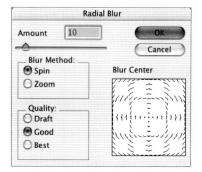

Figure 20.12

Click in the Blur Center box to position the Spin or Zoom starting point.

Lens Blur

In a photograph, depth of field is characterized by a variation of focus. When the photograph is taken, the subject's distance from the lens is the determining factor of its sharpness. Photoshop's new Lens Blur filter simulates this effect.

When you choose Filter → Lens Blur, the formidable Lens Blur filter dialog box is displayed (see Figure 20.14). From this control center, you can blur specific areas of an image while maintaining the sharpness of others. The dialog box presents the following options on the next page.

Preview Click the Faster radio button to generate faster previews. Choose it to preview the image while you make adjustments. Choose More Accurate after you've previewed the effect to see the final results.

Depth Map Choose a depth map to determine what parts of the image will be affected. You can choose a Layer Mask, Alpha Channel, Transparency, or None as a source. When you choose None the entire image or the contents of a selection will be affected. Black areas in an alpha channel or layer mask will remain in focus while, white will be blurred. Gradual blurring is achieved with a gradient mask. Drag the Blur Focal Distance slider to set the focal length. If your focal distance is set at 100 for example, pixels with brightness values of 1 and 255 are completely blurred, and pixels closer to 100 are blurred less. If you click the preview image, the Blur Focal Distance slider matches the location you clicked, setting that depth as in-focus.

Iris Choose a shape for the iris of the lens. This simulates the effect of the iris of a camera lens. The more blades on the iris the more precise the blur will be. You can change blades of an iris by curving them or rotating them. The effect of changing iris curvature, shape, or rotation is very subtle, so examine the preview closely.

Specular Highlights A specular highlight is an area of absolute white. The Threshold slider assesses the brightness value of the lightest areas of an image. Pixels that have higher values are treated as specular highlights. The Brightness slider lightens selected areas.

Figure 20.13

The hanging bulb: the original image (left); with Motion Blur (Angle: –9, Distance: 50) applied to a 300 ppi image (center); with Radial Blur (Amount: 18, Method: Spin centered at top-left corner, Quality: Good) applied (right)

Figure 20.14

The Lens Blur filter dialog box

Noise Film grain and noise are removed from the image when you apply the Lens Blur filter. Adding noise can help restore the grain and add consistancy to the image's tonal texture. Click either the Uniform or Gaussian radio button to choose a type of noise. Choose Monochromatic to avoid color shifts. The Amount slider controls the strength of the noise.

Figure 20.15 shows the result of applying the Lens Blur Filter. This image is on the CD. Open rebecca.psd in the Chapter 20 folder to experiment with the Lens Blur filter. It has a layer mask and an alpha channel that you can use as depth maps.

Figure 20.15

The results of the application of the lens blur filter.

Noise Filters

You'll find the next group of filters in the constructive category in Filter → Noise. Add Noise, Dust & Scratches, and Median all allow user control; the Despeckle filter is an automated effect that does its work without benefit of a dialog box. Like its "hands-off" counterparts in the Blur and Sharpen submenus, Despeckle's effects are easily surpassed by its more powerful siblings, Dust & Scratches and Median. These three filters work in various ways to eliminate noise; Filter → Noise → Add Noise, believe it or not, adds noise to an image.

Add Noise

When you Add Noise to an image, the result is a grittier, grainier look—a bit of texture. Noise can work wonders in helping to smooth tonal transitions; it can help prevent banding in gradations and stair-stepping in your tonal range. In a grayscale image, noise is added in black, white, and gray grains; in color images, noise is added individually to each color channel, producing natural-looking hues of noise that blend together at random. Figure 20.16 shows the Add Noise dialog box with its three option areas.

Amount Enter a number from 0.1% to 400% to set a color range for your noise. This controls how far the noise can differ from the existing pixel colors—the higher the number, the greater variation in color of the added noise.

Distribution Two options are available to define the way noise is distributed across an image. If you click the Uniform button, colors are applied at random throughout the image. Otherwise, Photoshop applies the noise in a Gaussian curve (you were warned that Carl Friedrich would turn up again). Gaussian generally results in a more pronounced effect than Uniform delivers.

Monochromatic Check this box if you wish to distribute noise uniformly across all color channels. Otherwise, Add Noise applies its effect randomly to each channel separately, resulting in more color variation. Monochromatic ends up producing grayscale noise; if you're working on a grayscale image, the effect is the same whether or not you check this option. Take a look at Figure 20.17 for some samples of noise in action.

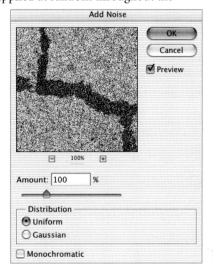

Figure 20.16

The Add Noise dialog box

Adding noise when retouching an image is a common task with little concern for RGB users, but it does have one small pitfall when working in CMYK. Noise is inadvertently added to the black plate, which can result in an overall graininess being added to the image.

To avoid this problem, Shift click the CMY channels in the Channels palette and apply the Noise filter only these channels

Dust & Scratches

The Dust & Scratches filter was created for the purpose of removing those spots and splotches that many old photos have acquired from years of neglect or abuse. Because it's used for photo restoration, the Dust & Scratches filter is covered at length in Chapter 19, "Photo Retouching," and further demonstrated in Hands On 7, "Restoring a Color Photograph."

Figure 20.17

The original image (left); and the image with the Add Noise, Gaussian filter, Amount: 64, applied (right)

Median

The Median filter is similar to Dust & Scratches, but its dialog box (see Figure 20.18) lacks the Threshold slider. Median is used to average the numerical values of adjacent pixels that are based on the Radius setting (with a range of 1 through 100). Median ignores pixels that are radically different so that the effect reflects a center-weighted average. The result is a softened, molded quality almost like a mild posterization. Higher values can destroy image detail, though, so take it easy on this one. Figure 20.19 provides one example of the Median filter at work.

Figure 20.18

The Median filter's dialog box

Sharpen Filters

The Sharpen group contains four filters: Sharpen, Sharpen Edges, Sharpen More, and Unsharp Mask. The first three of these are fully automated—that is, the user has no control over their effect. When you click one of these, no dialog box appears. Photoshop simply applies the predefined effect of increasing contrast. Sharpen increases contrast overall; Sharpen More has a stronger effect; and Sharpen Edges focuses on the areas of highest contrast in an image.

Much more powerful than any of these is Unsharp Mask, which we visited in Chapter 16. Unsharp Mask gets its unusual name from an old photographic technique of shooting through a blurred negative as a mask to increase the edge contrast in a film positive.

Figure 20.19

The original image (left), and the image with the Median filter applied with a Radius of 22 (right)

Photoshop's engineers have transformed that arcane bit of low technology into an incredibly useful enhancement tool. Its three-variable dialog box allows for minute adjustments and a very fine level of control. If the other three Sharpen filters were discarded, Photoshop users would still have all the sharpening capability they'd ever need with this one tool.

The Unsharp Mask dialog box (see Figure 20.20) appears when you choose Filter → Sharpen → Unsharp Mask. These options appear for your input:

Amount Values from 1% to 500% can be entered to define the degree of sharpening—the higher the value, the greater the effect.

Radius This setting defines the thickness (from 0.1 to 250 pixels) of an edge. As illustrated in Figure 20.21, lower values produce crisp, sharp edges, whereas higher values define edges as thicker and generate greater overall contrast throughout an image.

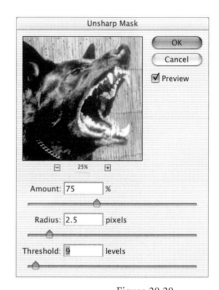

Figure 20.20

The Unsharp Mask dialog box includes options that are common to many filters.

Threshold Entering a value from 0 to 255 enables Unsharp Mask to determine what's considered an edge. The number indicates the difference in brightness values necessary to recognize an edge. Lower numbers include lots of pixels in the effect; the higher the number, the more exclusive the value.

These three variables work together to do the job of heightening focus and contrast. A little experimentation and practice might be in order to find the right combination of settings to achieve the desired effect. Subtle effects can be produced by keeping the Amount setting under 100%; raising it over 300% can create results that some might consider undesirable.

Sometimes repeated applications of a lower Amount setting can produce better results than a single application at a higher setting.

When identifying edges, Unsharp Mask uses the Radius setting as its criteria. The effectiveness of this setting depends entirely upon the resolution of the image. Screen images and Web graphics will require a much lower setting (say, in the 0.5 range) than high-resolution images intended for fine printing (usually nicely sharpened in the 2.0 range).

Radius values can be set all the way up to 250, but the higher values produce results more suitable for special effects than for day-to-day image correcting.

Raising the Threshold value has the effect of increasing the definition of an edge. In other words, higher values require more contrast between pixels to be recognized as an edge; lower values recognize edges between pixels with closer brightness values.

Figure 20.21

Unsharp Mask applied with various Radius settings. The original image (upper left); Radius of 2 (upper right); Radius of 100 (lower left); Radius of 250 (lower right).

Other Constructive Filters

Some other useful constructive filters reside in the Filter → Other submenu. Filter → Other → Offset (see Figure 20.22) is effectively a "Move tool in a (dialog) box." You enter numbers in the Horizontal and Vertical fields to tell Photoshop how far to move a selection. Positive numbers move the image to the right or down; negative numbers move it to the left or up. You can make the same precise moves by using the arrow keys in conjunction with the Move tool. The difference is that Offset enables you to determine what happens to the unselected areas by clicking one of its three radio buttons. Set To Background fills the emptied area with the current background color. If the image to be moved is on a layer, then the Set To Background option changes to Set To Transparent and the emptied area will become transparent. Repeat Edge Pixels fills the area with duplicates of the pixels at the edge of the selection, and Wrap Around takes pixels from the opposite side of the selection and duplicates them. These settings reappear frequently in some of the destructive filters you'll see shortly, particularly those in the Filter → Distort and Filter → Stylize submenus.

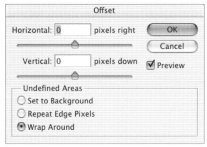

Figure 20.22

The Offset dialog box

Minimum and Maximum

The effect of the Minimum and Maximum filters will be familiar to anyone who has spent time in a lithography darkroom. To make colors in a printed image overlap, or *trap,* printers change the colors' borders to enable one of the colors (generally the lighter of the two) to spread into the other. When applied to a masking channel, the Minimum filter shrinks the selection. The number you specify using the Radius slider is the amount your selection contracts. Maximum does the exact opposite: input a Radius amount, and the filter expands your selection precisely by that number of pixels. This way you can create precise traps mathematically. Masks created using Maximum and Minimum can be used to overlap different colored areas so that just the right amount of trap is created. This prevents dreaded white space from showing where two colors meet during printing.

High Pass

The High Pass filter offers a tool for finding and isolating areas of high contrast. On its own, it seems at first glance an awkward and unlikely filter. But when applied to individual color channels or to selection masks, it can help create interesting line effects or imbue unremarkable images with added color. High Pass's Radius slider allows a range from 0.01 to 250 pixels. Lower numbers leave your image a flat, midrange gray. Higher values let the higher-contrast areas show through in lighter gray. This isn't so great when applied to an image as a whole, but try applying this filter to individual color channels and you have a completely different animal. If you increase contrast by applying High Pass to individual color channels, you end up adding color at either end of the scale.

You can achieve a line-drawing effect by using High Pass in combination with the Threshold command and then reapplying the modified image to the original. Figure 20.23 shows how this can be achieved. First, make a duplicate layer of your image, and apply High Pass to the duplicate, using the Radius to find a desirable effect. Choose Image → Adjust → Threshold at the desirable value. Then use the Opacity slider in your Layers palette to blend the line image with your original. Voilà! a line-drawing effect.

Many users favor variations on the basic High Pass sharpening technique. You can duplicate a layer and apply the High Pass filter from 0.3 to 3 pixels (depending on the image content and pixel dimensions). Blend the duped layer in a blending mode such as Overlay, Soft Light, Hard Light, or Linear Light and reduce the opacity until the desired effect is achieved.

Destructive Filters

Now that the constructive filters have displayed their image-correcting prowess, it's time for a little fun. The special effects in the Filter → Distort, Pixelate, and Stylize submenus take your precious pixels and shove them about with wild impunity. With these filters, you can turn images inside out, explode and reassemble them, or boil the life out of them, leaving you with an indigestible goo. Used with care, they can be useful friends; used unwisely, they'll turn on you viciously. These filters are undoubtedly the cool members of the gang; they look good and offer a fun night out, but ultimately they're not quite as responsible as the constructive filters. And some are just plain dumb.

Distort Filters

The common purpose of the filters in the Distort submenu is to transport pixels in your image across specifically defined patterns. For instance, Spherize gives the impression that your image has been wrapped around a ball. Twirl fixes the center point of your image and spirals the pixels around it, clockwise or counterclockwise. Shear provides an axis along which you can curve or lean your image.

The Distort filters are among the most memory-intensive of any of Photoshop's operations. To save yourself a lot of time watching the progress bar, do your experimenting with these filters on a lower-resolution version of your image. When you arrive at the effect you desire, make notes about the settings that produce the effect, and scale up those settings to apply the filter to your high-res version.

Filter values need to be greater for high-resolution images.

Diffuse Glow

Diffuse Glow seems to be misplaced in the Distort submenu, rather than among its kin, the Stylize filters. It gives the effect of viewing the image through a diffusion filter. You can set the level of Graininess, and define Glow and Clear parameters.

Glass

Glass, too, seems to belong elsewhere than with the Distort effects, perhaps among the Texture filters. Glass uses a hardwired variable displacement map effect similar to Distort → Displace (see the "Displace" section later in this section). Its effect approximates viewing your image through a glass lens (defined in the Texture pop-up menu). You also have the option of applying a texture of your own, using the Load Texture dialog box. You'll find this option in some of the Effects filters as well. Look for it in Artistic → Rough Pastels and Underpainting, Sketch → Conté Crayon, and especially Texture → Texturizer. These art effects offer a set of textures, but you can apply a pattern of your own making by saving it as a grayscale file in Photoshop format.

Ripple, Wave, and Zigzag Filters

Ocean Ripple, Ripple, Wave, and Zig Zag all offer methods of introducing degrees of wiggliness into your image. (Some might also include Glass in this group; it applies a rippling effect with the added element of texture.) Of these, Wave is by far the most powerful and the most mysterious. Compare Zig Zag's user-friendly dialog with Wave's scientific control panel (see Figure 20.24).

Wave

The Wave dialog is where some of Photoshop's mathematical underpinnings become most transparent. Too bad they couldn't provide a box with knobs you could twiddle like an old-fashioned synthesizer. You can

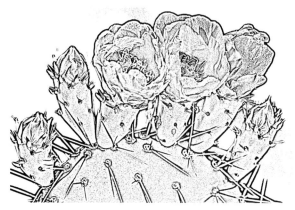

Figure 20.23

The High Pass filter is applied to a 300 ppi image. Step 1: High Pass, Radius 7 (top). Step 2: Threshold, Level 120 (center). Step 3: The Opacity slider in the Layers palette adjusted to 50% (bottom).

input the number of wave Generators, define minimum and maximum Wavelength and Amplitude levels, Scale the wave effect horizontally and vertically, and choose between three Types of waves. And when in doubt, just click the Randomize button; Photoshop will make up its own wave parameters.

Figure 20.25 shows some of the effects that these filters can accomplish.

Pinch and Spherize

Pinch and Spherize are opposite sides of the same coin. If you apply a negative Amount in the Pinch dialog box, you get a Spherize-like effect; if you go negative in Spherize, the result is a lot like a Pinch (see Figure 20.26). The difference is that Pinch maps your pixels onto a rounded cone, whereas Spherize maps the image onto—you guessed it—a sphere. Spherize offers the added option of enabling you to constrain the effect to the horizontal or vertical axis, or both. These two filters don't cancel each other out, though. Compare the effects of each in Figure 20.27.

Polar Coordinates

The Polar Coordinates filter takes the corners of your image and brings them together to form a circle (see Figure 20.28). Or the reverse: it takes the center and maps it out to the corners. Back in the old days, applying Polar Coordinates Rectangular to Polar was one of the few ways you could get type in a circle in Photoshop. Now that the Type tool offers that capability much more flexibly, Polar Coordinates can go back to what it does best: changing squares into circles.

Figure 20.24

Compare the Zig Zag (left) and Wave (right) dialog boxes.

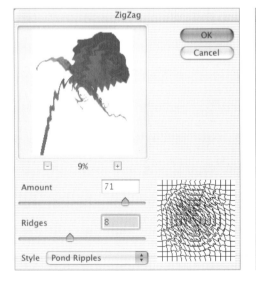
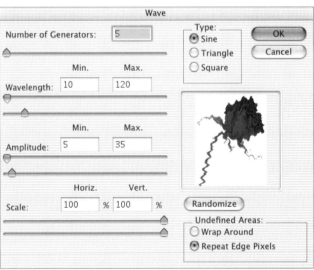

Figure 20.25

Comparison of filter applications, left to right: Ripple, Ocean Ripple, Zig Zag, (Around Center), Wave

Shear

Shear, as mentioned earlier, places your pixels along a curve. When you first open the Shear dialog box, you see a grid with a vertical line down the middle. You can take this vertical and angle it so it leans either way. This is akin to the Skew effect you get in the Transform functions. But if you click anywhere along the line, you can add points that turn the line to a curve. Now your image can distort along that curve in ways that Transform → Skew and Distort can't achieve, as I've done with the road in Figure 20.29. Radio buttons help you designate how the undefined areas will be treated: you can either wrap the image around or have the edge pixels repeat. If you don't like your curve, click the Defaults button and start over.

Twirl

The Twirl filter takes your image pixels and rotates them along a spiral. The center of the selection rotates while the edges remain in place. The Twirl dialog box (see Figure 20.30) offers two directions, expressed in minus and plus degrees, from 1 to 999. Because a circle is 360°, the full application of 999° gives you a spiral with almost three rotations. Applying a positive value maps the spiral in a clockwise direction, whereas applying a negative number twirls your image counterclockwise.

Figure 20.26

The Spherize dialog box is similar to Pinch, except for the extra Mode (axis) option at the bottom.

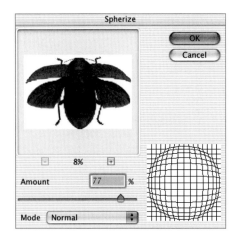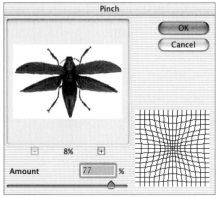

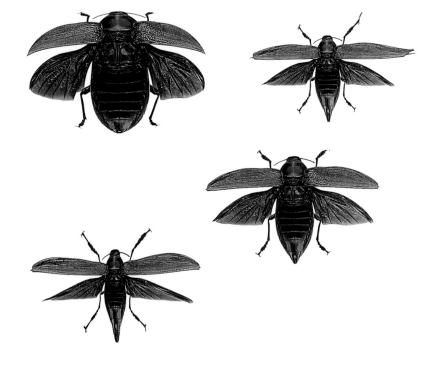

Figure 20.27

Pinched and Spherized images: (top left) Spherize, +100%; (top right) Spherize, –100%; (center) the original image; (bottom left) Pinch, +100%; and (bottom right) Pinch, –100%

Figure 20.28

The Polar Coordinates filter applied to the prickly pear

Displace

The Displace filter is a bit different from others in the Distort submenu. It relies on the use of displacement maps to reconfigure your image pixels. Like Distort → Wave, Displace retains quite a bit of its hard-science background, making it harder to predict without a lot of experimentation or mathematical know-how.

The Displace filter uses the brightness values in another image, called a *displacement map,* to relocate pixels. If the displacement map is a grayscale image with a single channel, pixels in the image that align with the black areas of the map are moved to the right and down, depending on your specifications in the dialog box. Pixels that align with the white areas of the map are moved to the left and up.

If the image has two or more channels, as in a grayscale image with an additional alpha channel or an RGB image, the first channel (Gray for grayscale and Red for RGB) determines horizontal movement and the second channel (an alpha channel for a grayscale image or the Green channel for an RGB image) determines vertical movement. The other channels in the image are not used. Areas of the image that align with the

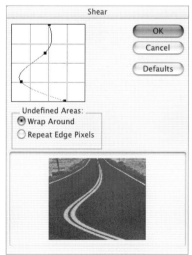

Figure 20.29

The Shear dialog box

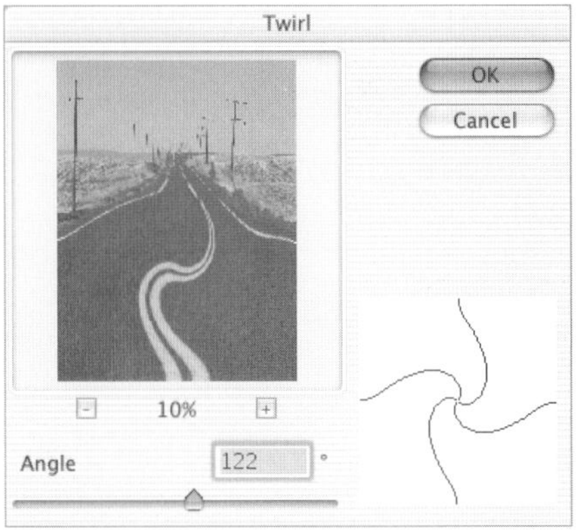

Figure 20.30
You can Twirl from
–999° to 999°.

black pixels on the first channel are moved to the right, and areas that align with the white pixels are moved to the left. Areas of the image that align with the black pixels on the second channel are displaced down, and the areas that align with white pixels are moved up. Of course, the amount of displacement depends on the specifications you enter in the dialog box.

You can access Photoshop's displacement maps (find them in the Plug-Ins folder in the Photoshop application folder) or create your own. Displace lets you define horizontal and vertical scale, and you get to say how you want undefined areas to be handled. You can also tell Photoshop whether to tile the displacement map or scale it to fit your image.

Pixelate Filters

In general, the Pixelate filters break up and rearrange your image into variously shaped groups of pixels. As I mentioned previously, it would be impossible to fully describe every effect, let alone demonstrate them all visually. I'll just hit the high points here.

Facet, Fragment, and Color Halftone

Neither Facet nor Fragment offers a dialog box; they simply apply their effects without so much as a by-your-leave. Of the two, Facet has a more pleasing, irregular, sort of hand-colored effect. Color Halftone's controls include a Radius input, and four screen angles boxes. It takes an awfully long time to apply this clunky effect, which can be achieved with more finesse by choosing Filter → Sketch → Halftone Pattern.

Crystallize, Mosaic, and Pointillize

Crystallize, Mosaic, and Pointillize all offer a Cell Size slider in their dialog boxes, which enables you to designate how many pixels will be used to create a cell or clump of grouped color. Larger values result in great big groupings of pixels that rob your image of detail. Smaller values can create more interesting artistic effects, mainly by increasing color contrast from cell to cell.

Mezzotint

The Mezzotint filter offers several ways of adding largely uncontrollable noise to your image, in the form of dots, lines, or strokes. It's like the bullyish big brother of Add Noise without the slider. Mezzotint turns grayscale images black and white; RGB images are reduced to six colors (red, green, and blue, and their complements cyan, magenta, and yellow) plus black and white.

Figure C30a–e in this book's color section shows the effects of some of the Pixelate filters.

Stylize Filters

Some filters in the Stylize submenu deal with the edges of your image in one way or another; others map image pixels into geometric shapes.

Solarize

Solarize is unique in dealing solely with color shifts. Its effect is similar to combining a photographic negative with a positive. All blacks and white become black, grays remain gray, and other colors become their negative equivalent. You have no control over this filter.

Tiles and Extrude

Tiles and Extrude are the two Stylize filters that map to shape. Tiles breaks your image up into squares. You can define how many tiles fill a row across your image, how far the tiles can offset from each other, and how the areas between tiles will be filled. But the effect is rather flat; the Texture → Mosaic Tiles filter creates a textured effect (with grouting options) that is much more realistic.

The Extrude filter is similar to Tiles, except that the mapping doesn't stay in two dimensions. The tiles or blocks extend into space. You can make your extruded elements block- or pyramid-shaped, and options are offered for the size and depth of the extruded shapes. In addition, you can decide whether you want incomplete blocks left out, and whether the fronts of square blocks should remain solid or contain image detail. Finally, you can arrange your extruded shapes randomly or arrange them by level. Figure 20.31 presents two sample Extrusions.

Figure 20.31

The Extrude filter set with different options: (top) Blocks, Random, Solid Front Faces, and (bottom) Pyramids, Level-based

Find Edges, Glowing Edges, and Trace Contour

Find Edges, Glowing Edges, and Trace Contour all provide ways of seeing a color outline of your image. (Remember the technique of using High Pass and Threshold to create line art, and include that method in this repertoire of edge-building tricks.) Find Edges is a no-options effect that draws colored lines around the edges of your image. Glowing Edges does the same, except that you can determine the width, brightness, and smoothness of your edges. Look at the examples in Figure C31b in the color section, and notice that Glowing Edges, if left to its defaults, is nothing more than an inverted-color version of Find Edges. Or vice versa: if you want control over Find Edges, just use Glowing Edges instead and then invert the results.

Trace Contour creates colored contours but leaves all non-edge areas white (see Figure C31a in the color section). You can define a threshold above or below which Trace Contour will determine what constitutes an edge. This one seems to require a bit of fading and blending to make it interesting, whereas Find Edges and Glowing Edges produce a more visually appealing effect.

To practice using Stylize filters, you can use the file stylize.psd in the Ch20 folder on the CD.

Diffuse

Diffuse works in a manner similar to the Dissolve brush or blending mode, in that it diffuses the edges of your selection. Because of this similarity, this filter's usefulness is rather limited; you can accomplish more by applying the brush or blending mode to an image. It does have a nice effect on type selections, though.

Wind

The Wind filter offers three "strengths" of wind effect: plain old Wind, a Blast of wind, or a Staggeringly strong wind, coming either from left or right. This filter is notoriously time-consuming, so try it on a grayscale or low-res image for a preview of the effect.

Emboss

And so we arrive at Emboss, perhaps Stylize's most interesting and entertaining offering. Figure 20.32 shows the Emboss dialog box with its Angle, Height, and Amount options. You can input your angle numerically, or slide the circle icon around to find the direction of light Emboss applies. Height is the distance of apparent bas relief you get, and Amount specifies the black-and-white value of edge pixels. Higher values create more contrast, and lower values give the image an overall gray cast.

Emboss is one of those filters people really like to overuse on its own. Look at magazine ads and you'll recognize this frequently used effect. Its true power comes when applied to blended layers, or when applied individually to color channels. For an effect of color relief, use the Fade command and apply it by using the Hue or Luminosity mode. This enables you to retain the colors in your image, while enabling the Emboss effect to reveal itself.

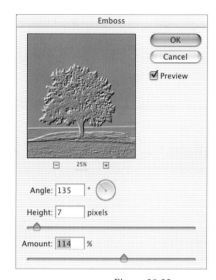

Figure 20.32

The Emboss filter dialog box

Effects Filters

This group of filters for the most part produce a variety of studio techniques traditionally achieved in drawing, painting, and photography. Artistic, Brush Strokes, Sketch, and Texture are the four groups of filters once called Gallery Effects. These all approximate different kinds of fine art, painterly techniques. With some of them, the results resemble effects that it would take several passes with standard Photoshop filters to achieve.

Artistic, Brush Strokes, and Sketch Filters

The Artistic effects attempt to reproduce the effects of traditional art media, such as Watercolor, Dry Brush, and Fresco. Brush Strokes filters convert the surface of the image into various styles of colored strokes, such as Crosshatch and Sprayed Stroke. Sketch filters use your foreground and background colors to replace your image colors while creating textures. If you want to get some of the original color back, just use your Fade command. Its usefulness is not to be underestimated.

Take a look at Figure 20.33, and the color version of these images as Figure C34a–e in the color section, for a variety of Artistic effects.

> Artistic, Brush Strokes, Sketch, and Texture filters are not available in Lab, Indexed, or CMYK modes. If you're working in any of those modes, you must convert to RGB or Grayscale mode before you can apply these effects.

Texture Filters

The Texture filters produce a a simulated surface on an image. Choose Filter → Texture or access these filters through the Filter Gallery. The Texture filters include Craclature, Grain, Mosaic Tiles, Stained Glass, Patchwork, and the Texturizer.

The Texturizer filter, gives you the most play, enabling you to choose from a list of surfaces including Brick, Burlap, Canvas, and Sandstone. You can also apply custom textures by clicking on the arrow in the upper right of the control panel to access the load texture command. Then you can regulate the scale, relief, and light source. The Texturizer filter is particularly useful for creating the effect that an image is painted on a surface (see Figure 20.34).

Figure 20.33

Examples of the Artistic filters

(a) Original image

(b) Artistic ➢ Watercolor

(c) Artistic ➢ Palette Knife

(d) Sketch ➢ Crosshatch

(e) Sketch ➢ Ink Outlines

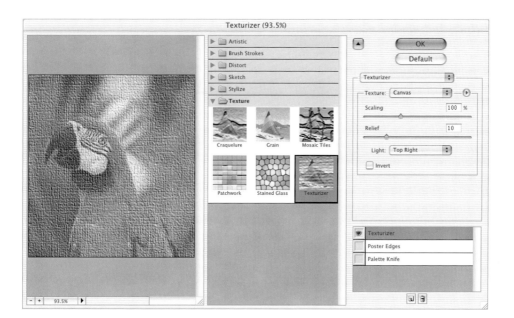

Figure 20.34

The Texturizer dialog box in the Filter Gallery

Render Filters

The Filter → Render submenu contains an interesting mix of lighting surface effects.

Clouds and Difference Clouds

These two Render filters produce ethereal, vaporous cloud formations. to apply either of these filters to your image, simply choose the command. A hazy mixture of foreground and background colors fills your selection. Choose the filter again, and the cloud pattern changes. Every time you choose this filter, the cloud patterns shift. If you hold down the Option/Alt key while choosing, the colors create a more pronounced effect. Difference Clouds works in the same way as Clouds, but you end up with inverted colors (if you started with blue sky and white clouds, you now get orange sky with black clouds). Apply the filter again and your colors reinvert, back to blue and white.

Fibers

This new filter automatically renders a surface resembling woven fiber in the foreground and background colors. In the Fibers dialog box (see Figure 20.35), you can control the variance and strength. The Variance slider controls how the fibrous texture is applied and how the colors are distributed. Lower values produce longer fibers, while higher values produce short fibers with a more varied distribution of color. The Strength slider controls the density of the fibers. Lower settings spread the fibers out over a larger area. Higher settings condense the width of the fibers and shorten their length. Click the Randomize button to see variations of the fibers. When you apply the Fibers filter, the image on the targeted layer is replaced with the effect. You can mitigate the effect after you've applied the filter and superimpose the fibers over an image by choosing Edit → Fade Fibers and moving the slider to the left.

Lens Flare produces a simple lighting effect. A preview box shows a replica of your image where you can move the pointer to find your flare center. The Brightness slider enables you to adjust brightness from 10% to 300%. Three lens shapes are offered: 50–300mm Zoom, 55mm Prime, and 105mm Prime. The result is a refraction, like light glinted back off a distant object.

Lens Flare and Lighting Effects, a much more powerful lighting tool, operate only on RGB images.

Some of these effects require a long time to compute and render.

Lighting Effects Filter

Figure 20.35

The Fibers filter dialog box

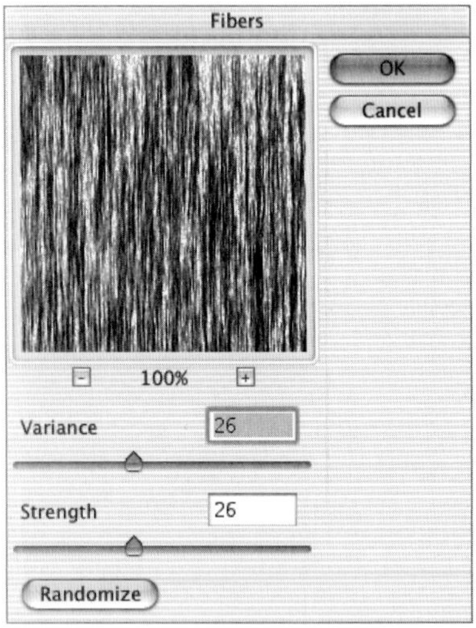

The Lighting Effects dialog box offers a wide range of options for simulating the play of spotlights or floodlights over your image (see Figure 20.36). Imagine you're hanging lights in a gallery, shining a flashlight into a dark cave, or driving down a wooded road at night. Any of these lighting situations can be duplicated with these versatile options.

At the top of the dialog box, the Style list provides a wide array of lighting styles. These preconfigured effects can serve as a starting point to add your own touches. In addition, the Light Type area enables you to create your own effects, which you can then save to the Style list. You're given options for Intensity and Focus, and you can choose a color for your light effect. You can define properties such as Gloss (Matte or Shiny finish), Material (ranges from Plastic to Metallic), Exposure, and Ambience. A color swatch lets you define the tint of the Ambience, which refers to ambient or overall lighting, separate from the spot or special lighting.

In the Texture Channel section, you can designate one of the channels (red, green, blue, or alpha) as a texture map—that is, a grayscale image in which the light areas become peaks and the dark areas become valleys. If you uncheck the White Is High box, the effect is reversed and the white areas become the valleys. Pick a Height somewhere between Flat and Mountainous, and you're set.

Inside the Preview area, you'll see a lighting footprint that shows you how the light source you've chosen will be applied. If you're working with a Spotlight or Omni, you can grab the handles and change the shape of the light. Clicking the Focus Spot (the end of the preview radius) enables you to change the angle of lighting. You can change the angle but not the shape of a Directional style of light. Keep in mind that the smaller the light footprint, the brighter or more intense the light. As you increase the size of the footprint, the light spreads out and dims accordingly. When you get an effect you like, click the Save button. Photoshop invites you to name your new lighting style, which will then appear in your Style list.

Figure 20.37 (also shown as Figure C38a–c in the color section) demonstrates a few lighting effects. `LFX_Dummy.psd` is included in the `Ch20` folder on the CD for you to experiment with lighting effects.

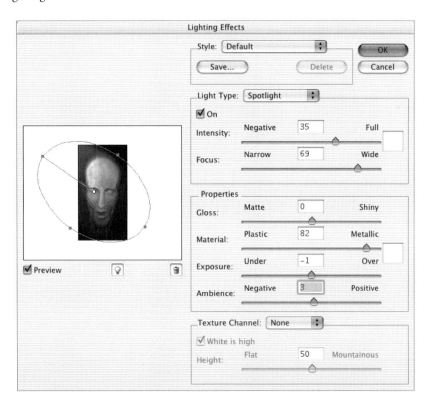

Figure 20.36

The Lighting Effects dialog box

Other Filters

Two filters—Video and Digimarc—exist in a category by themselves, being neither constructive, destructive nor effects for Render filters.

Video Filters

The Video → NTSC Colors filter has one purpose: to convert the colors of an image for transfer to videotape. This filter is not a color space. It converts your RGB images to NTSC (National Television System Committee)-compatible colors.

    If you continue to work on an image after using this filter, you might introduce incompatible colors. A better solution is to close the file, head to the Color Settings, and choose the NTSC RGB color space as your working RGB space. Then reopen the file and OK the profile conversion in the dialog box that appears.

    The Video → De-Interlace filter regenerates missing interlacing rows from video grabs. When you capture an image from a video device, the results might be less than satisfactory due to the interlacing used by the video program to compress file sizes. The De-Interlace filter restores the image by replacing pixel data. The result is that the image appears smoother. You can choose to replace interlaced fields by duplication or interpolation.

Figure 20.37

Examples of the Lighting Effects filter: The original image (left); default light expanded and rotated so that the source is from below (middle); RGB lights moved to various locations (right).

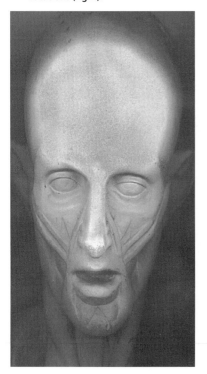

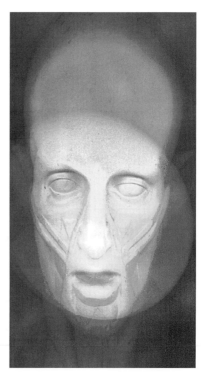

Digimarc Filter

The Digimarc filter lets you embed a digital watermark on your image to protect your copyright. It's particularly useful to professionals who license their work. Code is added to the document as noise and is usually imperceptible to the human eye. The watermark can endure most editing, even filters and file conversion.

To embed a digital watermark:

1. Choose Filter → Digimarc → Embed Watermark.

2. You must first register with Digimarc Corporation to get a creator ID. Click Personalize to launch your browser and access the Digimarc website at `www.digimarc.com`, or call the phone number in the dialog box.

3. Enter the PIN and ID number in the creator ID box. Click OK.

4. In each field, enter information about the image, including the copyright date and usage information.

5. Select a Visibility and Durability value. The more visible the watermark is, the more durable it is.

6. Click OK.

After you've embedded the watermark in an image, test its durability with the Signal Strength meter. Choose Filter → Digimarc → Read Watermark. The meter will tell you under what conditions the watermark will survive a specific intended use.

The Liquify Filter

The Liquify filter is, at its heart, a set of painting tools that distort and transform regions of an image by intuitively manufacturing pixels. If you can imagine applying the earth-shaking effects of the Photoshop's Distortion filters on the fly with a set brushes, then you understand the essence of this powerful subinterface (Figure 20.38). The Liquify filter dialog box contains sophisticated masking tools that protect the image from alteration and a complete set of reconstruction modes that correct unwanted distortions so you can apply a partial or complete reconstruction at will. There is an optional mesh grid overlay that enables you to gauge the effects of the distortion as you apply it. If desired, you can save the mesh and apply it to an entirely new image regardless of the image's size or resolution.

The Liquify filter has fully functional previewing capabilities and a set of transformation tools that let you experiment before actually applying their effects. You can configure everything exactly the way you want it without the risk of damaging the image, click OK, and your entire session is applied to the image.

Tools

Let's first look at the Liquify painting and masking tools, which work somewhat like a set of distortion filters.

Forward Warp tool This pushes pixels along as you drag. If you hold the mouse down and drag longer, the effect is enhanced. Short, gentle drags of the mouse can move changes along slowly and precisely. Generally applies the effect like a smudge tool.

Reconstruct tool If you change your mind after you've made some distortions, drag over the distortions with the Reconstruct tool to completely or partially restore your image to its initial state.

Twirl Clockwise tool This tool rotates pixels. Don't confuse it with the Twirl filter discussed earlier in this chapter. Unlike that filter, this tool causes pixels to rotate faster at the edges of the brush than at the center. The default tool twirls clockwise; press Option/Alt to twirl counterclockwise.

Pucker and Bloat tools These tools squeeze your pixels in or out. Pucker pinches pixels under its drag, and Bloat moves them away from the center of the brush.

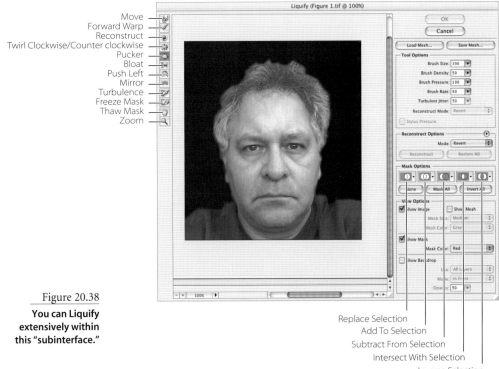

Figure 20.38

You can Liquify extensively within this "subinterface."

Push Left tool   This tool moves pixels at a 90-degree angle to the way you're moving the brush. Dragging moves pixels to the left of your mouse path; Option/Alt-drag moves pixels to the right.

Mirror tool   This tool drags along a mirror image of the pixels perpendicular to your brush.

Turbulence tool   This tool is another Liquify "brush" that applies the pixel-pushing effect more radically. If you click and hold the mouse, the pixels merge and melt like a piece of film burning in the projector. It's as if a randomizing Wave filter were at work inside the confines of the brush size. Changing the numbers on the Turbulent Jitter slider in the control panel slows down or speeds up this effect.

Freeze Mask tool   The Freeze Mask tool creates a mask to protect an area from distortions.

Thaw Mask tool   This tool unfreezes an area of an image so that are exposed to transformations.

Hand and Zoom tools   Notice in the toolbar the familiar Hand and Zoom tools. You can zoom in on a specific area of the image you are distorting and navigate anywhere you need to go inside the zoom. There is also a Zoom options menu at the lower-left corner of the window that lets you choose a zoom factor at which to display the image or you can click the plus or minus symblos to zoom in or out in specified increments. Incidentally, the interface displays the height and width of the entire image unless you have an area selected, in which case it will display only that area.

Options

On the right side of the Liquify window are Options that control that application of the distortions. Some of these options preprogram the tools in the Tool palette. The options are as follows:

Tool Options   These options configure the size, pressure, density, and rate of the brushes used to apply the distortion. Instead of individual brushes, you're provided with sliders that pop up when you click their arrow. They enable you to control the behavior of each tool's characteristics. The Turbulent Jitter slidercontrols the strength of the Turbulence tool.

Reconstruct Options   The Reconstruct Options area sets specifications for tool behavior. In the Mode pop-up list, there are seven options for regulating the degree and type of reconstruction, ranging from Rigid to Loose. Each one offers a slightly different degree of reconstructing capability. These options are applied to the Reconstruction tool. Choose the Reconstruction tool and then a brush size and pressure. Paint over the area and the reconstruction will be applied. If you want to reconstruct back to the original image, click the Restore All button. Or you can reconstruct it back to the original in steps by clicking the Reconstruct button.

Mask Options The Mask options give you various ways of creating masks to protect segments of your image from distortion. The icons enable you to create a new mask, add to a mask, subtract from a mask, intersect from a mask or invert a mask. Each icon's drop-down list enables you to load an active selection, a layer mask, or the transparent part of a layer as a mask.

View Options The View Options area provides options for the way you look at the liquification. Most important of these is the Show Mesh option. It displays a grid that is at first a regular square matrix, but as you apply distortions it takes on the shape of the transformations you apply. This can be useful when applying reconstructions, by letting you see how close to square you're able to return. At the top of the control area, you can save and load grids—which is useful if you want to apply the distortions made on one image to another image.

Show Backdrop The Show Backdrop feature enables you to superimpose the distortions over the original image so that you can view the liquified image on top of the original for comparison. When you click the Show Backdrop check box, choose a specific layer or all layers from the drop-down list and adjust the Opacity slider to compare the results.

Liquify can be used to create hilarious caricatures, as in Figure 20.39, or more subtle distortions that can improve the credibility of copied or composited regions of an image. For practice, you can open the Ch20 folder on the CD to obliterate and abuse sample files in the things-to-liquify folder.

Figure 20.39

These three images show the application of the Liquify filter and how it can be used to distort facial characteristics to produce wild caricatures.

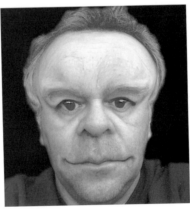

Remember, when using the Liquify filter, less is usually more. It's easy to get carried away with this feature and turn your image into a swirling amorphous galaxy of gray mud. With a little restraint and in the spirit of fun you can produce images that defy reality and have your audience wondering, "How'd they do that?"

The Pattern Maker

In the top section of the Filters palette under Extract Filter Gallery and Liquify is the Pattern Maker. With this interface, you can take any selection from any part of an image and generate repeating tiles based on the selection, the entire image, or the contents of the Clipboard. Figure 20.40 shows the Pattern Maker interface.

Like the Liquify tool, Pattern Maker offers you considerable control over its application. At the top-left corner of the window are the familiar Marquee, Zoom, and Hand tools. With Pattern Maker, the Marquee enables you to select an area of the image from which to generate patterns. However, the dialog box also gives you the options of using the Clipboard contents, the entire image (via the Use Image Size button), or an area you define with the handy Width and Height inputs.

Figure 20.40

The Pattern Maker interface

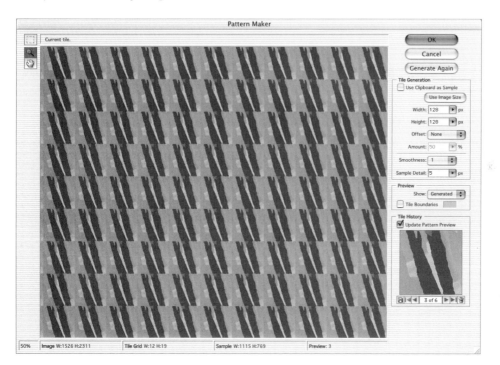

In addition, you can Offset the spacing of your tiles horizontally or vertically and specify an offset Amount percentage. Changing the Smoothness settings to 1, 2, or 3 can enhance blending of the edges of your tiles; increasing the Sample Detail allows greater precision in the formation of your sample. Keep in mind, though, that the farther you push the sample detail up, the more time Photoshop will take to generate the tiles. If you go all the way up to the maximum of 21, you could be in for a long wait while your sample generation grinds away.

After you've chosen a sample, click the Generate button to see elements of your sample repeated in place of your original image, tiled to fill the image area. Keep pressing Generate Again, and new patterns replace one another in the image window.

You can view the entire series of patterns you've generated in the Tile History area. The Tile History window shows the current generated sample as an individual unit. Up to 20 of these tiles can be stored (after that, the earliest ones are discarded as you produce more). By clicking the arrow buttons at the bottom of the dialog box, you can view each set of tiles sequentially. To delete one, click the trash can icon to the right; to save one, click the disk icon to the left. A dialog appears that shows you the pattern you've chosen and enables you to name it. Your new pattern will be saved at the end of Photoshop's list of default patterns, available for use with the rest, just as if you've made a selection and then chosen Edit → Define Pattern. You can use this option to save generated patterns without ever altering your image. If you click the Cancel button at this point, your saved patterns will remain, but your image will return to its original state.

Use the Preview area to see what you're doing. Choose either Original or Generated from the Show list to let Pattern Maker show you your original image or the current generated pattern, respectively. You can opt to view the tile boundaries as a line in the color (default green) you define. You can change this color just as you would the mask color in the Channels palette. Clicking the color swatch takes you to the Picker, where…well, you know what to do by now. If Tile Boundaries is checked, colored lines will show you the area covered by each individual tile.

Using any of the methods in the Tile Generation section will override any Marquee selection you might have made.

If you get lost in all this pattern generation, just look down at the bottom of the dialog, where all is displayed in an orderly fashion. You can check up on your zoom magnification, image size in pixels, and Tile Grid (how many tiles fit across and down in your image size). You can also see the size in pixels of anything you've stored in the Clipboard; under Preview, you can be informed of which of the generated tile patterns you're looking at. Figure 20.41 shows some sample patterns generated from the desert image.

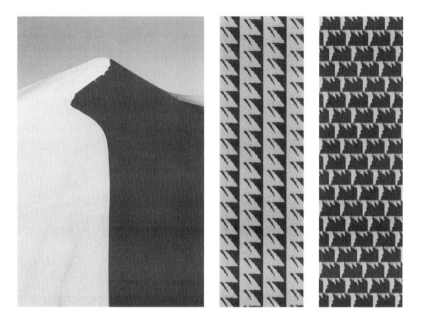

Figure 20.41

The original image (left) and two of the many possible patterns generated from it (center; right)

CHAPTER 21

Making Difficult Selections

Chapter 6 covered the basics of selection making. You saw that the selection tools, such as the Marquee and Lasso tools, provide several manual techniques to isolate areas of an image. Photoshop also has a few semiautomatic selection tools, such as the Magic Wand and the Magnetic Lasso, that select pixels based on their brightness or contrast values. The Quick Mask extends selection-making abilities to the painting tools for even more control, and the Pen tool makes accurate selections with Bezier curves.

Sometimes, however, areas of an image seem impossible to select because they have ambiguous surroundings or complex content. What do you do with these problem images, short of canceling all appointments, turning off the phone, and sitting in front of the computer for the next week, encircling each pixel one by one?

In this chapter, you will learn how to select those really tough areas with a few tools and techniques that, if they don't make these selections easy, at least get the job done with a minimum of effort. You will learn about:

- **Making selections with color channels**
- **Working with Color Range**
- **Selecting out-of-gamut colors**
- **Modifying selections**
- **Extracting images**

Making Selections with Color Channels

You can use an image's color information to make really difficult selections. The differences in the contrast levels of the red, green, and blue channels can often provide a method of isolating regions of the image that seem impossible to select. You'll use this technique and a combination of Photoshop's painting tools and filters to select from images in which the background and foreground are complex and almost indistinct. In Figure 21.1, for example, isolating the tree from the background would otherwise be virtually impossible.

Follow these steps to use color channels to make a selection:

1. Open the image `leaflesstree.psd` in the `Ch21` folder on the *Photoshop CS Savvy* CD.

2. Open the Channels palette (Window → Channels, or F7 on the keyboard if you still have it clustered with the Layers palette). Click the Red, Green, and Blue channel thumbnails to display each channel in grayscale in the image window. Determine which channel has the most contrast between the fine branch tips of the tree and the background. In this case, it's the Red channel.

3. Target the Red channel, and duplicate it by choosing Duplicate Channel from the Channels palette menu, or by dragging it to the New Channel icon at the bottom of the palette. The channel will be named Red Copy (see Figure 21.2).

Figure 21.1

It's close to impossible to select this tree with traditional selection tools, but you can use color channels to do it.

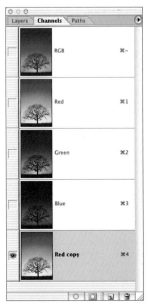

Figure 21.2

The copy of the Red channel in the Channels palette.

4. Choose Image → Adjustments → Levels and increase the contrast of the Red Copy channel by dragging the sliders inward. Click OK. I set the input levels in this image to 81, 1.00, and 186 (see Figure 21.3).

5. Choose the Lasso tool 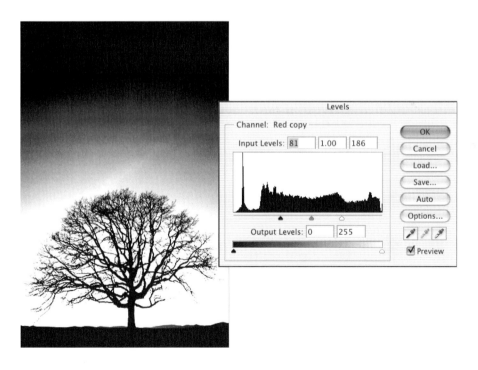. Encircle the tree as close to the branches as possible. Include the dark foreground at the base of the tree (see Figure 21.4).

6. Inverse the selection. Choose white as a foreground color and press Option/Alt-Delete/Backspace to fill the areas around the tree with white (see Figure 21.5).

7. Choose Image → Adjustments → Invert to make all the white areas of the channel black, and the black areas white. (See Figure 21.6).

8. Now that you've isolated the tree, you're going to place it on a different background. Open the file wasteland.psd from the Ch21 folder on the CD.

9. Click the leafless tree image. Target the RGB channel. Load the Red Copy by dragging it to the Load Channel As Selection icon in the Layers palette to select the tree.

10. Choose the Move tool ; drag the tree from the image window and drop it onto the wasteland image.

Figure 21.3

The Levels adjustment adds more contrast to the channel.

Figure 21.4

The Red Copy alpha channel with the areas around the tree selected

Figure 21.5

The Red Copy alpha channel with the areas around the tree filled with white

Figure 21.6

The Inverted Red Copy alpha channel

11.   The extremities of the branches are a red color. You'll adjust the color with the Hue/Saturation sliders. Choose Image →Adjust → Hue/Saturation. Drag the Hue slider so that it reads 33, and the Saturation slider so that it reads –41 (see Figure 21.7).

12.   Choose Layer → Matting → Defringe → Radius 1px to eliminate any unwanted edge pixels. See Figure 21.8 for the completed image.

Working with Color Range

Figure 21.7

The Hue/Saturation dialog box

The Select → Color Range command is ideal for selecting areas of similar color within an image or within a selection outline. In Chapter 17, Modifying and Mapping Color you used a similar technique, Image → Adjustments → Replace Color, to substitute colors.

Color Range operates in very much the same way, but instead of altering color it produces an accurate selection marquee around the specified areas of similar color.

This tool really helps you when you have a lot of small areas of similar color situated throughout an image. With so many scattered areas of color, a tedious task can be simplified, as you shall see.

When you choose Select → Color Range, the dialog box (see Figure 21.9) presents you with a mask of the image. The Select pull-down menu lets you choose a specific color range to sample, and it will automatically select all the pixels within the range. You can choose to select Reds, Yellows, Blues, Magentas, Greens, Cyans, Highlights, Midtones, Shadows, or Out-of-Gamut colors.

If you want more control, however, the best approach to making a selection is to choose the default, Sampled Colors. You use the familiar eyedropper tools to sample the colors you want to select from the image. I recommend that you change the setting in the Eyedropper tool Options bar to 3 By 3 Average. Click in or drag over the image with the Eyedropper to select colors. Drag over the image with the Plus Eyedropper to increase the range of colors selected, or with the Minus Eyedropper to decrease the range. The Fuzziness slider also extends the range of selection into adjacent pixels. Check the Invert box to invert the selection.

Figure 21.8

The finished image

The radio buttons under the mask let you view the selection mask on the image as you drag the eyedropper, or adjust the Fuzziness slider to accurately determine the range of the selection. The Selection Preview pull-down menu lets you choose from Grayscale, White Matte, Black Matte, Quick Mask, or None modes in which to view the mask in the image window. These preview modes help you better determine what areas of the image will be selected and what areas will be masked. Choose the one most appropriate to the tonal or color content of your image. For example, you'll probably choose White Matte if the image is particularly dark, because the mask will be more visible.

Selecting a Sampled Color Range

Let's try selecting part of an image by using Color Range.

1. Open the file sparks.psd in the Ch21 folder of the CD.

2. In the Tool palette, choose the Eyedropper tool. Change the setting in the Options bar to 3 By 3 Average.

3. Select the left portion of the image with the Rectangular Marquee.

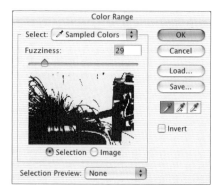

Figure 21.9

The Color Range dialog box

4. Choose Select → Color Range. With the Plus Eyedropper tool 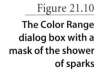, drag over a portion of the shower of sparks. Watch the mask in the Color Range dialog box (see Figure 21.10).

5. From the Selection Preview list, run through the masking options one by one to determine what part of the image will be selected.

6. Move the Fuzziness slider to extend the selection to include as much of the area that contains the sparks as possible.

7. Click OK to select the sparks.

Depending on the fuzziness and the range of color that was selected, portions of the welder might be included, in which case you'll need to deselect those areas by choosing the Lasso tool, choosing the Subtract From Selection icon in the Options bar, and encircling them.

Think about how much time you saved by using this technique. It certainly would have been labor-intensive to select these areas with the Magic Wand tool, even with the Contiguous option turned off. Color Range lets you collectively select those colors that are dispersed throughout the image simply by dragging over them. The finished selection is shown in Figure 21.11.

Selecting Out-of-Gamut Colors

Another unique function of the Color Range command is its capability to isolate unprintable colors. Chapter 15, "Color Management and Printing," describes Photoshop's color management features and shows how you can compensate for out-of-gamut colors. In the Edit → Color Settings dialog box, you can specify a CMYK profile for a device or printing

Figure 21.10

The Color Range dialog box with a mask of the shower of sparks

environment that has its own unique CMYK gamut. When you prepare an image for process color printing, the profile affects how the image is converted into CMYK from its working mode (usually RGB). If you choose View → Gamut Warning, Photoshop will display a gray mask that shows you which colors are out of gamut. If you choose View → Proof Setup → Working CMYK (Photoshop's default) and then View → Proof Colors, you can preview on-screen how the image will look when printed, before you convert it.

> Toggle in and out of Proof Colors by pressing ⌘/Ctrl-Y to compare the CMYK preview to the RGB display. You can also use Window → Arrange → New Window for soft-proofing CMYK.

You'll want to pull the out-of-gamut colors back into the CMYK range before you convert the image, so that you can perform final edits with the knowledge that what you see on-screen is as close as possible to what you'll get when you print. But first you'll have to select the out-of-gamut colors, and the method you'll use is buried deep within the Color Range dialog box.

To select and adjust out-of-gamut colors, for an image that will be printed on a web-fed printing press, follow these steps:

1. Choose Edit → Color Settings. From the Working Spaces, RGB menu choose Adobe RGB (1998). From the CMYK pull-down menu, choose U.S. Sheetfed Coated v2. Click OK.

Figure 21.11

The final selection

2. Open the file `chiles.psd` from the `Ch21` folder on the CD.

3. Make a duplicate of the document (Image → Duplicate). Name the copy `chiles_CMYK.psd`.

4. Place both images on the screen side by side.

5. Click `chiles.psd` to activate it. Choose View → Proof Setup → Custom. From the Profile menu (see Figure 21.12), choose Adobe RGB 1998 to display the original image in RGB mode. You'll keep this image on-screen for reference.

6. Activate `chiles.psd`. Choose View → Proof Setup → Working CMYK and then View → Proof Colors. You'll notice that the colors in the CMYK proof are less saturated than in the RGB image.

7. Choose View Gamut → Warning to view the out-of-gamut colors, as in Figure 21.13. They appear as gray shapes on the chiles. Press Shift-⌘-Y (Mac) or Shift-Ctrl-Y (Win) to turn the Gamut warning off.

8. Choose Select → Color Range. Choose Out Of Gamut from the bottom of the Select pull-down menu (see Figure 21.14). The dialog box displays a mask of the out-of-gamut colors.

9. Click OK. As shown in Figure 21.15, the marquee on the image displays a selection outline.

10. Choose Select → Feather → Radius type 3px to create smooth transitions between colors when you increase their intensity.

11. Press ⌘/Ctrl-H to hide the edges of the selection.

You can also experiment with other adjustments, including Levels, Curves, Color Balance, Selective Color, the Channel Mixer, or Variations to produce optimum results.

Figure 21.12

Use the Proof Setup dialog box to choose the current CMYK working space.

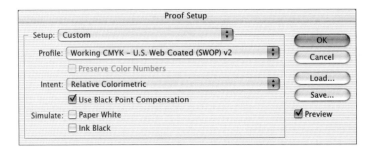

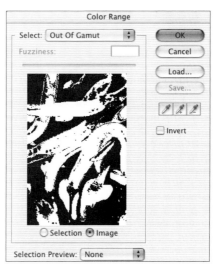

Figure 21.13

The Gamut warning displays the out-of-gamut colors as gray shapes.

Figure 21.14

Selecting out-of-gamut colors with the Color Range dialog box

Figure 21.15

The out-of-gamut colors selected

12. Choose Layer → New Adjustment Layer → Hue/Saturation. In the Hue/Saturation dialog box (see Figure 21.16), move the Hue slider to +8 and the Saturation slider to +61, to more closely match the RGB image.

13. You can compensate for diminished intensity by experimenting with variations of hue, saturation, and lightness to produce better results while maintaining the colors within the CMYK gamut. However, on most images you will never achieve the full intensity of the RGB image.

Extracting Images

Earlier you used RGB channels to isolate images with fuzzy, complex, or indefinable edges from their backgrounds. Another option is to use the Filter → Extract command for this purpose. The results might not be as precise as the channels method, but you can, by trial and error, isolate problem edges with much less effort. The Extract command is actually a mini-program, complete with a subinterface (see Figure 21.17), that measures subtle differences of the edge of an image by its color and brightness content and then determines how best to isolate the region.

Figure 21.16

Make adjustments in the Hue/Saturation dialog box so that the CMYK image matches the RGB original as closely as possible.

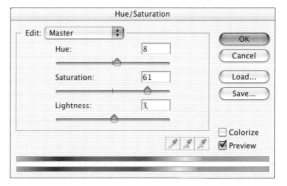

Figure 21.17

**The Extract
dialog box**

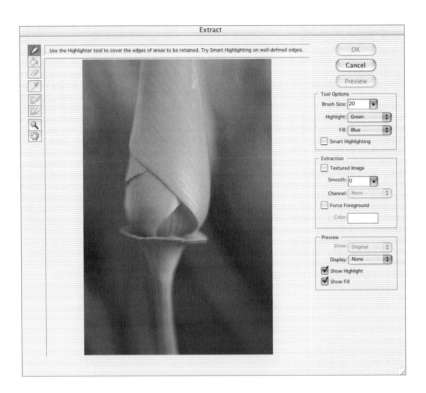

Use the Edge Highlighter to define the image's edges; you then fill its interior and preview it. You can refine and preview as many times as you like until you have all of the image and none of the background. You then extract it, which deletes undefined areas and places the image on a transparent layer.

Because of the radical transformation that Extract produces, you should first duplicate the image or make a snapshot of it.

Specify the following tool options in the dialog panel:

Brush Size Enter a value or drag the slider to specify the width of the Edge Highlighter tool, which defines the boundary of the image.

Highlight Choose a color to display the edge boundary that you draw with the Edge Highlighter tool.

Fill Choose a color to display the interior fill inside the boundary.

Smart Highlighting This option helps you keep the highlight on the edge, especially when the edge between the foreground and background is sharp with similar color or texture. To toggle Smart Highlighting on or off while you drag, press the ⌘/Ctrl key.

To practice extracting an image, choose Filter → Extract and open the file `iris.psd` in the `Ch21` folder on the CD. Then follow these steps:

1. Set the Highlight color to red and the Fill color to blue.

2. Choose a 24 px Brush Size. Select the Edge Highlighter tool ![icon] and drag along the edge of the flower to highlight the edge of the object you want to extract. Draw the highlight so that it slightly overlaps both the foreground and background regions around the edge, to cover areas where the foreground blends into the background.

3. Use a smaller brush to precisely highlight edges that are more defined, such as the area around the flower's base. Use a larger brush to highlight the fuzzy edges around the petals, loosely covering the soft transitions. Don't highlight the bottom or top of the flower, only the sides.

4. If you make a mistake, erase the highlight. Select the Eraser tool from the dialog box and drag over the highlight. This tool is available when a highlight exists. You can completely erase the highlight by pressing Alt-Backspace or Option-Delete.

> To toggle between the Highlighter and the Eraser while drawing an edge, press the Option or Alt key.

5. To fill the flower, select the Fill tool ![icon] . Click inside the outline to fill its interior (see Figure 21.18).

> If the image is especially intricate or lacks a clear interior, make sure that the highlight covers the entire edge. To highlight the entire object, press Ctrl-Backspace (Win) or ⌘-Delete (Mac), and then select Force Foreground. Use this technique with areas that contain tones of a single color.

Viewing the Extraction

Click Preview to view the extracted image. The edges of the flower will be soft, and the area around it will be transparent, like the one in Figure 21.19. You can better see the result of the extraction if you view it by using the following techniques:

-   In the Show menu, switch between previews of the original and extracted images.

-   Use the Display menu to preview the extracted object as a grayscale mask or against a white matte or a black matte. To choose a colored background, choose Other and a color from the Color Picker. To display a transparent background, choose None.

-   Select the Show Highlight or Show Fill option to display the object's extraction boundaries or interior.

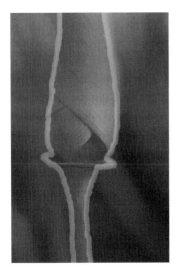

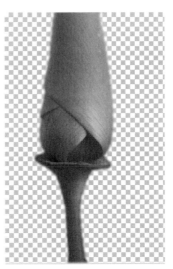

Figure 21.18

The highlighted and filled flower

Figure 21.19

Previewing the completed flower

Refining the Extraction

Several tools enable you to alter the edges and interior of the extraction, adding areas to the extraction or eliminating unwanted pixels.

The Cleanup Tool

You can edit and refine the extraction with the Cleanup tool , which is available only when you preview the extracted image. The Cleanup tool subtracts opacity. If you make multiple passes, it will have a cumulative effect. Drag over an area to erase it to transparency. Press the Option/Alt key while painting with the Cleanup tool to restore opacity.

> The Eraser and Fill tools can also be used to edit the previewed image. The Eraser restores the edge to transparency. Clicking a filled area with the Fill paint bucket removes the fill.

The Edge Touchup Tool

Use the Edge Touchup tool to edit the extraction boundaries. The tool, which is available when you show the extracted image, sharpens the edges of the extracted image. It has a cumulative effect as you make multiple passes over the edge. If there is no clear edge, the Edge Touchup tool adds opacity to the image or makes the background more transparent.

Textured Image

If the foreground or background of your image is textured, check the Textured Image box to better define the extraction.

The Smooth Control

To help remove stray artifacts in the extraction, click on the right arrow next to the Smooth field in the Extract dialog box. Enter a value in the field or drag the Smooth Slider. The higher the number, the greater the radius of pixels that will be affected. When you are finished editing, click Preview again to view the edited extraction. You can edit and preview the extraction as many times as you like until you achieve the results you want.

To apply the final extraction, click OK. All pixels on the layer outside the extracted image are eliminated. If necessary, use the History brush 🖌 or the Background Eraser 🖌 to touch up stray edge pixels and flawed areas.

CHAPTER 22

Advanced Layer Techniques

Chapter 7 introduced you to layers and how important they are to the Photoshop work flow. I compared a layer to a piece of transparent glass. You learned that you can separate areas of your image onto independent layers that can be edited at any time during the imaging process. You also learned how to reshuffle layers in the stack to reposition their plane of depth in the picture, and how to link layers or create layer sets to organize your work. You changed a layer's opacity to be able to see "through" it. You experimented with blending modes to dramatically alter the color relationships of layers, and applied cool special effects such as drop shadows and bevels. In Chapter 10 you learned to apply Fill layers and in Chapter 16 you discovered the power of Adjustment layers.

In this chapter, I'll introduce more of Photoshop's layer capabilities and show you techniques that empower you to combine visual elements in unique and rather surprising ways.

You'll learn about:

- **Creating and controlling layer masks**
- **Seamless compositing**
- **Grouping layers**
- **Casting shadows**
- **Creating multiple versions with layer comps**

Working with Layer Masks

When you work in Photoshop, you rely on masks to perform many of its editing tasks. Masking, as discussed in Chapter 6, is a way to isolate an area of an image. In Chapter 12, you worked with Quick Masks to extend the power of selecting to the painting tools. In the same chapter, you learned how to store selections as alpha channels so that they could be used at any time during the editing process. Selections, alpha channels, and Quick Masks all work to the same ends: to protect an isolated region from the application of a tool or operation. Layer masks are a little different. Instead of protecting an area of the image from the effects of an operation, they reveal or conceal areas of a layer from view.

When you adjust the Opacity controls on the Layers palette, you change the transparency of the entire layer so that the content of layers beneath it in the stack will be visible. But when you apply a layer mask to an image, you can control the transparency of a particular region of the layer. Layer masks use the same visual vocabulary as alpha channels to perform their tasks with a slightly different twist. On an alpha channel, by default, black fully protects an area, white fully exposes an area, and gray partially exposes an area. On a layer mask, black completely conceals an area, white fully reveals an area, and gray partially conceals an area.

Make a layer mask by choosing Layer → Add Layer Mask → Reveal All or Hide All. If you choose Reveal All, the mask thumbnail appears white and begins by *revealing* the entire layer. As you paint with black, you conceal areas on the targeted layer. If you choose Hide All, the mask thumbnail appears black and begins by *hiding* the entire layer. As you paint with white, you reveal portions of the layer. A thumbnail appears in the Layers palette to the right of the targeted layer's thumbnail. When you click the layer mask thumbnail, it displays a double border to indicate that it is ready for editing. By default, the layer mask is targeted after it is created and is indicated in the title bar of the document. By default, the layer mask is also linked to the layer, indicated by the chain icon.

> Not having the correct layer or layer mask targeted is perhaps the most common mistake made by users.

Controlling Layer Masks

After you've created a layer mask, you can control it in the following ways:

Activating and Deactivating a Layer Mask Press Shift and click the layer mask to turn it on or off, or choose Layer → Enable or Disable Layer Mask.

Viewing a Layer Mask Press Option (Macintosh) or Alt (Windows), and click the mask thumbnail to view the layer mask in the image window.

Making a Selection from a Layer Mask Press ⌘/Ctrl and click the layer mask to generate a selection outline.

Moving a Layer's Mask and Contents Click between the two thumbnails to reveal or conceal the chain icon. When the two thumbnails are linked and you drag on the image with the Move tool, both the image on the layer and layer mask move as a unit. When the link is not visible, only the content of the targeted thumbnail will move.

Applying a Layer Mask to Another Layer Target the destination layer. Drag the layer mask thumbnail icon from the existing layer to the Add Layer Mask icon at the bottom of the Layers palette.

Removing a Layer Mask Choose Layer → Remove Layer Mask → Discard or Apply. Discard removes the layer mask and does not apply the effect. Apply removes the layer mask and applies the effect directly to the pixels of the layer. You can also drag the Layer Mask icon (not the Layer icon) to the trash can on the Layers palette.

Making Layer Masks

To understand how layer masks work, you'll use one to conceal part of the contents of a layer. To practice creating a layer mask, follow these steps:

1. Open the file `coffee_time.psd` in the `Ch22` folder on the *Photoshop CS Savvy* CD (see Figure 22.1). The image is composed of two layers: the cup and the pattern layer behind it.

Figure 22.1

The `coffee_time` **image and its Layers palette**

2. Open the file `uninvited_guest.psd`.

3. Choose the Magic Wand tool . In the Options bar, set the tolerance to the default and select the white area around the beetle. (You might have to click more than once.)

4. Choose Select → Inverse or Shift-⌘/Ctrl-I to select the beetle.

5. Choose the Move tool ⊞. Place your cursor on the beetle, press the mouse button, and drag the selection onto the cup. Place it on top of the coffee. Name the new layer **Guest**.

6. Notice that there is a white fringe around the beetle, resulting from the anti-alias of the white background that was selected. To remove it, choose Layer → Matting → Defringe. In the Defringe dialog box (see Figure 22.2), enter **1** pixel. (To learn more about removing edge pixels, see the section titled "Seamless Compositing" later in this chapter.) See Figure 22.3.

Figure 22.2

Defringe dialog box

7. Choose Layer → Add Layer Mask → Reveal All. A Layer Mask icon appears in the Layers palette that is, by default, targeted for editing.

8. Choose black as the foreground color and white as the background color. Choose the Brush tool. Choose a 21-pixel Soft brush from the Brushes palette. In the Options bar, set the opacity to 100%. Pass over the topmost portion of the beetle's body. Set the opacity to 50% and make several passes as you work your way down the beetle's body. Reduce the opacity to 35% as you near the middle part of the beetle's body. The result should be a gradual fade on the layer mask, producing the illusion that the beetle is emerging from the depth of the coffee.

Figure 22.3

The two images combined

Figure 22.4

The transparency effect created by the layer mask

Figure 22.5

The layer mask

9. Apply the same technique to the legs. You can produce realistic transparency with this technique, as shown in Figure 22.4. Press Option/Alt and click the layer mask thumbnail to view the layer mask, seen in Figure 22.5.

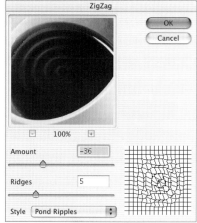

10. To enhance the effect, choose the Magic Wand tool. Set the feather radius in the Options bar to 1 pixel. Target the Cup layer and click on the coffee to select it. Choose Filter → Distort → Zig Zag → Pond Ripples; set the Amount to –36 and the Ridges to 5.

As an alternative technique, apply this filter again. During the second pass, adjust the amount to –42 and ripples to 4 to produce a very interesting reflective effect.

11. Double-click the cup icon to display the Layer Styles dialog box. Click on the name *Drop Shadow* to reveal the Drop Shadow controls. Set the opacity to 35%, the angle to 39 degrees, the distance to 22 pixels, and the size to 7 pixels.

If you make a mistake, choose white as a foreground color and erase it.

12. As a final touch, paint a shadow of the front leg on the cup in 30% gray; then blur it slightly with the Blur tool. The image should look like Figure 22.6, which can be seen here and in Figure C37 of the color section.

Figure 22.6

The completed image

Seamless Compositing

Sometimes you'll see an advertisement in a glossy magazine that you know has been "Photoshopped." Non sequitur and neosurreal images are dead giveaways, and sometimes they are amazingly clever. The image might have a brilliant concept, dazzling colors, and a truly dynamic composition and be perfect in every way—except for a few out-of-place edge pixels. It is unfortunate when a great work of commercial art is just short of perfection, especially when Photoshop has built-in bandages to cover every possible boo-boo.

Matting is the key to clean composites. When you select an image, the anti-alias programmed into the selection tool selects edge pixels. When you drag the selection onto another image, the stowaway edge pixels can't be seen until they reach their destination. When you see them, it's usually a row of one or two pixels that are significantly darker or lighter than the color behind them, as in Figure 22.7.

You can easily eliminate unwanted edge pixels by using Photoshop's matting functions. The matting functions eliminate those nasty little fellows and blend your image into the layers beneath it. There are three ways to matte an image, and if your edge pixels are particularly stubborn, there's also a workaround that does the job every time.

To matte an image, it must be on an independent layer surrounded by transparency. The three options are as follows:

Defringe Choose Layer → Matting → Defringe, and enter a value in the dialog box that is displayed (see Figure 22.2 earlier in this chapter). Defringe is an effective method of eliminating the off-color edge pixels selected by the anti-alias because it replaces the color of the edge pixels with the colors of the nearby pixels on the layer.

Remove White or Black Matte Choose Layer → Matting → Remove White Matte or Remove Black Matte to darken the white edge pixels or lighten the black pixels. This is helpful if you are moving a selection from a white or black background to another background.

Workaround for Stubborn Edge Pixels If neither of these operations works to your satisfaction—and sometimes you just can't eliminate enough of that edge—here's a neat workaround:

1. Select the image pixels on the layer by pressing ⌘/Ctrl and clicking the thumbnail.

2. Choose Select → Modify → Contract. Enter the amount (in pixels) to contract the selection. View the edge close-up to see how far into the image the marquee has contracted. Undo and enter different values if necessary.

3. Choose Select → Inverse.

4. Choose Select → Feather, and feather the selection 1 pixel.

5. Press Delete/Backspace to delete the edge.

    Or, choose Layer → Add Layer Mask → Reveal All to convert the selection into a layer mask that will conceal the edge pixels.

Figure 22.7

The hand grenade on the top is surrounded by light-colored edge pixels. On the bottom, the edge pixels were removed by defringing.

Using Clipping Masks

When you clip two layers together you create a clipping mask. Clipping masks enable you to perform some interesting graphic tricks such as literally "tattooing" one image onto the other. With the help of layer masks, layer opacity, and blending modes, you can mold and model the image into superbly realistic forms.

To join two layers into a clipping mask, the image on the bottom layer must be surrounded by transparency. The layer to be clipped will appear one step higher in the stack. When a layer is clipped, it fills the shape of the image on the layer below it; in other words, the bottom layer acts as a mask to clip the layer immediately above it.

To see how clipping masks operate, you'll clip two layers together to create an "electric" telephone, and then use blending modes and a layer mask to enhance the effect:

1. Open the `electric_telephone.psd` file in the `Ch22` folder on the CD. The image is separated into three layers: the topmost is the Lightning layer, the middle is the Telephone, and the bottom is the black Background (see Figure 22.8).

2. To create a clipping mask, press Option/Alt and click between the Lightning and Telephone layers (see Figure 22.9). Or target the top layer and choose Layer → Create Clipping Mask.

3. Experiment with blending modes to enhance the effect. Target the Lightning layer and choose Hard Light from the pop-up list at the top of the Layers palette. The lightning becomes more saturated. Try Pin Light and Linear Light, too. Adjust the Opacity slider to modify the effect.

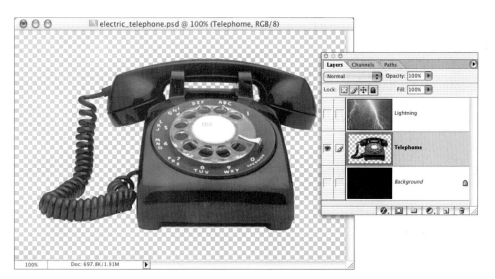

Figure 22.8

The beginning electric telephone image is composed of three layers.

4. You can also add a layer mask to subtly model the telephone. With the Lightning layer targeted, choose Layer → Add Layer Mask → Reveal All.

5. Be sure that the layer mask is targeted. Choose black as a foreground color. Choose the Paintbrush and set its opacity in the Options bar to 20%. Choose a Soft brush from the Brush panel. Paint on the telephone in various places to diminish the effect of the lightning and to enhance the phone's three-dimensionality. If necessary, paint multiple passes to achieve the effect shown in Figure 22.10. Look at the telephone in the color section (Figure C32) to see what happens to your telephone when a bolt of lightning hits a power line!

Figure 22.9

After Option/Alt-clicking between layers, the Lightning layer is shown as a clipping group to the Telephone layer.

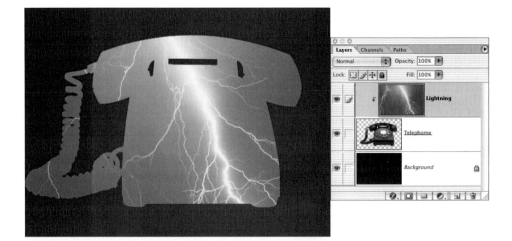

Figure 22.10

The final image altered with a layer mask

Casting Shadows

In Chapter 7, you looked at how to create realistic drop shadows by using Photoshop's built-in layer styles. Cast shadows are a little different. A *drop shadow* is quite simply a gray, semitransparent, soft-edged duplicate of the image from which it is dropped. A *cast shadow* has all the qualities of a drop shadow, except that it is distorted by the direction of light and the terrain on which it rests. Using layers, you can create a very convincing cast shadow and blend it perfectly into its surroundings.

You can see the beginning and end images from the following steps in the color section (see Figures C35 and C36):

1. Open the `black_cat.psd` file in the `Ch22` folder on the CD. The image is composed of two layers named Cat and Background (see Figure 22.11).

2. Duplicate the Cat layer by dragging it to the New Layer icon. Name the layer **Shadow**.

3. Check the Lock Transparent Pixels icon . Choose black as a foreground color and press Option-Delete or Alt-Backspace to fill the contents of the layer with black. Click the Lock Transparent Pixels icon again to deactivate it.

4. Drag the Shadow layer between the Cat layer and the Background layer (see Figure 22.12).

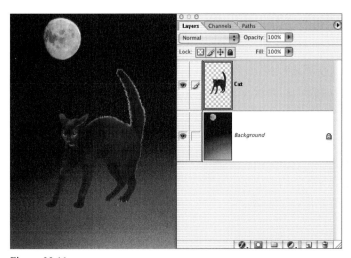

Figure 22.11

The shadowless cat

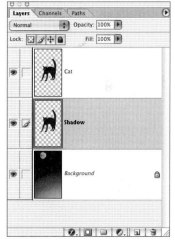

Figure 22.12

The stacking order of the layers in the Layers palette

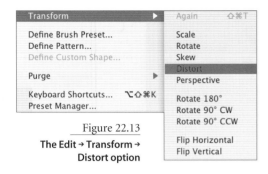

Figure 22.13

The Edit → Transform → Distort option

5. Choose Edit → Transform → Flip Vertical to flip the shadow. Then choose Edit → Transform → Distort (see Figure 22.13). Distort the marquee so that the contents of the Shadow layer appear to lie on the ground, as in Figure 22.14. You might have to play with this a little to get it to look convincing. After you're satisfied, commit your transformation by pressing Return/Enter.

6. Choose Filter → Blur → Gaussian Blur (see Figure 22.15). Drag the slider to 3.3 to soften the edges of the shadow. Click OK.

7. Move the Opacity slider on the Shadow layer to 40% to make it transparent, as you can see in Figure 22.16.

Advanced layer techniques extend your capabilities. These methods empower you to manipulate the image content and keep the editing process dynamic. Learn them and practice them—you'll find them indispensable.

Creating Multiple Versions with Layer Comps

The new Layer Comps palette is used to create multiple versions of a layered document. Designers can use this feature to present multiple comprehensives, or *comps,* to a client. In a sense, it's similar to the History palette but is entirely layers based. Unlike the History palette it is saved along with the document when the file is closed. A layer comp is a snapshot of a state of the Layers palette and records the palette's characteristics including layer visibility, opacity, position in the stacking order, content, and any styles that might be applied to the layers. The advantage of using layer comps is that you can build a document and display multiple versions quickly and efficiently.

To create a layer comp, follow these steps:

1. Choose Window → Layer Comps to reveal the Layer Comps palette (see Figure 22.17).

2. Click the Create New Layer Comp icon at the bottom of the Layer Comps palette. The default comp will be based on the current state of layers in the Layers palette.

3. In the New Layer Comp dialog box, name the comp. You can also add descriptive comments and choose options to apply to the comp. Then click OK.

Figure 22.14

Distort the cast shadow so that it appears to lie on the ground.

If you choose File → Scripts there are three Adobe supplied scripts to automatically save layer comps as PDF or WPG (web photo gallery) files.

Applying and Viewing Layer Comps

You must apply the layer comp to be able to see the comp in the image window.

In the Layer Comps palette, click the Apply Layer Comp icon next to a selected comp. You can apply the previous and next layer comp by clicking on the backward and forward arrows at the bottom of the palette.

You can cycle through all the layer comps by clicking the Next and Previous buttons at the bottom of the palette.

To cycle through a view of specific comps, highlight the comps in the Layer Comps palette by clicking them while pressing the ⌘/Ctrl key. Click the Next and Previous buttons at the bottom of the palette to cycle through only the highlighted comps.

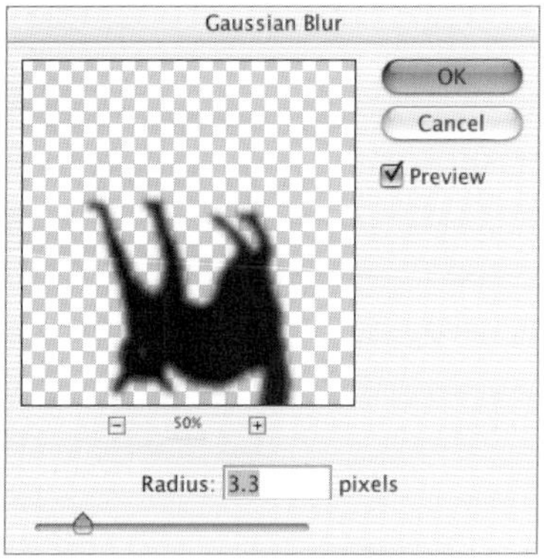

Updating and Restoring Layer Comps

You can save changes to a layer comp by highlighting it in the Layer Comps palette and then clicking the Update Layer Comp icon. This revises the targeted layer comp to reflect the current document.

After you've viewed how the changes affect your document, you can restore the document to its original state. Click the Apply Layer Comp icon next to the Last Document State, or with any layer comp selected, choose Restore Last Document State from the palette menu.

If you delete a layer, merge layers, or convert a layer to a Background, layer comps can no longer be fully restored. A caution icon appears to the right of the comp's name in the palette. You can ignore the warning, which might result in the loss of one or more layers, or you can update the comp. If you click the caution icon, an alert will appear (see Figure 22.18). Choose Clear to remove the alert icon and leave the remaining layers unchanged.

Figure 22.15

The Gaussian Blur dialog box

Figure 22.17

The Layer Comps palette

Figure 22.16

The cat with the cast shadow set to 40% opacity

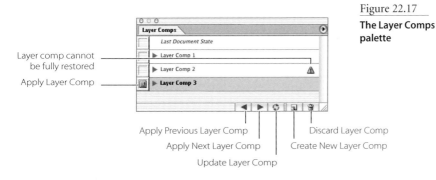

Layer comp cannot be fully restored

Apply Layer Comp

Apply Previous Layer Comp

Apply Next Layer Comp

Update Layer Comp

Discard Layer Comp

Create New Layer Comp

Deleting Layer Comps

To delete a layer comp, select the layer comp in the Layer Comps palette and either drag it to the trash icon, click the trash icon in the palette, or choose Delete Layer Comp from the palette menu.

Figure 22.18

The Layer Comps alert

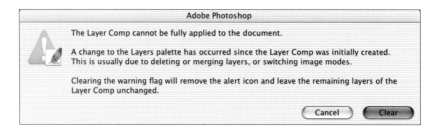

Adobe Photoshop

The Layer Comp cannot be fully applied to the document.

A change to the Layers palette has occurred since the Layer Comp was initially created. This is usually due to deleting or merging layers, or switching image modes.

Clearing the warning flag will remove the alert icon and leave the remaining layers of the Layer Comp unchanged.

Cancel   Clear

Advanced Layers

In this project, you'll try out some of the advanced layer techniques by making layer masks, clipping masks, and a drop shadow, and applying matting to clean up edge pixels. You'll also use layer comps to display three versions of a document.

Getting Started

In the H08 folder on the *Photoshop CS Savvy* CD, open the file `hotel_flamingo_start.psd`. Save the image to your disk. To view the beginning and completed versions of the Hotel Flamingo image, see Figure H8.1 (which is also presented as Figure C57 in the color section) and Figure H8.2 (Figure C58 in the color section).

Discard your preferences file before beginning this Hands On exercise. The "Modifying Photoshop's Settings" section in Chapter 5, "Setting Up Photoshop," details how to temporarily reset your preferences to Photoshop defaults. You can restore your customized personal settings when you're done.

Figure H8.1

The beginning image (left) with its Layers palette (right)

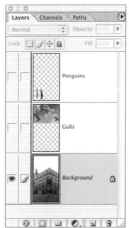

Placing the Parrot in a Window

The image has been divided into two layers and a Background. You'll start by dropping in an image from another document, and creating a layer mask to place the parrot in a window of the hotel:

1. Open the file `mr_parrot.psd` from the H08 folder on the CD.

2. Target the Parrot layer.

3. Choose the Move tool ![move tool icon]. Drag the Parrot layer to the hotel image. Align it on the fourth large window from the left, as seen in Figure H8.3.

4. Reduce the opacity of the Parrot layer to 60% so that you can see the window behind it.

5. Choose Layer → Add Layer Mask → Reveal All.

6. Choose the Brush tool ![brush tool icon] and a 19-point Hard-Edged brush from the Brush menu in the Options bar. Choose black as a foreground color. With the layer mask targeted, carefully paint out the background and portions of the parrot to give the appearance that the parrot is partially inside the window. Restore the opacity to see the result, as in Figure H8.4.

7. Save your work.

Figure H8.3

The parrot aligned on the window

Figure H8.4

With the layer mask targeted, paint out the background to give the appearance that the parrot is partially inside the building.

> Use the Burn tool to darken areas of the parrot closest to the window to heighten the effect.

Placing the Crane in a Window

Next you'll place the crane in a window by using a layer mask, but with a different twist for concealing the background:

1. Open the file `dr_crane.psd` from the H08 folder on the CD. Choose the Move tool. Drag the Background onto the hotel image. Align it on the second large window from the right. Name the layer **Crane**.

2. Choose Edit → Transform → Flip Horizontal.

3. Choose the Magic Wand tool ![magic wand icon]. Set the tolerance to 50. Click the blue areas around the crane to select them.

4. Choose Select → Inverse.

5. Choose Layer → Add Layer Mask → Hide All. The bird disappears, but you can see the selection marquee.

6. In the Tool palette, choose white as the foreground color.

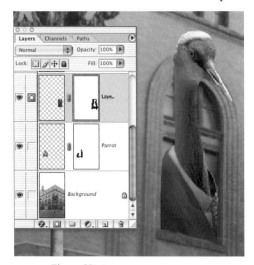

7. Press Option-Delete (Mac) or Alt-Backspace (Win) to fill the selected area on the mask and reveal the bird. Check carefully to be sure that all of the blue field has been removed. If there are any edge pixels showing, erase them with the Eraser tool.

8. Deselect. Reduce the layer's opacity to 60%. Choose the Brush tool and select black as a foreground color; on the layer mask, paint out the lower-right portion of the crane so it appears to be partially in the window, as shown in Figure H8.5. Restore the layer to 100% opacity.

9. To enhance the effect, target the Crane layer thumbnail and pass over it with the Burn tool to darken the bottom edge of the crane.

10. Save your work.

Figure H8.5

The crane in the window and the Layers palette displaying the layer mask

Casting the Penguins' Shadows

In these next steps, you'll make an additional layer and distort its contents to cast a shadow:

1. Target the Penguins layer and make it visible. From the Layers palette menu, choose Duplicate Layer; name the layer **Penguins Shadow**.

2. Drag the Shadow layer beneath the Penguin layer.

3. Check the Lock Transparency icon (see Figure H8.6). Choose black as the foreground color, and press Option-Delete or Alt-Backspace to fill the contents of the layer with black. Uncheck the Lock Transparency icon.

4. Choose Edit → Transform → Distort. Distort the marquee so that the contents of the Shadow layer appear to lie on the ground, as in Figure H8.7. You might have to play with this a little to get it to look convincing. After you're satisfied, press the Return/Enter key.

5. Choose Filter → Blur → Gaussian Blur (see Figure H8.8). Drag the slider to 2.3 to soften the edges of the shadow. Click OK.

6. Change the layer to Multiply Blend mode. Move the Opacity slider on the Shadow layer to 40% to make it semitransparent, so that it rests on the ground texture.

7. Save your work.

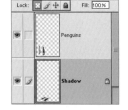

Figure H8.6

Layers palette with Lock Transparency icon

You can use this same shadow technique to create shadows for the flamingo, the parrot, and the crane.

Figure H8.7

Distorting the penguins' shadows

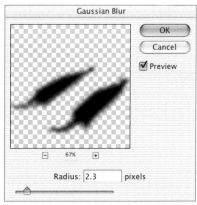

Figure H8.8

Gaussian Blur dialog box

Matting and Placing the Flamingo

Matting removes unwanted pixels that result from selecting and cutting or copying an image from another document or layer. Follow these steps to matte and place the flamingo:

1. Open the file `Flamingo.psd` from the H08 folder on the CD.

2. Choose the Magnetic Lasso tool ⌗. Drag around the edge of the flamingo, as in Figure H8.9, until you've selected it.

3. Choose the Move tool and drag the flamingo onto the hotel image. Name the new layer **Flamingo**.

4. The flamingo is too large, so reduce its size by 50%. Still using the Move tool, check Show Bounding Box in the Options bar. Place your cursor on the upper-left corner of the bounding box, click and drag inward a little bit, and release the mouse. The Options bar now changes to enable you to input numeric values for the transformation (see Figure H8.10).

5. Click the chain icon between the Width and Height fields to constrain the proportion of the flamingo. Enter 50% in the Width field. Click the Commit (check mark) icon on the Options bar to confirm the transformation.

6. Move the flamingo to the second row of windows from the top and align its neck with the eighth window from the left side.

7. Choose Layer → Matting → Defringe to eliminate the edge pixels. Enter **2** pixels in the dialog box and click OK (see Figure H8.11).

Figure H8.9

Selecting the flamingo with the Magnetic Lasso

Figure H8.10

**Width and
Height fields**

Figure H8.11

Defringe dialog box

8. Choose the Eraser tool and erase the bottom part of the flamingo so that it looks as though its neck is sticking out of the window (see Figure H8.12).

9. To enhance the effect, use the Burn tool to darken the bottom part of the flamingo's neck.

10. To further enhance the image, use the cast shadow technique to create a shadow for the flamingo.

11. Save your work.

Using Vector Masks

Vector masks are similar to layer masks in that they are designed to conceal parts of an image. (Read about vector masks in Chapter 9, "Drawing Paths.") Follow these steps to use one to conceal part of a seagull:

1. Open the file Gulls.psd from the H08 folder on the CD.

2. Select the frontmost gull by using the Magnetic Lasso tool. You might have to use the Lasso tool too to refine the selection.

3. With the Move tool, drag the selected gull and drop it on the top corner of the hotel. Name the new layer **VectorGull**. Defringe if necessary.

Figure H8.12

**The flamingo and
the cast shadow**

4. From the Layers menu, choose Add Vector Mask → Reveal All. A vector mask appears next to the VectorGull layer.

5. Choose the Pen tool  . Ensure that the paths and not the shape layer option is selected. Click along the top edge of the building. Encircle the gull to create a triangular path, as in Figure H8.13. The path will conceal the bottom of the gull.

6. After you've drawn the path, choose the Direct Selection tool and make adjustments to the path if necessary.

7. Save the image.

Figure H8.13

Creating the vector mask

Creating a Clipping Mask

The easiest and most flexible method of placing the gulls in the sky is to create a clipping mask with a Sky layer. Follow these steps:

1. Drag the Gulls layer immediately above the Background.

2. Target the Background. Choose the Magic Wand tool and set the tolerance to 50. Click on the white area above the hotel.

3. Choose Layer → New → Layer Via Copy. Name the new layer **Sky**.

4. Place your cursor on the line between the Sky layer and the Gulls layer above it. Press Option/Alt and click your mouse. The Gulls layer is now clipped to the Sky layer, taking its shape.

5. Target the Gulls layer. Choose the Move tool; drag the Gulls layer inside the clip until you are satisfied with its position.

6. Target the Gulls layer. Drop the opacity to 67% to subdue the gulls a little. The image should look like Figure H8.2, shown earlier in the chapter (see the image's Layers palette in Figure H8.14).

7. Save the image.

On the CD, in the MoreBirds subfolder, are additional images to add to the Flamingo Hotel to practice layer mask techniques.

Using Layer Comps

Now you'll make a few changes to the Flamingo Hotel and save the multiple versions as layer comps. Here are the steps:

1. Choose Window → Layer Comps. The Layer Comps palette appears (see Figure H8.15).

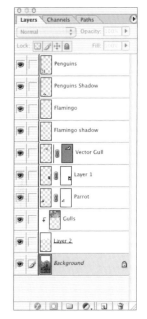

Figure H8.14

The Layers palette of the Flamingo Hotel image

Figure H8.15

The default Layer Comps palette

2. Choose Layers → New → Layer Comp, or click the New Layer Comp icon  at the bottom of the palette. The New Layer Comp dialog box appears (see Figure H8.16).

3. Name the comp **duckless**.

4. In the HO8 folder on the CD, in the MoreBirds subfolder, open the file duck.psd.

5. Select the duck with the Magnetic Lasso tool. Tweak the selection with the Lasso tool.

6. Choose the Move tool. Drag the selection and its contents and place it on the lower-right corner of the Flamingo Hotel image. Name the new layer **duck**.

7. Choose Edit → Transform → Flip Horizontal.

8. Click the New Layer Comp icon and name the comp **duck**.

9. Target the Background. Choose Layer → New Adjustment Layer → Hue Saturation.

10. In the dialog box, adjust the Hue slider to –59 and the Saturation to –79 to shift the hotel's color to a desaturated pink.

11. Click the New Layer Comp icon. Name the layer comp **HueSat**. Your Layer Comps palette should look like Figure H8.17.

12. Click the arrows at the bottom of the Layer Comps palette to cycle through the Layer Comps list. In the image window, the image will change to display the configuration of the layers in each comp.

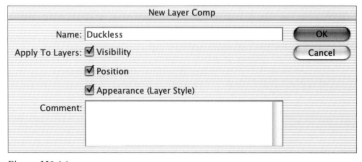

Figure H8.16

Creating a new layer comp

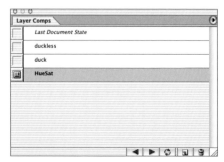

Figure H8.17

The Layer Comps palette with the addition of three new layer comps

Running a Script

A script is a sequence of commands that tell Photoshop to perform a set of specified operations. Scripts can automatically perform repetitive tasks. You will run a script to save your Layer Comps to separate files:

1. Choose File → Scripts → Layer Comps to Files.

2. From the Dialog box (Figure FH8.18) type a name, choose a format, and browse a location for the new documents.

3. As the script is running, the new documents appear on the desktop as separate files, and are then exported to the selected location.

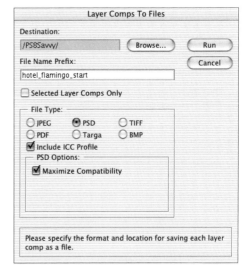

Figure H8.18

Layers Comps to Files dialog box.

CHAPTER 23

Automating the Process

When working in Photoshop, you often repeat tasks. For example, if you publish a lot of work on the Web, you might regularly convert files from PSD to JPEG format. Here's another: Let's say you want to place all of the images in a folder into a single document to make a contact sheet for comparison. Opening, sizing, and pasting the images can be tedious, time-consuming work.

Building a website is a lot of work too. Wouldn't it be nice if there was some way to accomplish this by simply pressing a button? This chapter is about Photoshop's magic buttons called Actions and automations. These operations can greatly accelerate your work flow by automatically performing tedious and repetitious tasks. You can perform most Actions and automations on either single or multiple documents, and you can save them and store them for later use.

You'll learn about these topics:

- ■ **Setting up an Action**

- ■ **Applying Actions to a batch of images**

- ■ **Creating contact sheets, picture packages, and a Web photo gallery**

- ■ **Creating Droplets**

Creating and Applying Actions

When a multimillion-dollar Hollywood movie is produced, everybody involved in the production, including the director, actors, and cinematographer, follows a script. A script is simply written dialog with accompanying directions. Just like the movies, computers also use scripts. Unlike actors, however, computers never ad-lib; they follow the script to the letter! When you record an Action, you are actually writing a script that tells the software what sequence of operations to perform. Fortunately, recording a script for Photoshop is a lot easier than writing a script for a movie.

Almost any single operation or sequence of operations can be recorded into an Action, except for some of the manual tools such as the Airbrush and Paintbrush. You can program an Action to select the Paintbrush, but you can't create an Action to paint with that brush. Likewise, the zoom tools, window commands, and view commands cannot be recorded. The tools from which you can record an Action are the Marquees, Polygon, Lasso, Magic Wand, Crop, Slice, Magic Eraser, Background Eraser, Gradient, Paint Bucket, Type, Shape, Note, Color Sampler, Healing Brush, and Patch. You can record many of the menu commands and you can insert many menu commands that can't be recorded.

Before you record an Action, envision the end product first. Try to imagine what you want the image to look like. Then ask yourself what processes need to be applied to accomplish that end. It's also a good idea to "walk through" and test the steps before recording them.

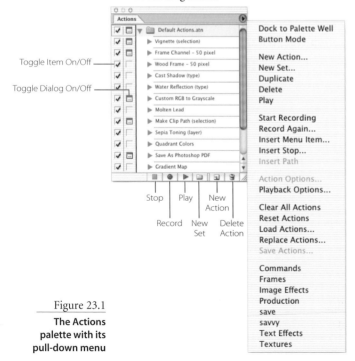

Toggle Item On/Off

Toggle Dialog On/Off

Stop   Play   New
Action

Record   New   Delete
Set   Action

Figure 23.1

The Actions palette with its pull-down menu

As you will see, Actions are flexible. You can create a sequence of Actions and then apply a single Action from the sequence to your image. Or you can apply the same Action with different settings to the image.

Understanding the Actions Palette

Actions are recorded and played in the Actions palette, shown with its pull-down menu in Figure 23.1. Choose Window → Actions to access the palette. When you first open the palette, you see a "set" called Default Actions.atn. A *set* is simply a folder in which groups of Actions are stored. Every Action must be contained within a set.

Expand the Default Actions set by clicking its down arrow. You'll see a list of Actions that Adobe includes with Photoshop. Actions are applied to the image in sequence from top to bottom. When a check mark appears in the Item On/Off box (in the far-left column of the palette) next to an Action or set's name, it will be applied to the image when played. If the item isn't checked, the Action will be skipped. By checking or clearing the Item On/Off boxes, you can determine which Actions will be applied in a sequence. When the Dialog On/Off box (in the second column of the Actions palette) is checked, the Action will pause to display a dialog box so that you can change the settings.

Figure 23.2

The toddler, selected

The pull-down menu provides commands to save, load, duplicate, and create new Actions and sets. Button mode displays a button interface on the Actions palette; in this mode, you simply click an Action's name to run it with the default or existing settings. The bottom section of the Actions pull-down menu provides many additional default Actions. Just click one of these Actions to load it in the Actions palette. Experiment with the default Actions and get to know their capabilities.

> Actions can be nested within other Action sets; you'll notice that the Actions inside the Default Actions set have, in turn, substeps. These are also Actions, but for clarity, I'll refer to these "sub-Actions" as *operations within an Action*.

Applying an Action Step by Step

To see how the Actions palette applies commands to an image, try running one of the Default Actions. In this exercise, you'll create a cameo vignette of an image:

Figure 23.3

The Vignette Action and its operations

1. Open the toddler.psd file in the Ch23 folder on the *Photoshop CS Savvy* CD. Duplicate the file (Image → Duplicate) and save the copy to your disk.

2. Choose the Elliptical Marquee ⬭ . Place your cursor on the center of the image. Click Option (Mac) or Alt (Win), and drag to generate an elliptical selection from a center point (see Figure 23.2).

3. Expand the Default Actions set. Target the Vignette Action and expand it to display the sequence of operations contained within the Action (see Figure 23.3).

4. You will use the default settings, so click each of the Dialog On/Off icons ... in the second column on the left, to turn off each one.

5. Target the Vignette Action and click the triangular Play button ▶ at the bottom of the Actions palette. When the Action has finished running, the image should look like Figure 23.4.

Recording an Action

Of course, you can create your own Actions and apply them to images. You can name, color-code, and specify a function key for an Action so that all you have to do is press the key to apply it. You'll go through making an Action step by step as you perform a tonal adjustment, eliminate moiré patterns, convert, and colorize an image. You'll work on two images cut from an old yearbook. Here are the steps:

Figure 23.4

The Vignette operations applied to the toddler image

1. Open the file Becky_1964.psd from the Ch23 folder on the CD.

2. Choose Window → Actions. From the pull-down menu, choose New Set. Name the set **Yearbook Photos**, as in Figure 23.5.

Figure 23.5

New Set dialog box

3. From the pull-down menu, choose New Action. In the dialog box, name the Action **Becky** (see Figure 23.6). From the Function Key list, choose F2. Click the Record button ● in the dialog box. The record button ● at the bottom of the actions palette turns red to remind you that your next steps will be recorded.

Figure 23.6

New Action dialog box

4. Choose Image → Adjustments → Levels. Drag the Black Shadow slider until the value in the box reads 10. Drag the White Highlight slider to 189 and the Gray Midtone slider to 1.34. Click OK.

5. Choose Filter → Blur → Gaussian Blur, and set the Radius to 1.0 to eliminate the moiré pattern.

6. Choose Filter → Sharpen → Unsharp Mask and set the following values: Amount: 66%, Radius: 3.4 pixels, Threshold: 2 levels.

7. Choose Image → Mode → RGB Color to convert the image so that you can colorize it.

8. Choose Image → Adjustments → Hue/Saturation and check Colorize. Enter 239 for the Hue, 12 for the Saturation, and 0 for the Lightness. Click OK.

9. Click the Stop Recording button ▣ . The Actions palette should look like Figure 23.7, and the image should look like the "after" version in Figure 23.8. You'll use this recorded set throughout this chapter.

Figure 23.7

The Actions palette with the Yearbook Photos Actions set and the Becky Actions

Watch out—you need to exercise caution when recording. Remember that almost anything you do is being recorded. If the image does not appear the way you want it to or if you make a mistake, stop recording, drag the Action or Action Set step to the trash, and rerecord it.

Figure 23.8

The Becky 1964 yearbook image before (left) and after (right) the Yearbook Photos set was applied

Applying Actions to Another Image

Obviously, the main purpose of using Actions is to repeat a command or series of commands. But because the settings often need to be readjusted to achieve good results on a different image, you can stop the Action during the process of applying it. In this exercise, you'll apply the Actions recorded in the preceding section to a second image, which will require that you change some of the settings as the Action is playing.

1. Open `Becky_1965.psd` from the `Ch23` folder on the CD.

2. In the Actions palette, click the Dialog On/Off icons (in the second column) next to Levels, Gaussian Blur, and Unsharp Mask to turn them on, so that the Action will pause and present the operation's dialog box. You can make the necessary changes to accommodate the different image and then continue to run the Action.

3. Target the Becky Action and press Shift-F2. The Play button turns red, and the Action begins to play.

4. As the Action runs, enter new values in the dialog boxes as they appear. Levels: 15 for the shadow and 220 for the highlight; Gaussian Blur: 0.8; Unsharp Mask: 47% for the Amount, 2.9 pixels for the Radius, and 4 levels for the Threshold. Click OK in each box. The new settings are applied, and the Action continues to run. The Convert Mode and Hue/Saturation operations are applied without interruption. The image will look like Figure 23.9.

Inserting a Stop

You can pause any Action in order to perform a task that is not recordable, such as painting a stroke with the Paintbrush. To insert a stop:

1. Select the Action or operation at the end of which you want to insert the stop.

Figure 23.9

The Becky 1965 image, before (left) and after (right) the Becky Actions have been applied

2. Choose Insert Stop from the Actions palette menu.

3. In the dialog box that appears, type a message that reminds you what to do manually (see Figure 23.10). Check the Allow Continue box if you want to display a dialog box that lets you choose to stop or continue. Click OK.

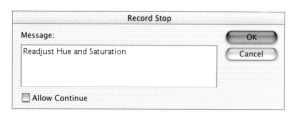

Figure 23.10

Record Stop dialog box

Undoing an Action

Because an Action is a sequence of operations, choosing Edit → Undo or pressing ⌘-Z (Mac) or Ctrl-Z (Win) will undo only the last operation in the sequence, not the entire Action. Instead, press ⌘-Option-Z or Ctrl-Alt-Z as many times as necessary to step backward through the operations. You can also undo a sequence of Actions by clicking the state in the History palette just above the first applied state of the Action.

> As some actions contain many more than 20 steps (the default number of history states), it's a good idea to take a snapshot before running the action.

Saving and Loading an Action

After you've compiled a series of operations into an Action, you'll want to save the Action to your disk. From the Actions palette, choose Save Actions with the Action set targeted. Then choose a destination on the disk. Add the extension `.atn` to the Action's name. (Even Mac users should do this, both to anticipate platform problems and to identify the file as an Action.) To load an Action, choose Load Action from the pull-down menu and locate the file where you saved it.

> Actions must be saved and loaded in sets.

Controlling the Speed of an Action

The Playback Options dialog box (accessed from the Actions palette menu) lets you control how fast an Action is played. Choosing Accelerated plays the Action as quickly as possible (see Figure 23.11). Step By Step waits until the Action is finished and the image redrawn before playing the next Action. Pause For lets you enter a number of seconds between operations within an Action.

Figure 23.11

Playback Options dialog box

Editing, Moving, and Discarding an Action

You can edit the settings of an operation within an Action when it's not running by double-clicking its name in the Actions palette. A document must be open (although you can insert a stop with no document open). The operation's dialog box appears so you can change the settings. The next time you run the Action, the new settings will be applied.

Actions can be repositioned in the stack. An Action's position in the stack can greatly affect the final outcome of the image. To reposition an Action, click and drag it within the Actions palette; release the mouse when it's positioned in the desired location.

To discard an Action, drag it to the trash icon in the Actions palette.

Inserting Unrecordable Commands

Some menu items that cannot be recorded as Actions can be inserted at the end of an Action. To insert a menu item:

1. Target an Action in the Actions palette by clicking it.

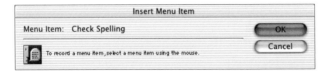

2. Choose Insert Menu Item from the Actions palette menu.

3. With the Insert Menu Item dialog box displayed, choose a command from the menu at the top of the screen.

Image Ready CS now features Conditionals, actions that bring the power of limited logic to choose whether an action step is performed. See Chapter 25.

Using Automation Operations

So far you've applied Actions to images manually. Hmmmm…manual automation? Sounds like an oxymoron, doesn't it? Wouldn't it be really cool if you could apply Actions automatically while you were away from the computer, maybe strolling in the park or dining out? "Why would he mention it if it couldn't be done?" you might be asking yourself right now. Yes, it can be done. And there are several ways to do it.

Batch Processing

You can apply Actions to multiple files within a folder by choosing File → Automate → Batch; the Batch dialog box is shown in Figure 23.12. This formidable-looking interface lets you apply a set, a group of Actions, or a single Action. You can batch-process a group of images within a folder, or from an external source such as a digital camera or scanner with a document feeder. (But note that your scanner or digital camera might need an Acquire plug-in to support batch processing.) You can then automatically save the images within the folder, or save them to new folders, leaving the originals unchanged.

> For better performance when batch-processing images, open the History palette. Turn off Automatically Create First Snapshot. In the General Preferences dialog box, decrease the number of saved History states.

To batch-process a group of images, choose File → Automate → Batch. Under Play, choose the Set and Action that you want to run from the pop-up lists. Then choose your input method from the Source list:

Import applies the images on a scanner or digital camera.

Opened Files plays the Action on open files.

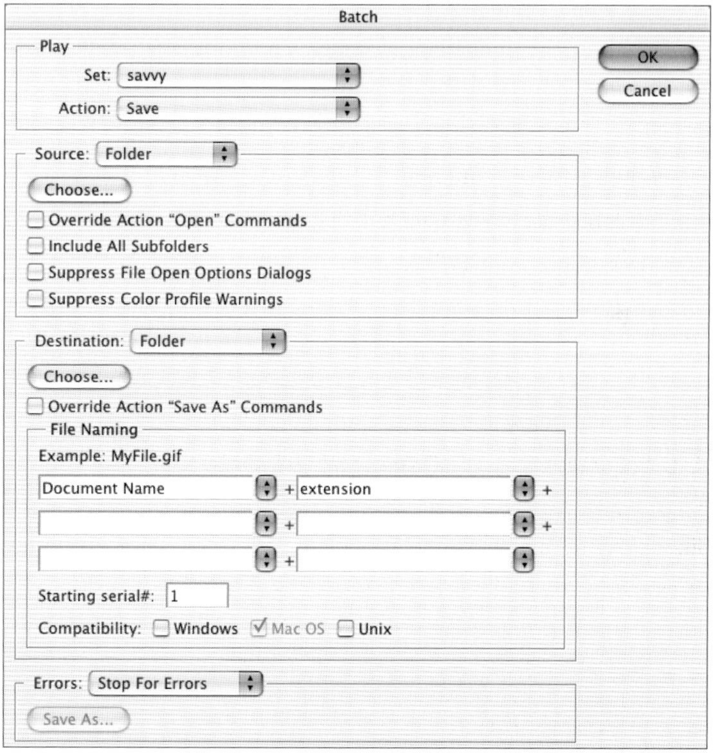

Figure 23.12

The Batch dialog box

Folder runs the Action on all of the images within a selected folder. Click Choose to locate and select the folder, and then select the following check-box options as desired. (You can also apply the Action within the File Browser.)

Override Action "Open" Commands ignores any Open commands that are part of the Action, to ensure that the images are opened from the specified folder. Select this option when you want Open commands in the Action to refer to the batched files, rather than to the filenames specified in the Action. If you enable this option, the Action must contain an Open command because the Batch command will not automatically open the source files.

Include All Subfolders affects the contents of any folders within the selected folder.

Suppress File Open Options Dialogs surpresses the display of the Open dialog box when opening a file.

Suppress Color Profile Warnings turns off the color policy and profile mismatch messages.

For the Destination, choose from these options for the batch-processed files from the Destination pop-up list:

None leaves the files open without saving changes (unless the Action included a Save command).

Save And Close saves the files in the source folder.

Folder lets you specify a new location for the batch-processed files. Click Choose to locate and select the folder, and enable the following check-box option if desired.

Override Action "Save As" Commands ignores any Save As commands that are part of the Action, to ensure that the specified files are saved to the destination folder. Select this option when you want the Save As commands in the Action to refer to the batched files, rather than to the filenames and locations specified in the Action. If you enable this option, the Action must contain a Save As command because the Batch command will not automatically save to the destination file.

The Batch command always saves the files in the same format as the original. To create a batch-processing operation that saves files in a new format, record the Save As or Save A Copy command. Designate a location within the Action, followed by the Close command. In the Batch dialog box, choose None for the Destination.

File Naming

File naming is available if you selected a folder as the destination. You can determine how batch-processed files will be named, as well as their platform compatibility.

Choose from pop-up lists or type into the fields to create file-naming conventions. Determine the naming convention for the document name, identification number or letter, date, and filename extension. The fields let you change the order and formatting of the filenames. For filename Compatibility, choose Windows, Mac OS, and/or Unix.

Error Processing

You can choose an option for error processing from the Errors pop-up list. Stop For Errors pauses the operation until you OK the error message. Log Errors To File records any errors in a separate log file. The error message appears after the process is complete. Click Save As and name the error file.

Creating and Using Droplets

A *Droplet* is a mini application that can play an Action. You can apply a single Action or series of Actions by dragging a file or folder onto the Droplet's icon. This way you don't even have to open the program to apply the Action—the Droplet will automatically do that for you.

The Create Droplet dialog box is quite similar to the Batch dialog box. To create a Droplet from an Action, choose File → Automate → Create Droplet (see Figure 23.13).

Under Save Droplet In, click the Choose button. Determine a location for the Droplet. Choose a Set and an Action from pop-up lists. Set the Play and Destination options for the Droplet as described for the Source and Destination options in the earlier section "Batch Processing".

Using a Droplet to Apply an Action

Now you'll make a Droplet from the Becky Action that you recorded in the previous section, "Recording an Action," and apply it to an image:

1. Choose File → Automate → Create Droplet.

2. In the Create Droplet dialog box, do the following: For the Save Droplet In option, click Choose and choose the Desktop of your computer. For Set, choose Yearbook Photos; for Action, choose Becky.

3. In the Play section, clear the check boxes for Override Action "Open" Commands, Include All Subfolders, and Suppress Color Profile Warnings.

Figure 23.13

**The Create Droplet
dialog box**

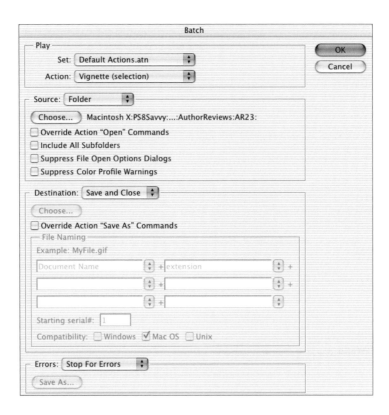

4. For Destination, choose Folder. Click Choose and determine a location for the Droplet's icon.

5. Leave the default filenames, and the Stop For Errors default.

6. Click OK, and the Droplet appears in the specified location.

7. On your desktop, open the Ch23 folder on the CD. Drag the icon of the Vicky.psd image onto the Droplet icon.

8. The adjustments for this photograph will be different from the ones recorded in the Action. As the Levels, Gaussian Blur, and Unsharp Mask dialog boxes appear, make adjustments to improve the image.

9. Open the image in the destination folder to observe the changes to the image. Your image should look better, perhaps something like Figure 23.14.

Using Other Automation Commands

The File → Automate commands are a group of commonly used Actions consolidated into a dialog box. You can configure options that vary the outcome of the image. Some of the Automate commands convert files to other formats or construct files into contact sheets.

PDF Presentation

The new PDF Presentation feature collects images and produces a multiple-page PDF file for presentations. The PDF Presentation dialog box (see Figure 23.15) presents several options for viewing your images—either as a multiple-page PDF or as a slide presentation complete with specific time intervals and a choice of graphic transitions.

To create a PDF presentation, follow these steps:

1. Choose File → Automate → PDF Presentation.

2. Click the Browse button to choose the images that you want to present.

3. If you have any open files on the Photoshop desktop that you want to include, click the Add Open Files check box.

Figure 23.14

Vicky before (left) and after (right) being dragged to the Droplet

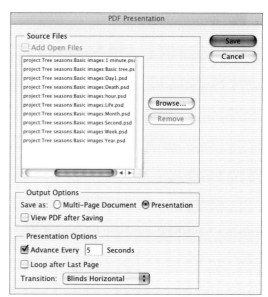

Figure 23.15

The new PDF Presentation dialog box

4. Choose an Output option: either Multi-Page Document or Presentation. You can check View PDF After Saving, which will automatically launch Adobe Reader to display the chosen images.

5. If you choose Presentation, enter an advance interval to determine how long the image stays on-screen.

6. Choose a Transition from the list.

7. Click Save, and choose a location and a name for the file.

8. In the PDF dialog box that appears (see Figure 23.16), enter the specifications for the PDF file. Choose a compression option: ZIP or JPEG. If you choose the JPEG option, then specify a quality.

9. Check the following boxes to determine other characteristics of the PDF file:

Save Transparency saves the transparent part of the image as a mask. If you reopen the PDF file in Photoshop, the transparency will be preserved.

Figure 23.16

The PDF Options dialog box

Image Interpolation enables other programs to interpolate the image when resampling its size and anti-aliases low-resolution images.

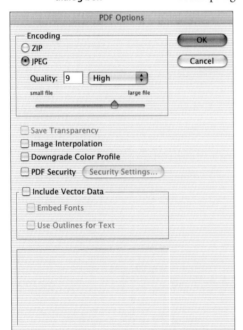

Downgrade Color Profile downgrades the profile to version 2 if you embedded a version 4 color profile when you saved the image. Choose this option if you are opening the file in a program that does not support version 4 profiles.

PDF Security specifies password protection and restricted access for a file. A 40-bit or 128-bit RC4 encryption will produce lower or higher levels of security, respectively.

Include Vector Data embeds vector data such as shapes or fonts to ensure smooth printing.

Embed Fonts attaches the font information to the file so that the fonts are displayed and printed, even on computers that do not have the fonts installed. Faux bold style and warped type cannot be embedded. If you use this option, the file size will increase.

Use Outlines For Text saves text as paths. Use this option if embedding fonts produces too large a file, if you are going to open the file in a program that cannot read PDF files with embedded fonts, or if a font fails to display or print correctly. You are unable to search for or select text saved in this manner.

Crop and Straighten Photos

This new feature automatically crops and straightens images. It will straighten an image that was scanned at an imprecise angle and eliminate its border. It will crop images that have been gang-scanned, and separate and duplicate them into individual documents. For best results the images should be placed on the scanner bed at least one-eighth inch or more apart. The background should be a solid color background, like the scanner's cover.

To use this feature to automatically crop and straighten a single image, follow these steps:

1. Open the file of an image that has been scanned at an imprecise angle.
2. Target the Background or layer that the image is on. Or select the image with a selection tool.
3. Choose File → Automate → Crop and Straighten Photos.
4. The image will be straightened and its border removed. It will be duplicated to a new document.

To try this feature out, open the file `big_city_night.psd` file in the Hands On 5 folder on the CD.

To use Crop and Straighten Photo on multiple images, follow these steps:

1. Open the file of the images that have been gang-scanned.
2. Target the Background or layer that contains the images or make multiple selections.

To try this feature out, open the file `black_rock_city_scan.psd` in the Chapter 23 folder on the CD.

3. Choose File → Automate → Crop and Straighten Photos.
4. The images will be cropped, the border will be removed and the images will be duplicated to separate documents.

Conditional Mode Change

You can change the color mode of a document while in an Action by choosing File → Automate → Conditional Mode Change. Choose the modes that you need changed, or click All to choose any mode. If your Action encounters a file in an unchecked mode, it will leave that file unchanged. Then choose a target mode. Click OK and the document's mode will be converted to the target mode. The

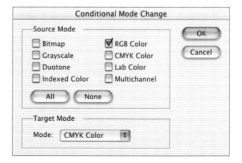

advantage of Conditional Mode Change (over, say, the Image → Mode submenu) is that this command enables your Action to avoid any error messages that occur when an image is required to be in a specific color mode, or is already in the desired mode.

Contact Sheet II

The Contact Sheet II command produces a new document of thumbnail previews on a single sheet from the files in a folder. Choose File → Automate → Contact Sheet II to display the Contact Sheet dialog box (see Figure 23.17). Choose a source folder from which to make the document, and specify a width, height, resolution, and mode for the document. In the Thumbnails section, Place determines whether the sequence of files will be placed horizontally or vertically. Choose the number of columns and rows. Check the box if you want to add the file's name as a caption, but be aware that this will make the images some-what smaller. You can also choose a font and a size for the caption. The preview on the right side of the dialog box displays the layout of the contact sheet.

I've provided a folder of images on the CD so you can try making a contact sheet. Follow these steps:

1. Choose File → Automate → Contact Sheet II.

2. Click Choose. On the CD in the Ch23 folder, click the Contact_Sheet folder; then click Choose.

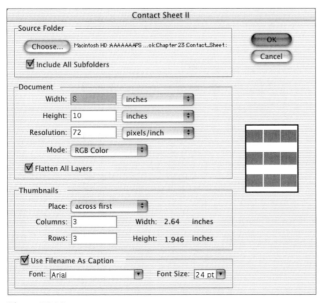

Figure 23.17
The Contact Sheet II dialog box

Figure 23.18
The contact sheet

3. In the Contact Sheet II dialog box, use these settings:

Width	8
Height	10
Resolution	72
Mode	Grayscale
Place	Across first
Columns	3
Rows	3

4. Check the Use Filename As Caption box. For Font, choose Arial; for Font Size, enter 10.

5. Click OK and…wait! This process can take a while. But eventually, an image that looks like Figure 23.18 will appear on-screen.

Fit Image

The Fit Image command will fit an image to a specified width or height without changing its aspect ratio. Keep in mind that this operation resamples the image, changing the amount of data in the image. When entering the Width and Height in pixels, the command chooses the smaller of the two numbers in which to configure the image.

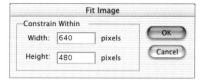

Multi-Page PDF To PSD

Use the Multi-Page PDF To PSD command to convert the pages of an Adobe Acrobat PDF document into separate Photoshop files. Choose the source folder and page range of the PDF file, specify the resolution and color mode of the new Photoshop documents, and choose a destination folder.

Picture Package

The Picture Package command creates a single-page document that has multiple copies of an active image. This feature is used to assemble a sheet of multiple copies of one image, the kind you might receive from a portrait studio, for example. The Picture Package dialog box lets you choose an image from a file, folder, or the frontmost document open in Photoshop (see Figure 23.19). Choose from a list of layout and size options and a resolution and mode for the new document. You can flatten the picture package document by checking the Flatten all layers box. The display on the right of the dialog box shows a preview of the picture package layout.

Figure 23.19

The enhanced Picture Package dialog box

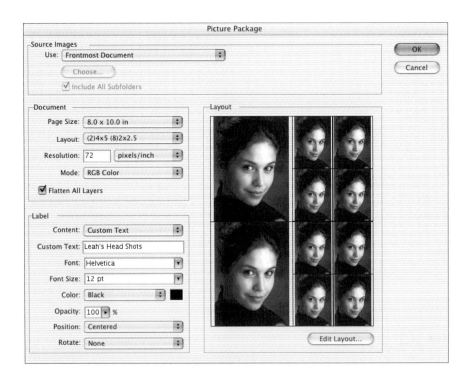

Figure 23.20

The Picture Package Edit Layout dialog box enables you to interactively build a custom layout for your picture package.

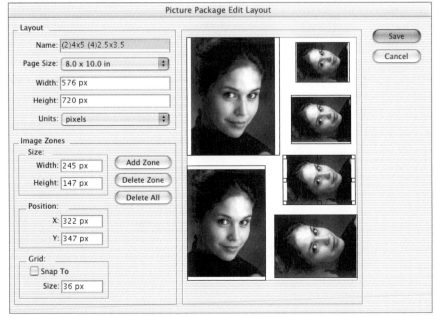

Labeling the picture package has been enhanced to enable you to edit the content font, size, opacity, color, position and orientation of the label.

Click the Edit Layout button to interactively reposition and scale the images in the picture package. The Picture Package Edit Layout dialog box is displayed (see Figure 23.20). The Layout field displays information about the page. The Image Zone field enables you to adjust the size and position of an image or reconfigure the grid of the page. Click Add Zone to add an image to the page. Click an image and click Delete Zone to omit it from the layout. Images can be scaled and repositioned manually. Place the cursor on an image and click and drag to move it or drag the corner of an image to scale it.

Web Photo Gallery

The Web Photo Gallery feature is a quick way to put your images online and offers a number of sophisticated navigational features that simplify Web publication. It automatically creates an HTML document, an index page, individual JPEG image pages, and hyperlinks to your specifications. Photoshop generates the code and the source files and places them in folders that can be uploaded to your FTP site. To create a website, choose File → Automate → Web Photo Gallery. A dialog box is displayed (see Figure 23.21).

Figure 23.21

The Web Photo Gallery dialog box

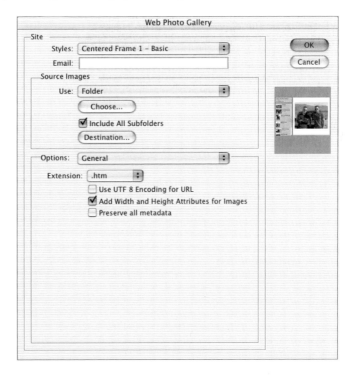

You can choose from these options:

Styles Choose from the new list of WPG templates with several variations of backgrounds and automated slide shows. The graphic on the right of the dialog box displays the layout.

Email This feature generates a mail link in the website with the e-mail address you specify.

Extension Choose from three characters (`.htm`) or four characters (`.html`) as a filename extension on your HTML-coded documents. Three-character extensions are a better bet for displaying your site on older browsers.

Folders Choose a source folder from which the JPEG images will be generated. Select a destination folder for the HTML documents and image folders that are created.

Options When you choose an option from this list, the field changes to display its specifications. Enter the desired configuration for the site's elements:

> **Banner** Specify a site name, photo credit, contact info, and copyright information. Date the site and choose type specifications for the HTML text that is generated.
>
> **Large Images** Choose the size and quality of the large JPEG images. You can also specify a border size and title content.
>
> **Thumbnails** Choose the size, layout, titles, and font usage for the site's thumbnail images.
>
> **Custom Colors** Select the gallery's background, banner, and link colors. Click a swatch and choose a color from the Color Picker.
>
> **Security** Enter labels and copyright information for the gallery images.

Figure 23.22

The 9 images on the desktop that will be stitched together.

Photomerge

The new Photomerge automation stitches together photos for panoramic effects. Choose from a group of open images as in Figure 23.22 or browse files or folders. When you choose File → Automate → Photomerge, the dialog box (Figure 23.23) asks you to choose the images you want to merge. You can also click the Attempt to Automatically Arrange Source Images checkbox. Photomerge will attempt to stitch and blend the images together. Results will vary. If results are not pleasing with the automatic arrangement, you still have full manual control of arranging the separate images. Click OK and the PhotoMerge interface is displayed (Figure 23.24). From the lightbox at the top of the screen, drag the images and place them in the panorama field. The display shows transparency where the images overlap so that you can align them precisely. You can utilize the tools in the tool palette to position and rotate the images or create a common vanishing point. Preview the image by checking the Advanced Blending button and clicking the Preview button. When you click OK, the images will be blended together where they overlap. If you decide to "Keep as Layers", the automated merge is not applied although the arrangement is maintained. You will then have to blend the images by hand. Depending on the photos, additional editing might be required as in Figure 23.25, to seamlessly blend the images together. See Chapter 14 to learn more about the Photomerge automation.

Figure 23.23

The Photomerge dialog box enables you to choose open images, individual files or folders

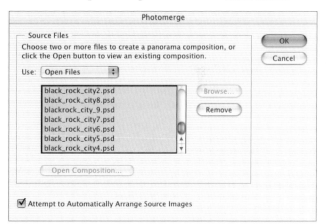

> To try out the new Photomerge feature, open the 9 `black_rock_city.psd` files in the Chapter 23 folder on the CD and stitch them together.

Keyboard Shortcuts

If you want to be a Photoshop power user I suggest you learn to use keyboard shortcuts. They can really speed up your workflow. Default keyboard shortcuts are listed in Appendix D. However, if you want to customize shortcuts, you can access the new Keyboard Shortcuts command. You can change existing shortcuts and create new ones.

To modify existing keyboard shortcuts, follow these steps:

1. Choose Edit → Keyboard Shortcuts. The Keyboard shortcut dialog box appears (Figure 23.26). Choose a set of shortcuts from the Set menu. Photoshop Defaults will be the only item in the list until you create a new set.

Figure 23.24

You can manually
align the images in
the Photomerge
interface.

Figure 23.24

You can manually
align the images in
the Photomerge
interface.

2. In the Shortcuts For: list, choose a type of shortcut. The options available are Application Menus, Palette Menus, or Tools. Clicking any one of these options will display a different list of shortcuts.

3. Choose the command or tool shortcut you want to modify, and a box will appear to the right of the name with the current shortcut displayed. If there is no current shortcut the box will be empty.

Figure 23.25

Often, additional
editing will be
required to seam-
lessly blend the
images together.

4. Type a new shortcut. After you make changes, the name in the Set menu will have (modified) after it.

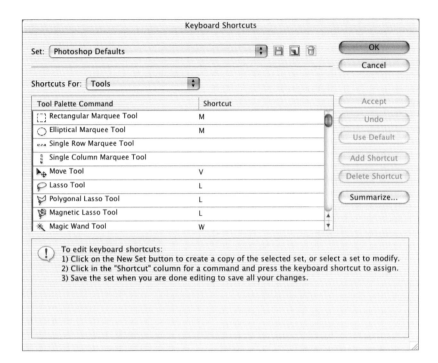

Figure 23.26

**The Keyboard
Shortcut dialog box**

You'll see an alert if the keyboard shortcut is already assigned to another command or tool. The alert tells you which command or tool has the shortcut. To assign the shortcut to the new command or tool click the Accept button. After the shortcut has been reassigned, click Undo Changes to cancel the shortcut, or click Accept and Go to Conflict to select the command or tool that has previously been assigned the shortcut to that you can reassign a new one.

The buttons at the right of the dialog box enable you to discard changes.

- To omit the last saved change click Undo.

- To reset a new shortcut to the default, click Use Default.

- To export the displayed set of shortcuts in an HTML browser, click Summarize.

To create a new set of shortcuts click the New Set icon. In the dialog box that appears, name the shortcuts, choose a destination and click the Save button (see Figure 23.27). You can delete a keyboard shortcut or a shortcut set by selecting its name the list and clicking the Delete Shortcut button.

Figure 23.27

**The Save Shortcut
dialog box**

CHAPTER 24

Overlay Techniques

One of Adobe Photoshop's greatest strengths is its capability to combine images. In Chapters 7 and 22 you became savvy to the potential of compositing with layers and how selected areas can be accurately positioned and superimposed. Images from multiple sources can be collaged together, their transparency can be precisely tuned with layer masks, and their shapes can be altered with clipping masks. You saw in Chapters 6 and 21 that, like layers, alpha channels can also be combined. The process of combining images from multiple sources takes many forms and is one of Photoshop's most useful features. In this chapter, you're going to look at industrial-strength image compositing.

You will learn about the following:

- **Superimposing images to enhance their quality**
- **Creating artistic effects by applying images**
- **Using calculations to combine complex selections**

Layer-Based Compositing

Imagine that you have two transparencies on a light table, one on top of the other. When you look at them through a magnifying loupe, you see the effect of combined colors on the two superimposed images. Opposite colors (for example, reds and greens) might cancel each other and produce areas of dark gray, and colors that are closer to each other on the color wheel (for example, reds and yellows) might produce richer, more saturated oranges.

Now imagine that you have duplicates of the *same* transparency on the light table, and you are able to "sandwich in" filters that produce a variety of color relations between the two superimposed images. In Photoshop, these are the *blending modes,* and you apply them to an image in the Layers palette. The blending modes, which are described in Appendix C and illustrated in the color section, can be used to enhance color on an image. When you superimpose one layer on another, you can apply a layer effect to alter the color relationships and then precisely control the result by adjusting the opacity of the layer.

To demonstrate this effect, follow these steps:

1. Open the file `Rinocerose.psd` from the `Ch24` folder on the *Photoshop CS Savvy* CD. Figure 24.1 shows before and after versions of the image. (See color versions, C53 and C54, in the color section.) The original image on the left is divided into two layers. It lacks rich colors and appears flat.

2. Hide the Rose layer by clicking the visibility indicator [image] next to it in the first column of the Layers palette. Target the Rose layer.

Figure 24.1

The original image (left) lacks rich colors and appears flat. Stacking layers with similar content and applying a blending mode and opacity and fill adjustments can greatly enhance an image's contrast and color (right).

3. Choose the Magnetic Lasso  and drag it around the rhinoceros. The Magnetic Lasso will most likely not make a perfect selection, so you'll need to add to and subtract from the selection with the Lasso tool or the Quick Mask .

4. Choose Layer → New → Layer Via Copy to copy the rhino to a new layer. Name the new layer **Rhino**.

5. Target the new layer and choose Linear Light from the Mode list. The layer looks more saturated but a little too "contrasty."

6. Drag the Fill slider to 65% to diminish the contrast. Drag the Opacity slider to 88% to bring out a little more detail in the shadow areas.

7. You'll now enhance the rose. Click the Rose layer's visibility indicator again.

8. Drag the Rose layer to the New Layer icon to duplicate it. Name the layer **Vivid Rose** and drag it to the top of the layer stack.

9. Choose Vivid Light from the Mode list, and reduce the fill to 55% to enhance the detail.

The image now appears much richer. The colors in the targeted areas are more saturated and have better contrast. Experiment with creating additional layers and applying different blend modes at varying degrees of opacity to vary the effect.

Excluding Colors

Use Photoshop's Layer Style dialog box (see Figure 24.2) to exclude colors in the image. Advanced Blending excludes targeted information in a specific channel. With the exclusion sliders, you can omit colors of a specific brightness value.

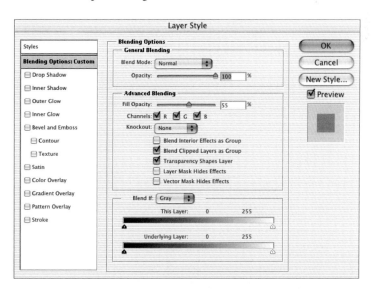

Figure 24.2

The Advanced Blending controls in the Layer Style dialog box

To demonstrate how these sliders work, follow these steps:

1. Open the file Heavenly_Roses.psd from the Ch24 folder on the CD (see Figure 24.3).

2. The image is divided into a layer and a Background. Double-click the Rose Layer icon, to display the Layer Style dialog box.

3. First, clear all of the Channels check boxes. The image of the roses disappears. Now check the red (R) box only. The channel information from the Red channel appears and affects the underlying layer. The Red channel appears to contain most of the detail of the red rose.

> If you were to look at the information for the Rose layer in the Channels palette, you would see that the Red channel contains most of the detail of the red rose and more pixels with higher brightness values.

4. Check the green box and uncheck the red and blue boxes. Notice that there is more detail on the green rose when the green box is checked. The same is true for the blue rose.

5. Check all of the boxes to display the roses in full color.

Figure 24.3

The Heavenly Roses image

You will now use the exclusion sliders to omit pixels of a specific brightness value within each channel:

1. Make sure Blend If is set to Gray.

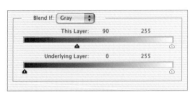

2. Move the black This Layer slider to the right until the shadow value reads 90, as in Figure 24.4. The darker pixels in the roses disappear.

3. Press Option (Mac) or Alt (Win) and click the Cancel button. It changes to the Reset button. In the Blend If list, choose Red. Move the black This Layer slider to the right until it reads 90. The dark pixels on the green and blue roses disappear, but almost all of the pixels on the red layer remain.

Figure 24.4

Setting the channel options to Gray and the This Layer black exclusion slider to 90

4. Press the Option/Alt key and click Reset. Now move the white slider to the left, until the highlight value reads 96. The red rose almost completely disappears.

If you use exclusion sliders to omit pixels of a specific brightness range from the layer, you force colors to disappear. This can produce harsh color transitions and jagged edges. You can diminish the effect by adjusting the Fuzziness setting, which softens the transition. Here's how: Press Option/Alt and click Reset. This time, press the Option/Alt key as you drag the *left half* of the white slider to the left. The effect on the red rose produces a softer edge, as in Figure 24.5.

Channel-Based Compositing

Adobe once counted channel-based compositing among Photoshop's most powerful features. The extensive layer compositing techniques introduced in recent versions of Photoshop have made this capability redundant. It still, however, enables you to apply additional modes that, even in Photoshop CS, have not been added to the Layers palette. Photoshop's two channel-based compositing techniques are the Apply Image command and the Calculations command.

Figure 24.5

You can achieve softer transitions by pressing the Option or Alt key while dragging half of a slider.

Apply Image

The Apply Image command applies a source image to the target image. To use Apply Image, both images have to be open on the desktop. The images must be exactly the same physical size and resolution.

First, look at the Apply Image dialog box (see Figure 24.6) to understand its commands. To access it, choose Image → Apply Image.

You can set these options in the dialog box:

Source This is the image that is applied, or overlaid. Choose the desired image from the pop-up list.

Layer The pop-up lists all of the layers and the Background in the source image. You can overlay all the layers if you choose Merged.

Channel Select the channels you apply to the image from this list. If you choose the composite channel (RGB, CMYK, and so forth), the entire channel will be mixed.

Invert Check this box to invert the contents of the selected channel. Pixels that are black will be applied as if they were white, and vice versa.

Target This is the image that is active. The target lists the channel(s) and layers that the image will be applied to.

Blending The pop-up list displays the blending modes in which the color will be applied (see Appendix C, "Blending Modes," for a description of each mode).

Opacity Enter the opacity of the mode.

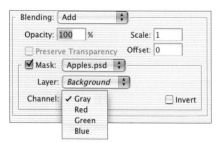

Preserve Transparency This check box leaves transparent areas on a layer unaffected.

Mask Checking this option masks off a part of the source image. When you choose Mask, the Apply Image dialog box expands. From the lists, choose an image and a layer. Choose a color channel, an alpha channel, or an active selection on the source image to isolate the application of the effect.

Scale and Offset If you choose either the Add or Subtract modes, you can enter values for scale and offset. These values are used in the calculation to determine the brightness values of the superimposed pixels. (See Appendix C.)

The Apply Image command can produce some beautiful artistic effects. You can vary the results by choosing different settings. In this example, you'll start with a sepia watercolor, and then apply a broadly painted version of the image and mitigate the effect by adjusting the blending modes and the opacity.

Figure 24.6

You can use the Apply Image dialog box for channel-based compositing.

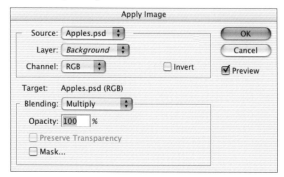

1. Open the `Apples.psd` file in the `Ch24` folder on the CD (see Figure 24.7). For this exercise, refer to the full-color versions of this image included in the color section (Figures C39a–e).

2. Choose Image → Duplicate to make a copy of the image. Name the new image **Paint**.

Figure 24.7

Use this sepia-toned watercolor to experiment with the Apply Image command.

3. With the painting tools, color the image with broad strokes as in Figure C39b.

4. Click the `Apples.psd` image to make it active.

> The image that is active will become the target image.

5. Choose Image → Apply Image. Enter the following and then click OK:

Source	Paint Image
Layer	Background
Channel	RGB
Blending	Subtract
Opacity	50%

6. Try different combinations of modes, channels, and opacities to produce vastly different results.

Overlaying Graphics

Apply Image can also be used to produce interesting overlay graphic effects. In Chapter 17, "Modifying and Mapping Color," you created a posterization and a halftone from the same image. You can combine these two types of images to produce a strong posterized halftone effect. You can vary the effect by applying different values, modes, and opacities. Follow these steps:

1. Open the images `Listerine_poster.psd` and `Listerine_halftone.psd` from the `Ch24` folder on the CD.

2. Click on `Listerine_halftone.psd` to activate it. Choose Image → Mode → Grayscale to convert the bitmapped image to a grayscale.

   Channel-based compositing techniques do not work on Bitmap images. It is therefore necessary to convert their mode.

3. Click `Listerine_poster.psd` to activate it. It will be the target document.

4. Choose Image → Apply Image. Enter the following specifications and click OK:

Source	`Listerine_halftone.psd`
Layer	Background
Channel	Gray
Blending	Add
Opacity	40%

   The halftone image is applied to the target. (Figure 24.8 shows the before and after results.)

5. Try different combinations of modes, channels, and opacities to produce different results.

Figure 24.8

The posterized image (a), the halftone (b), and the halftone superimposed on the posterized image by using the Apply Image feature (c)

(a) (b) (c)

Calculations

Despite the complexity of its dialog box, the Calculations command performs a rather simple operation—it creates only one channel. Image → Calculations works exclusively to combine two source channels into a new channel. Like the Apply Image command, it calculates the numerical values of pixels and applies a mode or mathematical formula to produce results. The difference is that it uses the information on individual channels to produce a new selection, a new alpha channel, or a new document. The Calculations command has three purposes: to create a new grayscale image, or to combine two masks into either a single alpha channel or an active selection.

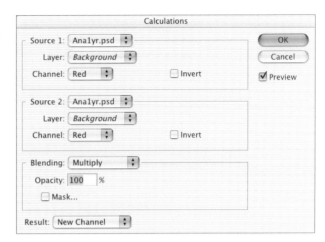

Figure 24.9

The Calculations dialog box

Like Apply Image, this command requires the images to be exactly the same height, width, and resolution. When you choose Image → Calculations, you see the Calculations dialog box (see Figure 24.9). It's quite similar to the Apply Image dialog box; the only difference is the additional source. The two source areas let you choose two channels to combine.

Here you'll combine a couple of alpha channels to see how the Calculations command works:

1. From the Ch24 folder on the CD, open the document Cowpoke.psd (see Figure 24.10).

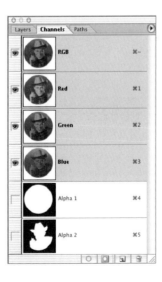

Figure 24.10

The cowpoke image and its Channels palette

2. Look at the Channels palette. Alpha 1 is a channel of the circle surrounding the cowboy; Alpha 2 is the outline of the cowboy. You are going to combine the two channels into a third.

3. Choose Image → Calculations. Enter the following:

Source 1	Cowpoke.psd
Channel	Alpha 1
Source 2	Cowpoke.psd
Channel	Alpha 2
Blending	Difference
Result	New Channel

4. Click OK, and Photoshop creates the Alpha 3 channel, which combines Alpha 1 and Alpha 2 (see Figure 24.11).

5. You can also use the Calculations command to blend channels from two source documents and create a new grayscale document. Open the file Cowboy_Sky.psd from the Ch24 folder on the CD. Then click Cowpoke.psd to reactivate it.

Figure 24.11

The new combined alpha channel

6. Choose Image → Calculations. Enter the following:

Source 1	Cowpoke.psd
Channel	Gray
Source 2	Cowboy_Sky.psd
Channel	Blue
Blending	Darken
Result	New Document

7. Click OK. A new document is created, combining the composite Gray channel of the Cowpoke.psd document and the Blue channel from the Cowboy_Sky.psd document (see Figure 24.12).

The Calculations feature is complex, to say the least, and as always there are several workarounds that perform the same operations. Mastering it, however, gives you the skills you need to quickly combine channels, and that can extend your selection-making capabilities.

Figure 24.12

This image was created by using Calculations to combine the Gray channel of the cowpoke with the Blue channel of the cowboy sky.

PART IV

Photoshop, WWW, and DV

As you've seen, *Photoshop is versatile at producing images for print media. It is the tool of choice for preparing files for CMYK conversion and for output to any printing device. Photoshop's versatility extends further into the world of electronic publications such as websites. Photoshop, in combination with its Web-authoring sibling ImageReady, can help you produce killer interactive websites with animations and rollovers. Furthermore, Photoshop is a great program for preparing files for output to digital video nonlinear editing systems such as Adobe Premier. The three chapters in Part IV will cover how you can use Photoshop for publishing images to the Web and with digital video.*

CHAPTER 25

Web Design with Photoshop and ImageReady

The Web is the world's most recent and dynamic publishing phenomenon. It gives you instant access to an enormous amount of information and entertainment. The Web is like having at your fingertips a several-million-volume encyclopedia that is revised hourly with the latest information. In addition to being able to access information, you can also publish your ideas and images instantaneously on the Web. Photoshop has many features that enable you to efficiently publish images to the Web.

Adobe, recognizing the need for streamlined, Web-specific software, bundles ImageReady with Photoshop to provide powerful tools to the Web designer. ImageReady can help you create images and animations and generate HTML code for browser-ready websites. ImageReady is fairly easy to learn because, in many respects, it closely resembles Photoshop. In fact, the two programs share many of the same capabilities.

This chapter will cover the cool Web-related stuff that Photoshop and ImageReady can do. It will take you through several step-by-step processes so that you can begin creating and optimizing images and animations for the Web.

This chapter will include these topics:

- **Creating Web page elements**
- **Optimizing images**
- **Slicing graphics**
- **Working with transparency**
- **Web-safe color and Web formats**

Web Features in Photoshop

Photoshop supports numerous image formats, which makes it ideal for importing scans and graphics from sources such as Photo CDs, digital cameras, and video captures. After you edit an image, you can easily save it or export it to a Web-compatible image format such as JPEG, GIF, or PNG. You can take advantage of the unique characteristics of each format including file size, progressive rendering, transparency, and compression.

Photoshop's user-friendly Layers palette is ideal for separating portions of an image so that they can remain editable throughout the creative process. This empowers designers to lay out entire websites within Photoshop and then use the elements created on the layers. The original files remain intact and can be modified as necessary. The Layers palette is also quite useful for creating and organizing simple animation sequences. These layer stacks are saved and reopened in Adobe ImageReady and have the capability of generating animated images.

ImageReady

When you open ImageReady, your first observation might very well be that it looks a lot like Photoshop, and indeed it performs in much the same way. It contains many of the same tools, filters, commands, and palettes as its bigger, older sibling. ImageReady's strength is its capability to prepare files for the Web, a capability it shares, in part, with Photoshop's Save For Web option. However, it also provides the additional capability of creating rollovers, image maps, and animations.

The primary difference is that in place of the extensive printing features of Photoshop, ImageReady has numerous powerful operations for Web file preparation. Instead of print-specific adjustments, color settings, and gamut tools, there are (among others) the Image Map tool, default browser preview, and the Slice, Rollover, Image Map, Animation, and Optimize palettes. Another major difference is Photoshop's capability to save a document to many different formats, including those that support printing and desktop publishing, video, and the Web. ImageReady, on the other hand, is designed to save optimized files exclusively to Web formats—GIF, JPEG, PNG, WBMP—and the Photoshop format, PSD.

> If you use the Export Original command, you can save in BMP, PCX, TGA, TIF, PICT, and PXR formats, and you can save an animation as a QuickTime movie.

ImageReady's Object-Based User Interface

ImageReady CS has made some significant changes to the user interface that aren't immediately apparent when you first fire up the program. The program is "friendlier"; it now works a lot more like simple print programs you might have used to create birthday cards and calendars. Multiple elements can be easily grouped together and aligned. Elements will snap into alignment with each other.

Let's see how it works by creating a simple button graphic:

1. In ImageReady, create a new document. Set the width to **250** pixels, set the height to **125** pixels, and name the document **Button**.

2. Select the Rectangle tool. From the Options bar, select Create A New Shape Layer. From the Style drop-down list, choose Green Gel.

3. Carefully drag from the upper-left corner to the lower-right corner. The cursor snaps to the edges of the canvas, making it easier for you to fill it exactly. Press F to enter Full Screen mode if the window borders are getting in your way.

4. Select the Text tool and choose a simple font. I've chosen Arial Black at a size of 48 px. Set the type color to white. Click the image with the Text tool and type the word **PUSH**. Don't worry about the positioning. Press ⌘/Ctrl+Enter to finish entering text.

5. With the Text tool still active, change the font size to 24 px, or half of your original font size. Click the image, away from the existing text, to create a new text element, and type the words **TO ENTER**. Don't worry about aligning the text just yet.

6. If the Layers palette is not open, open it now by choosing Window → Layers. You have four layers: the original Background, the green button shape, and the two text layers. In the Layers palette, ⌘-click (Mac) or Ctrl-click (Win) on both of the Type layers. ImageReady CS enables you to select multiple layers this way. You can also select multiple items by Shift-clicking on them in the canvas. You can drag these layers onto the Create A New Layer or Delete Layer buttons at the bottom of the Layers palette to duplicate or delete multiple layers, respectively.

7. With the text layers both selected, press ⌘/Ctrl+G. This groups the two layers, placing them together in a new layer group, called Group 1. To ungroup elements, select the group and press Shift+⌘/Ctrl+G. Groups can be nested—that is, you can have groups of groups of groups—up to five layers deep.

8. Double-click the name of Group 1 and rename it **Type** (see Figure 25.1).

9. With the Type group still selected in the Layers palette, choose the Move tool. When the Move tool is active, a number of alignment tools become available on the Options bar, enabling you to align and distribute layer elements at the push of a button (see Figure 25.2).

Figure 25.1

The text layers are grouped together.

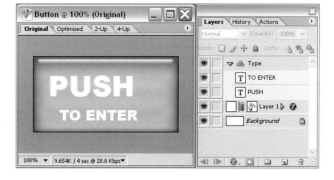

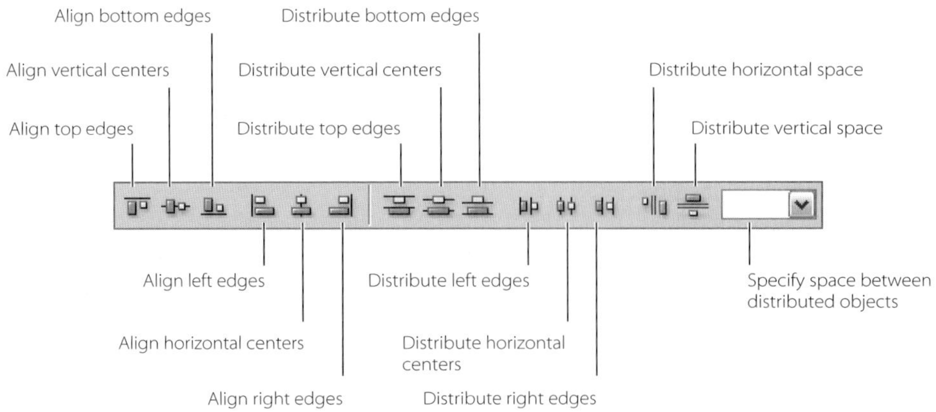

Align bottom edges   Distribute bottom edges

Align vertical centers   Distribute vertical centers   Distribute horizontal space

Align top edges   Distribute top edges   Distribute vertical space

Figure 25.2

These alignment options are available with the Move tool.

Align left edges   Distribute left edges   Specify space between distributed objects

Align horizontal centers   Distribute horizontal centers

Align right edges   Distribute right edges

10. On the Options bar, press the Align Layers Vertical Centers button and then press the Align Layers Horizontal Centers button. This centers the Type group within the button, but you'll notice it doesn't center the type within that group (see Figure 25.3). To align the text elements with each other, you must work within the group.

11. On the Layers palette, select the layer containing the text *TO ENTER*. With the Move tool active, click and drag the text *TO ENTER* within the image. (ImageReady "ghosts" the text as you move it.) Notice that, as it lines up with the left or right edge of the *PRESS* text, or when two layers' centers are aligned, ImageReady displays a thin blue line (a Smart Guide) to show you that the elements are in alignment (see Figure 25.4). A line also appears between the two text elements if they butt up against each other as you move them. Move the *TO ENTER* text so that its center lines up with the center of the *PRESS* text above. Leave some vertical space between the words.

12. Select the Type group in the Layers palette, and press the Align Layers Vertical Centers button and then the Align Layers Horizontal Centers button on the Move Options bar. Now everything is properly centered within the button.

Figure 25.3

Centering a group does not center individual layers within that group.

Figure 25.4

Smart Guides appear when elements are aligned with each other.

Designing Page Elements

Follow the exercises in this chapter to become accustomed to designing for the Web by using Photoshop and ImageReady. In this section, you'll build a few types of Web graphics.

Creating a Margin-Style Background in Photoshop

A margin-style background is a common visual element that helps unify the design of a Web page. It serves as a visual compass because it fills the entire vertical depth of the document no matter how tall it might be. Furthermore, a margin can help establish the ordered division of information by separating the background into vertical blocks. It is also a perfect way to infuse the page with interest and character by adding a splash of color or texture.

A margin background is simply a pattern that is configured so that the image repeats vertically but not horizontally. Because all Web backgrounds tile from the upper-left corner into the available space, you have to ensure that you create a strip long enough so that the tile doesn't appear to repeat along the horizontal axis.

To create a margin-style background:

1. Choose File → New.

2. Name the file **Margin**.

   Don't worry about the gif, jpg, or png extension at this point. Because the default Saving Files preferences is Append File Extension, Photoshop will automatically add the extension when the document is saved.

3. Enter a width of **1070** pixels and a height of **60** pixels (see Figure 25.5).

   The width of 1070 pixels in this image ensures that the image will not repeat at monitor resolutions of 1024×768 or lower. However, at higher resolutions, you run the risk of the image repeating. For this reason, some Web designers prefer to set their margin background widths to 1280.

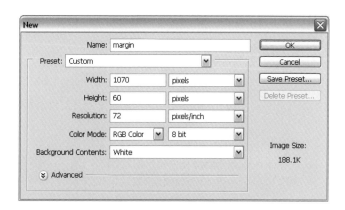

Figure 25.5

Choosing margin-style background settings in the New dialog box

4. Set the resolution to **72** pixels per inch.

5. Choose RGB Color for the mode.

6. For Background Contents, choose White. Ignore the Advanced button for now.

7. Click OK.

Now, fill a portion of the file with color:

1. Click the Rectangular Marquee tool to display its settings in the Options bar.

2. Choose Fixed Size from the Style list; enter **108 px** for the width and **60 px** for the height, as shown in Figure 25.6.

3. Click the image in the upper-left corner of the document.

4. Open the document `margin_texture.psd` from the `Ch25` folder on the *Photoshop CS Savvy* CD.

5. Choose Select → Select All. Choose Edit → Copy.

6. Click on the margin document title bar or choose Window → margin_texture.psd. With the Rectangular Marquee still active, choose Edit → Paste Into.

7. From the Swatches palette list, choose Web Safe Colors (see Figure 25.7). Click a light color to choose it.

8. In the Layers palette, target the Background.

9. Press Option-Delete (Mac) or Alt-Delete (Win) to fill the marquee with the foreground color.

You can now choose what to do with the file:

- Save the file in native Photoshop format, layers intact, for future use or modification in Photoshop (always recommended).

- Save it for the Web in GIF, JPEG, or PNG format (see "Saving for the Web" later in this chapter).

- Import the file into ImageReady for processing.

- After the file is optimized, load it into your HTML editor as part of your Web page. When the image is loaded as a background, it will repeat vertically as a pattern and appear to be a continuous design down the depth of the page (see Figure 25.8).

- When you open the Web page in the browser, it appears as a seamless margin, as in Figure 25.9.

Figure 25.6

Choosing the marquee size

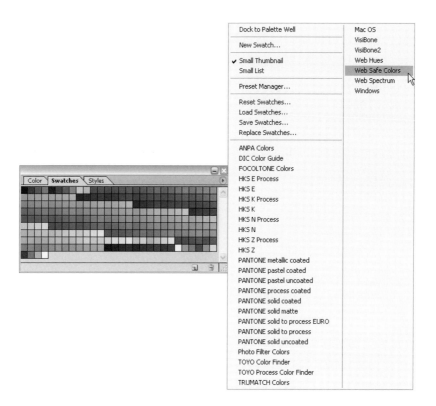

Figure 25.7

Choosing a color from the Swatches palette

CHOOSING A WEB-COMPATIBLE COLOR

There are three ways to choose colors that are Web-compatible:

- Choose Window → Swatches. From the pull-down list in the upper-right corner of the palette, choose Web Hues, Web Safe Colors, Visibone, or Web Spectrum. Any of these color palettes displays the 216 Web-safe colors; the palettes consist of the same colors organized differently. If you hover your cursor over any color in the palette, its hexadecimal name will be displayed.

- You can click the foreground color in the Tool palette to reveal the Color Picker and check the Only Web Colors box. Move the slider on the color bar to scroll through the hexadecimal hues and then pick a color from the color field.

- Choose Window → Color. From the pull-down list in the upper-right corner of the Color palette, choose Web Color Sliders. Drag the sliders to pick a color.

Creating a Seamless Background in Photoshop

Figure 25.8

The margin-style background as a Photoshop document

An alternative to the margin-style background is a background-repeating tile, also referred to as *wallpaper*. In most cases, you will want the pattern to be subtle so as not to compete with the information that floats on top of it.

Wallpaper patterns were the first wave of background graphics. You've probably seen lots of them, in all kinds of styles. They can be problematic for a number of reasons: if they're too dark or busy, for example, they interfere with the readability of images and hypertext. They're also demanding on the designer—making them completely by hand takes a bit of skill.

If you design them properly, however, seamless backgrounds can create an extremely attractive look for your site. The following are some general guidelines to use when creating tiles:

- Individual tiles should be at least 50 pixels by 50 pixels.

- Do *not* interlace background graphics.

- Use light colors so that images and text will float on the background.

Figure 25.9

The margin-style background as it repeats vertically in the browser

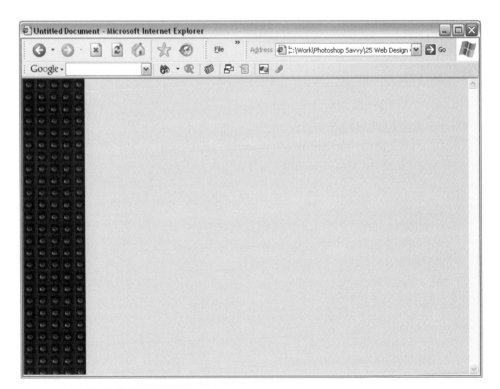

Follow along to create a tile by using Photoshop:

1. Open the file `Web_Clouds.psd` from the `Ch25` folder on the CD.

2. Display the Layers palette. Choose Layer → New → Layer From Background.

3. Name the new layer **Clouds 1**.

4. Drag the Clouds 1 layer to the New Layer icon to create a new duplicate layer. Name the layer **Clouds 2**. Repeat the process two more times, naming the additional layers **Clouds 3** and **Clouds 4**.

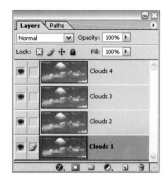

5. Choose Image → Canvas Size, and increase the width and height of the canvas to **200**% (see Figure 25.10). Anchor the image in the upper-left corner of the canvas. Don't worry about the Canvas Extension Color. Click OK.

6. Target the Clouds 2 layer. Choose the Move tool and drag the layer to the upper-right of the document.

7. Choose Edit → Transform → Flip Horizontal.

8. Target the Clouds 3 layer. Choose the Move tool and drag the layer to the lower-left of the document.

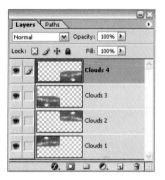

9. Choose Edit → Transform → Flip Vertical.

10. Target the Clouds 4 layer. Choose the Move tool and drag the layer to the lower-right of the document.

11. Choose Edit → Transform → Flip Vertical, and then Edit → Transform → Flip Horizontal.

Figure 25.10

Canvas Size dialog box

12. Zoom in close to the document to ensure that the layers butt up against each other and that there is no space between them. If there is, choose the Move tool and nudge them into place with the arrow keys. The image should look like Figure 25.11.

13. From the Layer Options pull-down list, choose Merge Visible.

14. Move the Opacity slider to 50%.

15. Save the document as a JPEG by using the Save For Web feature. (See the section titled "Saving for the Web" later in this chapter.) When displayed on the browser, the background should look like Figure 25.12.

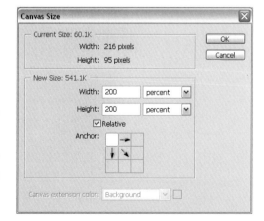

Using ImageReady's Tile Maker

ImageReady has a built-in tile maker that can help smooth out some problems that you might encounter when creating continuous, or seamless, background images. One such problem is that if each tile's edge is slightly different, those edges will show where the tile repeats. The effect is somewhat disturbing!

To correct or avoid this problem:

1. If Photoshop is running, click the Edit In icon 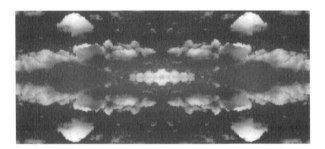 in the Tool palette to open ImageReady. Open the file `Tile.psd`.

2. Select Filter → Other → Tile Maker. The Tile Maker dialog box appears (see Figure 25.13).

Figure 25.11

The seamless background tile

Figure 25.12

The seamless background on a browser

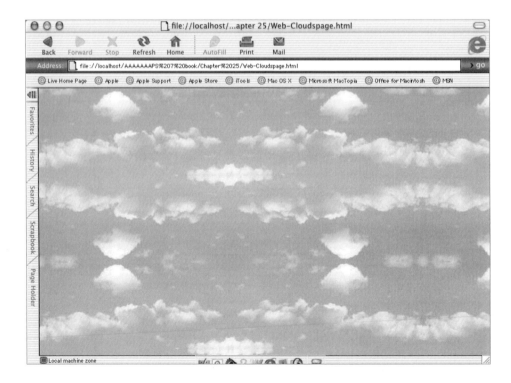

3. Click the Blend Edges radio button. You can select the amount of pixels for blending; I've left it at the default of 10%. I've also left the Resize Tile To Fill Image option checked. This expands the file where necessary to make the blending as seamless as possible.

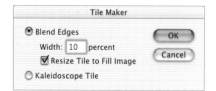

4. Click OK.

5. Optimize and save your file.

Figure 25.13

The Tile Maker dialog box

You can now view your file within an HTML page or import it into GoLive to begin designing your page. The result is a smoother, more attractive background (see Figure 25.14).

Creating Kaleidoscopic Tiles in ImageReady

While working to make your background tile seamless, you might have noticed the Kaleidoscope Tile option in the Tile Maker dialog box. This is a neat background effect with endless design possibilities.

To create a kaleidoscopic background:

1. Open or create an image. You can start with the textured tile developed in the previous section.

2. Choose Filter → Other → Tile Maker. When the Tile Maker dialog box appears, click the Kaleidoscope Tile option.

3. Click OK to create your tile (see Figure 25.15).

4. After you are done with the kaleidoscope effect, you can blend the edges of the tile. Select the Tile Maker filter again and blend the edges of the image for smooth results (see Figure 25.16).

Figure 25.14

The original image (left), and the image after the Tile Maker has been applied (right)

Figure 25.15

A kaleidoscopic tile

You can use a wide range of effects and source images before applying the kaleidoscope effect.

Choosing Web File Formats

Images need to be saved in one of several formats in order to be read by browsers. JPEG, GIF, PNG formats, and their variations are briefly described here. Look in Appendix B, "File Formats," for more detailed descriptions.

JPEG (Joint Photographic Experts Group)

JPEG is a lossy compression format. It supports 24-bit color and is used to preserve the tonal variations in photographs. JPEG compresses file size by selectively discarding data. A higher-quality setting results in less data being discarded. Low JPEG settings result in blocky areas within the image and a profusion of artifacts, or blotchy spots. JPEG compression can degrade sharp detail in images and is not recommended for images with type or solid areas of color. See Figure 25.17 for a comparison of JPEG settings.

Each time you save the file as a JPEG, you discard more data. To avoid progressive deterioration, you should save JPEG files from the original image, not from a previously saved JPEG.

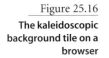

Figure 25.16

The kaleidoscopic background tile on a browser

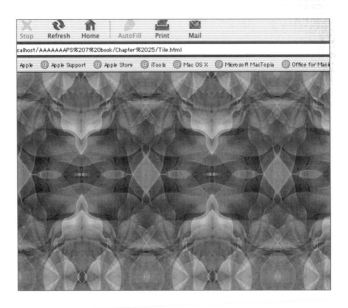

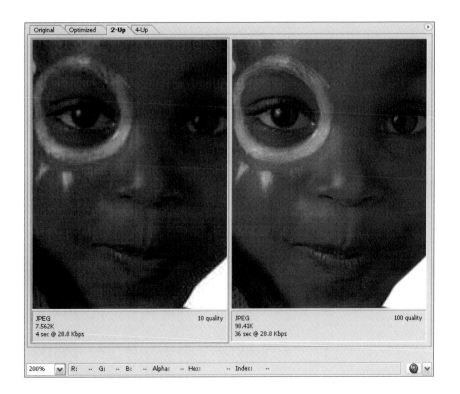

Figure 25.17

JPEG compression-quality comparisons: (left) Low and (right) Maximum

If you use the JPEG Options dialog box (File → Save As → JPEG) to save an image, you can specify characteristics of the JPEG (see Figure 25.18).

The JPEG format does not support transparency. When you save an image as a JPEG, transparency is replaced by the *matte* color. Use the background color of the Web page as the matte color to simulate transparency. Choose from the Matte list to select a color for the background of an image that is on a transparent layer. The color will fill the areas where there are transparent pixels when the image is seen on the browser. If your image is going to be displayed over a pattern or multiple colors, save it as a transparent GIF.

In the Image Options section, enter a quality value from 0 to 10, or choose Low, Medium, High, or Maximum from the pull-down list.

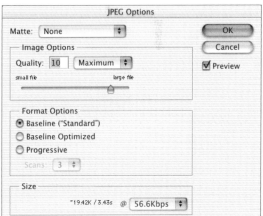

Figure 25.18

JPEG Options dialog box

Choose a format option by clicking the radio buttons:

Baseline ("Standard") This is the most widely supported format. It displays the image only after it has completely downloaded.

Baseline Optimized produces slightly smaller files than Baseline, but is not as widely supported. It displays the image from top to bottom as it downloads.

Progressive enables you to specify 3, 4, or 5 scans. These have the effect of displaying progressively higher-resolution versions of the image as it is downloading. Use this option to hold your viewer's attention while the image loads. Progressive is not as widely supported as Baseline.

In the Size section, the number on the left of the slash is the file size. The number on the right is the download rate, which you can determine by choosing a modem baud rate from the pull-down list.

GIF (Graphics Interchange Format)

The GIF format is used primarily for saving images with solid areas of color and sharp edges—for example, line art, logos, or illustrations with type. It is also the format for saving animations produced in ImageReady.

Unlike JPEG, the GIF format uses lossless compression. Yet because GIF files are 256 colors or fewer, optimizing an original 24-bit image as an 8-bit GIF can degrade the image. You can create lossy GIFs, which produce much smaller files but sometimes produce artifacts similar to those found in JPEG images. You can control the number of colors in a GIF image and adjust the dithering options to simulate the effect of blending.

You can save a file as a GIF in two ways. Choose File → Save As → CompuServe GIF to bring up the Indexed Color dialog box, where you can optimize the image. (See "Exporting to GIF" later in this chapter.) The second method is by using the Save For Web option.

PNG-8 and PNG-24 (Portable Network Graphics)

The PNG-8 format is similar to GIF 8-bit color. It uses 256 colors, supports transparency, and is lossless, but is not supported by older browsers, and doesn't support animation. PNG-24 is an excellent format because it combines the attributes of JPEG and GIF in lossless compression. It supports 24-bit color and is fine for saving photographs to the Web because it preserves tonality. Like GIF, PNG-24 preserves the sharp detail found in line art, logos, and type. It also supports transparency and matting.

Another great feature of the PNG-24 format is that it supports *multilevel* transparency, in which you can preserve up to 256 levels of transparency to blend the edges of an image smoothly into a background color. This seems like the dream format, doesn't it? The only (minor) drawback is that versions of the major browsers from 1999 and earlier don't support it, and it takes a while before the latest browsers are used by the majority of Web users. Take this into consideration when deciding to use the PNG formats.

Saving for the Web

Using Photoshop's Save for Web interface allows you to optimize your images for the best combination of size and appearance and save a copy, without altering your original image. In this section you'll learn how to optimize your images and save Web-ready copies in either Indexed or RGB color, as GIF, JPEG, or PNG format.

The Save For Web feature is a *subinterface.* It contains numerous options for saving files to Web formats, and can compare the effects of different settings on up to four images at once. Figure 25.19 shows the Save For Web dialog box. It behaves very much like a plug-in application, with full features contained within the dialog box itself.

The Save For Web dialog box contains the following tab options:

Original shows the image in its original state.

Optimized shows the image with whatever Web optimization features you select.

2-Up displays the original image next to the optimized image, or two optimized images side-by-side.

4-Up provides a look at the original image and three possible optimization results, or at four possible optimization results.

OPTIMIZING YOUR IMAGES

When it comes to optimizing Web graphics with Photoshop, you have several options. First, you can use the built-in Save For Web feature, which many Web designers opt to do; this has the advantage of preserving your original art and graphics. You can also choose to optimize in ImageReady, which provides the same capabilities as the Save For Web dialog, but in real-time, in the working environment. Another choice is to optimize 'by hand' in Photoshop, changing the original image's color mode to indexed then saving as CompuServe GIF (GIF86a) or PNG.

Ultimately Save For Web and ImageReady give you the most choices, the best previews, and the best information. Using the Save For Web feature or employing ImageReady puts some excellent power tools into your hands. Without them, you have to rely on testing and experience in order to make the best decisions.

The Preview list is accessible from the small arrow on the right of the image window. It has several options, including the capability to simulate what a graphic looks like on different computers. This feature enables you to make cross-platform decisions about your Web graphics. It also displays several baud rates (see Figure 25.20). Choose one to determine the amount of time your image will take to download. The value is displayed below the image window.

The right side of the Save For Web dialog box (see Figure 25.21) offers numerous file format and color controls:

Preset This option provides a pop-up list of preconfigured settings for saving images as GIFs, JPEGs, and PNGs.

Optimized File Format This option provides a pop-up list of possible file formats, including GIF, JPEG, PNG, and WBMP (for wireless Web surfers on mobile phones).

Color Reduction Algorithm This option is available for GIFs. In most cases, you'll want to select Web.

Figure 25.19

The Save For Web dialog "subinterface"

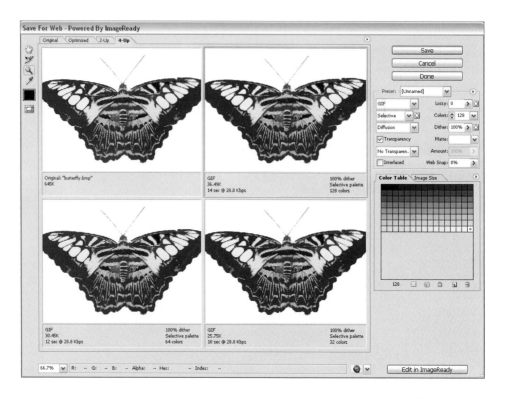

Dithering Algorithm Standard dithering options are provided for the GIF format. Work with these to see which gives you the best results.

Lossy This option enables you to create lossy GIFs. You'll sacrifice quality but you will reduce the file size.

Colors This pop-up list enables you to specify the exact number of colors you'd like to include in your image.

Transparency This option produces transparency if you are saving the image as a GIF or PNG image and the image is on a transparent layer.

Dither If you select a dithering algorithm, this slider enables you to precisely control the amount of dithering that occurs in the image.

Transparency Dither Algorithm This option allows you to choose between different methods for dithering partially transparent pixels. Try them all to see which gives you the best results for a particular image.

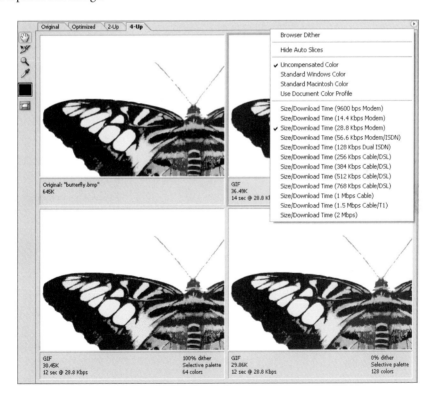

Figure 25.20

Baud rates

Figure 25.21

Options in the Save for Web sub-interface.

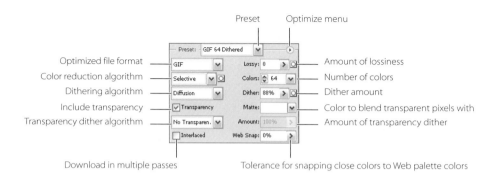

Transparency Dither Amount If you select a transparency dithering algorithm, this slider enables you to precisely control the amount of transparency dithering that occurs in the image.

Web Snap If you are using a color palette other than the 216 Web-safe colors, this slider enables you to adjust the number of colors that snap to the Web palette.

Interlaced Select this option if you want your image to be rendered progressively.

Color Table The color table enables you to see the exact colors being used in the optimized image when using PNG-8 and GIF images. Colors with dots in the center are Web-safe colors. The arrow to the right above the color table displays a list that enables you to select, sort, lock, shift, save, and load colors.

Image Size This palette enables you to change the physical dimensions of the image you are saving.

The annotations under the image(s) denote the format type, file size, download time on a selected modem, plus the various characteristics of a selected group of settings. Click the arrow at the top of the tabbed display to choose additional options for the display and annotations.

When working with the Save For Web dialog box, remember that the variations you apply to an image do not influence your original image. Instead, the image is saved as a new file. You can save your choices by using the Save Settings feature if you like the way that a particular combination of options worked for you.

I like to use the 4-Up option to display as many options at once as possible, so I can compare settings and results. The goal is to get the perfect balance of good-looking graphics and a low file weight.

Now let's go through the by-hand optimization process so you can effectively optimize your graphics to retain their good looks yet weigh little for fast load times. I'll use the same graphic, once with a solid background and once preserving transparency, but you can use the general process defined here to optimize any of your GIF and JPEG images.

Using Indexed Color

When you save an image, you can reduce the number of saved colors, and thus reduce its file size, by changing its color mode from RGB to Indexed. Converting the file to Indexed color substantially reduces the number of colors in the document. By reducing the number of colors, you reduce the image's file size. However … converting an RGB image to a Indexed image throws away much of the image information. It's better to save an optimized copy of your image using Save For Web, while keeping your original art intact.

See the practice steps in "Exporting to GIF," next, to learn how to save an image in Indexed mode.

> If the image you're working with naturally lends itself to transparency, you can save the image as a transparent GIF in the Save For Web dialog box. Images containing transparency need to be on layers surrounded by a transparent area. Because Indexed color does not support layers, check the Transparency box in order to maintain the transparency when the image is finally saved as a GIF.

Exporting to GIF

GIF (Graphics Interchange Format, or CompuServe GIF) is a common format used to optimize and export graphic files to the Web..

In this section, you'll save an image to GIF format by using Save For Web:

Figure 25.22

The Image Size palette

1. Open the `mallard.psd` file in the `Ch25` folder on the CD.

2. Choose File → Save For Web (see Figure 25.23). Click the 4-Up tab. The dialog box displays the original image in the upper-left and three additional images.

3. Click the upper-right image to select it. You will configure this image first.

4. There are a whole slew of optimization options available, letting you fine-tune everything from number of colors to the transparency dithering algorithm (see Figure 25.21). Choose GIF 64 Dithered from the Presets. This sets the file format to GIF, the color reduction algorithm to Selective, the dither algorithm to Diffusion, and so on. You can change any of these to suit. Change the color reduction algorithm to Adaptive. While the Selective algorithm creates a color palette which favors the colors your eye is most sensitive to, Adaptive creates a color palette favoring the colors appearing in the image.

5. Notice that reducing the number of colors to 64 hasn't changed the quality of the image significantly. Try different numbers of colors by scrolling down the Colors list, or typing a number in. Try different color reduction algorithms as well.

6. Dithering blends the areas of color together and helps the image look less posterized. Change the Dither amount to 0% to see the difference. The size of the resulting file is shown in the preview pane. Try numbers of colors with different dithering options to achieve the best possible image with the fewest number of colors.

Figure 25.23

Save For Web with the GIF option selected, displaying the color table

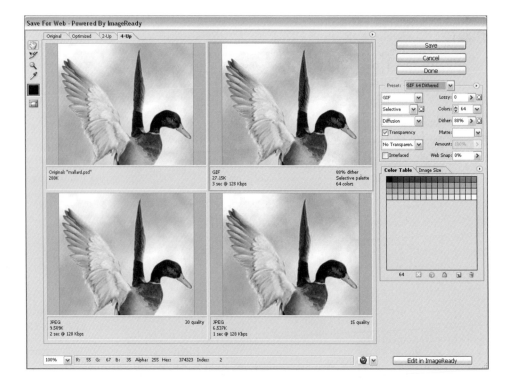

7. Click the other images and try different settings to compare the results.

8. Select the best image and click Save. The Save Optimized As dialog box appears. From the Save as Type list, you can choose to save the image only, the image plus an HTML page which references it (HTML and Images), or just the HTML page (HTML Only). Choose Images Only. Make sure Default Settings is selected and click Save to save your optimized file.

> Dithering increases a GIF file's size, so there is a trade-off between keeping the file small and preserving image appearance.

Saving the Image as an HTML File

1. In Photoshop, select the `mallard.psd` file and choose File → Save For Web. Your settings from the previous save will now be the default, displayed in the upper right preview pane.

2. Click Save to open the Save Optimize dialog box. Choose HTML and Images from the Save as Type list.

3. Choose Other from the Settings list.

When you saved your file in the last section, you used the Default Settings. But there are a wealth of options hidden in the Settings list. Most of these only apply when you are saving an HTML file.

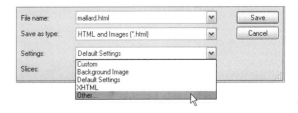

These appear in the list in the least intuitive order, so let's take them in a slightly different order.

- **Default Settings** uses Photoshop's default settings. More on these later.

- **Background image** the HTML file will use the saved image as a background for the Web page, rather than simply placing it in the Web page, as shown in Figure 25.24.

- **XHTML** Ensures that the HTML file contains XHTML-valid text.

- **Other** allows you to customize any aspect of the output settings from slice naming to copyright inclusion.

- **Custom** uses any changes you made to the default settings.

Let's explore customizing the output settings.

1. In Photoshop, select the `mallard.psd` file and choose File → Save For Web. Your settings from the previous save will now be the default, displayed in the upper right preview pane.

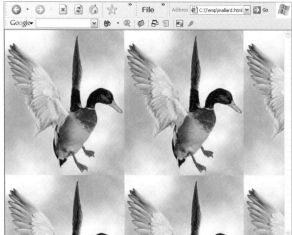

Figure 25.24

Gif image and HTML saved using Default Settings (left) and a Gif image and HTML saved using Background Image (right).

2. Click Save to open the Save Optimize dialog box. Choose HTML and Images from the Save as Type list.

3. Choose Other from the Settings list. The Output Settings dialog box is displayed (see Figure 25.25).

You can set options in four categories: HTML, Slices, Background, and Saving Files.

These options configure the preferences for files saved for publication to the Web. Choose a category from the pop-up list immediately below the Settings list.

HTML

Choose from these HTML formatting options:

Output XHTML Specifies that the HTML file will contain XHTML valid text.

Tags Case Selects the case for HTML tags: uppercase, initial cap, or all lowercase.

Attributes Case Selects the tag attribute case: uppercase, initial cap, second initial cap, or all lowercase.

Indent Determines a means for code indention: use the authoring software's default tab settings, a specific number of spaces, or no indention.

Line Endings Selects a platform for line-ending compatibility: Mac, Windows, or Unix.

Encoding Specifies a default character encoding for the Web page.

Use one of these options to embed comments into the HTML code:

Include Comments Embeds ImageReady comments in the HTML code.

Always Quote Attributes Places quotation marks around all tag attributes. This option is necessary for compatibility with some early browsers. It is not recommended to always quote attributes. Quotation marks are used when necessary to comply with most browsers, even if this option is deselected.

Always Add Alt Attributes Generates HTML with blank attributes when attributes are not specified.

Close All Tags Generates close tags for all elements.

Include Zero Margins on Body Tag The body tag code includes attributes to produce zero margins.

> The Load and Save buttons enable you to load and save custom output settings.

Slices

You can set HTML naming conventions for slices by entering text or choosing from the list items. This will configure the code to specific or universal browser compatibility. Choose from the following slice output options:

Generate Table Aligns sliced images in an HTML table.

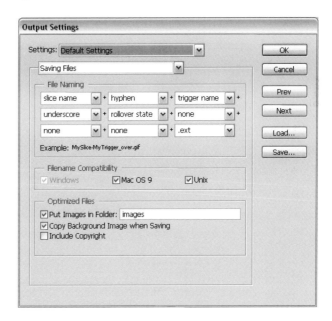

Figure 25.25

The Output Settings dialog box

Empty Cells Indicates how to fill empty table data cells (slices without content):

- Select GIF, IMG W&H to use a 1-pixel spacer GIF with width and height in the IMG tag.
- Select GIF, TD W&H to use a 1-pixel spacer GIF with width and height in the TD tag.
- Select NoWrap, TD W&H to code a nonstandard NoWrap attribute on the table data and place width and height in the TD tags.

TD W&H Determines when to place width and height attributes for table data: Always, Never, or Auto (recommended).

Spacer Cells Indicates when to place a row and a column of empty spacers around the table: Always, Never, or Auto (recommended). Spacer cells align slice boundaries in tables where slice borders do not line up to prevent the table from breaking apart in some browsers.

Generate CSS Creates cascading style sheets for slices.

Referenced Refers to how the cascading style sheet will be referenced in the HTML code: by ID, inline, or by class.

Default Slice Naming Determines naming conventions for slices.

Background

To designate the characteristics of a background, choose the Background preference category. You can specify the following configurations:

View Document As To designate the current image as a background, choose Background. To designate a background to be used with the current image, click Image. Specify the location path in the path field.

Background Image Identifies an image to display as the Web page's background.

Color Specifies the actual solid color that will be displayed while the image is downloading, and through transparent areas in the image.

Saving Files

Choose from these file-saving options:

File Naming Choose items from lists, enter values, or test for saving Web images. Items include preferences for saving the document's name, slice name if the image has been cut into slices, rollover state if the image contains a rollover created in ImageReady, file creation date, slice number, punctuation, and file extension. You can reconfigure the file-names, for example, using a different abbreviation to name the file.

Filename Compatibility Select one or more options to make the filename compatible with Windows, Macintosh, and Unix platforms.

For optimized files, choose from these options:

Put Images in Folder Consolidates sliced images into a separate folder when saving (not the folder with the HTML document). This folder is called Images by default, or you can rename it.

Copy Background Image when Saving Check this box to preserve the background settings of an image that is being used as a background.

Include Copyright Check this box to include copyright information with the image. You add copyright information for an image in the Image Info dialog box.

> These options can be set in ImageReady by choosing File → Save Optimized or File → Save Optimized As → Settings → Other.

Optimizing Images in ImageReady

Optimizing images in ImageReady is very similar to using the Save For Web feature in Photoshop. ImageReady's optimization capabilities include the following:

Live Preview Whenever you are working on a file in ImageReady, you can automatically see changes based on file type and optimization choices (see Figure 25.26).

Choice of File Types ImageReady supports GIF, JPEG, PNG, WBMP, and PSD. Depending upon the file and your needs, you can adjust accordingly.

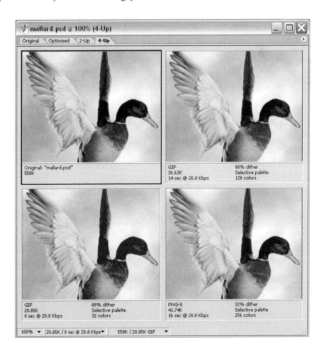

Figure 25.26

ImageReady's live preview enables you to see changes in a file as you make them. The Optimize palette enables you to format the image to your chosen specifications.

User-Level Control

Although you don't really need a working knowledge of optimization to use ImageReady, you will no doubt be empowered by understanding the basic rules of thumb when it comes to optimization:

- Use GIFs when working with line art, flat color, few colors, or with animations. Cartoons and text usually work best as GIFs.

- Use JPEGs for photographs and for art with many colors, shadows, or light gradations.

- PNGs are useful for broad application, but they are not supported by older browsers.

- SWFs are good for all kinds of animation, but they require a special browser plug-in and are not supported by older browsers.

Working with GIFs in ImageReady

The Optimize palette displays options for saving images as GIFs, JPEGs, or PNGs.

1. In ImageReady, open the file mallard.psd in the Ch25 folder on the CD.

2. Click the 4-Up tab to display four versions of the image. Click the top-right image. Choose Window → Optimized to display the Optimize palette.

Figure 25.27

The original mallard is at the upper left at 558 KB. The second image, at the upper right, displays the 128-color GIF at 36.63 KB. The image at the lower left is a 32-color GIF and is only 20.85 KB, and at the lower right is a 256-color PNG-8 with a file size of 41.74 KB.

3. Choose GIF 128 Dithered from the Presets. Compare the optimized version to the original. The original's size is approximately 558 KB, compared to the optimized version of about 36 KB (see Figure 25.27). In this particular image, there is no great variation in quality, but the file size has been substantially reduced.

4. Click on of the lower images. Choose GIF 64 Dithered from the Presets and reduce the number of colors to 2. Typically, this will be too few colors for most images, but it's a good idea to get a feel for how the image would look at the lowest possible file size of under 3 KB.

5. On the fourth image, bring the color number to 32, which gives you a great look but even better compression at about 30 KB than you had at the auto setting.

6. Choose File → Save Optimized As to save the GIF.

You can now make additional selections for your GIF, such as interlacing or transparency, by using the Optimize palette settings. Interlacing enables the GIF image to appear progressively on the page, and transparency is discussed later, in the "Matting" section.

Preparing JPEGs in ImageReady

For photographs and any image with significant amounts of gradations in light or shadow, JPEG is the file format of choice for the best look and compression. You can optimize an image as a JPEG to produce the best results for your photographs.

Follow these steps to prepare a JPEG in ImageReady:

1. In ImageReady, open the file Liberty.psd in the Ch25 folder on the CD.

GETTING INFORMATION ABOUT FILE SIZES

Information about the file size of your images is available in the Save For Web option in Photoshop or the image window in ImageReady. You can display different information in each of these windows:

- Select one of the tabs in the image window. Choose one of the options: Original, Optimized, 2-Up, or 4-Up. I like to set this option to 2-Up, which gives a comparison between the original file size and current file specifications.

- In Photoshop, the information is at the bottom of each image. By clicking the arrow at the upper-right of the window, you can choose a baud rate at which to recalculate the information.

- In ImageReady, choose information from the arrows at the bottom of the list. The first arrow indicates the size in which you are viewing the image. The second two arrows offer additional information, including the image's type, file size, and the possible speeds at which it will be downloaded.

2. When the file is open, go to the Optimize palette and choose JPEG from the File Format pull-down list.

3. Click the 2-Up tab on the image.

4. View the image by using Maximum, Very High, High, Medium, and Low JPEG settings in the Optimize palette. Try to find the setting that gives you the best quality and compression without causing artifacts on the image (see Figure 25.28).

   You can make further, custom adjustments by using the Quality slider bar. For example, if the quality at the Medium setting (30) is fine, but the Low setting (10) is showing artifacts, try moving the slider to a setting of 20 and seeing how the image's look and size add up.

Figure 25.28

The extremes of JPEG settings. Notice the deterioration and artifacts in the image on the right, which is set to JPEG Low to produce a file size of only 12.85 KB, but at the expense of image quality.

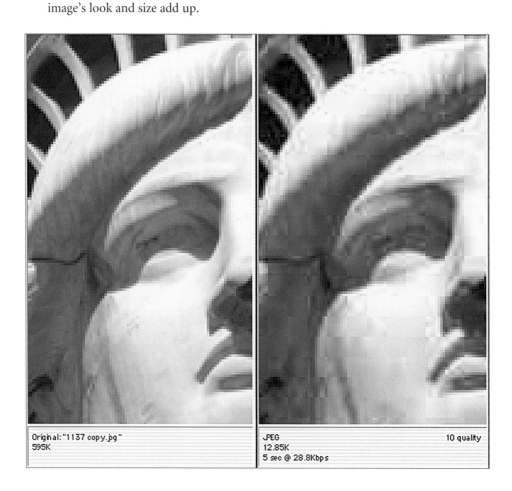

Original:"1137 copy.jpg"
595K

JPEG   10 quality
12.85K
5 sec @ 28.8Kbps

5. Choose File → Save Optimized. Name your file. The Format pop-up list provides the following options:

    HTML Only saves an HTML file with the images written into the code.

    HTML And Images saves an HTML file with the images written into the code and a separate folder of the image or slices.

    Images Only saves only the image or slices.

6. Choose HTML And Images to create a document and files that are Web-ready. ImageReady will generate the image in a separate folder as well as the HTML file. You can now view your HTML file in the browser of your choice.

These kinds of decisions are the heart and soul of image optimization for the Web. It's always a balance of good looks and quick load times, and always based within the context of the page with which you are working.

> To progressively render a JPEG, check the Progressive box. This enables supporting browsers to display the image incrementally.

Creating a Transparency Mask in Photoshop

If you'd like an image to appear seamless against a patterned or solid background, you need to either make an image transparent or matte the image on the background color. This technique is especially important to use whenever your image isn't a rectangle.

The streamlined features in File → Save For Web have replaced the GIF89a Export of former versions as the method of creating transparent GIF images. To create transparency on an optimized Web image, the image must be on a layer surrounded by transparency. Let's knock out the background of an image:

1. If `Liberty.psd` is still open in ImageReady, click the Edit in Photoshop button. Otherwise in Photoshop, open the `Liberty.psd` file in the `Ch25` folder on the CD.

2. Choose the Magic Wand tool. In the Options bar, set the tolerance to 32 and clear the Contiguous box. Click on the blue area surrounding the Statue of Liberty.

3. Choose Select → Inverse to select the statue.

4. Choose Layer → New → Layer Via Copy to isolate a copy of the statue on a separate layer.

5. Target the new layer. Click the Background's visibility indicator so that it is not selected.

6. Choose File → Save For Web (see Figure 25.29). Choose GIF from the pop-up list and enter 16 for the number of colors. Notice that the Transparency option is active and that the image is displayed on a checkerboard, indicating transparency.

7. Choose 2-Up.

8. Optimize the image as you did the opaque GIF. Try different settings and compare the results.

9. Click the best image and click OK. Name the image and choose a location in the Save File dialog box. The image should look like Figure 25.30 on the browser.

> Using the Magic Wand to select an object from its background, as you did in this example, leaves a 'fringe' of pixels tinted the background color. Select Layer → Matting → Defringe to recolor those fringe pixels with hues nearby pixels of the selected element. In this case, replacing sky blue with the green of Liberty's patina.

Matting

Browsers support either opacity or transparency. Unlike Photoshop, they do not display semitransparent layers. The idea of matting is to blend the edges of a shape with the background design of a page to simulate semitransparency and smooth out some of the rough

Figure 25.29

Choosing Save For Web and GIF with transparency

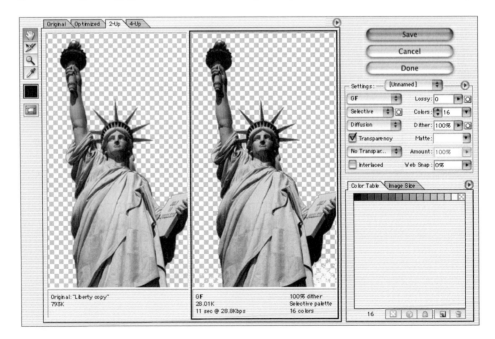

edges. Transparency in Photoshop is layer-based—in other words, the transparent areas that surround an area of a layer will be transparent in the browser. If you want an image to float on a patterned background, matting can help soften those edges. To apply matting to an image, follow these steps:

1. In Photoshop, open the file `Tile.psd` in the `Ch25` folder on the CD.

2. Choose the Eyedropper tool and sample a midtone green from the image. Click the foreground color swatch in the Tool palette to display the Color Picker. Check the Only Web Colors option. Write down the hexadecimal number of the color.

3. Choose File → New (see the dialog box in Figure 25.31). Name the file `emerald_forest`. Set the width to **468** and the height to **60**. Set the resolution to **72** pixels per inch, the mode to RGB Color 8-bit, and the contents to Transparent. Save the file in Photoshop format.

4. Choose the Type tool. Type the words **Emerald Forest**. I used Herculanum Bold, 64 point, but you can use any typeface you please.

5. Color the type yellow and add a Bevel and Emboss style to the text (see Figure 25.32).

6. Choose File → Save For Web. From the Settings pop-up list, choose GIF 32 Dithered, as in Figure 25.33.

Figure 25.30

The transparent GIF displayed on the browser with the clouds background tile

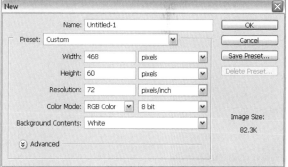

Figure 25.31

The New dialog box

Figure 25.32

The Emerald Forest text with the Bevel and Emboss layer style applied

7. Click on the matting swatch. Choose Other to bring up the Color Picker. Check the Web Colors Only option. Enter the hexadecimal value you recorded. This will place a green mat around the type to blend it into the pattern tile on the Web page.

8. Click Save. You can now display the image in the browser against the patterned background (as in Figure 25.34).

> If you frequently create images of a particular size that don't appear among the new file presets (for example, a 468×60 Web banner), create a new preset. Click the Save Preset option to save your current settings. They'll appear as a file preset from now on.

Slicing Images in Photoshop and ImageReady

A group of small images downloads more efficiently in a browser than one large image. In Photoshop or ImageReady, you *slice* a Web image in order to divide it into smaller files to accelerate download time or to assign different compression or file formats to various parts of an image, particularly animations. Slicing is the process of cutting an image into pieces, saving the individual parts as image files, and writing an HTML document that reassembles the slices on-screen.

Figure 25.33

The Save For Web settings

> Slices can butt up only against each other or against the top, bottom, or sides of the image. You cannot cut a slice out of the center of the image unless it is adjacent to other slices.

You can slice the image with the Slice tool in either program. To slice an image, choose the Slice tool from the Tool palette, click the mouse, and drag the cursor where you want the slice.

The individual slices are saved as separate files, and an HTML document with table code is written that reassembles them on the browser. You can select a slice with the Slice Select tool either from the Tool palette in Photoshop and ImageReady or within the Save For Web dialog box in Photoshop. The slice can be repositioned, or different options can be designated for the slice.

By default, when you choose the Slice tool, you see that the image is really one slice. The number 1 appears in the upper-left corner of the slice. Each time you create a slice, a new sequential number is assigned to it (see Figure 25.35).

Figure 25.34

The Emerald Forest text displayed without matting (above). The Emerald Forest text displayed with matting on a patterned background (below).

After you're satisfied with your slice arrangement, save the image by using the Save For Web option. You can select an individual slice by choosing the Slice Select tool. If desired, you can optimize the slices individually or, if no slices are selected, as a group.

Another method of creating slices is to set guides and convert them:

1. In ImageReady, open the image `Bio_Web_Site.psd` in the `Ch25` folder on the CD.

2. Choose View → Rulers.

3. From the horizontal and vertical rulers, drag a guide along the design to isolate the sidebar and other important areas of the image. In this example, the guides isolate the photo of the orangutan and areas that are naturally suited to being separated into rectangles.

4. Under Slices, choose Create Slices From Guides.

5. Choose File → Save Optimized. When the Save As dialog box appears, select HTML And Images from the Save As Type drop-down list, and All Slices from the Slice list. Click Save. Your image should now look like Figure 25.36.

You can make a slice into a link to connect it to another Web page or URL. Click the slice you want to make into a link. Activate the Slice palette (choose Window → Slice or, if the palette is visible, click the Slice tab). Enter the Name of the slice and the URL.

Figure 25.35

The image before slicing, with the guides in place

Figure 25.36

After slicing,
Photoshop and
ImageReady num-
ber the slices.

ImageReady saves the separate images, as well as the HTML code necessary, that are necessary to lay them out properly.

To view the results, open the HTML file in your browser, and you'll see that ImageReady maintains the integrity of your design while optimizing the sliced images in the best possible fashion.

Creating Tables in ImageReady

In ImageReady CS, you can create tables within slices. A table basically slices up one or more slices into smaller subslices. Follow these steps:

1. In ImageReady, open the image Bio_Web_Site.psd in the Ch25 folder on the CD, if the file is not already open.

2. Using one of the methods described in the preceding exercise, divide the image into at least two slices.

3. Select one of the slices, either by clicking it with the Slice Select tool or by clicking its thumbnail in the Web Content palette.

Figure 25.37

Converting
an image slice
into a table

4. From the list, choose Slices → Group Slices Into Table. Notice that a new, green table icon appears in the upper-right corner of the slice, indicating that this is a table. You can also create a table from a selected slice by changing its Type from Image to Table in the Slice palette (see Figure 25.37), or by clicking the Group Slice Into Table button at the bottom of the Web Content palette.

5. If it's not already open, open the Web Content palette by choosing Window → Web Content.

6. Under Slices in the Web Content palette, find the table you created. If you cannot see the subslice, expand the table by clicking the triangle to the left of the table's thumbnail.

7. Right-click the subslice in the Web Content palette and choose Divide Slice from the pop-up list (see Figure 25.38).

8. In the Divide Slice dialog box, divide the slice in two both horizontally and vertically (see Figure 25.39). The original slice has now been subdivided into four slices. This feature is useful if you have one slice containing multiple images or graphics that you might want to maintain individually (see Figure 25.40).

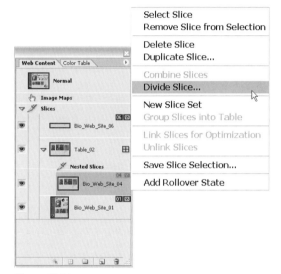

Figure 25.38

Using the pop-up list from the Web Content palette to divide a slice

Figure 25.39

Dividing the slice into four equal subslices

Figure 25.40

Use tables and sub-slices where your document has multiple individual images, closely grouped.

Subslices within tables act just like ordinary slices. You can create and modify them with the same tools and techniques, and use them as links to URLs.

You can group multiple slices into a single table by Shift-clicking the slices with the Slice Select tool or Shift-clicking the slices in the Web Content palette, and then choosing Slices → Group Slices Into Table from the list. Tables cannot be nested; you cannot create a table inside of another table.

CHAPTER 26

Creating Dynamic Web Elements

The Web is a dynamic and interactive environment. This chapter will cover the dynamic, interactive elements you can create in ImageReady. It will take you through several step-by-step processes so that you can begin adding interactivity to images and animations for the Web.

This chapter includes these topics:

- **Creating image maps**
- **Creating animations and rollovers**
- **Using data sets to automate image processing**
- **Embedding metadata**

Creating Image Maps in ImageReady

An *image map* is an area of an image that links the site visitor to another Web page or URL. You can set up multiple areas in the image called *hotspots*. Whereas slices let you define only rectangular areas as links, image maps let you define circular, polygonal, or rectangular regions.

> You can "float" the Image Map tools, or any of the drop-down subpalettes in ImageReady's Tool palette. Click and hold any of these tools, and select the small triangle at the bottom of the list at the bottom to create a new floating palette containing those tools.

To define an image map as a region of the entire image, use the Image Map tools:

1. Choose one of the Image Map tools from the Tool palette. The choices are rectangle, circle, or polygon.

2. Drag over the area you want to make into an image map.

3. Click the Web Content tab to display the Web Content palette. If it's not visible, choose Window → Web Content.

4. Double-click on the new thumbnail in the new image map layer to open the Image Map palette.

5. Name the image map and assign a URL to it. Now when visitors click that area of the image (as with the beetle in Figure 26.1), their browser will transport them to that URL.

You can also make a layer-based image map:

1. In the Layers palette, target the layer you want to make into an image map.

2. Click the Layer menu and choose New Layer-Based Image Map Area.

3. Click the Web Content tab to display the Web Content palette.

4. Double-click the new image map layer to open the Image Map palette.

5. Name the image map and enter a URL.

Using Photoshop to Prepare Animations

Because Photoshop's Layers palette enables you to successively stack one transparent layer on top of another in sequence, it serves as a very effective cell animation program.

You can target an image on one layer, copy the layer, and apply a small increment of a filter, movement, or other operation. Copy the layer again and apply the operation one more time. Continue this process until the animation is complete. Incidentally, you can record the entire operation as an action, and quickly automate your task.

Here is a step-by-step example of preparing a Photoshop animation:

1. Open the Beating_Heart.psd image in the Ch26 folder on the *Photoshop CS Savvy* CD. The Heart image has been separated from its Background and named Layer 1 (see Figure 26.2).

2. Choose Window → Actions.

3. From the Actions palette menu, choose New Set. Name the set **Animation**.

4. From the Actions palette menu, choose New Action. Name the action **Heart Beat**. Assign the F2 key as a key command. Click Record and OK.

5. In the Layers palette, control-click (Mac) or right-click (Windows) on Layer 1, the layer with the heart. Choose Duplicate Layer from the pop-up menu. A new layer called Layer 1 Copy is created.

6. Choose Filter → Distort → Spherize. Set the amount to 25% and the mode to Normal, as seen in Figure 26.3. On the new layer, the heart appears to have grown a little.

7. Stop recording.

8. Target the Layer 1 Copy. Run the action by pressing the F2 key. A new layer is created called Layer 1 Copy 2. On the new layer, the heart has grown a little more.

9. Each time you target the new layer, repeat the action. Repeat the process three more times by pressing the F2 key, until you have a total of five heart layers. The heart will grow a little bit each time as each new layer is created. Name each layer with a sequential numeric value from 1 to 5 (as in Figure 26.4), so that when you create the animation in ImageReady, you'll have no problem keeping the layers organized.

The animation file is complete. Save it as a Photoshop file named Beating_Heart_Layers.psd, with the layers intact. In order to create the beating heart animation and convert the file to animated GIF format, you'll import it into ImageReady.

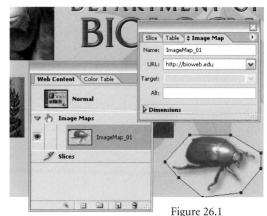

Figure 26.1

An image map defined by the Polygon Image Map tool and the Web Content palette

Figure 26.2

The Heart image separated from the Background

Figure 26.3

Settings on the Actions palette

Creating a GIF Animation in ImageReady

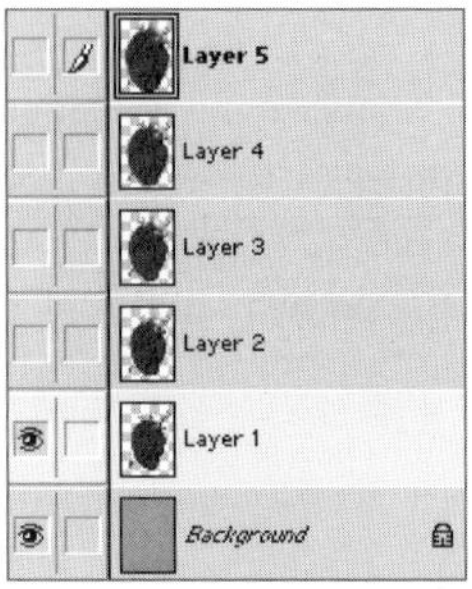

Another attractive aspect of ImageReady is that you can create layer-based animations. In Photoshop, you created the Beating Heart document; now, in ImageReady, you'll give it life. Follow these steps:

1. With Photoshop running and the layered Beating Heart document open, launch ImageReady by clicking the Edit In icon. If the Layers palette is not visible, choose Window → Layers to display it. The Layers palette shows five layers and the Background.

2. If the Animation palette is not visible, choose Window → Animation to display it. The frame in the Animation palette displays the visible portions of the image (see Figure 26.5).

3. Repeat the process, adding new frames for Layers 3, 4, and 5. Your Animation palette should look like Figure 26.6.

4. At this point, you might want to see the result. Click Play to see the first half of the beating heart animation: the heart expands and suddenly contracts. So for the second part of the animation, you'll create a smooth contraction. You will create the second half of the animation by using the same layers, but in reverse order.

5. Click the Duplicate Current Frame icon and make the contents of Layer 4 and the Background visible.

6. In the Layers palette, make sure the visibility indicator is turned off on all the layers except for the Background and Layer 1.

> Each frame in ImageReady's Animation palette displays the current visible layers. You create an animated sequence by making a new frame and then making visible only those layers that you want to appear in that frame.

Figure 26.4

The Layers palette after the animation action has been applied

Figure 26.5

The image, the Layers, and the Animation palette displaying the visible portion of the image

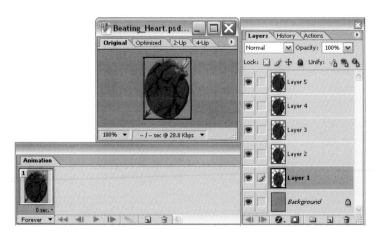

7. In the Animation palette, click the Duplicate Current Frame icon  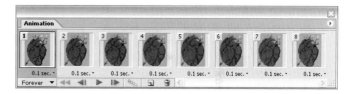 to insert a new frame, or choose New Frame from the palette menu. Click off the visibility indicator for Layer 1, and click it on for Layer 2. Leave on the visibility indicator for the Background.

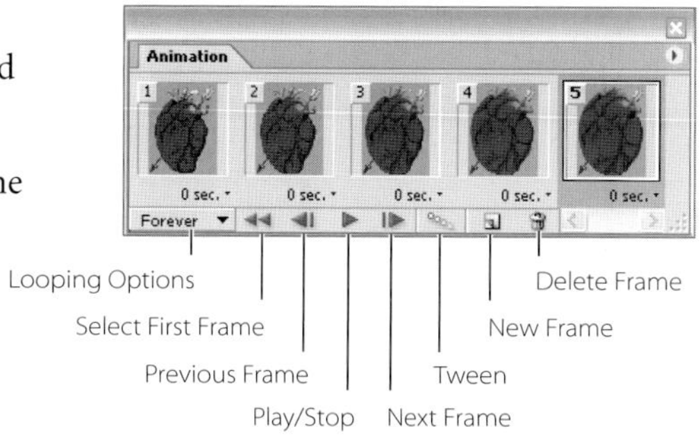

8. Repeat step 7 for Layers 3 and 2; the Animation palette should look like Figure 26.7.

9. To create a smoothly animated sequence, you want each frame to appear for the same amount of time. To set the speed between each frame, select all the frames by choosing Select All Frames from the Animation palette menu. Click the arrow on the lower-right of each frame, and set a uniform delay time for all frames (or choose a duration for each frame individually).

Figure 26.6

The Animation palette with the first half of the animation

10. Next, you'll want to set up the iterations of the animation, or the number of times it loops. The Forever option is appropriate only when the animation keeps looping in a constant motion, which is best for slower, subtler animations. Setting the animation to Once might be appropriate if the animation is particularly large and detailed. You can also set the animation to loop a custom number of turns. Choose Forever.

11. To add a smooth transition between points on an animation, use the Tween option from the Animation palette menu. Tweening, or "in betweening," will automatically add a blur so that a smooth transition occurs between frames.

12. To view your animation, click the Play button at the bottom of the Animation palette. The animation then cycles in the originating file. At this point, you can stop the animation by clicking the play button again and make any adjustments that you feel are necessary.

Figure 26.7

The Animation palette with the completed animation

13. After you're happy with your animation, save it as a GIF by choosing File → Save Optimized; then name the file and click Save.

Creating SWF Animations in ImageReady

A SWF (pronounced 'Swiff') animation is often called a Flash animation, because the SWF file format originated with Macromedia's Flash software. But, with version CS, ImageReady can create SWF animations, too.

Creating a SWF animation is similar to creating a GIF animation. In fact, in most cases, both the process and the results are virtually identical. SWF export is primarily useful if you are creating new elements for Flash-based websites. SWF files can be loaded dynamically by other SWF files. SWF files can also contain dynamic text, which can be changed via HTML, Flash ActionScripting, JavaScript, and PHP.

If the animation consists largely of vector shapes and text, SWF files are often more efficient than GIFs. Experiment and see what looks best, and weighs in with the lowest byte count.

In this section, you'll create a SWF animation and then take a closer look at some of the options used to do so.

Creating the Animation

To create a SWF animation, do the following:

1. Open the beating heart animation you saved in the preceding exercise, or open the Beating_Heart_Animation.gif file from Ch26 folder on the CD.

2. Select all the frames by choosing Select All Frames from the Animation palette menu. Click one of the arrows which appear at the lower-right of each frame, and set a delay of 0.1 seconds.

3. Choose File → Export → Macromedia Flash SWF.

4. Make sure Generate HTML is selected. Your settings should look like Figure 26.8.

5. Ignore the rest of the options for now, and click OK to save the file.

6. Save the animation as Beating_Heart_Animation.swf. ImageReady creates an HTML file called Beating_Heart_Animation.html with the SWF animation in it.

7. Open the newly created HTML file and preview the animation. It looks just like your animated GIF. The difference is that it's all ready to drop into a Flash-centric website.

Understanding the SWF Export Dialog Box

ImageReady SWF export offers you several options:

Preserve Appearance If you check Preserve Appearance, ImageReady will rasterize and flatten some vector layers, preserving the appearance of the animation, including layer effects, at the cost of a slightly larger file. If you leave Preserve Appearance unchecked, any effects, such as Drop Shadow, are dropped from vector (for example, text) layers.

SWF Bgcolor Use this option to specify the background color for the SWF.

Generate HTML Check this to tell ImageReady to create an HTML Web page "wrapper" with the SWF file within it.

Enable Dynamic Text Check the Enable Dynamic Text option if you want your SWF files to contain dynamic variable text.

Embed Fonts If you enable dynamic text, you can choose whether to embed your font in the file. The dynamic text will be displayed in the embedded font. If no font is embedded, the text will be displayed using a default system font. You can choose to embed the entire font or, to save file space, only selected characters. Click the buttons beneath the Embed Fonts drop-down list to individually embed uppercase characters, lowercase characters, numbers, and punctuation. You can also type extra characters to be embedded in the file.

Bitmap Options The following options are available from the Format drop-down list:

Figure 26.8

The SWF export dialog box in ImageReady

> **Lossless-8** encodes your bitmaps as 8-bit GIFs.
>
> **Lossless-32** encodes your bitmaps as 32-bit PNGs.
>
> **JPEG** encodes your bitmaps as 24-bit JPEGs.
>
> **Auto Select** tells ImageReady to choose the format it thinks will provide the best compromise between quality and file size.

If you choose Auto Select or JPEG, you can manually set the JPEG quality.

Working with Rollovers in ImageReady

A *rollover* is a mini animation that is triggered by your mouse. Rollovers add interactivity to your Web page. An example would be a button which changes shape or color when the cursor passes over it. In this section you'll learn how to create and change rollover states in ImageReady.

Creating Rollover States

Like animations, rollovers depend on layers for their behavior. You designate a rollover on an image by changing the visibility of a layer's content. To create a rollover, you should slice your image or create an image map so that the portion that contains the rollover is independent from the rest of the image. Follow these steps:

1. In ImageReady, open the file `Bio_rollover.psd` from the `Ch26` folder on the CD. To simplify the process, I have merged all the layers in the document except for the ones needed for the rollover. The Background and the Legs layer are visible, as shown in Figure 26.9.

Figure 26.9

The Background and the Legs layer are visible.

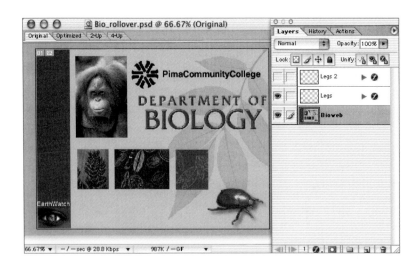

2. Choose the Slice tool ![slice tool] and drag a rectangle over the lower-right corner of the image to slice the beetle. Other slices will also be displayed. The beetle is the slice you want, so click it with the Slice Select tool, accessible by expanding the Slice tool in the Tool palette. It will be numbered Slice 03, as you see in Figure 26.10.

3. Choose Window → Web Content to display the Web Content Rollovers palette. It contains a layer for the new slice, a thumbnail of the entire image, named Normal, and a thumbnail of the slice, named Bio_rollover_03. This thumbnail displays the Normal, nonanimated, appearance of the slice. Rollover states will appear on new sublayers beneath it.

4. Target Bio_Rollover_03. Click the New Create Rollover State icon. A thumbnail appears beneath the Bio_Rollover_03 layer, in the Rollovers palette, named Over State. Click *off* the visibility indicator next to the Legs layer, and click *on* the indicator next to the Legs 2 layer, as in Figure 26.11.

Figure 26.10

The document showing the beetle slice

5. To see the rollover, choose File → Preview In and choose a browser. Place your mouse on the beetle, and the legs move. Remove the mouse, and the legs are restored to the Normal state.

6. When the rollover is complete, you can optimize the image slice by slice. Choose the Slice Select tool from the Tool palette, click the individual slices one by one, and optimize them individually with the Options palette.

7. Save the entire page as an HTML document: choose File → Save Optimized → HTML And Images.

Changing Rollover States

You can program other states into a rollover and create additional rollover frames. The rollover might be triggered by the viewer pressing (or releasing) the mouse button, by moving the mouse over it, or by moving the mouse off of it.

Control-click (Mac) or right-click (Win) the name of a rollover state, and choose a different rollover state from the Set State pop-up list.

The Rollover State Options list (see Figure 26.12) gives the following State options:

Normal The image doesn't change; this is the default, or nonanimated, state.

Over The state changes when the mouse is hovered over the image or slice. Over is the default setting for the first rollover state.

Down The state changes when the mouse is clicked and held down in the area.

Selected This option implements a rollover state when the user clicks the mouse on the slice or image map area. The state is maintained until you activate another selected rollover state, and other rollover effects can occur while the selected state is active. Note that if a layer is used by both states, the layer attributes of the Selected state override those of the Over state.

To activate a state initially when the document is previewed in ImageReady or loaded into a Web browser, double-click on the name of the rollover state and check Use as Default Selected State.

Out The state changes when the mouse is moved off the area.

Up The state changes when the mouse is released within the area.

Click The state changes when the mouse is clicked and released over the area.

Web browsers, or different versions of a browser, might process clicks and double-clicks differently. Some browsers leave the slice in the Click state after a click, and in the Up state after a double-click; other browsers use the Up state only as a transition into the Click state, regardless of single- or double-clicking. Be sure to preview rollovers in various Web browsers.

Custom This option lets you enter a custom behavior. You must write JavaScript code and add it to the HTML file in order for this to work.

None The state does not change.

Figure 26.11

The Layers palette and the Rollovers palette

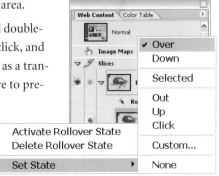

Figure 26.12

Rollover State Options

Using Data Sets in ImageReady

ImageReady CS introduces data sets. What exactly is a data set? The ImageReady Help file tells us that a data set is "a collection of variables and associated data," and, further, that you can "switch between data sets to upload different data into your template." But what, exactly, does that *mean*? It's a whole lot easier to show you than to try to explain it.

Creating Data Sets

Follow these steps to create some ImageReady data sets:

Figure 26.13

Each layer contains a photo.

1. In ImageReady, open the file headshots.psd from the Ch26 folder on the CD. This file consists of five named layers, each containing a small photo, as seen in Figure 26.13.

2. Choose Image → Variables → Define to open the Variables dialog box. From the Layer list, select Darren, as shown in Figure 26.14.

3. Under Variable Type, check Visibility. Leave the Pixel Replacement option unchecked. Notice that an asterisk (*) appears next to the layer name to show that there is now a variable associated with that layer. The dialog box should look like Figure 26.15.

4. Under Layers, select the next layer, Jenn. Click the Visibility option. Continue by selecting each layer in turn and checking Visibility for each of them.

5. Click the Next button, or choose Data Sets from the drop-down list at the top of the Variables dialog, to begin defining data sets. You should see a data set like the one in Figure 26.16. There are five variables, each of which defines the visibility of one of the five layers in the document (see Figure 26.16).

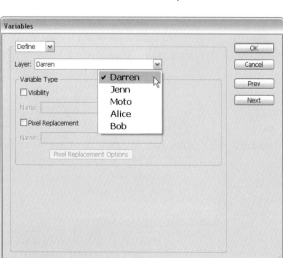

Figure 26.14

The Variables dialog box

Figure F26.15

Creating a Visibility variable for a layer

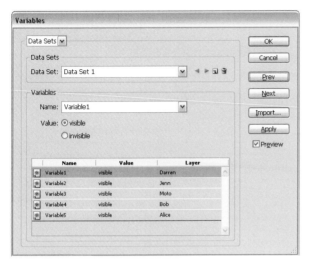

Figure 26.16

Your first data set

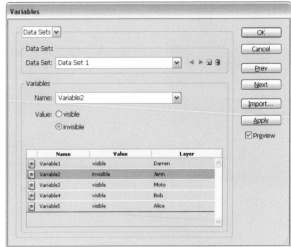

Figure 26.17

Variable2 set to Invisible

6. Select Variable2, the variable for the Jenn layer, at the bottom of the dialog box, and check the Invisible radio button under Value, as shown in Figure 26.17.

7. Select each of the remaining variables in turn, clicking Invisible. Leave the variable for the Darren layer, Variable1, set to Visible, as shown in Figure 26.18.

Name	Value	Layer
Variable1	visible	Darren
Variable2	invisible	Jenn
Variable3	invisible	Moto
Variable4	invisible	Bob
Variable5	invisible	Alice

Figure 26.18

Only one layer is visible in the finished data set.

8. Click the New Data Set button to the right of the data set name, as shown in Figure 26.19. This creates a second data set, called Data Set 2. Each data set has the same variables, but those variables can have different values in each data set.

9. In Data Set 2, select Variable1 and change its Value to Invisible.

10. Select Variable2 and change its Value to Visible.

11. Repeat steps 8-10 to create Data Set 3, Data Set 4, and Data Set 5. Set the values for each variable so that only Variable3 is set to Visible in Data Set 3, only Variable4 is set to Visible in Data Set 4, and so forth. When all five data sets are complete, press OK to close the Variables dialog box.

12. Choose Image → Preview Document. From the Data Set Options bar, select the various data sets to see the changes (see Figure 26.20). Every data set should display a different layer and photo. You can also scroll through the various data sets by clicking the triangle buttons to the right of the data set name.

Figure 26.19

Creating a second data set

Importing Data Sets from External Files

What, you might be asking, is all this actually good for? Data sets are most useful for automating the production of large numbers of images, especially when combined with

ImageReady's capability to import data sets. Suppose that you maintain the internal website for a company with 500 employees. For each of the employees, you need to create a banner graphic featuring their photo, their name, their department, their employee number, and assorted graphics. That's a lot of Photoshopping!

But data sets can automate that process for you. You can build a template file in ImageReady and then import information about how to change that file, replacing graphics and text, and turning layer visibility on or off.

Figure 26.20

Reviewing the data sets

Suppose that the company personnel department has given you a CD that includes photos of each employee, and a text file exported from their database that includes each employee's name, number, and department. You can use data sets to combine these files with your PSD template to automatically generate a new banner for each employee.

The syntax of the external text file is as follows:

```
VariableName1<sep>VariableName2<sep>VariableNameN<nl>
Value1-1<sep>Value2-1<sep>ValueN-1<nl>
Value1-2<sep>Value2-2<sep>ValueN-2<nl>
```

The first line contains the variable names. Subsequent lines contain the actual variable values for each data set. <sep> can be either a comma or a tab. <nl> is the new line character.

Here is the actual file you'll be using in this exercise:

```
EMPNUM, DEPT, ITICON, IT_BG, MGMTICON, MGMT_BG, NAME,
    PHOTO, SUPPORTICON, SUPT_BG
857911, "IT Ctr.", true, true, false, false, "Bob Smith",
    headshot_Bob.jpg, false, false
400215, "Mgmt.", false, false, true, true, "Darren Smalls",
    headshot_Darren.jpg, false, false
403320, "Mgmt.", false, false, true, true, "Jenn Sward",
    headshot_Jenn.jpg, false, false
111203, "Supt.", false, false, false, false, "Moto Sugai",
    headshot_Moto.jpg, true, true
137684, "Supt.", false, false, false, false, "Alice Rowe",
    headshot_Alice.jpg, true, true
```

The variables in an external data file do not have to appear in the same order as they were defined in your PSD, but they do have to have the same names.

This file contains only five employees, not 500, but the principles are the same. The word true dictates that a given layer will be visible; false dictates that it will be invisible. The number at the beginning of each line, and the quoted text, will all be used to replace text within the image. The .jpg files will replace the image on one layer of the file.

Follow these steps to see how it all works:

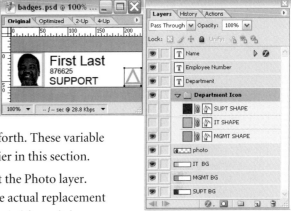

Figure 26.21

The badges.psd file

1. In ImageReady, open the file badges.psd from the Ch26 folder on the CD. This file consists of 10 layers—a combination of text, shapes, and a photo, as seen in Figure 26.21.

2. I have done the work of setting up the variables for you. Choose Image → Variables → Data Sets to see them (see Figure 26.22). Notice that I've named the variables NAME, PHOTO, DEPT, and so forth. These variable names match those in the text data file presented earlier in this section.

3. Click Next to examine the variables themselves. Select the Photo layer. PHOTO is a pixel replacement variable; it controls the actual replacement of the photo on the Photo layer with another image, loaded from disk. Each data set will load a different JPEG file into this layer (see Figure 26.23).

Figure 26.22

The data set contains 10 variables.

Figure 26.23

Pixel replacement replaces the current layer with an image loaded from disk.

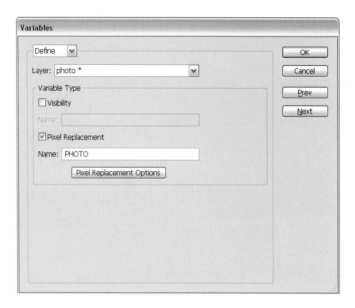

Table 26.1

Employee Data Set Layers

LAYER	VARIABLE	TYPE	DESCRIPTION
Name	NAME	Text replacement	This text will be replaced with the actual name of each employee.
Employee Number	EMPNUM	Text replacement	This text will be replaced with each employee's number.
Department	DEPT	Text replacement	This text will be replaced with the department name of each employee.
Department Icon (Layer Set)	*no variable*	—	—
SUPT SHAPE	SUPPORTICON	Visibility	Determines whether the support department icon is visible.
IT SHAPE	ITICON	Visibility	Determines whether the I.T. department icon is visible.
MGMT SHAPE	MGMTICON	Visibility	Determines whether the management icon is visible.
Photo	PHOTO	Pixel replacement	The image in this layer will be replaced with a new photo from the hard disk.
IT BG	IT_BG	Visibility	Determines whether the I.T. department background is visible.
MGMT BG	MGMT_BG	Visibility	Determines whether the management background is visible.
SUPT BG	SUPT_BG	Visibility	Determines whether the support department background is visible.

4. Select the Name layer. NAME is a text replacement variable. It enables the text on this layer to be replaced with new text, in this case, the name of each employee. Examine each layer in turn to inspect the variable associated with it; the layers are listed in Table 26.1. Note that Department Icon is a Layer *Set*, containing three separate shape layers, and has no variable associated with it.

Figure 26.24

The Import Variable Data Sets dialog box

5. It's time to import those files and create the Web banners. Click Next, or select Data Sets from the drop-down list at the top of the Variables dialog box. Click the Import button and select the file `employee_data_set.txt` from the `Ch26` folder on the CD. Check the Use First Column For Data Set Names and the Replace Existing Data Sets options, as shown in Figure 26.24. By selecting Use First Column For Data Set Names, you tell ImageReady to create data sets whose name is the same as the value of the first variable in the data file, in this case the employee number, rather than Data Set 1, Data Set 2, and so forth. Click OK.

6. To review the data sets, click the two triangle buttons to the right of the data set name, as shown in Figure 26.25. Notice that ImageReady loads in new photos, changes text, and hides and reveals graphics elements.

Figure 26.25

Scrolling through the data sets

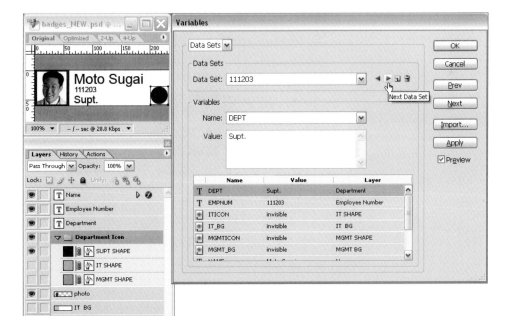

Figure 26.26

Data set file naming

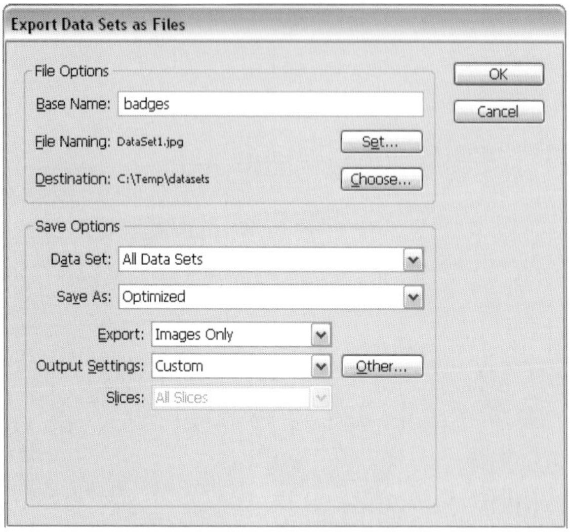

Figure 26.27

Data Set Export settings

7. Press OK again to close the Variables dialog box.

8. From the Optimize palette, choose JPEG Medium from the Presets list.

9. Choose File → Export → Save Data Sets As Files. In the Export Data Sets as Files dialog box, click the Set button under File Options to tell ImageReady what to name your new images. Choose Data Set Name from the first drop-down list. Leave the last drop-down list set to .ext, and set all the other lists to None, as shown in Figure 26.26. Click OK.

10. Choose a destination for your new images to be saved to. Under Save Options, select All Data Sets from the Data Set list, Optimized from the Save As list, and Images Only from the Export list. The dialog box should look like Figure 26.27. Click OK to export the files. ImageReady creates five new images in your destination directory. Each file will have the same name as the employee's employee number, plus the .jpg extension, as shown in Figure 26.28. This exercise created only five Web banners, rather than 500, but the principles are the same.

Figure 26.28

Each data set exported as a JPEG

Embedding Metadata

ImageReady can also embed metadata in your image files. What, exactly, is metadata? *Metadata* is data that describes other data. In the case of, say, a GIF image, metadata would be additional information, other than the actual pixel data, that describes the file, such as a description and copyright notice. ImageReady can embed this metadata within the GIF file itself.

Saving the Data

Let's take a look at how metadata is saved by ImageReady:

1. In ImageReady, open the file `tomatoes.jpg` from the `Ch26` folder on the CD.

2. To add metadata to the file, choose File → File Info to open the File Info dialog box. Click Description in the left column and add some text for Document Title, Author, Description, and Copyright Notice, as seen in Figure 26.29. When you are finished, click OK.

3. If the Optimize palette is not open, open it by choosing Window → Optimize. By default, ImageReady does not save metadata with your optimized images. To turn saving of metadata on, reveal the Options section at the bottom of the Optimize palette. Check the Add Metadata box, as shown in Figure 26.30.

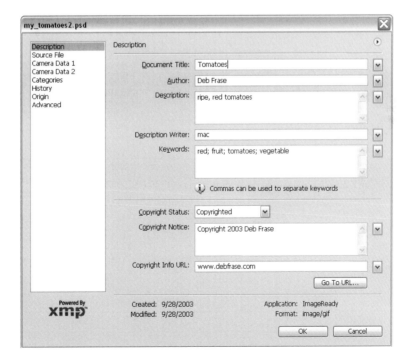

Figure 26.29

Add some metadata to the file.

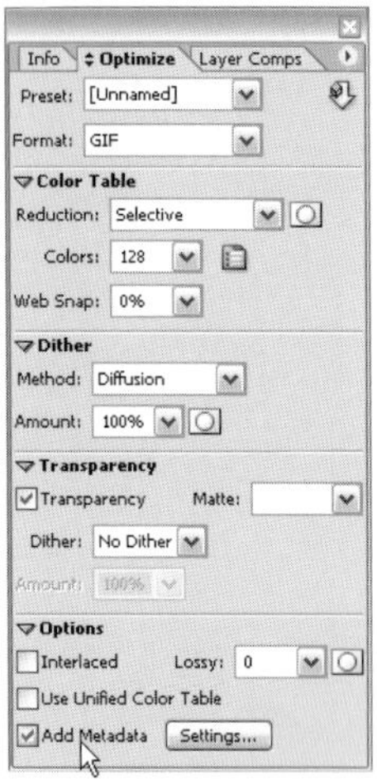

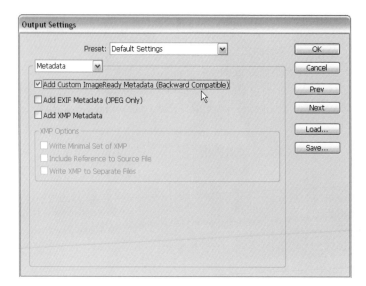

Figure 26.30

Enable the saving of metadata from the Optimize palette.

4. Click the Settings button next to the Add Metadata box to open the Output Settings dialog box. Make sure that Add Custom ImageReady Metadata is checked, and all other options are not checked, as shown in Figure 26.31. Click OK to close the Output Settings dialog box.

5. Choose GIF 128 Dithered from the Preset list at the top of the Optimize palette.

6. Choose File → Save Optimized As to save your image. Name the new file **my_tomatoes**, and choose Images Only from the Save As Type list. Save the image. Leave toma-toes.jpg open.

7. Choose File → Open Recent and select my_tomatoes.gif from the file list to reopen the file you just saved.

8. Choose File → File Info to review the embedded metadata. Notice that some of the metadata you typed in was *not* saved with the file. Only the Description and Copyright Notice appear, as shown in Figure 26.32. By default, these are the only pieces of metadata ImageReady saves with your optimized files.

9. Close my_tomatoes.gif and return to the original file, tomatoes.jpg. On the Optimize palette, click the Settings button at the bottom of the Options section. This time, check the Add XMP Metadata option so it is selected. Click OK.

10. Choose File → Save Optimized As to save your image. Again, name the file **my_tomatoes**, and choose Images Only from the Save As Type list. Save the image.

11. Choose File → Open Recent and select my_tomatoes.gif from the file list. Choose File → File Info to review the embedded metadata. Notice that, this time, all the data has been saved with the file.

Figure 26.31

Metadata output settings

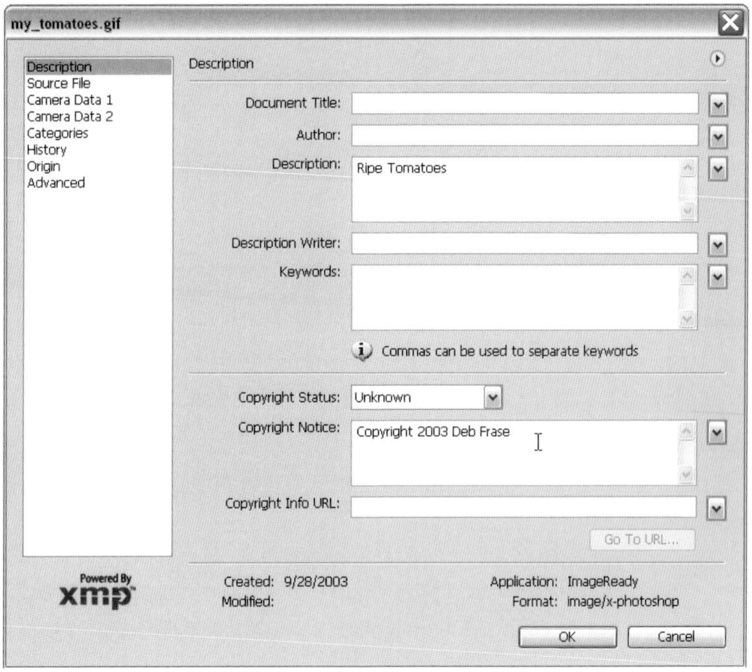

Figure 26.32

By default, ImageReady saves only the description and copyright notice.

In ImageReady, metadata is saved with optimized JPEG, GIF, and PNG files. It is not supported in WBMP.

Embedding metadata into a file naturally makes the file larger. Generally, you want the smallest possible optimized files. Metadata (especially XMP metadata) can get quite large. If you just spent half the day optimizing an animated GIF to get it under the 64 KB limit your client requires, you don't want to add 16 KB of metadata.

To combat this problem, ImageReady gives you the option of saving your metadata as a separate XMP file that gets referenced in the HTML code it creates. So, instead of making each image larger, ImageReady abstracts the metadata and saves it in a format that's easy for a search engine to find.

Here's an example of HTML code that references an XMP data file called `tomatoes.xmp`:

```
<html>
<head>
    <title>Tomatoes</title>
    <!-- copyright 2003 sybex -->
    <meta http-equiv="Content-Type"
          content="text/html; charset=iso-8859-1">
</head>
```

```
<body bgcolor="#FFFFFF" leftmargin="0" topmargin="0" marginwidth="0"
    marginheight="0">
  <!-- ImageReady Slices (tomatoes.gif) -->
  <img src="tomatoes.gif" width="250" height="250" alt=""
      xmpmetadata="tomatoes.xmp">
  <!-- End ImageReady Slices -->
</body>
</html>
```

Understanding the Metadata Output Settings

When you check the Add Metadata option on the Optimize palette, ImageReady saves metadata with your image. You can control just what metadata is saved with your image by clicking the Settings button next to the Save Metadata checkbox, which gives you the following options:

Add Custom ImageReady Metadata Includes simple copyright and description information from the File Info dialog box.

Add EXIF Metadata Includes information stored with digital photographs, including camera type, date and time of photo, and file size. EXIF is supported only for JPEG files.

Add XMP Metadata By default, ImageReady saves only the description and copyright notice. Checking the Add XMP Metadata option enables you to include a wider range of data with your image.

> **Write Minimal Set of XMP** Includes only a small subset of the complete XMP metadata set, including file modification and output times, file dimensions, and format.
>
> **Include Reference to Source File** Adds to the XMP a block of information that points to the original document.
>
> **Write XMP to Separate Files** XMP data for the file is written to a separate file, instead of being embedded in the image file.

Web Design and ImageReady

In this Hands On project, you'll lay out a website and use ImageReady to prepare the files for publication. The project is intended to take you through some of the Web features of ImageReady, but you will also use image-editing commands covered in previous chapters. The goal of this project is to assemble a home page for Ballet Bleu, an international ballet company (see Figure H9.1).

To see the finished version from this exercise, see Figure C59 in the color section.

Figure H9.1

The finished home page

Getting Started

Launch ImageReady and choose File → New. Name the new document `ballet_bleu.psd` in preparation for saving to disk. Enter **768** for the width and **480** for the height, and set the color to white, as in Figure H9.2. (These pixel dimensions work for displaying a browser on a 17′ monitor.)

Opening the Ballerina Image

The beautiful ballerina is a large part of the background image on the website. In these first steps, you'll drag it from its window onto the Web page:

1. Open the file `ballerina.psd` in the H09 folder on the *Photoshop CS Savvy* CD. Choose the Move tool  and drag and drop the image to the new document. Use ImageReady's Smart Guides to snap it to the left side of the canvas.

2. Open the Layers palette; a new layer is created. Name it **Ballerina**.

3. Adjust the opacity of the Ballerina layer to 40%.

Creating a Background

Because you're going to slice the image in ImageReady, you don't have to worry about creating a seamless background. But you will fill the empty portion of the background:

1. Choose the Magic Wand tool . Click the transparent area of the Ballerina layer to select it.

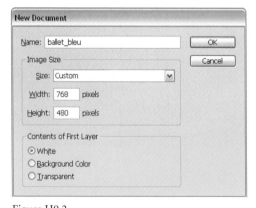

Figure H9.2

Settings for the new document

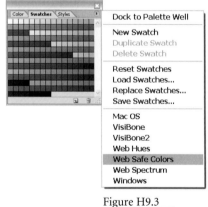

Figure H9.3

Choosing Web-safe colors

2. Choose Window → Swatches. From the Swatches palette menu, choose Web Safe Colors, as seen in Figure H9.3. Click the Replace button to replace the current swatches with Web-safe colors. The Web Safe Colors swatches let you choose from the 216 colors that are displayed uniformly on the World Wide Web.

3. Choose black (#000000) from the Swatches palette. Black is the very last swatch in the palette.

If you hover your mouse over a swatch, the color's RGB value will be displayed.

4. In the Layers palette, target the Background. Press Option-Delete (Mac) or Alt-Delete (Win) to fill the background with black.

5. Deselect by pressing ⌘/Ctrl-D. The image should look like Figure H9.4.

Figure H9.4

The image with the ballerina and black area filled

Entering the Type

Another way to choose Web color is with the Color palette. Here, you'll color the type with a hexadecimal that you choose from the Color palette:

Figure H9.5

The Color palette

1. In the Layers palette, target the Ballerina layer.

2. Choose the Type tool, and click on the canvas but don't type yet. To specify a hexa-decimal value for the type color, open the Color palette by choosing Window → Color. The Color palette has three drop-down boxes, one each for red, green, and blue. Select values from the drop-down lists. The Web Safe palette limits you to the following hexadecimal values for red, green, and blue: 00, 33, 66, 99, CC, and FF, so these are the only values offered by the drop-down lists, making the selection of Web-safe colors quick and error-free. The sliders under the red, green, and blue color bars also snap to these six values. You can also type hex values directly in the boxes. As you can see in Figure H9.5, I chose #FF0033.

3. I used 160-point Edwardian Script ITC for the font, but you can use another typeface. Type the words **Ballet Bleu** in the lower part of the image.

4. Click the Move tool and select Align Layer Horizontal Centers from the Option bar to center the text.

5. In the Layers palette, ⌘/right-click the Type layer and choose Layer Style → Drop Shadow from the pop-up menu to display the Layer Style dialog box (ImageReady).

6. Set the opacity to 50%; use all of the other defaults. Don't click OK yet.

7. Check the Bevel & Emboss option and choose the Inner Bevel style. I used the Smooth technique with a depth of 201%. Click OK to close the Layer Style dialog box. The type should look like Figure H9.6.

> The color swatches in the Type drop-down list include only Web-safe colors. You can safely choose any one of these colors.

Figure H9.6

The styled text

You can drag and drop a color from ImageReady's toolbox, color selection box, Color palette, Color Table palette, or Swatches palette onto a Type layer or any layer. This will add a Color Overlay layer style of that color to the layer.

Adding the Logo

The logo is a graphic element that will later be used as a rollover on an image map in ImageReady. Follow these steps to create two layers, one for each state of the rollover:

1. Open the file titled Logo.psd from the H09 folder on the CD. Choose the Move tool and drag the Logo layer from the Layers palette onto the Ballet_Bleu image so that the logo appears to the left of the *B*. Leave some space beneath the logo; you'll be adding another element here later.

2. In the Layers palette, drag the Logo layer and place it under the Type layer, as in Figure H9.7. Name it **Logo Black**.

3. Duplicate the layer by dragging it to the New Layer icon. Name the new layer **Logo Blue**.

4. With the new layer selected, choose Image → Adjustments → Hue/Saturation. In the Hue/Saturation dialog box, check Colorize.

5. Move the Hue slider to 215, the Saturation slider to 100, and the Lightness slider to 21, as in Figure H9.8. Click OK.

6. Press ⌘/Ctrl-S to save the document.

Figure H9.7

The logo in position

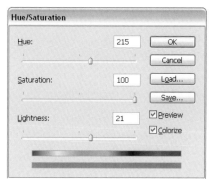

Figure H9.8

The Hue/Saturation dialog box

Adding the Animation Images

Next, you'll prepare the images for an animation sequence. Follow these steps:

1. Target the Ballerina layer.

2. Open the file animation_images.psd in the H09 folder on the CD.

3. Target the topmost layer (1) in the stack. Click the second column in the Layers menu of each layer to link all eight images together.

4. Choose the Move tool. From the image window, drag the layers and drop them on the Ballet Bleu image.

5. In the Layers palette, click the Create A New Set button to create a new layer set. Double-click the set's name and rename it **animation**.

6. Click the topmost animation layer (1); then Shift-click the bottommost animation layer (8) to select all eight layers. Release the Shift key and drag the selected layers into the animation set.

7. Target the animation set. In the image window, use the Move tool to drag the images to the upper-middle of the black rectangle, as in Figure H9.9.

8. Press ⌘/Ctrl-S to save the document.

Slicing the Image

Now you can slice the image into smaller, more manageable pieces. You'll then create an animation, a rollover, and an image map. Finally, you'll save all the elements as an HTML document for publication to the Web.

Here are the steps for slicing the image:

1. Choose the Slice tool ✎ and use it to divide the image into six rectangles (slices), as shown in Figure H9.10. One slice should contain the images you will use for the animation. One slice should contain the logo at the bottom right. Make the lower-left slice as small as possible, while still containing the entire image.

2. Use ImageReady's Smart Guides to snap your slices to the edges of the images. If need be, you can readjust or reposition the slices by dragging their edges with the Slice Select tool.

> Another method of creating slices is to drag guides into the position where you want the image to be sliced. Then choose Slices → Create Slices From Guides.

Animating the Images

ImageReady can create layer-based animations. Follow these steps to animate the numbered layers:

1. In the Layers palette, turn off the visibility indicators next to all the layers within the animation set.

2. Choose Window → Animation. The frame in the Animation palette displays the visible portions of the image. For the first frame, click the visibility indicator next to Layer 1 in the animation set to make that layer visible.

   Remember that each frame in the Animation palette in ImageReady displays the current visible layers. You create an animated sequence by making a new frame and then making visible only those layers that you want to appear in the frame.

3. Click the Duplicate Frame icon  to insert a frame in the Animation palette. In the Layers palette, click the visibility indicator next to Layer 1 in the animation set to conceal it, and the indicator next to Layer 2 to reveal it.

4. Repeat the process, adding new frames for Layers 3, 4, 5, 6, 7, and 8 and changing the layer visibility for each. When completed, your Animation palette should look like Figure H9.11.

Figure H9.9

The Web page with the ballet images

Figure H9.10

The sliced image

Figure H9.11

The Animation palette displaying the eight frames

Figure H9.11

The Animation palette displaying the eight frames

5. At this point, you might want to see the animation. Click the Play button ▶ to display it in the image window.

6. Currently, the animation runs too fast. To slow it down, go to the Animation Options pull-down menu and choose Select All Frames. Click the small arrow next to one of the frames and set the delay to 2 seconds.

7. Target Frame 1. Set the delay to 20 seconds. This means that the animation will stop for 20 seconds on the Frame 1 image and then repeat.

8. You might want to set the *iterations* of the animation, or the number of times it loops. The Forever option is appropriate only when the animation keeps looping in a constant motion. Setting the animation to Specific might be appropriate for certain animations such as this one. From the Looping Options menu, enter **5**, which means that the animation will display five times on the browser and then stop.

Creating an Image Map

An image map defines an area on the image that will be interactive. Follow these steps to make the logo a link to another Web page:

Figure H9.12

Identifying the image map

1. Choose the Polygon Image Map tool 🖑 . Draw a shape around the logo, as in Figure H9.12.

2. Choose Window → Image Map. In the URL field, enter **http:// cyberdance.org** (see Figure H9.13). Choose _self from the Target drop-down list. This links the image map to another website. (Note that the URL must include the entire address, as in `http://cyberdance.org`.)

If you want to link the logo to another Web page on this site, you will have to create a place for that page in the same folder as the Ballet Bleu Web page. The title of the page should include the HTML extension, as in `aboutballetbleu.html`.

Creating a Rollover

Like animations, rollovers depend on layers for their behavior. You designate a rollover on an image by changing the visibility of a layer's content. Follow these steps to create a rollover and change the color of the logo:

1. In the Layers palette, be sure that the Logo Black layer is displayed and the Logo Blue layer is concealed.

2. Choose Window → Web Content to display the Web Content palette, seen in Figure H9.14.

3. In the Web Content palette, select the slice that includes the Logo layers, the one labeled slice 04 in Figure H9.14. Click the Create Rollover State button  at the bottom of the Web Content palette. A new rollover state appears beneath the slice, labeled Over, as shown in Figure H9.15.

4. In the Layers palette, conceal the Logo Black layer and reveal the Logo Blue layer (by clicking the visibility icons so they are selected and deselected, respectively). When the mouse is within the boundaries of the new slice, the black logo will be hidden and the blue logo revealed.

Figure H9.13

The Image Map palette

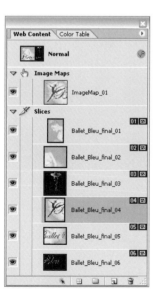

Figure H9.14

The Web Content palette

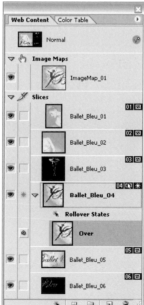

Figure H9.15

Rollover states

Creating a Remote Rollover

By default, rollovers affect only the rollover slice itself. But rollover slices can remotely control other slices, so that moving or clicking the mouse in one part of the screen causes changes in another part of the screen.

Follow these instructions to create a rollover that alters the appearance of two slices:

1. In the Web Content palette, select the Over rollover state layer you just created and drag it to the trash icon at the bottom of the palette to delete it.

2. Still in the Web Content palette, right-click the slice that contains the logo image, the slice you just deleted the rollover state from, and choose Group Slices Into Table from the pop-up menu, as shown in Figure H9.16.

3. Select the new subslice you just created, right-click it, and choose Divide Slice from the pop-up menu to bring up the Divide Slice dialog box. Divide the slice horizontally into **2** slices, as shown in Figure H9.17.

4. In the Layers palette, select the Ballet Bleu text layer and drag it to the Create A New Layer button at the bottom of the palette.

5. With the new Type layer still targeted, choose the Type tool and choose 36 px from the font size drop-down list in the options bar—about ¼ the size of the original text.

Figure H9.16

Group Slices Into Table

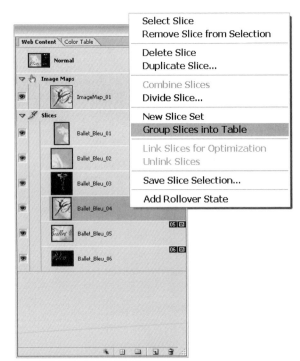

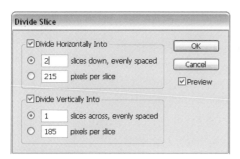

Figure H9.17

Divide Slice dialog box

Figure H9.18

Position the *Enter* text beneath the logo.

6. Click on the new type with the Type tool and change the text to read **Enter**.

7. Choose the Move tool and drag the new type to the bottom of the canvas, below the logo, as shown in Figure H9.18. Make sure the top of the text is *below* the lowest point in the logo.

8. Choose the Slice Select tool. Drag the boundary between the two subslices down, until it is between the bottom of the logo and the top of the word *Enter*. The word *Enter* and the logo should be on two different slices, as shown in Figure H9.19.

9. In the image window, use the Slice Select tool to click the top subslice, the one containing the logo. In the Layers palette, be sure that the Logo Black layer is displayed and that both the Logo Blue layer and the newly created Enter layer are concealed.

Figure H9.19

Divide the subslices between the logo and the text.

10. Click the Create Rollover State button at the bottom of the palette. Target the newly created Over rollover state layer. In the Layers palette, conceal the Logo Black layer, and reveal the Logo Blue layer and the Enter layer (by clicking the visibility icons).

11. By default, rollovers affect only the rollover slice itself. To make the Logo slice control the visibility of the Enter slice as well, you'll use the Pickwhip button ⬚ . In the Web Content palette, click and drag the Pickwhip button to the left of the Over rollover state, and drag the end of the line onto the Enter slice in the menu, as shown in Figure H9.20. This tells ImageReady that this rollover state will remotely control the state of the second subslice. Notice that a target icon appears next to the Enter slice. You can select and deselect remote control by clicking this icon on and off.

Previewing the Page

Before saving the optimized file, it's a good idea to look at it in your browser and to test the animation, the rollover, and the image map. Choose File → Preview In and choose a preferred browser from the submenu. The preview displays the Web page and the source code for the document, as shown in Figure H9.21. When the image opens, the animation will run. Place your mouse on the logo; the dancer will change color and the word *Enter* will appear. Click your mouse, and you will be transported to the cyberdance.org website.

If you get a warning and your animation doesn't run, don't worry about it. You'll fix that in the next step.

Optimizing the Images

After the image is complete, you can optimize it slice by slice. To do this, select slices one by one, either by clicking on the image with the Slice Select tool or by clicking on them in the Web Content palette. Optimize the slices individually with the Optimize palette, or select them as a group and apply the same settings.

Follow these steps to reduce the file sizes of your slices:

1. In the Web Content palette, use ⌘/Ctrl-click to select every slice *except* the slice at the top right, which contains the animation. Select only the slices, not the rollover states or image maps.

2. In the Optimize palette, choose JPEG Medium for the Preset setting, as in Figure H9.22.

Figure H9.20

Selecting a slice to be remotely controlled by the rollover

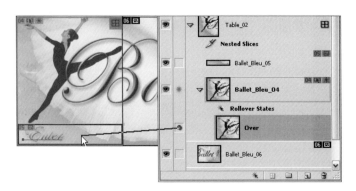

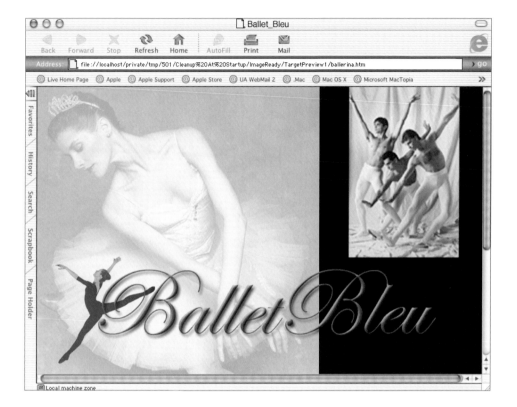

3. In the Web Content palette, select the remaining slice, or click on the upper-right slice with the Slice Select tool. In the Optimize palette, choose the setting GIF 64 Dithered (see Figure H9.23) to decrease the file size of the animation and preserve its appearance.

4. Choose File → Save Optimized As → HTML And Images. The slices and animation are divided into separate images and inserted into an image folder. It's important not to remove the images from the folder, because the HTML code refers to these images within the folder hierarchy.

Animations need to be saved as GIF or SWF.

Figure H9.22

Optimize palette showing a JPEG setting

Web Authoring Alternatives

Having brought your page to life, you are ready to publish it to the Web. ImageReady is a good tool for creating simple Web pages with slices, as well as straightforward cell animations and rollovers. For more complex animations, you might want to try Macromedia Flash or Adobe LiveMotion. To create and manage larger, more sophisticated websites, you'll find what you need in programs such as Adobe GoLive, Macromedia Dreamweaver, or Microsoft FrontPage.

Many professional Web designers still prefer to assemble their Web pages in HTML code. They claim the code is cleaner than that generated by WYSIWYG (What-You-See-Is-What-You-Get) editors. I recommend that you at least learn basic HTML code, so that you can understand the structure of Web pages and troubleshoot any problems that might result from code that is too complex or that is not universally compatible with all current browsers.

Figure H9.23

Optimize palette showing a GIF setting

CHAPTER 27

Photoshop and Digital Video

A new movement of visual expression is in play, and it's the digital movement. The computer encompasses all artistic mediums including music, drawing, photography, painting, sculpture, and video. This final chapter will cover how Photoshop enables you to handle still images and titles for video formats to be used in nonlinear video-editing programs. As an extra bonus, if you have Adobe After Effects, you'll learn how Photoshop stills can easily be composited into your movies.

This chapter will cover the following topics:

- **Nonlinear editing**
- **Understanding video formats, pixels, and video aspect ratios**
- **Preparing Photoshop images for digital video**
- **Working with alpha channels for compositing**
- **Pulling it all together in After Effects**

Brief Insight into Nonlinear Editing

Imagine that before the advent of digital video, you just finished shooting a short film in 35mm format with the intention of it being 20 minutes in length. The project is on a deadline, but you are nowhere near finished because the film must be previewed and edited—not only to fit the 20-minute time constraint but also to tell your story more effectively. Of course you understand that less can often be more, so you use this philosophy to your advantage. After taking the film to the lab to be processed, you get in return several large reels with hours of footage. Now you are ready to sit at the editing machine and edit through hours of your story to determine what is relevant to the story line and what should be discarded.

With the reel on one side of the editing machine, the length of the film is fed through a preview window, where the technician can physically assess and cut away any irrelevant scenes. Now if you want to add a scene from a different reel, you would have to preview the location to start your sequence and then physically tape together the two ends of the film so it will look like you are cutting from one sequence to the next on the big screen. This is normally referred to as *splicing*.

Well, that's video editing in a nutshell. It's just cutting and pasting scenes to better illustrate the final story. But notice that by using the old way, you have to work in the same chronological order as you filmed your scenes to edit your reels. The luxury of accessing different scenes in your short film randomly is not an option. You have to go through every frame to get to the location that you want to access. You are working in a linear fashion!

So what is the big deal about nonlinear editing? *Nonlinear editing (NLE)* is the random access of video storage, and this is synonymous with digitized film imagery. After your material is digitized, you can use your video-editing program to place on your hard disk only the sequences that are needed to tell a better story. Once on your system's disk, the footage is brought into a video-editing suite such as NewTek's Video Toaster or Adobe's Premiere to enable you to further organize and enhance your story with digital ease and speed. Not only does this give the editor greater creative options, but time is money and that's the business. All software packages will enable you to edit on a timeline, and most will have a suite of special effects to visually enhance your story. After the story is edited on the timeline, you can save it to the editing systems format.

Exploring Video Formats

Because of the variety of video-editing systems on the market, each has its own proprietary format for preserving timeline edits and special-effects information so the user can save and continue to edit their footage at a later date. For example, Adobe Premiere uses a `.ppj` file extension, NewTek's Video Toaster uses `.rtv` files, Video Delux uses `.mtv` , and Adobe

After Effects uses `.aep`, to name a few. There are some universal formats such as Targa (`.tga`), MPEG (`.mpg`), and AVI. Most editing programs will support those formats. Some will use their own codecs (compression-decompression schemes)—for example, Apple's QuickTime or Microsoft's AVI. Some, but not all, formats will incorporate codecs to compress and decompress the video images and sound. This process reduces storage requirements and data rates, enabling you to save the project for distribution via the Web, CDs, or DVDs. Almost all video-editing systems will enable you to export to various formats.

All video editing will use interlaced or (on occasion) noninterlaced formats. Interlaced files record video imagery in even and odd horizontal fields of data that each display half of the image frame (see Figure 27.1). The purpose of separating this data into even and odd fields is simple: it's a bandwidth issue. Video images are sliced up into fields for the same reason that Web designers slice up a single image for preparation of a website—because smaller amounts of data will transfer faster and more efficiently than larger ones. Also, just like Web graphics, the resolution is 72 ppi (pixels per inch). Be aware that unless traditional film was scanned in at user-defined settings, it is conventional for any files imported from any digital and/or video camera to be at a resolution of 72 ppi with the width and height changing accordingly.

The larger alternative is noninterlaced, which is composed of one complete image per frame and takes up a greater amount of bandwidth. This improves the visual quality of each frame. However, not all video-editing programs will recognize and edit noninterlaced file formats. Recently, Avid, Apple's Final Cut Pro, and Video Toaster 3 software and systems are a few that will edit this format. All software packages will edit the standard interlaced frames.

Figure 27.1

(left) A noninterlaced image, and (right) an example of interlaced technology

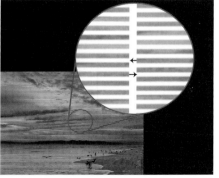

Understanding Pixels

The more pixels that are added to a file, the higher the resolution of the image. In other words, 150 pixels per inch is twice the resolution and file size of the same image that is 72 pixels per inch. So what does this have to do with video aspect ratios? Most of us have been working with square pixels, but now Adobe has given us the ability to format our images for rectangular video formats. Let's discover how this works.

Figure 27.2 is 5″×5″ with a resolution of 72 ppi that is completely square and is measured by five square objects of equal dimensions. For this example, consider the small square objects your pixels. Keep in mind that the file size is 379 KB.

Now choose Image → Pixel Aspect Ratio and view the variety of square and rectangular pixel aspect ratios (see Figure 27.3). Choose D1/DV PAL Widescreen 1.066 for an extreme view of the original. Look what happened (see Figure 27.4)! The once square file is now stretched—but the file size is still 379 KB! The reason is simple: You have not added any more or taken away any less pixel information in this file. You simply took the existing square formatted pixels and stretched them to be rectangular; thus the file size remains the same but formatted to video dimensions of your preference.

So what does this mean to the digital video artist? Understand that anything that is scanned into your computer will take on the square pixel format. That means any flatbed, film, or drum scanner will produce square pixels. However, digital video cameras that produce digital footage natively will produce rectangular pixels. Now Photoshop CS can accommodate the video format without adding more pixel information.

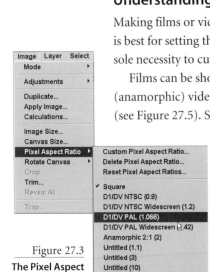

Understanding Video Aspect Ratio

Making films or video is an art. The ideal situation would be to choose a format ratio that is best for setting the mood of film. However, sometimes formats are chosen out of the sole necessity to cut costs.

Films can be shot in frame aspect ratios of 4:3 (4 width by 3 height) or widescreen (anamorphic) video formats of 16:9 (16 width by 9 height) to gain a more cinematic feel (see Figure 27.5). Some of the newer formats include HDTV (high-definition television) for both NTSC (American formats) and PAL (European video format standard).

Table 27.1 shows the dimensions of several video aspect ratios as well as some of the presets Photoshop allows when you create a new file. And don't forget that the resolution of the video formats are screen resolution at 72 ppi. This means that the dimensions of your file will change in width and height as needed while the resolution will remain at 72 ppi. In essence, you are working with the normal resolution of your monitor of 72 pixels per inch.

Figure 27.2

Image at square pixel dimensions

Figure 27.3

The Pixel Aspect Ratio submenu

FORMAT	SQUARE PIXEL PHOTOSHOP	RECTANGULAR PIXEL
NTSC 4:3 analog	640×480	N/A
NTSC 4:3 digital	720×534	720×480
NTSC 16:9 anamorphic	864×540	720×480
PAL 4:3	768×576	720×576
PAL D1 DV Widescreen (with Guides)	720×576	
PAL D1 DV Widescreen (with Guides)	768×576	
HDTV (with Guides)	1280×720	
HDTV (with Guides)	1920×1080	

Table 27.1

Dimensions of Selected Video Formats

Preparing Photoshop Images for Digital Video

There are a variety of tools for working with files from video, and Adobe has placed a couple of these tools in the Filter menu. They are the De-Interlace and NTSC Colors filters located under Filter → Video.

Using the De-Interlace Filter

When working with video, it is important to prepare your files so that they are compatible with the environment that they are going in. Let's say that you really liked a particular frame from previous video footage and you would like to use it for the background of your current project. Photoshop can prepare a still image from interlaced frames to look as if it were originally a noninterlaced image, to give the background a much cleaner look. Let's start with a digital video image exported to a single JPEG file as shown in Figure 27.6. Notice that you can see the horizontal fields used to create this image; however, your goal is to fill in the empty lines so that the image looks as if it were noninterlaced.

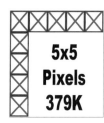

Figure 27.4

The image at rectangular pixel dimensions

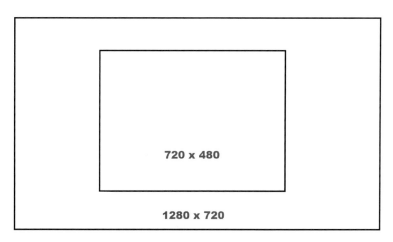

Figure 27.5

The smaller box has a 4:3 aspect ratio; the larger one is 16:9.

Figure 27.6

The image before De-interlacing

Figure 27.7

The Filter → Video → De-Interlace dialog box

To do this, choose Filter → Video → De-Interlace. A dialog box appears with options to duplicate or interpolate the fields, as shown in Figure 27.7. It also gives you the choice to work with the even or odd fields. Selecting either one simply will shift the image up or down by a negligible percentage.

Click the Interpolation radio button to have Photoshop add more pixels around each pixel until the missing gaps are filled in, or click Duplication to have Photoshop duplicate existing information to fill in the gaps. The interpolated version gives smoother results, as shown in Figure 27.8.

Figure 27.8

The image after De-interlacing

Using the NTSC Colors Filter

After you have improved the look of your background image, you should consider altering its colors to be more compatible with video. Colors that can be seen in NTSC formats are more limited than those that your computer screen has the capability to display. Just as there are gamut differences between monitors and print devices, so there are differences between what your monitor and what the television can display. To facilitate this process, Photoshop has a filter called NTSC Colors. You can access it by choosing Filter → Video → NTSC Colors (see Figure 27.9).

Once applied, the colors in your image are changed to be more compatible with the way that video and television will display color. If you pay close attention to the highlight areas of the image, you will see a slight color shift. On the computer monitor this might be a slight disappointment; however, the loss of color and detail will not be perceptible on a television screen.

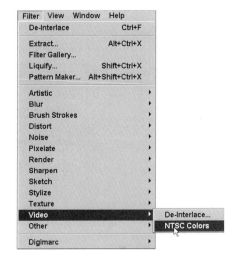

Figure 27.9

Choosing the NTSC Colors filter

> To some extent, the NTSC Colors filter is a legacy tool. With the Convert To Profile command, you can choose NTSC (1953), PAL/SECAM, or SMPTE-C ICC profiles for the conversion.

Working with Alpha Channels for Compositing

The film industry uses compositing to enhance the visual effects of a story. In short, *compositing* is the layering of images or other video footage over the main story line for effects purposes. Essentially this is exactly what you do in Photoshop with layers when you blend two or more images together to portray a concept.

In this section, you are going to get a little experience applying alpha channels to isolate a subject from its background.

The standard image format that all video-editing programs can read and apply an alpha mask to is Targa. Targa files are associated with a .tga extension, and Photoshop CS will save to this extension.

I created the image shown in Figure 27.10 in a 3-D program called LightWave by Newtek (www.newtek.com). When I exported into a bitmap, Photoshop placed the object on its own layer. You can take advantage of this to create a selection of your object. Try this:

1. From the *Photoshop CS Savvy* CD, open the file starship.psd from the Ch27 folder.

2. Open your Layers palette and ⌘/Ctrl-click the Star Ship layer. Photoshop has now made a selection based on the existing pixels. In this case, it's the ship itself.

3. Now you will create your alpha channel from this selection. Choose Selection → Save Selection. Click OK to save it as an alpha channel. The additional channel will designate transparency in your image file (see Figure 27.11) that any video-editing program will read and honor. Take note that the black areas in the channel designate transparency.

Figure 27.10

My 3-D spaceship

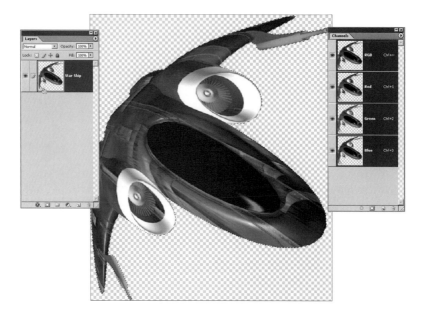

Figure 27.11

Saving a selection adds an alpha channel to the file.

Figure 27.12

Format dialog box

4. Now you are ready to save the file to the universal Targa format. Choose File → Save As and save it under a new name. From the Format list, choose the Targa format (see Figure 27.12). Your file will be given a .tga extension.

5. Choose Select → Save Selection and click OK.

In another page or so, you'll use this starship file, with the saved selection, to add a flying spaceship to a still image.

ALPHA CHANNELS

Alpha channels are nothing more than imagery made up of 256 shades of gray in Photoshop. What does this mean to us as artists? It simply means that we now have 256 levels of transparency. The black areas designate transparency, whereas the white areas will leave the image unaffected. The grays in between give us various levels of transparencies. This alpha channel can be edited with any of Photoshop's painting tools to alter how it will appear in the video-editing program.

Understanding Title-Safe Areas for Video

Photoshop provides most of your video format as a preset in the New File dialog box. Choose File → New, click the down arrow for the preset button, and browse all of the video formats that Adobe has provided. Also notice that guides are listed next to each of the video formats. Choose the NTSC DV 720×480 (With Guides) option. Now look at Figure 27.13 to see what Photoshop CS has given us.

What are these guides for? Your television set is really closer to a square format, but many DV and big-screen movie formats are more rectangular. So something will have to be cropped off, and the guides show you the areas that are going to be viewed on the television set. The center is also known as *safe areas.* The center rectangle is known as the Inner Title Safe Area. You want to make sure that all titles are within these borders so that your audience will get the full view of credits without any cropping. The outer rectangle guide is called the Outer Action Safe Area. You want to ensure that your visual imagery will fit within these borders. This will allow the video editor to choose what areas of the film will be seen by the audience for the normal TV set formats. If you would like to see the entire movie format as filmed according to the director's vision, then you just have to wait for the director's cut to be released or purchase an expensive HDTV television. Personally I think the movie theatre is much more fun.

Figure 27.13

**Video format
with guides**

Pulling It All Together in After Effects

If you have Adobe After Effects, you can apply all that you've learned and create a sample special-effects clip.

In the Ch27 folder on the companion CD, you will find a sample AVI video clip of the Golden Gate Bridge (GoldenGateBridge.avi). You can use the starship Targa file created earlier in this chapter to composite the starship bitmap onto the video clip and make it appear as if it's flying from the background out toward the camera and then zooming out of view.

Open After Effects and begin with the projects box, which is by default on the upper-left corner of your interface. Then follow these steps:

1. Right-click/Ctrl-click within its interface, choose New Folder from the pop-up menu, and name the folder whatever you like (see Figure 27.14).

2. You need to create a new composition that will create the timeline information that you need to create your very short movie. So right-click/Ctrl-click again on the projects box interface and select New Composition (see Figure 27.15).

3. Import your two files into the projects box by right-clicking/Ctrl-clicking once again and choosing Import → Multiple Files. You can use the ⌘/Ctrl key to select multiple files; then click OK. Notice that you get an Interpret Footage dialog box for your starship.tga file (see Figure 27.16). This is because you saved an alpha channel with it, and After Effects recognizes that fact. Keep the default (Straight - Unmatted), click OK, and After Effects will designate the transparency of this file.

Figure 27.14

Creating a new folder for your project

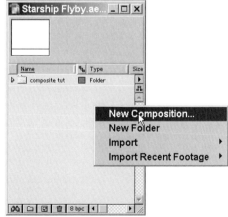

Figure 27.15

Creating a new composition

Figure 27.16

Tell After Effects how to interpret the alpha channel.

4. To stay organized, drag the composition files and the two imported files into the folder you created earlier (see Figure 27.17).

5. Before you start compositing, right-click/Ctrl-click your preview area, select Composition Settings, and make sure that you are using DV format of 720×480. Make sure the aspect ratio is set to DV/D1 NTSC (0.9), as shown in Figure 27.18.

6. Now drag your Golden Gate Bridge file from its folder onto the preview area. Do the same for the starship file (see Figure 27.19).

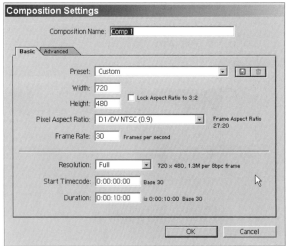

Figure 27.17

Drag the project files into their folder.

Figure 27.18

Composition settings

Figure 27.19

Drag both files into the Comp window.

You have the beginning of your composited short. After preparing `starship.tga` in Photoshop CS and saving it with an alpha channel, After Effects blocked the areas that were designated as black in the alpha channel. As a result, you see only the starship. Now let's make it fly!

Make It Fly, Baby!

Now let's have some real fun! If you look at your timeline, you will notice that both of your files were placed in their own layer and organized just as you would have done in Photoshop. With the starship on top, you can now make it look like it will fly from the background to the foreground and out of view while in front of the Golden Gate Bridge.

If you adhere to the rules of perspective, you know that anything in the background will appear smaller and anything in the foreground will appear larger, so let's animate the starship to be smaller in frame 1 and large in the last frame.

1. Put your playhead on frame 1, open the Transform properties (next to the `starship.tga` title on the left side of the timeline), and choose Scale.

2. Click the keyframe symbol on the left side of the Scale timeline (see Figure 27.20). A diamond appears at frame 1, designating a keyframe at frame 1.

Figure 27.20

Setting a Scale keyframe

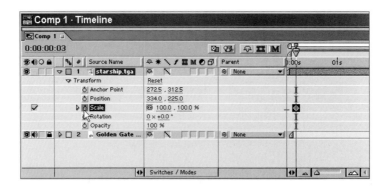

Figure 27.21

Resize the starship and move it up.

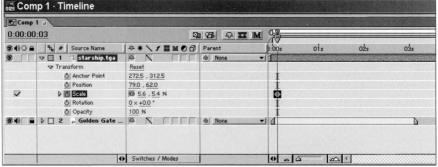

3. Click on the starship to activate it in the preview area. You will see a box with handle bars surrounding the object. Click and hold one of the corner handle bars and drag it to resize the ship smaller—about 1/10 the size of the viewing frame. Finally, place the ship in the upper-left side of the frame (see Figure 27.21).

4. Now place the playhead on the last frame and resize the starship to be 2/3 the size of your preview frame.

5. Place the playhead back on frame 1, and press the spacebar to preview your animation. The ship resizes but it doesn't move (see Figure 27.22).

6. Select the Position property underneath the Starship layer. Once again, place the playhead at the first frame and make a keyframe (see Figure 27.23).

7. Place the playhead on the last frame and drag the starship down to the right corner and off the frame. A keyframe will automatically be set for you (see Figure 27.24).

8. Go back to frame 1 and press the spacebar again. Now your ship is really flying!

Figure 27.22

The starship grows large but in the same place.

Figure 27.23

Place the ship in the upper left when the Scale is small…

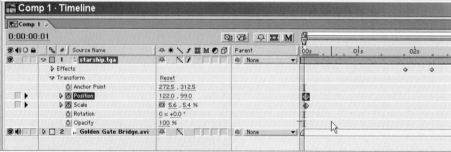

Figure 27.24

…and then place it in the lower right when the Scale is large.

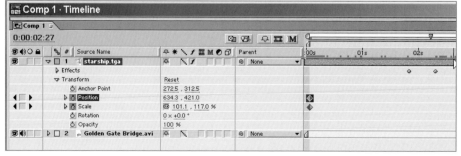

A Little More EFX!

Now you'll add just a little more of an effect by adding some motion blur to give the spaceship some movement:

1. Click the Effects palette and double-click Directional Blur. In Figure 27.25, notice that the dialog box enables you to specify the direction as well as the length of the blur. In addition, it enables you to specify when and how much of the effect will take place. Set these options according to your vision.

2. Specify when you would like the effect to begin and end by setting your playhead to the desired frame and then selecting a keyframe in the Directional Blur dialog box. Notice that the effect settings are transferred to the timeline on its own layer as a subset of the Starship layer. Figures 27.26 and 27.27 give an example of how the effects were applied in the beginning and end of the ship movement on the timeline.

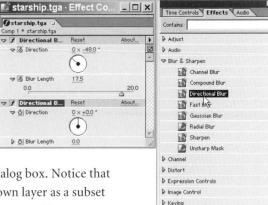

Figure 27.25

After Effects Directional Blur options

Figure 27.26

Directional Blur applied to the ship's starting position

Figure 27.27

**Directional Blur
applied to the ship's
ending position**

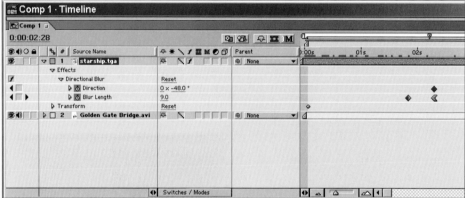

Figure 27.27

**Directional Blur
applied to the ship's
ending position**

Don't be afraid to play with these effects because the best way to learn about After Effects is to experiment.

The only thing that remains now is to render the effect into the format and dimensions that you see fit. To begin a simple render:

1. Choose File → Export and, from the submenu, choose your format (see Figure 27.28). I chose the QuickTime format in this example.

2. A Save As dialog box appears; tell After Effects where you would like the file to be saved to. Make sure that you have plenty of disk space available.

3. A Save As dialog box appears; tell After Effects where you would like the file to be saved to. Make sure that you have plenty of disk space available.

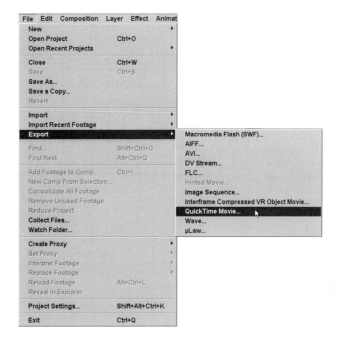

Figure 27.28

Exporting your composited movie

4. All you have to do now is specify the format, color, and compression settings in the Movie Settings dialog box (see Figure 27.29). This is another area where experimentation will serve you best. To test these, in the beginning render only short clips so that you don't have to endure the long render times.

Now that you have a fairly good understanding of how Photoshop CS can aid you for video production, the galaxy is truly the limit.

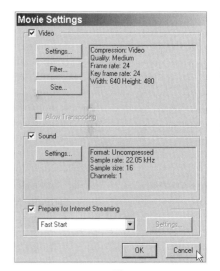

Figure 27.29

Choosing video settings on export

Appendices

This section of the book will provide a window to the power of the World Wide Web in expanding your Photoshop skills. It includes an introduction to third-party plug-ins and descriptions of many useful Web links. This section will conclude with a glossary of terms related to the world of digital images.

APPENDIX A ▪ Plug-Ins

APPENDIX B ▪ Online Resources

GLOSSARY

Plug-Ins

The power of Photoshop is multiplied by the many third-party plug-ins available. These plug-ins integrate themselves into Photoshop and operate as components every bit as much as those that originally come from Adobe.

A plug-in can operate as a filter on the filter's menu, affecting the current image, or as an add-in that gives new functionality such as the ability to import and export in new file formats.

There are far more plug-ins than can be covered in any appendix, and new ones are being written every week. This appendix showcases some interesting and useful ones tested with Photoshop CS: Eye Candy 4000, Image Doctor, and the Windows-only Impressionist filter.

Some plug-ins are sold, and others are given away free. Trial and demonstration versions with limited functionality are often available for testing before purchase. As such, you are always encouraged to shop around for the best deal on the functions that you need to perform. Internet searches for Photoshop plug-ins or Photoshop filters provide many sources.

DISCLAIMER

Third-party plug-ins cannot be warranted by the authors or publisher of this book. It is always up to the purchaser to ensure that all such products function correctly for their needs.

Eye Candy 4000

Eye Candy 4000 is a set of 23 special-effects filters from Alien Skin Software. They can be found on the Web at www.alienskin.com.

Eye Candy 4000 contains improved Eye Candy 3 filters, plus several new ones. Some Eye Candy 3 filters have been combined into single, new Eye Candy 4000 filters.

Getting Started

Figure A.1

The Eye Candy submenu

Eye Candy 4000 contains setup programs for both Macintosh and Windows. It attempts to locate known graphics programs and allow installation for any program it recognizes. When it doesn't recognize a program (such as a too new version of Photoshop), you can manually select it to be installed in its own subdirectory for Windows under the Plug-Ins subdirectory in your Photoshop directory.

After it is correctly installed, restart Photoshop and you should see the list of Eye Candy filters in the Filter menu (see Figure A.1).

The Filters

To show the transformations performed by Eye Candy 4000, a simple graphic of letters with a gradient fill has been created (see Figure A.2). This *Normal* graphic is the starting point for the following transformations, and has both white and black backgrounds to better highlight some features.

Figure A.2

We'll use this base image to apply the various filters.

Antimatter

The Antimatter filter inverts a selection, but gives more control over a simple Photoshop invert. Adjustments allow tweaking of the inversion for better results. One use is for creating dramatic rollover images.

Bevel Boss

Bevel Boss enables you to create a wide variety of beveled images.

Chrome

Chrome does what the name says. Using a variety of textures and options, a wide range of shiny metal effects are easily created.

Corona

Corona easily creates the effect of solar flares, gaseous clouds, and other astronomical effects around your selections.

Cutout

Cutout creates the effect of cutting out your selection, complete with shadowing. Here I cut through the black layer to reveal the white layer below.

Drip

This filter does what it says, with a wide variety of options to control the final results.

Fire

Set your image on fire for dramatic effect.

Fur

Fuzzy, wavy, or curly. Long or short, it's up to you.

Glass

Create the effect of transparent or colored glass over a selection.

Gradient Glow

Create mild to wild gradients around selections. There are many options for every situation.

HSB Noise

HSB Noise enables you to add textures based on the underlying image. It's easy to use, and the results are hard to duplicate with standard tools.

Jiggle

Distort entire selections far more than you can easily do with Photoshop alone.

Marble

Create marble textures in a variety of colors, sizes, and features.

Melt

This one does what you expect, with a variety of different settings available.

Motion Trail

This filter provides dramatic variations on motion blurs. Create your own roadrunner effects.

Shadowlab

This provides far more flexible shadowing—including perspective shadowing—than you can achieve using layer styles.

Smoke

Heat up your presentations with some smoke. It also creates haze, fog, and fume effects.

Squint

Blur the areas outside your selection to create the effect of poor vision.

Star

Create all kinds of stars quickly and easily.

Swirl

Smear your selection with randomly placed whirlpools for an amazing variety of texture effects.

Water Drops

Apply water drops to your image more easily than leaving it out in the rain.

Weave

Weave re-creates a selection, giving a woven appearance.

Wood

Turn a selection to wood with great control over rings, knots, and grain.

Image Doctor

While some plug-ins are fun, others perform serious image repair. Such is the case with Image Doctor from Alien Skin Software. They can be found on the Web at `http://www.alienskin.com`.

Although only four filters are included with this package, they are powerful in the right circumstances.

Getting Started

Like Eye Candy 4000, Image Doctor contains setup programs for both Macintosh and Windows. It attempts to locate known graphics programs and allow installation for any program it recognizes. When it doesn't recognize a program (such as a too new version of Photoshop), you can manually select it to be installed in its own subdirectory for Windows under the `Plug-Ins` subdirectory in your Photoshop directory.

After it is correctly installed, restart Photoshop and you should see the list shown in Figure A.3 under the Filter menu.

The Filters

JPEG Repair

JPEG Repair mitigates the compression artifacts from overly compressed JPEG images. It is adjustable so that only the necessary amount of correction is applied. The results can be seen in Figure A.4.

Smart Fill

Smart Fill removes an object or defect from the image and re-creates a background based on the surrounding image. Although it can't restore exactly missing data, it provides a surprisingly realistic re-creation. In addition, because it randomly creates the new background from sampling nearby image material, the filter allows easy stepping through numerous possible replacement fills until a good match is found. Removing light poles, telephone lines, and similar distractions becomes a snap.

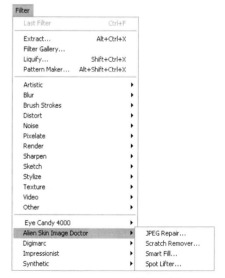

Figure A.3

The Image Doctor submenu

Figure A.4

(left) Before and (right) after the application of JPEG Repair

Consider Figure A.5, where several ugly black lines mar the image. Smart Fill automatically identifies them and removes them in the after image.

Figure A.5

(left) Before and (right) after the application of Smart Fill

Scratch Remover and Spot Lifter

Also included in this package are Scratch Remover and Spot Lifter filters:

Scratch Remover automates repair of small scratches, folds, creases, wrinkles, and other defects. Removal of time codes from digital images is quick and clean with this filter.

Spot Lifter removes and blends backgrounds for moles, birthmarks, and even watermarks, stains, and dust.

The Microsoft Impressionist Filter (Windows Only)

The Microsoft Impressionist filter is legendary—or at least the stuff of some legends—in the Photoshop community. Some call it the finest piece of software ever released by Microsoft.

Though never known to be sold as a Photoshop add-in, and not sold at all at this time, this Microsoft Windows–only filter was written to the Photoshop filter interface standards and has operated well with the last several versions of Photoshop. Capable of hundreds of variations, the Microsoft Impressionist filter's effects are limited primarily by the user's imagination

Getting It

The Microsoft Impressionist filter is included in the now discontinued Microsoft Image Composer product. This product was shipped as part of Microsoft Front Page 97, 98, and 2000.

A legal way to acquire this product is through purchase of a new or used copy of Microsoft Front Page 97/98/2000. Listings for this software regularly appear on auction sites (for example, eBay) at low prices.

Installing It

Because the Impressionist filter was never sold as a stand-alone product, it must be installed by hand. The complete package even includes a Help file.

1. Locate the Image Composer plug-ins on the Front Page CD by searching for `Impres_1.8bf`.

2. Create the following subdirectories under your Adobe Photoshop `Plug-Ins` subdirectory:

        ..\Plug Ins\Impressionist Accessories
        ..\Plug Ins\Impressionist Accessories\Brushes
        ..\Plug Ins\Impressionist Accessories\Factory Settings
        ..\Plug Ins\Impressionist Accessories\Paper

3. Copy the following CD files to the indicated locations:

        ..\Plug Ins\Impres_1.8bf
        ..\Plug Ins\Impressionist Accessories\imprsnst.cnt
        ..\Plug Ins\Impressionist Accessories\imprsnst.GID
        ..\Plug Ins\Impressionist Accessories\imprsnst.hlp

4. Copy the CD contents of `\Brushes`, `\Factory Settings`, and `\Paper` to the corresponding subdirectories for Photoshop.

Figure A.6

The Impressionist submenu

Using It

After the Impressionist filter is installed properly and Photoshop CS is restarted, the filter appears on the Filter menu, as shown in Figure A.6. After it is started, you are presented with the opening window shown in Figure A.7.

The best way to learn about this filter is to use its Run Demo and Help buttons. Run Demo causes the filter to sequence through default settings for its major effects. After that, just have at it. The combination of different brushes, papers, styles, and settings allow for nearly infinite variations.

Figure A.7

Using the Impressionist filter

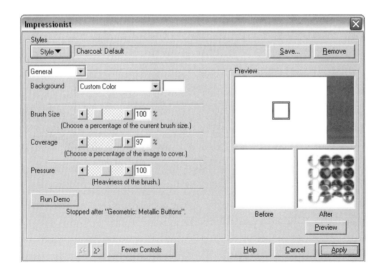

Here are some samples of effects quickly and easily generated by using the Impressionist filter:

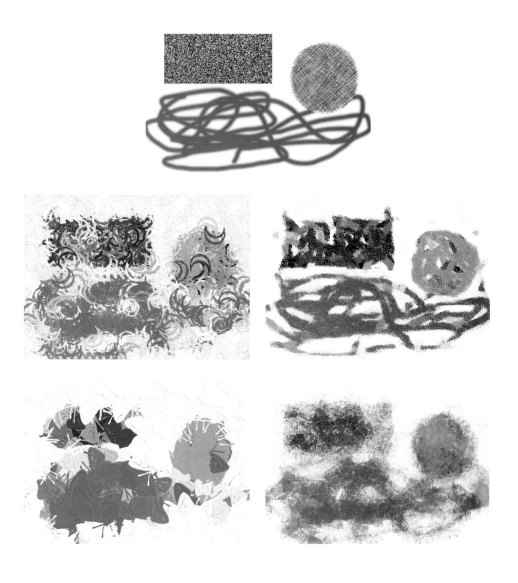

To see it do something a bit more serious, look at Figure A.8, which shows a seashell turned into a fine pencil drawing.

Figure A.8

The Impressionist filter can produce a fine pencil version of your art.

Online Resources

Now that you've loaded Photoshop and read this book, you have taken only the first steps toward finding all the information, marvelous tips, tricks, and tutorials available to the Photoshop user.

Websites and Usenet newsgroups provide additional resources. You can find all kinds of useful information by going online. The type of help varies from site to site.

Note that the Web is dynamic, and websites and newsgroups come and go without notice. The sites listed here have survived for some period of time and are valid as of publication of this book.

Websites

Photoshop-related websites fall into the following general categories:

Art sites showcase what can be accomplished with Photoshop.

Competition sites sponsor Photoshop image contests in which you can demonstrate your creativity in competition with others. Many competitors at these sites are happy to share their techniques.

Forum sites have user forums where your questions can be answered by other users.

Links sites give links to other useful sites, and are updated more often than this book can be.

Plug-ins sites offer downloadable plug-ins or information about plug-ins.

However, because many sites fall into more than one category, it is impossible to group them. Instead I offer a quick summary of what you can expect to find on each site listed here.

These websites are the property of their owners. No warranty of fitness for your application is expressed or implied.

Action FX Photoshop Resources A large site of Photoshop actions contributed by members for Windows and Macintosh platforms.

> http://www.actionfx.com

Adobe Studio Exchange The Adobe source for Knowledgebase answers to questions and downloads of updates, new brushes, and additional software.

> http://share.studio.adobe.com/Default.asp

Adobe User to User Forums The Adobe Web-based list for discussing Adobe products and associated issues with other users and Adobe staff.

http://www.adobe.com/support/forums/main.html

ClarkVision.com Art, digital photography information, and insights.

http://www.clarkvision.com

Creativepro.com Articles, plug-ins, tutorials.

http://www.creativepro.com/front/home

DesignsByMark.com Tutorials, art, and links.

http://www.designsbymark.com

Digital Creativity UK Many tutorials.

http://www.digital-creativity.org.uk

Fantastic Machines Filters, free demo downloads.

http://www.fantasticmachines.com

FilterMeister A package for writing your own filters for Photoshop.

http://www.filtermeister.com

Flaming Pear Software Plug-ins, free demos, links.

http://www.flamingpear.com

Fnord Free Jpeg 2000, SuperPNG, and xMeta plug-ins.

http://www.fnordware.com

Fonte Free artistic fonts and clip art.

http://www.webgate.dk/klaus/Fonte/newfonts/nyefonte.htm

Free Photoshop Free plug-ins and filters.

http://www.freephotoshop.com

GFX Many tips and tutorials.

http://user.fundy.net/morris

Jeff T. Alu Digital fine art photography. Pay attention to his My Process pages.

http://www.animalu.com/pics/photos.htm

My Janee Forum, competition, tutorials, links, this site has it all, from the Graphics Goddess.

http://www.myjanee.com

National Association of Photoshop Professionals NAPP has the largest membership of any Photoshop organization. The site offers resources, discounts and special conferences.

> http://photoshopuser.com

Nebulus Designs Tutorials.

> http://www.nebulus.org

Phong Tutorials.

> http://www.phong.com/tutorials

Photoscientia Articles, especially on grain aliasing as related to film scanning.

> http://www.photoscientia.co.uk

Planet Photoshop Tutorials.

> http://www.planetphotoshop.com

Plugins World Attempts to cover every Photoshop plug-in.

> http://www.pluginsworld.com

Pluginz.com Articles, plug-ins.

> http://www.pluginz.com

PhotoshopCafe.com Art, forum, links, tutorials.

> http://www.photoshopcafe.com

Reindeer Graphics Digital photography tools, plug-ins, some free.

> http://www.reindeergraphics.com

RetouchPRO Tutorials in photo retouching, competition.

> http://retouchpro.com

ScanTips by Wayne Fulton Everything you want to know about how to properly use your scanner with Photoshop.

> http://www.scantips.com

Telegraphics Donation-ware (but very cheap) plug-ins, fonts, art.

> http://www.telegraphics.com.au

The Great Illusion A fascinating example of web-page image technology.

> http://www.thegreatillusion.com

The Imaging Resource A great amount of information and reviews on digital photography.

> http://www.imaging-resource.com

The Photoshop Guru's Handbook Tutorials, forum.

> http://photoshopgurus.info

TutorialHunt.com Large index of tutorials covering many programs.

> http://www.tutorialhunt.com

The Unofficial TIFF Home Page Lots of information about TIFF files. Useful to people who really need to know the internals of this format.

> http://home.earthlink.net/~ritter/tiff

Wacom Technology Information, driver updates, and Photoshop plug-ins for people using Wacom tablets. You are using a tablet with Photoshop, aren't you?

> http://www.wacom.com

Wetzel & Company Art and tutorials, some tied into their textures.

> http://www.wetzelandcompany.com

WhatTheFont A site that seeks to identify fonts for you from image files. Haven't you ever wondered just what that fascinating font is that an artist used on that page?

> http://www.myfonts.com/WhatTheFont

This is just a start. Follow links from these sites to still more resources, or type **photoshop tutorial** into your favorite search engine. You will continually be amazed at what new tricks someone has gotten this program to perform.

Newsgroups

There's nothing like finding personal support when you run into a problem you can't solve or a question you can't answer immediately. Usenet newsgroups not only give you a great place to get help, but also enable you to answer questions yourself and be part of the Photoshop community. Usenet is the oldest widely distributed discussion forum on the Internet.

For Photoshop-oriented Usenet groups, try the following:

- adobe.photoshop.windows
- alt.graphics.photoshop
- comp.graphics.apps.photoshop (recommended)

You can also search for other groups with *Photoshop* in the group name. Some of these offer discussion in languages other than English.

The Google search engine keeps an archive of all Usenet newsgroup postings in searchable form. Go to the Google site (www.google.com) and click the Groups tab for free access to this wealth of information.

Glossary

Action A Photoshop operation that automates a single operation or a sequence of operations. Photoshop comes with default Actions, and you can create and save custom Actions to a file. When you need a particular Action or Action sequence, you can play it and apply its operations to any image by pressing a function key.

Actions palette The Photoshop palette that contains controls for recording and playing back Actions.

additive primary colors Red, green, and blue, which are used to create all other colors when direct, or transmitted, light is used (for example, on a computer monitor). When pure red, green, and blue are superimposed on one another, they create white.

Adjustment layer In Photoshop, a separate layer containing the mathematical data for an adjustment operation applied to an image. You can re-edit the Adjustment layer at any time during the imaging process.

Adobe Gamma calibration package A package that includes Adobe Gamma software, the Gamma Wizard, and ICC (International Color Consortium) color profiles for some RGB devices. You can use the Gamma software to calibrate your monitor on the Windows operating system.

alpha channel An 8-bit, grayscale representation of an image. Alpha channels are selections that have been stored for later use. The values of gray can represent tonality, color, opacity, or semitransparency. Image formats that support alpha channels include Photoshop (PSD), Photoshop 2.0, Large Document Format (PSB), BMP, JPEG 2000, Photoshop PDF, PICT, PICT Resource, PIXAR, Photoshop Raw, Targa (TGA), and TIFF.

analog Signals made up of continuously varying wave forms.

anti-alias A process that adds a 2- or 3-pixel border around an edge that blends into the adjacent color to create a small transition zone. Without the anti-alias, an image would look stair-stepped and not have smooth transitions between colors. The width of an anti-alias is determined by the resolution of the image; you have no control over its size.

artifact An unintentional image element produced in error by an imaging device or inaccurate software. Dirty optics are one common reason for artifacts.

aspect ratio The height-to-width ratio of a selection, an image, or—in the case of digital video—a frame.

Background In Photoshop, the area behind layers. The contents of all layers float on top of the Background. Unlike a layer, the Background is opaque and cannot support transparency. If the document contains more than one layer, the Background is always at the bottom of the stack and cannot be moved or placed in a higher position. When new layers are added to the document, their content always appears in front of the Background.

baseline An imaginary line on which the bottom of most textual characters are placed. Some characters, such as *g* and *y*, have descenders that extend below the baseline.

baseline shift The movement of the baseline of a character horizontally or vertically from its default starting position. Unlike leading, which affects all of the characters in a paragraph, baseline shift affects individual characters.

Batch Action An Action that will be applied to all of the images in a folder automatically, also known as *batch processing*. You can batch-process a group of images within a folder or from a different source, such as a digital camera or scanner with a document feeder.

Bezier curves Lines and shapes composed of mathematically defined points and segments. Bezier curves are used in vector graphics.

bit depth Refers to the amount of information per color channel. Photoshop can read images with 16 bits of information per channel, such as a 48-bit RGB or a 64-bit CMYK color image. Even though images with higher bit depths contain more color information, they are displayed on the monitor at the bit-depth capability of the computer's video card, which is 24 bits in most cases.

Bitmap mode A Photoshop mode that displays and converts images that are composed of pixels, each containing 1 bit of information. The pixels are either black or white. Bitmap images are used to create line art and digital halftones. Bitmap image file sizes are smaller than grayscale images, which contain 8 bits per pixel, or color images, which contain 24 bits per pixel. Bitmapped images do not support layers, alpha channels, filters, or any operations involving color.

black point The darkest pixel in the shadow areas of an image. In Photoshop, you can set this point in the Levels and Curves dialog boxes.

blending mode A preprogrammed color formula that determines how the pixels in an image are affected by painting or image-editing and overlay operations. In Photoshop, the Mode menu on the Options bar offers a choice of several blending modes.

brightness The relative lightness or darkness of a color, measured from 0 to 100 percent. Brightness is also referred to as *value*. Colors with low brightness values are dark; colors with high brightness values are light.

burn A technique used by photographers in the darkroom to underexpose or darken areas of an image. Photoshop's Burn tool darkens by lowering the brightness values of pixels as you move the tool over the image.

calibrated monitor The foundation from which all other color settings are determined. You can use a calibration device or the Adobe Gamma calibration package to calibrate your monitor.

calibration bars The grayscale or color indicators that appear on printed output. When you print a CMYK color separation, the calibration bars appear only on the black plate. On a color image, the calibration bars are the color swatches printed at the sides of the image.

Camera Raw A proprietary digital camera file format specific to each camera manufacturer and often to the make/model of a camera. Photoshop CS can process Camera Raw files from many popular digital cameras.

canvas In Photoshop, the surface on which your image resides.

capture Specific to digital video, the transfer of video information via FireWire to a computer environment for nonlinear editing.

channel Analogous to a plate in the printing process, the foundation of an image. Some image types have only one channel, whereas other types have several channels. An image can have up to 24 channels. See also *color channels*.

Channel Mixer A Photoshop feature that enables you to adjust the color information of each channel. You can establish color values on a specific channel as a mixture of any or all of the color channels' brightness values.

Channels palette The Photoshop palette that enables you to work with an image's color information, or channels, and create alpha channels.

Character palette The Photoshop palette that contains settings for type, such as size, tracking, kerning, and leading.

chroma See *saturation*.

CIE (Commission Internationale de l'Eclairage) An international organization of scientists who work with matters relating to color and lighting. The organization is also called the International Commission on Illumination.

clipping mask Layers grouped together to create effects. In order to join two layers into a clipping group, the image on the bottom layer must be surrounded by transparency. When a layer is clipped, it fills the shape of the image on the layer below it so that it acts as a mask to clip the layer immediately above it.

clipping path A path designed to be used as a mask in other applications. In Photoshop, the Clipping Paths option in the Paths palette menu enables you to create a path that will knock out the area outside the path when it is opened in another program. The interior portion of the path will be displayed, and the area outside the path will be transparent.

cloning In Photoshop and other image-editing programs, a feature that enables you to copy a part of an image and use that copy to replace another part of the image. Cloning is accomplished with the Clone Stamp and Pattern Stamp tools.

CMYK The colors used in process printing. Each color plate contains tiny dots of cyan, magenta, yellow, or black (CMYK). The densities of the colored dots on each plate influence the surrounding colors when the eye mixes them together.

CMYK color mode A color mode that produces a full range of color by printing tiny dots of cyan, magenta, yellow, and black ink. Because the colored dots are so small, the eye mixes them together. The relative densities of groups of colored dots produce variations in color and tonality. CMYK is referred to as a *subtractive* color system.

CMYK image A four-channel image containing a cyan, magenta, yellow, and black channel. A CMYK image is generally used to print color separations.

CODEC An acronym for the compression/decompression process. Reducing storage requirements and the data rate required to retrieve video from a disk for decompression and playback.

color channels Color information from an image. The number of color channels depends on the image's color mode. For example, Photoshop configures the information for an RGB image into three color channels (for the red, green, and blue components) plus a composite RGB channel, which displays the entire image in full color. The computer processes the information in each channel as an independent grayscale image. Each pixel is assigned a specific numeric gray value, where black equals 0 and white equals 255. Each color channel is actually an 8-bit grayscale image that supports 256 shades of gray.

color correction Changing the colors of pixels in an image—including adjusting brightness, contrast, mid-level grays, hue, and saturation—to achieve optimum printed results.

color depth The number of shades that an imaging device can capture at once. The more bits there are per pixel, the more hues you can represent. The most common color depth, 8 bits per color, can produce 256 shades of each hue.

color management module (CMM) The color management engine used by software to convert colors. The Adobe engine is ACE (Adobe Color Engine). Others you might encounter include Agfa, Apple ColorSync, Apple, Heidelberg, Imation, Kodak, Microsoft, and X-Rite.

color management policies Policies that determine how Photoshop deals with color profiles when opening RGB, CMYK, or Grayscale files.

color mapping Operations that can radically alter existing colors in an image. Color mapping provides the means to alter the basic characteristics of color while maintaining the image's detail.

color mode or model A system of displaying or printing color. Photoshop supports the HSB color model and RGB, CMYK, Lab, Indexed, Duotone, Grayscale, Multichannel, and Bitmap color modes.

color separation (process) An image that has been separated into the four process colors: cyan, magenta, yellow, and black (CMYK). The image is then printed on four separate plates, one for each of the process colors.

color working space The colors produced by a specific device, such as a printer or monitor. Photoshop enables you to edit and store an image with a color space other than that of your monitor. The image is embedded with an ICC (International Color Consortium) profile that describes the working color space. The image can then move from one computer to another with its profile, and it can be displayed on two different monitors and appear the same.

colorimeter A device used to calibrate a monitor by measuring the temperature of its color characteristics.

colorize To convert gray pixels to colored pixels. Before a black-and-white image can be colorized in Photoshop, you must change its mode from Grayscale to a mode that supports color (RGB, CMYK, or Lab). By colorizing, you apply color to the image without affecting the lightness relationships of the individual pixels, thereby maintaining the image's detail.

conditional A statement of a situation that must be met before the next step of an action can take place. You set both the condition situation and the steps to take if the condition is met. Inserting conditional steps is supported only in ImageReady CS.

continuous-tone image An image containing gradient tones from black to white.

contrast The tonal gradation between the highlights, midtones, and shadows in an image.

crop To select part of an image and discard the unselected areas.

crop marks The marks that are printed near the edges of an image to indicate where the image is to be trimmed.

Curves A Photoshop color-adjustment tool that enables you to lighten, darken, add contrast to, and solarize images.

densitometer An instrument used by print shops and service bureaus to measure the tonal density of printed halftones.

density The capability of an object to stop or absorb light. The less the light is reflected or transmitted by an object, the higher its density.

density range The range from the smallest highlight dot that a press can print to the largest shadow dot it can print.

digital video (DV) The configuration of video into a pixel-based media that can be interpreted and displayed on a computer monitor.

digitize To convert analog image or video information to a digital format.

digitizer board A special-purpose computer card that transforms video signals into image data. Image sources for this technology include television signals and the output from VCRs and traditional analog video cameras. Digitizer video boards are also called *frame grabbers,* because they receive the frames sent by the video image sources.

distort To stretch a selection or layer contents along either of its axes. Unlike skewing, distortion is not restricted to a single border at a time.

dither A method of distributing pixels to extend the visual range of color on-screen, such as producing the effect of shades of gray on a black-and-white display or more colors on an 8-bit color display. By making adjacent pixels different colors, dithering gives the illusion of a third color.

dodge A technique used by photographers in the darkroom to overexpose or lighten specific areas of an image. In Photoshop, the Dodge tool performs a similar function by increasing the brightness values of pixels as you paint with it.

dot gain A phenomenon in printing that causes dots to print larger due to the absorbency of the paper they are printed on. Dot gain creates darker tones or colors. Dot gain is reflected in an increase in the density of light reflected by an image.

dots per inch (dpi) The measurement of the number of dots produced by a printer that defines the tonal elements of a halftone dot or stochastic screen. The dpi determines the resolution of printed output.

Droplet A mini application that contains Actions. A Droplet can sit on the desktop or be saved to a disk file. You can apply an operation to a file or group of files by dragging the file or folder onto the Droplet's icon.

drum scanner A type of scanner that uses a spinning drum. The image is taped to a drum that spins very rapidly while the scanner's sensors record its color and tonality information.

Duotone An image that uses two inks. Duotone can add a wider tonal range in a grayscale image by using more than one shade of ink to fill in the gaps. Duotone curves let you control the density of each shade in the highlights, midtones, and shadows. Photoshop creates Duotones by applying the various curves that you've defined to a single image.

Duotone mode A Photoshop mode that displays Duotones, which are images that have been separated into two spot colors. Duotone mode also supports Monotone (images with one color), Tritones (images with three colors), and Quadtones (images with four colors). The Duotone Mode color information is contained on one color channel. Photoshop displays a preview that is an RGB simulation of the ink combinations.

DV See *digital video*.

emulsion The photosensitive layer on a piece of film, paper, or plate.

EQ (equalization) Specific to digital video, the altering of the frequency/amplitude response of a sound source or a sound system.

equalization A technique for distributing image data across a greater range of pixel values. Typical equalization techniques include gamma correction and adaptive histogram equalization.

fade-out rate The rate at which the Photoshop Paintbrush and Airbrush tools fade out as you paint with them to simulate an actual brush stroke.

feather A process that creates a gradual transition between the inside and the outside of image borders. When you apply an effect to a feathered selection, it diminishes and becomes more transparent, producing a softening or blurring effect. Feathering gradually blends colored pixels into each other and eliminates hard edges. Feathering differs from anti-aliasing in that you can determine the size of the soft edge in pixels.

feather edge The area along the border of a selection that is partially affected by changes you make to the selection.

File Browser The Photoshop File Browser lets you view, sort, and process image files.

fill To paint a selected area with a gray shade, a color, or a pattern.

Fill layer A Photoshop method for filling an area. Fill layers combine the action of the Fill command with the flexibility of layers. You can create Fill layers with colors, gradients, or patterns.

filter A software method for applying effects to images. With filters, you can adjust focus, eliminate unwanted artifacts, alter or create complex selection masks, and apply a wide range of artistic effects.

Filter Gallery A Photoshop CS feature that consolidates the 47 separate Photoshop 7 Effects filters into a single interface with filter effect previews and multiple filtering operations.

FireWire A cable that allows the capture of DV (digital video) images and audio via an IEEE 1394 port.

Flag A File Browser command to simplify the process of viewing only flagged or unflagged image assets.

Flash (SWF) A Macromedia Flash application file format export option supported by ImageReady CS.

flatbed scanner A type of scanner that reads a line of an image at a time, recording it as a series of samples, or pixels, by bouncing light off the area it needs to digitize. The scanner directs the bounced light to a series of detectors that convert color and intensity into digital levels.

floating selection In Photoshop, a selection that has been moved or pasted on an image The selection floats above the pixels in the underlying image until it is deselected, and it can be moved without affecting the underlying image.

font The style or appearance of a complete set of characters. The four main categories of fonts are serif, sans serif, cursive, and display or decorative.

font obliqueness Refers to whether the characters in a font lean, as does italic-style type.

font weight The thickness or heaviness of the characters in a font.

frame grabber See *digitizer board*.

full-color image An image that uses 24-bit color. A full-color image uses three 8-bit primary color channels—for red, green, and blue—each containing 256 colors. These three channels produce a potential of 16.7 million colors ($256^3 = 16,777,216$). Photo-realistic images that consist of smooth gradations and subtle tonal variations require full color to be properly displayed.

gamma A measurement of midtone brightness for a monitor. The gamma value defines the slope of that curve halfway between black and white. Gamma values range from 1.0 to about 2.5. The Macintosh has traditionally used a gamma of 1.8, which is relatively flat compared to television. Windows PCs use a 2.2 gamma value, which has more contrast and is more saturated.

gamut The range of viewable and printable colors for a particular color model, such as RGB (used for monitors) or CMYK (used for printing). When a color cannot be displayed or printed, Photoshop can warn you that the color is "out of gamut." In terms of color working spaces, the gamut of a monitor is a triangular space with its corners in the red, green, and blue areas of an industry-standard color gamut chart. The gamut chart plots the device's available colors compared to the gamut of colors that humans can see.

GIF87a and GIF89a The Graphics Interchange Formats (GIFs), used for Web applications and for saving animations produced in ImageReady. GIF is a *lossless-compression* format that compresses the image through reduction of the available colors. GIF87a does not support transparency. GIF89a is used to omit the visibility of selected colors on a Web browser.

gradient Variations of color that subtly blend into one another. Photoshop gradients blend multiple colors into each other or into transparency over a specified distance.

gradient fill A fill that displays a gradual transition from the foreground color to the background color. In Photoshop, gradient fills are added with the Gradient tool or a Gradient Fill layer.

gray-component replacement (GCR) An operation that removes a neutral mixture of cyan, magenta, and yellow from colored and neutral areas, and replaces them with black. GCR is generally more extreme and uses more black than the related undercolor removal (UCR) separation method.

grayscale image An image that use an 8-bit system, in which any pixel can be one of 256 shades of gray. Each pixel contains 8 bits of information. Each bit can be either on (black) or off (white), which produces 256 possible combinations.

Grayscale mode A Photoshop color mode that displays black-and-white images. A grayscale image is composed of one channel consisting of up to 256 levels of gray, with 8 bits of color information per pixel. Each pixel has a brightness value from 0 (black) to 255 (white). Grayscale pixels can also be measured in percentages of black ink, from 0 percent (white) to 100 percent (black). When color images are converted to Grayscale mode, their hue and saturation information is discarded and their brightness (or luminosity) values remain.

grid In Photoshop, a series of equally spaced horizontal and vertical lines that create a visual matrix. A grid helps you see the global relations between aligned elements on a page. Grids do not print.

GUI (graphical user interface) A software program's way of interacting with users. The GUI (pronounced "gooey") of Photoshop lets you perform virtual operations that mimic real-world tasks such as painting, compositing, or filtering.

guide In Photoshop, a horizontal or vertical line that can be positioned anywhere on the image's surface. Guides do not print.

halftone The reproduction of a continuous-tone image, which is made by using a screen that breaks the image into various-sized dots. The resolution, or number of lines per inch (lpi), of a halftone depends on the printer's capabilities. The tonal densities of an image are determined by the size of the dots. The larger the dot, the more ink deposited, and the darker the area appears. When you send an image to a printer, Photoshop, in tandem with the printer driver software, automatically converts the tonal information contained in pixels into dot-density information that the printer uses to construct the image.

halftone screen Refers to the dot density of a printed image, measured in lines per inch (lpi). A halftone screen, also called *screen frequency,* is a grid of dots.

highlight The lightest part of an image, represented on a digital image by pixels with high numeric values or on a halftone by the smallest dots or the absence of dots.

histogram A graph of the brightness values of an image. The more lines the histogram has, the more tonal values are present in the image. The length of a line represents the relative quantity of pixels of a particular brightness. The taller the line, the more pixels of a particular tonal range the image will contain. Histograms are displayed in Photoshop's Levels and Threshold dialog boxes and the Histogram palette.

History log A Photoshop CS feature to record the edit history of a work session to a text file, file metadata, or both.

History palette The Photoshop palette that records all of the changes that you make to an image during a session, as a series of individual states. You can use the History palette to revert to former versions of an image and to create special effects. The History palette also works in conjunction with the History Brush and Art History Brush tools.

hotspot In an image map, an area that links to another Web page or URL.

HSB color model A color model that uses hue, saturation, and brightness characteristics to define each color.

HTML (Hypertext Markup Language) The programming language used to create Web pages.

hue The color of light that is reflected from an opaque object or transmitted through a transparent one. Hue in Photoshop is measured by its position on a color wheel, from 0 to 360 degrees.

ICC See *International Color Consortium*.

image caching A mechanism that accelerates screen redrawing during the editing process.

image link A link on a Web page activated by clicking an image.

image map An image on a Web page that has multiple links to another Web page or URL. Each link is called a hotspot. Image maps let you define circular, polygonal, or rectangular areas as links.

image size The physical size and resolution of an image. The size of an image specifies the exact number of pixels that compose a picture.

ImageReady A companion program to Photoshop, used to create dynamic Web graphics.

Indexed color image A single-channel image, with 8 bits of color information per pixel. The index is a color lookup table containing up to 256 colors.

Indexed color mode A color mode that uses a maximum of 256 colors to display full-color images. When you convert an image color to Indexed mode, Photoshop stores the color information as a color lookup table. You can then use a specific palette to display the image to match the colors as closely as possible to the original. Because it contains fewer colors, Indexed color mode creates smaller file sizes than the other color modes produce.

Info palette The Photoshop palette that shows information about the current image. By default, the Info palette displays Actual Color and CMYK fields, the x and y coordinates of the position of the cursor, and the height and width of the selection. This palette can display values in different modes, including Web, HSB, Lab, Total Ink, and Opacity.

interlacing A technique used to display a GIF image progressively on a Web page.

International Color Consortium (ICC) An organization that sets standards for color management systems and components.

interpolation In Photoshop, the setting for how the program resamples, or sizes, images.

inverse In Photoshop, to reverse the selection; that is, to change the selected area to the portion that you did not select with a selection tool.

invert To remap the brightness values of a channel to its opposite value. When you invert a channel, the white pixels with a value of 255 become black with a value of 0. Dark gray pixels in the channel with a value of 20, for example, will be remapped to a value of 235.

JPEG (Joint Photographic Experts Group) A *lossy-compression* file format that supports 24-bit color and is used to preserve the tonal variations in photographs. JPEG compresses file size by selectively discarding data. JPEG compression can degrade sharp detail in images and is not recommended for images with type or solid areas of color. JPEG does not support transparency. When you save an image as a JPEG, transparency is replaced by the matte color. See also *matting*.

kerning The space between two individual characters in text.

knockout An area that prevents ink from printing on part of an image, so that the spot color can print directly on the paper. Knockouts keep a spot color from overprinting another spot color or a portion of the underlying image.

Lab color mode A color mode that is device-independent. Lab color consists of three channels: a luminance or lightness channel (L), a green–red component (a), and a blue–yellow component (b). Lab can be used to adjust an image's luminance and color independently of each other.

labels A Photoshop printing option that prints the document and channel name on the image.

Large Document Format (PSB) A Photoshop CS–only compatible file format that supports resolutions up to 300,000 pixels in either direction.

layer A software feature that enables you to isolate image elements so that you can work on each one individually. You can also rearrange the positions of layers, enabling parts of an image to appear in front of other parts. Versions of Photoshop prior to 7 supported 99 layers, but more recent versions support an unlimited number.

layer comp A specific saved state of the Layers palette

layer mask A mask that conceals an area from view. When you apply a layer mask to an image, you control the transparency of a particular part of the layer.

layer set A Photoshop layer-management tool. Layer sets let you consolidate contiguous layers into a folder on the Layers palette. By highlighting the folder, you can apply certain operations to the layers as a group. For example, the layers in a layer set can be simultaneously hidden, displayed, moved, or repositioned.

layer styles Predefined Photoshop effects, such as drop shadows, neon glowing edges, and deep embossing. Layer styles apply their effects to the edges of the layer. Because they can be translucent or soft-edged, the colors of the underlying layer can be seen through the effects.

Layers palette The Photoshop palette that contains controls for working with layers, including creating and deleting layers, reordering layers, merging layers, and many other layer-related functions.

leading The typographic term to describe vertical spacing between lines, measured from baseline to baseline.

Lens Blur A Photoshop CS command that adds blur to an image to give the effect of a narrower *depth of field* so that some objects in the image stay in focus while others areas become blurred.

Levels A Photoshop tool that enables you to adjust an image's tonal range. When you perform a Levels adjustment, you are actually reassigning pixel values.

ligature A set of two characters that is designed to replace certain character combinations, such as *fl* and *fi*, to avoid spacing conflicts.

linear gradient A gradient that is projected from one point to another in a straight line.

lines per inch (lpi) A measurement of the resolution of a halftone screen.

Liquify A Photoshop feature that enables you to distort pixels and transform areas of an image by using a special set of distortion and transformation tools.

lossless compression An image-compression scheme that preserves image detail. When the image is decompressed, it is identical to the original version.

lossy compression An image-compression scheme that creates smaller files but can affect image quality. When decompressed, the image produced is not identical to the original. Usually, colors have been blended, averaged, or estimated in the decompressed version.

lpi See *lines per inch.*

margin-style background A background that is configured so that the image repeats vertically but not horizontally. This type of background appears as a continuous design down the depth of the page. It is a common visual element that helps unify the design of a Web page.

mask An element that isolates and protects portions of an image. A masked area is not affected by image editing such as color changes or applied filters. Masks are stored as 8-bit grayscale channels and can be edited with Photoshop tools.

Match Color A Photoshop CS image adjustment command for color matching based upon statistical data.

matting Filling or blending transparent pixels with a matte color. Matting can be used with GIF, PNG, and JPEG files. It is typically used to set transparent image areas to the background color of a Web page.

metadata Information about the file that is embedded in the document.

midtone A tonal range of brightness values located approximately halfway between white and black.

moiré pattern An undesirable pattern in color printing, resulting from incorrect screen angles of overprinting halftones. Moiré patterns can be minimized with the use of proper screen angles.

monitor profile A description of a monitor's characteristics used by Photoshop to display images correctly on that monitor. One way to create a monitor profile is to make a visual calibration of your monitor by using Adobe Gamma and then save the resulting information as a color profile.

monitor resolution The number of pixels that occupy a linear inch of your monitor screen. The resolution for most Macintosh RGB monitors is 72 ppi. Most Windows VGA monitors have a resolution of 96 ppi.

monospaced type Type in which all of the characters are the same horizontal width.

Multichannel mode A Photoshop mode that enables you to view the spot-color channels in color separations. The number of channels in a Multichannel document depends on the number of channels in the source image before it was converted. Each channel in a Multichannel document contains 256 levels of gray. Multichannel mode will convert RGB to cyan, magenta, and yellow spot color channels, and CMYK into CMYK spot color channels.

Navigator palette The Photoshop palette that shows a map of the current image displayed as a thumbnail. It indicates the exact location of what appears in the image window relative to the entire image and provides features for scrolling and zooming.

noise In an image, pixels with randomly distributed color values. Noise is primarily a result of digitizing technology. Noise in digital photographs tends to be the product of low-light conditions.

nonlinear editing (NLE) The random access of video storage.

NTSC (National Television System Committee) system The video standard for television used in North and South America and many Asian countries.

object-oriented software Vector-based illustration applications (such as Adobe Illustrator, Macromedia Free-Hand, and CorelDRAW) and page-layout programs (such as QuarkXPress, Adobe PageMaker, and Adobe InDesign). Vector-based illustration software is appropriate for creating graphics such as charts, graphs, maps, cartoons, architectural plans, and other images that require hard edges and smooth blends. Vector-based page-layout software is suitable for creating books, pamphlets, brochures, flyers, and other documents that combine images and text. Photoshop is *raster-based software,* rather than vector-based illustration software; it does not print object-oriented graphics as vectors.

one-quarter tone A tonal value located approximately halfway between the highlight and midtone.

optimization settings In Photoshop and ImageReady, features that put images in the best possible form for Web applications, such as the file format, color-reduction method, and matting settings. In Photoshop, optimization settings are available in the Save For Web dialog box. In ImageReady, these settings are on the Optimize palette.

Optimize palette The ImageReady palette that contains controls for optimizing images for Web applications.

Options bar In Photoshop, the area that contains settings for tools. When you select a tool in the Tool palette, the Options bar changes to reflect the options available for the selected tool.

overprint colors Two or more inks that are printed one on top of the other.

PAL (Phase Alternation Line) system The video standard for television used in Western Europe, Australia, Japan, and other countries.

PANTONE A brand name of spot color inks. The PANTONE Matching System is a group of inks used to print spot colors. PANTONE inks are solid colors used to print solid or tinted areas. The PANTONE system is recognized all over the world.

Paragraph palette The Photoshop palette that contains settings that apply to entire text paragraphs, such as alignment and hyphenation.

path A vector object that mathematically defines a specific area on an image. Vector objects are composed of anchor points and line segments known as *Bezier curves.* Paths enable you to create straight lines and curves with precision. If a path's two end points are joined, it encloses a shape. A path can be filled with color, stroked with an outline, or stored in the Paths palette or the Shape library for later use. A path also can be converted into a selection.

Paths palette The Photoshop palette that contains controls for working paths, including creating and deleting paths, filling paths, stroking paths, and saving work paths.

PDF Portable Document Format (PDF) is a flexible, cross-platform, cross-application file format that can contain raster and vector data, including embedded fonts.

PDF Presentation A Photoshop CS command that can create a multipage PDF document or a PDF slide show with transition effects between each image.

perspective In Photoshop, a transformation that squeezes or stretches one edge of a selection, slanting the two adjacent sides either in or out. This produces an image that mimics the way you perceive a picture slanted at a distance.

Photo Filter A Photoshop CS image adjustment that mimics the traditional technique of using a colored gel on a camera lens to alter color balance and/or temperature.

Photomerge A Photoshop CS automation for creating a single, seamless, panoramic image from multiple source images.

pixel An individual square of colored light, which is the smallest editable unit in a digital image. The pixels (short for *picture elements*) in a digital image are usually so small that, when seen, the colors blend into what appears to be a *continuous-tone* image.

pixels per inch (ppi) The number of pixels that can be displayed per inch, usually used to refer to pixel resolution from a scanned image or on a monitor.

plug-in A modular mini program or filter, usually developed by a third-party vendor, that adds functions to Photoshop.

PNG-8 A lossless-compression file format that supports 256 colors and transparency. PNG-8 is not supported by older Web browsers.

PNG-24 A lossless file format that supports 24-bit color, transparency, and matting. PNG-24 combines the attributes of JPEG and GIF. PNG-24 is not supported by older Web browsers.

point A measurement system for type. There are traditionally about 72 points in 1 inch.

ppi See *pixels per inch.*

preferences In Photoshop, settings that affect the appearance and behavior of the program, which are stored in the preferences file.

Preset Manager A library of palettes that can be used by Photoshop. As you add or delete items from the palettes, the currently loaded palette in the Preset Manager displays the changes. You can save the new palette and load any of the palettes on the system.

printer resolution The number of dots that can be printed per linear inch, measured in dots per inch (dpi). These dots compose larger halftone dots on a halftone screen or stochastic (random pattern) dots on an ink-jet printer.

process color The four color pigments used in color printing: cyan, magenta, yellow, and black (CMYK).

progressive JPEG file A file that displays a low-resolution version of the image while the full image is downloading.

Proof Colors A Photoshop control that enables the on-screen preview to simulate a variety of reproduction processes without converting the file to the final color space. This feature takes the place of the Preview In CMYK feature in earlier Photoshop versions.

Quadtone An image that has been separated into four spot colors.

Quick Mask mode A Photoshop mode that enables you to edit a selection as a mask. This mode provides an efficient method of making a temporary mask

by using the painting tools. Quick Masks can be converted into selections or stored as alpha channels in the Channels palette for later use.

radial gradient A gradient that is projected from a center point outward in all directions.

random access memory (RAM) The part of the computer's memory that stores information temporarily while the computer is on.

raster image An image that consists of a grid of pixels. Raster images are also called *bitmaps.* The file sizes of raster images are usually quite large compared to other types of computer-generated documents, because information needs to be stored for every pixel in the entire document. See also *raster-based software.*

raster image processor (RIP) Software on a computer or a device inside an imagesetter or PostScript printer that interprets a vector curve by connecting a series of straight-line segments.

raster-based software Photoshop and other programs that create raster images. Raster-based software is best suited for editing, manipulating, and compositing scanned images, images from digital cameras and Photo CDs, continuous-tone photographs, realistic illustrations, and other graphics that require subtle blends, soft edges, shadow effects, and artistic filter effects such as Impressionist or watercolor.

rasterize To convert vector information into pixel-based information. For example, you can rasterize type so that you can apply filters and other effects that do not work on vector-based type. Rasterized type cannot be edited as individual characters and appears at the same resolution as the document.

red eye An effect from flash photography that appears to make a person's eyes glow red.

registration mark A mark that appears on a printed image, generally for color separations, to help in aligning the printing plates.

rendering intents Settings established by the International Color Consortium (ICC) under which color conversions can be made. Rendering intents cause the color of an image to be modified while it is being moved into a new color space. The four rendering intents are Perceptual, Saturation, Relative Colorimetric, and Absolute Colorimetric.

resample To change the size or resolution of an image. Resampling down discards pixel information in an image; resampling up adds pixel information through interpolation.

resolution The number of units that occupy a linear inch of an image—measured in pixels per inch (ppi) on an image or monitor, or dots per inch (dpi) on a printer. The resolution of an image determines how large it will appear and how the pixels are distributed over its length and width. Resolution also determines the amount of detail that an image contains. High resolutions produce better quality but larger image file sizes. Resolution can also refer to the number of bits per pixel.

resolution-independent image An image that automatically conforms to the highest resolution of the output device on which it is printed.

RGB color mode A color mode that represents the three colors—red, green, and blue—used by devices such as scanners or monitors to display color. Each range of color is separated into three separate entities called *color channels.* Each color channel can produce 256 different values, for a total of

16,777,216 possible colors in the entire RGB gamut. RGB is referred to as an *additive* color model. Each pixel contains three brightness values for red, green, and blue that range from 0 (black) to 255 (white). When all three values are at the maximum, the effect is complete white.

RGB image A three-channel image that contains a red, a green, and a blue channel.

rollover A mini animation that is activated by mouse behavior. Rollovers add interactivity to a Web page. Rollovers depend on layers for their behavior. You designate a rollover on an image by changing the visibility of a layer's content.

safe action A defined area for video display that indicates the space where the video action will be displayed on standard television screens.

safe title A defined area for video display that indicates the space where the image is not distorted or cropped by the curve of standard television screens.

saturation The intensity of a color. Saturation, or *chroma,* is determined by the percentage of the hue in proportion to gray, from 0 to 100 percent. Zero-percent saturation means that the color is entirely gray.

scanner An electronic device that digitizes and converts photographs, slides, paper images, or other two-dimensional images into pixels.

scratch disk An area of memory that Photoshop uses as a source of virtual memory to process images when the program requires more memory than the allocated amount.

screen angles The angles at which the halftone screens are placed in relation to one another.

screen frequency The density of dots on the halftone screen, commonly measured in lines per inch (lpi). Also known as *screen ruling.*

scrub slider Photoshop CS enables users to "scrub" text fields found in pop-up slider interface controls as a shortcut to accessing the underlying slider interface (scrub behavior is indicated via a hand icon).

SECAM (Sequential Color and Memory) system A video standard for television used in some European and Asian countries.

shadow The darkest part of an image, represented on a digital image by pixels with low numeric values or on a halftone by the smallest or absence of dots.

Shadow/Highlight A Photoshop CS command that lightens or darkens based on the brightness levels of surrounding pixels; this gives separate control to the process of adjusting exposure problems in shadows or highlights, as in the case of lightening a backlit image.

sidecar XMP and THM files A sidecar file stores image-specific metadata and aids other applications in processing the metadata associated with an image file without increasing the size of the image file.

skew To slant a selection along one axis, either vertical or horizontal. The degree of slant affects how pitched the final image appears.

slice To cut an image into pieces, saving the individual parts as image files and writing an HTML document that reassembles the slices on the screen. Slicing increases the efficiency of displaying images with a Web browser by decreasing the download time. Slices also enable you to define rectangular areas as links to other Web pages or URLs.

SMPTE-C A movie industry standard, compliant with the Society of Motion Picture and Television Engineers standards for motion picture illuminants.

snapshot In Photoshop, a saved image's state. By default, when the image is opened, the History palette displays a snapshot of the image as it appeared when it was last saved. You can save the current image to a snapshot to preserve that state.

soft proof An on-screen document that appears as close as possible to what the image will look like if printed to a specific device. Image formats that enable you to embed a soft proof profile in the saved document are Photoshop EPS, Photoshop PDF, and Photoshop DCS 1.0 and 2.0.

spectrophotometer A device used to measure the color gamut of a printed page. From the data that the spectrophotometer collects, a profile can be written that can be used as a color working space.

splash screen A screen that appears when you first load a program. For example, the default Photoshop splash screen indicates the components that are loading and program-specific data, such as the registered owner's name and the program's serial number.

spot color Ink used in a print job in addition to black or process colors. Each spot color requires a plate of its own. Spot colors are printed in the order in which they appear in the Channels palette. Spot color channels are independent of the color mode of the image, which means that they are not blended with the other channels in a Grayscale, RGB, or CMYK image. Spot color channels are also independent of layers, which means that you cannot apply spot colors to individual layers. Image formats that support spot color are Photoshop (PSD), Photoshop PDF, TIFF, and Photoshop DCS 2.0.

sRGB color space A color space designed for corporate computer monitors and images intended for Web applications. sRGB is the default color working space in Photoshop, but other color spaces are available.

state In Photoshop's History palette, a stored version of an image. Each time you perform an operation, the History palette produces a state with the name of the operation or tool that was used. The higher the state appears in the stack, the earlier in the process the state was made.

stroking Outlining a selection border with a color. In Photoshop, strokes can vary in width and relative position on the selection border.

subtractive primary colors Cyan, magenta, and yellow, which are the printing inks that theoretically absorb all color and produce black. Because pigments subtract light components from the white light in the environment, they reduce its intensity, making it less bright than unfiltered light. Subtractive colorants reduce the amount of light reflected back at the viewer.

timeline The window that provides a schematic view of your program including all video, audio, and superimposed video tracks in nonlinear editing programs such as Adobe Premier.

tolerance A parameter of the Magic Wand and Paint Bucket tools that specifies the color range of the pixels to be selected.

Tool palette In Photoshop, the area that contains icons for tools, also called the Toolbox. Some of the tool icons expand to provide access to tools that are not visible, bringing the entire number of tools to 50, plus paint swatches, Quick Mask icons, view

modes, and the Edit In command. The Tool palette is a floating palette that you can move or hide.

tool tip A GUI identifier that appears when you hover your cursor over a screen element and wait a few seconds. Photoshop includes tool tips for the tools on the Tool palette, as well as for many of its operations accessible from other palettes, the Options bar, dialog boxes, and windows.

tracking The global space between selected groups of characters in text.

transparency scanner A type of scanner that passes light through the emulsions on a piece of negative film or a color slide. A transparency scanner's dynamic range determines its capability to distinguish color variations.

trap A technique used in preparing images for printing color separations. Misalignments or shifting during printing can result in gaps in images. A trap is an overlap that prevents such gaps from appearing along the edges of objects in an image.

Tritone An image that has been separated into three spot colors.

tweening From "in betweening," a method for adding transitions between frames in animations.

undercolor removal (UCR) The process of reducing the cyan, magenta, and yellow inks from the neutral or darkest neutral shadow areas in an image, and replacing them with black.

Unsharp Mask (USM) A mask that exaggerates the transition between areas of most contrast, while leaving areas of minimum contrast unaffected. It can help increase the contrast of an image and fool the eye into thinking fuzzy areas of the image are in focus.

value See *brightness.*

vector graphics Images that are composed of lines and objects that define their shapes. The objects created in vector-based software are made from *Bezier curves,* which are composed of mathematically defined points and segments. Vector images take up less space on a disk than raster images of comparable dimensions. See also *object-oriented software.*

vector mask An area that is defined by a path and hidden from view.

virtual memory The memory space that is separate from the main memory (physical random access memory, or RAM) in a computer, such as harddisk space. Virtual memory helps to increase the amount of memory available to work on large documents.

wallpaper tiles A background that is configured so that the image is displayed as repeating tiles.

Web colors Colors that are browsersafe, meaning that all Web browsers can display them uniformly. Photoshop's Web-Safe Colors feature lets you choose colors that will not radically change when viewed on other monitors of the same quality and calibration as the one on which you are working.

Web Photo Gallery A Photoshop automation that automatically builds a website gallery from selected source images. Photoshop CS ships with professionally designed gallery templates with feedback options.

white point The lightest pixel in the highlight area of an image. In Photoshop, you can set this point in the Levels and Curves dialog boxes.

work path In Photoshop, a temporary element that records changes as you draw new sections of a path.

Index

Note to the Reader: Throughout this index **boldfaced** page numbers indicate primary discussions of a topic. *Italicized* page numbers indicate illustrations.

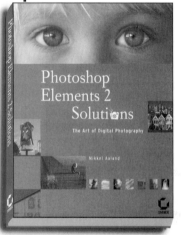

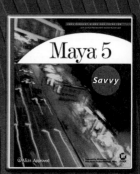

ABOUT THE AUTHOR

Stephen Romaniello is an artist, educator, and writer. He began his career in graphics in 1980 as a production artist and typesetter; soon he was promoted to designer and then art director. In 1982, he became a partner in Armory Park Design Group. Three years later he founded Congress Street Design, a full-service design firm. In 1987, at the beginning of the digital revolution in graphics technology, he purchased his first computer. Romaniello accepted a faculty position in 1990 in the Advertising Art program at Pima Community College in Tucson, Arizona, with the intention of developing a state-of-the-art digital graphics program. He served as chair of the renamed Communication Graphics department for eight years.

Romaniello has developed curriculum and training materials for many of the mainstream graphics programs, and has offered seminars at the Maine Photographic Workshops, the League for Innovation and National Business Media. A certified instructor in Adobe Photoshop, he currently teaches digital art at Pima Community College. He is the coauthor of *Mastering Adobe GoLive 4* and the author of *Mastering Photoshop 6, Photoshop 7 Savvy*, and *The Perfect Digital Portfolio*. His column, "The Digital Eye," appears monthly in *Digital Graphics* magazine. Romaniello is the founder of GlobalEye Systems, a company that offers onsite training and consulting throughout the country. His home and studio are in Tucson, Arizona.

Sybex has been part of the personal computer revolution from the very beginning. We were founded in 1976 by Dr. Rodnay Zaks, an early innovator of the microprocessor era and the company's president to this day. Dr. Zaks was involved in the ARPAnet and developed the first published industrial application of a microcomputer system: an urban traffic control system.

While lecturing on a variety of technical topics in the mid-1970s, Dr. Zaks realized there wasn't much available in the way of accessible documentation for engineers, programmers, and businesses. Starting with books based on his own lectures, he launched Sybex simultaneously in his adopted home of Berkeley, California, and in his original home of Paris, France.

Over the years, Sybex has been an innovator in many fields of computer publishing, documenting the first word processors in the early 1980s and the rise of the Internet in the early 1990s. In the late 1980s, Sybex began publishing our first desktop publishing and graphics books. As early adopters ourselves, we began desktop publishing our books in-house at the same time.

Now, in our third decade, we publish dozens of books each year on topics related to graphics, web design, digital photography, and digital video. We also continue to explore new technologies and over the last few years have been among the first to publish on topics like Maya and Photoshop Elements.

With each book, our goal remains the same: to provide clear, readable, skill-building information, written by the best authors in the field—experts who know their topics as well as they know their audience.